CHINESE INTELLECTUALS
AND THE WEST

1872-1949

THE UNIVERSITY OF NORTH CAROLINA PRESS · CHAPEL HILL

Y. C. Wang was born in Peking, China, and holds degrees from the London School of Economics and the University of Chicago. Recipient of many distinguished fellowships and honors, he has held teaching positions in a number of American universities and colleges and has published widely in Chinese and English journals. Now a United States citizen, Dr. Wang is an associate professor of history at The University of North Carolina at Chapel Hill, where he has taught since 1962. During the academic year 1965-66, he is a Visiting Scholar with the East Asian Institute at Columbia University.

CHINESE INTELLECTUALS AND THE WEST

1872-1949

By Y. C. WANG

Copyright © 1966 by
The University of North Carolina Press
Manufactured in the United States of America
Library of Congress Catalog Card Number 66-10207
Printed by The Seeman Printery, Durham, N. C.

Foreword

One of the most striking phenomena in the recent history of China is the large number of Chinese youths who went abroad to study. Each year, from the beginning of this century, hundreds and then thousands of young men and women broke away from the confines of their own culture and immersed themselves for a few years of study in the modernizing worlds of Japan, the United States, Western Europe, and Russia. Most of the nation's leaders during the twentieth century had this experience, or at least learned from teachers who had studied abroad. This group of leaders was the driving force in nearly every aspect of the multifaceted process of China's modernization—military, technological, scientific, diplomatic, financial, political, ideological, and literary. Study abroad was also part of the process through which the Chinese began to adjust to the realities of the world outside the Middle Kingdom. Without taking into account this phenomenon of Western education, modern China is incomprehensible.

Yet, strange to say, until the publication of the present book, there has been no comprehensive and systematic study in a Western language of this aspect of China's recent history. Professor Y. C. Wang has explored the subject intensively, if not exhaustively, using a formidable array of historical data to trace the movement from the closing decades of the nineteenth century to mid-point in the twentieth.

During these seven or eight decades, about one hundred thousand students went abroad for extended periods. Most returned to China eager to use their knowledge to contribute to the country's social transformation. Some had distinguished careers and some were misfits. Some used their knowledge for personal aggrandizement. What effect did they have upon their own society? To bring coherence to a subject of such complexity, Professor Wang has used a variety of approaches—socio-historical, statistical, descriptive, and biographic. He has explored many neglected aspects of China's modern history in which the foreign educated were leaders of political revolution, guides to social reform, managers of the country's finances, ideologists, cultural leaders, and entrepreneurs. Finally, he has tried to appraise the impact upon China of this massive drive for foreign education.

If some of his conclusions are pessimistic, this may not be inappropriate in view of the agonizing cultural readjustment China has gone through in the twentieth century. Leaders with part of their education acquired abroad were unable to prevent this cultural confusion; indeed, they contributed to it. On the whole, they neglected the problems of rural China where most of the population lived. Was this the fault, or at least the result, of their foreign education? Was this education, generally speaking, ill-suited to China's needs? Was the turmoil an inevitable by-product of modernization? Japan seems not to have suffered so traumatic an experience. What other factors bore upon the Chinese case? These are some of the questions to which Professor Wang addresses himself.

Questions such as these have an import far beyond China. Most of the world is undergoing a process of modernization disruptive of established mores and attended by conflict. Thousands of young men and women from Asia and Africa are studying today in foreign countries—in America, Western Europe, Russia, and now in China— seeking eagerly to enhance their own knowledge with the hope of contributing to the modernization of their own societies. Will their education abroad, and the conflicting ideologies various of them may absorb, serve them and their nations well or ill? Must the transplantation of knowledge, belief, and technical skill create social confusion? American youths, too, are studying abroad in ever-increasing numbers. What judgments will future historians come to in appraising the inter-cultural education which so many of the world's future leaders are experiencing?

Professor Wang's study of the Chinese historical case does not attempt to answer these latter questions. For this he may surely be forgiven, since he has pioneered in one important field affecting something like a fifth of the human race. But certainly his book has much to say not only to students of China but also to those concerned with education in the modern world.

C. MARTIN WILBUR
Professor of Chinese History
Columbia University

October, 1965

Preface

This study has several purposes. The principal ones are to describe the circumstances surrounding the beginning and development of the Chinese movement to study abroad, to demonstrate what the students accomplished both abroad and after their return, and to determine the impact these students later made upon Chinese society and government. A broader purpose is to shed light on problems that arise when a society, deeply embedded in tradition, attempts to shake off the tyranny of habit and adapt itself to an entirely different way of life within the shortest possible time. Because my hope is to reach a circle of readers beyond Sinologists, well-known events in Chinese history are upon occasion described briefly in order to make them more intelligible to readers not familiar with the country's past.

Although the term *intellectuals* is difficult to define when it is used to denote a certain group of men in an industrial society, it takes on a clear-cut meaning when applied to the elite in China. It simply means "educated men" in distinction to the masses who are uneducated. Given this fact, one can speak of the "higher" or "lower" intellectuals, meaning men who had much or little formal education. Since the word *intellectuals* has a modern connotation, I have reserved it for the Chinese of the twentieth century and have used another term, *literati*, to denote the educated peoples before this time.

As I point out in the introductory chapter, it is my belief that the ruling group in Chinese society was made up of scholars who assumed the dual task of preserving traditional ethical values and attending to the chores of government. Because of their pivotal and exposed position, they were the first group to feel deeply the impact of Western penetration into China in the nineteenth century. This situation was unprecedented in China's long history, and the reaction of her ruling elite provided both a symptom of the crisis and a cause for further changes in Chinese society. In one way or another, a study of the changing intelligentsia is thus a key to the understanding of modern China.

The scope of this central idea has led to many practical problems in presentation. To begin with, the very reference to Chinese educated abroad implies the view that they shared certain common traits that can be isolated for discussion. This view is commonly accepted in China, and I find no objection to it. It is one thing, however, to observe a separate fact and quite another to isolate it for cause-and-effect discussion, and the difficulty is compounded by the scope of my attempt. Nearly all of the writers on cross-cultural education are anthropologists and sociologists who are interested in individuals as members of a group rather than in individuals themselves. In contrast, I have attempted not only to describe the Chinese movement to study abroad as a group phenomenon but also to discuss the impact on China of certain individual foreign-educated Chinese. This, not unnaturally, has created some organizational problems. Aside from the introductory Part I, the two main parts in my book have quite different frameworks and are only loosely connected. Part II is primarily a "sociological" study of a factual, objective nature, while Part III is a more subjective analysis of the achievements and failures of selected returned students. I could either have condensed one of the two parts to achieve a higher degree of unity, or broken Part III into a series of monographs devoted to single events. But each of these approaches had its own limitations. The first would have involved the sacrifice of much information that is relevant to the general topic, while the second would have sacrificed an understanding of the over-all movement to the elucidation of a small part of it. I therefore felt it better to proceed as I did, as the most likely way of gaining new historical perspective. If my present endeavor leads to more useful contributions from others along the same path, I shall be more than satisfied.

Several other methodological problems must be mentioned. First, in some instances I found it necessary to cover events in which the returned students played only certain parts. An example is the Revolution of 1911 discussed in Chapter 9. To my knowledge there is no adequate account of this event in English, and it is difficult to summarize the role of a group when the episode itself remains obscure. I also suspect that most authors have a tendency to overstress the importance of their heroes. In the present case it seemed better to paint the whole canvas and let the reader make his own evaluation of the individual components than to focus on one issue or personality in which I had a special interest.

Second, several important groups of those who studied abroad and who were influential upon their return to China are not brought clearly into my analysis. Obviously, an author is limited by his own taste and competence and by the availability of materials. If I may express an opinion on the groups not specifically discussed in this book, I would first comment on the paucity of materials left by the diplomats of the Republican era. Their noticeable reluctance to leave any personal record is in itself unusual and is a phenomenon upon which I have commented elsewhere.[1] Hopefully, more will be

1. See my article "Intellectuals and Society in China, 1860-1949," CSSH (July, 1961), 422.

known about these diplomats once the Chinese government opens its archives.[2] At the present time I feel that the diplomats, while technically competent, were alienated from the Chinese cultural tradition. Since this was true of all Western-educated Chinese, the omission of the diplomats from my discussion should not affect my general conclusions.

Another group I left out was the militarists. While many of them underwent training in Japan, few really spoke the Japanese language and even fewer assimilated Japanese culture in more than a superficial sense. Their outlook was thus probably little different from that of the militarists trained entirely in China. A third group omitted from my account consists of the professional political workers. Here a sharp difference seems to have existed between the Kuomintang organizers and the Communist leaders. Relatively few of the former were Western-educated, and the careers of those who did study abroad were apparently not dependent on their Western education. By contrast, many of the Communist leaders were trained in Russia, and their subsequent careers were largely determined by their training. Certainly they might have formed an important part of the present study, but they were excluded for two reasons. First, to my knowledge no Chinese has rendered an account of his experiences in Russia. The extreme scarcity of biographical materials is mitigated, so I understand, by a body of confessions exacted from captured Communists and still preserved by the Kuomintang regime; but despite repeated attempts, I have had no success in eliciting information from the government in Taiwan. A second and quite different reason for excluding those trained in Russia is the ambiguous position of Russia herself. When a Chinese speaks of the West, he is thinking primarily of America and Great Britain, with France, Germany, Belgium, and other European powers on the fringe. Japan is not a part of, or even adjacent to, this composite whole but occupies a half-way house between it and China, while Russia is set completely apart. This should suggest something of the nature and importance of the gulf between Western education and Russian training.

Some readers may also question the sharp contrast I draw between the highly ethical traditional elite and the new amoral elite that resulted largely from education in the West. Briefly, three considerations are involved: first, whether the traditional elite was actually ethical; second, whether the new elite was amoral; and third, if it was amoral, whether Western education was a causative factor. Of

2. The political changes of the last few decades have probably resulted in the preservation of fewer documentary materials for the Republican period than for earlier ones. I understand that the only important single body of diplomatic archives that has been left intact is the file of official papers at the Chinese embassy in Washington, D.C. It is hoped that the Chinese authorities will soon make these papers available for research.

these, the first and the last are probably the most controversial. Largely because of the changes that have occurred in the social environment of China in the last fifty years, it has become fashionable to condemn the traditional order and to depict the scholar-officials as ruthless exploiters of the peasants. Indeed, this interpretation has gained so much currency that it is often accepted as an immutable truth. Yet I have seen little more than fragmentary evidence to support this charge. While the issue is admittedly one that cannot be answered easily, any judicious investigation would require at least a balancing of the services rendered by the scholar-officials to society against the abuses they committed. If we adopt such a procedure, it is not at all clear that the general picture is in their disfavor. For one thing, the whole body of Chinese literature, including the local gazetteers and dynastic histories, contains many accounts of outstanding deeds performed by the scholars; and unless one takes the extreme view that all such reports are falsehoods perpetuated in the interest of the ruling class, it is difficult to see how these scholars can be depicted as greedy and grasping exploiters of the people. Moreover, in the study of any society, the meaning behind its institutions must be understood. In China all social mechanisms have worked toward a single aim: the inculcation of Confucian values from childhood, the severe social condemnation of deviant behavior, the stress on individual responsibility to a family that included ancestors as well as posterity, the lack of physical mobility and the resulting attachment to a man's native community, the lack of a mercantile class bent on creating and stimulating the consumers' demand—all these and more have shaped Chinese character and reduced the acquisitive instinct. Unless one argues that man's evil nature rises above the influence of his environment, it is difficult to see why the traditional elite should have failed to respond to the appeal of their culture. Finally, the scholar-peasant relationship in China had a long history and was one of the most lasting of the world's institutions. Its longevity alone casts doubt on the proposition that it was used by one class for the exploitation of another.

Against these considerations we have only miscellaneous reports from a few rural areas showing that in the decades preceding 1949 the peasants suffered deeply from the exactions of their landlords.[3] Even if all these reports are true and unexaggerated, how far the picture can be generalized remains in doubt. Furthermore, sound methodology does not permit us to project the present into the past. Because of the vastly changed social environment, it is virtually certain that the landlord class of 1949 had little in common with its counterpart of 1800. There is therefore little evidence to combat the tradi-

3. See for instance HCYNT, *passim;* AC, 15-17.

tional view that the scholars lived to serve the people and performed useful functions for them.

Apart from the evidence presented in my book, several broader considerations may be advanced to substantiate the existence of an amoral elite in modern China. In the first place, amoralization is an inevitable tendency in modern society. A severely moral orientation has always been the hallmark of a privileged group, either religious or intellectual; it is not a characteristic of cultures devoted to mass production and the average man. As life becomes more pluralistic, morality by definition can no longer be its sole or dominant concern. Furthermore, as specialization leads to greater skill and productivity, an individual is correspondingly subjected to more technical training and is left with less time for philosophical speculation. This is universally true, and it applied to China as she moved toward industrialization. More specifically, to be moral presupposes a moral code, and such a code hardly existed in China between 1919 and 1949. With the discredit of Confucianism in the May Fourth Movement, the Chinese intelligentsia moved into a period of moral and ethical vacuum. Communism, although growing in strength, was still poorly adapted to Chinese conditions and the Chinese temperament. The only teaching with even limited popular appeal was the Three Principles of the People of Sun Yat-sen. But this doctrine was less ethical than political, suffered from numerous inconsistencies, and above all, despite formal promulgation, was ignored by the Kuomintang government. There was thus nothing in Chinese life to serve as a standard of values, and under such circumstances it is hardly conceivable that the intelligentsia could have had the same moral fervor as its predecessors.

In regard to the Chinese students abroad, the situation was even worse. Although Western civilization is basically as steeped in spiritual values as the Chinese, these values are extremely difficult for a foreign visitor to assimilate. For one thing, Christianity is at variance with Chinese culture and is unattractive to most Chinese. For another, Western secular values are generally rather implicit. They are not explicitly taught at the college level or above, and are often meaningless when deprived of the support of accompanying social institutions. Furthermore, foreign students not only lack the intimacy with a culture that can come only from birth or childhood; they also tend to have rather limited social experiences. Among conscientious students, such cultural barriers almost inevitably cause them to become more absorbed in their studies. Because their courses are usually of a highly technical nature, greater devotion only contributes to a more detached attitude toward life. In this way a visitor can become even more amoralized than a native of an industrial society.

This "exaggerated" impact on foreigners points to the unsuspected difficulties of semantics. When we say a Chinese is "Westernized," we do not mean that he has actually become a Westerner. Rather we mean that he has deviated from the Chinese pattern as a result of his Western experiences. In other words, the result of Westernization may well be a pattern of behavior that bears some traces of both Chinese and Western culture, but that in itself is neither Chinese nor Western. This situation is one that easily causes confusion and misunderstanding, and the views of various commentators differ sharply according to their bias. Those who are critical toward Chinese culture advocate more Westernization on the part of the Chinese students, while those ill disposed toward the West argue just as sincerely for an opposite course. In reality such disagreement would disappear if we purged the word "Westernization" of all moral connotation and used it simply to denote the change following upon cultural contact. An attitude is "Westernized" because it was derived from Western sources. This does not imply that it has the same functions in China as it has in the West. In all likelihood they are completely different. Yet we cannot on this account deny that Western influence was the initial causative factor in the changing attitudes of the Chinese.

A related factor that should be mentioned is the presence of indigenous elements in any borrowed institution. When an attitude was derived from the West, it still generally had its Chinese components. On what grounds and in what proportion can we then attribute Chinese developments to Western influences? This question is an exceedingly interesting one. But because of limitations of time and space, my book will not undertake to measure the various Chinese and non-Chinese elements in any given situation. Nor will it be particularly concerned with what might have happened in China had her culture been different from what it was. My purpose is to inquire into the actual events that occurred in China as a result of Western penetration. In order to accomplish this, I will attempt to establish that Western influence was the initial catalytic agent, but I will not try to measure the cultural factors in every situation that later arose.

Despite its obvious interpretative nature, the view that the Chinese elite became increasingly amoral and detached from society from 1902 to 1949, is, to my mind, an indisputable statement of fact. As a social scientist, I hold that this is an inevitable result when modernization is imposed from above and when different segments of society experience grossly uneven degrees of modernization. In so far as subsequent events were not anticipated or desired by the reformers in China, the movement was a failure, but unless we make further assumptions on man's ability to rise above his environment, we cannot blame the failure on any particular individual. My stand in this regard thus differs radically from that of the authorities in Communist China, who, despite their assertion that "existence determines consciousness," have unreservedly condemned the Westernized "high-class Chinese" as a group. But the point is, whatever their political affiliation, few Chinese observers believe that the movement to study abroad was a success.[4] In this sense my book yields no startling new discoveries. It is merely an attempt to examine the phenomenon more systematically.

I do not think my work has proved that Western education has had no benefit for China, nor have I demolished the case for cross-cultural education as such. All I am suggesting is that certain types of cross-cultural programs can yield very undesirable results. If the Chinese experience is of any general significance, it would seem that foreign study has a maximum chance of success only if the students are mature in age, have definite objectives in mind, and limit their sojourn to fairly short periods. Only in this way are they likely to acquire new knowledge without being uprooted from their own cultural tradition. On a more abstract level, I wish to stress that the Chinese movement to study abroad failed primarily because of its misconceived and unattainable goal, which was no less than national rejuvenation and achievement of major-power status within the shortest possible time. Even more illogically, the Anglo-American experience inspired the Chinese to believe that they could foster democratic institutions at the same time they were attaining national power. Actually, of course, the Anglo-American model was inapplicable because the institutions of both countries had evolved over a long period of time, a process which, because of foreign pressure, China was unable to follow.

Despite the failure of the Chinese attempt, other developing nations are unrealistically aspiring to the same goal. They desire democracy, but they long for national power even more. This is an objective that may well plunge the world into chaos. From the example of China—and of Japan—one may safely conclude that democracy and national power are often incompatible aims, that neither can be attained overnight, and that even if major-power status could be achieved, it might well be a curse in disguise. Only

4. Significantly, the intellectuals of Communist China are now confessing their sins of being detached from the masses and are atoning for them by living among the peasants. To be sure this action is politically induced, but it does not follow that the feelings are necessarily insincere. Virtually all the recantations are marked by cogent reasoning, internal consistency, and careful attention to details. Probably the most plausible explanation of this phenomenon is that because of their psychological vulnerability, these intellectuals were susceptible to coercive persuasion. Once the initial resistance was broken, they expressed their emotions readily. The self-condemnation may take an extreme form partly because the feelings are genuine.

on the foundation of such understanding can a nation properly conduct its educational programs. On the other hand, it should be noted that a developing society is rarely dependent upon itself alone. In China's case, her political and educational development was almost entirely a response to foreign pressure. If the West finds the present state of affairs in China unpleasant and menacing, it should scrupulously refrain from repeating elsewhere the mistakes it made in that country.

Y. C. WANG

October, 1965

Acknowledgments

I am grateful to Professors F. A. Hayek and Earl H. Pritchard for their constant interest in this work, which I began during my student days at the University of Chicago. I am indebted to Professor C. Martin Wilbur, who read the entire manuscript, made valuable comments, and wrote the Foreword. I am also obliged to Professors H. G. Creel, Edward Shils, George E. Taylor, T. H. Tsien, L. Carrington Goodrich, George V. Taylor, Edwin McClellan, and E. A. Kracke, Jr., who each read part of my manuscript and gave me many helpful suggestions. I additionally thank my friends on the Committee on Social Thought and in the Department of History at the University of Chicago, and at the East Asian Institute of Columbia University, as well as my colleagues at The University of North Carolina at Chapel Hill, for interesting and illuminating discussions of the subject.

For stylistic improvements I am particularly indebted to Michael Alexander, who, interestingly, is a student of English history but who so quickly grasped the essentials of my subject that he had much to do with the final revision of Part II of this book. I am obliged to the staff of The University of North Carolina Press for their highly skillful assistance in editorial and production matters. I wish to thank the editors of the following journals for permission to use portions of articles which appeared previously, in somewhat different form, in *The American Sociological Review, Comparative Studies in Society and History, Foreign Affairs, Monumenta Serica, The Pacific Review,* and *Sinologica.*

I must acknowledge the generous financial assistance I received from the Volker Fund, the Earhart Foundation, the Social Science Research Council, and the Institute for Research in Social Science of The University of North Carolina at Chapel Hill, which together made it possible for me to finish my work. I must also mention my indebtedness to the Alumni Annual Giving funds and the University Research Council of The University of North Carolina at Chapel Hill for aid in publication of this book.

Finally, but very importantly, I wish to thank my daughter Hui, who saved me from many errors in my English, and my wife Kay, who has shared with me the hardships of a scholar's life. Obviously, those who have helped me are not in any way responsible for the mistakes that may remain.

Contents

Tables

[Part I]

INTRODUCTION

[1] *Ideas and Men in Traditional China*

For more than two thousand years before the twentieth century, Chinese society was strongly influenced by moral principles. While this fact is generally recognized by Sinologists, the degree to which these principles influenced Chinese politics has received little attention. This introductory chapter will establish these points. First, certain dominant ideas, which can be stated fairly concisely, profoundly influenced the behavior of the scholar class and, through it, society at large. Second, the scholar-officials constituted an elite, since as individuals they served as leaders in various fields and since as a group they were more powerful than any other class. Third, ideas, men, and institutions must be viewed as a whole; without Confucianism there would have been no scholar class of this particular type, and Chinese society would have had a different structure. In so far as the scholar-officials played a key role in society, a change in their function would have reflected a change in the whole social structure. Thus an understanding of this group, which was the predecessor of the modern Chinese intelligentsia, will aid in our study of contemporary China.

This chapter is not intended as a brief history of the various schools of Chinese thought. Instead it will be devoted to a summary of the essentials of traditional Chinese thought, to those dominant ideas accepted by most scholars regardless of their stand on more sophisticated issues. Although these essentials served as the framework of man's behavior, certainly all men did not conform to the ideal. Deviation naturally existed, and even in conformity men's motives often differed from what the ideal assumed. But in so far as the ideal formed the framework of human behavior and was thus a force in history, it should be understood in its pure form. Accordingly, I shall first analyze the ideas themselves and then indicate the most frequent deviations from them.

DOMINANT IDEAS

The main current of Chinese thought was devoted to the realization of true good for all mankind. "True good" meant the attainment of happiness in the here and now. Little concern was shown for such questions as the beginning of human life, man's position in the universe, and the relation between the natural and the supernatural.

Man was what he was. The only meaningful question was how he should live.

Like the Greeks, Chinese philosophers recognized that man was a social animal. To live meant to live with one's fellow men; there was no happiness unless it was shared by others. What then was happiness? First, certain material needs must be met. "Only when food and clothing are sufficient will men think of glory and humiliation." Once these were met, affluence was neither essential nor conducive to the good life. Happiness was primarily moral, although its specific meaning varied from one individual to another. For the most gifted, it meant the achievement of a contemplative life when in seclusion and the establishment of a good social order when knowledge was applied to statecraft. Although human nature was considered to be good and all men capable of achieving some degree of saintliness, man was nevertheless restricted by his innate intellectual capacity and his external surroundings. For the masses, the good life meant a life in peace and harmony with others through the fulfillment of their role in the perpetuation of social life.

Postulation of the ends of life dictated the means of best serving them. Society was essentially a hierarchy of intelligence over ignorance. Knowledge was virtue, and those who were deficient in knowledge could lead a higher life by following the guidance of the sages. The position of the ruler was a trust: it was his duty to elevate the moral status of the ruled and, indirectly, to further their material well-being. He was expected, in so far as possible, to avoid compulsion in all forms, for moral elevation could come only through introspection and could not be secured by coercion. A true prince was a saint who ruled by teaching and the power of example. His position depended not on the accident of birth but on the will of heaven as expressed through the support of the masses.

This ideal of the philosopher-king was symbolized in Chinese history by the three legendary kings Yao, Shun, and Yü who were frequently referred to in political essays and who became a standard for all subsequent rulers. At least five or six princes between Yü and the Warring States (403-221 B.C.) abdicated in favor of men they admired.[1] Toward the end of Western Han (206 B.C.-24 A.D.) many scholars supported Wang Mang because they accepted his moral worth and hence his right to the throne.[2] Several subsequent dynasties came into being, ostensibly at least, by the abdication of a previous ruler, notably the T'ang (618-905 A.D.), which was in many respects the greatest in Chinese history. The precept that merit alone justified power became a universally accepted truth and developed into the

1. LIC:CK, I, 75-76.
2. CM:KSHL, 72; CM:KSTK I, 105-8. For a discussion of the idea of abdication, see HCY:KTCK II, 471-72.

theory that all offices were held pending the advent of the virtuous. Thus the most frequent reason for resigning from a post was that "I withdraw in order to clear the path for a worthier man."

But the idea of co-opting or electing the most virtuous did not develop into a regular system. Succession by inheritance is said to have existed during the legendary Hsia. How then could the powerful also be the righteous? The answer was gradually found in accepting an authority and making his teachings binding on all.[3] Such seems to have been the development of Confucianism after the reign of Han Wu-ti (140-87 B.C.). After that time the humanistic doctrines of Confucius, as interpreted by later philosophers who were often influenced by other schools of thought, became the mores by which the Chinese lived for some twenty centuries. The word *mores* is not exact. The Confucian code at its broadest was a combination of mores, ethics, precedents, *Weltanschauung,* and institutions which permeated the fabric of society and governed the life of each individual. The authority of the ruler depended on and was limited by his conformity to the Confucian code, which was accepted as the standard precept of life. A philosopher-king was both desirable and desired, but the definition changed from one who philosophized to one who followed and who sometimes interpreted the prevailing philosophy. The role became narrower and the need less urgent.

What then was the essence of Confucianism? Only a very broad generalization can be given here. Concerning itself with mundane happiness, defining the good life as a minimum of material wants and a maximum of moral cultivation, and recognizing the unequal intellectual capacities of men, Confucianism prescribed a body of elaborate rules governing man-to-man relationships. The essence was to pro-

3. The need of a moral authority and the qualifications of Confucianism to fill this need were apparently discovered gradually by experience gained through the sensible choice of alternatives. Two historical incidents can best illustrate my point. Shortly after the first emperor of Han came to the throne, he boasted that he had conquered the world on horseback. A Confucian scholar thereupon replied: "You have conquered it on horseback, but you cannot rule it on horseback." The truth of these words must have deeply impressed the emperor, especially because he was soon to be rescued from an embarrassing situation by another Confucianist. The emperor, who was a rascally person of plebian origin, had had in his gang many ruffians who all became high officials upon their leader's ascension to the throne. Yet they had no manners and behaved in an extremely unseemly fashion at court. After having tried and failed to instill some decency into their behavior, the emperor finally turned to Shu-sun T'ung, who assembled a band of scholars, conferred with them upon proper court etiquette, rehearsed certain procedures with music, and introduced them to the court. The unruliness disappeared, and the dignity of the throne was saved. The popular view that Confucianism was arbitrarily decreed the orthodox cult by Kao-tsu's grandson, Wu-ti, is therefore not entirely correct. Perhaps it is more plausible to view this decree as the outcome of a long process of deliberation undertaken by the Han court.

mote harmony by means of self-abnegation and consideration for others. The rules of conduct emphasized love—not a universal love bestowed equally upon all, but reasoned benevolence apportioned according to the proximity of one man to another. Thus unbounded love was for parents; loyalty, for the prince; frankness, but not vengeance, for enemies; and relative indifference, for strangers. The idea of obligation was ingrained in the minds of all. Like love, obligation was hierarchical; the heaviest fell upon the most exalted, in terms of morality, intellect, or political power. Normally, the last presupposed the first two, for only those with high moral standards and intellectual ability were entitled to power. However, the moral and the intellectual might on occasion prefer a contemplative life and elevate others by teaching or by example rather than by assuming the reins of government.

The whole Chinese socio-political structure can be viewed as an application of the concept of *jen*. The central idea in this concept is that man is by nature good, that he has an inner feeling of sympathy for others, and that as this feeling develops, he will share their joys and sufferings as part of his own experiences. In actual practice, the process of commiseration began with the family; hence it was the basic unit in the system. Because the duty of all statesmen was to nurture the people, the state became merely an extended form of the family. But as the basis of social relationships shifted from the biological to the political level, obligations of those in authority were correspondingly increased and penalties for their nonfulfillment became heavier. Whereas children were expected to have unceasing love for their parents, subjects were allowed the right to rebel against leaders who had clearly failed according to the Confucian standard. The specific sanction of rebellion was a cardinal feature of the Confucian order. Among other things, it indicated that political office was dependent on moral conformity. The ultimate authority was thus Confucianism; political personalities and institutions stood or fell in accordance with their measurement by this standard.

What then were the sustaining forces of Confucianism itself? One was its demonstrated worth as a practical system. Adherence to Confucianism produced peace and prosperity, while negligence brought chaos and misery. Repeated demonstrations of this practicality produced the so-called dynastic cycles from the Han (206 B.C.-220 A.D.) to the Ch'ing (1644-1911 A.D.), a time-span of some twenty-one centuries. While each cycle had certain peculiarities of its own, the one feature characteristic of all of them was the resurgence of the basic Confucian spirit.

Culture has, however, no meaning apart from material conditions. The preservation of the Confucian order depended largely on the lack of rapid changes in the material modes of life. For the Confucian virtues were no mere principles in abstraction but were embodied in concrete institutions and rules of conduct which could not retain their meaning and validity in vastly different circumstances. Furthermore, Confucianism emphasized education and habituation but deprecated law and compulsion. For such means to suffice as the unifying force of society, there had to be a maximum acceptance of common values by the sophisticated elite as well as by the uninitiated masses. The habituation of the latter came about by their constant exposure to the same ideals in all aspects of life. For instance, a man, whatever his station, was told from childhood to be filial to his parents as they were to theirs. He saw that the majority of other people were in fact filial. Indoctrination and exemplification were reinforced by praise and punishment. Outstanding sons and daughters received homage from the highest in the realm and became immortal in history, while the few violators were censured and ostracized. In all activities—art, drama, folklore, and popular stories—the same theme was always present. Unity of purpose led to a common outlook. In spite of great differences in the degree of sophistication, the masses understood their leaders and were able to judge them on the basis of a common heritage. This cohesiveness could not persist in the face of complex and changing modes of life, in which social groups might differ both in their interests and in their moral orientation.

To avoid rapid changes, technology and commerce were discouraged. To what degree the discouragement was designed and to what degree it merely resulted from institutional factors such as the family, which by its collectivism discouraged adventure and enterprise, need not be discussed here. That there was some hostility toward commerce and technology is abundantly clear. Under many dynasties merchants were subject to discriminatory and restrictive measures by the government. Industry, where it existed, was concentrated in the hands of the state for revenue or military purposes and, to a lesser extent, for the purpose of providing the court with luxury articles unobtainable in the market. In spite of important sparks of inventiveness in Chinese history, the general attitude toward technology seems to have been that "the artifice in making clever things would have a degrading influence on morals."[4] Agriculture was accepted as the only true form of production. Farmers produced and supported the rulers; the latter, freed from material wants, devoted themselves to the elevation of mankind. Each class thus performed the role best suited to it. The doctrine of specific function, which the Greeks also spoke of, was perhaps nowhere so completely realized as in the Confucian model.

4. CML:TFW, 32.

The exaltation of morals over politics naturally lent great influence to the scholar-moralists. While the evolution of this group was a gradual process and cannot be dated precisely, the general trend was fairly clear. Before Confucius no such group existed. In the Spring and Autumn period (722-404 B.C.) some hereditary officials seemed to have developed a humanistic attitude toward politics characteristic of the later scholars.[5] By the Warring States period a group of wandering and arguing intellectuals appeared, armed with doctrines, policies, and intrigues, seeking power and office from the feudal lords but as yet possessing no common ideology and group consciousness. By the early part of the Western Han, these had disappeared and the scholar-moralists were beginning to emerge. The main characteristic of this group was their knowledge of and belief in Confucianism. As the doctrine became more widely accepted in court circles, the scholar-moralists gradually became the ruling group in society. Broadly they acted in three capacities: as moralists, as government officials, and as gentry. To facilitate discussion, each of these will be discussed separately, although in many ways they were so interrelated as to make distinction difficult.

The Moral Function. The education of a scholar-moralist usually began at the age of four or five under private tutors. Poor children often shared a teacher with their wealthier relatives. Occasionally, they shared a teacher among themselves and paid according to their abilities. Some pupils had learned a few words at home; others started by filling out the strokes of the simplest characters printed on paper. In many cases the first textbook was the *Three Character Classic,* which in verse begins:

> A man is born with a nature that is originally good. Men's natures are very much alike; through habit they become widely different. If a person is not educated, his nature will deteriorate. The way of education needs devotion. In days of old the mother of Mencius made a [careful] selection of the neighborhood in which to live. When her son would not study she broke a rod of her weaving instrument [as a sign of despair and a warning to her son of the danger of approaching starvation]. Tou Yen-shan had the right method [of education]. He educated [his] five sons [in such a way that] all of them became famous. To bring up children without educating them is the fault of the father. If teaching is not strict, the teacher neglects his duties. A youth who does not study inflicts harm on himself. If one does not study when young, what will he do in old age? A gem

5. CM:KSHL, 65.

uncut makes no jewel; a man uneducated knows not what is right.[6]

After the *Three Character Classic* came the *Hundred Family Names,* the *Thousand Character Essay,* and the *Classic of Filial Piety.* In the case of bright students, these were often omitted in favor of the Four Books—*Confucian Analects, Mencius, The Great Learning,* and *Doctrine of the Golden Mean*—all of which were devoted to morals. These were followed by the Five Classics, of which even a somewhat rudimentary knowledge took a number of years to acquire. At the same time that these books were being read, the pupil was taught calligraphy, essay writing, and political history. In the last subject heavy emphasis was placed on the deeds of past emperors and scholar-officials and evaluation of them in the light of Confucian ethics.

In addition to these standard curricula, correct composure and mannerism were traditionally a part of learning. These as well as ascetic practices symbolized by such manual labor as cleaning the yard were particularly stressed by scholars of the Sung School. The respect due to one's elders was also taught in the form of waiting upon parents and teachers. Such teachings were sometimes known as the "Small Learning *(hsiao-hsueh),*" meaning "the base of moral cultivation."

Broadly, the object of education was two-fold: to imbue the pupil with a sense of right and wrong and to awaken in him a sense of mission toward the masses. By the nature of the system, right and wrong were merely deductions from Confucian axioms. The deeply felt sense of mission found its classical expression in the words of Fan Chung-yen: "A scholar worries over the world before the world worries over itself; he is happy only after all mankind has achieved happiness."[7] To reduce the effect of the human acquisitive instinct, the accumulation of wealth was reproved in Confucian classics. The emphasis on morals, coupled with the need to maintain stable social conditions, eliminated grounds for inculcating mechanical or scientific knowledge in the minds of youth.

When a student set out to apply his knowledge, he found the most natural outlet in government service, for it was there that he could best guide the masses and seek advancement for himself. However, there was an area of tension in this role. As a bureaucrat, a scholar owed allegiance to the prince, but as a moralist he often felt compelled to oppose him. The possibility of conflict was early recognized by Mencius, who maintained that the nobility of heaven, which was virtue, enjoyed precedence over the nobility of earth, which was rank.[8]

6. Translation based on CFT:EW, 15-16, with slight modifications of my own.
7. KWKC, 9, 138.
8. MENCIUS, 2b.2, 6a.16.

Whenever a conflict arose, Mencius contended, an official should remonstrate with his prince and, in extreme cases, rebel against him.[9] Although the doctrine was only rarely followed unreservedly, its spirit, the exaltation of morals over politics, became the essence of Confucianism.

As a defender of the faith, the scholar at times showed astounding intransigence. When Prince Yen of the Ming proclaimed himself emperor, Fang Hsiao-ju, a Han-lin scholar, not only refused to draft his accession edict but also denounced the conqueror as a usurper, knowing that in doing so he would perish by torture and cause all his relatives and pupils to die with him.[10] The causes for which scholars risked their lives were often seemingly trivial. Thus in 1879, a minor official named Wu K'o-tu took his own life because it was the only way he could hope to have a memorial presented to the throne. His point was that the Dowager Empress had erred in selecting, as heir to the throne, one of the same generation as the deceased emperor instead of one of the next generation as proper ritual demanded.[11] Such examples, which can be extended ad infinitum, indicate a basic characteristic of the scholar-moralist, a determination to defend his faith for the sake of good social order. Whether principle could be accomplished only at the risk of his life or the lives of others, or whether he was faced with a *vis major* which he could not effectively oppose, often appeared as irrelevant questions to him.

The intense moral feeling of the scholar-moralists resulted in a latent sense of sin. Since it was their mission to save mankind, imperfection in reality often brought them a sense of frustration. Self-examination and self-condemnation were rigorously pursued by all genuine Confucianists. Traditionally, in times of crisis, not only were high officials often held responsible and removed but also the throne itself issued edicts admitting its own responsibility. Even in more normal times, the dictum of Confucius was "to treat the people as if they had been wounded."[12] This basic humanitarian attitude was often combined with still another trait of the literati, namely, their love for dramatic effect and overstatement.[13] As a consequence, existing evils were often seen in greatly exaggerated dimensions, sometimes with grave political results. Although a sense of sin was shared by all Confucianists, by its nature its burdens fell on those who were

9. *Ibid.*, 1b.8, 5b.9.
10. See Fang's biography in MS.
11. HA:ECCP, 874-75.
12. MENCIUS, 4b.20.3.
13. It is on record that Tu Yen, a famous statesman in the Sung, often described existing evils in exaggerated fashion to the emperor (CKLT, 571). Cheng Hsia once submitted a painting portraying the misery of the people to the emperor under the false pretense that it was a military dispatch (CKJM, 1562). The famous poet-official Su Shih and his friends loved to indulge in hyperbole (CM:KSTK II, 427).

in power, who could and should do good but who, because of their own weaknesses, had neither resigned nor made good use of their power. The awareness of their unfulfilled mission often made government leaders sensitive to criticism and apologetic in the defense of their own position. By contrast, critics often saw in attacking the government the only righteous course to follow. Because they had no administrative and therefore little moral responsibility, they naturally tended to believe in their own superiority over those in power and felt no compunction about giving advice. The situation sometimes went so far that government activities became paralyzed. Thus, in the Sung of the eleventh century, it was said that "government ministers could do nothing but comply with the wishes of the censors."[14] When Fan Chung-yen, a man of noted ability, was prime minister, he dared not make proposals for reform, even at the urging of the throne. When finally he submitted a ten-point memorial, it was accepted by the emperor but defeated by the opposition of critical scholar-officials.[15] Essentially the same fate awaited Wang An-shih, who introduced his reform under another insistent emperor.[16] After that time similar attempts during several reigns were also unsuccessful. In the Ming of the seventeenth century, grand secretaries customarily resigned when they were attacked by the censors and literary groups outside the government.[17] In 1870, even Tseng Kuo-fan, the man who had shortly before saved the dynasty from being toppled by the Taipings, came under vitriolic attack by the literati for his handling of the Tientsin massacre. To all criticisms, Tseng's reply was a confession of remorse, and there is little ground to believe that his confession was insincere. The exaltation of morals over politics thus had unforeseen consequences. The inner sense of sin tended to lead to strong opposition and weak administration.

On the critics' part, since determined efforts often won them public acclaim and not infrequently personal gain, the moral motive became in many cases indistinguishable from ulterior purposes. In the T'ang, the famous Niu-Li feud originated from a censor's impeachment of a prime minister who was a conscientious official. Yet the stricture earned fame for the censor and served as the basis for his rise.[18] In the Sung the censors who were critical of the men in power usually became their successors in a matter of years.[19] In the late

14. TFK:CKCC, 77.

15. CM:KSTK, II, 399-401.

16. *Ibid.*, II, 402-3.

17. WTL:CKLT, 202. An interesting dialogue between Ku Hsien-ch'eng, the critic, and Wang Hsi-chüeh, the minister, ran as follows: Wang asked Ku why the people objected to all government decisions, to which Ku replied, "I only see that the government has objected to all the decisions of the people," *Ibid.*, 197-98.

18. *Ibid.*, 57-81. See also CTS, 172.122; 176.126; and HTS, 180.105; 223.148.

19. TFK:CKCC, 226.

Ming, political feuds were inextricably linked with appointments and patronage.[20] In the Ch'ing during the 1880's, the censors known as the Puritan Clique *(ch'ing-liu-tang)* caused the removal of four Board Presidents on unsubstantiated charges and themselves gained rapid promotion.[21] Even mass student demonstrations, which took place in both the Later Han and the Sung, often concerned some specific political figures, either in support or in protestation.[22] It would be rash to conclude that behind every banner of moral crusade there were ulterior purposes, yet there is no doubt that the prospect of personal gain contributed to the opposition of the literati.

Probably a related feature was the literati's tendency to disagree and disparage one another. This propensity was well-testified by many proverbs, one of which maintained that "others' wives may look more attractive, but one's own sons and writings are decidedly better." The reasons for this attitude were probably manifold. In the first place, the exalted position of the scholars made them ambitious, and since each was a potential leader, none needed to feel inferior to another. This feeling of equality was well suited to the ideological precept that all men are potentially sages. On a more practical plane, however, employment was difficult and competition intense. Frustration, or the fear of it, thus engendered envy and jealousy, which were in turn rationalized into criticism of various kinds. Under the traditional structure, this tendency toward atomization was balanced by two forces. On the ideological plane there was Confucianism; while on the political plane, rigid civil service procedure imposed orderliness in the competition for power. Even then doctrinal disagreement was at times extremely lively, and rivalry in politics intense. When both Confucianism and the civil service structure collapsed, the atomizing propensity was seriously to undermine the strength and influence of the intellectuals as a group.

Political Function. Although the Chinese emperor theoretically had absolute power, in practice it was the bureaucracy that governed the country. Since the bureaucracy wielded such extensive power, it is necessary to consider its composition in some detail. Civil servants were recruited in many ways but by the tenth century the civil service examinations had become the most important route. Continued emphasis on this particular method naturally led to a tightening of procedure. Under the Ming the examinations were divided into three categories, each consisting of a series of tests. The main test of the first series was held at the prefectural level about twice in every

20. WTL:CKLT, 171-209; CM:KSTK, II, 483-87; C. O. Hucker, "The T'ung-lin Movement of the Late Ming Period," in FJK:CTI, 132-62.

21. HA:ECCP, 48.

22. WTL:CKLT, 120, 124-25, 135, 144-47.

three years; that of the second, triennially at the provincial level; and that of the third, triennially at the capital.[23] The number of successful candidates varied from one period to another. In 1440 the court set quotas of 150 and 900 for the metropolitan and provincial examinations,[24] and a much larger, but not strictly determined, number for the prefectural examinations.[25] Later, the quotas were increased, and this liberal trend continued until by the late nineteenth century more than 300, 1,500, and 30,000 were passed at the metropolitan, provincial, and prefectural levels each time the examinations were held.[26]

The examination system has been described as a pillar of the traditional order. Of the numerous purposes it served, the most obvious was a practical and impartial means of recruiting government officials. By testing men on the basis of a clearly defined body of knowledge, the system reduced to a minimum the incidence of favoritism; and by opening officialdom to all educated men, it broadened the base of power and helped promote political stability. The extent to which the Chinese bureaucracy was open to rich and poor alike is controversial but available statistical evidence seems to affirm that the civil-service system was conducive to social mobility. Thus, an analysis by E. A. Kracke, Jr., of 931 individuals who passed the metropolitan examinations in 1148 and 1256 reveals that nearly 60 per cent lacked a family tradition of civil service, defined as the holding of office by father, grandfather, or great-grandfather.[27] Research by P'an Kuang-tan and Fei Hsiao-t'ung on 915 degree-holders during the late Manchu dynasty shows that more than 41 per cent came from rural areas and well over 30 per cent had no family tradition of civil service.[28] A detailed study by Chung-li Chang indicates that at least 35 per cent of the gentry in the nineteenth century were "newcomers," that is, neither their fathers nor grandfathers had held gentry status.[29] Using an entirely different method, Francis L. K. Hsü made a study of 7,359 prominent individuals mentioned in the gazetteers of four widely separated districts in China, and found that roughly 50 per cent of these men came from unknown origins and that roughly 80 per cent of their descendants beyond the grandson generation were also unknown. Hsü therefore concluded

23. HWHTK, 35.2.
24. CCC:CKWK, 85.
25. CCL:CG, p. 77, footnote 17.
26. *Ibid.*, 123, 124, 143.
27. E. A. Kracke, Jr., "Family vs. Merit in Chinese Civil Service Examinations Under the Empire," HJAS, X (September, 1947), 103-21.
28. "Civil Service Examinations and Social Mobility," SHKH, Vol. X, No. 1, pp. 1-21 (in Chinese).
29. CCL:CG, 214-16.

that a high degree of social mobility has existed in China during the last thousand years.[30] More recently, Ping-ti Ho studied some 30,000 successful candidates of the advanced and intermediate civil service examinations during the Ming and the Ch'ing (1368-1911), concluding that "probably more careers ran 'from rags to riches' in Ming and Ch'ing China than in modern Western societies."[31]

Assuming the accuracy of these findings, we must consider the factors that led to this high degree of social mobility. First, educational costs were low because all that was needed to pass the examinations was an intimate knowledge of the Confucian classics, which could be secured through perseverance and intelligence at little monetary cost. To be sure much time was required, but time was not a valuable item in a country where there were far fewer jobs than men. Furthermore, society provided many institutional devices to overcome the financial obstacles in the path of promising students. Because of the collective way of life, the clan, the village, and all of the relatives had much to gain from a man's rise to officialdom. Hence they were usually willing to lend a hand to a needy student and often exempted him from tuition charges or contributed to loans to finance his trips. Moreover, lower literati received aid from the government, and many received monthly stipends. All who intended to participate in higher examinations were given travel expenses and subsidies, and successful candidates were provided with further allowances. In times of famine, relief to needy literati was handled apart from the general relief to commoners.[32] In addition, students in private colleges, which were established during the Five Dynasties (907-960 A.D.) and became numerous during the Ming and Ch'ing, were often given stipends as well as cash prizes for outstanding performance, sometimes large enough even for family maintenance.[33] Thus it does not seem strange that the examination system, while confining its requirements to classical subjects, succeeded in making the Chinese political system a comparatively open one.

But to achieve political stability more was needed than social mobility. Another advantage of the examination system was its success in placing government service on a partially geographical basis through the use of geographical quotas for successful candidates at various levels. Originating in the eleventh century, this system had increasingly wider application until the Manchus established strict quotas for all three levels. The primary aim of the policy was to

30. Francis L. K. Hsü, "Social Mobility in China," ASR, XIV (November, 1949), 764-71.
31. Ping-ti Ho, "Aspects of Social Mobility in China, 1368-1911," CSSH, I (June, 1959), 330-59.
32. CCL:CG, 41-43.
33. SLH:CKSY, 1, 198-205.

assure a certain quota of officials from all regions. Within a province the less developed counties would have a number of men possessing the provincial degrees, and within the country the less developed provinces would have several metropolitan graduates. In this way all areas would be represented in the central bureaucracy, and a more balanced policy could be promoted at the national level.

Some modern scholars question the extent to which such a geographical balance in the government was realized. It is true that under both the Ming and the Ch'ing top officials were primarily men who had received high marks in the examinations, and that in this group men from a few provinces predominated because the quota system merely limited the numbers of regional groups but not their grades relative to those of men from other areas. Nevertheless, this imbalance at the top does not prove that the quota system had no effect on the bureaucracy. On the contrary, since practically all metropolitan graduates became officials, the quota system must have increased comparatively the opportunities of men from less developed regions. This situation becomes abundantly clear if we compare it with that which existed after the quota system was abolished in 1905. By the 1930's the richer provinces had practically monopolized the country's educational opportunities. Thus, in 1932, Kiangsu has 35 per cent of all Chinese college students, while Kansu had none.[34] In 1943 students from Kiangsu accounted for 20.9 per cent of all Chinese students in America,[35] while those from Kansu and Kweichow together probably numbered less than one-third of 1 per cent.[36] As those educated abroad had far better opportunities for advancement than those who had no higher education, clearly the abolition of the quota system severely reduced the chances of men from the less developed regions.

To return to our analysis of the bureaucracy, a cardinal feature of the old system was the relative strength of the scholars in regard to the monarchy. Here the common impression of Western observers that the Chinese emperor was a despot with unlimited power over his ministers is clearly wrong. In fact, it is more correct to characterize the average ruler as an isolated, helpless man very much at the mercy of his ministers. As the recent memoirs of the last emperor of China, Aisin Gioro P'u I, vividly show, the emperor was a very lonely man. He was confined to the palace and had no contact with the outside world. If he were a minor, he was not allowed to see his elders for more than a few minutes each day.[37] For the rest of the time he was in the company of either the eunuchs or his tutors. Here the tradition

34. KYC:GHE, Tables 96-99.
35. WYC:CIW, 410.
36. SURVEY, 33.
37. PI:WTC, I, 21, 55.

of a reigning house could make a sharp difference in the emperor's inclinations. If, as during the Ming, education were not emphasized in the training of a ruler, he would remain with the eunuchs and shun the scholars. If, as during the Ch'ing, education were stressed, the emperor would lean heavily on his tutors for advice, since they were virtually his sole source of information. Even in such a case, however, the substance of their communications was likely to be limited. By force of circumstances the scholars would stress only two themes—that the emperor occupied a unique position in the realm and that he had a moral duty toward his subjects. The emphasis could be carried so far that scarcely any other impression was left on the pupil's mind: according to P'u I, he did not even know the location of Peking or the origin of rice, the staple food of China.[38] Obviously, such a man was in no position to exercise power but had to rely on others for guidance.

In contrast, the literati generally came from the people and knew their living conditions. While direct information is meager, circumstantial evidence points clearly to a fairly close relationship between the scholars and the peasants. Thus a survey by Fei Hsiao-t'ung and P'an Kuang-tan of 758 *chin-shih* (metropolitan graduates) in the second half of the nineteenth century showed that 52.5 per cent resided in cities, 6.34 per cent in towns, and 41.16 per cent in rural areas.[39] Clearly, the literati were closer to the peasants than the emperors could be. Furthermore, farming was by tradition a respected occupation in Chinese society. Many men, after rising to officialdom, still insisted that their families not give up farming and continue to lead a simple, frugal life at home, in conformity with the ideal of an "honorable family of farming-study tradition *(keng-tu ch'uan-chia)*." Confucian ideals as well as legal restrictions forbade officials to engage in industry and commerce. While these injunctions were often surreptitiously violated, the general tendency was for an official to invest his earnings in land, usually on a scale that assured him of some contact with the actual cultivators. Thus by their choice of residence, their relative exaltation of farming, and their tendency to become landowners, the literati were usually fairly well acquainted with conditions at the grass-roots level. On top of all this, they were the most widely traveled men in the realm. By reason of the rule that a man could not hold office in his own province nor remain in one post for too long a time, the officials frequently traveled from one place to another. They also attended examinations in different cities, and, in addition, they returned home when mourning for their parents.

38. *Ibid.,* 59-60.
39. SHKH, Vol. IV, No. 1, p. 8.

They knew the country at first hand and could therefore handle state affairs better than their royal masters.

As part of the design to maintain their position in society, the scholars were entitled by tradition to certain privileges. A graduate of the prefectural examinations was addressed by special titles, wore distinct garments, enjoyed a degree of legal immunity, and was exempt from certain taxes.[40] Such privileges became greater as a man passed the provincial examinations. Even those metropolitan graduates with the lowest grades became county magistrates or prefectural directors of studies, while those with higher ones served as secretaries to various boards. Those with the highest grades were admitted to the Han-lin Academy, where they would undergo another test in three years' time. The most brilliant younger scholars were then retained at the academy. After a few tours of duty as provincial director of studies, they would rise to such important posts as provincial governorships or vice-presidencies of administrative boards.[41] By tradition only they could become the highest officials of the land, the grand secretaries of the Ming and Ch'ing era.

To a large extent the promotion of officials was independent of the royal will. At least during the Ming, personnel matters were the exclusive concern of the Board of Civil Office. Regular promotion took place according to a detailed merit-rating system, and extra promotion depended largely on the higher officials, who were required to make specific recommendations from time to time. Appointments below the fifth rank were as a rule made by the Board, while those above were subject to a special consultative process: grand secretaries, presidents of board, and governors were named by a conference of senior court officials *(t'ing-t'ui)*; vice-presidents of boards and provincial administrative commissioners, by consultation between the Board and the third-rank officials and above; lesser posts, by appropriate procedures of a similar nature.[42] Officials who received appointments by special edicts bore a stigma and seldom survived the continual attacks of their colleagues.[43] Such institutional devices vividly demonstrate the independence of the scholar-official group.

A further evidence of their strength lies in the history of the office of prime minister. As early as the Han it was recorded that "the emperor would descend from his chariot when passing the prime minister, and leave the throne when he came into the room."[44] During the T'ang, imperial decrees were issued by the ministers in the

40. CCL:CG, 32-42.
41. CM:CKLT, I, 96.
42. CCC:CKWK, 192-93.
43. MS, 240.26b.
44. TFK:CKCC, 47.

emperor's name, while personal edicts were written in a different form and carried less weight.[45] This tradition of ministerial responsibility was resented by later emperors, and repeated attempts were made to curtail it. At the beginning of the Sung, the ministers were deprived of their seats in the imperial presence;[46] but even this strategem failed to produce substantial political results, for, throughout the Sung, the personal edicts of the emperor were strongly criticized as improper.[47] Consistent with the trend toward centralization of power, the first emperor of the Ming abolished the office of prime minister and re-placed it with a Secretariat *(Nei-ko)*. Originally given only a clerical function, this office in a matter of decades regained practically all the powers that had belonged to earlier prime ministers. It composed imperial edicts and made recommendations on policy matters. Even more striking, remonstration with the emperor became an important part of its duties. While a few members rebuked the emperor in only a perfunctory way many went beyond the common bounds of decency and became positively insulting.

In order to clarify the position of these men, I have surveyed 118 grand secretaries who held office between 1403 and 1628,[48] e.g., all those who served the Ming emperors except for the first and last, whose reigns were too unsettled to give us a view of the normal func-tioning of the bureaucracy. The average tenure of these 118 men was 7.6 years, and a breakdown of their reasons for leaving office shows: natural death, 30; retirement because of illness or old age, 34; resigna-tion as a result of feuds with colleagues, 13; resignation or dismissal because of troubles with eunuchs, 13; resignation in protest to royal misbehavior, 3; killed in action, 2; dismissal for involvement in struggles between two emperors, 3; resignation demanded by the emperor, 4; miscellaneous (including unknown), 16. The large number of deaths in office suggests a lasting tenure, while the small number or resignations demanded by the emperor (always by subtle hints rather than open threats) can only mean the relative weakness of the court. Looking at the matter in another way, only one of the 118 was executed while still in office, for siding with a deposed emperor; two others lost their lives after retiring as a result of plots masterminded by enemies within the bureaucracy; and seven others suffered punishment after leaving office for various offenses, trumped up by their bureaucratic enemies. As far as is known, none of the other 108 men encountered any serious trouble after leaving office. On the other hand, by protocol most of them were bestowed high

45. CM:CKLT, 32-33.
46. LT:STT, 70-71.
47. TFK: CKCC, 59.
48. The list is taken from SCT:CM, chüan 23.

honors even though they had not been popular with the court or their colleagues. In spite of the cursory nature of this survey, the general situation is clearly one of great bureaucratic strength and little imperial power.

Another device that was apparently designed to curb royal caprices was the censorial system. Like many others, this arrangement became institutionalized during the Han.[49] The general principle was that a censor should be young in age, low in rank, and aggressive in spirit. On the one hand, he was required to find fault with the court and the officials, while on the other, totally unsubstantiated charges could lead to his own dismissal. With the support of many dynasties the system developed into an essential feature of Chinese politics. Significantly, as the bureaucracy became larger and more complex, the censorate tended to concentrate more on the ministers than on the emperor. By the Sung and the Ming, the censors were so powerful that they influenced not only policies but also the tenure of prime ministers and grand secretaries.[50] During the Ming each censor was given authority over matters pertaining to a specific government board. All edicts relating to that board passed through his hands, and he virtually had the power of veto *(k'o-ts'an)*. Since most of these edicts represented the decisions of the board, the censor influenced both the throne and the board.[51] In one case the censor in charge of military matters actually supervised a campaign and interfered with the military command. Toward the end of the dynasty, a key issue was the question of whom to fight first, the rebels or the Manchus. At the suggestion of the Board of War, the court decided to concentrate on the rebels, but the court was then opposed by the censors and as usual yielded to their insistence. The immediate result was a rapid deterioration in the military situation which hastened the downfall of the dynasty.[52]

Clearly, in spite of the fiction of the emperor's omnipotence, the Chinese system was normally a government of bureaucrats. That the mechanism worked fairly well is illustrated by the long imperial era, but like all other schemes, it had serious drawbacks. The critical moment was to arrive in the nineteenth century when China was confronted by Western power. At this juncture the underlying weaknesses of the system came to the surface, and China floundered helplessly before the rising tide of Western imperialism.

The Functions of the Gentry. The traditional political theory had many implications. One of these bore directly upon the scope of

49. CCC:CKWK, 225-26.
50. TFK:CKCC, 77.
51. CM:CKLT, 78; CCC:CKWK, 235.
52. CM:CKLT, 110.

government. Since the essence of politics lay in teaching the masses and directing them to the righteous path, the personal behavior of the ruler was more important than his administrative actions. In fact, the more the masses were elevated, the less was the need for government. Hence the expansion of government activities was always an ominous sign that the ideal had not been achieved. Furthermore, in the tradition of Han philosophy, natural elements were held to echo human behavior. Harmony among men extended to harmony between mankind and nature. Amid the abundance of moral good, natural calamities could not occur; on the other hand, the occurrence of such events indicated a grave failing in the morals of the rulers. Thus, visible government beyond a certain minimum was unnecessary in good times and inept in evil times.

The restriction of government activities went hand in hand with a limitation in the number of officials dealing directly with the masses. The authority of the central power stopped at the county *(hsien)* level. The power of the magistrate was extensive, but his tenure short—averaging less than two years in the nineteenth century[53]—and his staff small. Thus the potentiality of the magisterial function was limited. In a negative sense the system was beneficial to the illiterate masses who in any contact with the government were likely to be exploited by the petty bureaucrats. Yet at the same time there had to be some organ to take charge of the necessary communal activities. Consequently, below the county level, the literati residing in the district led the peasants.

The functions of these men, whom we may call the gentry for want of a better term, were not related to the ownership of land. As in the case of the bureaucrats, leadership was justified on the basis of morals and scholarship. Generally speaking, the gentry were either retired officials or men qualified to become officials. In the latter case, the status of a gentry member corresponded closely to the degree he held. A *sheng-yüan,* or prefectural graduate, would function within his own county, a *chü-jen* (provincial graduate) within his prefecture, and a *chin-shih* (metropolitan graduate) within his province. The residence of a gentry member was an indication of his status; a minor one usually lived in his own village, and a major one in the provincial capital. Because of the geographical quotas of all civil service examinations, the gentry resided everywhere and played an integral role in community life.

The functions of the gentry were varied. They organized schools, raised funds to subsidize worthy students, and promoted the maintenance of Confucian temples and examination halls. They compiled local gazetteers and were often requested by the government to

53. CCL:CG, Table 2.

expound politico-moral maxims to the masses. They initiated famine relief, arbitrated in civil disputes, encouraged the building and repairing of dikes and dams, roads and bridges; and they organized associations in provincial and national capitals to further the interests of their traveling townsmen. They helped in the collection of taxes and often took charge of local defense.[54] The famous Taiping rebellion of 1850-65 was crushed not by regular government forces, who were routed by the rebels, but by forces organized by the gentry, who received government support but who retained command throughout the campaign.

Because they had excellent connections with the official hierarchy and yet occupied no formal status, the gentry formed a pressure group par excellence. They functioned to protect the local populace against government exactions. If the magistrate sent an order to a village levying special taxes or demanding labor services, the local headman, often a minor gentryman co-opted by his peers, would announce the order in the village teashop and discuss it with all concerned. The opinion of the gentry in particular would be ascertained and a decision reached as to whether the order should be followed. If the decision was not to accept it, a process of lobbying would be initiated immediately. The elders of the village would call on the magistrate, or appeal to someone of high standing to intervene. Pressure from local interests was seldom without effect, for even high provincial officials feared the gentry, who had good connections in court circles and might find the means of ousting officials they intensely disliked.[55]

As members of the literary hierarchy, the gentry had definite privileges. They were the social equals of local officials, and special forms of hat buttons and garments distinguished them, along with the officials, from the commoners. Only the gentry could participate in certain official ceremonies. When clans observed ancestral rituals, the gentry among them were specially honored. The gentry were exempt from labor conscription and from payment of head tax. They were also immune to corporal punishment as long as they were not officially deprived of their examination degrees. They could not be involved by commoners as witnesses in law suits. When they themselves were party to litigation, they were not required to attend the trial but could be represented by their servants.[56]

These privileges naturally led to abuses. The most common were evasion of the land tax, obstruction of payment of such taxes by others and pocketing what should have been handed over to government, aid to others in avoiding labor service, division with officials of

54. *Ibid.*, 51-70.
55. Hsiao-t'ung Fei, "Peasantry and Gentry," *AJS* (July, 1946), 1-17.
56. CCL:CG, 32-42.

the spoils of public projects, and infringement upon the judicial authority of the government.[57] In so far as they occurred, abuses were at the expense of the government and involved no naked exploitation of the masses. It is true that the evasion of taxes could result in increasing the burdens of the peasants who did pay; but in Chinese public finance the rule was not to tax according to budgeted expenditure figures, but rather to spend what had been received, except perhaps in time of war and major crises. Tax rates remained unchanged for centuries.[58] Although county magistrates were required to turn in so much revenue each year, the quota was somewhat elastic. Thus evasion by one did not necessarily increase the burden of another. Moreover, if the best government was the least, why should anything more than the unavoidable minimum be paid into the public purse? In the same light perhaps can be explained the gentry's effort to help others evade labor service. The tendency for the gentry to interfere with litigation appeared even more natural. In the traditional system contentiousness was always discouraged; no civil code in the Western sense was developed; and litigation was known to be a ruinous course for all parties, mainly because of the corruptible nature of the underclerks and runners through whose hands all litigants must pass. Hence arbitration by the gentry was by far the preferred method. Once this became the accepted practice, the line of demarcation between judicious proceedings and improper infringement of authority became a matter of moral judgment. Some overstepping perhaps was to be expected.

Granted the fact that rulers were economically supported by those they ruled in Confucian society, the role of the gentry seemed on the whole highly beneficial to the masses.[59] The question is, then, what sustained the gentry-peasantry relationship?

It seems that in addition to the sense of mission inculcated by Confucianism, institutional forces were at work. Chief among these was the high degree of social mobility that resulted from the examination system. The idea of an aristocracy of merit was very old. In the fourth century B.C., Mencius once mentioned six statesmen of ancient times, all of whom had come from humble origins, one rising from "among the channeled fields," one from "the midst of his building frames," one from "his fish and salt," one from "the hands of his jailor," one from "his hiding by the seashore," and still another from "the market place."[60] By the T'ang, the examination system had entrenched the aristocracy of merit more deeply than ever before. Among others, Wang Po, a commoner who rose to be prime minister,

57. *Ibid.*, 43-51.
58. CM:KSHL, 57.
59. Fei Hsiao-t'ung, *op. cit.*, 7-10.
60. MENCIUS, 6b.15.1.

had lived on the charity of a monastery whose monks were so disgusted with him that they sounded their dinner bell only after they had eaten.[61] Fan Chung-yen, in the Sung, had lodged free in a monastery and had barely kept himself alive on lean rations of rice-porridge.[62] In later eras the statistical analyses of scholars cited earlier reveal a high proportion of men of humble origin among the degree-holders, who in all probability had come from peasant stock. After an official's death, his descendants might, for lack of literary talents, revert to peasant status after a generation or two.[63] Thus there was a two-way safety valve between the elite and the peasants which could not fail to promote understanding and sympathy, even though the gentry did not derive their power from the masses.

The gentry-peasantry structure was sustained by still other factors. One was the sedentary nature of Chinese life which, by severely restricting geographical mobility, promoted men's attachment to their native areas. It was not unusual, particularly among the well-to-do, for a family to have been in the same area for centuries. Although functionaries did not hold office in their home provinces, their absence in no way decreased their attachment. There were specified occasions on which they would return and stay for years. After decades of public life an official almost invariably retired to his place of birth. In fact, to return in official garments and be bathed in glory was traditionally regarded as one of the main motives for entering officialdom.[64] This eagerness for public praise of course tended to reduce any motive for exploiting the masses in one's native area. On the contrary, it often led the more enlightened gentry to view their own interests within the compass of communal well-being. Cases were not unknown where a single man was responsible for the development and prosperity of a whole area. The last and best known was Chang Ch'ien of Nan-t'ung in the early twentieth century.[65]

Another factor was the frugal life that most Chinese lived, regardless of their station. Occasional legends of luxurious lives merely proved the exception to the rule. With technology, industry, and commerce discouraged, and the acquisitive instinct of man reduced to a minimum, the material amenities of life were largely absent. The decentralized cellular form of Chinese economy meant that life in the city and in the country differed relatively little. As a consequence, not only did the city and the rural dwellers understand each other but to move from a large city to a town involved

61. CKJM, 145.
62. SS, 314.73.
63. CM:KSHL, 132-33.
64. Ou-yang Hsiu, "Notes on Chou-Chin Hall," KWKC, *chüan* 10.
65. CHJ:NTCC, *passim.*

no basic change in living habits. Only thus could an urban-rural flow be maintained. Unless this condition continued, the officials would tend to settle down in large cities, the vitality of rural life would be sapped, and the geographical quotas of the examination system would lose their meaning.

Still another factor was the paramount importance of the family. The continuity of the family line extended the tie into another dimension. As Tocqueville puts it: "All generations, as it were, become contemporaneous." The individual willingly imposed duties on himself and often sacrificed his personal desires either to his ancestors or to his descendants. In the best tradition, the most filial act a man could perform, and the most precious legacy he could provide his descendants, was not to accumulate great wealth but to make his name an immortal symbol of virtue. Compared to such an achievement, even the perpetuation of the family line was secondary in importance. On the other hand, descendants of an infamous man were shunned by society, and in order to live a normal life, they had to disown their ancestry. In such circumstances, virtue and respectability often appeared more practical than wealth to those mindful of their posterity. Actually in China's long history there seem to have been few cases where wealth was perpetuated in a family beyond two or three generations, while the names of illustrious ancestors were known by their descendants at all times. Thus one's duty toward his family acted as a powerful safeguard against unscrupulous acts of the gentry. When traditional family life crumbled under Western impact, one of the chief pillars of Chinese society disappeared.

ON THE EVE OF CHANGE

Although effective under certain conditions, the Chinese social structure was not without serious shortcomings. These will become clear as we analyze the role of the scholar class more closely. Of the three levels of society—the emperor, the scholars, and the masses—the scholars were by far the most important, for it was they who circumvented the power above and directed the masses below. Yet their position and usefulness were derived solely from Confucianism and the social order that developed from it. To begin with, they could not possibly check the imperial power except by acting as defenders of the faith. Similarly, Confucian thought influenced their relationship with the masses in two ways. On the one hand, it provided a basis for their role as shepherds; and on the other, by restraining their acquisitive instincts, it strengthened their position among the masses. Finally, the ability of a scholar to serve in a variety of capacities—as lawyer, engineer, or militarist—depended strictly on the maintenance of the Confucian order. If material conditions of life became less simple, or social changes more rapid, intelligence alone would no longer qualify a man for all positions. The need for specialized training would arise, and the type of universal leader would disappear. Thus, it is probably correct to say that Confucianism shaped the social existence of the scholar.

The very fact that a single force should mold a social group and indirectly a whole society necessarily has important ramifications. In the first place, a change in the composition of this force, however slight, was likely to have a great social impact, and the collapse of this force would almost certainly lead to social disintegration. Second, for such a scheme to function, one system of values must be exalted above all others. It is true that Chinese traditional thought was not merely the philosophy of Confucius, or even the theories of Confucian scholars, but a synthesis of Confucianism, Taoism, Legalism, and, later, Buddhism—with a sprinkling of still other theories, such as Mohism and the Yin-Yang astrological beliefs. Nevertheless, the process of syncretization had gone on since the Han. By the Sung a relatively homogeneous tradition had emerged, and by the Ming and Ch'ing it had become rigid and intolerant, replete with an extensive set of rules for human behavior on all occasions.

The sanctification of one scheme of values had ominous social consequences. While providing man with a maximum feeling of security, it precluded a sense of objectivity from his habits of thought. Right and wrong were deducted from a priori concepts, and facts, in order to be accepted, had to conform to established values. In a limited sense, the Sinitic universe was not unlike the modern Marxist-Leninist system: nothing could be neutral in life. Any event, any activity was either conducive to the given ends and therefore good, or contrary to the values of society and therefore bad. In the absence of relativity and objectivity, strong ethnocentric feelings developed, and no attempt was made to study and learn from other civilizations.

The belief that their faith was ultimate truth and the acceptance of allegorical legends as proofs of attainment committed the Chinese scholars to the position that no progress was possible beyond revival, and that degeneration inevitably resulted from deviation. As a result, Siniticism (the so-called Confucianism) acquired a conservative element perhaps in spite of its own intention. Thus Chinese scholars were deeply suspicious of and hostile to all innovations, even those couched in revival terms. The few reformers among them were always condemned as evil-doers in the histories composed by orthodox classicists.

Another characteristic of the highly integrated Chinese ethos was the stress laid on symbolism, which covered the wide spectrum from the practice of rituals to the use of words expressing judgment where mere factual descriptions might suffice (e.g., the habit of calling a rebel chief "thief" [*tse*] or "bandit" [*fei*]). One drawback of this excessive reliance on symbolism was a drift toward hypocrisy. In the end, outward appearance became more important than inner content; so long as the former was preserved, the latter was left unexamined. The discrepancy between theory and practice in turn paralyzed social organization and deprived it of its capacity to adjust to external stimulation.

Still another attribute of an integral ethos was the unity of religion and politics. In the case of China, Siniticism was eminently pragmatic. The scholar-moralist was not interested in life beyond this world. Rather his religious fervor was directed toward the realization of a Utopia on this earth in accordance with his preconceived values and plans for action. As long as these remained workable, they offered a similar kind of consolation and protection as other religions. But once a change in circumstances rendered these schemes and values inoperative, not only political chaos but also social and psychological collapse would ensue. For the purpose of adaptation to new conditions, such a system was far less effective than a polycentric scheme with ethics, religion, and politics separated into different compartments.

Still another feature of the Chinese ethos was the absence of any nationalistic concept. This peculiarity seems to have resulted from the postulation of Siniticism as the ultimate truth and from the Sinitic position that political order was merely a reflection of more basic social and ethical orders. If Chinese values were ultimate, then any society that embraced them was by definition at the peak of human ingenuity. The only problem was how China could best spread the gospel and share her beneficence with other peoples. The relationship between China and other societies was exactly like that which existed between Chinese scholars and the masses. Neither race nor political unity was important. If the primary social units were the family and the neighborhood, the most encompassing one was the world. It was in such a spirit that from the sixteenth to the early eighteenth century, merchants from Portugal and later from England were received and granted trade concessions, even though, in the words of a Manchu emperor, China had never set much store by strange objects or had any need for foreign manufactures.[66]

At a more practical level, one of the most important consequences of Siniticism was the absence of science and technology. While it is impossible to venture here into the history of science, several generalizations may perhaps be made. One of the most basic conditions for the growth of science is an interest in nature, and intellectual curiosity

66. TSY:CRW, 19; MHF:MCH, 405.

that has no immediate utilitarian motives behind it. With their excessive concern for human relations, the Chinese seemed to have developed little such curiosity. To their minds, the result was far more important than the process by which it was achieved. Perhaps this mentality explained the curious fact that in spite of their early and brilliant achievements in mathematics the Chinese never "spontaneously invented any symbolic way of writing formulae" but wrote their mathematical statements in characters without the use of an equals sign.[67] Even worse was the Chinese tendency, as earlier indicated, to rule out neutrality and classify all things into the two categories of good and evil. This characteristic clearly indicated their lack of objectivity, and without such an attitude no science could develop. That China's weakness in science was related to her pervasive sense of values is suggested by the periods of Chinese mathematical achievements. In this regard we may observe that the two periods especially known for mathematical achievements were the Han and Sung,[68] the eras when the so-called Confucianism and Neo-Confucianism were on their way to dominance after a period of competition with other schools; whereas the Ming, a period of intolerance under the full sway of Neo-Confucianism, witnessed the low ebb of Chinese science. Thus it is quite possible that scientific developments were closely related to the value orientations of Chinese society and that intellectual fermentation, even of a limited nature, was conducive to scientific developments.

Another result of China's pervasive sense of values was the lack of technological progress. That this lag followed from limited scientific development is quite obvious, but there are reasons to believe that Chinese policy-makers purposely discouraged technology. A notable example was the water-mill, which was invented in the third century and became widespread by the eighth. But instead of benefiting the peasants, it seriously threatened their livelihood because its owners, all men of means, claimed exclusive use of the streams. On the grounds that social harmony was infinitely more important than increased productivity, the government stepped in and ordered the destruction of the mills.[69]

Still another argument against technology was the belief that such artifices had a degrading influence on morals. While the exact reasoning behind this feeling is not clear, the prejudice was probably based on the traditional anti-commercial stand. From the Han to our own times, Chinese merchants were always of low social status and often suffered severe legal discrimination. The perennial opposi-

67. NJ:SCC, III, 152.
68. *Ibid.*, 153.
69. Wu Han, "The Use of Water-Power in Medieval Times," CKCS, Vol. VI, No. 1. For a more technical discussion of the water-mill, see LKP:CKKH, 170-85.

tion to this group had a deep root in traditional thought, which held that men should think of others first and themselves last and that moral cultivation was far more important than material pursuits. By these standards merchants were evil-doers who pursued their own interests at the expense of their fellow men. Because technological knowledge was usually sought by merchant-venturers who were seeking inordinate profits, it too became suspect and was rejected in the interests of social stability.

Anti-commercialism not only discouraged technology but also produced important social effects. By turning talents away from industry and commerce, it limited the potentiality of both men and enterprise. The poor regard accorded commerce was such that even when a firm—a pawnshop, for instance—was actually owned by an official, he could not manage it openly but had to entrust it to someone of much lower social status. Such limitations could not but reduce the range of possible expansion. Furthermore, the social atmosphere caused most scholars to avoid all types of association with artisans. This gulf further reduced the chances of technological advance and indirectly contributed to China's military weakness. At the same time, by limiting their thought to abstract topics, the literati lost their ability to pursue "the investigation of things" in any meaningful way. A striking example of this failure was the famous experiment conducted by Wang Yang-ming (1472-1528) and a friend. Wishing to study the principle behind the growth of bamboo, Wang's friend sat before the plant and gazed intently at it. After three days of unswerving concentration, he learned nothing but became quite ill. Blaming his friend for insufficient perseverance, Wang then took over and began his vigil. After seven days of unrelenting labor he too became ill, whereupon he decided that knowledge must be gained through intuition rather than investigation and experimentation.[70]

A somewhat different result of anti-commercialism was the confinement of talented men to government service. At first this occurred presumably by design; later, after printing popularized learning, it became a more serious problem. From then on employment difficulties always plagued the literati because their numbers perennially exceeded the available bureaucratic posts. Thus no less than 120,000 men were qualified for 18,805 regular government posts at the beginning of the ninth century,[71] and more than a million degree-holders competed for 20,000 government posts at various times during the latter part of the nineteenth century.[72] It is true that the number of posts did not include such employments as teaching, gentry

70. FYL:HCP, II, 597n.
71. TT, 15.3.85.
72. CCL:CG, 116, 138.

service, and supernumerary government assistants, which were probably many times greater. But the fact remains that the more desirable posts were so few that jockeying for positions became extremely important to men who were not supposed to be concerned with mundane considerations. Among the results that followed was the outbreak of factional conflicts, which became a prominent feature of Sung and Ming politics. Although it would be incorrect to describe these fights as struggles for position alone, there can be no doubt that personal gain was a powerful contributory factor. Furthermore, because efforts to pursue material goals violated moral precepts, there was a tendency to seek psychological subterfuges and to sweep the seamier side of life under the carpet, with the consequence that such efforts became more underhanded than ever.

Another result of employment difficulties was the tendency to increase the number of employed by reducing the salary paid to each. Thus in the early part of the sixteenth century no less than 20,000 civil servants, 55,000 government clerks, 35,800 students, 100,000 army officers, and 896,000 soldiers were kept on the government payroll, all at salaries below that required for subsistence living.[73] As a consequence, corruption became an accepted fact in society, and the morals of the Confucian order were openly violated while they were nominally exalted. Yet in spite of such infractions, the literati owed their status to the Confucian faith and were psychologically unprepared to admit the validity of other value systems. Indeed, they could scarcely do so without at the same time renouncing their own position. Thus, instead of being a crusading force, Confucianism became a protective shield for entrenched interests.

A similar ambivalence existed in the scholar's relationship with the masses. Originally, Confucianism insisted that the scholars should teach the masses so that they could be elevated to a higher moral level. In actual fact, the teaching that was done took the form of moral exhortations having little to do with the mastery of the language or the technique of passing examinations. Consequently, beyond a general understanding of the basic Confucian virtues, the masses had little means of broadening their knowledge. To be sure, they could study the classics and join the gentry by means of the examination route. But this required more perseverance and will power than most people had. For the great majority, the exaltation of Confucianism and the sanctification of the difficult classics certainly did not help to make knowledge any more accessible. As long as the old order remained intact, no basic change in the institutional framework of learning—the language medium, for instance—was likely to

73. CM:KSTK, II, 504. For a list of Ming officials' salary scale, see PHW: CKHPS, 466.

occur. Thus, the very success of Confucianism tended to produce results contrary to its own ideals.

So far my discussion has mainly been confined to the period before the rise of the Manchu regime. What effects did this alien dynasty introduce into our picture? A preliminary question is the degree to which the Manchus assimilated Chinese culture. Controversies have long been waged on this point, with one school maintaining that the Manchus became culturally well assimilated and another school arguing just the opposite. The truth is that the Manchu reigning house demonstrated two contrasting tendencies in their behavior. On the one hand, it was conscious of its alien origin and jealous of its prerogatives. Under its rule, high court officials were reduced to servility; the consultative process of appointment was abolished; the censorial functions were weakened; and the literati were discouraged from commenting on current affairs. Chinese suffered discrimination, and officials of even the highest rank were sometimes openly insulted by their Manchu colleagues.[74] Worse still, severe punishments were imposed on the scholar-gentry group whenever occasion arose, particularly in the South. In 1657 seven officials were executed in Peking for irregularities in the provincial civil service examinations and nineteen more in Nanking on the same charge.[75] In 1661 eighteen literati lost their lives merely for complaining about the harsh acts of the magistrate of Soochow, and 18,000 persons suffered various degrees of punishment for tax evasions, some as little as a penny.[76] In 1663 the first of a series of literary inquisitions resulted in the death of 221 persons.[77] It is easy to see that all of these practices violated the spirit of Confucianism and undermined the strength of Chinese society.

On the other hand, the Manchu monarchs were in many ways the most Confucian of all the rulers in Chinese history. In the first place, they not only patronized learning but also pursued it themselves. According to an eyewitness account, the royal princes regularly studied Chinese from dawn until three o'clock in the afternoon and devoted the rest of their day to archery, cavalry, and Manchu studies.[78] Practically all of the emperors had their own printed works of prose and poetry. Even if the authorship of these works is doubtful, they still bear eloquent witness to the importance attached by the dynasty to learning. Life within the palace was, by comparison with other dynasties, frugal, and few problems occurred in connection with eunuchs or members of the families of consorts. In the economic

74. HTS:CKCT, I, 523.
75. SYL:CTKC, 301-4.
76. JKS:CY, I, 204; HIS:CTTS, I, 427.
77. HTS:CK, I, 78.
78. LIC:CK, III, 88-89.

realm the Manchus pursued the strikingly Sinitic policy of favoring agriculture and discouraging industry and commerce. While the tax burdens of the farmers were extremely light, industrial and commercial activities were severely hampered by exactions and restrictions.[79]

In social policy, too, the regime aimed at promoting equality. In 1723 an edict bestowed commoners' rights on a large number of "mean people"—notably the "beggars" of Kiangsu, the "boatmen" of Kwangtung, the "hereditary servants" of Anhwei, and the "singers" of Chekiang.[80] Most characteristic of all, the Manchu monarchs always thought of China as the Middle Kingdom and all foreigners as barbarians. This attitude finds ample expression in both the communication of Ch'ien-lung to King George III in 1793 and the erratic, almost irrational, behavior of Hsien-feng during the wars with England and France of 1856-60.[81] Thus, using Confucianism to support the monarchy, the Manchu rulers themselves fell victim to some of its less wholesome influences.

The over-all effects on the literati of the contradictory dynastic policies is more difficult to assess. Politically, their role remained largely unchanged, even though their power was radically curtailed. As a result of their unique position in society, they continued to serve as teachers, bureaucrats, and local gentry leaders, professing altruistic ideals but enjoying considerable economic privileges. Intellectually, however, a new movement took place in the seventeenth century. For various reasons leading scholars of the time began to approach the classics in a more detached manner. Using the inductive method of assembling evidence from the broadest range of materials and testing against certain hypotheses, these scholars initiated a revolution in Chinese scholarship. Many examples can be cited. The most notable is probably the achievement of Yen Jo-chü (1636-1704). By textual analysis as well as historical reasoning, Yen proved that certain parts of the *Classic of Documents,* which had generally been accepted for over a thousand years, were forgeries by a man in the fourth century.[82]

Furthermore, even though it continued to emphasize the classics, the new scholarship was not confined solely to them. Distinct new approaches could be found in such fields as physics, medicine, phonetics, mechanics, geography, astronomy, and mathematics. Progress in the last was particularly noteworthy and had a discernible pattern. A brief survey reveals three periods: a formative one from 1610 to 1640, in which Hsü Kuang-ch'i (1562-1633) and Li Chih-tsao (d.

79. *Ibid.,* 72-74; SY:CK, 386-88.
80. HIS:CTTS, I, 866-67.
81. FWL:CK, I, 193-96.
82. LCC:YPSCC, 17.75.68-70.

1630) published mathematical texts under the direction of Jesuits; a period of maturation from 1640 to 1820, in which Mei Wen-ting (1632-1721), Mei Ku-ch'eng (d. 1763), Tai Chen (1724-1777), and Chiao Hsün (1763-1820) recovered many Chinese texts and sought a synthesis with Western techniques; and a high period between 1820 and 1901, in which further progress was made despite China's falling further and further behind the West. Several specific events can be cited to illustrate the general development. In 1774 a work appeared under the name of Ming An-t'u, which gave several formulae on analytical circle-measurement and is "highly deserving in the mathematical history of the Chinese."[83] In 1846 a book by Li Shan-lan (1810-1882) on the principles of logarithms was described by Alexander Wylie as a work that would have been sufficient to raise the author to distinction "in the days of Briggs and Napier."[84] Around 1854 a work on logarithmic calculations by Tai Hsü (1805-1860) so intrigued the English mathematician Joseph Edkins that he not only sought an interview with the author but also published a translation of the work in an English journal.[85]

Aside from its continuous growth, Chinese mathematics was also marked by an intimate connection with classical studies. During the eighteenth century practically all the classicists knew mathematics, and a few of them, notably Tai Chen and Chiao Hsün, were outstanding mathematicians. Partly because of their dual interests these scholars devoted much of their efforts to the recovery of lost Chinese mathematical texts, thus accentuating the revival tendency of eighteenth-century Chinese scholarship. On the other hand, toward the end of that era a group of men appeared whose life interests were concentrated on mathematics.[86] This trend continued into the nineteenth century and attracted not only such men as Li Shan-lan but also a son of Tseng Kuo-fan and a nephew of Tso Tsung-t'ang.[87] In one significant respect these specialists were quite unlike the scholar-moralists: they were willing to associate with, or even play the role of, artisans. An example was Hsü Chien-yin (1845-1901), a mathematician and chemist who sacrificed his life in carrying out a chemical experiment.[88]

Before we can examine the nature of the impact of this remarkable reorientation of Chinese scholarship, it is necessary to inquire into the causes of the movement. The earliest was undoubtedly the arrival of Europeans in the sixteenth century. In the wake of the merchants

83. MY:DMCJ, 149.
84. WA:CR, 194.
85. MY:DMCJ, 128.
86. LCC:YPSCC, 17.75.344.
87. Ibid., 17.75.346.
88. CWHK, 52.5b-8a.

came Jesuit priests. The most notable among them, Matteo Ricci (1552-1610), reached Macao in 1582. First garbed in the robes of a Buddhist monk and later in the dress of a Confucian scholar, Ricci sought to spread religion by way of scientific knowledge.[89] He especially impressed the Chinese with his grasp of mathematics and geography, while his associates imported clocks, gauges, glass prisms, and astronomical and musical instruments. By accommodating themselves to Chinese customs, notably in such matters as ancestral worship, the Jesuits made good progress in their main goal, proselytization. The number of converts increased from one in 1583 to 100 in 1596, 2,000 in 1608 and 150,000 in 1650.[90] According to contemporary sources, there were among the converts 114 imperial clansmen, 40 eunuchs, 14 high officials, 10 *chin-shih*, 11 *chü-jen*, and 300 *sheng-yuan*.[91] Perhaps the most well-known were Hsü Kuang-ch'i and Li Chih-tsao, both of whom were Ricci's pupils. Hsü was the first Chinese to translate European books into Chinese, and his work on Euclid's *Elements* was particularly influential. Two outstanding works that he helped to compile were the *Ch'ung-chen li-shu,* a compendium of current scientific knowledge (1635), and the *Nung-cheng ch'uan-shu,* a handbook on agriculture and irrigation.[92] Li was famous for his achievements in geography, arithmetic, philosophy, and logic.[93] Another early convert, Wang Cheng (1571-1644), was one of the few scholars well versed in mechanics.[94] Between them, these men initiated a new trend in scientific studies.

An added impetus was the downfall of the Ming. True to the pattern of dynastic change, a number of loyalists refused to concede defeat and continued to work for a Ming restoration. To sustain them in such a forsaken cause they naturally needed an abiding faith, a profound conviction encompassing both an examination of past failures, and a plan for future action. After much soul searching, Ku Yen-wu (1613-1682), the leader of the loyalists, rather characteristically placed the responsibility for the overthrow of the Ming on the sterile and abstract philosophizing of Sung and Ming Neo-Confucianism, which, he said, discouraged true learning and prevented the officials from coping with political realities. Prescribing a remedy of learning from the widest possible sources, Ku pursued this goal for the rest of his life. He not only traveled widely in order to gather information but also studied the classics by the inductive method, which had been initiated somewhat earlier by another scholar, Ch'en

89. LKS:HCMC, 91-98; CCE:CC, Chapter IV.
90. FH:CHCT, V, 100.
91. LIC:CK, III, 17.
92. HA:ECCP, I, 316-18, 489.
93. *Ibid.,* 452-53.
94. *Ibid.,* II, 807-809.

Ti. Ku was so successful in his work on ancient pronunciation that the new method was adopted by other classicists.[95] Thus began a new era of "empirical research."

Paradoxically, still another factor that contributed to the intellectual awakening was the inquisitions of the Manchu regime. Conscious of their ethnic origin and jealous of their power, the monarchs took ruthless steps to eradicate Chinese hostility toward barbarians. In 1663, because a deceased writer had alluded to the Manchu emperors as if they had remained under Ming rule after 1644, the writer's family and the families of his collaborators were executed.[96] Countless similar cases occurred in the ensuing hundred years, and fear of political persecution drove the scholars toward such specialized fields as textual criticism, mathematics, archeology, and geography. By concentrating on more tangible subjects and by using improved methods, these scholars made important contributions to knowledge and pushed their achievements far beyond all previous levels.

At least on the surface, eighteenth-century China had high hopes of emulating earlier European scientific developments. With the appearance of Catholicism, a rival value system was provided. Hand in hand with the growth of inductive method, there was a notable trend toward a revival of ancient learning, going back from Ming to Sung, Han, and finally pre-Ch'in antiquities.[97] Among the scholars, a group appeared that spent most of its time on specialized studies. Contrary to common belief, not all Chinese scholars refrained from physical activities or association with artisans. Thus, Wang Cheng (1571-1644), Chu Shun-shui (1600-1682),[98] Wang Ch'ing-jen (1768-1831),[99] and Hsü Chien-yin (1845-1901)[100] were all adept with their hands, while Yen Yüan (1635-1704) and Li Kung (1659-1733) went so far as to denounce book-learning in favor of practical training.[101]

Why, then, did modern science fail to develop in China? Among the commentators who have discussed this issue, some note the absence of any idea of rigorous proof and the lack of a system of formal logic.[102] Some see the reasons in the "eight-legged" essays, the proscription of Catholicism during the mid-eighteenth century, and even the outbreak of the Taiping rebellion (which caused the death of many mathematicians).[103] Some criticize imperialism[104] and the backwardness of

95. *Ibid.*, I, 421-25.
96. *Ibid.*, I, 206.
97. HICY:ITCP, 26-27.
98. LCC:YPSCC, 17.75.83.
99. KHSCK, 6, 66-74.
100. CWHK, 52.5b-8a.
101. HA:ECCP, II, 912-15.
102. Notably Fu Ssu-nien and Mikami as noted in NJ:SCC, III, 151.
103. LCC:YPSCC, 17.75.17-19, 349-50.
104. YHC:CK, 4, 298.

China's economy.[105] Some place the blame on the conservatism of Ming officials and on the Manchu conquest of China.[106] Still others maintain that, in the first place, the Jesuits did not bring the most up-to-date knowledge to China, and in the second, that the Chinese were not really interested in science as such.[107]

While most of these points have a certain validity, they fail to provide a completely satisfactory explanation for China's poor scientific development. Especially weak were the arguments blaming the "eight-legged" essays, the Manchu conquest, and the Chinese economy; for most of the Chinese mathematicians, including Hsü Kuang-ch'i and Tai Chen, were products of the examination system, and it was under the Manchus that Chinese scholarship on the whole reached its climax. The stress on economic conditions seems to be a tautology, for one can argue with equal validity that China was poor because science and technology were undeveloped. Perhaps Joseph Needham was on the right path when he stressed the fact that because Chinese society was dominated by the bureaucracy, little or no profit could be gained from technological improvements and a powerful incentive for the development of science was lacking. "Apparently," he maintained, "a mercantile culture alone was able to do what agrarian bureaucratic civilization could not—to bring to a fusion point formerly separated disciplines of mathematics and nature-knowledge."[108]

But how had an agrarian-bureaucratic system come into being in the first place? Since the bureaucracy was founded on Confucian ideals and anti-commercialism was deeply rooted in Chinese philosophy, ideology was a decisive factor in shaping the institutional circumstances that prevented the development of science and technology. One way to view Chinese history between 1600 and 1850 is in terms of two groups of forces, one favoring the growth of science and one opposing it, the latter being represented by the integral ethos that I discussed earlier, with all of its hostility to new ideals. Logically, the scholarly advances made after 1600 indicated a breakdown of this integral ethos, but because of the over-all circumstances these achievements were lonely outposts in a vast wilderness. In order to understand the situation one needs only to remember that even during its height "empirical research" did not engage the attention of more than a tiny fraction of the literati, most of whom still confined their interests to the "eight-legged" essays. The decisive factor in this regard was the double-edged policy of the Manchu monarchs. Both K'ang-hsi and Ch'ien-lung patronized "empirical researchers," but the

105. Chu K'o-chen in HKCCN, 7.
106. HKC:CKC, IV, 578-79.
107. Chang Yin-ling in CKCTLC, II, 23-24.
108. NJ:SCC, III, 168.

dynasty continued officially to support Sung philosophy. Not only did the commentaries of Chu Hsi remain the sole authority for civil-service examinations, but men dedicated, or supposedly dedicated, to Neo-Confucian ideals also received praise and reward from the throne, to such a degree that the "sterile and abstract" Sung philosophy actually provided a quick path to preferment.[109] Undoubtedly motivated by political considerations—loyalty to the prince was especially counseled by Sung philosophers—the dualistic policy of the Manchus probably reinforced the traditional ethos far more than it promoted the rising scientific spirit. Furthermore, the sources that had inspired the new movement soon dried up. By the mid-eighteenth century, Jesuit activities had ceased, literary inquisitions had slackened, and anti-Manchu feelings among the Chinese had become dormant. Under such circumstances it would indeed be strange if the experimental movement could gather enough momentum to bring about a change in the social landscape.

As highly resistant as it was to cultural change, the Confucian order finally crumbled under crushing military defeats coupled with economic penetration that undermined the material foundations of the whole social structure. This deterioration occurred in the nineteenth century. Beginning in 1699 the English East India Company regularly dispatched ships to Canton. By the close of the next century the Canton trade had become in large measure a British trade. Anxious to acquire larger profits, the British were intensely dissatisfied with the Chinese trading system and repeatedly tried to bargain for more privileges. From the Chinese point of view, foreign trade was a concession and gesture of generosity in return for political suzerainty. Commercial negotiations on an equal footing with foreigners were therefore unthinkable. This basic divergence in viewpoints soon led to friction. Added to this difference was the explosive issue of opium, of which imports increased from one thousand chests a year in 1779 to sixteen thousand chests in 1830, and to thirty thousand chests in 1839.[110] When China took drastic measures to halt the opium trade, war ensued.

By its very nature Confucian society was a closed system that sought stability at the expense of material progress. It could not compete effectively with a civilization that had sufficient scientific knowledge to challenge nature. The series of wars after 1839 shook China to her foundations and nearly resulted in her dismemberment as a nation. Yet the response of the reigning house and the scholar-officials was painfully slow.[111] In fact, because the political situation

109. LCC:YPSCC, 17.75.103-4.
110. HTS:CK, I, 175.
111. One complicating factor was the internal disorder. Even though the Confucian order had reigned supreme for two thousand years, it was subject to

was so serious, the officials clung tenaciously to ideological orthodoxy. Only belatedly did they begin to seek corrective measures. At first the key factor was assumed to be technology, and efforts were made to transplant technological procedures to Chinese soil. When these proved unavailing, political reforms of various sorts were launched, but with equally disappointing results.

Finally, China's problems were traced to the literati themselves. It was realized that all reforms had to be carried out by human agents, and, given a ruling group that was completely ignorant of world affairs and rival value-systems, no basic improvement could be made. Thus nearly all of the reform proposals made after 1895 stressed the need to re-educate the educators.[112] Stage by stage the process moved toward its logical but momentous conclusion, for with the reorientation of the literati, the defenders of the faith disappeared and a group of intellectual rebels rose in their stead. Confucian values were rejected, and traditional models were demolished. What had been launched as a program of conservation ended by becoming a giant wrecking project. The turmoil was immense, and the effect has since been felt all over the world. Whether the storm is over, whether China's social metamorphosis has given rise to a new order, still cannot be judged. But at least one thing is certain: the scholar-moralists have disappeared for good. Who are their immediate successors? How have the newcomers played their social role as compared to their predecessors? These questions must be raised, even though there may not be definitive answers.

---

painful periodic readjusting processes known as dynastic cycles. This circumstance arose essentially from two factors. Because of the extreme emphasis on human qualities, there were few institutional checks on political corruption. As a dynasty grew older, incompetent emperors came to the throne, and the administrative machine became cumulatively weaker. At the same time the prevalence of peace brought about an increase of population without any commensurate increase in farmland or improvements in the techniques of production. When a series of natural calamities struck the country, the peasants were ruined, and riots developed into major rebellions. This downward phase of the dynastic cycle coincided approximately with the occurrence of the Opium War in 1839-42.

112. See the memorials to the throne in CPT:WHPF.

THE GENESIS OF A NEW ELITE

文
士
在
詩
與
昔
時

[2] The Period
1872-1895

The year 1860 marked a turning point in Chinese history. Before that time, tradition reigned supreme, and all foreigners were considered distant and uncivilized peoples, whose best fortune lay in becoming vassals of the Middle Kingdom. A preliminary sign of change occurred in the years from 1839 through 1842, when China was defeated in the Opium War by Great Britain. The defeat, humiliating as it was at the time, proved insufficient to shake China's intertia and was soon almost forgotten. But the age of change had nevertheless arrived. Internal rebellion flashed up in the next decade. By 1853 the Taiping rebels had reached Nanking, and the Manchu empire was almost split in half. In addition, a new war with Britain and France broke out in 1856. Four years later foreign troops stormed the gates of the Chinese capital, and the emperor fled to Jehol. The imperial summer palace, hitherto a sacrosanct place, was burned to the ground by the invaders in order to impress the government that it must not violate a flag of truce. The wound to China from these events was too deep to be ignored, and the way was prepared for reform.

In 1861-62 a foreign legion was formed in Shanghai to aid the imperial troops against the Taipings. Equipped with western weapons and steamships, this legion became a powerful arm of the imperial forces and won battle after battle against numerically superior opponents. While the blow to the Taipings was severe, the demonstration of Western prowess produced an even greater effect on the minds of the Chinese scholar-generals. When the shrewd Governor Hu Lin-l saw a fast-moving steamer on the Yangtze River, he at once realized the immense difficulties China would face in coping with the West.[1] Another scholar-general, Li Hung-chang, was no less impressed by the might of Western weapons. In his memorials to the throne, he repeatedly emphasized that Western artillery and steamships had caused "an unprecedented change in China's situation in the world."[2] He and his more enlightened colleagues were convinced that in order to survive, China must obtain knowledge of these weapons from the West. It was largely through the efforts of these officials that China began to adopt Western learning.

1. Hsueh Fu-ch'eng, "Ching-ch'en Yu-kuo" ("A Loyal Official Worried about His Country"), quoted in HTS-CK, II, 488.
2. LWCTK, 19.45a, 24.11b.

In order to acquire Western technology, it was first, of course, necessary to know Western languages. Beginning in 1862 language schools were opened in several cities. In 1866 two arsenals were established, and attached to each were schools devoted to the study of Western technology.[3] These schools undertook a program of translating Western books.[4] As a logical extension of these measures, students were sent abroad to secure technological knowledge at its source. The first group of students sent to the United States sailed in 1872. Since then the movement to study abroad enjoyed various degrees of success and support, but on the whole it remained a permanent feature of the Chinese educational system. Broadly, the movement can be divided into four periods: (1) the initial period from 1872 to 1895, of which the second half witnessed a low ebb in the movement; (2) the period from 1896 to 1911, in which the Chinese reform movement gathered momentum and Western superiority became increasingly apparent; (3) the period from 1912 to 1927, in which Chinese intellectuals showed great interest in Western ideas; and (4) the period from 1928 to 1948, of which the first phase—before 1937—was marked by more stringent government control of foreign study, and the second—after 1937—by an exhausting war with Japan and a renewed exodus of students to the West, particularly to the United States, toward the end of the period.

THE CHINESE EDUCATIONAL MISSION TO AMERICA

In modern times the first Chinese lay student[5] to return to China after study abroad was Yung Wing, who had been brought to the United States by an American missionary, Samuel Robbins Brown. After Yung's graduation from Yale in 1854, he returned to China in order to help the rising generation enjoy similar educational advantages.[6] Between 1872 and 1875, mainly because of Yung's efforts, 120 Chinese students were sent by the Chinese government to study in the United States. The plan was for them to learn military science, navigation, ship-building, and surveying.[7] But because of the indiffer-

3. TCP:CKC, 1-2; John Fryer, "Chinese Education—Past, Present, and Future," CRR, XVIII (1897), 381-82.
4. Ibid.; T. H. Tsien, "Western Impact on China through Translation," FEQ (May, 1954), 314-18.
5. In the eighteenth century Turgot wrote his Essai sur la Formation et la Distribution des Richesse for two Chinese students in Paris whom he befriended. A recent writer, Fang Hao, unearthed the names of some 113 men who went to the West between 1650 and 1870 (FH:WL, pp. 169-88). Even this list is not complete, for names outside it can be seen in the diaries kept by various Chinese diplomats abroad in the last quarter of the nineteenth century. However, these Chinese were mostly Catholic clergy who had little general impact on China; hence they are not part of my study.
6. YW:MLCA, 41.
7. CPIWSM, III, 82.46b-52a.

ence of the Chinese public, considerable difficulty was experienced in recruiting students. Nine-tenths of the students came from southern China.[8]

That was the first time a group of students had been sent abroad by the government, and great pains were taken by the officials to draw up proper regulations for the mission. According to the regulations finally adopted, the age of the students was limited to between ten and sixteen years. After being recruited, they were to undergo preliminary training in Shanghai, which was to last for six months. Their study in the United States was to last about fifteen years, and during that time quarterly and annual examinations were to be conducted by the commissioners. After their arrival in the United States, the students were expected to continue their study of the Chinese classics under special tutors attached to the mission; and at specific intervals the commissioners were to summon the students together to read the "Sacred Book of Imperial Edicts." In the eighth month of each year, Chinese calendar books containing information on rituals were to be issued and sent to the students through the customs service. The customary rituals were to be performed by both the commissioners and the students in order to preserve and develop their sense of propriety and reverence.

After the completion of their studies, the students would be allowed two years for travel before returning and reporting to the Chinese Foreign Office *(Tsungli Yamen)*. Awards of official rank and appointments to government service would then be made on the basis of evaluation reports submitted by the commissioners. As dependents of the government, the students were not permitted to withdraw before completing their studies, to seek naturalization abroad, or to secure their own employment after completing the program.[9] Generally speaking, these regulations reveal the great importance attached by the government to the continuation of Chinese studies while the students were abroad. At first the regulations were complied with, but later they were ignored.

As devised by Tseng Kuo-fan and other officials in 1871, the plans for the educational mission called for 120 boys to be sent to America for a period of fifteen years. Since the students' expenses were to be paid by the government, a budget of 1,200,000 taels was established to finance their stay abroad. Although the number of students taking part in the mission had by 1877 been reduced from 120 to 111, the Chinese authorities were compelled by unforeseen expenses to increase the budget to 1,489,800 taels.[10] This total meant that each student's

8. YW:MLCA, 186.
9. CPIWSM, *loc. cit.*
10. William Hung, "Huang Tsun-hsien's Poem," HJAS (June, 1955), p. 65, footnote 65.

annual expenses amounted to between 1,340 and 1,240 taels depending on whether 111 or 120 students are used in the calculation. Since one tael was then worth $1.40, each student's annual expenses came to approximately $1,200. Clearly the cost of education in the United States was extremely high in terms of the Chinese income level.

After their arrival in the United States, the students were placed by twos and threes in American families in the towns and villages of the Connecticut Valley.[11] There they learned English and were taught such refinements as singing, dancing, piano playing, drawing, and oil painting.[12] The headquarters of the Chinese Educational Mission was at Hartford, where the Chinese classes were conducted. A contemporary account of 1876 records that:[13] "There are now only 113 [Chinese] boys who live by twos in gentle families and study with their children under special tutors. Each boy's annual expenses amount to four hundred taels. There are two Chinese teachers in the Headquarters. Each boy comes to the Headquarters to study Chinese for fourteen days in every three months. The boys are grouped into classes of twelve each and come by rotation. Every day they get up at 6 A.M. and go to bed at 9 P.M. . . . I have observed that the boys get along very nicely with the Americans with whom they stay. . . ."

Although the mission made a good beginning, criticism of it soon developed. Toward the end of 1878, Tseng Chi-tse, the enlightened Chinese Minister to England and France, observed that the Chinese Educational Mission had "yielded less result" than the T'ung Wen Kuan[14] and the Foochow and Shanghai arsenals. Tseng implied that the C.E.M. boys were being steadily denationalized, owing to their youth and lack of basic Chinese training.[15] In 1879 the same criticism was repeated in accentuated form.[16] Moreover, in the following year, 1880, Li Hung-chang learned that the students were neglecting their Chinese studies. According to the information Li received, Yung Wing, the supervisor of the C.E.M. boys abroad, firmly believed that the students should not spend too much time on Chinese learning and would not agree to have them review their Chinese lessons even during the summer vacation. Worried by this development, Li sought official support and planned to write directly to Yung, urging him to change his course so that the students might return to China able to

11. LTE:CFH, 34.

12. YL:A, 33 ff.

13. LK:THJC, entry under the twenty-fourth day of the fifth intercalary month of the fourth year of Kuang-hsü (1878).

14. For a description of the T'ung Wen Kuan, see Knight Biggerstaff, "T'ung Wen Kuan," CSPSR, XVIII, 307-40.

15. TCT:CSYF, entry under Kuang-hsü 4/10/11 (1878).

16. Letter to Ch'en Lan-pin, in PLHK, 18.31b-32a.

fulfill the original purpose for which they were sent abroad.[17] The neglect of Chinese studies was confirmed in all contemporary accounts bearing on the mission.[18] A number of the students were also converted to Christianity,[19] and all of the boys were said to be popular with American girls.[20]

Considering the conservatism of the Chinese scholar-gentry at that time and the immense difficulties the country experienced in handling missionary activities,[21] it was natural that the attitudes of the students should arouse the ire of the official class. The conflicting ideas of Yung and his colleagues led in 1881 to a government decision to recall the students.[22] In violation of the mission's regulations, between five and ten students either remained in the United States or returned there soon afterwards. These students violated another regulation by marrying American girls and settling down in the United States.[23] Academically, at the time they were recalled, only two boys had completed their college education. Of the rest, half a dozen were enrolled in college courses and others were in high school. In spite of a somewhat chilly reception upon their return, most of the students were later able to find good jobs. A number of them achieved great prominence after the turn of the century.[24]

CHINESE STUDENTS IN EUROPE

The first Chinese students were sent to Europe in 1875. In that year Commissioner Shen Pao-chen placed several students of the naval schools at Foochow under the care and supervision of Prosper Giquel, a Frenchman who had fought against the Taipings and had served as director of the Foochow arsenal from 1867 to 1874.[25] In the following year, 1876, Li Hung-chang sent seven army officers to Germany under the care of a German who represented the Krupp interests in China.[26] Of these officers, two were recalled in 1878 because of slow progress.[27] Three returned to China in 1879 after undergoing infantry

17. *Ibid.*, 19.21a.
18. LTE:CFH, 44; Ts'ui Kuo-ying's diary quoted in William Hung, "Huang Tsun-hsien's Poem," HJAS (June, 1955), 71. See also the text of American educators' protest to the Tsung-li Yamen against the recall, as quoted in RAG:TSRS, 18.
19. LTE:CFH, 44-45.
20. PWL:AL, 56-59.
21. HTS:CKC, III, 1-44.
22. William Hung, *op. cit.*
23. Yung Kwai's unpublished papers. I am indebted to Mrs. Gertrude Tong, of Washington, D.C., for the use of these papers.
24. Biographical notes of Chinese Educational Mission students in LTE:CFH, 173-76; Yung Shang Him, "The Chinese Educational Mission and Its Influence," THM (October, 1939), 225-56.
25. GP:TFA, *passim.*
26. LWCTK, 27.4a. For the regulations of this mission, see ISHK, 4.41a-43.
27. LWCTK, 35.35a.

training in the German army,[28] one became sick in Germany and died soon after his return in 1880,[29] and one continued his studies under special tutors in Berlin after receiving infantry training in the German army. The last returned to China in 1881 and was appointed captain (*tu-ssu*) in the Peiyang army.[30] The training of these officers appears to have been extremely varied, consisting of military strategy, ammunition manufacturing, cartography, artillery, and other subjects.[31] But their achievement was described as meager "on account of their mature age."[32]

In 1876 Li Hung-chang, Shen Pao-chen, Ting Jih-ch'ang, and other officials secured imperial permission to send students and apprentices of the Foochow arsenal to England and France.[33] The plan was to send forty-nine trainees abroad for a period of five years at a cost of 420,000 taels.[34] In addition, Kuo Sung-t'ao, the Chinese Minister to England, suggested that ten students be sent from Hupeh and Hunan to the West to study "subjects more basic than military science,"[35] such as mining. But this plan failed to materialize because of financial difficulties, and for a time it was doubtful that students could be sent to Europe at all.[36] Finally, through the efforts of Governor Ting Jih-ch'ang, it was decided to send thirty students and apprentices at an estimated cost of 200,000 taels.[37] According to the regulations established for the mission, fourteen students and four apprentices were to study naval construction in France for three years. They were to be directed by special tutors and were to do practical work in arsenals and workshops; and in the second and third years they were to spend sixty days annually in touring French arsenals and dockyards. In addition to the students sent to France, twelve others were to study navigation in England. After devoting their first year to learning English, taking academic courses, and touring mines, forts, and arsenals, they were to spend two years aboard royal warships. At the end of their study, they were expected to be able to pilot ironclad ships and to know the principles of naval strategy.

The students were to be examined quarterly by special commis-

28. *Ibid.*, 35.33a-35a.
29. *Ibid.*, 32.24a.
30. *Ibid.*, 41.23a-24a.
31. *Ibid.*, 35.33a-35a.
32. A remark by the German Minister of Peking recorded in ISHK, 8.28a-29b.
33. LWCTK, 28.20a-23a. Students sent abroad in 1876 differed from those sent in 1875 in that the latter group merely toured Europe but did not pursue any study there.
34. ISHK, 6.28a-29b.
35. PLHK, 16.26b-27a.
36. *Ibid.*, 16.32a.
37. *Ibid.*, 16.35a, 16.36b; ISHK, 6.37b-38b. The reduction in budget was strongly opposed by Prosper Giquel, the foreign supervisor of the mission, but Ting overruled him.

sioners, or foreign experts appointed by them, and any test papers were to be subject to inspection by the Chinese government. The students were required to continue their Chinese studies, supervised by a Chinese commissioner. If any of the students should demonstrate an aptitude and desire to learn chemistry, metallurgy, international law, or similar subjects, the commissioners were authorized to make the necessary arrangements and hire additional instructors. Both the commissioners and the students were expected to keep diaries of their experiences, which were also to be submitted to the government for inspection. The commissioners were further instructed to secure blueprints of new machinery and information relating to the techno-logical progress of other nations.[38] Detailed rules were also established to govern relations between the Chinese and the French commis-sioners, the welfare of the students and apprentices, and the financial procedures of the mission. The regulations were to remain in force for three years, and any revision at the end of that period was con-sidered a Chinese matter "not subject to the intervention of any foreign party."[39]

The mission sailed in the early months of 1877. In addition to the two commissioners and thirty trainees, there were three attachés who took part in the program and later became diplomats. In the same year five more apprentices were sent to France in the company of L. Dunoyer de Segonzac, an employee of the arsenal.[40] The mission was completed in the second half of 1880, and Li Hung-chang's report to the throne stated that:

> On arrival in England three students were placed aboard warships and nine were admitted to Royal Greenwich College. In time they all went on practice tours to Africa, America, the Atlantic, the Indian Ocean, and the Mediterranean Sea. After they left the ships, they studied, under special instructors, electricity, the handling of torpedoes, and gunnery. Their proficiency was certified by the captains concerned. In accor-dance with regulations, they also toured various workshops and dockyards.
>
> Four of the students to France joined Cherbourg college; five entered the Toulon dockyard; the rest went to the St. Étienne mining school and the Creuset plant. In these places they learned mining, casting, and molding. Five students sub-sequently entered the official mining school in Paris to learn manufacturing. The apprentices were sent first to privately owned factories to learn industrial crafts and then entered the official Sai-lung and Pai-hai-shih-teng [The original French names cannot be identified]. They also received certificates of

38. LWCTK, 28.24a-27a.
39. CCTI, 14.16a-17b.
40. *Ibid.*, 15.24b.

proficiency from foreign experts and finished their study with a tour of arsenals and dockyards in England, France, Belgium, and Germany.[41]

Li's report shows that the students were given special training and that emphasis was placed on practice rather than academic knowledge. Whether they fulfilled the purpose for which they were sent abroad is difficult to determine, for the goals of study were couched in ambiguous terms in the regulations, probably because the officials had no awareness of the depth of Western knowledge. If the mission is to be judged on the basis of the students' subsequent careers, it should be noted that the Foochow students became the nucleus of a new naval force after their return to China.[42] In this sense their training abroad was of considerable value, even though the new navy suffered a crushing defeat in the war with Japan in 1894.

In 1881 ten more students were sent to Europe from the arsenal.[43] In 1886 another thirty-three students were sent, eighteen to England and fifteen to France.[44] Recognizing that Western technology could not be mastered in three years, Li Hung-chang proposed that the students of manufacturing remain abroad for six years and that the students of navigation, while continuing to pursue a three-year course, spend six months each year aboard warships instead of two months as previously.[45] Another change in the arrangements required that ten of the thirty-three students sent abroad be chosen from among the graduates of the Tientsin Naval School,[46] an institution established in 1880.[47]

An official estimate of 1886 called for a budget of 300,000 taels to cover the expenses of thirty-four students, of whom twenty would remain in Europe for three years and fourteen would remain for six years.[48] This was equivalent to 2,085 taels (about $2,900) per student per year, or nearly two and a half times the annual expenses of the Chinese students in the United States during the 1870's. Since the students' expenses were so high and the Foochow arsenal had limited funds,[49] it was not until 1897 that another educational mission was sent to France.[50] The mission of 1897 was composed of only

41. LWCTK, 40.1a-3a. A more detailed report on the study of the trainees is found in CCTI, 15.24a-25a. See also the account given in BK:EMGS, 233.
42. PLHK, 19.4b, 20.6a-7a.
43. LWCTK, 42.25a-26a.
44. *Ibid.*, 55.14a; CCTI, 41.8 f.
45. LWCTK, 55.14a.
46. *Ibid.*; CCTI, 32.3.
47. TCP:CKC, 3.
48. CCTI, 32.3.
49. *Ibid.*, 47.20b-21a.
50. *Ibid.*, 49.1a-4b.

six students and was provided with a budget of 107,000 taels, or approximately 3,000 taels per student per year.[51] Because of the ever-increasing financial difficulties of the arsenal, the students were recalled three years later, before they had completed their program.[52]

OTHER STUDENTS ABROAD

Between 1881 and 1892 four Chinese girls went to the United States under the sponsorship of American missionaries. The four received medical degrees from American colleges and became not only the first women to study abroad but also the initial women doctors in China.[53]

In 1885 a censor, Hsieh Tsu-yüan, petitioned the court to send more officials on foreign tours.[54] In its reply to this memorial, the Chinese Foreign Office accepted the proposal and emphasized that foreigners had long been acquainted with Chinese conditions and that China urgently needed to know "foreign laws, conditions, manufacturing and surveying, naval and military strategy, taxation, tea and sericulture industry, animal husbandry, and mining, etc."[55] In 1887 a fourteen-point regulation was drawn up to govern study tours for the officials. Each official was permitted to be accompanied by a translator and a servant. The tour was to take between eighteen and twenty-four months, and special attention was to be paid to military topography, social and political conditions, the navy, forts, dockyards, torpedo operation, artillery, steamers, and railways. The study of foreign languages, mathematics, astronomy, and other sciences was also encouraged. Promotion would be granted to those who, upon their return, could demonstrate their knowledge in written work or in some other way.[56]

Because of the large number of volunteers, an examination was necessary to determine who should be sent. Ten officials were eventually chosen and sent abroad in two groups, one to the United States and one to Europe and Africa.[57] In 1890 the court directed that Chinese envoys to the United States, Germany, England, France, and Russia each should take with them two students from the T'ung Wen Kuan, a school established in 1862 in Peking for the study of foreign languages and, later, sciences.[58] In 1895 the number of such

51. *Ibid.*, 49.1.
52. *Ibid.*, 53.3a-4b.
53. WKCWLT, 488, 521-22; TMTZ:CA, 24; Rubby Sia, "Chinese Women Educated Abroad," WCSJ (November-December, 1907), 27-32.
54. HFC:CSYF, 36b.
55. *Ibid.*
56. *Ibid.*, 36b-37a.
57. SHC:CTCK, 121.
58. Biggerstaff, *op. cit.*, 307-40.

students accompanying these envoys was increased from two to four.[59] Quite a few of the students later joined the diplomatic service and eventually became envoys themselves.

Generally speaking, the last quarter of the nineteenth century witnessed an increasing awareness in China of the necessity of modernization along Western lines. But this realization was limited to a narrow circle of enlightened officials and was not supported by public opinion. During the last decade of the century there was a noticeable slackening of efforts to send students abroad. Several factors were responsible for this lull. The first was that the government had expected too much from the returning students. Without fully knowing the depth of Western science, it had hoped that the young men could make China technologically independent of the West, a goal that was, of course, unrealizable. Although the results were disappointing, the high hopes entertained for the mission had led the students to expect good salaries and immediate promotions upon their return.[60] Thus, neither their performance nor their aspirations encouraged the officials to send more students abroad.

Apart from all of this initial misunderstanding, the cost of the earlier missions to Europe was inordinately high in terms of the total expenditures of the Chinese navy. Although an imperial rescript of 1878 fixed the annual expenses of the navy at 4,000,000 taels, actual allocations were always in arrears and never fully made in any year. As a result, only one of two squadrons proposed was formed, and total expenditures in 1890 were only 1,420,000 taels, of which two-thirds covered salaries and only one-third was available for operational expenses.[61] Against such a background the proposed budget of 300,000 taels for the arsenal's educational mission in 1886 seemed extremely large. Actually, the high cost of the missions contributed to the difficulties of the arsenal, for as more funds were spent on education, fewer were available for construction of ships. After 1890 no new ships were acquired by the Chinese navy,[62] and the Foochow arsenal practically ceased operation. Many of the men trained abroad were forced to seek employment elsewhere. Whatever skills they had acquired were of little benefit in their new jobs, and the heavy investment in their education was largely wasted.

59. SHC:CTCK, 21.
60. PLHK, 20.3b, ISHK, 12.7a.9a.
61. CCTI, *passim;* "Foochow Arsenal," THP (August, 1932).
62. See list of Chinese naval vessels as of 1895 in HTS:CK, III, 592-94.

The years from 1896 to 1911 were a critical period in modern Chinese history. The significance of the period lay not so much in the overthrow of the dynasty but in the decline of traditional values and authority. Before 1895 reform measures were limited in extent, and articulate Chinese opinion did not tolerate any semblance of Westernization. Kuo Sung-t'ao, China's first envoy to England, was severely censured for observing that Western civilization was also two thousand years old.[1] Hostility toward him was so great that when he returned from England in 1878, he did not dare go to the capital but retired instead to his native province.[2] His political life was ended, in spite of the friendship and high esteem Li Hung-chang had for him.

But the situation began to change after 1894. China's defeat by Japan conclusively demonstrated the necessity of Westernization on a large scale. The Chinese literati were jolted into action, and a real reform movement developed[3] in which the Emperor himself was an active figure. In 1898 a series of edicts was issued for the purpose of modernizing China's political structure.[4] Although the reform failed, it furthered the progressives' cause in an ironical way. In 1898 the Empress Dowager considered having the Emperor put to death, but she restrained herself because of the fear of foreign intervention.[5] The wounded pride of the old Empress contributed to the Boxer uprising of 1900, which in turn led to the full-scale reform that followed.

In essence the Boxer rebellion was the last stand of the conservatives who wished to repulse Westerners as well as Western ways of life. When foreign forces crushed the Boxers, they also destroyed China's resistance to change. In August, 1900, the Empress Dowager issued the first of a series of decrees calling for basic reforms in all fields.[6] By 1902 more reforms had been decreed than had even been contemplated by the Emperor in 1898.[7] Between 1903 and 1906 the old civil service examinations were abolished, a modern educational

1. HTS:CK, II, 438-39.
2. HA:ECCP, I, 438.
3. HTS:CK, II, 534-64.
4. CPT:WHPF, II, 1-122.
5. *Ibid.*, I, 325; III, 433, 444-46, 500.
6. CM:TRM, 57.
7. HTS:CK, III, 512.

system was established, intermarriage between Chinese and Manchus was allowed, and constitutional government was granted in principle.[8] Nevertheless, these changes failed to save the dynasty, for China's faith in traditionalism had disappeared. The years to come were characterized by blind worship of the West and a process of indiscriminate imitation. The Manchu regime, as a symbol of tradition, was the first to fall, while Confucianism as the dominant ideology was rapidly undermined.

EDUCATIONAL REFORM AND GOVERNMENT POLICY

Most of the reforms undertaken between 1896 and 1911 fell into three main groups: military, educational, and constitutional.[9] Of these, the educational reforms were probably the most fundamental, since they were intended in part to develop a new kind of civil servant to implement future reforms. Moreover, the educational reforms were endorsed by both the radicals and the conservatives at court and consequently enjoyed much more support than the other reforms.

To a large extent the educational reforms were shaped by one man, the scholar-official Chang Chih-tung. In a monograph of 1898 entitled *Exhortation to Learning,* he asserted that while Chinese moral values should be preserved, they should be coupled with "Western politics and technology." His essay was divided into two parts, the first preaching traditional Chinese values and the second discussing the means, necessarily Western, to preserve those values. Besides the usual arguments for railways, mines, and new military forces, Chang stressed the importance of broadening the outlook of the scholar-official class. He maintained that "Knowledge alone can save us from destruction, and education is the path to knowledge. The literati ought to take the lead and then instruct the farmer, the workman, the merchant, and the soldier; but if the educated class remains ignorant, how can this be done? If we do not know the [Western] principles of government, we shall be unable to practice their technology."[10] Accordingly, Chang recommended several specific educational measures: first, study abroad by Chinese students; second, establishment of a modern school system in China; third, translation of Western books, especially from Japanese sources; and fourth, acquisition of knowledge from foreign newspapers.[11] In regard to foreign study Chang made further suggestions. First, "much more benefit can be derived from study abroad by older and experienced men than by the young, by high mandarins rather than by petty

8. *Ibid.,* 512, 516.
9. CM:TRM, Chapters IV, V, VI.
10. CWHK, 203.3a.
11. *Ibid.,* 203.6-18.

officials."[12] Second, "Study should be in Japan rather than in the West [because] (1) Japan lies nearer than the West and more students can be sent there for a given cost, (2) the geographical proximity of Japan facilitates the supervision of our students there, (3) the Japanese language is easier to understand, and (4) a selection of Western books has been made by Japan and the countless volumes of less importance have been weeded out."[13] In other remarks Chang implied that students sent abroad should be carefully selected and that they should be granted official titles upon their return.[14]

In 1901, Chang further developed his views on how to cope with the national crisis. In the first of three famous memorials to the throne, he blasted the ignorance and narrow-mindedness of the official class as China's basic evil and proposed to overcome it through study abroad. He believed that Japan should be the place of study and that special attention should be paid to pedagogy, political and military science, and the technical disciplines of industry, commerce, and agriculture.[15] Since the need for enlightenment was great and the number of students the government could support was small, he proposed that self-supporting students be encouraged through the reward of government degrees upon their return. Chang's second and third memorials included twenty-four measures touching all aspects of Chinese government.[16] Among them was a proposal to send government officials abroad in order to cure their bigotry. On their return the touring officials were to be rewarded on the basis of the length of their tours and the number of countries visited. As a negative check, all government appointments beyond a certain rank were to be withheld from those who had not been abroad.[17]

Chang Chih-tung's three memorials as well as his book *Exhortation to Learning* achieved great fame and became classics of the period. Their success was due to the fact that they stated with great insight the growing sentiments of a powerful segment of the Chinese ruling class. Even the most conservative elements at court now supported educational reform. Immediately after the *coup d'état* of 1898, the Empress Dowager ordered the provincial officials to continue their efforts to establish new schools.[18] In 1899 another decree was issued prescribing a broad educational program. It instructed envoys to

12. *Ibid.*, 203.6a.
13. *Ibid.*, 203.7a.
14. *Ibid.*, 203.7b.
15. *Ibid.*, 52.28a.
16. These memorials were written by Chang but presented jointly by Chang and Liu K'un-i. The latter was then governor-general of Liang-kiang.
17. CWHK, 67.16b, 54.3a-4a; USFR (1905), 201; TCP:CKC, 18.
18. Imperial edict, November 13, 1898 (Kuang-hsü 24/9/30), quoted in SHC:-CTCK, p. 28, footnote 1.

encourage Chinese students to acquire knowledge in agriculture, industry, and mining; and it ordered both envoys and officials at home to follow the Japanese pattern in seeing that technical books were translated into Chinese, with their nonessential sections eliminated. The decree called for more advanced students to be sent abroad by the provinces, with directions for them to pay particular attention to note-taking and the translation of foreign books. It encouraged Chinese diplomats with requisite linguistic skill to pursue technical studies in foreign colleges and promised rapid promotion to those who returned and made practical contributions. The program also provided for the establishment of technical schools throughout the country, and it demanded that foreign-trained Chinese replace Western teachers at the earliest opportunity. In addition, it granted government positions to Chinese graduates of foreign schools in accordance with merit, and increased the term of government students abroad uniformly from three to six years. It also urged students to make every effort to graduate with honors from foreign colleges. Envoys were then to make specific comments on each student, and officials at home were to examine returning students and try them in appropriate positions before making formal recommendations for their employment to the throne.[19]

Even the Boxer uprising did not cause more than a temporary delay in most of the educational projects. In 1899, the university at Tientsin decided to send a number of students to the United States. They were able to sail in 1901, after making a direct appeal to Sheng Hsüan-huai, the sponsoring official, in Shanghai.[20] In the same year an imperial edict urged the provincial governors to send more students abroad.[21] A year later the court sent a number of imperial clansmen to foreign countries[22] and directed the governors to send more students to the West.[23] In 1903, when Peking University sent thirty-one students to Japan and sixteen to various Western countries,[24] Chang Po-hsi, the imperial commissioner of education, personally went down to see the students off.[25] In the same year Governors-General Chang Chih-tung and Tuan Fang sent twenty-four students to Belgium,

19. YCCA, 32a.22-28.
20. I am indebted to the late Mr. Ch'ung-yu Wang for this information. Mr. Wang, a mineralogist of international fame, was one of the five sent abroad.
21. SHC:CTCK, 34. In reply the governor of Kiangsu memorialized that he had done his best, but because of the lack of volunteers, only twenty government scholarships had been created for study in Japan. See KHYC, 21.30.
22. HPTT, Memorial of Kuang-hsü 33/11/1.
23. Quoted in SHC:CTCK, p. 35, footnote 1.
24. *Ibid.*, 34.
25. Lo Tun-jung, "The Establishment of Peking University," reprinted in SHC:CKCY, I, 160.

sixteen to Germany, eight to England, and four to Russia.[26] In 1904, Yang Chao-yün, the envoy to Belgium, petitioned the court to send more students to Belgium, on the grounds that expenses there were low and that the technical courses—mining, railway operation, manufacturing, and allied subjects—were excellent. Attached to Yang's memorial was a draft of regulations including a provision that would require each province to send from ten to forty students to Belgium. Yang's memorial received the imperial assent.[27]

The strenuous efforts of the government led to an increase in the number of students sent to Western countries on government scholarships. In 1906 out of some 15,000 Chinese students in Japan, 8,000 were recipients of scholarships,[28] mainly provincial ones. In 1908 Hupeh province alone maintained 475 students in Japan and 103 in Europe and America.[29] In some provinces the governors were so interested in sending students that scholarships were awarded to applicants who possessed only the slightest qualifications. Students who already held scholarships in Japan were allowed to petition the governor-general or governor for relocation in Western countries, and if they were found to be good students in interviews with lesser officials appointed for the purpose, their requests almost always were granted.[30] There was unbounded enthusiasm for Western education throughout the Chinese bureaucracy, and because the provincial authorities were in an excellent position to raise needed funds, they became the patrons of those who wished seriously to acquire learning abroad, as well as of those whose purpose was not so earnest.

The first groups of provincial students sent abroad were placed under supervisors appointed by the sponsoring officials. Students in Western countries were sometimes supervised by Westerners; the four students sent to England by Nanyang College in 1900 were placed under Professor Lambert, a man described by contemporary sources as one who "had had much to do with the educational missions since 1876 and had received a fur coat from Li Hung-chang in recognition of his services."[31] The Peiyang group sent to the United States in 1901 was for a time supervised by John Fryer, who soon found the task of managing the immature, highly sensitive, and somewhat recalcitrant students rather tedious.[32] In 1907 the Peiyang students

26. YCCA, 32b.32b-28a.
27. Reprinted in SHC:CTCK, 36-39. Shu and the source he quotes mistake Yang Chao-yün, minister to Belgium, for Yang Ch'eng, minister to Austria.
28. J. A. Wallace, "Chinese Students in Tokio and the Revolution," NAS (June, 1913), 171.
29. "Education," EM, Vol. V, No. 3, p. 94.
30. *Ibid.*
31. C. P. Hu, "Chinese Students in England," WCSJ (November, 1907), 41-43.
32. I am indebted to the late Mr. Ch'ung-yu Wang for this information.

were placed under the supervision of C. D. Tenney.[33] But most supervisors were chosen from among the provincial officials. Numerous difficulties resulted thereby because the Chinese supervisors knew no foreign languages and were as ignorant of foreign conditions as their wards. In many cases the supervisors departed after a few months and left the students under the care of Chinese envoys, who were thus compelled to deal with different groups of students, often recalcitrant, on the basis of very different procedures. In 1904, at the suggestion of the Chinese Minister to Belgium, a single supervisor, chosen by the Liang-chiang, Hu-kuang, and Szechuan governors-general from among the junior Chinese diplomats abroad, took charge of all of the students from those provinces in Europe.[34]

Meanwhile, the envoy Yang Chao-yün suggested that the throne promulgate uniform rules governing Chinese students abroad.[35] As a result, a six-point regulation was issued specifying that students chosen to go abroad should know a foreign language and be between fifteen and twenty-five years of age; and that whenever students with these qualifications were not available, boys of fourteen to fifteen who did not know a foreign language should be chosen. When young boys were sent abroad, an interpreter was to accompany them and guide them through their preliminary studies. Concerning the choice of subjects of study, technical disciplines were especially emphasized. Detailed rules were established regarding stipends and the disbursement of funds for tuition and other student expenses at various academic levels.[36]

Since students were often sent abroad by agencies that were uninformed of the practices of other government departments, the need for a standard scale of assistance to the students was soon felt. Therefore, a schedule proposed by the Board of Education received the imperial assent in 1906. By this schedule, uniform annual stipends were established for students in various Western countries. Students in England were to receive £192; students in France and Belgium, fr. 4,800; students in Germany, RM 3,840; students in Russia, R 1,620; and students in the United States, $960.[37] These annual stipends included tuition fees but not clothing allowances, emergency medical fees, or travel expenses to and from China, all of which were paid by the government. At the discretion of the supervisor, a student's

33. WCSJ (Chinese edition), Nos. 5-6 (second month of Ting-wei), pp. 82-83.
34. Wu Tsung-lien, "Reminiscences," JW II (March, 1931), 1-4.
35. "Education," EM, Vol. I, No. 3, p. 36.
36. Ibid.,
37. These were for students enrolled in colleges. Those in preparatory schools were subject to reduction of one-fifth.

laboratory fees and miscellaneous travel expenses might also be paid by the government.[38]

Actually, the cost of foreign educational missions during this period was much higher than indicated by the above figures, for two reasons. First, the schedule of stipends did not include government expenses in maintaining missions abroad. For example, one of the major items in the budgets of many missions was the salary of a foreign supervisor, who served as a chaperon and guide to the Chinese students. And second, the schedule of stipends established the minimum, not the maximum, amounts to be paid to the students. A common practice during this period was for the students to overdraw their stipends, and by 1909 a student from Hupeh province had anticipated his annual payments by 30,000 francs, or by more than six entire years. Since this sum was much too large to be deducted from current payments, the government could only accept his pledge to repay the money after he returned to China.[39]

Perhaps as a result of the generally confused conditions, the court decided late in 1907 to appoint a general supervisor for all Chinese students in Europe.[40] The only man to hold this position was Kuai Kuang-tien, who resigned as a circuit intendant to devote himself to the cause of education.[41] On his arrival in Europe, Kuai found the conditions of Chinese students there highly unsatisfactory, morally as well as academically.[42] In his attempts to improve the situation, he incurred the displeasure of the students and was on one occasion either pushed or assaulted by them.[43] In 1909 Kuai resigned after urging the Board of Education to establish stricter supervision over the students. Kuai proposed three changes: first, students should not be allowed to change courses and schools at random; second, the practice of allowing them to overdraw their stipends should cease; and third, government students should not be permitted to "audit" courses, and "auditing" students should not be granted scholarships.[44] Furthermore, Kuai suggested that a supervisor be appointed for each country and not for all of Europe. His proposals were well received by the Board of Education, and the last suggestion was put into effect immediately.[45]

In 1908, at the suggestion of a censor, an imperial decree was issued specifying that all government students should henceforth study

38. HPTT, circular letter dated Kuang-hsü 32/10/5.
39. *Ibid.*, circular letter dated Hsuan-t'ung 1/2/26.
40. TCP:CKC, 22.
41. Wu Tsung-lien, *op. cit.*, 4.
42. HPTT, circular letter to the provinces dated Hsüan-t'ung 1/2/26.
43. Wu Tsung-lien, *op. cit.*, 5.
44. HPTT, circular letter to the provinces dated Hsüan-t'ung 1/2/26.
45. SHC:CTCK, 166.

such practical subjects as engineering, agriculture, and natural science and that self-supporting students abroad could not be awarded scholarships unless they were enrolled in these disciplines.[46] In 1910 a series of regulations governing Chinese students in Western countries was promulgated: (1) Government scholarships were to be confined to students in the practical disciplines and at the university level; (2) government students were not to be allowed to change courses or schools; (3) the length of study abroad should not be shorter than three years or longer than seven, though university graduates doing post-graduate work were not to be subject to this limitation; and (4) self-supporting students enrolled in practical disciplines in the universities as regular students were to be entitled to government subsidies.[47] These regulations differed substantially from those of 1906 governing students in Japan (see p. 65). In the first place, the earlier regulations did not stipulate that holders of government scholarships must enroll in "practical" disciplines. The difference was not due to a general change of policy in 1908 but rather to the fact that Chinese students went to different countries for different purposes. If they wanted to study politics or law, Japanese schools were deemed adequate; but if they wanted to specialize in the natural sciences, a longer trip to the West was usually felt necessary. Unlike the regulations of 1910, those of 1906 made no mention of graduate study, probably because nearly all the Chinese students in Japan were enrolled in elementary courses, while some in Western countries were engaged in research.

A prohibition not embodied in the regulations but separately proclaimed was the ban on marriage between Chinese students and foreign girls. A memorial issued by the Board of Education in 1910 reads in part:

> Recently, students to Japan and Western countries have married foreign girls. While there is no good reason to prohibit intermarriages as practiced by ordinary people, in the case of students the disadvantages are very serious. First, with a family burden on him, a student can hardly pay as much attention to his studies. Second, since foreign girls are accustomed to luxuries, a student with large family expenses would have difficulty meeting his tuition fees. Third, a student with a foreign wife tends to become an expatriate, in which case he would not serve China even if he had talent. . . . Hence all students abroad must be prohibited from becoming engaged to or marrying foreign girls. . . .[48]

46. HPTT, joint memorial by three Boards dated Kuang-hsü 33/9/21 (1908).
47. Quoted in SHC:CTCK, 166-68.
48. Quoted in *ibid.*, p. 178, footnote 1.

The same prohibition was later proclaimed on at least two occasions by the educational authorities of the Republic.[49] But most Chinese envoys felt little inclination to interfere in the personal affairs of the students, and the prohibition was rendered effective more by social and cultural barriers than by official decrees.

CHINESE STUDENTS IN JAPAN

Before the last quarter of the nineteenth century, the Chinese considered Japan as a kind of vassal state. In 1877, in line with the current policy of establishing legations abroad, the first Chinese minister arrived in Tokyo. Later, in order to recruit translators, a school was established in the legation with five or six pupils.[50] But it was not until 1895 that the achievements of the Meiji Restoration deeply impressed the Chinese. In 1896 when the new envoy Yü Keng went to Japan, he took along thirteen students chosen by the Foreign Office for study in Japan. Of the thirteen, four returned to China after a few weeks, two others withdrew before completing their studies, and only seven finished the three-year course.[51] Three of the seven continued their studies and secured a college education.[52] In 1898 Liu K'un-i and Chang Chih-tung sent thirty students each to study military science in Japan.[53] Chekiang province sent six more for the same purpose.[54] In the same year Japan invited more Chinese to study in her schools and offered to pay the expenses of two hundred of them. In response to this friendly gesture, the Foreign Office, while declining the offer of financial assistance, sent several students from the Japanese class of the T'ung Wen Kuan to Japan. In addition, it initiated a search in the provinces for students with a rudimentary knowledge of Japanese, hoping to send them to Japan.[55] The Chinese students received much attention in Japan, and by 1898 several schools had been established especially for them.[56]

In 1901 there were about 280 Chinese students in Japan, including several women.[57] In the bustle of the more modern Japanese cities, the students quickly began to lose their reverence for Chinese traditions and to defy the Chinese authorities. In August, 1902, several self-supporting students besieged the Chinese legation when the minister hesitated to allow them to enroll in a military preparatory school, the Seijō Gakkō. They dispersed only after the Japanese

49. *Ibid.*, footnotes 2 and 3.
50. HCC:TYJC in HFHC, 86.9a, entry under the date of Kuang-hsü 19/5/23.
51. SK:KNBR, 187.
52. SHC:CTCK, 22.
53. 1st CYNC, II, 1110.
54. SHC:CTCK, 276.
55. *Ibid.*, 24.
56. 1st CYNC, II, 1110; CMS:JPWH, 58.
57. SK:CNRS, 348.

police were called out to restore order.[58] Subsequently two of the student leaders were deported, of whom one was Wu Chih-hui, later a prominent politician of the Kuomintang.[59] This incident prompted the Manchu Court to send a special envoy, Prince Tsai Chen, to investigate. On his recommendation, an educational commissioner was appointed to take charge of all Chinese students in Japan.[60]

In 1903 a series of regulations was set forth,[61] of which one contained several provisions relating to student behavior: first, endorsement by the Chinese government was declared a prerequisite for admission to all Japanese schools; second, extracurricular activities were made subject to the supervision of Chinese officials, who were authorized to request Japanese schools to dismiss undesirable students; and third, students were forbidden to interfere in politics on pain of expulsion from classes and deportation from Japan. For the execution of this regulation, Chang Chih-tung secured the co-operation of the Japanese government.[62]

Another set of regulations dealt mainly with the self-supporting students. The cultivation of moral integrity was emphasized, and limitations were placed on both the kinds of schools students might attend and the subjects they might study. The number of Chinese students in private Japanese schools, which were considered academically inferior, was limited to one-half the number in government schools. No self-supporting students were allowed to study military science, and only a limited number each year could begin the study of law and political science. Students on provincial funds were required to work five years in their provinces after their return to China.[63]

The third set of regulations provided for the recognition of students after the successful completion of their studies abroad. Upon graduation, Chinese students were to apply for certification of good conduct from Chinese officials in Japan, and those securing it would be examined on their return by high-ranking court officials. Successful candidates would be entitled to the following awards:[64]

58. According to the report of special envoy Tsai Chen, the reason for the minister's hesitation was that too many students were involved, but not that self-supporting students could not study the art of war. The stipulation that only government students were allowed to study military science did not come into being until 1903. On this point, Roger F. Hackett is incorrect. See his paper "Chinese Students in Japan, 1900-1910," HPC, III, 151.

59. YCCA, 32b.18a-22a.

60. *Ibid.*

61. CWHK, 61.1a-10a.

62. *Ibid.,* 61.1a-2a.

63. *Ibid.,* 61.7b-10a.

64. *Ibid.,* 61.5b-7b.

Academic Qualifications	Chinese Titles Awarded
1. Honor graduates of Japanese secondary schools	*Pa-kung* (B.A.)
2. Honor graduates of Japanese government high schools or their equivalents	*Chü-jen* (M.A.)
3. Graduates of certain selected programs in Japanese universities	*Chin-shih* (Ph.D.)
4. Graduates of Japanese government universities	*Chin-shih* and *Han-lin* (Academician)
5. Doctors of Japanese government universities	*Chih-shih* and *Han-lin* plus promotion

The regulation also provided that candidates who possessed such official titles before going abroad would be awarded additional appointments.

These enactments clearly indicate the dilemma faced by the Chinese government in regard to the students abroad. On the one hand, the government regarded the education of students abroad as the only way of achieving the modernization of the country; on the other hand, its dependence on the students weakened its position and encouraged a defiant attitude on the part of the students, which the government could hardly countenance. The regulations compiled by Chang Chih-tung with the co-operation of Japan were designed to keep the students in their place by the use of rewards and punishments. Yet subsequent events showed that this purpose could not be attained. In the summer of 1905, Hunan province sent a group of students to Japan. When they passed through Wuchang, Governor-General Chang Chih-tung decided to grant them an audience but insisted that they perform the traditional ritual of obeisance. The students objected, and after ten days of protracted negotiations, Chang was compelled to give way. A few days after their arrival in Tokyo, the students went on strike because their luggage was inspected by the Japanese police, an act they regarded as an insult.[65] Finally, an incident later in the year caused many Chinese to give up their studies and return home.

In 1903 the Japanese government had agreed to enforce the regulations governing Chinese students in Japan. Toward the end of 1905 the Japanese Ministry of Education promulgated its own regulations for the supervision of Chinese students and the schools in which they studied. According to these regulations, the Japanese Minister of Education would prepare and submit a list of schools suitable for Chinese students to the Chinese envoy. The minister was also

65. CMS: JPWH, 68-69.

authorized to appoint officers to supervise the examinations of Chinese students and to make changes in the examinations whenever necessary. On their part, the accredited schools were required to furnish the minister with information regarding their programs, to keep a complete record for each Chinese student, to supervise the dormitories and boarding houses inhabited by Chinese students, to keep the Chinese legation regularly informed of the conditions of Chinese students, and to refuse admittance to any Chinese who had been expelled by another school for moral reasons or who was not otherwise recommended by the Chinese legation.[66]

The Japanese regulations, although paternalistic, were neither insulting nor malicious in intent. Yet after they had been in effect for a month, the Chinese students became highly critical and declared a strike on the grounds that the regulations violated personal freedom, insulted the Chinese, and interfered with the internal politics of China. Many students did not even read the regulations but merely went along with their cohorts. Amid the turmoil a Chinese committed suicide and left a long letter expressing his views on future Sino-Japanese relations, protesting against the rights of foreigners in China, and stressing the necessity of revolution against the Manchus.[67]

In spite of Japanese explanations regarding their intent, a large number of Chinese students withdrew and went home; but most of them returned to Japan after a few months. Those who did not established and maintained a college in Shanghai with the support of such officials as the Governor-General Tuan Fang. The financial aid advanced by Tuan was requested and granted on the grounds that the college would prepare students properly for education abroad.[68]

The defiant attitude of the students contrasted strikingly with the government's leniency toward them. The government continued to regard Western education as its only hope and felt an urgent need for civil servants with modern training. In January, 1904, a comprehensive series of educational regulations was drawn up by Chang Chih-tung[69] and agreed to by the court. The regulations, eight volumes long, consisted of nineteen separate parts and additional appendices, each dealing with a section of the planned national education system. Primary schools were to be established in each community of one hundred or more families, higher primary schools in each county, middle schools in each prefecture, and colleges in each province. In the summary preceding the regulations, Chang Chih-tung emphasized the problems of personnel, both teaching and administrative,

66. *Ibid.*, 65-82; SHC:CKCY, I, 233-62.
67. *Ibid.*, 240.
68. *Ibid.*, I, 262-63; SK:CNRS, 80-82; SHC:WHCY, 176-77.
69. With two other officials, Chang Po-hsi and Jung Ch'ing.

and suggested a program to send prospective staff members on study tours abroad: "Distance and expenses involved render it impossible to send more than a handful of men to Western countries. It is nevertheless imperative for the educational personnel to go to Japan. This is the only way to get started and no consideration of the expenses involved should stand in its way. Even the distant and poor provinces should at least each send two men to Japan. . . ."[70] Chang's suggestion was adopted and included in a regulation to promote study tours by officials at their own expense.[71] A definite scale of promotion was established for officials returning from foreign tours: those who studied in both Japan and Western countries for at least three years received the highest positions; those who toured two or more Western countries for two years were ranked next; those who went to one Western country for a year ranked third; while those who toured Japan for a year came fourth. Tours of less than a year were not counted.

One of the interesting features of the educational enactments of 1904 was that it provided for the award of titles and appointments to graduates on an even more liberal basis than in 1903.[72]

Academic Standing	Title	Position
1. Higher primary school graduates	*Sheng-yuan*	none
2. Graduates of Industrial middle schools	*Pa-Kung-sheng, Yu-kung-sheng, Sui-kung-sheng*	Assistant Chou magistrate, assistant to prefect (*fu-ching*), assistant to *hsien* magistrate (*chu-pu*)
Junior Normal school graduates	*Kung-sheng*	Prefectural supervisor of studies, assistant *hsien* supervisor of studies
3. Graduates of normal college, college of law and political sciences, technical colleges	*Chü-jen*	Clerks in the Grand Secretariat (*chung-shu*), clerks in the boards (*ssu-wu*), *hsien* or *chou* magistrate, assistant prefects
4. University graduates	*Chin-shih*	Various positions in the Han-lin Academy or clerks of the boards (*chu-shih*)

70. TTHSCC.   71. TCKHHF, *chüan* 11.
72. "Regulations for the Encouragement of Study," reprinted in SHC:CKCY, IV, 63-74.

If the grades of a graduate of the first or second category reached a certain standard, he was sent to the capital for a government examination. While titles were bestowed on all graduates regardless of grades, substantive appointments varied according to a candidate's total score, that is, his grades at school plus the result of the examination in the capital.[73] The examination system was later extended to cover students returning from study abroad.

In 1904, at the persistent request of a number of provincial officials, the time-honored civil service examinations were abolished.[74] Thereafter study abroad became the shortest route to officialdom. Japan's emergence as a world power after the Russo-Japanese War gave added impetus to study abroad, and hundreds of Chinese flocked to Japan. The number of Chinese students there jumped from 1,300 in 1904, to 2,400 in January of 1905, and to 15,000 in September of 1906.[75] But most of these students were interested only in acquiring titles and not in actual study. According to a survey made by the Board of Education, approximately 60 per cent of the Chinese students were enrolled in short-term training courses, 30 per cent in elementary courses, 3 to 4 per cent in high schools, and only 1 per cent in universities. The remaining 5 to 6 per cent were perpetually transferring from one school to another.[76]

To meet China's educational problems, the Board of Education resorted to various measures. First, it continued to encourage the program of reorienting officials. In May, 1906, a plan was approved to send from forty to fifty Han-lin academicians abroad for formal study or study tours.[77] Later, it announced that all provincial commissioners of education were to spend three months on foreign tours before taking office.[78] In August a group of *chin-shih* of 1904 was sent to Japan to enroll in courses lasting a year and a half.[79] On the other hand, the board sought to limit the number and improve the caliber of students going abroad. In the spring of 1905 it enacted regulations requiring that students intending to study in Japanese technical schools and colleges must be graduates of middle schools in China and well-acquainted with the Japanese language, while those wishing to undertake short-term training in Japan must know Chinese thoroughly, be twenty-five years of age or more, and have some experience in the political or educational field in China.[80] In the summer of

73. Memorial of the Board of Education in CCKP, No. 997 (Hsüan-t'ung 2/7/4).
74. SHC:CKCY, IV, 117-28.
75. CM:TRM, 78, JY (1919-1920), 270. Cf. Hackett, *op. cit.*, 142.
76. TCHTHF, Vol. XV, Appendix.
77. HPTT, memorial dated second of the fourth moon.
78. TCKNC, 1998.
79. HPTT, memorial dated seventh of the seventh moon.
80. *Ibid.*, circular telegram to the provinces dated nineteenth of the second moon.

1905 the board directed the provinces to stop sending students to Japan for short-term training.[81] Less than a month later, it specified that all students going abroad must be graduates of middle schools or above.[82]

Meanwhile, efforts to supervise the students already in Japan were not successful. The 1903 regulations were dependent on the Japanese for enforcement, and they had little interest in closely supervising the Chinese students. Moreover, because the Chinese educational commissioner to Japan was recalled in 1903 to assume a post in the Foreign Office,[83] student affairs fell by default to the charge of the Chinese Minister in Tokyo.[84] Dissatisfied with these conditions, the Board of Education introduced a new forty-point regulation in late 1906.[85]

The fourth section of the regulation, dealing with the supervision of students, was divided into three parts. The first pertained to all students and stipulated that they might enroll only in schools recognized by the Chinese minister in Tokyo, that they must obtain permission from him before enrolling in or withdrawing from a particular school, and that enrollment in a school would be permitted only if the student had graduated from another at an appropriate level. Violators of these rules would not be allowed to attend the metropolitan examinations or become teachers in government schools in China, while students of low moral and academic standing would be ordered to leave Japan. The second part of Section Four dealt with government students and authorized the supervisor to encourage them to enroll in specified fields of study and allowed him to order them to avoid certain undesirable hotels and hostels. The third part was concerned with self-supporting students and provided for the awarding of government scholarships to all who were accepted by Japanese government high schools or universities and for the granting of loans under certain conditions. The new regulation also provided for a deputy supervisor of students to assist the Chinese Minister.[86]

The policy of tighter control was extended even to study tours. In the summer of 1906 the Board of Education stipulated that all persons going abroad on study tours must be "righteous, learned, in the prime of life, free from bad habits [drug addiction], and experienced in politics, education, or industry"; that they must have

81. *Ibid.*, telegram dated eighteenth of the sixth moon.
82. TCP:CKC, p. 19.
83. PCCP, Appendix, 27a.
84. See the memorial of Minister Yang on student affairs, E.M., Vol. I, No. 5, p. 113.
85. HPTT, memorial dated Kuang-hsü 32/10/17.
86. *Ibid.*, memorial dated seventeenth of the tenth moon.

definite plans regarding their proposed tours; and that such tours were not to last for less than three months in Japan or six months in Western countries.[87]

The policies of the Board of Education led to a decline in the number of Chinese students in Japan. From some 15,000 in September, 1906,[88] the number decreased to 8,000 at the end of 1906 and to about 5,000 in 1909.[89] A large number of these students returned to China after the revolution of 1911, and only 1,400 remained in 1912.[90]

THE SPECIALLY-APPOINTED SCHOOLS

One of the measures taken by the board in the interests of the students was to arrange for their enrollment in Japanese government schools. Toward the end of 1907 an agreement with Japan specified that five Japanese high schools should accept 165 Chinese per year, with each of the schools to receive an annual subsidy of 190 Japanese yen per student. Eligibility to compete in the examination for the quota of 165 was to be determined by the Chinese envoy to Japan on the basis of good character and proficiency in Chinese. Successful candidates would automatically become government scholars. Every year sixty-five students were to enter the First High School for eight years of study, including a college course, and one hundred were to enter four other schools for four years of study. The funds for the subsidy and scholarships were to be contributed by the provinces, the larger ones supporting nine scholarships each year and the smaller ones six. Each province was to be entitled to retain the services of as many returning students as the number of scholarships it contributed. The period of service was to be the same as the number of years the student had enjoyed government support. The allocation of individual students among the provinces was to be made by the Board of Education acting upon information furnished by the Chinese envoy in Japan.[91]

Between 1908 and 1910, 460 Chinese enrolled in the five appointed schools. This was below the quota of 165 a year, and the scarcity of students eligible for scholarships was largely due to the fact that English, and not Japanese, was the foreign language taught in the new Chinese school system. As a remedy the Board of Education proposed to open a special preparatory Japanese language school in Peking for middle-school graduates so that they could later study in

87. *Ibid.*, circular memorandum to the provinces, dated twentieth of the seventh moon.
88. WCSJ (Chinese edition), No. 3 (1906), p. 84.
89. SK:CNRS, 350; Hackett, *op. cit.*, 142.
90. Report of the Japanese Ministry of Education, quoted in SHC:CTCK, 70.
91. HPTT, memorial dated Kuang-hsü 33/11/30.

Japan. But this plan was shelved when the revolution broke out in 1911.[92] After the founding of the Republic, the provinces fell behind in their contributions, and the system of appointed schools did not operate in full.[93] In 1922 the project finally came to an end.[94] But many provinces continued to accept enrollment in one of the five schools as a mark of promise and allocated scholarships on that basis.[95]

CHINESE MILITARY STUDENTS IN JAPAN

As indicated earlier, the humiliation of the Sino-Japanese War of 1894-95 spurred China to make new efforts toward reform. Under the circumstances it was natural that military science should be emphasized as a subject of study. In 1898 sixty-six students went to Japan to study the art of war, but it was not until 1904 that Chinese military students were sent regularly to Japan in large numbers. Early in that year, Yang Shu, the Chinese envoy to Japan, petitioned the throne to send more students to study military science there. Yang noted the proficiency and high standards of the Japanese army and proposed that between one and two hundred students be sent to Japan each year to study military organization and tactics. Since the expenses of military training were several times greater than those of liberal arts courses, he believed that the government should assume the financial burden.[96] Yang's memorial received the imperial assent, and in the summer of 1904 a series of regulations for such an educational program in Japan was drawn up by the Bureau of Military Training.

The regulations provided that one hundred boys between the ages of eighteen and twenty-two were to be sent each year to Japan for a four-year course of study. Each province was allocated a definite quota of students, varying from three to six, and was asked to contribute approximately half the funds needed by the students, with the Bureau of Military Training furnishing the other half. Only those students endorsed by the government would be allowed to study military science. Self-supporting students already enrolled in such a program would be granted government scholarships only if they demonstrated promise as well as exemplary character, and in the future no self-supporting students would be allowed to enroll in this field.

The Chinese envoy to Japan was authorized to supervise the students, and a special military attaché was appointed to aid him. Since the Shinbu Gakkō had been established as a military preparatory

92. 1st CYNC, II, 1110.
93. SHC:CTCK, 68-69.
94. 1st CYNC, II, 1111.
95. *Ibid.*
96. YCCA, 32b.45a-b.

school especially for Chinese students, the Minister to Japan was instructed to consult with Japanese officials on ways of improving its program. The teachers of the Shinbu Gakkō were to be subsidized by the Chinese government, and the teachers in other schools were to receive prizes after the graduation of each class. After returning to China, the graduates of the Cadets' School, the Japanese military academy, would be required to take an examination. Those who received the mark of first grade would become second captains in the Chinese Army, those who received second grade would be commissioned as lieutenants, and those who received third grade would serve as sergeants. Graduates of Japanese military universities would be awarded even higher ranks, and all returning students would be assigned to the provinces and military installations by the Bureau of Military Training.[97]

Until 1905 the program of the Shinbu Gakkō lasted only fifteen months. In that year it was increased to eighteen months, and in 1906 to three years. According to a report of 1907, 521 Chinese had graduated in the past six years from Japan's two leading military preparatory schools, the Shinbu Gakkō and the Seijō Gakkō, and 330 others were currently enrolled. A majority of these students continued their training at the Japanese Cadets' School, and most of China's military leaders during the next twenty years came from the group that studied in Japan.[98] Even as late as 1932, half of the members of the military commission of the Nationalist government had received their training in Japan.[99]

EXAMINATIONS FOR RETURNING STUDENTS

An important event for students returning from abroad was the metropolitan examination that was held annually between 1905 and 1911. The idea of an examination for returning students was implicit in the regulations of 1903, but it was not until 1905 that the Board of Education examined fourteen men who had studied in Japan. Afterwards they were granted an audience by the Emperor and awarded titles and positions in the government. The two highest-ranking men became *chin-shih* and members of the Han-lin Academy; five others, *chin-shih* and board clerks (*chu-shih,* 6th rank) ; one, *chü-jen* and clerk of the Grand Secretariat (*Nei-ko-chung-shu,* secondary 7th rank) ; the last six, *chü-jen* and expectant magistrates.[100]

In 1906 another examination was held on a more formal basis.[101]

97. *Ibid.,* 32a.
98. Report of Shinbu Gakkō, quoted in SHC:CTCK, 63-64.
99. SK:KNBR, 236-37.
100. KHYC, edict dated Kuang-hsü 31/6/12.
101. Unless otherwise noted, the account of the 1906 examination is drawn

Advance notice of the examination was sent to the provinces, and through them it reached the public. All graduates of foreign schools above the level of a Japanese "high school"—equivalent to the last two years of an American high school and the first two years of college—were allowed to compete in the examination. Forty-two candidates entered but only thirty-two passed. The examination consisted of two papers: one dealt with the candidate's special subject as specified on his diploma, and the other with languages, one question being written in Chinese and another in a foreign language. The candidate was required to answer only one question in the second paper, which meant that no Chinese was required. Eighteen candidates who had studied in Europe and America answered in English; one who had been in Germany, in German; and twenty-three who had studied in Japan wrote in Chinese.[102] Many Western-trained candidates were said to be poor in Chinese, and at least one could not "write his own name in Chinese decently." The academic qualifications of the candidates varied from a Ph.D. from Yale to a mere high school diploma from Japan. Five of the successful candidates received the coveted *chin-shih* and twenty-seven the *chü-jen*. Of the twelve highest places, eleven were awarded to students who had studied in the United States,[103] although among those who failed one had received an M.A. in analytical chemistry from the University of Chicago. The purpose of the examination was merely to confer Chinese degrees upon the successful candidates, not to accord government positions. Nevertheless, about ten candidates subsequently joined the government when several boards petitioned to retain them.

One difficulty the government faced in regard to the examinations was the dearth of competent examiners. Among those finally chosen for the task were three former C.E.M. boys and one Foochow arsenal graduate. In general, the examination was considered to be too lenient by the public, and severe criticism was leveled at the government, particularly in regard to the optional use of Chinese.[104] As a result, beginning in 1907, the composition of a Chinese essay was made mandatory and led to the failure of many candidates.[105] In addition, graduates of Japanese schools established primarily for Chinese students were no longer allowed to sit for the metropolitan examination.[106] In 1908, the examination was divided into two stages: the

from W. W. Yen, "The Recent Imperial Metropolitan Examinations," CRR (1907), 34 ff.

102. "Educational Comments," WCSJ (November-December, 1906), 8; WCSJ (Chinese edition), ninth moon of 1906, frontispiece.

103. CM:TRM, 82.

104. WCSJ (May, 1908), 40; SHC:CTCK, p. 184, footnote 3.

105. WCSJ (November, 1908), 167.

106. HPTT, memorial dated Kuang-hsü 33/5/13.

first was a test given by the Board of Education, which if successfully completed, entitled the candidate to an academic degree; the second was an examination "held in the presence of the emperor," which led to a substantive appointment. In the second examination a candidate was required to write two papers, one technical and one literary. The latter, confined in scope to the Chinese classics, was not compulsory for candidates in the sciences. Nevertheless, only candidates who showed aptitude in both papers were awarded the highest grades. Those proficient in science but only fair in Chinese were ranked second, and those who could not write in Chinese came last. Official appointments were made on the basis of the grades the candidates received.[107]

In 1908 all graduates of private Japanese universities were required to undergo a preliminary test in both Japanese and general knowledge before becoming eligible for the metropolitan examinations. A year later, the regulations were made even more restrictive. In order to qualify, a candidate was required to have studied for at least three years in the institution where he secured his diploma and must have covered at least three-fourths of the required courses in that institution. In addition, he must have had his transcript sent by a Chinese envoy to the Board of Education; he must have secured references from either Chinese envoys, provincial governors, or senior board officials; and he must have passed a preliminary test in foreign languages and basic knowledge relevant to his academic specialty, at a grade no lower than 50 per cent of the full mark.[108]

In spite of these regulations, the number of successful candidates in the metropolitan examination increased from 38 in 1907,[109] to 107 in 1908,[110] and to 400 in 1911.[111] In the last year, 1911, the Board of Education had difficulty placing all the men and finally assigned over three hundred to the provinces as county magistrates.[112] Meanwhile, the total number of graduates from higher primary schools and beyond, who were entitled to official recognition according to promotional measures enacted in 1904 and amended in subsequent year,[113] increased to about 300,000 in 1909-10, causing the widespread comment that soon "there would be no commoners in the country."[114] Because of this situation, the government decided in 1911 to stop awarding

107. *Ibid.*, memorial dated Kuang-hsü 33/12/20.
108. SHC:CTCK, 188-90.
109. CRR (January, 1908), 12.
110. WCSJ (November, 1908), 167.
111. *Ibid.* (September, 1912), 59.
112. SHC:CTCK, 190.
113. CM:TRM, 86. The number of Chinese college graduates in 1911 was 3,184, of whom 76 won the *chin-shih* and an unknown but far larger number won the *chü-jen*. See 23d CKTC, 8n; SYL:CTKC, 175-76.
114. WCSJ (July, 1911), 451.

official positions to graduates of Chinese schools and directed that the palace examinations for returning students cease in 1912.[115]

STUDENTS IN AMERICA

In 1905 the Manchu Court sent five high commissioners abroad to investigate constitutional forms of government. During the commissioners' visit to the United States, scholarships were promised to Chinese students by Yale, Cornell, and Wellesley.[116] After the officials returned to China, a competitive examination was held in Nanking in 1907 and another in Hangchow a year later. In the first, ten boys and three girls were chosen from about six hundred candidates,[117] and in the second, which included both a physical examination and a strict test in Chinese, twenty were chosen out of two hundred contestants. Seventeen of the grantees went to the United States and three to Europe.[118]

In 1908 the United States began to return the Boxer indemnity to China, and the Chinese government decided to use the funds for sending students to America. In order that the students would have no difficulty in entering American colleges, a preparatory school, later known as Tsinghua College, was established in 1909 and was run entirely in the American way, with American personnel and an American curriculum. The students were divided into two categories: those between the years of fifteen and twenty and those less than fifteen. At first it was intended to recruit one hundred students from the first category by competitive examinations, and two hundred from the second category by means of recommendations from provincial authorities. Both categories were to be filled according to quotas patterned on the provincial burdens of the Boxer indemnity, with some vacancies reserved for the Bannermen, Mongolians, and Tibetans.[119] Later, the quota for the advanced category was eliminated, and the number of younger students increased to three hundred.[120]

The school opened in the fall of 1911, and when it reopened in May of 1912 after the interruption of the Revolution, there were a hundred students in the advanced group and more than three hundred

115. SHC:CTCK, 190.
116. "Education," EM, seventh month, 1907, p. 178. In this connection Harvard has often been mistakenly substituted for Cornell, see TMTZ:CA, 24; WCSJ (September, 1912), 58.
117. WCSJ (September, 1912), 58-59.
118. *Ibid.* (September-October, 1908), 105-8.
119. Joint memorial by the Board of Education and the Wai-wu-pu, quoted in SHC:CTCK, 75-78.
120. Circular letter to the provinces by the Board of Education, dated Hsüant'ung 2/3/6. The letter is in a collection of official papers kept at the China Institute in New York. For the use of these papers I am indebted to Dr. C. P. Cheng of that Institute.

in the junior course.[121] Initially the advanced group was divided into two classes, one to sail for the United States in 1912 and one to sail in 1913.[122] Meanwhile, other students selected through competitive examinations were sent to America in 1909, 1910, and 1911.[123] A number of these students had studied in America independently but had returned to China to compete for the Boxer indemnity scholarships, which carried attractive stipends.[124] Several other groups of students who did not compete in the examinations were awarded scholarships by government order. A large number of the Boxer indemnity scholars later achieved prominence in China. The two best-known men among them were perhaps Hu Shih and T. V. Soong, the former securing his scholarship through the examinations of 1910 and the latter being one of those appointed by the government in 1912 for "meritorious work in the cause of the Revolution."[125]

WOMEN STUDENTS ABROAD

A noteworthy feature of the Chinese movement to study abroad was the inclusion of women at an early stage in the program. Apart from young girls adopted or sponsored by Christian missionaries, the first Chinese women to go abroad for foreign study were probably women of wealthy families in the company of their husbands. In 1900 there were such women students among the Chinese in Japan.[126] But it was not until a few years later that the provinces began to select single women to study abroad. In 1905 Hunan sent twenty women to Japan to take short training courses in education,[127] and in the same year Fengtien arranged with a Japanese girls' school, the Jissen Jogaku, to send fifteen girls there each year for courses in education.[128] In fact, the number of women students in Tokyo increased so rapidly in the early years of the twentieth century that two girls' schools decided in 1905 to establish special Chinese departments.[129]

In 1903, when Liang Ch'i-ch'ao traveled through America, he noted the names of three women, two single and one married, among the fifty Chinese students he could remember.[130] A contemporary account of 1905 records that nineteen Chinese girls were enrolled in

121. LSC:PSTC, 31, 35.
122. Ibid., 32.
123. THTHL.
124. I am indebted to the late Dr. Hu Shih for this information.
125. THTHL.
126. SK:CNRS, 204.
127. "Education," EM, Vol. II, No. 8, p. 202.
128. SHC:CTCK, 130.
129. TCP:CKC, 15, 17.
130. LCC:YPSCC, 5.22.127-30.

American intermediate and secondary schools,[131] and more than ten girls attended the 1908 summer conference of Chinese students at Ashburnham, Massachusetts.[132] A report of the Chinese Students' Alliance in 1910 records that thirty-six women were among the Chinese students in the eastern states during that year.[133] In 1907 three women were awarded scholarships by Kiangsu province, and one by Chekiang province, for study in America.[134] By 1910 self-supporting female students abroad were competing on equal terms with males for government scholarships. In 1914, 94 out of 847 Chinese students in America were women;[135] and in 1925 no less than 640 out of 1,637.[136]

131. FJ:ACS, 180.
132. CSM (November, 1908), 48-49.
133. *Ibid.* (March, 1910), 267-72.
134. WCSJ (September, 1912), 58-59; *ibid.* (July-August, 1907), 30.
135. CSD, 1914.
136. Ch'ang Tao-chih, "Conditions of Chinese Students in America," CHCYC, Vol. XV, No. 9. The 1,637 were members of the Chinese Students' Alliance, not all of the Chinese students in America, who numbered about 2,500 in 1925.

[4] *Aspects and Effects*
of the New Education, 1872-1911

GOALS OF STUDY ABROAD

When the Chinese government sent 120 students to the United States from 1872 to 1875, the goal of foreign study was for them "to learn about the sciences related to army, navy, mathematics, engineering, etc., for ten-odd years, so that after they have completed their study and returned to China all the technological specialties of the West may be adopted in China, and the nation may begin to grow strong by its own efforts."[1]

The regulations of the mission further clarified the intention of the government. Special emphasis was placed on Chinese studies, and various methods were devised to "foster a sense of propriety and deference" among the students. For this purpose, Chinese calendar books containing information on customary rituals were to be delivered to the mission in America each year.[2] Thus the students were expected to acquire certain specific technological skills but were not to become Westernized in their outlook. Upon their return they were to serve as experts, but not necessarily as political leaders.

These stipulations were, however, opposed by Yung Wing, the co-commissioner of the mission. Yung was convinced that China's only hope lay in scrapping her ancient philosophical civilization and adopting as rapidly as possible the progressive, technological culture of the West. He believed that the government must send abroad a constant stream of carefully selected youth for education in the schools of America and Europe, and that they should remain abroad long enough to attain a thoroughly Western education and a completely "Western viewpoint." In fact, Yung maintained that only by being de-Sinicized would they be able to overcome the great difficulties of introducing Western machinery and technology into the hostile Chinese environment.[3] Thus in Yung's scheme, the C.E.M. boys were to become Westernized in both outlook and values, were to acquire knowledge useful for government service, and, upon their return, were to "make a new China of the old, and to work out an Oriental civilization on an Occidental basis."[4] Nothing could have been

1. ISHK, 1.19b-22a.
2. LWCTK, 19.9a-9b.
3. LTE:CFH, 23.
4. YW:MLCA, 177.

further removed from the government's plans than the ideas of Yung Wing. The gap between them was so great that one wonders how Yung was able to accept the responsibility of directing the mission. Probably he had such a poor opinion of Chinese institutions[5] that he felt the mission's regulations could be conveniently ignored.[6] At any rate, because the mission was established at Yung's suggestion and because he knew infinitely more about America than his colleagues, he became the moving force behind it. Under his direction, a marked change developed in the boys' attitude and conduct: they played baseball, dated American girls, refused to show respect to the head of the mission,[7] and neglected their Chinese studies to such an extent that they forgot how to speak the language.[8] Some became Christians. These developments were resented by the other officials, and a conflict between them and Yung quickly developed. Criticism of the students' conduct was soon heard in China, and the mission was recalled in 1881. At that time only two of the 120 boys originally sent abroad had graduated from college. One of them became China's first railway engineer and a prototype of the technician-official that became prevalent in later decades. He was the only C.E.M. student to fulfill the goals of foreign study as set forth by the government.

The students sent to Europe in 1877 were directed to learn primarily about navigation and manufacturing, with an emphasis on their naval aspects. Specifically, the students of manufacturing were expected to learn, during their three years' stay abroad, how to build a naval vessel and all of its parts; and the students of navigation were instructed to learn about naval strategy and the art of commanding ships.[9] As a secondary objective, the students were directed to study mining, chemistry, and international law. Although the students had all graduated from the Foochow arsenal school and shown promise in their fields, the technological goals aimed at were beyond their reach. This fact was recognized by the sponsoring officials after they became better informed about foreign study.[10] When the third group of students was sent abroad in 1886, the plan of study was changed in an effort to enable them to learn more.[11] No specific goals were established for those who were to study mining and international law. A number acquired the licentiate's degree in France and later joined the Chinese diplomatic service.[12] As in the case of the Chinese Educa-

5. *Ibid.*, 236.
6. Cf. Yung's attitude toward the appointment of Ch'en Lan-pin as head of the mission. *Ibid.*, 181.
7. LIC:CK, II, 447.
8. LTE:CFH, 55.
9. See Chapter 2, section on students to Europe.
10. CCTI, 46.24a.
11. LWCTK, 55.14a.
12. CCTI, 41.8a-12a.

tional Mission to America, the official goal was to acquire specific skills in order to serve China's immediate needs, and there was no intention to train them as leaders or to encourage their general absorption of Western culture.

As a result of these missions to Europe and other related efforts, many Chinese felt that their national security had been reinforced.[13] Thus the defeat by Japan in 1894 came as a great shock to the literati-officials and led them to conclude that more Western knowledge must be sought by China. What they had in mind was not a mere re-doubling of efforts already being made, but the adoption of new measures qualitatively different from the old. As one memorialist put it, China had failed because the elite had not taken Western learning seriously[14] and because the scope of study had been too narrowly confined to "a single art," that of war.[15] Thus to save China, not only must the program be broadened, but a different kind of student—those who would become China's future political leaders—must be trained.

This opinion was shared by men of different political affiliations. For example, those who accepted the necessity of training future political leaders included the Emperor himself, who was hostile to the conservative officials of the court;[16] Chang Chih-tung, who supported the Empress Dowager but emphatically denounced the bigotry of the official class;[17] and T'ao Mo, a governor-general in the border provinces, who believed that an improvement in the standards of the bureaucracy was China's most urgent need.[18] This consensus profoundly influenced the goals of foreign study. When the exodus to Japan and the West began shortly after the turn of the century, the objective was no longer limited to securing technical experts. It was now broadened to include the training of able government officials and educators who would in turn contribute to the enlightenment of the masses.[19] The basic formula for this program of leadership training was "Chinese learning as the essence; Western knowledge as the practice."[20] In other words, Western knowledge would be used as

13. The main argument of the war party in China in 1894 was that China was militarily stronger than Japan. See HTS:CK, II, 216.

14. Sun Chia-nai, "Memorial Relating to the Establishment of a Government Printing Office," HCCS, III, *chüan* 1.

15. Sun Chia-nai, "Memorial Relating to the Establishment of Peking University," *ibid.*

16. CPT:WHPF, I, 268-73.

17. CWHK, 52.10b.

18. CPT:WHPF, II, 269-77.

19. CWHK, 203.3a.

20. The phrase has been widely attributed to Chang Chih-tung, but was actually coined by Sun Chia-nai in his memorial relating to the establishment of Peking University written in 1896, quoted above.

a means of preserving Chinese moral values. The earlier goal of selective absorption was thus broadened and attempted at a much higher level.

However, unforeseen problems soon arose in the attainment of the new goals. Since the aim in the past had been only to train experts in a few prescribed fields, a limited number of students had sufficed. But, now that China had begun to depend on foreign study for her hierarchy of officials and educators, the number of students to be sent abroad became extremely large. Moreover, as long as the goal was limited, most of the students sent abroad were fairly young; with the new program, mature men, including those already in government service, needed to be sent. The foreign danger to the country, which prompted the government to adopt the program in the first place, also led it to look for quick results; thus many officials were sent hastily to Japan for short-term training. How was such a vast project to be financed? For a partial solution the government took vigorous measures to encourage students to pay their own way. In 1905 it abolished the civil service examinations and took several other steps to make foreign study a prerequisite to official appointment.[21] These measures led to a tremendous increase in the number of students going abroad, of whom a sizable proportion now paid their own way. The emergence of a large group of self-supporting students at this time was significant, for the government's efforts had caused foreign study to be regarded primarily as a means of personal advancement rather than as a way to acquire knowledge. Haste and a rigid emphasis on study abroad tended to preclude any serious consideration of the quality of foreign training.[22] Thus, the meaningfulness of study abroad was fundamentally impaired.

Throughout the period in which the main objective of foreign study was to develop political leadership, the government retained an interest in having students acquire knowledge of practical matters, particularly technology. In 1899 the throne urged students abroad not to confine themselves to languages and military science but to devote some attention to commerce, industry (i.e., engineering), and agriculture.[23] In 1903, twenty-four men were sent to Belgium to acquire industrial training.[24] A year later a large number of students were sent there to study mining and railway engineering.[25] Meanwhile, the government was disappointed at the large number of students who had gone to Japan, ostensibly to study law and politics, but who

21. TCP:CKC, 18; CWHK, 67.16b; USFR (1905), 201.
22. *Supra,* Chapter 3, sections on Chinese students in Japan and examinations for returned students.
23. YCCA, 32a, 22a-28b.
24. *Ibid.*
25. *Supra,* Chapter 5, section on educational reform and government policy.

instead devoted their time and energy to political agitation.[26] In the hope of decreasing the number of revolutionaries while increasing the number of technicians, the government decided in 1908 to limit all future scholarships to technical disciplines.[27] The same goal found expression in a stipulation of 1909 that 80 per cent of the students going to America on Boxer indemnity funds must enroll in technical fields. Had there been no revolution in 1911, the effect of this policy would probably have been very great.

THE SOCIAL BACKGROUND OF CHINESE STUDENTS ABROAD

As noted in Chapter 2, the cost of foreign study, especially in the West, was extremely high in terms of the Chinese income level. The annual expenses of each student sent to America during the 1870's amounted to approximately $1,200, and the expenses of each of the students sent to Europe in 1886 by the Foochow arsenal were almost $3,000. Thus, only persons from very wealthy families or with financial aid from a sponsoring organization could afford to undertake a course of study in the West. Actually, a majority of those educated abroad in the late nineteenth century were probably from poor families, and their expenses were largely paid by the government.

Before 1900 sponsorship by Christian churches was an important source of support for the few Chinese who studied abroad. As early as 1650 Chinese students were sent to Rome under the aegis of the Catholic Church.[28] In the nineteenth century the first Chinese graduate of an American college was sponsored by a missionary, as was probably the first Chinese who received a master's degree in the United States. After 1900, government scholarships, awarded at both the central and provincial level, became the predominant form of support for students abroad, and after 1909 the Boxer indemnity fellowships sent a steady stream of students to America.

The earliest Chinese lay students in Europe appear to have been inhabitants of British colonies. Two of the better known were Ku Hung-ming (1856-1927) and Wu T'ing-fang (1842-1922). Ku left his native Penang for Europe in 1860,[29] and Wu journeyed from Hongkong to England about a decade later,[30] both probably as self-support-

26. After 1906 the Manchu government became weary of the students in Japan on account of their political enthusiasm and academic indolence. In 1907, a censor suggested the recall of all Chinese students in Japan and the dismissal of all of the Japanese-educated from government service. See "Miscellaneous," EM, Vol. IV, No. 8, p. 19.

27. HPTT, memorial dated twenty-first of the ninth moon.

28. FH:WL, pp. 169-88. Fang Hao has unearthed the names of some 113 men, mostly Chinese Catholic clergymen, who were sent to the West between 1650 and 1870.

29. Johnson Tsou, "The Life of Ku Hung-ming," CHC (June 9, 1936), 33.

30. Wu was probably called to the bar in 1876 and was practicing law in Hongkong in 1879. See LHH:YS, 7b, under the date of Kuang-hsü, 2/12/10 (1877).

ing students. The first Chinese students from China proper were sent to England by the government, and during the early years of the twentieth century a large proportion of the students there received financial aid. In 1908, 65 per cent of them held government scholarships,[31] and in 1910, 50 per cent.[32]

What do we know about the self-supporting students abroad? Our earliest account of the expenses of a self-supporting student in America comes from the pen of Hsü Jun, a merchant-compradore who became an official in Shanghai.[33] Writing in 1908, he noted that his son had spent four years studying Western learning in China under Dr. Tenney and five years in America under the supervision of Professor Fryer. The total expenses incurred during these nine years amounted to 30,000 taels. Hsü's other son studied in England for nine years, and his expenses were approximately twice as great, or 60,000 taels.[34] These examples are undoubtedly atypical of the self-supporting students at this time, for Hsü Jun was a rich man and his son in England was dubbed the "Prince" by his fellow Oxonians because of his lavish hospitality.[35]

Nevertheless, there is little doubt that during these years almost all self-supporting Chinese students came from well-to-do families, and many of them were relatives or close friends of one another. Furthermore, since few prospective students knew anything about conditions abroad, they had to be chaperoned by foreigners on home leave from China or by Chinese who had been abroad before. The difficulty of making the trip tended to make it an infrequent affair, but when a family group went abroad it was often accompanied by close relatives. Thus, Hsü's son-in-law and grandson were both trained in the West, as his two sons had been before them.[36]

Another pioneer Chinese student during this period was Alfred Sao-ke Sze, who traveled to America with his brother in 1894 as a member of the Chinese legation. During the next ten years seven members of the Sze family visited the United States.[37] In addition, the Szes brought along two other families, the Piens and the Suns. Five members of the Pien family, a gentleman and his four nephews, reached America by 1903. They were close relatives of Li Han-chang, a brother of the powerful Li Hung-chang. The Sun family, which also

31. WCSJ, Vol. III, No. 3, p. 167.
32. CSM (June, 1917), 408-14.
33. See Hsü's biography in WCY:CKKYS, II, 966-67.
34. HJ:TC, entry of 32/9/2.
35. I am indebted to Dr. F. T. Cheng for this information. Cheng was the first Chinese to get an LL.D. from University College, London, in 1916.
36. HJ:TC, entry under the twenty-eighth and thirty-fourth years of Kuang-hsü.
37. SCC:TN, p. 3.

visited the United States in the wake of the Szes, was related to the grand Secretary Sun Chia-nai. The Suns acquired their wealth through the salt trade, but toward the end of the nineteenth century they shifted their interests to flour mills and banking. The mercantile and bureaucratic connections of the Sze, Sun, and Pien families seems to have been typical of the self-supporting students abroad during this period.[38]

ACADEMIC ACHIEVEMENTS

The 120 students sent to America during the years from 1872 through 1881 had little previous education in China, since they were for the most part from poor families and were only ten to sixteen years of age when they sailed for the United States. Because Commissioner Yung's idea was to Westernize them under the most favorable conditions, they were placed in New England families where they learned English as well as such refinements as singing, drawing, and oil painting, in conformity with the educational pattern of well-bred American youth. The comfort of their new environment probably facilitated their integration into local community life but did not necessarily promote high academic achievement. At the time the mission was recalled in 1881, many of the students had barely finished high school, and with two or possibly three exceptions, none had progressed beyond the second year of college.

The situation of the early students in Europe was somewhat different. The naval students and apprentices had been trained in the Foochow arsenal and had demonstrated an aptitude for their task.[39] A number of this group studied languages and international law, and at least seven secured the licentiate's degree in France. The earliest to receive the baccalaureate was Ma Chien-chung, in 1878, and a part of his report reads:

> The examination took place in the École Libre des Sciences Politiques in the second half of the fifth moon. There were eight papers. The first was on international law, as seen from 1,800 pages of diplomatic records. . . . The second paper was on treaties . . . the third on foreign exchange and money and credit . . . the fourth on diplomatic history . . . the fifth on similarities and differences between the political institutions of France, England, and the United States . . . the sixth on the political systems of Prussia, Belgium, Austria, and Switzerland . . . the seventh on the doctrine of the separation of powers as practiced in various countries . . . and the eighth on public finance. . . .
>
> The written examination lasted three days, and I wrote out

38. I am indebted to S. C. Thomas Sze for this information.
39. CCTI, 46.24a; TCT:CSYF, 22b.

my answers in over a hundred sections in twenty-odd examination papers. The examiners lavished their praise on me and published my papers in the newspapers, with the comments that I had demonstrated both a broad perspective and a subtlety of thought. Actually, I surprised these Westerners precisely because they, in their spasmodic dealings with us, had come to view us with contempt. Their praise of me therefore originated from their contempt of China.

Since my arrival in Paris, I have kept company with the government officials, especially some Academicians . . . who often advised me to be a candidate for some French degrees. . . . After I had taken the examination at the École Libre des Sciences Politiques, I sat for the examination for the *baccalauréat des lettres*. This examination lasted two days. The first day was devoted to Latin and Greek . . . and the second to geography, history, and Latin and Greek literature. The examiners again congratulated me saying that they wished to have more French candidates like me. This remark was greeted with applause by an audience of several hundred people and was subsequently quoted by nearly all Parisian newspapers. It was pointed out that never before had an Oriental obtained a *baccalauréat des lettres*. . . .[40]

The Chinese students in Europe during this period showed various patterns of adjustment to their new environment. One, Ch'en Chi-t'ung, who joined the Chinese diplomatic service as soon as he reached Europe, became a popular figure in Paris and was said by Henri Cordier to know more about France than China.[41] A number of others, on the other hand, had considerable difficulty in adjusting themselves to conditions abroad. Some suffered poor health; five out of about eighty-eight men sent abroad between 1877 and 1886[42] died either in Europe or upon their return to China, and another two were compelled by illness to interrupt their studies to go home.[43] One apprentice was so impressed with the luxuries of Western life that he stole a gold watch, for which he was sent to prison.[44]

The seven military men sent to Germany in 1876 also encountered difficulties. They had disagreements with their German supervisor, and two were recalled for lack of progress in their training.[45] One became ill and died upon his return in 1880.[46] At least three of the

40. *Ibid.*, 2b.-4a.
41. CH:HDR, III, 68.
42. This number includes ten men sent abroad in 1886 in connection with the purchase of some warships. See CCTI, 32.7a.
43. *Ibid.*, 32.9, 41.13; HFC:CSYF, 49a.
44. HCY:OY, 36a.
45. LWCTK, 35.33a; LHH:YS, 15a-15b.
46. LWCTK, 32.24a.

other four had linguistic difficulties and derived few benefits from their training.

Probably the first Chinese postgraduate student in America was Yen Yoong Kiung, a Christian from Shanghai, who obtained a master's degree from Kenyon College in 1869.[47] All of his four sons later went to America, presumably with church support. One of them, W. W. Yen (Yen Hui-ch'ing), later a premier of China, went in 1895, took a college preparatory course at Episcopal High School, and graduated from the University of Virginia in 1900.[48] Self-supporting students probably went first in the late nineties. Alfred Sao-ke Sze went in 1894 as a student attaché of the Chinese legation in Washington, D.C., and secured an M.A. from Cornell in 1902. His brother S. C. Thomas (Shih Chao-hsiang) went in 1897 after graduating from St. John's College in Shanghai. He enrolled in Central High School in Washington, D.C., and graduated in engineering from Cornell in 1905.[49]

A group of nine postgraduate students was sent to the United States by Peiyang University in 1901. One of them obtained an M.S. from the University of California in 1902 and a Ph.D. from Yale in 1906.[50] Another obtained the degree of D.C.L. from Yale in 1904,[51] for his translation of the German Civil Code into English, which was widely acclaimed as a scholarly and remarkable contribution.[52] Another obtained his doctorate from Columbia in 1905.[53] A fourth achieved considerable fame by a book on antimony in 1908.[54] However, the scholarship of this group was not representative of the Chinese students in America as a whole. In most cases, Chinese students were enrolled at the high school level, and from there they slowly climbed the academic ladder. In 1905, out of some two hundred Chinese students in the United States, nineteen were graduate students, fifty-one were undergraduates, and the rest were enrolled at the preparatory level.[55] In 1910, when Prince Tai T'ao was touring the United States, Chinese circles presented him with a petition that made a number of illuminating comments on the students:

> In recent years [among] Chinese students in America . . .
> quite a number misbehaved and wasted the tuition fee. The
> majority of government students sent by the provinces are

47. I am indebted to S. R. McGowan, Registrar of Kenyon College, for this information.
48. WWAR (1917), p. 203.
49. I am indebted to S. C. Thomas Sze of New York for this information.
50. TDCS, 3.
51. WWCS, 7.
52. Lin Yu-tang's introduction, CKS:CD.   53. *Ibid.*, 105; TDCS, 3.
54. WCY:A.   55. FJ:ACS, 180.

deficient in foreign languages and not admitted to universities. Hence the name "preparatory students." This is already shocking and deplorable. Yet, the worst ones, while being on government scholarships, loaf around but do not study, indulging in wine, women, and gambling. When their funds are exhausted, they either force the [Chinese] Supervisor of Students to give them a loan or actually swindle the merchants of money and goods. . . .

Most of the self-supporting students work hard. When they are in primary and high schools, they generally work part time. When they join the universities, the pressure of their studies makes this impossible. Some students have to study one term and work another term. Students from wealthy families, however, under the pretense of study, fool around with the government-supported students. . . .

Last year over forty students were sent out by the Board of Education and the Board of Foreign Affairs. Their academic standards varied. The intention had been that all of them should enroll directly in colleges. Yet after their arrival it was found that the English of some of them was much lower than the requirements of the colleges. Hence they had to be relegated to the preparatory course. Some older students who have families even go as far as to keep back their tuition fee [and remit it] to their families. . . .[56]

When the movement to study abroad was at its peak in China, provincial authorities competed with one another in sending students abroad. In the midst of all the enthusiasm and fervor, quantity was preferred to quality, and many of the students were improperly selected. In 1904 it was discovered by chance that one of the Szechuan students en route to America was completely illiterate.[57] A year later the Chinese Minister to Belgium complained that the students from Hupeh had apparently undergone no pre-selection, since many of them were inferior academically as well as morally, and often indulged in fights and menaced others with pistols.[58] In a lengthy report to the Board of Education in 1909, the Chinese Commissioner in Europe painted a very gloomy picture of the students under his supervision. Most of them, he maintained, were only "auditors" in the universities and had few serious academic interests. Yet they loudly demanded more money from the government, ostensibly to pay for books and private tuition but actually to be used in dissipation. Furthermore,

56. Letter No. 3106 from Prince Tai to the Board of Education dated the twenty-third of the seventh moon (handwritten copy in the files of the China Institute in America, for the use of which I am indebted to Dr. C. P. Cheng).

57. "Comments," EM, Vol. I, No. 4, p. 12.

58. *Ibid.*, EM, Vol. II, No. 1, p. 6.

many students repeatedly changed their fields, schools, and even countries of study, with the result that their graduation was indefinitely postponed.[59]

OCCUPATIONS AND ACADEMIC SPECIALTIES

Of the three Chinese students sent to the United States in 1847 by the Reverend S. R. Brown, one eventually became a medical doctor in Canton, and another returned within a year to work in a printing house and eventually to serve as an interpreter for the Chinese legation in Washington, D.C. The third, Yung Wing, was for many years connected with the Chinese government.[60] Only eight of the 120 students sent to America during the years from 1872 to 1875 eventually obtained college degrees. Twenty-two served in the diplomatic corps or were in some way connected with the conduct of China's foreign relations, and twenty-one were associated with the administration of the navy. Thirteen others served as railway officials and engineers, while ten became executives of banks and telegraph companies. Six were employed as merchants and businessmen, and eleven became professional politicians. In addition, four were employed as British and American diplomatic and commercial agents in China, and three pursued careers as mining engineers.[61]

Of those eight who did obtain degrees, two graduated in 1881, and two others remained in America to complete their studies after the mission was recalled in that year. At least four later returned to resume their education, and one was sent to London by Li Hung-chang to study mining. But only one, Jeme Tien Yau, pursued a professional career in China and thereby used his technical training for the benefit of the country. One other who was trained as an engineer subsequently entered the diplomatic service, and another who continued in the field of mining was employed for most of his life by a British-dominated concern. Little is known about the fourth who became a mining engineer, although the fact that he died in Hongkong seems to indicate that he neither practiced his profession nor accomplished much for China. The remaining four of the college-trained became expatriates in the United States, and one served as a consulting engineer and was credited with several important inventions. Another became a free-lance worker in various fields until he returned to his native country at an advanced age; and the other two served as Chinese diplomats while maintaining permanent residence in the

59. HPTT, circular note to the provinces dated Hsüan-t'ung 1/2/26.
60. YW:MLCA, 251-53; LTE:CFH, Chapter II.
61. Yung Shang Him, "The Chinese Educational Mission and Its Influence," THM (October, 1939), 225-56; LTE:CFH, particularly pages 173-76; unpublished notes of Yung Kwai, for the use of which I am indebted to Mrs. Gertrude Tong of Washington, D.C.

United States. Thus so far as China was concerned, the training provided the C.E.M. boys seemed to produce few tangible results.[62]

Of the eighty-four students sent to Europe by the Foochow arsenal during the years from 1876 to 1897, three died at early ages, two were recalled to China, and one failed the examinations for returned students. Of the remaining seventy-eight, thirty-one studied shipbuilding, mining, and the manufacturing of explosives; twenty-six studied navigation; twelve studied international relations; and nine became engineering apprentices.[63] Upon their return to China, these students served mainly as teachers in government schools, naval officers, and technicians. Before 1890 the number of students retained at the arsenal was very large, but after that date the arsenal became much less active in naval construction and many of the foreign-trained dispersed. According to an official report of 1896, the arsenal was suffering extreme financial hardships and could not afford to purchase new machinery or to stockpile needed materials. Work at the dockyards therefore came to a halt, and many of the students were driven to seek employment in foreign firms or in other parts of China.[64] Although many of them entered the service of foreigners or returned to their native districts to teach or to assume positions among the lesser gentry,[65] it seems likely that others continued to work for the government in some capacity.[66] Those who did so probably found their general knowledge of Western countries more useful than the technical training they had acquired. Of the ten men who subsequently became diplomats, two had studied mining and manufacturing, one had specialized in admiralty law, and one had concentrated on chemistry and mathematics. Only one of the ten had studied international law and a modern foreign language.[67] Thus, like the C.E.M. boys, the Foochow students had little opportunity after 1890 to put their technical training to good use. However, a small number of them continued to serve as the nucleus of the modern Chinese navy, and from that time until 1949 natives of Foochow controlled most of the Chinese naval squadrons.

In the first decade of the twentieth century, the number of students who studied in Japan was extremely high, possibly as great as 30,000 if those who took short-term courses are included. In one way or

62. *Ibid.*

63. HFC:CSYF, 486-96. The seventy-eight men do not include those sent abroad in connection with the purchase of ships and who subsequently studied in Europe.

64. CCTI, 46.22, 47.20a-21a.

65. One of the students, Cheng Wen-ying, returned from England in 1890 and began teaching English in his native province in 1897. See CFT:EW, 70; for a description of the lower gentry, see CCL:CG, 6, 51-70.

66. EM, Vol. V, No. 8, pp. 32-33; Vol. V, No. 1, p. 42.

67. HFC:CSYF, under the dates of Kuang-hsü 16/8/4 and 16/10/21.

another most of the students educated in Japan were subsequently connected with the government, and the major fields of employment were politics, administration, education, and the armed forces. In the educational field, there were by 1909 about 57,000 modern schools with a total enrollment of 1,626,000 students. Of these, about 1,000 with an enrollment of 190,000 were at the level of middle schools or above.[68] Within their faculties all except 356 were Chinese.[69] According to the educational regulations of 1904, teachers in colleges and universities were required to be graduates of foreign universities or the Chinese research academy. But since the latter institution existed only on paper, this stipulation effectively made teaching in China's colleges the exclusive domain of foreign-trained students.[70]

In the military field, the government drafted plans in 1907 to establish within the next five years a standing army of thirty-six divisions, 460,000 men for all of China.[71] Since the new army would have to be trained from the ground up, military education was of the utmost importance. By 1912 twenty-seven primary schools, four middle schools, fifteen surveying schools, a military college for nobility, and a staff preparatory school had been established in connection with the military training program. Most of the teachers in these schools were Chinese who had studied abroad, the majority of them in Japan.[72]

In the political field, several broad segments can be distinguished. In the upper echelon of the civil service, there were a few bona fide students who had studied in Japan, and most of them had passed the metropolitan examination for returned students. T'ang Pao-ngo, one of the fourteen honored in the examination of 1905, studied law at Waseda University in Japan. He became a *han-lin* in 1905 and accompanied the five high commissioners abroad in 1905-1906. Later, he became president of a high normal school, deputy director of a provincial bureau of foreign affairs, head councilor of the Board of War, and a member of the Northern peace delegation during the revolution of 1911.[73] Another one of the fourteen honored in 1905 was Ts'ao Ju-lin, who became a *chin-shih* in 1905 and joined the civil service and served as vice-president of the Board of Foreign Affairs in 1911.[74] While few others ascended the nine-rung mandarin's ladder as rapidly as T'ang or Ts'ao, most of the Japanese-educated men did fairly

68. CM:TRM, 86.
69. SK:CNRS, 170.
70. Ho Ping-sung, "Chinese College Education in the Last Thirty-five Years," SSWN, 86.
71. *Ibid.*, 177-78.
72. *Ibid.*, 182; CY (1912), 247.
73. SK:KNBR, 183-84.
74. *Ibid.*, 204-6.

well. According to a report of the Board of Education in 1908, many of them became officials even before they unpacked their luggage.[75]

After October, 1909, a new outlet was found for the foreign-trained in the recently established provincial councils. These councils consisted of 30 to 140 members each,[76] and most of the councilors had been students in Japan.[77] Another employment that had close connections with politics was writing. The report on foreign conditions submitted by the five high commissioners of 1906 was reputedly written by Liang Ch'i-ch'ao and Yang Tu, both of whom were in Japan at the time.[78] The regulations pertaining to the establishment of provincial councils were drafted in 1908 by two Chekiang students who had studied in Japan.[79] Between 1898 and 1911 the Chinese published over fifty student journals in Japan;[80] and the newspapers they edited, all anti-dynastic in attitude, found ready audience in China in spite of a government ban. The situation so infuriated the officials that in 1907 a censor suggested the banishment of all Japanese-educated persons from the civil service.[81] Thus, whether in or outside the government, the students wielded immense political influence.

No complete information is available about the employment of students trained in Europe and America before 1917. But we do know that in 1910 some eighty-two Western-trained persons were employed in Peking. Out of these fourteen were not connected with the government. One was employed in Y.M.C.A. work; thirteen were engaged in miscellaneous fields, of which the details are unknown. Of the rest thirteen were teachers or administrators in government schools, and the others were bureaucrats. In regard to the academic status of these men, information is available in only forty-four cases. Of these, two received doctoral degrees; one, a master's degree; and four, bachelors' degrees. One had been called to the bar in London,[82] and the rest had either traveled in Western countries or had obtained some kind of general education there. Although the academic standards of this group seem to have been higher than those of the earlier students, our data is not sufficient to reveal if their training aided them in their specific occupations. My general impression is that, like the C.E.M. and Foochow students, the Western-trained persons in Peking derived few practical benefits from their education abroad.

75. HPTT, Memorial dated Kuang-hsü 33/12/20.
76. HTS:CK, III, 538.
77. CM:TRM, Chapter VI, particularly pages 122-35.
78. TCY:LCT, 14-17.
79. BJOP:RE, 127-38.
80. SK:CNRS, 228-31.
81. EM, Vol. IV, No. 8, p. 19.
82. Wu Lu, "A List of British Returned Students in Peking," WCSJ (January, 1910), 199-200.

PROMINENCE

As far as we know, nearly all of the C.E.M. students who did not die early in life or become expatriates abroad were fairly successful in their subsequent careers in China. A large number of them became provincial heads of the telegraph service or senior railway officials. Of the seventy-eight who went into government service, six or seven attained the rank of cabinet minister or its equivalent, and seven or eight others achieved national fame in one way or another. The pattern of their success was much the same. Most of them were sponsored by powerful officials, notably Yüan Shih-kai, under whom half-a-dozen C.E.M. men rose to prominence.[83] Others served under Chang Chih-tung or Sheng Hsüan-huai. Still others were regular companions of Manchu princes on official missions abroad and in this way became plenipotentiaries themselves.[84]

On the whole the Foochow group was far less successful, even though there were among them a prime minister, several admirals, and a writer-translator of outstanding fame. While it is difficult to account with certainty for the greater success of the C.E.M. students, several factors seem to have nevertheless been relevant. For example, the Foochow students received a far more technical education and stayed abroad for a shorter period than Yung Wing's students. As a consequence, they probably acquired less general knowledge of foreign countries and developed less skill in foreign languages than the C.E.M. boys. Moreover, the Foochow students went abroad in small groups and at different times. Thus they did not develop a strong *esprit de corps* as the C.E.M. students did.[85] Probably the most famous member of the Foochow group was Yen Fu, who in spite of his literary fame, lacked political support and was unsuccessful as an official.[86] Neither he nor any others demonstrated the same trait as the C.E.M. students in holding a number of official posts in succession.[87]

For one reason or another Western training always enjoyed more

83. LTE:CFH, 116; Wu Lu, *op. cit.*, WCSJ (July, 1919), 363.
84. A typical example was the life of Sir Chengtung Liang Cheng. Liang was a member of the Chinese mission to Queen Victoria's Diamond Jubilee, secretary to Prince Ch'un upon his expiatory mission to Germany in 1901, tutor to Prince Tsai Chen, and Chinese Minister to the United States in 1903. This biographical sketch is taken from a newspaper clipping in Mrs. Gertrude Tong's possession. The title and date of the newspaper cannot be identified, though it probably appeared in New England sometime in 1903. The newspaper clipping has a reprint of a photograph of Sir Chentung Liang Cheng and Prince Tsai Chen, which originally appeared in *Harper's Weekly*.
85. An example was the execution of Fang Po-ch'ien in September, 1894, at the instigation of Liu Pu-shan, who went to England with Fang in 1877. On Fang's execution, see CYL:WC, 195.
86. WS:YFC, 14-15.
87. LTE:CFH, Chapters V-VIII.

prestige than education in Japan. During the early years of the twentieth century, the number of Western-trained men in China was relatively small and high positions were within the reach of all. Of the eighty-two Western-trained people in Peking in 1910, half a dozen were board presidents or vice-presidents, and the rest were councilors to boards, professors in government colleges, or directors of such government departments as the mint.[88] When the Republic was established in 1912, the stock of the Western-trained group rose even higher. One commentator wrote in 1917 that "from the government down through all walks of Chinese life, the returned man or woman is sought after to direct, or to assist in, the realizing of the potentialities of this nation. . . . The number and character of the men and women educated in alien lands and returned to China have become a new factor— I had almost said a new class. . . . It is evident that the returned student has, under the Republic, come into his own."[89]

The first cabinet in Peking under the Republic was composed of some twelve men,[90] of whom two were trained in Japan and eight were educated in the West.[91] Of the latter, one, who held the post of premier, had returned from the United States in 1881; another had returned from England in 1889; one had graduated from an American college in 1897 and been awarded his master's degree in 1902; one had studied in Germany during the academic year 1889-90; one had secured his doctorate from Yale in 1904; one, a *han-lin*, had been in Germany between 1907-11; and one, an acting minister, had graduated from Yale as late as 1910. The eighth member of the Western-trained group had left China as a student attaché in 1893, been promoted while abroad, and returned in 1912 to become minister of foreign affairs. Three months later he became the second premier of the Republic.[92]

An indication of the high positions held by the Western-trained is the salary they commanded. In 1881, each of the students recalled from America received from four to twelve taels per month.[93] In the nineties the monthly salaries of the Western-educated ranged from forty to one hundred taels.[94] By the first years of the Republic,

88. WCSJ (January, 1910), 198-200; (July, 1910), 362-66.
89. Mei Hua-Chuan, "The Returned Student in China," CRR (March, 1917), 158-59.
90. The exact number is difficult to determine because some members were appointed but never took office, some took charge of more than one portfolio, and some portfolios were in the charge of vice-ministers.
91. The eight were T'ang Shao-i, Alfred Sao-ke Sze, Ts'ai Yüan-p'ei, Tuan Ch'i-jui, Wang Ch'ung-hui, Liu Kuan-hsiung, and Lu Cheng-hsiang. The two Japanese-trained were Sung Chiao-jen and Chen Ch'i-mei.
92. LK:LCH, 301.
93. LTE:CFH, 59.
94. CCTI, 31.1a-27a; WCSJ (May, 1910), 365.

students returning from the West accepted offers of no less than two to three hundred dollars a month.[95] By the second decade of the century, even the few industrial and commercial concerns in China had great respect for Western training. An interesting example is the Commercial Press, the leading publishing house in China, whose practice it was to pay its editorial staff at five levels. A Chinese college graduate with some experience received $80 a month and was provided a desk three by one and a half feet in size, whereas a graduate of a Japanese college was paid $100 to $200 and was allowed a desk three by two feet. Those who had graduated from Japanese imperial universities received $150 and were permitted a desk four by two and a half feet, in addition to book shelves, a rattan chair, and a crystal ink well; and graduates of western colleges received monthly salaries of $200 and were provided the same physical perquisites as the Japanese graduates. At the apex of the scale were the graduates of Harvard, Yale, Oxford, and Cambridge, who received $250 a month and were supplied with a custom-made desk in addition to the standard perquisites. According to eyewitness reports, this scale was rigidly applied, regardless of the ability of those employed.[96] The practice probably began in the early years of the Republic and persisted until 1927, when a more flexible policy was adopted by the firm. While few concerns had such rigid practices, a high regard for students trained in the West seems to have been widespread.

EXALTATION AND UNEMPLOYMENT

Although the students who returned to China had better employment opportunities than the Chinese-trained, they were not completely free from difficulty and frustration. In fact, the complaint that they were not adequately appreciated in China was as old as the movement to study abroad. In 1881, the C.E.M. boys, upon returning to China were highly dissatisfied with the treatment they received and the jobs to which they were assigned. In their letters to American friends, vitriolic attacks were made on the conventional mandarin-official, who they thought was the cause of their plight.[97] Although such complaints were not made by the Foochow students, they were generally less successful than the C.E.M. students, and a number of them were reported to be unemployed in 1896.[98]

Even in the first decade of the twentieth century, when men with Western training were sorely needed by the government, frustration

95. Mei Hua-chuan, *op. cit.*, 170.
96. Tao Hsi-sheng, "A Story of the Desk," TYT, Vol. IX, No. 9, p. 8; SHC: WHCY, 95.
97. LTE:CFH, 55-59.
98. CCTI, 47.20a.

seemed to be the lot of many of them. Their reactions can be seen clearly from the *World Chinese Students' Journal*, a magazine published in English[99] and controlled by a group of Western-trained men in Shanghai, more or less as a mouthpiece for themselves and their peers. Although politically loyal to the Manchus, the journal was sharply critical of what it considered to be the government's insufficient appreciation of the Western-trained and its annoying tendency to treat the Western-trained on an equal basis with the Japanese-trained. On the latter score, it complained of "the incompetence and partiality" of officials who examined returning students and of their "arbitrary methods of grading papers."[100] The success of many Japanese-trained in the examination of 1907 was attributed to the "sympathetic attitude" of the chief examiner Chang Chih-tung.[101] Even the system of examinations for returning students did not satisfy the journal. On one occasion it pointed out that "only a few successful candidates in the . . . examination had been retained by the government" and asked what had become of the great majority who had not been retained.[102] On another occasion a writer complained that the examination questions had been either "too difficult or too simple."[103] Perplexed by the increasing number of foreign-educated, the journal called in March, 1910, for a wholesale reorganization of provincial institutions "with a view to giving suitable employment to returned students."[104]

After the Republic was established in 1912, even though "the returned students had come into their own,"[105] five hundred of them were reported unemployed in Peking alone, with one hundred more unemployed in Shanghai and another fifty in Canton in June, 1916.[106] Conditions seemed to become even worse as time went on, for successive writers on the subject pointed to earlier years as the golden age for returning students. Thus, M. T. Z. Tyau, writing in 1922, stated that while the returned students had been in great demand in 1908, there was now an overabundance of them.[107] Shu Hsin-ch'eng, the

99. The most complete set of this interesting publication that the writer has seen runs from 1906 to 1913, of which the issues in 1906 were published in both Chinese and English, but the rest were only in English.

100. "The Recent Metropolitan Examination for Returned Students," WCSJ (September-October, 1907), 38-40.

101. "Educational Comments," WCSJ (November-December, 1908), 167.

102. Editorial, WCSJ (March, 1910), 209.

103. "The Value of the Peking Examination of the Foreign-Educated Students," WCSJ (May-June, 1909), 372.

104. Editorial, WCSJ (March, 1910), 210.

105. Mei Hua-chuan, "The Returned Student in China," CRR (March, 1917), 158.

106. *Ibid.*, 167.

107. TMTZ:CA, 25.

author of a special treatise on the problem of returned students, maintained in 1931 that "ten years ago the foreign-educated had no worry of employment, but now over two thousand of them are unemployed in Shanghai alone.[108]

What were the factors that underlay the perennial frustration of the foreign-educated in general and the Western-trained in particular? In Chapter 7, we shall see in statistical terms that few Western-trained held poor jobs and that they fared better than the Chinese-trained in most fields.[109] If, in spite of their comparative advantages, many Western-trained continued to feel frustrated, the indications are that they were poorly adjusted to the situation in China. An examination of the historical circumstances seems to confirm this situation.

The movement to study abroad began under circumstances that forced China to recognize Western superiority in an increasing number of fields. The movement did not consist of a continuous stream of students to the West, seeking knowledge for its own sake. It was closely related to the turn of political events in China, and the final blossoming of the movement coincided with a spectacular breakdown of the old order in 1900. These circumstances engendered, on the part of Chinese in general and the Western-educated in particular, a sense of the inferiority of China and an awesome respect for Western civilization. These psychological complexes were diametrically opposed to the belief, long held by Chinese literati, that China was by far the most civilized country on earth; and the very tenacity with which this belief had been held now gave way to violent reaction. A deep inferiority complex characterized most Chinese intellectuals in the first three decades of the twentieth century and probably still influences a number of them. These feelings were sometimes bluntly expressed. Thus, when a Chinese student in England was asked to address a gathering in 1910, he began by saying, "Being a world-despised Chinaman, I could not help feeling, when I cast my eyes upon myself, how unworthy I am for such a great honor."[110] But candid expressions of this type were comparatively rare. More commonly the psychology was expressed in an increasing lack of interest in China's past and a painful effort to avoid identification with Chinese institutions that had strong traditionalist features. Thus, Chinese students abroad almost invariably took pains to distinguish themselves from the men in Chinatown. On a higher level, but in the same vein, Wu Chih-hui, who later became an elder statesman of the Kuomintang, once emphatically declared that "all Chinese string-

108. Shu Hsin-ch'eng, "Preface to the Special Issue of Whither Chinese Education," CHCYC, Vol. XIX, No. 3, p. 3.
109. See pp. 174-82.
110. C. C. Lu, "China of Today," WCSJ (January, 1910), 269.

bound books (i.e., books printed and bound before the Western impact) should be thrown into the toilet and not read for thirty years."[111]

The counterpart of this feeling of inferiority was a painful effort to imitate the West in every possible way. In 1897, Hsü Ching-ch'eng, then Chinese Minister to St. Petersburg and later a martyr in the Boxer uprising, asserted that over-Westernization was quite impossible for a Chinese; hence he advised Lu Cheng-hsiang, a future prime minister, to become a Christian in order to Westernize himself thoroughly. Lu not only accepted this advice but subsequently married a Belgian lady, spent a great many years abroad, and finally, after his wife died, became a priest in Belgium.[112] The earlier Chinese students in America showed the utmost concern about mastering English and apparently spent an enormous amount of time and effort on this task alone.[113] A number of them competed with Americans in oratorical contests and carried off many signal honors. Some even became chief editors of their college papers. Yet on the whole the scholastic standing of these students did not extend beyond the undergraduate level. The assiduous efforts at imitation reached a climax in 1917, when a group of top-ranking professors in China advocated with great seriousness the complete abandonment of the Chinese national heritage and the "total Westernization of China."[114]

The loss of faith in Chinese institutions and the worship of Western practices generated a highly inflated ego on the part of the returned students. If China could be saved only through the adoption of Western knowledge, who would be able to perform this mission but those trained in the West? This way of thinking led to the accepted notion that "the returned students are the leaders and saviors of the nation." By virtue of their contacts with the West, these students were assumed to be fully equipped—morally and technically—for the task of redeeming the fallen nation. Though the myth was somewhat discredited after 1925, the prestige of the Western-trained remained remarkably high.

Because of the prevalence of these ideas, many of the Western-trained became extremely arrogant. Their overbearing attitude can be seen in two statements made in 1909 and 1913. From Cambridge, Massachusetts, it was reported in 1909 that "a few men intend to return to China this Summer. . . . Their return means an increase of that force

111. WCH:HSLC, 122-24.
112. LK:LCH.
113. E. K. Moy, "Thirteen Years of Chinese Students," *CSM* (December, 1923), 7.
114. The phrase "total Westernization of China" *(Ch'uan-p'an hsi-hua)* did not seem to appear in the writings of the New Cultural leaders, but the thought is commonly attributed to them. For a more thorough discussion of the subject, see CKY:CHWH, 302-20; CHC:CKWH, particularly Chapter V; SHC:CTCK, 208-9.

in China which represents integrity, efficiency, and, above all, patriotism."[115] Four years later a notable passage appeared in the *World Chinese Students' Journal:* "Happily for China, when the nation was on the verge of disintegration, a slight balance on the right side of the wheel of fate prevented its final ruin. And this balance was undoubtedly made possible through the element of the early students returning from abroad, to whom we owe the quick awakening of the nation in the last fifteen years."[116]

It is interesting to note that the highly inflated ideas of the Western-trained in China were shared by many eminent Westerners. Bertrand Russell, writing in 1922, maintained that callousness was a native Chinese vice and that "for the sake of money all except a few foreign-trained will be guilty of corruption."[117] Five years later Paul Monroe contended that the solution of China's problems lay "in the hands of the modern generation of students,"[118] that "many of the best of the returned students" would serve to guide and restrain the country,"[119] and that "when the time of deliberation and negotiation comes . . . the returned students will take a not insignificant part."[120] Professor Arthur N. Holcombe, in the Lowell Institute Lectures of 1930, dwelt at length on the number of leading men in China who had received their education abroad and observed that "all the principal bureau chiefs in the [Chinese] Ministry of Finance were Harvard graduates."[121]

The inflated egos of the Western-trained naturally found expression in material terms. As early as 1881, the Foochow students were determined to use their knowledge to secure high positions and good pay.[122] A different and more arrogant attitude was adopted by Yung Wing. In his management of the Chinese Educational Mission, Yung completely ignored his instructions and the basic purpose of the mission. Yet, when it failed, he would concede no other cause than the ignorance and reactionary stand of his colleagues.[123] Though an official of the Chinese government, he corresponded in English with the Chinese Minister to Washington, who knew no language other than Chinese.[124] Appointed in 1895 by Chang Chih-tung as "secretary of foreign affairs in Kiangnan," Yung resigned three months later on the

115. "Harvard News," CSM (March, 1909), 310.
116. Hyne Sun, "The Returned Student and the Coolie," WCSJ (July, 1913), 397.
117. RB:PC, 223.
118. MP:CN, 412.
119. *Ibid.,* 294.
120. *Ibid.*
121. HAN:SC, 3-7.
122. PLHK, 20.3b.
123. *Supra,* Chapter 2.
124. TKY:CS, 28a (Kuang-hsü 16/2/17)

grounds that Chang failed to accept his ideas for the modernization of China.[125] That Chang, a veteran reformer and statesman of great note, was expected to yield to Yung, who had lived in America but knew little about his native country, indicates the mood of the Western-trained in the early stages of the movement to study abroad.

The exaggerated sense of self-importance on the part of the returned students was naturally inimical to their employment. The role of leadership to which they aspired implied a concomitant desire to secure high positions. The success of many of the returned students in the bureaucracy toward the end of the Manchu regime no doubt set the pace that the majority sought to emulate. But the number of such posts was limited and could not be attained by all. A contemporary account in English described the situation thus:

> As education has in China always been identified with official career, the new educational system in spite of its Western influence, has not been successful in separating the two from the minds of our students; and whatever may be the profession, the magnetic pole of the returned student's ambition has been Peking with its glamor of official distinction. This idea has certainly been encouraged by the easy way in which a student fresh from college can push himself into official circles. The result, as must naturally be expected, is a contempt for the ordinary routine of work; and apart from the teaching profession and official position, the returned student considers it below his dignity to undertake an enterprise which savors of ordinary and commonplace occupation. He is too high for a small position, but too inexperienced to fill any responsible position. Hence he will get neither.[126]

That the difficulty was not unforeseen by the government is clear from a memorial presented by Sun Chia-nai in 1898 mentioning employment as an important aspect of the educational problem.[127] But little could be done, for the government realized the urgent need for newly-trained personnel and understood that they were the last hope of the tottering regime. Through strenuous efforts, the regime made thousands of new men available, but not unsurprisingly they had very little practical training. The government was now in an even greater quandary. Whereas the initial promise of employment had exposed its perilous situation and bred secret contempt, subsequent amendments constituted, to those who had answered the call, a breach of faith. Resentment turned both the unemployed and the unemployable against the regime.

125. LTE:CFH, 63.
126. "Editorials," WCSJ (July, 1911), 388.
127. See Sun's memorial relating to the establishment of a university in HAWP, *chüan* 15.

EXPATRIATION

From the very beginning of the movement to study abroad there was a tendency for Chinese students to forsake their native country and become citizens of the countries in which they studied. Yung Wing, the first Chinese to graduate from an American university, became a United States citizen in 1852 while he was still at Yale.[128] Although he returned to China in 1854, he refused to marry a Chinese and for a number of years was perturbed by the thought that no American lady would marry him.[129] Finally, in 1875, while he was in charge of the educational mission from China, he married Miss Louise Kellogg of Hartford.[130] After several trips to China, during which he sought unsuccessfully to introduce various reform proposals, he returned permanently to Hartford. Before he died in 1911 he was a large shareholder in the Gatling Gun Factory in the Connecticut capital.[131]

Yung's expatriation was emulated by a number of his pupils. Two of them, Yung Kwai and Tan Yew Fun, refused to return to China when they were recalled in 1881. Tan died soon afterwards, but Yung graduated from Yale and remained in the United States. In May, 1894, he married Miss Mary Burnham of Springfield, Massachusetts. This event caused a social furor, for there was great popular disapproval of the marriage. However, several of Yung's journalist friends rallied to his defense. They maintained that his family in China was "next to that of the emperor"[132] and stressed that Yung himself was all but American. In a letter to a newspaper, one of Yung's friends, C. T. Whittlesley, quoted the *Springfield Weekly Republican* approvingly: "He [Yung Kwai] is an American gentleman in education, culture, and dress. He does not betray his nationality in speech, and the only remnant of China is the body—that heritage of ancestry which no man can escape. What can be done to escape heredity, has been done by Mr. Kwai in intellectual and ethical advancement."[133]

Yung received his A.B. from Yale in 1884 and later took several postgraduate courses in biology and chemistry. From 1890 until 1893, he served as an interpreter for the Chinese legation in Washington. From 1893 to 1897 he lived in New York, working as a reporter and managing a Chinese club.[134] From 1897 until his death in 1943, he

128. LTE:CFH, 42.
129. *Ibid.*
130. *Ibid.*
131. V. P. Suvoong, "Yung Wing," WCSJ (September, 1912), 63-67.
132. BDG (May 24, 1894). The legend apparently lasted, for a clipping from some New England newspaper in 1908 repeated it. The clipping was shown to me by Mrs. Gertrude Tong, to whom I am greatly indebted for many materials.
133. A clipping in Mr. Burnham Yung-Kwai's possession. The letter is dated June 8, 1894, but the newspaper in which it appears cannot be identified.
134. BDG (May 24, 1894).

was a member of the Chinese diplomatic service and was stationed in Washington. Yung's thorough knowledge of the United States and his long years of experience made him unique among Chinese residents in the United States.[135] In an obituary notice, the *New York Times* called him "the permanent Chinese diplomat."[136]

Another of the original C.E.M. students, Jang Ting Seong (Cheng T'ing-hsiang), returned to China in 1881 but was determined to visit the United States once again. In 1883 he stowed away on an official junk, hoping thereby to reach America. Luckily for him, he encountered T'ang Shao-i, one of the C.E.M. students who had become prominent, and T'ang agreed to help him return to America.[137] Jang resumed his studies and graduated from the Worcester Polytechnic Institute in 1887. He subsequently became well known in New York as a consulting engineer and participated in the construction of the Brooklyn Bridge. He devised the "Jang method" of coupling railway cars and made many other technical inventions. He was twice offered responsible positions in the Chinese government but accepted none. He died in July, 1909, and was survived by his American wife and children.[138]

Several other C.E.M. students forsook their Chinese nationality. In fact, it has been estimated that between 5 and 10 per cent of the original 120 boys became citizens of other countries.[139] Their expatriation had been strictly forbidden by the regulations of the mission and was carried out at great hazard and under difficult circumstances.[140] Their determination to become American citizens indicates their irresistible attraction to the United States. Although all of the expatriates reared families in the United States, information about their descendants is difficult to obtain, for many adopted American surnames and became reluctant to reveal their Chinese background. Among the descendants of the C.E.M. expatriates, we know that one man was killed in France during World War I while serving in the United States army. Another became a prominent American citizen and served as Dean of the Sheffield Scientific School of Yale University.

It is interesting to compare the educational status of the C.E.M. expatriates to that of the students who returned to China. Of the 120 original students, four of the eight who eventually received college degrees were expatriates. At the same time, out of the more than one

135. ES (March 19, 1943).
136. NYT (March 21, 1943).
137. LTE:CFH, 142.
138. Y.S.C., "Life of Jang Landsing," CSM (January, 1910), 186-87.
139. According to Liang Chi-ch'ao ("*Hsin-ta-lu yu-chi*," LCC:YPSCC), some ten C.E.M. boys were still in the United States in 1903. If this was true, the percentage would be ten.
140. TKY:CS, entry dated Kuang-hsü 15/11/4.

hundred students who did not finish college, only one subsequently returned to live in the United States. Thus a correlation seems to exist between education and expatriation, for the general educational level of the expatriates was considerably higher than that of the returning students. However, there seems to have been no causative effect between the two, for those who sought foreign citizenship had apparently made up their minds to leave China before they received any college training. A contemporary observer attributed their alienations to poor family backgrounds and inferior material conditions surrounding them at home.[141] As far as material conditions are concerned, the American way of life was probably very attractive to a Chinese, regardless of whether he came from a poor family. At the same time, in the traditional Chinese social structure, family ties were generally weaker among the poorer classes than among the wealthier; hence a student from a poor family probably felt less emotional attachment to his native society. In the case of the C.E.M. students, the most decisive factors seem to have been the age at which they were sent to the United States and the length of their study abroad. College education was also probably a factor to the extent that those who received higher training were more easily assimilated into American society and were better prepared to meet the demands of foreign citizenship.

141. William Hung (trans.), "Huang Tsun-hsien's poem 'The Closure of the Educational Mission in America,'" HJAS (June, 1955), 53.

[5] The Period
1912-1927

The period from 1912 to 1927 can be divided into two sub-periods by the death of Yüan Shih-kai in 1916. Before that time the government, although beginning to undergo many changes, retained a basic continuity with the past; after 1916 the militarists whom Yüan appointed as provincial officials to reinforce his own power became virtually independent of the government in Peking. Civil wars were waged for the personal interests and aggrandizement of various warlords. After 1920 the cabinet members in Peking became virtual appointees of the warlords in power, and they rose and fell according to the fortunes of their masters. The central government exercised little power, and, because it was unable to collect revenues from the provinces, it was hard pressed to pay even the salaries of its civil servants. Certain ministries were more fortunate in this regard than others because they enjoyed direct sources of income. The Ministry of Communications, for example, ran the railways and received revenue from them. But the Ministry of Education was one of the least solvent government departments. For months and years its employees received only a fraction of their salaries, and they repeatedly went on strike in protest. The same situation prevailed in the eight government schools in Peking.[1] The educational program, which had received so much government attention during the last decade of Manchu rule, now became a forgotten project, as far as the central government was concerned. Leadership in education passed largely to private educators, most of whom had studied in America. Particularly prominent were those trained in the Teachers College of Columbia University.[2] A striking example of the influence of the American-trained in this period was the new educational system promulgated by the government in 1922, which was patterned after the American system. The whole project was first embodied in a resolution of the Federated Educational Association of China, a private organization of educators. The Ministry of Education simply adopted the resolution and put it into effect.[3]

1. Li Chin-hsi, "The Kuo-yu Movement in the Last Thirty-five Years," in SSWN, 121, 131; TCP:CKC, 91, 102, 103, 108, 132.
2. KLY:APA, p. 140; Yi-yi, "The Problem of Returned Students," CHCYC, Vol. XIII, No. 10, p. 4.
3. Ho Ping-sung, "Chinese College Education in the Last Thirty-Five Years," in SSWN, 102.

GOVERNMENT EDUCATIONAL POLICY

In the first years of the Republic, government policy in regard to study abroad closely followed the line pursued by the Manchus, that is, the government maintained a large number of scholarships for foreign study, mostly in Japan. But records were poorly kept, if at all, and few details are known. The following excerpt from the educational report of Szechuan province in 1914 indicates a typical situation.

After the fall of the dynasty, there were changes in administrative personnel. Files and records disappeared. The students [abroad] returned or changed schools. Hence it was difficult to keep track of them. . . . There used to be three kinds of scholarships tenable in Japan: the Five Schools scholarships, provincial scholarships, and local scholarships. The last consisted of agricultural students and were handled by the Intendent for Industries during the Ch'ing dynasty. . . . After the downfall of the Manchus, . . . the only information we had was the number of provincial scholarships listed in the provincial budget of 1911, 64. We did not know the names of these students. Under the circumstances we decided to grant 270 dollars to each student then in Szechuan who was going back to Japan. Another four thousand dollars were remitted to the legation in Tokyo to be distributed at its discretion among the Szechuan students there. . . . [Later] the legation sent us the names of 64 Five Schools scholars and 22 agricultural students. Upon examination, however, the list proved to be untrustworthy since many on the list were known to have [left Japan and to have] come home. . . . Thus we were compelled to remit 29,977 dollars [to the legation in Tokyo to be distributed as it saw fit]. . . . Only in the spring of 1913 did the legation send us a more reliable list of students. As of December, 1912, there were 118 provincial scholars in all three categories, of whom 70 were in Japan and 48 on leave in Szechuan. There were in addition 73 self-supporting students.

There were no provincial students from Szechuan in America. According to the record of remittances, as of the sixth intercalary moon of 1911, there were six students in France, three in Belgium, two in Great Britain, and one in Germany. In 1912 the Chief of Civil Affairs decided to send 40 more students to Europe and America. Thirteen were selected in April, 1913, but the rest of the proposed scholarships were canceled at the order of the Ministry of Education. As of June, 1914, there are 17 students in the West: America, 7; Germany, 4; Great Britain, 2; France, 3; Belgium, 1. These do not include the self-supporting and the scores of students sent to Belgium by the Bureau of Railways.[4]

4. SSCYHC, 161-88.

Theoretically, the award of provincial scholarships was subject to the supervision of the central government. Under the Manchus the Board of Education had been content to establish general regulations. Between 1912 and 1916 the selection of provincial students was made by the Ministry of Education in Peking. A regulation of 1916 required all provincial students to undergo two examinations, one at the provincial level and one in Peking. But the ministry was to determine the number of scholarships to be awarded, the subjects to be studied, and the countries in which study would be allowed.[5] However, when China's agreement with Japan in regard to the specially appointed schools expired in 1922, the Ministry of Education relaxed its control over provincial scholarships for students in Japan and, in so far as its directives had any effect on the provinces, limited its attention to scholarships in Western countries.[6]

In 1916 the Ministry also directed the provinces to maintain the same number of scholarships that they had reported in 1914.[7] The exact number of scholarships reported in that year cannot be ascertained, but a list published in 1926, which is probably representative of the period from 1914 to 1926, indicates 358 scholarships for study in Europe and America and 1,045 more for Japan.[8] However, it should be noted that these scholarships were probably fully awarded only in the early years of the Republic when the political situation was fairly stable and government officials retained a keen interest in education. In addition to the regular scholarships, special fellowships were awarded from time to time. Thus about a hundred "revolutionary workers," including T. V. Soong, Jen Hung-chün, and many others who later became prominent, were sent abroad in 1912 in response to their wish not to become officials but to engage in further academic endeavor.[9] In 1917 the Ministry of Education provided twenty-four scholarships for secondary and college teachers to study abroad. In 1918 a group of college professors, including Chu Chia-hua, Liu Fu, Teng Ts'ui-ying, and Yang Yin-yü, were sent to Europe and America.[10] In 1922 the Ministry announced that no awards would be made for that year.[11]

Chinese government fellowships abroad were subject to one great inconvenience, the failure of stipends to arrive on time. The delay

5. "Educational News," CYTC, Vol. IX, No. 3.
6. CKCYHI, see in particular the motion submitted by Ch'en Li-chiang.
7. "Educational News," CYTC, Vol. IX, No. 3.
8. For the detailed listing, see WYC:CIW, 135.
9. WCSJ (September, 1912), 87; Chiang Wei-ch'iao, "From the Ministry of Education in Nanking to the Ministry of Education in Peking," CYTC, Vol. XXVII, No. 4, p. 4. See also THTHL for the names of the men sent abroad. Apparently the fund came from the Boxer indemnity returned by the United States.
10. CYTC, Vol. X, No. 8, p. 64.
11. TCP:CKC, 97.

seems to have occurred first during the revolution of 1911. From London, the Chinese Supervisor of Students, Ch'ien Wen-hsüen, reported: "Literary Chancellors were wont to supply the students abroad regularly with . . . funds . . . but since the revolution two lifelong months have rolled by without even a word from them. We were constrained to apply for a loan of £5,000 at the China-Belgian Bank in London, which was granted only after lengthy and difficult negotiations. . . ."[12] From America, a student reported that "provincial students are cut off from their support" and that he himself had already discontinued his studies.[13] The temporary financial difficulties of 1911 appeared again in 1917 as political chaos spread in China. By 1921 a number of provinces were some two years behind in their remittances to students in the United States.[14] At first the supervisors of students abroad secured loans from banks, but eventually the situation became so hopeless that the supervisors either resigned or went into hiding to evade the needy students.[15] These difficulties dampened the spirit of provincial authorities, and the number of scholarships decreased. In 1914 there were 164 provincial students in the United States;[16] in 1922, 167; but in 1925, only 110.[17] In December, 1923, the Ministry of Education directed the provinces not to send students abroad for a year.[18] But because the provinces were independent of one another and the central government as well, the practice of sending students abroad did not cease immediately. In some cases, provincial authorities were pressed by candidates to make awards regardless of actual financial conditions, because the students were attracted by the prestige accorded foreign study and were willing to go abroad in the hope that stipends would be forthcoming at a future date.[19]

Under the Republic the government moved away from paternalism toward less supervision of students abroad. In March, 1913, the office of Supervisor of Students in Japan and European countries was abolished.[20] In August a single "Manager" was appointed to take charge of fellowship payments to students in all European countries except Russia.[21] But in 1915, the office of Supervisor was restored and remained in existence until 1924, when it was finally abolished.[22] A

12. WCSJ (March, 1912), 738-39.
13. *Ibid.*
14. "Chinese Students and Government Support," CSM (May, 1925), 39-41.
15. "Government Education," ER (1921), 291; ER (1922), 97-99, 221, 316, 405-6; CSM, Vol. XX, No. 7, pp. 39-41, and Vol. XX, No. 8, pp. 6-7.
16. CSD (1914).
17. HCS (1922).
18. TCP:CKC, 108.
19. CSM, Vol. XX, No. 8, p. 7.
20. SHC:CTCK, 169.
21. "Chronology of Events," CYTC, Vol. V, No. 8.
22. 2d CYNC, 896.

"Manager" for Japan was appointed in January, 1914, with the authority to supervise the study and behavior of Chinese government students there. His title was changed back to "Supervisor" in December, 1914.[23] Under the Supervisor were "Managers" appointed by each province to oversee their own students.[24] The larger supervisory groups in Japan continued in existence until the outbreak of war in 1937[25] and reflected both the greater number of Chinese students there and the common opinion in China that stricter supervision was needed for students in Japan. In America, when the Boxer indemnity students began to arrive in 1909, a special mission was established in Washington, D.C., for their supervision. In 1913 the Ministry of Education appointed the supervisor of Tsinghua students to take care of all recipients of Chinese central and provincial government scholarships. In 1916 a separate office, known as the Chinese Educational Bureau, was established;[26] and in 1917 it began to assume the character of a loan-contracting agency. Finally worn out by this tedious chore, the director of the bureau resigned in 1925 and left America, unnoticed by the stranded students.[27] The organization was never revived.

In 1915, an examination for the returned students was held. Candidates were graded upon the basis of degrees received while abroad and upon performance on the examination. Degrees from Western universities and Japanese government universities ranked first, those of Japanese private universities and government high schools came second, and the diplomas of the two-year courses in Japanese private universities or government high schools ranked last. Of the 192 candidates, 151 completed the examination successfully.[28]

All of those who passed received official appointments, but at a lower level than those awarded under the Manchus. Among the candidates, the best known was perhaps Weng Wen-hao,[29] the geologist, who became premier under Chiang Kai-shek but later reverted to his role as a scientist under the Communist regime. The examination of 1915 was held at the personal order of Yüan Shih-kai and was not continued after his death. In 1918 the Ministry of Education promulgated regulations offering cash rewards to Chinese students in Japan for good attendance at school and superior performance on examinations. But the amount of the rewards was not large, and they seem to have had little effect.[30]

23. SHC:CTCK, 172.
24. *Ibid.*, 171-72.
25. 2d CYNC, 896.
26. *Ibid.*
27. CSM, Vol. XX, No. 7, p. 39.
28. SHC:CTCK, 191.
29. "Current Events," CYTC, Vol. VII, No. 4, p. 41.
30. SHC:CTCK, 192-93.

A significant feature of government policy between 1912 and 1928 was the absence of efforts to induce students abroad to concentrate on technical disciplines. In 1914 the Ministry of Education officially announced that all self-supporting students must be middle-school graduates or teachers in middle schools or above.[31] In 1916, an eighteen-article regulation was issued by the Ministry of Education in regard to the selection of government students to be sent abroad.[32] All candidates were required to be graduates of Chinese or foreign colleges, or teachers of two years' standing in Chinese colleges. In the case of provincial scholarships, candidates were required to undergo two qualifying examinations, one in their native province and another in the capital under the Ministry of Education. Significantly, the fields of study were left to the discretion of the Minister of Education. There was thus a tacit de-emphasis on technology, which reflected the prevailing opinion that all Western learning was superior. Not until the rise of the Kuomintang to power in 1928 was technology again emphasized by the government. In this respect, as in a number of others, the "warlord era" from 1916 to 1927 witnessed a liberal tendency in government policy, albeit a very ineffective one.

In general, the government adopted a laissez-faire attitude toward self-supporting students except in special circumstances. In 1914, because self-supporting students in Japan were demanding subsidies from the government, regulations were established for their supervision.[33] In 1917, an executive order of the ministry reaffirmed the provision that all students going abroad must secure an authorization-certificate from the ministry beforehand.[34] In 1923, when it was learned that a number of Chinese were using student passports in order to engage in non-academic activities abroad, the Ministry of Foreign Affairs made the authorization-certificate a prerequisite to the issuance of student passports.[35] In July, 1924, regulations were issued for the supervision of self-supporting students because of reports that a large number of them, poorly prepared academically as well as financially, were having difficulties abroad. Among other things, the need to secure an authorization-certificate from the ministry was again emphasized.[36] But Chinese opinion continued to favor a hands-off policy toward self-supporting students,[37] and the requirement of a certificate from the Ministry of Education was largely inoperative.

31. CYTC, Vol. XVI, No. 9, p. 8.
32. *Ibid.*, Vol. IX, No. 3.
33. *Ibid.*, Vol. XVI, No. 9.
34. TCP:CKC, 70.
35. HCHSH (1923), Appendix, letter from the Commissariat of Foreign Affairs.
36. "Laws," CYPKP, 11th Year, No. 8, p. 3.
37. See, for instance, Ao Yüan-huai, "A Discussion of the Post-War Policy of Study Abroad," CYTC, Vol. XXXII, No. 2, p. 34.

CHINESE STUDENTS IN FRANCE

The enthusiasm of the intellectuals for Western civilization naturally gave impetus to the movement to study abroad. In 1912 a number of Kuomintang leaders who had studied or stayed in France, including Wang Ching-wei, Wu Chih-hui, Li Shih-tseng, Chang Ching-chiang, and Ch'u Min-i, established a Thrift-Study Society in Peking for the purpose of encouraging Chinese to study in France in an economical way.[38] Similar societies were founded in Szechuan and Shanghai for the promotion of study in France as well as in other Western countries. According to the society in Peking, a student needed only 600 dollars in Chinese currency anually for all his expenses in France.[39] At the prevailing exchange rate, this sum was equivalent to approximately 1,400 francs (or U.S. $270),[40] which was actually far from adequate for a student's needs in France at that time.[41] The scheme reflected the eagerness of certain individuals to encourage the movement to study abroad, and in 1912-13 some eighty students went to France under the sponsorship of the Thrift-Study Society in Peking.[42]

In 1914, because several Chinese laborers in France were studying at their own expense, the society conceived the idea of sending students who would support themselves by working part time. A new organization, the Diligent-Work-Thrift-Study Society, was formed, but the plan could not be launched because of the war in Europe. In 1916 the French government began to recruit laborers in China, mainly through the Hui Min Company in Peking[43] and to a lesser extent through the Thrift-Study Society.[44] About 200,000 Chinese laborers were sent abroad and among them in the later batches were "quite a few students and teachers."[45]

The presence of such students in France and the great demand for Chinese labor fired the imagination of the Diligent-Work-Thrift-Study leaders, and the movement was vigorously promoted. First, Li Shih-tseng and other officials stressed China's need to send students abroad

38. "Regulations of Peking Society of Thrift Study in France," LJ, Vol. III, No. 2, pp. 1-4.
39. *Ibid.*
40. CY (1939), 255.
41. I am indebted to the late Dr. Tsien Tai for this information. Dr. Tsien took his doctorate in Paris in 1914 and was at one time Chinese ambassador to France.
42. "Regulations of the Peking Society for Thrift Study in France," LJ, Vol. III, No. 2, p. 2.
43. LYSNP, I, 447-54.
44. SHC:CTCK, p. 89, footnote 2; Judith Blick, "The Chinese Labor Corps in World War I," HPC, IX, 115.
45. CKCYTT, 353-54. For a general discussion of Chinese laborers in France during the first world war, see CT:CM, Chapter IX.

as well as the advantages of study in France, where "one year's work could pay for two years of study."[46] A number of schools were established in various Chinese cities in order to prepare students for study in France. Second, the Société Franco-Chinoise d'Éducation was organized in Paris for the purpose of promoting cultural relations between the two countries. This organization assumed a large role in the work-and-study movement.[47] Third, Li Shih-tseng, Ts'ai Yüan-p'ei, Wang Ching-wei, and others solicited the support of important government officials. Large sums of money were donated by the President, the cabinet ministers and vice-ministers, and various provincial officials. The head of the Chinese Emigration Bureau, established in connection with the Chinese labor corps abroad, was one of the most enthusiastic supporters of the work-and-study movement. Provincial authorities and civic leaders made strenuous efforts to advance the movement; in some cases, not only the travel expenses of the worker-students but also regular subsidies were paid by provincial treasuries.[48]

On the French side, the Chinese were welcomed with open arms. Various factories competed in the recruiting of Chinese, and some went to the trouble of securing special dormitories and food for the worker-students. The arrival of Chinese in Paris became the occasion for special welcoming editorials in the newspapers.[49] Even Americans in Paris helped to provide the Chinese with adequate accommodations on their arrival.[50] The daily wages of Chinese worker-students varied from fifteen to forty francs,[51] and many of them were able to make sizable savings.[52] Hence the number of such students increased from a few score in May, 1919, to over four hundred at the end of the year,[53] and to some seventeen hundred at the beginning of 1921.[54]

Meanwhile the situation in France began to change for the worse in the second half of 1920, as the postwar depression led to mounting unemployment. By the beginning of 1921 practically all of the worker-students were in need of financial assistance. For a time emergency loans were made to them by the Société Franco-Chinoise d'Éducation out of funds remitted from China,[55] but the situation soon became critical. The environmental difficulties were complicated by administrative problems. The worker-student movement had been initiated

46. SHC:CTCK, 89.
47. Pien Hsiao-hsüan, "Materials on the Diligent-Work-Thrift-Study Movement," CTST, 174-204; SHC:CTCK, 95-96.
48. *Ibid.*, p. 90, footnote 4.
49. Pien Hsiao-hsüan, *op. cit.*, 180.
50. "Government Education," ER (April, 1920), 189-90.
51. A report by Shen I-chia quoted in SHC:CTCK, 92.
52. Pien Hsiao-hsüan, *op. cit.*, 179.
53. *Ibid.*, 192.
54. SHC:CTCK, p. 98, footnote 1.
55. Pien Hsiao-hsüan, *op. cit.*, 185.

by several Kuomintang leaders, but none of them remained in France to supervise the students. The actual management of the Society was left in the hands of subordinates who enjoyed little prestige among the students and were probably not equipped to handle this difficult assignment.[56] The funds were soon exhausted, and the relations between the Society and the students became very strained. When the situation finally deteriorated beyond repair, the sponsors of the movement lost interest and left the students to shift for themselves.[57]

In January, 1921, the head of the Society, Ts'ai Yüan-p'ei, who had arrived in France somewhat earlier, declared that after February 28 the Society would terminate all financial connections with the students. Greatly alarmed, the students appealed to the Chinese Minister to France for help. In response to pleas from the legation, the government in Peking promised to provide all the needy students with return passage to China.[58] But the students refused this offer and proposed that the legation should grant each of them a sum of four hundred francs per month for four years. In spite of this excessive demand, the legation solicited financial assistance wherever possible, and in May, 1921, a Franco-Chinese relief committee was established with a fund of fr. 906,500 donated by both Chinese and French.[59] In August, because the number of working students was continuing to decrease and the burdens of the committee were correspondingly mounting, it was decided to ask the students to apply for admission to regular schools. According to this plan, those who gained admission to schools would be supported by the committee, those who failed would be asked to secure employment, and those who could neither study nor work would be sent back to China. But before the plan could be carried out, a rumor began spreading among the worker-students that a political loan was being negotiated by the Chinese and French governments to the detriment of China's national interest. The students promptly declared their opposition to such "treacherous transactions" and staged demonstrations in Paris against both governments. In the resulting melee, several officials of the Chinese legation were assaulted by the students.[60] In September, the French government withdrew its support of the relief committee but, upon the Chinese legation's protest that its notice was too short, allotted an additional 100,000 francs to delay the effective date of its withdrawal to October 15, 1921. On September 21, the students announced their intention to enroll in

56. *Ibid.*, 184-86.
57. *Ibid.*, 185, 198; ER (1921), 191. According to the latter source, Li Shih-tseng, who originated the movement, was asked by the Chinese Ministry of Education to go to France to seek a settlement of the matter, but Li refused.
58. "Correspondence," HCHSH (1921).
59. SHC:CTCK, 98.
60. SC:HHKT, 62 ff.

the newly founded Franco-Chinese Institute at Lyon. To achieve this end, they transferred their union to Lyon and occupied the buildings of the Institute by force. They refused all orders to vacate the premises and had to be driven out by the police. The French Communist party supported the students and exerted political pressure on their behalf. As a consequence the French government decided to deport several of the worker-students.[61]

As soon as it learned of this development, the Chinese legation lodged a protest with the French government and sought contacts with other Chinese leaders in France in order to arrange a solution to the problem. Several proposals were advanced calling for the students to be classified into different groups so that the talented could be retained in France for study or work while the others would be sent home. But the effort met with little success, and over a hundred students were deported from France on October 13, 1921.[62] After that date the whole movement sponsored by the Diligent-Work-Thrift-Study Society collapsed. Out of some two thousand worker-students, a majority returned to China of their own accord, but four or five hundred remained in France.[63] A large number of the latter group became permanent settlers.

The Diligent-Work-Thrift-Study movement reflected the extraordinary Chinese enthusiasm for study abroad as well as an astounding absence of proper planning. There had been almost no screening of the students sent to France. The level of their education varied from students who had studied in Japan to students in primary schools. Some of these students had been technicians in Chinese factories[64] while others were mere riffraff. A number of them suffered from tuberculosis,[65] and about two hundred died in France.[66] The sending of such a heterogeneous group to France can be understood only in relation to the theories of the sponsors of the movement, who maintained that China must be "totally Westernized" and that the more Chinese who were sent abroad, the greater would be the results for China.[67] Overenthusiasm on the part of the sponsors made them disregard all foreseeable difficulties, and their prominence and their French educational backgrounds helped to convince the Chinese public of the soundness of the project. Because study abroad was a path to fame and success, the students accepted the plan without realizing what was involved. Most of them had no knowledge of the

61. SHC:CKCY, I, 333.
62. *Ibid.*, I, 334.
63. Li Huang, "The Problems of Study in France," CHCYC, Vol. XV, No. 9.
64. Pien Hsiao-hsüan, *op. cit.*, 192-95.
65. Li Huang, *op. cit.*
66. SC:HHKT, 61.
67. SHC:CTCK, 205-9.

heavy physical exertions expected of factory hands in Western countries, and a large number would have been unable to work their way through college even if there had been no depression in France.[68] But a minority did succeed in making the necessary adjustments and enjoyed moderate success during their sojourn in France. According to a writer in 1926, about a hundred of the worker-students learned enough in French factories to serve as technicians after their return to China, and another two hundred saved enough from their wages to pursue some kind of further study in France.[69]

A significant feature of the Diligent-Work-Thrift-Study movement was its connection with the Chinese Communist movement. Mao Tse-tung was one of the organizers in Peking of the Hunan students who were sent to France. One of the first cells of the Chinese Communist party was established in Paris by Chou En-lai and other worker-students.[70] As far as can be ascertained no less than thirteen prominent Chinese Communists were at one time worker-students in France.[71] Li Li-san, once the leader of the Chinese Communist party, was among those deported from France as agitators.[72] Thus the French passion for political radicalism seems to have had an important influence on the development of Chinese Communism.[73]

Another outgrowth of the Diligent-Work-Thrift-Study movement was the establishment of the Franco-Chinese Institute at Lyon. In 1917 the Thrift-Study Society established a preparatory school in a suburb in Peking. Later, the school was expanded into the Franco-Chinese University.[74] In 1921, through the efforts of Li Shih-tseng, Wu Chih-hui, and others,[75] the Chinese and French governments agreed to sponsor an institute in the University of Lyon. The original aim in establishing this institute (and a similar one at Charleroi in Belgium) was to provide the worker-students with a dormitory and facilities for learning French.[76] But by the time the Franco-Chinese Institute opened in 1921, the relations between the worker-students and Li

68. SC:HHKT, 67.

69. Li Huang, *op. cit.;* Shen I-chia, "Conditions of Chinese Students in France," CHCYC, Vol. XIII, No. 7.

70. HCKJWC, I, 32.

71. Chou En-lai, Ts'ai Ho-shen, Hsiang Ching-yü, Wu Yü-chang, Hsü T'e-li, Li Li-san, Li Fu-Ch'un, Ch'ien I, Ts'ai Ch'ang, Chang K'un-ti, Lo Hsüen-tsen, Wang Jo-fei, Lo Man (Li Wei-han).

72. SC:HHKT, 67.

73. It is interesting to note that the founder of the Chinese Communist Party, Ch'en Tu-hsiu, was also an admirer of France (see his article "The Frenchman and Modern Civilization," LJ, Vol. I, No. 1). Ch'en's passion against all traditional institutions and his eulogy of violence and bloodshed seemingly bear the influence of the French Revolution.

74. 1st CYNC, Section III, "Educational Conditions," p. 92.

75. SHC:CTCK, 99.

76. CYTTS, 74; Pien Hsiao-hsüan, *op. cit.,* 202, 204.

Shih-tseng's group had become strained. As a result, the worker-students were completely barred and recruitment was carried out in other areas. The first group of students were Chinese middle-school graduates brought to France by Wu Chih-hui himself.[77] By arrangement the Franco-Chinese University in Peking and the Chung-shan University in Canton each year sent five of their best graduates to the Institute.[78] Several Chinese students already residing in France were also admitted.[79] The students were divided into three classes: full scholars who were exempt from all expenses and provided with pocket money and transportation to and from China; scholars who were exempt from all expenses but not given pocket money; and students who were expected to pay their own way.[80] At one time the Institute had approximately 150 students, but by 1947, its last year of operation, its enrollment had fallen to eighty-five. Between 1932 and 1945 some seventy-six doctoral dissertations were submitted to and approved by the four faculties of the University of Lyon. The achievement of the students is said to have been high, and a majority of them secured the degree of *Licencié* or *Docteur*.[81]

The establishment of the Institute at Lyon involved heavy financial outlays. The initial expense of converting the premises, which had been built as a fort, amounted to over two million francs. Although it housed a maximum of only 150 students, the Institute had an annual budget of six hundred thousand francs, of which a large part was contributed by the Peking and Canton governments.[82] After 1925 the Institute was supported by refunds from the French Boxer indemnity.[83] Many Chinese educators criticized the project as unwise and a whimsical child of Li Shih-tseng and his supporters.[84]

In the years after World War I, the number of Chinese students in France, even excluding the worker-students, was large. An estimate made in January, 1920, placed the total number of Chinese students in France at six thousand, as compared to less than three thousand in the United States.[85] The factors that led Chinese students to select France were manifold, including the current Chinese aversion to Japan and Germany, the immigration restrictions of the United States, French

77. CYTTS, 74.
78. LFC, 1. I am indebted to Professor Georges Dubarbier of Lyon, France, for this material.
79. CYTTS, 74.
80. LFC, 2-3.
81. Information given by Professor G. Dubarbier.
82. SHC:CTCK, 99.
83. 2d CYNC, 1584.
84. Shen I-chia, *op. cit.*
85. CSM (January, 1921), 189-90. Among the six thousand in France were about two thousand worker-students.

hospitality to the Chinese,[86] low expenses in France, and the rising prestige and influence in China of men educated in western Europe.[87] The academic standards of the Chinese students in France were on the whole very low. Most Chinese were "auditors" in the universities, and the work of Chinese government students was even poorer than the rest. The political passion of these students was very high, in sharp contrast to the situation in other Western countries, especially Great Britain and the United States. In February, 1922, a former worker-student attempted to assassinate the Chinese Minister to France, Ch'en Lu, on the vague suspicion that he had betrayed the interests of the worker-students and was in general a traitor to his country.[88]

CHINESE STUDENTS IN AMERICA

During the years from 1912 to 1929 a steady flow of students traveled to America through the auspices of Tsinghua College. The first group of sixteen Tsinghua graduates sailed in 1912, but no students were sent in 1913 because the government was short of funds.[89] Beginning in 1914, Tsinghua graduates were sent each year to the United States. By the time the college was reorganized in 1929 and the practice of sending all graduates abroad had ended, some 1,268 Tsinghua students had studied in the United States with the support of appropriations from the American Boxer indemnity funds.[90]

According to regulations set forth in the joint memorials of the Board of Education and the Wai-wu-pu in 1909, 80 per cent of the students sent to the United States were required to study technical subjects—agriculture, engineering, commerce, and mining—and 20 per cent, law, finance, and education. As it turned out, the fields of study of Tsinghua students in 1909-29 were as follows:[91]

Field of Study	Percentages of Students
Engineering	32.33
Science	10.99
Medicine	5.19
Agriculture	3.63
Military Science	1.94
Humanities	5.54
Music	.25
Social Sciences	23.84
Law	2.77

86. "Government Education," ER (April, 1920), 189-90.
87. Hsün-yü, "The Problem of Study in France," CYTC (1929), 107-8.
88. SC:HHKT, 67; CPH:HW, 190-214.
89. LSC:PSTC, 38-39.   90. THTHL.
91. Computed from THTHL.

Political Science	9.15	
Economics	10.38	
Sociology	1.54	
Education		5.04
Business		11.25
Total		100.00

This pattern was not appreciably different from the distribution of fields of study among all Chinese students in the United States, and it indicates the large degree of free choice allowed to the students themselves.

During their stay abroad, the Tsinghua students were expected to complete the requirements of a course with collegiate standing, but there were no restrictions placed on postgraduate study. At first the number of years allowed to students abroad was not prescribed, although there seems to have been a tacit understanding that students could remain abroad for seven years at the expense of the college. In 1913 or 1914, a new ruling came into effect which limited scholarships abroad to six years. The intention of this ruling was to prevent the students from "loafing."[92] Later, the scholarships were shortened to five years,[93] and then to four years. To a certain extent, the shortening reflected an advance in the academic standards of the Tsinghua students before going abroad. The students sent out from 1909 to 1911 were youngsters, of whom a number entered American high schools. The Tsinghua graduates of later years were usually admitted to American colleges as freshmen or sophomores, and after 1921 as juniors.[94]

The original plan as devised by the Board of Education and the Wai-wu-pu called for the sending of two kinds of students to America, a senior as well as a junior group. Twelve junior students were sent abroad in 1914,[95] but none were sent thereafter.

Beginning in 1914, since Tsinghua students were men, ten scholarships were offered every other year to women students from other schools. Competitive examinations were regularly held for these scholarships, and between 1914 and 1929 fifty-three girls were sent to the United States, generally for four years. If the goal of study abroad was to meet China's immediate needs, the award of scholarships to women probably served little purpose, for in most cases they did not go beyond the undergraduate level.[96] Nevertheless, the matter at-

92. F. Chang, "The Effects of the Six Year Limit," CSM (May, 1914), 551-53.
93. Regulation of Tsinghua College quoted in SHC:CTCK, 79. No date is given.
94. I am indebted to the late Mr. Y. C. Mei for this information.
95. LSC:PSTC, 51.
96. According to the Tsinghua Alumni Register of 1937, about two-fifths of these students became housewives, one-fifth college professors, one-fifth medical

tracted considerable public interest. When Tsinghua College temporarily halted the awards in 1920, violent protests came from women students throughout China.[97] This episode amply symbolized the spirit of Chinese intellectuals at the time: an unbounded enthusiasm for Western education and a strong wish to promote equality between men and women.

Between 1916 and 1929 scholarships were also awarded by Tsinghua on the basis of competitive examinations for male students at large. All candidates were university graduates, and those who received grants were sent to the United States to do postgraduate study. The duration of these scholarships was generally limited to three years. Sixty-two scholarships were awarded between 1916 and 1929, with two-thirds of them for study in the fields of engineering and the natural sciences. More than a third of the students received doctoral degrees and another half earned masters' degrees. In terms of their later careers, as of 1937 slightly less than one-half were university teachers and over one-fourth were in government service, the two major outlets for all Chinese intellectuals.[98]

In addition to these scholarships, Tsinghua College also made grants-in-aid to needy students in American colleges who had reached the rank of sophomore or above. These grants usually amounted to $480 a year, with three years as the maximum period of award.[99] Between 1914 and 1929, nearly five hundred men received such grants.[100] All of the scholarships and grants were administered by a supervisor of studies appointed by the Chinese Minister of Foreign Affairs, to whose jurisdiction Tsinghua College was subject until 1929. The supervisor's office, known as the Chinese Educational Mission, was located in Washington and remained in existence until September, 1933, when it turned its affairs over to the China Institute in America.[101] It is interesting to note that the supervisor or director usually exercised little control over the students' academic progress and was concerned mainly with disbursements. Nevertheless, the directorship was usually held by a man of standing and prestige in the Tsinghua group. The last two directors were Y. C. Mei, who relinquished the post in 1931 to become president of Tsinghua University, and Y. R. Chao, a well-known Chinese philologist who later became an Agassiz professor at the University of California.

---

doctors, and one-fifth workers in various fields such as the Y.W.C.A. Most of them had done their work abroad in pre-medicine, the humanities, science, or music.

97. "Home News," CSM, Vol. XVI, No. 2, p. 131.
98. Information derived from THTHL.
99. Regulations of Tsinghua College quoted in SHC:CTCK, 81.
100. Information derived from THTHL.
101. CBY:ACW, 255.

The fact that all graduates of Tsinghua College were provided scholarships for foreign study naturally enhanced the attractiveness of its program and made it a very special institution in China.[102] But as the number of its students in the United States increased to 440 in 1921 and 470 in 1923,[103] the college experienced financial difficulties. Meanwhile, the Chinese public became hostile toward an institution whose sole purpose was to prepare Chinese youth for American education.[104] They viewed the returned students with skepticism and found their knowledge shallow and their ability mediocre.[105] Even the alumni themselves advocated reform.[106] Accordingly, the college decided to admit no more "junior" students after 1920 and no more "senior" students after 1924. Instead, it enrolled one hundred freshmen in 1923 and became a full-fledged university in 1929. In the same year it ceased to send all of its graduates to the United States.[107]

Although the original program did not last, its impact was considerable. Because of family and other connections, the Tsinghua students tended to bring other Chinese with them to the United States, thus increasing the number and the influence of the American-trained in China. Second, on their return these men formed a select group whose influence was felt in both political and academic circles. Third, in spite of the unfavorable public image, a number of Tsinghua students became first-rate scientists and left important marks on the Chinese world of learning.[108]

But this last effect was unknown at the time. On the contrary, far more apparent was the fact that Tsinghua College went to great expense to remain a preparatory school on the American model. Such a course seemed unwise to the Chinese public, for two main reasons. First, American scholarship was not then considered fully equal to European, and second, the Chinese resented the immigration policy of the United States. In a bill passed on May 26, 1924, Congress placed severe restrictions on all Chinese, including students. In order to be admitted, a student was required to be at least fifteen years of age,

102. A song among Chinese girls ran: "Peita [Peking University] boys are old; Shih-ta [Normal University] boys are poor; only Tsinghua boys are eligible suitors." See EM, Vol. XL, No. 11, p. 57.

103. 2d CYNC, 599.

104. *Ibid.;* SHC:CTCK, 248-54.

105. *The Chinese Educational World* (CHCYC), a leading educational journal in China, had a special issue on study abroad in 1926. Most of the papers have a critical tone toward the returned students. A biting satire was written by K. C. Wu, then a student at Princeton, in "Thus Spake Adam," CSM (March, 1926), 79-81. See also E. M. Anderson, "Returned Western Students," in CMY (1932-33), 325.

106. THCK, Nos. 289 and 300, contain many such expressions.

107. 2d CYNC, 599.

108. See *infra,* Chapter 12.

to have been accepted by an accredited college approved by the Secretary of Labor, and to see that the institution in which he was enrolled kept the Secretary of Labor informed of the progress of his studies. Furthermore, the student was expected to leave the country upon graduation and was not allowed to be employed in a factory for practical work.[109] These provisions seemed so unjust to the Chinese that the Ministry of Education issued the following memorandum to the provinces.

This Ministry was in receipt of a telegram from our Education Commissioner in the United States to the effect that our government students were treated very harshly and that no more such students should be sent to that country. The contents of this telegram have already been communicated to you.

In recent years there has been an increasing stream of self-supporting students to the United States. Last year, students who went to that country numbered 176 as against 2 to the Philippines, 62 to Germany, 37 to France, and 2 to Belgium. In the first six months of this year 90 students went to the United States as against 1 to Honolulu, 2 to the Philippines, 2 to Canada, 2 to Germany, 20 to France, and 3 to England. In the last 18 months, therefore, self-supporting students to the United States numbered two-thirds of all self-supporting students to Western countries.

The cause of students' preference for the United States lies in the fact that admission to American colleges is easy to obtain and that credits earned at Chinese schools are recognized. In many cases a student can graduate with a degree in less than two or three years. . . . Among the self-supporting students [who go to the U.S.] there are unavoidably those whose only concern is to get a degree and who are not interested in study as such. Worse still, some are so alienated as to have adopted Western names and surnames, thus making it extremely difficult to identify them by their diplomas.

This Ministry is of the opinion that even if American scholarship is so superior that it cannot be excelled by other nations, the number of Chinese students to the United States still needs to be limited lest American influence predominate in China. Restrictions now imposed by the United States furnish a good occasion for us to take measures to forestall this danger. Beginning in this year, all provincial scholarships should be made tenable in countries other than the United States. The stipends due students now in the United States should be remitted without delay.[110]

109. Immigration Act of 1924, Sec. 4 (e) and Sec. 15, as reprinted in CAE:ILUS, 170, 184; Ruth Crawford Mitchell, "Foreign Students and the Immigration Laws of the United States," IIEB, No. 1, pp. 5-30; Chao-ying Shill, "The Effects of the Immigration Bill of 1924 on Chinese Students," CSM, Vol. XX, No. 2, pp. 16-19.
110. Reprinted in SHC:CTCK, 85-86.

Because of a later Chinese impression that provisions concerning Oriental students in the Immigration Act of 1924 had been temporarily suspended, the suggestion embodied in the memorandum of the Ministry of Education was not vigorously pushed and had little practical effect.[111] But the contents of the document are interesting because of the light they shed on the Chinese attitudes toward foreign study.

STUDENTS IN JAPAN

On the whole there were more Chinese students in Japan than any other country.[112] This was due in part to the Manchu policy of encouraging study in Japan by offering large numbers of scholarships, which was continued under the Republic for several years. But there were other factors as well. Among those mentioned in contemporary accounts were: (1) the geographical proximity of China to Japan, (2) the lower time and financial requirements of study in Japan, (3) the similarity between the Chinese and Japanese languages, (4) the social prestige of returned students in China, and (5) the desire to escape from chaotic conditions in China. Little need be said about the last two factors which were equally applicable to study in all foreign countries.[113] Some of the rest did not always hold true. The similarity in language was the result of the use of Chinese characters in Japanese writings. With the increasing use of kana by the Japanese, the similarity became less pronounced, and Chinese students in Japan were usually compelled to undergo lengthy preparation in the language. A writer in 1926 pointed out that it normally took a Chinese two years to learn enough Japanese to be able to enter a high school, five years to be proficient in the language, and eight years, from the time he entered high school, to finish college.[114]

Geographical proximity was an important factor. Low travel costs attracted many students who wanted a foreign education but could not afford a heavy initial outlay. But the same factor had other ramifications. The ease of travel meant that many who went to Japan, upon encountering initial difficulties, were likely to give up and return to China. The closer contacts of the Chinese in Japan with their families and friends at home tended on the whole to be a disturbing factor in their studies. Among other things, it increased their active response to political events in China. In 1911, for instance, a great majority of them returned to participate in the revolution, while in the years 1913 and 1914 the failure of a campaign against Yüan Shih-

111. SHC:CTCK, 86.
112. SK:CNRS, 351.
113. Chung-chiu, "The Question of Study in Japan," CHCYC, Vol. XV, No. 9.
114. Chung-chiu, *op. cit.*

kai brought a large number of Chinese political exiles to Japan, most of them as students. Immediately after Yüan's death in 1916, there was another exodus from Japan to China.[115] During some of the frequent diplomatic crises between China and Japan—which also resulted from geographical proximity—many Chinese students felt compelled to interrupt their studies and return to China, as a gesture of protest. This kind of exodus occurred in 1915, on the occasion of the Twenty-One Demands;[116] in 1918, when Japan forced a military defense pact on China;[117] and in 1931, on Japan's occupation of Manchuria.[118] Mass withdrawals also took place in 1905, in protest of the educational regulations issued by the Japanese government,[119] and in 1923, on the occasion of a severe earthquake in Japan.[120]

Because of geographical proximity, Japan was a haven par excellence for Chinese political refugees, who during their stay either became students or developed relations with bona fide students. In addition to all of these factors, the Japanese police force was a source of disturbance. Ever vigilant against radical thought, it never hesitated to act against a suspected person, and many Chinese suffered arbitrary arrests. Thus in May, 1919, several were imprisoned for their sympathy toward student demonstrators in Peking.[121] In March, 1923, four Chinese students were wounded and over twenty arrested by Japanese police for political demonstrations.[122] In September and October, 1929, approximately 130 Chinese students were arrested for alleged Communist activities.[123] In 1933, several Chinese were imprisoned in connection with student union activities.[124] Thus political activities regularly interfered with the academic work of Chinese students in Japan.

Contemporary sources also reported discrimination against China in some of the schools and limited facilities for study in general. One student said that Chinese were not admitted to the best courses and were assigned, in an anatomy course, disease-carrying bodies.[125] Another mentioned that Chinese were not allowed to visit industrial plants.[126] Still another said that even the Imperial University of

115. WCSJ (January, 1912), 729; SK:CNRS, 247.
116. CBY:ACW, 145.
117. SK:CNRS, 248; ER (July, 1918), 272.
118. CYTC, Vol. XXIII, No. 11, p. 111.
119. CMS:JPWH, 65-82.
120. *Ibid.*, 106.
121. WNK:HSYT, 11.
122. "Educational News," CYTC, Vol. XV, No. 4.
123. *Ibid.*, Vol. XXII, No. 1, p. 161.
124. HPY:TJP.
125. CBY:ACW, 142, 143, 147.
126. Li Ju-mien, "Criticism of the Movement to Study Abroad and a Suggested Future Policy," CHCYC, Vol. XV, No. 9.

Tokyo had a library of only 660,000 volumes, that because of the scarcity of books students often had to depend solely on notes taken in class, and that the Chinese were especially handicapped because they could not write Japanese fast enough to take down all a lecturer said.[127] Other complaints included the lack of creativity of Japanese scholars because of the absence of academic freedom and the prevalence of a conservative moral code that involved rigorous loyalty to the emperor and utmost deference to the head of the family.

In common with other nations, Japan paid considerable attention to Chinese students. Shortly after the Twenty-One Demands, the Japanese government decided on a campaign of friendship among the Oriental races. A special official, Okubo Shintaro, was sent to arrange with the Chinese Supervisor of Students for the implementation of the new policy. Several students were chosen as representatives from China and were granted certain privileges in visiting places and gaining practical knowledge.[128] Beginning in 1918, questions were asked repeatedly in the Japanese Diet about Chinese students. As a consequence, the Japanese government undertook to create a special fund for the aid of Chinese students. It also waived Chinese subsidy to the specially-appointed schools and established a Sino-Japanese cultural society, the Nikka Gakai, to render service to Chinese students and visitors. After a tour of the United States, a Japanese industrialist, Mochidbuki Gunshiro, endowed the Seijō Gakkō with half-a-million yen in order to emulate American hospitality to Chinese students.[129] In 1921-22, when stipends to Chinese government students fell into arrears, Japanese bankers loaned up to 500,000 yen for the maintenance of the students, while schools delayed the collection of fees and lodging houses deferred rents.[130] Yet such generous gestures could not efface the ill will nurtured by the constant friction between the two nations.

In 1923 Japan decided to return part of the Boxer indemnity to China for cultural purposes. An agreement was subsequently concluded by which 320 scholarships were to be awarded each year to Chinese students in Japan. Then the method of selection became a bone of contention among various groups of Chinese students in Japan.[131] Finally, the Ministry of Education in Peking decided that 10 scholarships should be reserved for professors of Chinese government universities and that the rest would be awarded to Chinese students in Japan according to quotas based on provincial origins. One-half of the scholarships would be awarded to self-supporting

127. Chung-chiu, *op. cit.;* CBY:ACW, 140-41.
128. CBY:ACW, 145-46.
129. CMS:JPWH, 62.
130. "Government Education," ER (1922), 99, 316, 405.
131. SHC:CTCK, 100-4.

students and the other half to Chinese government students. Monthly stipends were to be seventy yen per student, and priority would be given to students who had attained high academic levels in institutions of recognized standing. For the latter purpose a list was composed giving the order of all of the accredited colleges in Japan.[132]

The Boxer indemnity scholarships were first awarded in October, 1924.[133] By that time, Chinese estimates of the worth of Japanese education were quite low. Chinese provincial authorities therefore attempted to transfer their own scholarships in Japan to Western countries. For every Indemnity scholarship awarded to a provincial student, the Chinese government reduced one of its own scholarships to Japan.[134] Thus Japan's aim of securing more Chinese students was largely defeated. Furthermore, the management of the Indemnity refunds was unsatisfactory to China because Japan retained control of the funds. As anti-Japanese feelings continued to rise in China, the Kuomintang government in 1929 abrogated the agreement with Japan and stopped awarding Indemnity scholarships.[135] During the short time the agreement was in force, Chinese professors and students were on several occasions invited to tour Japan. In 1926 Japan expressed the hope that three student tours could be exchanged by China and Japan each year.[136] But in 1929 the Chinese government prohibited its subjects to accept further subsidies from Japan for travel purposes.[137]

Perhaps a word should be said of the number of Chinese students who were educated in Japan. An accurate estimate is difficult because many of these students traveled constantly and had no definite academic status. On the other hand, fairly reliable information is available about the number of all Chinese students who were in Japan at particular times in the years from 1900 through 1937.[138] If we interpolate for the few missing years by using the mean of the figures immediately preceding and following, the gross total for the period is 136,326. On the assumption that the minimum stay in Japan for any serious Chinese student was four years, we can divide the total by four and reach a net figure of 34,081.[139] This makes the Japanese-

132. *Ibid.*; "Boxer Indemnity and Education and Culture," 1st CYNC, II, 112-14.
133. SHC:CTCK, p. 104, footnote 1.
134. CHMK, 135.
135. TCP:CKC, 193.
136. "Educational News," CYTC, Vol. XVII, No. 5.
137. "Boxer Indemnity Funds and Education and Culture," 1st CYNC, II, 114.
138. The figures are taken from a variety of contemporary sources. For full documentation, see WYC:CIW, 279. The missing years are 1912, 1915, 1916, 1919, and 1926.
139. Professor Saneto Keishu, who has done the most research on Chinese students in Japan, believes that more than 100,000 Chinese had been trained in Japan by the early 1940's. This is probably true if we include all who stayed in

educated the largest group among foreign-trained Chinese, exceeding by a considerable margin the American-educated, who, according to a survey conducted by the China Institute in America, numbered 20,906 during the period from 1854 to 1953.[140]

Japan for short periods. The number of Chinese students in Japan was small after 1937 on account of the war.

140. SURVEY, Table E, p. 37.

[6] The Period
1928-1949

The twenty years between 1928 and 1949 fall naturally into three sub-periods because of a single major event, the Sino-Japanese War of 1937-45. The prewar years were marked by the ascendancy of the Kuomintang and especially of Chiang Kai-shek, while the postwar years witnessed a rapid disintegration of the party apparatus and a popular repudiation of Chiang's leadership. The steady growth of the power of the central government from 1928 to 1937 was in marked contrast to the weakness of the Peking regime in previous years. Not only did the government exercise greater control over the provinces but there was also a change in the basic concepts underlying the exercise of state power. The ideological foundation of the Kuomintang was the Three Principles of the People of Sun Yat-sen. According to Sun, there should be three stages in the period of national reconstruction. During the first stage, military campaigns were to be waged to crush the warlords. During the second, the masses were to be educated and taught how to practice political democracy; and in the third, a democratic government was to be installed. In the first and second stages, the Kuomintang was to act as the guardian and take the country under its tutelage. Obviously, a political doctrine such as this one, if put into practice, would lead to a party dictatorship. Actually, this theoretical inclination toward political totalitarianism was reinforced by another circumstance, namely the Kuomintang's alliance with the Russian and Chinese Communist parties from 1923 to 1927 and its adoption of their organizational practices. The pyramidal structure of the party with a Politburo at the top, a secret police, a committee system for all political units, political commissars in the army, the sanctification of the Leader, and the suppression of all opposition as counterrevolutionary activity—all these and more characteristics of the Russian party were adopted by the Kuomintang. Although some of these features were either abolished or subsequently became mere formalities, the spirit of party dictatorship persisted and profoundly influenced the whole Chinese scene during the two decades of Kuomintang rule.

Before and during the Northern Campaign of 1925-1927, agrarian reform was one of the main objectives of the party. But as the entente with the Communists disintegrated, the work of the Kuomintang among the peasants visibly slackened. In the continuous struggle for power after 1927, Chiang drew support from the rich coastal provinces of Kiangsu and Chekiang, and particularly from the port of Shanghai, where Western influence was predominant. Perhaps this was one of the main reasons for the Kuomintang's decision to alter its foreign policy from a rather violent anti-Western stand to a rapprochement with Europe and America. With Western support, or at least its acquiescence, China was able to achieve tariff autonomy, make progress toward jurisdictional autonomy, and recover six concessions or leased territories from Britain and Belgium.[1]

In contrast, Sino-Japanese relations became steadily worse. In 1915, Japan presented China with the Twenty-One Demands, and three years later, at the time of the Siberian Campaign, Japan forced a military alliance on China. In 1919, China waged a valiant but unsuccessful struggle against Japan at the Paris Peace Conference. In 1925 the May Thirtieth Incident broke out after a Japanese police guard killed a Chinese worker in Shanghai. Three years later Japanese militarists murdered a high Chinese official in Tsinan. In 1931, Japan occupied Manchuria, and in the following year China and Japan fought a local war in Shanghai. After the Manchurian incident of 1931, tremendous pressure was exerted on Chiang by all segments of Chinese opinion to confront the Japanese with force. When the war finally broke out in 1937, the whole nation rallied behind the government, and Chiang became the symbol of national survival. As long as the war lasted, the intense national consciousness was sufficient to hold the nation together under his leadership.

In the meantime, difficulties arose as a result of the war. China lost her rich coastal provinces; her industrial production sagged; and inflation threatened the entire national economy. The intelligentsia, the most influential class, suffered more than any other group. In the face of rapidly rising prices, its real income dwindled to almost nothing, while war profiteers prospered and government corruption increased. Furthermore, the power of the secret police was felt everywhere, and overt critics of the government were often jailed and, in some cases, assassinated. Violent criticism of the Kuomintang developed and reached extreme proportions by the time the war was over.

When Japan capitulated in 1945, the Kuomintang apparatus, strained by the long years of war, had become ineffectual, and the ideological fervor of the Northern Expedition had completely disappeared. Most government workers were now concerned only with how to relieve their own financial distress. Consequently, the administrative change-over in areas occupied by the Japanese was marked by corruption seldom equaled in Chinese history.[2] Parallel to the

1. M. T. Z. Tyau, "Foreign Relations, 1928-1935," CHY (1935-36), 348-52.
2. A novel written by Chang Hen-shui in 1946 entitled *Wu-tzu-teng-k'o (Grab-*

Japanese situation after the Mongol invasion in the thirteenth century, the Kuomintang regime gained victory while at the same time it was drained of all inner strength and cohesion.[3] When Chiang Kai-shek, mistaking outward grandeur for actual popularity, proceeded to crush the Communists by force, the façade of his power rapidly disintegrated. By the second half of 1948 the Kuomintang was forced to resort to naked coercion for the enforcement of its orders.[4] But soon the agent of coercion—the army—collapsed, and the regime quickly withered away.

EDUCATIONAL CONDITIONS

Before 1928, the government in Peking exercised little active control over the educational system, but this situation was reversed under the Kuomintang. The liberal educational principles embodied in the school system of 1922 were blamed for the rapid expansion of the universities, the generally declining academic standards, and the numerous student strikes.[5] Accordingly, strict government control was imposed. In line with the general political orientation of the Kuomintang, education was declared to be an ideological weapon in the hands of the party.[6] A weekly meeting in memory of Sun Yat-sen was held in all schools, and "Party Doctrine" became a required course in place of Social Studies. A standard curriculum for middle schools was set up, and compulsory military training was introduced in secondary and higher educational institutions.[7] From 1932 to 1944, annual public examinations for all middle-school graduates were conducted by the government.[8] In 1931 the credit system in Chinese universities was standardized, and a minimum of 132 credits was required for a four-year bachelor's degree.[9] Beginning in 1928 the Ministry of Education made efforts to standardize all university curricula; and in 1938 the government announced a series of required courses for students in various disciplines.[10]

In accordance with Sun's concept of a five-power constitution, the Kuomintang established in 1930 an Examination Yüan to take charge of the civil-service administration in general and the recruitment of

bing the Five Kinds of Wealth) gives a detailed description of the pattern of corruption. See also KC, Vol. I, No. 3, p. 15; Vol. I, No. 5, p. 20, for some sample cases of corruption.

3. WC:TK, *passim.*
4. An example is the currency reform in August, 1948. See KC, Vol. V, No. 6, p. 5.
5. TLL:RC, 73 ff.
6. 2d CYNC, 6.
7. *Ibid.*, 1331-33.
8. *Ibid.*, 373.
9. *Ibid.*, 495.
10. WSC:EC, 18; "Laws and Statutes," CHCYC, Vol. XXX, No. 2, p. 93.

civil servants through competitive examinations in particular. Broadly speaking, there were three kinds of examinations, one for higher official appointments, one for ordinary civil-service positions, and one for specialists and professionals.[11] The first was open to college graduates or their equivalents, the second to middle-school graduates or equivalents, and the third to candidates fulfilling qualifications on an *ad hoc* basis. From 1931 to 1937 four examinations for higher official appointments were held, and 596 candidates were successful. In 1939 the regulations were changed and all who passed the examination were required to undergo further training at the Central Political Institute in order to increase their knowledge of practical conditions in China and to become better versed in party ideology. Between 1939 and 1947, 3,150 persons passed under the new regulations.[12] Success in the examination for higher official appointments not only entitled one to a position but constituted a kind of academic qualification in itself. But, because such qualifications were not required for an official appointment under the Kuomintang, the examination system on which Sun laid so much emphasis was of little practical importance.

An important feature of this period was the gradual growth of postgraduate training at various universities. Although graduate study had been a part of the educational system from the very beginning, few graduate programs actually existed until the late 1920's. One of the pioneers, Tsinghua College, established a type of research institute in Chinese studies in 1925 with Liang Ch'i-ch'ao as supervisor,[13] but it was not until 1930 that graduate training was available in other disciplines.[14] In 1934 the Ministry of Education promulgated a provisional regulation pertaining to the granting of higher degrees, and by the time the Sino-Japanese War broke out in 1937 graduate study was being conducted at twelve universities.[15]

When the Kuomintang first came to power, rigorous rules were laid down for the registration of mission schools in China. Between 1927 and 1929 all of the Christian colleges supported by missionary boards experienced difficulties under the increasing rigor of government control.[16] But with the reorientation of foreign policy and

11. After 1940 there was another kind of examination which aimed at qualifying a candidate for an elective office. Actually, the examining was done by correspondence and no formal examination was held. See CHNC (1948), I, 518-19.
12. *Ibid.* (1948), I, 513, 519-20, 522-23. The figure for 1947 is not complete.
13. LJKHS, III, 666.
14. 2d CYNC, 600. The first M.A. in sociology was granted to Fei Hsiao-t'ung by Tsinghua in 1934, according to Dr. Shu-Ching Lee, to whom I am indebted for this information.
15. 2d CYNC, 574. The graduate training at the time was all at the M.A. level. No Ph.D. seems ever to have been granted by a Chinese university until 1961 in Taiwan.
16. See, for instance, CCH:SC, 162-82; SR:FC, 45-46.

through improved relations with the Western powers during the 1930's, the movement for the recovery of educational rights from the missionaries died down. One of the most widely known Christian colleges, St. John's University, did not register until November, 1947.[17]

In the early 1930's, China solicited technical assistance from the League of Nations. The fields in which foreign expert services were sought included economic reconstruction, public health, and education. In their report published in 1932, the League experts on education severely criticized the educational system as a poor imitation of American methods and advocated a complete reorientation.[18] The report was taken very seriously by the Chinese government and was translated into Chinese for wider circulation.[19] A special educational mission was sent to Europe in August, 1932,[20] and two of its members, upon their return, were appointed provincial commissioners of education in order to put into practice the recommendations of the League experts.[21] In December, 1933, the Chinese government requested the League to appoint a permanent liaison officer between China and the International Institute of Intellectual Co-operation. A Chinese National Committee on Intellectual Co-operation was created, as well as an Intellectual and Technical Employment Bureau and a Chinese Institute of Educational Cinematography.[22] But very little was achieved before Japan attacked China in 1937, and with the outbreak of war the educational reforms suggested by the League experts came to an end.

An important characteristic of modern Chinese education that seems to have had a particularly close connection with the Kuomintang was the student strike. In the early years of Sun Yat-sen's struggle for power, much political agitation occurred among the students.[23] The May Fourth Incident of 1919 was particularly welcome to Sun and Ts'ai Yüan-p'ei among the Kuomintang leaders.[24] During the Northern Campaign of 1925-27 student movements continued to favor the Kuomintang,[25] but as soon as the party came into power, the tables were turned. Student unrest now became a source of unabated embarrassment. An incomplete survey made in 1931 for the previous

17. LM:SJ, 234.
18. TRE, Chapters I and II.
19. TCP:CKC, 257.
20. Tzehsiung Kuo, "Technical Co-operation between China and Geneva," IB, Vol. I, No. 6, p. 12.
21. Tzehsiung Kuo, "China and International Intellectual Co-operation," IB, Vol. II, No. 1, p. 8.
22. *Ibid.*, 10, 12.
23. TL:CKKS, II, 587; W. C. Tsao, "The Nationalist Government and Education," ER (January, 1928), 191.
24. "Editorial," CSM (December, 1919); PTP:CKC, II, 26.
25. "Educational News," CYTC, Vol. XVIII, No. 11, p. 1.

year recorded twelve strikes in Chinese universities in eight different cities. In at least seven cases, the head of the college concerned or his immediate subordinate was forced to resign to pacify the students. In one case a personal feud between the Minister of Education and the president of the leading government university was openly aired. In another case, the Kuomintang headquarters in Shanghai openly sided with the students in their attack upon the head of a college. In two cases students brought legal suits against college authorities, in addition to declaring strikes and assaulting professors.[26] After 1931, the student movement became distinctly political. Large-scale demonstrations during 1935 and 1936 urged the government to undertake military action against Japan.[27] In the meantime Communist influence spread among the students. Soon after the end of the war, student agitation resumed and continued until 1949 with the single objective of overthrowing the "reactionary" regime.[28] The Kuomintang's use of students for political purposes had backfired and helped to bring about its own downfall.

A notable event during the war with Japan was the inauguration of a large number of scholarships in the middle schools and above. Before 1938 scholarships were practically unknown in Chinese schools. In that year, as many of China's provinces fell under Japanese control and large numbers of students fled from the occupied to the unoccupied areas, the Ministry of Education began granting loans to refugee students. At first the grants were restricted to those in government schools and took the form of loans covering either all the normal needs of a student or half of that amount, but beginning in 1943 the aid was greatly extended. Under the revised system, students in government schools still received preferential treatment: graduate students in all disciplines and undergraduates in pharmacology, engineering, medicine, and education were entitled to full scholarships, while 80 per cent of those in the natural sciences, 60 per cent of those in the social sciences, and 40 per cent of those in other disciplines were given half-scholarships. In private colleges, 70 per cent of the undergraduates in medicine, engineering, and pharmacology, and 50 per cent of those in the natural sciences and in agriculture received half-scholarships. At the secondary level, all students in normal schools were awarded full scholarships, and from 70 to 90 per cent of the others received half-scholarships.

Although the grants were intended for students from occupied China, enforcement of this restriction proved to be difficult. In 1944

26. Hsu Shih-chien, "A Study of the Student Strikes in the Universities in 1930," CHCYC, Vol. XIX, No. 1, pp. 21-38.

27. PRL:TC, 1-64.

28. See reports on student strikes in KC, Vol. V, No. 1, p. 17; Vol. V, No. 4, pp. 1, 17; Vol. V, No. 16, p. 12. See also WNK:HSYT.

the regulation was further revised to include needy students in the interior, to fix the total number of full and half-scholarships at 40 per cent each for all freshmen, to grant full scholarships to students in public schools who had received earlier grants, and to provide free meals for all students in private schools who had received earlier grants.[29]

Instituted as a temporary relief measure during wartime, the program continued until 1949 because the government was afraid of alienating the educated public in the bitter struggle against the Communists. While there is no evidence that the mass distribution of grants influenced the political opinions of the students in any way, the measure did increase social mobility by opening school doors far wider than before.

GOVERNMENT POLICY IN REGARD TO STUDY ABROAD

In line with its general policy, the government exercised increasing control over foreign study. Regulations issued in February, 1929, contained two main provisions.[30] First, all future self-supporting students abroad were required to be at least senior middle-school graduates or middle-school graduates with two years' experience in the educational field.[31] Second, all students going abroad were required to secure certificates from the Ministry of Education, and those who failed to do so would become ineligible for scholarships and would not receive official recognition for their diplomas.[32] This regulation was very similar to a statute enacted five years earlier and therefore represented no change in official policy.[33]

In the first National Educational Conference of May, 1928, five motions were submitted in regard to study abroad. Basically these motions suggested that only students who had demonstrated their potential in examinations should be sent abroad; that funds should be used to bring foreign professors to China; and that full-time university professors in China should enjoy the opportunity of going abroad from time to time.[34] These proposals reflected the growing concern of the educators for the future of study abroad and thus explained their clamor for government control. In September, 1931, the Central Executive Committee of the Kuomintang set forth its *Basic Policy of Education According to the Party Principles*.[35] This important document was divided into eight sections, and the last dealt with foreign

29. 2d CYNC, 52-57.
30. MKFK, V, 131-34.
31. *Ibid.*, 131.
32. *Ibid.*, 132.
33. "Statutes," CYTC, Vol. XVI, No. 9.
34. CKCYHI.
35. 2d CYNC, 9-10.

study. It emphasized that the Three Principles of the People were to serve as the basis of a new culture. Other regulations specified that government students must be college graduates chosen by examination and that self-supporting students must be senior middle-school graduates who had passed suitable tests before they were allowed to go abroad.

These stipulations seemed inadequate to most commentators. In November, 1932, the Minister of Education, Chu Chia-hua, expressed his views in these words:

> According to the statistics of this Ministry, there are about 5,400 Chinese students abroad costing twenty million dollars per year, which is double the total budget of all Chinese universities. . . .
> There has never been any limitation on students going abroad. Even middle-school graduates are free to go abroad. There are no restrictions on age, academic qualifications, and subjects of study. They (the middle-school graduates) go abroad merely to receive elementary education. From now on, the sending of government scholars must be made more strict and confined to university graduates with two years of practical experience and to university instructors. The fields of study must also be specified by the government. Provincial scholars must be examined by the Ministry. Self-supporting students must be college graduates.[36]

Accordingly a new regulation containing forty-six articles was issued in April, 1933.[37] The provinces and municipalities were urged to promote study abroad by granting subsidies to self-supporting students with good grades (article 3). Students on government scholarships were limited to college graduates with two years' experience in their fields. They were to be selected by competitive examinations (article 11) and encouraged to enroll in "practical" disciplines—agriculture, engineering, science, and medicine—not in the liberal arts (article 8). The term of foreign study was fixed at from two to five years (article 5). Self-supporting students were required to be college graduates or graduates of technical schools with two years' experience in a technical field (article 27). All students were instructed to secure authorization certificates from the Ministry of Education before applying for their passports (articles 33 and 37).

This regulation embodied the Kuomintang's policy before the Sino-Japanese War. How far the regulation was actually carried out is difficult to determine. It seems to have been strictly applied in regard to most government scholarships. From 1933 to 1947, 194 students

36. Quoted in 1st CYNC, Sec. C, p. 7.
37. "Statutes," CHCYC, Vol. XXI, No. 2, pp. 91-93.

went to England as Boxer indemnity scholars.[38] Between 1933 and 1938, 135 Tsinghua University scholarships were awarded,[39] and in 1934 twenty-one students were sent abroad by eight provinces. All these fulfilled the requirements of the central government.[40] Although students with scholarships were expected to conform to the regulation, it was not strictly enforced in cases of self-supporting students. My own experience in going to England as a student in the winter of 1935 revealed no difficulty in the securing of a passport, although I was not a college graduate. Furthermore, none of the self-supporting students whom I knew appeared to have bothered with the requirements of the Ministry.

After the war with Japan began in 1937, the Chinese government placed severe restrictions on students going abroad. In June, 1938, the Executive Yüan laid down the "Provisional Regulations for the Limitation of Chinese Students Abroad," which virtually confined students going abroad to men of established standing in the fields of engineering and of military, natural, and biological science. Because the regulation was strictly enforced, the number of students leaving China dwindled to a fraction of the prewar average. Between July, 1937, and October, 1942, only 665 permits were issued by the Ministry of Education for students abroad, compared to an average of 755 per year before that period.[41] Furthermore, the difference is accentuated by the fact that the 665 permits probably included all who went abroad, while the prewar average of 755 covered few of the self-supporting students.

Another measure taken by the government was to recall students already abroad. Some 462 students, mostly in Europe, received government subsidies to return home.[42] Aside from these restrictions, there seemed to be a tendency for Chinese students in Europe to transfer to America after the outbreak of war in Europe.[43] Those already in America remained, permanently in some cases.

After the Pacific War broke out in late 1941, the Chinese government, feeling that ultimate victory was in sight, looked forward to postwar reconstruction and reversed its policy of restricting foreign study. In Chiang Kai-shek's *China's Destiny*, published in 1942, it

38. Letter from Mr. A. G. Morkill, Secretary, Universities' China Committee, London, November 9, 1955. See also CYWCC (March, 1947).
39. 2d CYNC, 600.
40. 23d CKTC, Table 164, p. 276.
41. CLF:CE, 3.
42. *Ibid.*
43. According to the census of the Institute of International Education (quoted in SURVEY, 18), the number of Chinese students in the United States decreased during the war. The number given by the census is much smaller than that stated in CLF:CE (p. 5) and perhaps needs to be treated with caution.

was clearly stated that talents in all fields were needed. This stand was immediately implemented by government action and marked an important change from the previous policy of emphasizing technical education alone.[44]

THE QUALIFYING EXAMINATIONS FOR SELF-SUPPORTING STUDENTS ABROAD

In lifting restrictions on foreign study, the government decided to institute a new system to select those who would be allowed to go abroad. Consequently, a qualifying examination was instituted for all graduates of recognized institutions of higher learning who had done research or practical work.[45] The first examination took place in December, 1943. There was a paper for each of three basic subjects: party doctrine and Chinese history and geography, Chinese, and a foreign language. There was also a paper on the candidate's special subject. Of the 751 applicants, 327 were successful and went to the United States.[46] Although most fields were represented, engineering was easily the most important, making up a third of the total. Partly because of the Communists' rise to power in China, a number of these men subsequently settled in America.

Another examination was held in July, 1946, with some revisions in the requirements. The most important changes were that the candidate was allowed to choose English in lieu of the language of his prospective country of study, and that two papers instead of one were required for the special subject. Of the 2,774 candidates, 1,216 suc-cessfully completed this examination.[47] By October, 1947, 1,163 of the successful candidates in the 1946 examination had been granted certif-icates to go abroad by the Ministry of Education. Of these, 1,018 went to the United States; 57 to France; 30 to England; 32 to Switzerland; 11 to Canada; 3 to Holland; 2 to Australia; 4 to Belgium; 1 to Mexico; and 5 to Sweden.[48]

According to the regulations, the term could not exceed four years in the case of self-supporting students.[49] Each of the successful candi-dates in the 1943 examination was allotted U.S. $5,000 at the official rate of exchange before leaving China,[50] and another $2,400 a year

44. 2d CYNC, 879.
45. Chu Ching-nung, "Survey of Chinese Studying Abroad," CAW (December, 1944), 18.
46. 2d CYNC, 880.
47. *Ibid.*, 882-86. The fields were: engineering, 291; sciences, 109; medicine, 88; agriculture, 78; liberal arts, 146; social sciences and law, 337; business, 131; educa-tion, 45. The total 1,216 is as stated in the source quoted; it should be 1,225 according to the item figures.
48. *Ibid.*, 882.
49. *Ibid.*, 894.
50. "Readers' Column," KC, Vol. V, No. 6, p. 2.

later.[51] The candidates in the 1946 examination were less fortunate. A rapid inflation took place in China after November, 1946, and the official rate of exchange between Chinese and U.S. dollars increased from 2,020:1 in November, 1946, to 474,000:1 in May, 1948,[52] and to 12,000,000:1 after the currency reform of August, 1948. Under the circumstances, the students had great difficulty securing the exchange they needed. The amount of Chinese money needed to purchase a certain number of U.S. dollars increased rapidly, and some students were unable to raise it. They therefore claimed the right to purchase the foreign exchange at a rate prevailing at an earlier date, for example, the day on which they passed the examination or the day on which the Central Bank notified them of their eligibility to purchase the exchange. Yet from the point of view of the government, any allotment of foreign exchange was a giveaway since the official rate was far below the free market rate. Thus the students' demand could not be granted and dispute between them and the government dragged on until 1949. The outcome varied in individual cases, but most of the students secured between U.S. $2,000 and U.S. $5,000 in foreign exchange.[53] The strain on the resources of the government was considerable, since as early as 1946 over four thousand government and self-supporting students were on record as having gone abroad.[54] Even in 1949, when the Kuomintang regime was fleeing from city to city in the face of rapid Communist advance, a number of students in America secured a last government subsidy amounting to U.S. $400 for each person willing to return to China and U.S. $100 for persons not returning home.[55] The generosity accorded the students was highly indicative of their privileged position in China.

When the new regulations were put into force in 1943, one of the stipulations required the students to abide by the Three Principles of the People.[56] Furthermore, students were directed to undergo a two months' training program consisting largely of indoctrination courses.[57] These practices were much resented in the United States. In March, 1944, the Steering Committee of American Defense, a group of Harvard professors, wrote to the United States Department of State in protest to the Kuomintang's efforts to control the thought of Chinese students abroad.[58] The protest created a great stir at the time

51. I am indebted to Mr. Tso-chou Shen of Chicago for this information.

52. KC, *loc. cit.*

53. Information gathered from students who came to the United States in that period.

54. KC, Vol. III, No. 20, p. 20.

55. I am indebted to Mr. Min-sun Chen of Chicago for this information.

56. I am indebted to Mr. Chen Li-fu for this information.

57. Ou Yüan-huai, "The Post-War Policy of Study Abroad," CYTC, Vol. XXXII, No. 2, pp. 32-33.

58. NYT (March 31, 1944), 6:4; (April 5, 1944), 18:3; (April 13, 1944), 8:1.

but was apparently based on a misconception. In theory Chinese students abroad had always been subject to government supervision in regard to their studies and behavior, but in practice such supervision had never been effective. Thus there were no real grounds for the American protest. But, coming at a time when the Chinese government was dependent on American support, the protest was not without its effect. The indoctrination courses, a common feature of many Kuomintang programs, were dropped from the agenda of a group of government workers leaving for the United States in 1944.[59]

SCHOLARSHIP EXAMINATIONS

Toward the end of World War II, the international status of China reached a new peak. As a gesture of friendship, Great Britain and the United States offered a large number of scholarships to Chinese students. In 1943 nine postgraduates and thirty-one trainees went to England at the invitation of the British Council and the Federation of British Industries.[60] In December, 1944, in response to offers of scholarships from abroad, the Ministry of Education held a special examination for the award of 199 scholarships donated by British and American organizations.[61]

The examination was open only to college graduates and to persons who had passed the Higher Civil-Service Examination with two years of practical experience. The examination was divided into two parts, written and oral, each lasting for two days. The written examination consisted of three papers on basic subjects and two papers on special subjects. The oral section was a test of the candidate's personality in general and of his ability to speak English. Some 1,824 persons applied to take the examination.[62]

A second examination was held in 1946 for the award of another 190 scholarships for study in the United States, Europe, and Australia.[63] Except for the 20 Boxer indemnity scholarships to England and the 50 exchange scholarships to France, all of the scholarships were offered by the Chinese government. Some 3,300 candidates applied, and of these only 148 were successful. But an additional 718, while failing to qualify for scholarships, did well enough to qualify as self-supporting students. Thus they were allowed to go abroad on their own funds, an option that many of them accepted.[64]

Beginning January, 1948, all examinations were suspended, and

59. Ou Yüan-huai, *op. cit.*, p. 32.
60. 2d CYNC, 889-90. The Annual Reports of the British Council for the years concerned give slightly different numbers of scholarships.
61. For details, see WYC:CIW, 191.
62. 2d CYNC, 889.
63. Seventeen of these were British indemnity scholars.
64. 2d CYNC, 882, 886-89.

only students who had their own foreign currencies were allowed to go abroad. Forty such students went abroad during January and February, 1948,[65] and probably many more later as the Communist advance provided people of means with an additional reason for leaving China.

YOUTH ARMY AND INTERPRETER SCHOLARSHIPS

In 1944 the Chinese government announced in Chungking that an elite army was needed to rejuvenate the depleted military forces. This new army was to be organized of youths from colleges and high schools, and the recruiting goal was set at 100,000 men. Eventually, nine divisions were organized.[66] When the war ended, the Chinese government decided to allow these student-soldiers to compete in the 1946 examination for scholarships to study abroad, provided that they were college graduates and could prove their ties with the Youth Army. The candidates were examined on four basic subjects—Chinese history and geography, the Chinese language, a foreign language, and the Three Principles of the People. In addition, there were three papers on special subjects and an oral examination. Twenty-five candidates in various disciplines were successful.

During the war, the Chinese Air Force first employed interpreters for the benefit of American pilots who were members of Chennault's Flying Tigers. In 1941 these interpreters were formally organized, and in 1943 they were attached to the Bureau of Foreign Affairs under the Military Commission. At that time the total number of interpreters did not exceed four or five hundred, but in March, 1944, the government conscripted the 1,224 seniors in foreign languages departments of Chinese universities.[67] In April, 1945, fifty of these men were sent to the United States to help in the training of American fliers. In June of the same year another group of fifty was sent "on loan" to the American government. A number of them have since settled in the United States.[68]

According to regulations decreed in March, 1944, not more than one-tenth of the interpreters were to be allowed to study abroad after the end of the war.[69] In 1947 a qualifying examination was held for them in seven Chinese cities. The examination was open to all of those who were interpreters in good standing under the Bureau of Foreign Affairs of the Military Commission and who were graduates of senior middle schools or above. Ninety-seven candidates were successful and were granted permission to go abroad, supposedly for a period of from two to four years.

65. *Ibid.,* 895.
66. I am obliged to Professor K. Y. Hsü for this information.
67. 2d CYNC 567.
68. I am indebted to Professor K. Y. Hsü for this information.
69. 2d CYNC, 567.

EXCHANGE OF STUDENTS AND PROFESSORS

In 1936, China instituted an exchange program with Poland and Italy. In 1937, Germany proposed to exchange six students with China, but the Sino-Japanese War ended the proposal. In 1942, India proposed an exchange of ten students. A year later the Indians, who were all postgraduate students and in some cases mature scholars, arrived. The subjects they studied were Chinese history, philosophy, anthropology, chemistry, mathematics, and agriculture. The majority of the ten students sent by China to India specialized in engineering. In 1944, five of these exchange students on each side stayed on for another year.

In 1943, Turkey proposed an exchange of ten students. Iran also invited Chinese students to seek practical knowledge in oil works there; and four scholarships in medicine were offered by the University of Montreal in Canada. But these proposals were not carried out because of transportation difficulties. In 1947, India sent eleven more students to China. In the same year Turkey again brought up the subject of exchange, and the Chinese Ministry of Education began to select Muslim students. In 1946, France and China agreed to exchange forty students. Twenty-four of the forty Chinese students sailed for France in the fall of 1947, and the remaining sixteen went in 1948.[70]

In 1940 the Universities' China Committee in London requested the Chinese government to send a professor to England to speak on conditions in China. Both Oxford and Cambridge proposed an exchange of professors with China. In the spring of 1941 the Chinese psychologist Kuo Jen-yüan went to England and succeeded in securing from the British Council a promise of scholarships for Chinese students. In 1942, the Sinologist E. R. Hughes of Oxford went to China, and from that time a number of exchanges took place. In 1943, Professor Chou Hou-fu went to England at the invitation of the British Council. In the same year the United States Department of State requested six Chinese universities each to send a professor to the United States. As a result, six Chinese scholars, including Fei Hsiao-t'ung and Chang Ch'i-yün, later Minister of Education in Formosa, spent a year in the United States. In 1944 another six Chinese professors went to America, while five others went to Britain. Later in the same year two Chinese professors in the field of radiology were invited to England.

In the same period many Western scholars visited China. Two well-known Englishmen in China were E. R. Dobbs, the Oxford classicist, and Joseph Needham, who established the Sino-British Science Co-operation Office in Chungking. Among the Americans in China were a number of technical experts who worked as a team with

70. *Ibid.*, 878-79.

various Chinese government departments.[71] Other eminent Americans, including Roscoe Pound of Harvard, G. B. Cressey of Syracuse, and Henry Sloane Coffin of Union Theological Seminary, also visited China. After the Pacific War broke out in 1941, the Chinese government became more actively interested in cultural relations with the West, and in 1943 ninety-five men were sent abroad. Of these, seventy-five were senior college professors; ten were research workers of the Academia Sinica, all in the fields of engineering, science, medicine, or agriculture; and the other ten were experts in educational administration selected by the Ministry of Education. Of the countries visited, seventy-four went to the United States, six to Canada, and thirteen to Great Britain. The period of study was two years; but in the case of those whose departure was delayed until 1945 or later, the period was shortened to one and a half years because of the growing shortage of foreign exchange in the hands of the government.[72]

In May, 1941, the Ministry of Education issued a regulation that granted sabbatical leaves to college professors under certain conditions. In 1943-44 ten faculty members of Chinese national universities were permitted to spend their leaves in the United States at a total cost to the government of $84,000.[73] In addition, a large number of cultural missions were exchanged between China and other countries, particularly the United States and Great Britain. Between 1943 and 1947 a group of Chinese professors journeyed each year to the United States under the Cultural Co-operation Program of the State Department.[74] A number of Chinese became visiting professors in American universities by direct arrangement. Among them was Francis Wei, who was appointed in 1945 as the first Henry W. Luce Visiting Professor at Union Theological Seminary.[75] Fellowships were offered to ten Chinese professors by the United Service to China in 1947.[76] In the same year, eleven Chinese scientists joined the faculty of six major American universities, including the Massachusetts Institute of Technology and the University of Chicago.[77] At one time or another during the war and immediate postwar years, the presidents of all major Chinese universities visited the United States, and many remained there for a number of years. By glancing through the bulletins of the China Institute in America during those years, one can find almost the entire *Who's Who* among China's Western-educated elite.

71. For names of these people, see "Notes on Personnel," QBCB (1943-47).
72. 2d CYNC 895.
73. *Ibid.*, 521-22.
74. *Ibid.*, 878; see also CIB (1943-47).
75. *Ibid.* (October, 1945), 11.
76. *Ibid.* (October, 1947), 2.
77. *Ibid.* (May, 1947), 2.

The large number of Chinese who taught abroad prompted the government to take legislative action, and in 1945 a nine-article regulation was promulgated.[78] Scholars going abroad for teaching purposes were limited to those who had held the rank of associate professor or above in Chinese universities for more than five years and had published important scholarly works. Those going abroad for research were required to have been university lecturers for two years, or instructors for five years. Moreover, each scholar leaving China was required to secure prior permission for his trip from the university where he was employed and from the Ministry of Education. The number of professors on leave was not to exceed 2 per cent, and the number of research workers was not to exceed 4 per cent of the faculty in any university. The subjects taught abroad were to be "pertinent to Chinese culture or in the interest of a communion of Chinese and foreign scholarship"; and the fields of research were confined to those "deemed necessary by the Ministry of Education." The term of stay abroad was limited to one year for teaching professors and two years for research workers, any prolongation being subject to the Ministry's consideration and approval. Progress reports were to be submitted to the Ministry by all touring scholars. The number of Chinese who went abroad under this regulation was 130 in 1945, 270 in 1946, and 450 in 1947.[79] Thereafter the political situation probably rendered government control inoperative. In the meantime, the number of Chinese on the faculties of American colleges and universities continued to increase: the total reached 500 in 1954,[80] and 660 in 1956.[81]

OTHER CHINESE GROUPS IN THE UNITED STATES

Academic men were not the only group of Chinese in the United States. Enthusiastic aid in the medical field was rendered China by the United States. Various organizations, notably the Rockefeller Foundation and the American Bureau for Medical Aid to China, donated large sums of money during the war. In addition, Chinese medical personnel were brought to the United States for training. From 1945 through 1947, 129 medical scholarships were granted to Chinese by American sources.[82] Other technical personnel also came to the United States in large numbers. In the three months ending October, 1947, more than one thousand technicians were sent to the United States under Lend Lease arrangements to undergo a year of

---

78. 2d CYNC, 895.
79. *Ibid.*, 895.
80. SURVEY, 22.
81. CSAS (March, 1956), 7.
82. 2d CYNC, 897. See also Frank Go Tui, "The Doctors Point the Way to Sino-American Co-operation," NRJ (January, 1946), 57-67.

intensive practical training.[83] Some four hundred senior officials of the National Resources Commission visited America in the years from 1945 through 1947.[84] The trip across the Pacific was popular even with politicians and militarists. Among numerous others, Feng Yü-hsiang went to the United States in 1946 for the purpose of "studying irrigation problems." The Chinese government paid him more than $130,000 for less than two years' stay.[85] In 1948 he left to join the Chinese Communists via Soviet Russia but died as a result of an accident on the way.[86] The vogue of visiting America in the 1940's was reminiscent of the Chinese exodus to Japan in 1905 and 1906. A curious historical coincidence was that in both cases the Chinese government in power soon met its downfall.

CHINESE STUDENTS IN THE UNITED STATES AFTER THE
OUTBREAK OF THE PACIFIC WAR

Shortly after Pearl Harbor, the United States Department of State took active steps to relieve the difficulties of Chinese students in America. In the first place, the students were allowed to accept employment. Secondly, $800,000 was appropriated from the President's Emergency Fund for the aid of Chinese students.[87] The Secretary of State appointed a committee of two to screen the applications for grants and to recommend awards, which were made on the basis of three criteria: first, the immediate importance to China of the student's field of study; second, the student's ability; and third, his financial need. The two members of the committee were the director of the Institute of International Education and the director of the China Institute in America.[88] The grants were worth up to seventy-five dollars a month for minimum living expenses, and they were awarded for periods of from one month to a year and were renewable.[89] The number of grants outstanding was 89 in April, 1942; 279 in May, 1943; and 122 in May, 1945.[90] In June, 1946, the Department of State announced the inauguration of a program of travel grants to Chinese students who had completed their education in the United States and who were returning to China to fill teaching posts in colleges and universities.[91] A few months later, thirty-five scholarships and nine

83. Chu Ching-nung, *op. cit.*, 19; CIB (October, 1945), 1-2.
84. Letter of Weng Wen-hao, quoted in KC, Vol. III, No. 17, p. 6.
85. Letter of Hsüeh Tu-pi, quoted in KC, Vol. III, No. 17, p. 6.
86. NYT (September 5), 28; (September 6), 1; (September 12), 9, all in 1948.
87. DSR, 1.
88. CIB (March-April, 1942), 1.
89. *Ibid.* (November-December, 1942), 4. The upper limit of the stipends was later changed to one hundred dollars. See *ibid.* (April, 1943), 3.
90. *Ibid.* (March-April, 1942), 1; (July-August, 1943), 3; (May, 1945), 1.
91. *Ibid.* (June, 1946), 9.

special agricultural scholarships were awarded to Chinese who were in China at the time. Four other Chinese in China were appointed to research assistantships or instructorships. The travel expenses of all forty-eight were paid by the United States.[92]

Before the American government made its appropriation of $800,000 only fifty Chinese students in the United States were recipients of Chinese government or quasi-government scholarships. The action of the United States prompted China to appropriate a similar sum.[93] Under the chairmanship of T. V. Soong, the Committee on Wartime Planning was formed in the United States in June, 1942, for the purposes of rendering aid to Chinese students and organizing special projects by groups of students under the leadership of Chinese and American experts.[94] Awards were made on the same basis as the State Department grants and carried the same terms. No report appears to have been issued summarizing the operation, but according to published lists of the awards, at least 318 scholarships were granted between June, 1942, and October, 1947. In addition to these, a large number of Chinese were placed in industries and departments of the United States government, and were engaged in teaching the Chinese language. In May, 1943, 347 Chinese students or former students were reported to be employed;[95] in May, 1945, the number had risen to 654.[96]

In recognition of the importance of research, the Committee on Wartime Planning organized seven group projects dealing with various aspects of postwar reconstruction in China. The committee hoped to co-ordinate the training of Chinese students with the "present and future needs" of China. It also sought the elevation of Chinese academic and professional standards through the establishment of national reconstruction forums in the United States. There were thirty-eight such forums in existence in September, 1944, and forty-three in February, 1945.[97] A *National Reconstruction Journal* was published quarterly to air the views of Chinese scholars and the results of their research. However, few scholarly papers appeared in the *Journal,* and no specific results can be traced to the seven group projects.

Throughout the war years the American people and government showed great enthusiasm for the training of Chinese technicians. An example was the aerial survey scholarships conceived by Dr. W. C. Lowdermilk of the U.S. Department of Agriculture, who felt that China would need men trained in making land capability maps after the war, when airplanes and photographic equipment previously used

92. *Ibid.* (October, 1946), 3-4.   93. DSR, 1.
94. CIB (July, 1942), 1.   95. *Ibid.* (July-August, 1943), 3.
96. *Ibid.* (May, 1945), 1.   97. *Ibid.* (June, 1945), 1.

for war purposes would become available. In 1943 the Department offered twenty training scholarships to Chinese students with stipends of $1,200 per year.[98] Six months later, the stipends were increased to $120 a month[99] and still later to $150 a month, plus expenses.[100] Numerous offers were made by industrial concerns to employ Chinese trainees. The extent of these offers was shown by a message of President Chiang Kai-shek on January 27, 1947, to American corporations. No less than 102 concerns were specifically mentioned in Chiang's scroll for their services in providing special training for Chinese students. Many of these concerns were major manufacturers in American industry.[101]

The spirit of fraternity was also demonstrated by the American academic world. Numerous colleges and universities offered scholarships to Chinese. In 1947, the University of Washington awarded thirty scholarships to Chinese, out of forty-nine available to foreign students.[102] The spirit of Sino-American friendship was so widespread that in April, 1947, the teachers, parents, and school children of Hackensack, New Jersey, devoted a whole week exclusively to the study of China.[103] Such manifestations of friendship further stimulated the regard that Chinese young people held for an American social environment. Between December, 1944, and May, 1945, self-supporting students from China flocked to the United States at the rate of 120 a month, in spite of great transportation difficulties.[104] The number in the United States rose from 823 in 1944-45, to 3,914 in 1948-49, exclusive of officials and visiting professors.[105]

Beginning in 1948, the condition of these students became precarious as Communist forces advanced in China and remittances ceased to reach them. In January, 1948, the Department of State set aside $8,000 as aid to Chinese students. The universities and colleges also made tuition loans and assisted in other ways. But it was obvious to those concerned that greater efforts were needed.[106] In February, 1949, at the request of the Chinese Ambassador, the Economic Co-operation Administration provided the Department of State with $500,000 to aid Chinese students.[107] Even this sum was regarded only as a stopgap measure. By the Foreign Appropriations and China Area Aid Acts of 1950, Congress allocated $10,000,000 to assist Chinese intellectuals in the United States and to bring advanced

98. *Ibid.* (September-October, 1943), 8.
99. *Ibid.* (April-May, 1944), 4.
101. *Ibid.* (February, 1947), 1-3.
103. *Ibid.* (April, 1947), 2.
100. *Ibid.* (January, 1945), 4.
102. *Ibid.* (December, 1947), 8.
104. *Ibid.* (May, 1945), 1.
105. Census of the Institute of International Education quoted in SURVEY, p. 18. As noted earlier, the census is incomplete and is an underestimate. The actual number in 1949 was probably larger.
106. DSPE, 4.   107. *Ibid.*, 5.

students and scholars to the United States from East Asia.[108] Some 3,641 Chinese had received grants under this program by the time it was terminated in 1954-55.[109]

The China Area Aid Act of 1950 also opened the way for students to secure part-time employment and to become self-supporting after they completed their study.[110] On the other hand, the act also provided for the use of program funds by grantees returning to China. In fact, during the first phase of the program in 1949, a grantee was required to sign a statement that "upon termination of the award I promise to return to China."[111] In June, 1949, the pledge was altered to read: ". . . I will return to China as soon as practicable."[112] In 1949 and 1950 approximately 1,000 Chinese students returned to Communist China, 637 of these at American expense.[113] But beginning in January, 1951, the policy was changed, and American-trained Chinese were no longer encouraged to return to China. Instead, a large number of Chinese were granted permanent residence under the Displaced Persons Act of 1948 and the Refugee Relief Act of 1953.[114]

After the entry of the Chinese "volunteers" into the Korean conflict, the departure of Chinese with certain types of technical training was prohibited. During 1950-51, 150 detention orders were issued by the Immigration Service. For a time the government apparently had no fixed policy but considered each individual case on its merit. Thus, while some of the detention orders were lifted beginning in the summer of 1951, strong restraints were imposed in other cases. In September, 1951, nine Chinese, including Tsien Hsüeh-shen, an internationally known authority on aerodynamics, were forcibly removed from the *S. S. President Cleveland* in Honolulu en route to the Far East. The incident provoked wide comment in both the American and the foreign press.[115] Perhaps as a result of the unfavorable publicity concerning this case, the American government soon decided on a more liberal course. By 1955 it had rescinded all of the 150 detention orders. Strikingly, only 39 of the 150 Chinese concerned had chosen to leave the United States.[116]

BRITISH SCHOLARSHIPS

By returning to China the unused portion of the Boxer indemnity, the United States accomplished a diplomatic feat much admired and emulated by other nations. In December, 1922, the British government announced that the remainder of the Indemnity due from China would be waived for use in cultural and educational enterprises of

108. *Ibid.*, 8.
110. CSUS, 8-10.
112. *Ibid.*
114. *Ibid.*
116. *Ibid.*

109. *Ibid.*, 18.
111. DSPE, 16.
113. DSR, 11.
115. CSUS, 10-11.

mutual advantage to both countries. After sending an exploratory mission to China in 1925-26, the British finally concluded an agreement with the Chinese authorities in September, 1930.[117] In the exchange of notes, it was stipulated that the whole fund—some eleven million British pounds, including accumulated interest—should form an amount to be loaned to various productive enterprises in China, and that the interest deriving therefrom would be devoted to educational and cultural purposes. To handle this work, a board of trustees was appointed in April, 1931, with ten Chinese and five British members.[118] Among other cultural activities, the board awarded twenty scholarships a year on the basis of competitive examinations for study in Great Britain. The courses in which the scholarships were awarded varied from year to year, although they were mostly in science and technology; and selection was made on the basis of the needs of China and the facilities for training available in Great Britain.[119]

The scholarships were for two years of study in England, although in many cases the students were allowed to remain for longer periods of time. From 1933 to 1939 and from 1945 to 1947 a total of 194 scholarships were awarded. With only one or two exceptions all of the students obtained advanced degrees from British universities, and as a group the British indemnity scholars were highly respected in Chinese university circles. Because of the war, the group of 1939 was diverted to Canada and eventually to the United States. No awards were made between 1940 and 1944.[120]

The Federation of British Industries Apprentice Program was financed by grants from the Universities' China Committee and the Board of Trustees in charge of the British Boxer indemnity refunds. The objects of this program were to develop trade relations between China and Great Britain and to enable selected Chinese apprentices to secure practical training in British engineering works. The choice of apprentices was made by a selection committee in Shanghai consisting of local British merchants and engineers. The period of training was approximately two years for each apprentice. The first two began their training in January, 1934.[121] From then until 1945, over 150 apprentices were sent to Great Britain.[122]

117. 2d CYNC, 1575.
118. Han Li-wu, "The British Indemnity for Education and Culture," CR (November, 1935), 24.
119. Han Li-wu, *op. cit.*, CR (March, 1937), 9.
120. Letter of Mr. A. G. Morkill, Secretary of the Universities' China Committee, London.
121. CR (December, 1933), 7; (July-September, 1935), 40; (September, 1936), 19.
122. Letter from Mr. A. G. Morkill. According to Chinese official sources, thirty more apprentice scholarships were offered by the Federation in 1947. See 2d CYNC, 879.

CHINESE PROVINCIAL GOVERNMENT SCHOLARSHIPS

Under the Kuomintang, the number of provincial scholarships continued to decrease—in the case of Japan, from 1,073 in 1923 to 321 in 1929 and to 51 in 1936, and in the case of America and Europe, from some 242 in 1923 to only 31 in 1936.[123] In 1934 the Kuomintang conducted an examination for provincial scholarships that was open to students who had passed the first qualifying examinations in their home provinces. Twenty-six candidates from four provinces completed the examination successfully[124] while twenty-six from another five provinces were exempted from it.[125] Beginning in 1935, the Ministry contented itself with checking over the examination papers of provincial candidates and approving or disapproving their scholarships on that basis.[126] In 1944 it was decided that henceforth all government scholarships should be handled by the central government.[127] But this ruling was implicitly reversed in 1947 when regulations by the Ministry of Education again made provisions for provincial scholarships.[128]

In 1944, just as the provinces were being deprived of the function of sending students abroad, the governor of Yunnan, a warlord, announced that he would send forty-four students to the United States to study. The embarrassed Ministry of Education then initiated a prolonged negotiation with the governor in order to dissuade him. Finally, a compromise was reached whereby all but four of the students selected were allowed to go abroad.[129] All of these students were undergraduates, and the four whose academic status was found to be deficient were admitted to a Chinese university as sophomores.[130] This incident marked the termination of overseas study under the sponsorship of great provincial leaders.

The sending of provincial students abroad bore two distinct

123. TTYLTT, 20; CKTC (1930-35); CYTC, Vol. XXII, No. 4 and Vol. XXVI, Nos. 7, 8, 11; CHCYC, Vol. XVIII, No. 12; SSCYHC.
124. Announcements of the Ministry of Education, Nos. 8340 and 8341, dated July 7, 1934 (hand-written copies in the possession of Dr. C. P. Cheng). I am indebted to Dr. Cheng for their use.
125. 23d CKTC, Tables 145 and 146.
126. Ministry of Education, note to Hupeh Province, No. 9386, dated July 8, 1935, directive to the Bureau of Education, Shantung, No. 8921, dated May 15, 1937, note to Shensi Province, No. 16331, dated September 1, 1937. (All are copies in the possession of Dr. C. P. Cheng).
127. Ministry of Education, note to Hupeh Province, No. Kao 15798, dated March 31, 1944. (Copy in Dr. C. P. Cheng's possession.)
128. "Regulations Pertaining to Study Abroad," Article 4, 2d CYNC, 894.
129. Report to Generalissimo Chiang by Minister Ch'en Li-fu, No. Kao 16771, dated April 7, 1944. (Copy in Dr. Cheng's possession.)
130. Ministry of Education, directive to Bureau of Education, Yunnan, No. Kao 48537, dated September 12, 1944. (In Dr. Cheng's possession.)

features from the beginning. One was that what was done depended much on the personal inclinations of the provincial authorities. It was not an established practice regularly carried out according to plan. Even during the height of provincial activities in the movement to study abroad, some provinces sent many more than others. In 1916 the Ministry of Education in Peking attempted to put the matter on a sounder institutional basis by decreeing that all provinces should maintain the same number of scholarships as there were in 1914. This decree probably had little effect. The second feature was the personal way in which most of the provincial scholarships were awarded and administered. With few exceptions, selection was made more on the basis of personal relations than on academic merit. Even in the 1930's when more control was exercised over the scholarships than ever before, this situation persisted. Thus in 1935 only three candidates competed in the examinations held by Hupeh province.[131] In many cases there were no limitations on the duration of scholarships and no requirements on minimum academic achievements. With the right kinds of connections, a student could linger abroad for many years. During the 1920's, when scholarship stipends fell into arrears, the families of the luckier students secured the money from the Bureau of Education and then sent it to them.[132] A scholarship was also occasionally divided and given to two or more students.

In one particular sense, the decrease of provincial scholarships was significant. Almost without exception these scholarships were open only to natives of the province awarding them. In China, where some provinces were much more backward economically and educationally than others, the award of scholarships tended to serve as an equalizer of educational and social opportunities. This was particularly true because the poorer provinces often offered large numbers of scholarships, thus affording their residents an opportunity of education and advancement which they would not otherwise have had. The decrease and eventual disappearance of provincial scholarships meant that all students had to compete on a national basis. Under such conditions, students from an underdeveloped province were at a severe disadvantage. Thus few of the Tsinghua scholarships and the British indemnity scholarships went to natives of inland provinces. Unequal educational opportunities in turn aggravated and perpetuated the urban-rural cleavage, which was a basic problem in modern China.[133]

131. Ministry of Education, note to Hupeh Province, No. 9386, dated July 8, 1935. (In Dr. Cheng's possession.)
132. I am indebted to Mr. Cheng-fu Wang, of New York, for this information. Mr. Wang was a Honan provincial scholar to America and Europe in 1918-27.
133. FHT:HTCC, particularly pages 65-98.

CHINESE MINISTRY OF COMMUNICATIONS SCHOLARSHIPS

Established in 1906, the Ministry of Communications exercised jurisdiction over the four fields of mails, telegraphs, railways, and steamships.[134] Even though it had little voice in the management of the postal service, which was controlled by Westerners, the Ministry was largely a technical service. It administered three engineering colleges and had a large foreign study program. Between 1906 and 1911 approximately 800 men were sent abroad—639 to Japan, more than 80 to Belgium, about 60 to the United States, and a few to Great Britain.[135] Under the Republic, the ministry continued this policy but on a smaller scale. In 1912-13 five men were sent to America and three to Europe.[136] In August, 1913, a new regulation of twenty articles established minimum requirements for the scholarships and placed greater emphasis on practical training than academic studies.[137] Between 1917 and 1919 more than twenty trainees were sent to America, and more than ten to Japan. Their training lasted from one to three years.[138]

In 1925 another revision of policy took place. The regulation of July of that year fixed the number of scholarships at seventy and divided them into three categories. First, every year the four best graduates of the three colleges under the Ministry were to be sent abroad to study for five years. Second, every year twenty workers in the services controlled by the Ministry, who had graduated from one of the three ministerial colleges and who had had two years' work experience, were to be selected to study abroad for two years. These students were normally to be evenly distributed among the four fields of railway management, and civil, mechanical, and electrical engineering. Third, ten scholarships were to be awarded to self-supporting students abroad who were sophomores or above and whose fields lay within the scope of the services of the Ministry. The duration of these scholarships was for two years. At the discretion of the Ministry, the stipends of the second and third categories of scholarships could be reduced to half the regular term.[139] Between 1921 and 1927, thirty-five men were sent to Europe, twenty-seven to America, and four to Japan.[140]

In January, 1930, new regulations were promulgated by the Ministry of Railways under the Kuomintang government.[141] The number of scholarships was now increased to one hundred, of which not more

134. CM:TRM, 106. The Chinese name of the Ministry changed under the Republic, but this semantic difference is ignored here.

135. TTNC (1933), I, 568.   136. *Ibid.*

137. Reprinted in SHC:CTCK, 107-8.   138. TTNC (1933), I, 568.

139. SHC:CTCK, 109-14.   140. TTNC (1933), I, 568.

141. *Ibid.* The Ministry of Railways came into existence in November, 1928, but was again amalgamated with the Ministry of Communications during World War II.

than thirty were partial scholarships. The required qualifications of the scholarship candidates were slightly changed. The length of study was limited to three years for full scholarships and to two years for partial scholarships, with an extension of one year permissible in both cases. All scholars were to acquire both practical and theoretical knowledge. Between 1928 and 1932, seventeen scholars were sent to Europe, thirty-one to America, and one to Japan.[142] Beginning in 1933, the government decided to send more students to Europe, particularly to England and Germany, rather than to the United States; and none were sent to Japan.[143] The situation underwent further changes during the war. At the beginning of 1946, there were at least forty-one railway trainees in the United States who had been sent by the Ministry of Communications for training with the American railroads.[144]

One particularly noticeable feature of the Ministry's training program was the degree of high integration between training and employment. The trainees were sent abroad to acquire specific knowledge, and when they returned, they received appointments in which their training was of immediate value to them. Such integration was possible because the Ministry of Communications controlled large-scale technical services that were run along Western lines. The same conditions did not exist in regard to other Chinese educated abroad—thus a man trained in one field might be hired for work in an entirely different field. In such cases, a man's experience abroad was of value only as it enriched his general educational background; it would not serve the specific purpose for which many Chinese scholarships were awarded.

142. *Ibid.*
143. *Ibid.* (1936), III, 1001.
144. CIB (February, 1946), 2.

[7] *Aspects and Effects*
of the New Education, 1912-1949

The Manchu educational policy, with its emphasis on selective adaptation from Western civilization, was basically retained after the establishment of the Republic. But as the government became increasingly passive in educational matters, public opinion began to favor a more general absorption of Western culture. In 1912 a group of prominent persons organized the Thrift-Study Society in order to encourage study in France. The statement announcing the organization of the society read in part:

In the task of improving our society, we must assign first priority to education. . . . Now that the Republic has just come into being, *study abroad is the only way to build a new society and a new citizenry.* It is particularly desirable to study in a country where democracy had an early start. . . . Again, social progress depends much on the improvement of the family system. Vital to both is education for women, which can best be obtained abroad. Hence we have also organized a Women's Thrift-Study Society and a Family Thrift-Study Society.[1]

In 1917, Wu Chih-hui, a leading figure in the movement, encouraged whole families to travel abroad.

Improvement in our life can be made in ten thousand ways and our need is not limited to academic knowledge. Only by seeking multifarious knowledge from the outside world and by following the trend of the times can we survive among mankind. To take the whole family abroad will enable all the members to live in a progressive city of the world, to remodel their habits by those of a progressive society. . . . Academic knowledge and facilities in our country cannot reach a satisfactory level in a short time . . . . nor is the social environment felicitous. Hence the best graduates from our schools are often not as good as an ordinary returned student. . . . It is because in one case the student hears and sees nothing beneficial outside the school, and in the other he sees and hears much outside it.[2]

1. "Regulations of the Peking Thrift-Study Society," LJ, Vol. III, No. 2, p. 1. Italics mine.
2. Wu Chih-hui, "On Study Abroad," *ibid.*, Vol. IV, No. 2, p. 170.

Although few families heeded his plea, Wu's unreserved condemnation of China's national heritage and ardent admiration for Western civilization helped prepare the way for a major intellectual upheaval throughout the country. This powerful tide engulfed China's youth and had important repercussions. The worker-student movement flourished. A Sino-French institute was established at Lyon, and a Sino-Belgian institute at Charleroi.[3] In Europe, the number of Chinese students increased from 565 in 1914 to approximately 3,180 in 1923.[4] And in the United States, the number increased during the same period from 847 to 2,600.[5]

The influence of Wu's denunciations of China's past on the attitude of the students was especially significant, although difficult to document. In conformity with the theme that nothing Chinese was good and everything Western was worth emulating, the students abroad tended to feel unconstrained by traditional Chinese values and redoubled their efforts to adopt Western ways of life—under the circumstances, in a superficial way. Among the Chinese students in America, fraternities grew rapidly in the 1920's.[6] Christian names and Western surnames were adopted by many in place of their Chinese names.[7] Directories of Chinese students ceased to list the students' provincial origins in China. Many students also took great pains to dissociate themselves from their compatriots in Chinatowns because the latter were far less Westernized than they.[8] All of these symptoms reflected the dominant trend of thought in China.

It should be noted that the theory of total Westernization did not in itself negate the concept of service to the country. From the standpoint of those who advocated it, the reverse was true; it was precisely in order to serve the country that a general absorption of Western culture was felt to be necessary. During the 1920's, the idea that it was the mission of the students educated abroad to save the country remained widespread. Influential officials and qualified observers continued to express this feeling. In 1917, Dr. V. K. Wellington Koo declared in a speech, "Whatever courses they [the Chinese stu-

3. 2d CYNC, 654, 1585. Enquiry from Belgian sources in Chicago reveals that L'Université de Travail de Charleroi was operative in 1921-32. Further details are unavailable.

4. WTC:TYM, 54.

5. Figures for 1914 to 1918 are compiled from the student directories concerned. The 1923 figure is taken from a speech by Y. T. Tsur quoted in WTC:TYM, 52.

6. Quentin Pan, "Evaluation of Chinese Student Fraternities in America," CSM, Vol. XX, No. 8, p. 26; "Educational News," CYTC, Vol. XVIII, No. 1, pp. 5-6.

7. A list of names taken from CSM, Vol. XVI, No. 2, pp. 145-46 (1920-21) reveals the interesting fact that out of 454 students listed, 36 had Western names and surnames and another 85 had Western first names.

8. See, for instance, SYC:HY, 29.

dents in America] selected for their study, they did it with the primary object of serving their country in their respective fields."[9] In 1921 the sailing of Chinese students for America was still an occasion for great entertainment in Shanghai. The students were feted for days by various civic organizations, and every speech delivered at the public banquets bore the theme "The fate of the new China depends on you."[10] In 1920 a Chinese weekly in New York severely censured the summer conference of Chinese students meeting at Princeton, New Jersey, for the participants' lightheartedness and clear lack of interest in affairs at home.[11] In 1927 the Chinese Minister to Belgium, in a preface to a student yearbook, deplored the political situation at home and accused the returned students of not fulfilling their duty to the country.[12] The high moral purpose behind these statements was characteristic of the era between 1900 and 1930. After that period such pronouncements became increasingly rare.

In 1931 the Kuomintang government laid down three goals for the movement to study abroad: first, to create a Sun Yat-senist culture (*San-Min-Chu-i te hsin-wen-hua*) ; second, to provide for China's academic needs by producing specialists in various fields; and third, to meet China's material needs by producing talents useful for the country's reconstruction.[13]

The stress on specialist training reflected an interesting change in the goals of study abroad. In the mid-1920's Chinese opinion began express dissatisfaction with the imitative character of Chinese higher education and to urge that "academic independence" be achieved.[14] The Kuomintang also endorsed this stand. Finally, after World War II, Hu Shih, who had once "unreservedly praised the modern civilization of the West," also came to the conclusion that China should seek "academic independence."[15] The precise meaning of this phrase varied from one writer to another. Some merely sought to downgrade the importance of study abroad, while others wished to allocate more resources to Chinese universities. However different their basic emphases, all of them maintained that academic originality was desirable and that China had not developed this characteristic in spite of the large number of students sent abroad.

The stress on the academic tasks of the foreign-educated amounted,

9. Reprinted in CSM, XIII, 20-28.
10. WTC:TYM, 55.
11. CSM (November, 1920), 89-91.
12. Wei Ch'en-tsu's preface, LTHH.
13. 2d CYNC, 10.
14. Yi-yi, "The Problems of Study Abroad," CHCYC, Vol. XIII, No. 10; Yü Chia-chü, "Nationalist Education," quoted in Li Ju-mien, "Criticism of Study Abroad and a Suggested Policy for the Future," CHCYC, Vol. XV, No. 9.
15. Hu Shih, "A Ten-Year Plan to Gain Academic Independence," KC, Vol. III, No. 7, p. 23.

of course, to a de-emphasis on their other public duties. In particular, their possible role in political affairs was discounted. The hope once so widely held in China that a man educated abroad would be able to perform political miracles was based on the popular identification of intellectuals with public service. This coupling of the two was a characteristic of the traditional society that had almost disintegrated. Although the civil service continued to absorb a high proportion of the returning students, many of them remained outside of the government and had few connections with politics. Old bonds loosened and traditional values disappeared. As a result, personal motivation became the first consideration of Chinese students abroad. Writing sometime around 1937, George H. Danton observed: "A mature man of my acquaintance, studying for an advanced degree, frankly confessed that his *main* object in coming was not primarily to get a better job, but a better wife. 'With an A.M. I can get a better wife than if I have nothing but the Chinese A.B.; if I get a Ph.D. I can get a still better one.'"[16] In an open letter to students preparing to study in America, Quentin Pan, a professor at Tsinghua University, stated that some of the students were going abroad to seek degrees, that some did not intend to secure degrees but were relying on their sojourn abroad to provide them with the prestige of returning students, and that still others were leaving China merely to escape from unpleasant realities, such as their inability to find employment.[17] Another prominent educator declared in 1948 that foreign study had become a routine part of higher education for those students who could afford it—"just as they proceeded from the primary school to the middle school, so they went abroad after they finished college."[18] Thus by implication, foreign study had become associated more with a student's means and social status than with any particular goal or mission. Clearly, the concept of foreign study was radically altered during the years after 1920. Whereas in 1920 the goal of study abroad was to prepare a student for service to his country, by the 1940's personal motives had become the foremost consideration of students going abroad.

Viewing the history of the entire period from 1872 to 1949, the primary aim of foreign study before 1900 was to acquire certain specific skills, particularly in the military and naval fields. After 1900, study abroad was intended to foster better political leadership. This broadened view led to greater attention being given to all branches of knowledge useful for government service, in addition to technology. This condition more or less continued until the Kuomintang came

16. DGH:CP, 266. The italics are mine.
17. PKT:CHTY, pp. 185-91; for a confirmative opinion, see Chi Hsien-lin, "The Existing Policy of Study Abroad," KC, Vol. III, No. 7, p. 9.
18. Ou Yüan-huai, *op. cit.,* 33.

to power, when technology once again became the focus of government attention. Beginning in the mid-1920's, a specific new goal was defined as gaining "academic independence," that is to say, students going abroad were urged to achieve a measure of academic originality and not to echo the words of their Western professors in all cases. Thus political leadership, technical know-how, and academic achievement were the specific objectives of foreign study; and it is by these three objectives that the results of the movement can be evaluated.

Personal motivation, another goal of foreign study, was recognized in the Manchu educational policy from 1903 to 1911. It was at that time that large numbers of students first began going abroad on their own funds. But there was no obvious difference between their motivation and the motivation of government students; all were popularly regarded as having a mission to perform. It was not until the 1930's that qualified observers began to explain the motivation behind foreign study entirely in terms of personal ambition and interest.

As far as official policy is concerned, the aim was always to absorb Western culture selectively. But the concept of total Westernization was advanced by Yung Wing and later revived by Ch'en Tu-hsiu, Wu Chih-hui, and their friends, most of whom received some training abroad. Yung's concept deeply influenced the 120 C.E.M. students under his supervision, and the statement of Ch'en and Wu had a great impact on Chinese students at home and abroad. Ironically, the wholesale condemnation of China's national heritage was meant as a way of saving China. Whether it worked as intended is of course another matter.

SOCIAL BACKGROUND OF CHINESE STUDENTS ABROAD

The period from 1912 to 1927 was marked by political confusion, increasing curtailment of government expenditures on foreign study, and, above all, a changing attitude toward education on the part of ranking government officials. The number of provincial scholarships began to decline rapidly, and this circumstance not only caused non-fellowship students to predominate among those who studied abroad but also altered the proportion of students from different parts of the country. Students of poorer provinces now had even less opportunity to go abroad; consequently, natives of the richer areas predominated.

Government expenditures for study abroad began to decline after 1912. In the years 1909 and 1910, more than five times as much was spent on foreign study as on higher education in China. In 1917, approximately twice as much was spent on foreign study; but in 1931 only 9 per cent as much was spent on foreign study as on higher education at home, mainly because fewer government scholarships were being awarded.

As noted in Chapter 4, the first Chinese students from China proper were sent to Great Britain by the government. Although the number of Chinese students in Great Britain increased after 1900, the number with government fellowships declined steadily until the mid-1930's. In 1906, 65 per cent of the Chinese students held fellowships; in 1910, 50 per cent; and in 1916-17, only 20 per cent. During the 1930's the proportion increased somewhat, and between 1929 and 1936, 36 per cent of those who applied for permission to study in Great Britain were fellowship holders. After World War II, the proportion continued to rise, and in the academic year 1946-47, 62 per cent of the Chinese students there received government aid. The tendency after 1930 for more students to hold fellowships was owing largely to the initiation in 1933 of the British indemnity scholarships for Chinese students, and the high proportion of fellowship-holders in 1946-47 was largely a result of the increased number of British grants.

As in Great Britain, the proportion of fellowship students in the United States steadily declined during the first three decades of the twentieth century. In 1905 approximately 61 per cent of the Chinese students in America held government scholarships; in 1910, about 32 per cent; in 1925, 20 per cent; between 1929 and 1935, approximately 19 per cent; and in 1942, only 3 per cent.[19] Because the figures for the years from 1929 through 1935 were based on student applications for permission to study abroad, and because few self-supporting students applied for such permission, the proportion of fellowship-holders during these years is undoubtedly too high. In all probability, after 1925, when provincial scholarships virtually ceased, fellowship students constituted a small minority of the Chinese studying in America.

After the American government instituted a scholarship program for Chinese students in 1942, the proportion of fellowship students rose to 52 per cent late that year,[20] and to 80 per cent in 1950.[21] However, it must be noted that this program was intended mainly for the relief of Chinese already abroad and rarely included students still in China. Between 1949 and 1954 a large number of Chinese girls, many of whom have since married Chinese in America, came from Formosa under Catholic scholarships. But the essential fact is that during the years from 1925 through 1945, which witnessed the rise of the Communist movement in China, self-supporting students predominated among the Chinese studying in the United States.

The proportion of fellowship students in Japan suggests a striking parallel to the situation in the United States. In 1906 approximately

19. CIB (January, 1942), 1-3.
20. *Ibid.* (October, 1942), 3; (November-December, 1942), 3.
21. SURVEY, 20.

53 per cent of the Chinese students in Japan held government scholarships, but the proportion began to decline after the downfall of the Manchus. In 1920, 32 per cent of them received government aid, and in 1929,[22] about 30 per cent. During the years from 1929 through 1935, only 3 per cent of those who applied for permission to study in Japan were awarded fellowships.[23]

Although the number of government scholarships was severely curtailed during the first three decades of the twentieth century, the number of Chinese students abroad continued to increase. Occasionally there were cases where students of small means were able to study abroad by dint of sheer will power or extraordinary luck. At least one is known to have borrowed every cent of his fare and to have landed in America almost penniless.[24] Others owed their opportunity to wealthy philanthropists in China.[25] But these were rare exceptions, for a prerequisite to foreign study was previous education in China. After the establishment of the modern school system in 1902, tuition fees were instituted, and these together with the geographical location of the primary and secondary schools virtually placed education beyond the reach of a large majority of the Chinese people. A few simple statistics will illustrate this point.

The largest social class in China was the farmers, who comprised 75 per cent of the population.[26] According to a report of 1936 that covered sixteen provinces, their landholdings, and consequently their incomes, were distributed as follows:[27]

Size of Holdings (in Units of mou or one-sixth of an acre)	Percentage of Total Households
10 and under	59.6
10-29.9	29.4
30-49.9	6.2
50-99.9	3.5
100 and over	1.3
Total	100.0

22. NAS (June, 1913), 171; SHC:CTCK, 148; Yü Lü-fu and Ch'en Chu-t'ung, "Recent Conditions of Chinese Students in Japan," CYTC, Vol. XXII, No. 4, pp. 79 ff.

23. 23d CKTC, 284-85.

24. STH:KN, *passim.*

25. One of China's foremost economists used to be a kind of page to China's cotton king who sent him to America to study economics. In 1919 the chairman of the Nanyang Brothers Tobacco Company sent five students to America at his own expense. See LTW:WS, 24.

26. The term "farmers" is used here in a general sense. It includes both landlords and peasants, but excludes those who had important diversified financial interests.

27. Report of the National Land Commission, quoted in LSC:SIF, 114.

In central China in the 1930's, only farmers having 30 *mou* of land could afford to send two children to primary school.[28] Another report in 1935 noted that "only a family having about 50 *mou* could afford to send one child to the higher primary school," and only families with over 200 *mou* could spare 150 dollars per year to send a son to secondary school.[29] In 1930, the expenditure of an average college student in Shanghai was about 500 Chinese dollars a year.[30] An investigation made by the China International Famine Relief Commission in the 1920's reported that only .2 to 1.6 per cent of China's agricultural population received annual incomes of between 2,000 and 5,000 dollars per family, and only .2 to .4 per cent had annual incomes of over 5,000 dollars.[31] On the assumption that self-supporting students spent as much as the scholarships provided by the Chinese government, not including travel or medical expenses, a student in the United States needed 2,035 Chinese dollars in 1909, 2,025 dollars in 1924, and 3,280 dollars in 1933. On the same basis a student in Great Britain needed 2,150, 2,160, and 4,104 dollars respectively in the same years.[32] It is extremely doubtful that even a family with 5,000 dollars a year could afford these sums without outside help, since it traditionally supported a large number of kin and was unable to sacrifice everything in order to send one son abroad.

The second largest group in China was the factory workers, who were estimated to number between two and five million at any time between 1927 and 1947. During the years from 1917 through 1931, more than eighty surveys were made of their living conditions, and these placed the yearly incomes of this group at 100 to 400 dollars per family.[33] In one study, the yearly educational outlay per family was reported to be 77 cents;[34] in another 1.45 dollars.[35] Therefore, it may be safely concluded that, except in special cases like those involving the patronage of a missionary, no Chinese student in the West came from a working-class family.

28. Ho Jih-pin, "Chinese Education," CHCYC, Vol. XIX, No. 3, pp. 10-11.
29. AC, 171.
30. Chou Yung, "The Reconstruction of Chinese Education," CHCYC, Vol. XXVIII, No. 12.
31. J. B. Taylor, "A Study of Rural Economy in China," CSPSR (April, 1924), 251.
32. Standard stipends paid by the Chinese government to students in Japan were 400 yen in 1909 and 840 yen in 1924 and 1933. Stipends paid to students in the United States were 960 American dollars in 1909 and 1,080 American dollars in 1924 and 1933. Stipends paid to students in England were £192 in 1909 and £240 in 1924 and 1933. To facilitate comparison, these sums were converted into Chinese currency at the average exchange rates prevailing in the respective years. As the rates fluctuated, so the sums in Chinese currency changed.
33. In Chinese currency; TLK:SL, 4-5.
34. *Ibid.*, 25.
35. SKJ, 75.

The social origins of the Chinese students in America are suggested by the occupations of the heads of the families of Tsinghua College students—all of whom, for two decades, were sent to the United States after graduation. Of the 389 family heads in 1924, over 32 per cent were government employees, almost 31 per cent were educators, 13 per cent were lawyers or members of other professions, more than 20 per cent were industrialists, and only 3.7 per cent were farmers.[36] In 1947, questionnaires were sent to nearly 2,300 Chinese students in the United States. Of the replies received, 660 were by students from China, whose fathers' occupations were distributed as follows:[37]

Profession	Percentage
Businessmen	30.3
Professionals	27.4
Government Workers	17.0
Farmers	6.2
Landlords	5.3
Clergymen	3.8
Technicians	1.2
Others	5.9
Unknown	2.9
Total	100.0

In neither survey were the terms precisely defined, and in the second the respondents were free to choose their own description.[38] For the reasons indicated above, it could be that the "farmers" and "landlords" in the 1947 listing were people who owned land but who, having diversified financial resources as well, were not farmers in the strict sense of the term. On the other hand, during the Sino-Japanese War of 1937-45 the Kuomintang government awarded a large number of scholarships to students, and these undoubtedly enabled many without adequate resources to continue their studies and to go abroad.[39] At any rate the data indicate the predominance of three groups— businessmen, professionals, and government officials—among the fathers of Chinese students in Western countries.

The same cannot be said of Chinese students in Japan, where the cost of study was much lower than in the West. In 1925, for instance, while a Chinese government student in the United States received $80

36. Ts'ao Yung-hsiang, "The Way to Improve Tsinghua," THP, Tenth Anniversary Special Issue, p. 67.
37. Sun Zen E-tu, "A Poll of Chinese Students in the United States," EM, Vol. 44, No. 9, pp. 11-18.
38. I am indebted to Mrs. E-tu Jen Sun for this information.
39. I am indebted to Dr. Ch'ang-yün Fan of the University of Chicago for bringing this point to my attention. Dr. Fan was one of those who benefited from those scholarships.

per month, which was equivalent to 143 Chinese dollars at the current exchange rate, a student in Japan received only 70 yen or about 50 Chinese dollars.[40] Actually the difference was even greater because travel expenses from China to Japan were low and because a student could live more cheaply in Japan than the size of the stipend indicates. An account of 1917 records that a third-class steamship ticket from Shanghai to Yokohama cost U.S. $7.50 and that a Chinese needed only U.S. $10 per month to study in Japan, with tuition fees and incidentals included.[41] Often it was cheaper for Chinese students to live in Tokyo (and even more so in the Japanese provinces) than in Peking or Shanghai, where many Chinese colleges were clustered.

In the early years of the twentieth century, when government scholarships were available for study in all countries, the family background of Chinese students in Japan and in the West probably differed little in general. While no direct survey seems to have ever been made in this respect, circumstantial evidence strongly suggests that in the 1920's and 1930's Chinese students in Japan were not nearly as well off as their counterparts in the West. An indirect indication was the effect of a change in the expenses on a number of Chinese studying in Japan. During the academic year 1918-19 their number sharply declined because of a rise in the Japanese price level.[42] On the other hand, their number increased in 1935, as a result of a sharp appreciation of the Chinese currency vis-à-vis the Japanese. Previously, in September, 1931, the Sino-Japanese exchange rate had been .48 yen to 1 Chinese dollar. In that month the Japanese army occupied Manchuria, and, aroused by a spirit of patriotism, most Chinese students in Japan returned home. By the first quarter of 1933 the exchange had moved to par and from then to the end of 1937 Chinese currency was at a premium, reaching a high of 1.46 yen to 1 Chinese dollar in May, 1935.[43] With little improvement in the political situation, Chinese students in Japan increased from 1,421 in June, 1932, to 4,500 in June, 1935, and to 8,000 in November of that year.[44]

This case contrasted sharply with that of Chinese students in the West. United States currency averaged 93 cents to 1 Chinese dollar in 1919 and 56 cents to 1 Chinese dollar in 1925.[45] Between these years, Chinese currency lost 65 per cent of its value in terms of the American dollar; yet the number of Chinese students in this country increased from 955 in 1919 to 1,561 in 1925-26.[46] As members of China's

40. CY (1939), 255.
41. Howard S. Chang, "Chinese Students in Japan," CSM (1917), 323.
42. SK:CNRS, 535.
43. *Ibid.*, table facing p. 312.
44. *Ibid.*, 309.   45. CY (1939), 255.
46. SURVEY, 18.

wealthiest class, the students in America were far less sensitive to cost factors than those in Japan; and perhaps because study in America was so expensive, much more value was attached to it. It appears that the prestige accorded foreign education was not unrelated to snobbish motives, even though this was only one of the factors involved.

NATIVE ORIGIN

A person's native origin was a matter of importance in traditional China. Not only was it a primary item in a man's *vitae,* but even casual acquaintances did not fail to inquire of one another's "honorable provinces and counties." Under Western impact, however, old customs disintegrated; individuals were no longer tied to their native districts, and the concern for a man's place of birth came to be regarded as parochial. Nevertheless, the native origins of returning students are of significance for us. For one thing, as Western influences bore unevenly on different parts of China, patterns of life began to vary more widely from one region to another. At one extreme were the highly Westernized seaports, and at the other were the rural areas where tradition scarcely changed.[47] These differences in turn influenced the people's outlook and behavior. While a key factor was the question of urban-rural relations, these relations to a large extent ran parallel to provincial divisions. In the second place, since study abroad was a means of personal advancement, the predominance of certain native groups among the foreign-educated naturally affected the geographical distribution of leadership in China. A radically new pattern of distribution soon came into existence, and it not only indicates important social changes but also provides us with a key to the understanding of such changes.

Our inquiry will begin with the Chinese students in the United States to determine whether their native origins reflect a pattern. A series of comparisons will then be made between the Chinese students in the United States and those in Europe, Japan, and China. The purpose of these comparisons is to establish whether Chinese students in one country persistently differed from those in another country in regard to native provinces, and, if so, what the implications of these differences were.

The distribution of Chinese students in the United States in terms of native province is shown in Table 1. In the table Kwangtung stands out as the province sending the largest number of students to the

47. A good description of the difference may be found in CHC:ESC. The author views the modern and the old ways of life in China as a mixture of the East and the West. Actually, what he describes so vividly is not a mixture but represents the urban and rural patterns of life. Of course the two come in contact, but perhaps they are less a mixture than two forces pulling apart from each other. See FHT:HTCC, *passim.*

United States, since it provided from 24 to 51 per cent during the years 1909 to 1945. Kiangsu was second, accounting for 13 to 28 per cent. The commanding position of these two provinces changed very little over the years and the consistency is worth noting. Third place belongs to Chekiang, although it was slightly eclipsed by Hopeh in 1943 and 1945. Traditionally, Kiangsu and Chekiang were considered as one region in China. Together they furnished from 22 to 40 per cent of the students between 1909 and 1945. With Kwangtung they provided between 57 and 82 per cent of all of the Chinese students in the United States while having only about 16 per cent of China's population.

The position of Kwangtung may have been boosted considerably by the fact that many Chinese-Americans claimed to be, or were designated as, natives of Kwangtung, following the Chinese custom of taking the birthplace of one's parents as one's own. Since our study is primarily interested in the native-born Chinese, these should ideally be excluded. Yet the citizenship status of Chinese in America is a baffling problem: men who had been there for fifty years were often not American citizens, while those who were citizens frequently had every intention of returning to China. At any rate, information contained in the student directories, on which this study is based, is not sufficiently clear to make the exclusion of Chinese-Americans possible. That there were Chinese-Americans listed in the directories and that they served to boost the position of Kwangtung is, however, quite clear. In the 1914 *Directory of Chinese Students,* for instance, the presence of American citizens is specifically mentioned by the compiler; and if we follow his indication and remove the names of the 120 students most likely to be American-born, Cantonese students will constitute only 37.6 instead of the original 47.2 per cent.

Statistics compiled in China on students leaving for America confirm the importance of these three provinces but give first place to Kiangsu. Thus between 1921 and 1934 the percentages of students from Kiangsu, Chekiang, and Kwangtung were respectively 24.9, 12.8, 12.8.[48] A comprehensive survey made by the China Institute in America for the period from 1854 through 1953 gave Kiangsu 29.3 per cent, Chekiang 5.0 per cent, and Kwangtung 15.3 per cent.[49]

The considerable variations shown by these figures may, to a limited extent, be attributed to the differences of the periods covered and, in a more important way, to the scope and method of compilation. The China Institute survey is based on files of American colleges and universities, thus including no students below the college level,

48. WYC:CIW, 412.
49. SURVEY, Table C.

while the directories are usually compiled from membership lists of student unions and have no such limitation. One probable result is that the survey includes proportionately fewer Chinese-Americans than other sources. But the significant point is that all give prominence to the same three provinces.

TABLE 1. *Native Provinces of Chinese Students in the United States*[a]

	1903[b]	1909	1910	1911	1914	1918	1921[c]	1943	1945
Kwangtung	58.0	38.1	38.0	51.2	47.2	43.0	24.2	36.9	33.6
Kiangsu	4.0	28.5	23.2	22.0	13.9	13.4	21.9	20.9	22.3
Chekiang	6.0	11.3	11.6	9.2	8.3	9.2	10.8	8.4	7.5
Fukien	2.0	4.6	5.1	3.7	5.3	8.8	7.8	6.4	5.5
Hunan	—	.4	2.1	1.0	8.0	4.7	5.2	2.6	3.0
Hupeh	12.0	1.7	3.1	1.6	2.4	3.7	2.8	1.9	3.2
Hopeh	—	8.4	8.2	4.3	2.2	3.7	9.7	10.6	10.9
Anhwei	16.0	3.4	4.1	2.0	—	2.8	2.3	2.0	1.6
Kiangsi	—	1.3	1.4	.4	4.1	2.6	2.4	1.5	1.7
Szechuan	—	—	—	1.0	—	1.6	1.8	1.5	2.2
Shantung	—	—	.4	2.1	2.7	1.4	2.2	2.2	2.5
Honan	—	.4	.4	—	—	.8	3.8	1.2	1.5
Shansi	—	.4	.7	—	—	.5	.9	.8	1.1
Liaoning	—	—	—	—	—	.1	.9	1.3	1.3
Kirin	—	—	—	—	—	.8	.1	—	.4
Heilungkiang	—	—	—	—	—	—	—	—	—
Others	2.0	1.5	1.7	1.5	5.9	2.9	3.3	1.8	1.7
Total in %	100.0	100.0	100.0	100.0	100.0	100.0	100.0	100.0	100.0
Total in number	50	239	292	490	830	990	679	1191	1972
Including unknown	50		292	650	847	1124	805	1295	3066

a. 1903 compiled from Liang Ch'i-ch'ao, "Hsin-ta-lu yu-chi."
  1909 compiled from CSM (November, 1909), 28-30.
  1910 compiled from CSM (March, 1910), 267.
  1911 compiled from WCSJ (September, 1911), 486.
  1914 compiled from CSM (February, 1914), 344-45.
  1918 compiled from CSD, 1918.
  1921 compiled from WWCS.
  1943 and 1945 compiled from DCUG, 1943 and 1945 editions.

b. The information is not complete, only fifty out of "some two hundred students" being listed. The sample seems, however, fairly representative.

c. After 1921 the native origin of a student is no longer listed in directories of Chinese students, except during the years from 1943 to 1945 when a great expansion of the activities of the China Institute caused it to issue directories much more comprehensive in scope than was customarily the case.

A related matter is the educational background of the Chinese students in America. In the first place, a Chinese education generally indicates that a person was born in China and not in America. In the second, education received in one place normally signifies a long period of residence in that place. Thus, by knowing the last schools attended by Chinese students in China, we may derive a fairly accurate picture of the regions where they lived. This last connection need not be their native region, but since we are more concerned with a student's background than with his place of birth, such information is useful.

According to the survey, no less than 49.36 per cent of the native-born Chinese last attended schools in four cities in Kiangsu and Chekiang, 30.72 per cent in two cities in Hopeh, and 7.89 per cent in Kwangtung.[50] Since a portion of those educated in one region were undoubtedly natives of other regions and maintained contacts with those regions, it may be presumed that over one-half of the Chinese students in the United States were in one way or another connected with the Kiangsu area. This fact is significant because Kiangsu is geographically a very small part of China, and life in Shanghai, from which most Kiangsu students came, was Westernized and differed a great deal from that in other parts of the country.

Our inquiry thus leads to several important observations. Among the Chinese students in America, natives of Kwangtung, Kiangsu, and Chekiang accounted for between 57 and 82 per cent during the years from 1909 through 1945. The dominant position of these provinces was maintained throughout this period. Whether Kiangsu or Kwangtung was in the leading position is not altogether clear. Indications are that Kwangtung was in first place if Chinese-Americans are included, but that Kiangsu led in regard to the native-born Chinese. Finally, many Chinese students in America last attended schools in Kiangsu.

Statistics for Chinese students in Europe between 1921 and 1934 show that 20.0 per cent came from Kiangsu, 13.9 per cent from Chekiang, and 9.16 per cent from Kwangtung.[51] Direct surveys are available in only three cases:

Native Province	Per Cent in Germany[52]		Per Cent in Belgium[53]
	1902?-26	*1927*	*1929-30*
Kiangsu	28.2	27.4	21.5
Chekiang	19.4	17.7	11.3
Kwangtung	14.4	10.6	8.0
Fukien	7.6	8.0	9.5
Szechuan	6.6	9.7	7.7
Rest of China	23.8	26.6	42.0
Total	100.0	100.0	100.0

50. *Ibid.*, Table E.
52. LTHH
51. WYC:CIW, 412.
53. CHCYC, Vol. XVIII, No. 11, p. 20.

In the case of Chinese students in Germany, Kwangtung was behind Kiangsu and Chekiang. This fact does not conflict with our supposition that students from Kwangtung were especially prominent in the United States because Chinese-Americans were also included, and that wherever (as in Germany) such a native-born group did not exist, Kiangsu and Chekiang would come first. Taking the three provinces together, their prominence was as high in Germany as in the United States. But the same was not true in Belgium, where students tended to come from more widely scattered parts of China. A major difference in regard to Belgium was the lower level of educational costs there. Thus we may conclude that the pattern of native origin was based in part on the cost of study in foreign countries: if the cost of study was high, there would be a larger number of students from China's richest provinces. This conclusion can be tested by the data available to us. Among the Chinese students in Europe, the poorest were the worker-students of 1921, many of whom arrived in France almost penniless. According to our conclusion there should have been relatively few natives of the three coastal provinces among this group. The data, based on an actual survey, bear this out.[54]

Native Province   Per Cent of 1,862 Worker-Students in France

Szechuan	25.13
Hunan	18.58
Kwangtung	13.48
Kiangsi	12.24
Hopeh	7.89
Fukien	4.78
Chekiang	4.56
Kiangsu	3.71
Hupeh	2.15
Anhwei	2.15
Others	5.33

Among the Chinese students in Japan, where expenses were low, natives of Kiangsu and Chekiang were again inconspicuous. The percentages of students from various provinces were as follows:

	1913[55]	*1928-29*[56]	*1930*[57]
Kwangtung	12.8	17.1	18.4
Kiangsu	3.5	4.6	5.5

54. SHC:CTCK, p. 89, footnote 1. The percentage computation is mine.
55. Compiled from WCSJ (November, 1913), 112. The addition in this source is wrong and has been corrected.
56. Compiled from Yü Lü-fu and Ch'en Chu-t'ung, *op. cit.*
57. Compiled from 17-20th CKTC, Table 106.

Chekiang	6.5	9.2	6.4
Liaoning	1.9	16.2	18.0
Kiangsi	11.9	8.3	7.3
Szechuan	5.7	6.8	6.7
Fukien	3.0	4.3	5.4
Hunan	18.0	5.6	5.1
Hupeh	12.4	4.3	4.4
Rest of China	24.3	23.6	22.8
Total	100.0	100.0	100.0
Total in number	1,674	2,635	3,064

Significantly, a large number of the students in Japan were from Kwangtung and Liaoning. This points to two factors other than the cost of study. One was the presence of a large overseas Chinese group from a single province in China. Because this particular group tended to bring many acquaintances and relatives to their country of residence, the result was an increase in the percentage of that group among the Chinese students there. This factor seemed responsible for the importance of the Kwangtung group among the Chinese students in Japan. The other factor was the prevailing system of spheres of influence in China. The comparatively large number of Manchurian students in Japan contrasts with their virtual absence in Western countries and points to the dominance of Japanese interests in Manchuria before World War II. To a certain extent the same relationship undoubtedly existed between the large number of Kiangsu and Kwangtung students in the United States and the importance of Anglo-American influence over central and Southern China. However, the political factor is less clear in this case than in the case of the Manchurian students in Japan.

A correlation between the students' native origins and the level of educational expenses can be observed even in the Chinese educational system. From primary school to university, as the level of education advanced and as expenses mounted, the percentage of students from the richer provinces increased (Table 2).

A word should be said of the relation between scholarships and native origins. A great deal depended on the nature of the scholarships offered. In the case of competitive scholarships awarded on a national scale, students from the interior had little chance of doing as well as those from coastal areas. A comparison can be made between the Tsinghua scholars in 1909-1929 and those of 1933-35 as well as the British indemnity scholars of 1933-47. Because the 1909-29 group was at first recruited partly on a provincial basis, the recipients tended to come from more widely scattered areas than the members of the two

TABLE 2. *Native Provinces of Chinese Students in China and Abroad*

	CHINA			Chinese Students in Japan 1930	Chinese Students in Belgium 1929-30	Chinese Students Leaving for USA 1931	Chinese Students in Germany 1927	Chinese Students in USA 1943
	Primary School 1930	Middle School 1930	College 1931					
Kwangtung	9.46	11.74	13.24	15.2	8.0	17.8	10.6	36.9
Kiangsu	7.29	15.16	15.06	5.5	21.5	11.6	27.4	20.9
Chekiang	5.98	4.51	7.73	6.4	11.3	17.1	17.7	8.4
Sub-total	22.73	31.41	36.03	27.1	40.8	46.5	55.7	66.2
Rest of China	77.27	68.59	63.97	72.9	59.2	53.5	44.3	33.8
Total	100	100	100	100	100	100	100	100

other groups, both of which were chosen on a national basis. Among
the 1909-29 Tsinghua group, natives of Kiangsu, Chekiang, and
Kwangtung accounted for 46.5 per cent of the total[58]; among the 1933-
35 group, for 70.6 per cent[59]; and among the 1933-47 indemnity group,
for 57.1 per cent.[60]

Without attempting a complete analysis at this stage, two larger
implications of these findings should be mentioned. In the first place,
better educational opportunity contributed to the high incidence of
leaders among the natives of these three provinces. This result became
very clear under the Kuomintang when the capital was moved to
Nanking and when the remaining influence of the old mandarinate
rapidly declined. Among the central government leaders, the number
of men who hailed from these provinces was only four out of twelve
in 1915 and one out of eleven in 1923, but nine out of eighteen in
1932, nine out of sixteen in 1937, nine out of twenty in 1943, and
thirteen out of twenty-four in 1947.[61] That this increasing domination
was related to educational qualifications is shown by the lack of such
domination among the provincial heads, who generally had little
formal education. In other words, where circumstances did not place
a premium on educational qualifications, the incidence of leaders

58. Compiled from THTHL.
59. Compiled from 23d CKTC. Of course even the lowest figure of 46.5 per cent
was much higher than that intended by the Manchu Government in 1910, when
the American Boxer indemnity scholarships were initiated. According to current
regulations, all provinces and minority groups—including Sinkiang (Chinese Tur-
kestan) and Mongolia—were to be given quotas, but this scheme was never fully
implemented.
60. I am indebted to Mr. A. G. Morkill of the Universities' China Committee
in London for this information.
61. Computed from the lists of government leaders in CY (1916, 1923, 1931-32,
1939); CH (1937-45); WHJP (1947).

among natives of the three coastal provinces was correspondingly low. Two corroborating examples may be cited. During the years between the first and sixth Kuomintang congresses, natives of Kwangtung constituted the largest group among the Central Executive Committee, rising from 16.7 per cent in 1924 to 25.0 per cent in both 1929 and 1931. Thereafter the proportion declined to 19.3 per cent in 1935 and 14.4 per cent in 1945.[62] Similarly, natives of Chekiang and Kiangsu, increased from 8.4 per cent in 1924 to 30.8 per cent in 1931, and declined somewhat thereafter to 19.4 per cent in 1935 and 24.7 per cent in 1945.[63] Closer examination reveals that the decline in the number of men from these three provinces in 1935 was owing to a great expansion in the size of the Central Executive Committee in order to absorb provincial militarists into the top echelon of the party organization. Thus the major fact was that leaders who started at the center, as distinguished from those whose power base was in the provinces, were largely natives of Kwangtung, Chekiang, and Kiangsu.

If we use listings in *Who's Who* as an index of national leadership in general, the steady increase of these native groups becomes even more striking, from 30.24 per cent of the total in 1916, to 32.41 per cent in 1923, 45.28 per cent in 1931, and 50.54 per cent in 1939. Significantly, the proportion of returned students in the same *Who's Who* also increased from 49.5 per cent in 1916 to 71.0 per cent in 1939, and of this, the increase of the American-trained alone was from 9.5 per cent to 36.2 per cent. The persistent concomitant variation in the proportion of coastal natives among the foreign-educated and among leaders at the national level cannot but point to opportunity of formal education as a key factor governing both classifications.

Another phenomenon that was closely connected with the native origins of returned students was their known habit of congregating in China's port cities. Our survey of the Tsinghua alumni indicates that in 1925, 34 per cent lived in Shanghai, 39 per cent in six other cities, 3 per cent each in Hongkong and the United States, but not a single member of this group settled in a city smaller than a county seat. The situation was broadly similar in 1937.[64] This was a notable departure from the traditional practice in China, according to which the most cherished ambition of a successful man was to return to his native district. The survey made by Fei Hsiao-t'ung and P'an Kuang-tan referred to in Chapter 1, it will be remembered, reveals that 52.50

62. NR:KCC, Appendix D, Table 4.
63. Computed from the listings of the "Who's Who" sections in the *China Yearbook*.
64. Compiled from THTHL.

per cent of 758 *chin-shih* lived in cities, 6.34 per cent in towns, and 41.16 per cent in rural areas.[65]

The changed residential pattern of China's elite is a significant phenomenon that deserves careful attention. Essentially, it indicates a process in which many factors converged. Under Western impact certain provinces became centers of wealth and areas where Western ways of life prevailed. Because certain groups among the inhabitants were financially well off, they could afford to secure more advanced education and thus enjoyed increased chances of becoming leaders. Having come from Westernized surroundings and having been exposed to Western ways of life while abroad, they almost inevitably chose to settle in metropolises upon their return. Against this natural tendency there was no institutional counteracting force—as there had been in imperial China in the form, for instance, of a geographical quota in the civil-service examinations. Yet with a leadership that was essentially Westernized and urbanized, policy at the national level inevitably reflected an ignorance of rural conditions and a neglect of rural interests. Thus, an abyss was created between the leaders and the great rural masses of people, with serious political consequences.

ACADEMIC ACCOMPLISHMENTS

After the revolution of 1911, the government continued to require a certain minimum academic standard of all students going abroad, particularly of government scholars. But official policy had little effect, and the educational level of Chinese students abroad continued to be very low. An extreme example was the worker-student movement in France; of 1,340 students, 741 were refused admittance by all schools, another 522 were enrolled only in secondary schools.

In 1924 a Chinese student in France reported that few of his compatriots took their studies seriously. There were approximately three thousand Chinese students in France, including the worker-students; yet counting all the Chinese who ever studied there, only three secured the *Doctorat d'état*—all in natural science—and less than twenty, the *Doctorat de l'université*. Only five Chinese ever graduated from *écoles supérieures*. Most Chinese government students behaved so badly that the term "government students" acquired a connotation of academic incompetence. Several students sent to France by Governor-General Chang Chih-tung remained in Paris for more than two decades. One student became the "king of billiards"; another knew enough about men's wear to be known as "the tailor." Some specialized in rendering service to visiting Chinese dignitaries; some lived on the earnings of prostitutes; some purchased their

65. SHKH, Vol. IV, No. 1, p. 8.

diplomas; and some were sent to prison for burglary.[66] Severely critical in tone, the report appeared in one of China's leading educational journals and went unchallenged.

In November, 1926, the *Ostasiatische Rundschau* published a report on the Chinese students in Germany. It maintained that during the hyper-inflation of 1924 numerous Chinese were attracted to Germany by the favorable exchange rate. In the middle of 1924 there were almost a thousand Chinese students in Berlin alone. Of these only a small number were registered in academic institutions; the rest "preferred to spend their time outside the schools and lecture halls, a circumstance which did no credit to the Chinese students as a whole." When the inflation ended, most of the Chinese students left Germany, and only 250 to 300 remained to pursue their studies.[67]

In a yearbook published in Berlin in 1927, 119 persons were listed as members of the Chinese students' union. Of these, 6 had graduated from German universities, 1 from a Japanese university, 5 from Chinese universities, and 3 from Chinese colleges. The other 104 members had attended only middle schools in China and were pursuing undergraduate courses in German. Excluding the 26 about whom little is known, the average age of the students was 26.8 years, and many of them had been in Germany for more than four years. Their academic record as a whole was unimpressive.[68]

Conditions among Chinese students in Japan were no better. In 1907 only 3 to 4 per cent were enrolled in technical schools and only 1 per cent in colleges.[69] In 1914, out of 70 students from Szechuan, 47 were pursuing preparatory courses.[70] In October, 1929, a comprehensive survey revealed that there were 2,635 Chinese students in Japan, of whom more than 67 per cent were graduates of Chinese middle schools, less than 8 per cent were graduates of Chinese colleges, and the rest had educational backgrounds varying from virtually no formal training to undergraduate training in Chinese universities. As for their academic status in Japan, nearly 42 per cent were only beginning to learn the language, and none of those registered in universities was on a graduate level. There were 250 girls among the students, of whom 80 per cent were just learning Japanese.[71] In 1930, another survey of 3,064 students revealed that 1,268 were enrolled in preparatory courses, 686 were studying in technical and normal schools, 463

---

66. Shen I-chia, "Conditions of Chinese Students in France," CHCYC, Vol. XIII, No. 9.

67. Max Linde, "Chinese Students in Germany," OR, Vol. VII, No. 11, pp. 234-35.

68. LTHH.

69. HPTT, memorial dated thirtieth of the eleventh moon.

70. SSCYHC, 168.

71. Yü Lü-fu and Ch'en Chu-t'ung, "Recent Conditions of Chinese Students in Japan," CYTC, Vol. XXII, No. 4, pp. 79-104.

were pursuing special two-year college courses, and 647 (or only 21 per cent) were enrolled in regular university courses.[72] Not only was the percentage of preparatory students very large but a number of them were reportedly doing very little.[73] Low academic standards characterized the Chinese students in Japan during the years from 1896 to 1937.

Throughout China there was great dissatisfaction with the performance of Chinese students abroad. Several Tsinghua students bitterly criticized the low academic standards of their schoolmates, and one critic even declared that "prudent and conscientious men do not wish to admit that they are from Tsinghua."[74] In 1917 a group of Chinese students in the United States embezzled thousands of dollars donated for flood relief in China.[75] Two years later the supervisor of Tsinghua students in the United States, T. T. Wang, and his two assistants were shot to death by a student who was refused a loan.[76] In 1924, a Tsinghua student at the Yale law school was sent to prison for forging his professor's signature on a check.[77] As more than isolated phenomena, these incidents reflected a severe personality maladjustment on the part of the students who, because they felt attached neither to Chinese nor to American culture, tended to drift into dissipation and decadence.

This is not to say that all Chinese students in the United States were delinquents. Several of them made notable contributions to knowledge;[78] others set good examples in their extracurricular activities. Between 1917 and 1919, a group of students devoted themselves to social work among Chinese laborers in France, a task that demanded much dedication on their part.[79] Nevertheless, most of the Chinese students abroad compiled mediocre academic records, and a few were morally degenerate. According to a survey made by the China Institute, American colleges and universities awarded Chinese students 4,463 degrees between 1854 and 1929, and 9,334 more between

72. 19-20th CKTC, Table 107.

73. Yü Lü-fu and Ch'en Chu-t'ung, "Recent Conditions of Chinese Students in Japan," CYTC, Vol. XXII, No. 4, pp. 79 ff.

74. Liang Ch'ao-wei, "Exhorting Our Schoolmates in America," THCK, No. 289, p. 2; "Summaries of Conditions of Tsinghua," *ibid.*, No. 301, pp. 39-50.

75. "Educational News," CYTC, Vol. XVIII, No. 1, pp. 5-6.

76. HSK:AS, 63; CSM (March, 1919), 287-89.

77. "Educational News," CYTC, Vol. XVIII, No. 1, p. 5.

78. Some examples are: Chen Huan-chang, *The Economic Principles of Confucius and His School* (New York, 1911), 2 vols.; Chen Shao-kwan, *The System of Taxation in the Tsing Dynasty, 1644-1911* (New York, 1914); Mabel Ping-hua Lee, *The Economic History of China, with Special Reference to Agriculture* (New York, 1921); Ta Chen, *Chinese Migrations, with Special Reference to Labor Conditions* (Washington, 1923).

79. W. W. Lockwood, "Chinese Students from America Serve in France," INT, Vol. XXXVI, No. 7, pp. 9-10.

1930 and 1954. Of this number, 4,590 were bachelor's degrees, 7,221 were master's degrees, and 1,727 were doctorates.[80] Because a number of students received more than one degree, it appears that between 40 and 50 per cent of the 22,000 Chinese who studied in the United States received no degrees at all.

A marked improvement in the academic status of the Chinese students in the United States took place during the 1930's. The years from 1930 through 1937 were the golden era of the Kuomintang regime, and rapid strides were made in a number of directions, including education. By 1932 all of the students going abroad were required to be college graduates. Although this regulation was enforced only in regard to government students, it nevertheless had a generally beneficial effect. After 1938 government control became even stricter, and study abroad was restricted to postgraduate students. As a result the academic status of Chinese students abroad reached a peak during the 1940's, and graduate students in the United States outnumbered undergraduates by more than two to one. After 1950 the trend was reversed, and by 1953-54 undergraduates again accounted for more than one-half of the total.[81]

To a large extent this change reflected the policy of the Chinese government. In 1949, in the face of the rapid Communist advance on the Chinese mainland, many well-to-do Chinese sought feverishly to escape to the United States. One of the easiest ways to go was as a student. Probably under heavy pressure, the Ministry of Education in 1949 waived the requirement of college graduation and allowed any student with two years' college training to go abroad on scholarship or at his own expense. The requirements were further reduced by the Nationalist government in 1950 to allow middle-school graduates to go abroad on foreign scholarships.[82] Between 1949 and 1954 nearly a thousand undergraduate scholarships were awarded to Chinese by Catholic universities in America and Europe, through the personal efforts of Archibishop Paul Yupin.[83] The policy of the government in Formosa provided and added impetus; among other things, middle-school graduates were required to undergo only four months of military training before leaving the country, whereas a full year of training was required of all university students remaining at home.[84] This policy was, however, of an emergency nature. As the political situation became stabilized in Formosa, the government once again

80. SURVEY, 40-50. A recent work by Dr. T. L. Yüan lists 2,789 doctoral dissertations by Chinese students in America in 1905-60. This is a definitive figure for the period. See YTL:GDD, 237.

81. WYC:CIW, 273.

82. Tien-fang Cheng, *op. cit.*, 15-16.

83. Wu Chün-Sheng, *op. cit.*, 17-20.

84. I am indebted to Mrs. Jeannette Yin Mo of Indianapolis for this information.

reversed its stand, and no middle-school graduates were granted permission to go abroad in 1956. Thus educational policy remained at the mercy of political circumstances in China.

After World War II, and particularly after 1949, a large number of Chinese students settled permanently in the United States. The average academic standards of this group were probably the highest among all Chinese educated abroad. A directory of Chinese students and graduates in Chicago in 1954 listed nearly five hundred persons. Information is available on 237 of these. At least 65 had received doctoral degrees, while 48 others held master's degrees. The number of undergraduates was extremely small, probably not more than a dozen.[85]. Again in 1955-56, 587 Chinese were on the faculties of American colleges and universities.[86] Of this number, 35 were full professors—mostly in engineering and natural science—in major centers of learning, and 13 held the same rank in smaller colleges. In 1960 there were no less than 1,124 Chinese faculty members in America. Of this number, 20 were deans; 14, full professors; 103, associate professors; 150, assistant professors; 157, instructors; and 433, research assistants.[87]

ACADEMIC SPECIALTIES AND OCCUPATIONS

The Chinese Ministry of Education grouped all subjects of study under eight headings: engineering, sciences, medicine, agriculture, humanities, social sciences, commerce, and education.[88] An examination of the fields of study among the Chinese students in America between 1905 and 1954 reveals that engineering was by far the most popular field.[89] Engineering of various kinds accounted for some 30 to 44 per cent of the Chinese students in America between 1905 and 1924; 24 to 30 per cent between 1927 and 1941; 35 to 41 per cent

85. *Chinese Students and Professional Directory*, published by the Chinese Student Association of Chicago, April, 1954. It should be noted that this directory covered almost all Chinese students and graduates in Chicago, while the directory published by the China Institute covered primarily students enrolled in academic institutions.

86. *Directory of Chinese Members of American College and University Faculties, 1955-1956*, published by the China Institute in America.

87. CYYWH (March 31, 1961), 73.

88. The first four headings constitute the "practical disciplines" and the others the "arts disciplines." The division is probably based on the common belief in China that "practical" knowledge was subject to laboratory tests while the "arts" knowledge was not. To facilitate comparison this method of grouping is followed in this study.

89. For a detailed listing see Appendix B, Table 10. These statistics were obtained primarily from college directories, which vary considerably in format and content. For the purpose of this study the sample years used are assumed to be representative.

between 1942 and 1945; and 25 to 30 per cent between 1949 and 1953.[90]
While engineering remained the most popular subject through the years, the natural sciences increasingly attracted students: 8 to 10 per cent between 1904 and 1924; 5 to 13 per cent between 1927 and 1941; 10 to 15 per cent between 1942 and 1945; and 14 to 18 per cent between 1949 and 1953. To the Chinese engineering and the natural sciences were closely related fields, representing in their minds both technology and Western civilization. In the early years engineering seemed most important since China's immediate needs required men in this area. But as time passed the natural sciences grew in popularity. Combined, the two fields accounted for some 34 per cent of the Chinese students in the United States in 1931-32 and for some 52 per cent in 1945.

On the other hand, agricultural studies were the least popular of all the major fields. Between 1905 and 1953 agricultural students constituted a mere 3.38 per cent of the total.[91] Indicative of the lack of practicality on the part of some Chinese students was the fact that after 1935 such subjects as theology, music, and fine arts attracted more students than did agriculture.

Among the "arts" disciplines, the social sciences were most popular among the Chinese students, particularly economics, political science, and education. These were areas of study thought imperative for the reconstruction of China, as indeed they were.

Information on the jobs held by the returning students is difficult to obtain before 1917, but after that year we can reconstruct a fairly detailed picture from the various *Who's Who's*. During the period from 1917 through 1937 the most important field of employment for returning students was education, which accounted for approximately 32 to 40 per cent of all the positions held between 1917 and 1934. The next most important field of employment was government service, which accounted for another 16 to 42 per cent during the same years.[92] Regrettably, very few students secured employment in their fields of academic training. A study has been made of the careers of 580 Tsinghua students who returned from the United States before 1925 (see Appendix B). It reveals that in 1925, 70 per cent of the students trained in agriculture were engaged in educational work; a few were

90. For comparison one may note that only 9.8 per cent of all American college students were enrolled in engineering courses in 1947-48 and only 7.8 per cent of all earned degrees were awarded to students in engineering in 1954-55. See BSE, 1946-48, Chapter 4, Table 7, pp. 78-79; EDC, 1954-55, Circular No. 461, p. 4.

91. Between 1905 and 1924 they accounted for 4.98 per cent; between 1927 and 1941, 3.60 per cent; between 1942 and 1945, 2.65 per cent; and between 1949 and 1953, 2.96 per cent. Agricultural studies, as understood in China, included forestry, horticulture, agricultural economics, and animal husbandry. Yet in spite of this grouping, the enrollment was very small.

92. WYC:CIW, 319.

employed by the government; a few were unemployed; and none were connected with rural work or farming. That these students were unable to use their training to practical advantage was well known. In the words of a student in 1918: "It may be said with no hesitation that a great part of the total energy spent by former students of American agriculture has become wasted, since only a small percentage of the returned agriculturalists are working in agricultural occupations. The principal cause of this unforeseen misfortune is probably the fact that their training is not actually applicable to Chinese agriculture on account of the many differences between the Chinese art of agriculture . . . and the American science of farming. . . ."[93]

During the 1920's competent observers began to note that returning students were not using their training for the benefit of the country. In 1926, J. H. Reisner, a missionary educator connected with the University of Nanking, declared, "I don't know of a single graduate of an American college of agriculture who has returned to a strictly rural community and made himself an important factor in the life of that community."[94] In a speech delivered in 1933 to a meeting of Western-educated persons in Shanghai, Pearl Buck made a poignant appeal to all "modern men and women" to put aside their comforts and settle in the towns and villages of the interior.[95] After the outbreak of World War II, when circumstances forced many Chinese intellectuals to live in rural areas, Fei Hsiao-t'ung observed that Chinese peasants often poked fun at Western-educated agriculturists on the grounds that their farming was a "mere expensive hobby."[96] These examples suggest that during the course of the movement to study abroad Chinese students of agriculture did not practice their knowledge after returning to China,[97] but used their training abroad merely as a stepping stone to teaching or government posts.

Among the engineers, 28.7 per cent were employed in educational work, 16.7 per cent in government service, and over 30 per cent in industry and commerce. Thus their occupations were varied, and this group indicates a better utilization of their Western training. But it should be noted that the proportion of unemployed and of those employed by foreigners was higher among the engineers than among any other group. Whether these two phenomena were related has not been determined; but the explanation might be that unlike the

93. D. Hoe Lee, "The Chinese Student of American Agriculture," CSM (1918), 33.

94. J. H. Reisner, "Wanted—Rural Leaders in China," CSM (February, 1926), 12.

95. Pearl Buck, "The New Patriotism," CR (January-March, 1934), 15.

96. FHT:HTCC, 73.

97. One reason for their inability was their habit of living in larger cities, where farming was not possible.

medical doctors, who could and did set up their own practice in port cities, the engineers had to depend on industrial and construction activities that did not generally flourish in China during the 1920's. As a consequence a number of them accepted foreign employment and some even became unemployed.

The case of business students provides another illustration of the importance of environment in the employment of the Western-trained in China. The major source of employment for these students was banking, and nearly 43 per cent of them worked in that field. The crucial factor here was that modern banks in China were developed along Western lines and needed American-trained experts.

Both the natural scientists and the educators depended heavily on teaching for their means of livelihood. Although this was the educators' own field, it should be noted that few of them—only about 5 per cent—taught in and administered schools below the college level. The reason was that school work carried no prestige in the larger cities and was generally considered less than appropriate for a Chinese educated in the West. Our study shows that the two groups with the highest proportion of school workers among them were the humanists and agriculturists (see Appendix B), but neither group was trained for that kind of work. Extremely few schools in China offered agricultural courses, and the anomaly of few educators but many agriculturists in school work indicates that study abroad was not geared to social needs and that the agriculturists went into teaching after having failed to find more suitable jobs.

To a certain extent the position of the natural scientists was similar to that of the agriculturists. Little scientific research was done in China in 1925. The only major outlet for the scientists was educational work, and when university positions were filled, they turned to the secondary schools. Our study reveals that next to the humanists and agriculturists, more scientists went into school work than any other group of American-trained, and that when some scientists entered government service, it was not as technicians but as white-collar workers (see Appendix B).

In Tables 3 and 4 the connection between employment and academic training is further traced. A person's job is considered "suitable" if it demanded the full utilization of the training he acquired abroad. It is "related" if his training was immediately applicable to the performance of his duties. It is "unsuitable" if the performance of his job involved no direct connection with his academic training. Thus, if an engineer worked as an English secretary, his job was "unsuitable," even though his stay in the United States might have been a key factor in his securing the position. On the other hand, a mechanical engineer who taught electrical engineering comes under the "related" group, since without his training he could hardly have been prepared to teach in that general field. According to Table 3, only about 52 per cent of the students fully utilized their American training in their work in China, while 34.5 per cent— composed of the "unsuitable," "unemployed," and "housewives"— presumably made no use of the academic training they had received in the United States.

TABLE 3. *The American-Trained in China in 1925: Suitability of Their Preparation as Measured by Their Occupations*[a]

Occupation	Training								
	Suitable	Related	Unsuitable	House-wives	Unem-ployed	Sub-Total	Sub-Total in Number	Suitability Unknown	Total in Number
Educational work									
College	86.8	7.5	5.7	—	—	100.0	174	17	191
School	13.8	17.2	69.0	—	—	100.0	29	4	33
Government Service									
General	23.1	23.1	53.8	—	—	100.0	26	10	36
Technicians	55.6	22.2	22.2	—	—	100.0	36	3	39
Diplomats	30.0	50.0	20.0	—	—	100.0	10	3	13
Militarists	—	100.0	—	—	—	100.0	2	—	2
Foreign Employ	54.5	27.3	18.2	—	—	100.0	22	1	23
Bankers	75.8	15.2	9.0	—	—	100.0	33	2	35
Merchants	16.7	16.7	66.6	—	—	100.0	24	2	26
Industrialists	46.2	23.1	30.7	—	—	100.0	26	6	32
Industrial technicians	75.7	18.9	5.4	—	—	100.0	37	—	37
Professionals	76.5	11.8	11.7	—	—	100.0	17	2	19
Social and religious workers	—	40.0	60.0	—	—	100.0	5	2	7
Housewives	—	—	—	100.0	—	100.0	13	—	13
Unemployed	—	—	—	—	100.0	100.0	78	—	78
Total in %	52.2	13.3	17.5	2.3	14.7	100.0	532	52	584
Total in number	278	71	92	13	78	532	—	52	584

a. Source: Computed from the special section on 584 American-educated persons in *Who's Who in China*, 1925 (Shanghai: *China Weekly Review*).

Of the rest, the correlation between employment and training varied widely from group to group, from nearly 100 per cent in the case of medical students to only 40 per cent (counting both the "suitable" and "related") for humanities students, and from nearly 94 per cent in the case of college professors to as low as 31 per cent for educational workers. The key factor accounting for such variation seems to have been the relationship of certain types of Western

TABLE 4. *Suitability of the Occupations of the American-Trained as Measured by Their Preparation*[a]

				Occupation					
Training	Suitable	Related	Unsuitable	Housewives	Unemployed	Total in %	Sub-Total in Number	Suitability Unknown	Total in Number
Engineering	54.3	13.5	16.3	—	15.9	100.0	208	2	210
Sciences	62.5	7.1	12.5	5.4	12.5	100.0	56	—	56
Agriculture	51.4	8.6	28.6	—	11.4	100.0	35	—	35
Medicine	89.5	10.5	—	—	—	100.0	19	—	19
Social sciences	36.2	20.4	30.4	1.4	11.6	100.0	69	—	69
Business	73.2	16.1	7.1	—	3.6	100.0	56	—	56
Education	51.4	16.2	10.8	10.8	10.8	100.0	37	—	37
Humanities	31.3	9.4	37.5	12.5	9.3	100.0	32	—	32
Military sciences	—	100.0	—	—	—	100.0	2	1	3
Training unknown	—	—	—	5.6	94.4	100.0	18	49	67
Total in %	52.2	13.3	17.5	2.3	14.7	100.0	532	52	584
Total in number	278	71	92	13	78	—	532	52	584

a. Source: Computed from the special section on 584 American-educated persons in *Who's Who in China*, 1925 (Shanghai: *China Weekly Review*).

training to existing conditions in China. If a student's training was immediately utilizable, his employment opportunities were good, and the correlation between training and occupation was high. In addition, many students trained in the United States accepted jobs where their training was most readily applicable to local conditions and where their formal qualifications were most easily recognizable. These conditions existed particularly in regard to college teaching, which therefore became the most important source of employment for students in all fields. Other suitable occupations existed only for certain groups of students, notably those of medicine and business. Students for whom no such specific occupations existed relied heavily on teaching, but they were often compelled to accept the less desirable jobs such as lower school work. In professions where success was heavily dependent on local knowledge and personal relations, correlations between foreign training and occupation at home were apt to be very low. Conversely, where jobs were of a specialized nature, a high positive correlation between training and occupation usually resulted. As was pointed out earlier, agricultural students did virtually no farming and very little rural work, but were largely engaged in teaching. The extent to which agricultural students failed to utilize their training cannot be seen from Tables 3 and 4 because teaching in their own field at the college level was regarded as "suitable." But it should be observed that the proportion of "suitably employed" was lower than the proportion of college professors among the agricultural students. Thus it seems that, outside of college teaching, very few agriculturists were suitably employed.

PROMINENCE

In order to assess the prominence of Western-trained students who returned to China, we must make a study of their careers after they accepted employment at home. To do this, I grouped the 1,736 persons covered by the *Who's Who* of 1925 and the Tsinghua Register of 1937 into seven categories. The "prominent" category included college presidents, heads of major railways, department chiefs in various ministries, bureau directors in provincial governments, managers of large banks, executives of business concerns operating on a national scale, and professors who were recognized authorities in their fields of study. The second or "good" category included headmasters of reputable high schools, managers of smaller banks, section chiefs in various ministries, licensed engineers, college professors, accountants, lawyers, and physicians, except in those cases where a higher classification was justified. The third category, "fair," included civil servants below the rank of section chiefs, assistant managers of smaller banks, college instructors, and engineering assistants.[98] Persons whose positions were not included in the first three categories—in terms of salary, security, and prestige—were classified as "poor." In addition, there were the "housewives," "unemployed," and "unknown."

The survey made in 1925 gives neither the length of a student's stay in America nor the year of his return to China. But it appears that most of the persons included had returned from abroad between one and nine years earlier, with an average of about six years. During this period, a number had secured positions of responsibility, and nineteen of them, or 3.9 per cent, were ranked in the "prominent" category. Of the others, 353, or 71.6 per cent, were classified as "good," and 41, or 8.3 per cent, were considered "fair." Only 80 persons, or 16.2 per cent, were found to be poor or unemployed. The remaining ninety-one included in the survey were either housewives or persons whose exact positions were not determined.

Altogether, 78, or 15.8 per cent, of the 1925 group were found to be unemployed. This high rate of unemployment can be explained in two ways: first, many of the Western-educated came from wealthy families and chose not to work; and second, many who desired work held out for "good" positions and refused to accept jobs below their

98. The positions listed may appear somewhat incongruous by American standards, but they seem to have been appropriate in China.

expectations. The latter situation occurred frequently in China[99] and was more often a manifestation of frustrated ambitions than an indication of society's low regard for such men.

If we use the same occupational divisions used in Table 3 and correlate them with the degrees of prominence, we will find that more than 25 per cent of the "social and religious workers," 10.7 per cent of the "bankers," and 10 per cent of the government workers reached the "prominent" category. The first group was composed of only seven men who had achieved prominence in other fields and then assumed leadership in philanthropical works.[100] The prominence of the American-trained in government and banking work calls for no special comment. What is interesting is the relatively poor showing of the university professors, of whom only 5.3 per cent reached prominence. Actually, all college teachers above the level of instructor were automatically classified as "good" because of their prestige. To be "prominent" in our sense, they needed only to have contributed serious publications or to have acquired another kind of recognition, such as the holding of a visiting professorship abroad or the enjoyment of widespread fame in China. One reason for their failure to achieve prominence was the transient nature of the profession. College teaching was often merely a stepping stone: as soon as a professor secured recognition he was no longer content to teach. Thus at any given time there were few college teachers who were "prominent." If we correlate other fields of study with degrees of prominence, we will find that students of education and business made the best showing, with 8.3 and 8.2 per cent, of them, respectively, classified as "prominent," and that all of the medical students were ranked as "good."[101]

In comparing the 1925 group with the 1937 group, we find that the relative number of "poor" and "unemployed" was almost unchanged; that the incidence of prominence was greater (9.9 per cent in 1937 as against 3.9 per cent in 1925); and that the proportion of "fair" was greater (22.3 per cent as against 8.3 per cent).[102] Thus a process of polarization was clearly at work between 1925 and 1937. The longer working experience of the 1937 group—an average of eleven years, with a range of from three to twenty-one years—probably contributed to the greater incidence of prominence. The decrease in the "good" category might be explained by two factors. First, as the number of college graduates and returned students continued to increase, the American-trained were confronted with more competition and enjoyed fewer opportunities of starting with a good job. Second, as their work experience increased, the American-trained were increasingly forced to stand on their own performance rather than on

99. For example, see CSM, XIII (1918), 20-28.   100. WYC:CIW, 350.
101. *Ibid.*, 352.
102. For detailed tabulation, see WYC:CIW, 355.

their initial formal qualifications. Consequently, men of ability rose while those with less capacity drifted downward. The extremely small percentage of "poor" in 1937 indicates that the American-trained continued to enjoy favorable treatment in regard to employment, but at a lower level than before.

Another way of studying the problem is to examine the proportion of foreign-educated men among the top leaders in various walks of life in China. For this purpose, four specific fields have been examined: "general prominence" as revealed by listings in *Who's Who*; "political importance" by occupancy of certain offices in the central and provincial governments; "academic leadership" by faculty membership in two universities as well as Fellowship in the Academia Sinica; and "business prominence" by listings in the most authoritative sources available. Where little biographical data accompanied the names in the listings, supplementary information was sought from other sources.

General Prominence. The "Who's Who" contained in *The China Yearbook*, edited by the British journalist H. G. W. Woodhead, is the only such listing that was issued consecutively from 1912 to 1939, and therefore it has been used. (The findings derived from this source are cross-checked with two other listings below.) The sample years selected for examination were 1916, 1923, 1932, and 1939, each falling within a different sub-period but otherwise chosen at random. The findings, as displayed in Table 5, point not only to the high percentage of the foreign-educated cited in "Who's Who" but more importantly to the steady increase of this percentage through the years. Furthermore, this increase was confined to men trained in America and Europe.

In order to cross-check the data, the "Who's Who" published by *The China Weekly Review* in 1925-1927 and 1931 and that published by Liang Yu Book Company (in Chinese) were used, and the results are shown in Table 6. Comparisons of Tables 5 and 6 indicate the essential similarities of all three "Who's Who's." In spite of the enormous expansion of the Chinese school system between 1912 and 1939, when the aggregate number of Chinese college graduates increased by some 250-fold,[103] in 1931-1932 there were fewer Chinese-trained than foreign-educated among the men listed in "Who's Who" in China. Among the returned students, those educated in America easily led the field, while those trained in Japan trailed at a distance. Since at that time there were probably five times as many Japanese- as American-trained in China, the individual advantage enjoyed by the latter was considerable.

103. CHMKT, 314 ff.

TABLE 5. *Educational Background of Listees in "Who's Who" by Country of Study and Selected Years*

Country of Study	1916	1923	1932	1939
China only				
Classical education[a]	35.0%	27.3%	7.8%	5.8%
Modern schools	13.4	15.4	10.8	13.5
Militarists[b]	2.1	4.8	12.6	9.7
Sub-total	50.5	47.5	31.2	29.0
Abroad				
Japan	33.7	29.5	20.3	15.4
United States	9.5	12.9	31.3	36.2
England	1.6	2.0	3.2	6.4
Other countries	4.7	8.1	14.0	13.0
Sub-total	49.5	52.5	68.8	71.0
Total	100.0	100.0	100.0	100.0
Total, numbers[c]	380	689	591	638

a. Classical education refers to persons with no formal schooling, but who either held an old civil-service examination degree, or were renowned classical scholars, or were known to have pursued classical studies.

b. A militarist is defined as one whose official position was derived largely from his hold on the army. Such persons generally had little formal education but often acquired some kind of formal academic qualifications after they had reached prominence. There being no way to determine the illiterate militarists in spite of the academic qualifications listed, all of them are placed in a special group.

c. These numbers exclude the educationally unknown, of whom there are 144, 188, 87, and 56 in 1916, 1923, 1932, and 1939, respectively.

The three "Who's Who's" do show several differences in the percentage of the Chinese-trained for the years 1931-1932: 40.8 per cent in the Liang Yu, 37.0 per cent in the *China Weekly*, and 31.2 per cent in the Woodhead editions. The discrepancy suggests bias on the part of the two latter listings in favor of the foreign-educated in China. However, further examination shows that the numerical strength of the Chinese-trained in the Liang Yu listing was derived from the inclusion of a large number of militarists, of whom most had received little formal education. As to those educated in Chinese schools, the percentage is actually higher in the Woodhead than in the Liang Yu listing—10.8 against 9.6. Because the coverage of the Liang Yu edition is far more comprehensive than that of the Woodhead, some difference in percentages is to be expected. The very small difference actually found seems to indicate that the Woodhead edition is an adequate indicator of general prominence in China. Comparing the 1927 and 1931 issues of the *China Weekly* edition, the gain of the American-trained group and the decline of both the Chinese- and Japanese-trained groups during these five years are notable (see Table 6). A

TABLE 6. *Educational Background of Listees in Two Other "Who's Who's" by Country of Study and Selected Years*

Country of Study	China Weekly Edition 1925-27	1931	Liang Yu Edition 1931
China only			
Classical education	—	—	11.9%
Modern schools	—	—	9.6
Militarists	—	—	19.3
Sub-total	38.0%	37.0%	40.8
Abroad			
Japan	17.3	14.4	18.0
U.S.A.	29.1	35.7	28.4
England	5.2	5.5	4.3
Other Countries	10.4	7.4	8.5
Sub-total	62.0	63.0	59.2
Total	100.0	100.0	100.0
Sub-total	519	827	3,320
Unknown	41	133	779
Total, numbers	560	960	4,099

similar trend between 1923 and 1932 is shown by the Woodhead edition.

Government Leaders. These men of political prominence may be divided into two categories: (1) the central government group, which included, under the old Peking regime, the President and the cabinet members, and under the Kuomintang, the Chairman of the national government, the heads of the five "Yüan," and the ministers in the Executive Yüan—roughly the equivalent of the cabinet; and (2) the provincial group, which included only the provincial heads. The number of foreign-educated persons among the leaders of the central government tended to increase during the years, and this increase became particularly pronounced after 1927, when the Kuomintang came to power. In 1915, five out of twelve central government leaders were foreign-educated; in 1923, seven out of twelve; in 1932, fourteen out of eighteen; in 1937, twelve out of sixteen; in 1943, sixteen out of twenty; and in 1947, seventeen out of twenty-four, with one unknown.[104] While the distribution of various foreign-educated groups followed no established pattern, the Western-trained as a whole outnumbered the Japanese-trained in all years except 1923 and 1937. The success of the latter group in becoming government officials seems to

104. Computed from the lists of government leaders in CY (1916, 1923, 1931-32, 1939); CH (1937-45); WHJP (1947).

have varied according to the course of Sino-Japanese diplomatic relations: whenever Japanese influence over China's domestic politics increased, more persons trained in Japan would be employed by the central government. On the other hand, the political opportunities of the Western-educated suffered no such limitation and were far better than those of the Japanese-trained, especially in proportion to their respective numbers in China.

Among the provincial leaders, the proportion of foreign-educated was much lower. During the six selected years between 1916 and 1947, 151 persons served as provincial heads. Of the 146 whose careers have been studied, only 3 were Russian-trained and 6 Western-trained (see Table 7). The Russian-trained were professional revolutionaries

TABLE 7. *Educational Background of Chinese Provincial Heads by Selected Years**

	1916 Civilians	1916 Militarists	1923 C.	1923 M.	1932 C.	1932 M.	1938 C.	1938 M.	1943 C.	1943 M.	1947 C.	1947 M.	Total
China	7	5	2	8	1	16	—	14	—	16	1	21	91
Japan	—	3	—	3	—	4	1	7	1	6	—	6	31
Western countries	1	1	1	—	1	—	—	—	—	—	2	—	6
Soviet Russia	—	—	—	—	1	—	—	—	—	—	1	1	3
No formal education	—	2	—	5	—	2	—	—	—	2	—	—	11
Unknown	—	2	—	—	—	2	—	—	—	—	—	—	4
Total	8	13	3	16	3	24	1	21	1	24	4	28	146

* The list of government leaders is taken from *The China Yearbook*, 1916, 1923, 1931-32, and 1939; *The China Handbook*, 1937-1945; and *Wu-han jih-pao nien-chien*, 1947.

who were, in almost all respects, quite distinct from the Western-educated. Only three of the six Western-trained were appointed after 1932, and none of the three was a normal case. The single official serving in 1932 answered directly to a military overlord; the other two were appointed to office in Manchuria in 1947 for special political reasons and probably never exercised power. If these three cases are regarded as exceptions, the backgrounds of provincial leaders appear to have run counter to the backgrounds of central government leaders: not only were few of the provincial heads Western-trained, but the Western-trained also decreased in number and ultimately disappeared between 1916 and 1947.

Two factors may have accounted for the dichotomy between the central and provincial leaders. First, after 1916 the inland provinces fell increasingly under the control of militarists, some of whom were Japanese-trained, but most of whom had received little formal education. Second, the Western-educated tended to congregate in the largest coastal cities, with only a handful returning to the provinces: thus there were few civilian provincial heads and even fewer Western-educated ones. Thus the result was a tendency for the Western-educated leaders and the militarists to become mutually exclusive groups, one dominating the central government and the other the provinces.

Academic Leaders. In the University of Amoy, a small, privately endowed institution, there were 81 Chinese faculty members in 1927-28, of whom the American-trained accounted for 67 per cent of the full professors and 58 per cent cent of the associate professors; and the Western-educated teachers in general held 86 and 83 per cent of the same ranks, respectively.[105] There were no Western-trained lecturers (assistant professors) and instructors. A Western degree seems to have been sufficient in this case to assure its holder of a senior faculty rank. In 1937, on the faculty of Tsinghua University, a nationally famous center of learning, there were 94 Chinese full professors who had studied in the following countries: the United States (69), both the United States and Europe (5), Germany (7), France (4) England (3), Japan (3), Hongkong (1), China (1), unknown (1). The only man trained solely in China was a professor of Chinese, who later spent a year on a study tour in Europe.

The educational backgrounds of the Fellows of the Academia Sinica in 1948 show a pattern similar to those of the college faculties. The 81 Fellows were distributed among three divisions: physical sciences (28), biological sciences (25), and humanities (28). Seventy-five of the 81 were trained in the West, and 52 in the United States. All 6 of the Chinese-trained taught in the humanities: 4 had received classical educations, and only 2 were products of the modern Chinese educational system.

Business Leaders. This survey includes 564 merchants,[106] 40 industrialists, and 29 leading bankers.[107] The first two groups were selected

105. During the Kuomintang era, the government recognized three kinds of higher educational establishments: universities (with three or more faculties), colleges, and technical schools. In 1934 scholars trained abroad accounted for about 56 per cent of university teachers, over 51 per cent of college teachers, and almost 41 per cent of technical school faculties. The better known institutions generally had more foreign-educated men on their faculties, and institutional prestige depended to some extent on the presence of such men.

106. Under the Kuomintang, commerce was classified into seventeen types, ranging from "business of purchase and sale" to "room renting," "publishing," "warehousing," and "manufacturing and finishing" (CM [1944], 404-405)—"merchant" has a very broad meaning.

107. The banking resources were highly concentrated. In 1937 the Chinese national government had a three-quarter share in the capital of ten banks which held 61 per cent of the combined resources of all banks (TF:BFC, 185-186). Four-

from the official *Chinese Economic Yearbook,* 1933-1934, and the last group from a series of articles on "Contemporary Chinese Industrialists" written by a well-known Chinese journalist between 1944 and 1948.[108]

The 564 merchants were for the most part officers of Chambers of Commerce in various parts of China. Ten of them had been educated abroad: four in Japan, three in the United States, two in England, and one in Germany. But, of these ten, nine were bankers "by profession," and there were practically no foreign-educated men among the other merchants. This finding seems to confirm the popular Chinese notion that, in commerce, "book knowledge" was far less useful than practical experience.[109]

The predominance of government-controlled industries in China was reflected by the fact that most of the industrialists were state officials rather than private entrepreneurs. The forty cases studied may be divided into four sub-groups: engineers, politicians, private industrialists, and businessmen-in-government—each type showing a different educational pattern. Of the thirty engineers, the educational backgrounds of eighteen are known. All of these men were trained abroad, thirteen in the United States, three in Europe, and two in Japan. They all began as engineers but soon became executives of governmental industries. This pattern possibly indicates the high prestige of technical training and the lack of a sharp division between technology and industrial management in China. The three political heads of government industries who made up the second sub-group were educated abroad but had neither business training nor private business interests. Of the three private industrialists, none was Western-trained and only one was Japanese-trained.

The four businessmen-in-government included one Western-educated, one Japanese-educated, and two Chinese-trained, a distribution that appear to reflect their marginal role as both officials and merchants. Interestingly, a similar educational pattern existed among the twenty-nine leading bankers: Chinese-trained (12), Japanese-trained (6), American-trained (4), European-trained (4), no formal education—old-style bank apprentices (3).[110] Technically the bankers

teen banks controlled four-fifths of the total assets of all commercial banks (*ibid.,* p. 161). In addition, most large commercial banks in China were founded and dominated by single individuals. Hence the highly important bankers were few.

108. Hsü Ying, "Contemporary Chinese Industrialists," HCH, Vols. 2, 3, 5, and 6.

109. Except in modern banking, import-export, and a few other new fields, trade in China was conducted largely according to the traditional practices, which had to be learned through apprenticeship. Formal schooling presumably did not give merchants the training they needed.

110. There were two kinds of banks in China, native and modern. The former had been in existence for centuries. The native bankers all began their careers

were merchants, but they had a good deal to do with the government and depended heavily on official connections. Their diverse educational backgrounds do not seem to be accidental. Because the officials of the central government were highly educated, at least in a formal sense, those who had dealings with them also tended to be formally educated. Whether this was owing to the similar class origins of many of the bankers, businessmen-in-government, and government officials need not be discussed here. The significant finding is that highly-educated men dominated the central government; and even the businessmen who were close to the central government showed better educational qualifications than those who had little to do with it.

EXALTATION AND UNEMPLOYMENT

Problems of readjustment and unemployment, which had confronted returning students since the very beginning of the movement to study abroad, improved only slightly after the establishment of the Republic. In 1912, Dr. Wellington Koo, a leader of the American-trained group, delivered a lengthy address on the subject to Chinese students in the United States. The frustration of returning students, Koo declared, was owing to five causes: first, superciliousness in demeanor and arrogance in thought; second, expectation of high position and refusal to start at the bottom; third and fourth, inattention to detail and unwillingness to undertake hard work; and fifth, lack of steadfastness of purpose. Koo emphasized that he was speaking from five years' experience in organizing and administering the American-European Returned Students' Association in Peking, and he illustrated his points with a specific example of an American-trained student who, a few days after his arrival in Peking, rejected an offer of a junior secretaryship in a Ministry because it was too "small" for him.[111]

Another factor that contributed to the difficulties of the returning students was their tendency to congregate in urban centers. The reasons for this development are not difficult to understand. Under Western influence, the way of life in Chinese port cities became very different from life in the interior. In 1924, Shu Hsin-ch'eng, a noted writer, toured four provinces and described the conditions as follows:

> The cost of living in Hsü-pu of Hunan, an average county of a prosperous province, is only one-tenth of that in Shanghai.

---

as apprentices and had no formal schooling. Leading native bankers were sometimes employed by modern banks, but native banks never employed a person who had not begun as an apprentice. This is the reason that the native bankers are not included in this survey.

111. Address of Dr. V. K. Wellington Koo, CSM, XIII (1918), 20-28.

Since all books are published and priced in Shanghai, they are prohibitively expensive to students in Hsü-pu. In Shanghai, an office clerk pays six dollars for his food [Chinese currency, as are all dollars referred to in this report] and a dollar for his newspaper every month. In Hsü-pu, a dollar suffices to pay for a man's food for the whole month and hence the Shanghai newspaper becomes much too expensive for him. Furthermore, the ways of life in Shanghai and Hsü-pu are so different that a man in Hsü-pu feels no interest in reading about events in Shanghai. Consequently, in all Hsü-pu, an area of three hundred square miles with a population of 300,000, there are only nine copies of a Shanghai newspaper and some six copies of the *Educational Review* [the leading Chinese educational journal published in Shanghai]. In the Bureau of Education, Shanghai newspapers, always a month late because of slow communication, can be read free but few people bother to do so. Teachers in Hsü-pu are ignorant of national events. They have heard of the "New Educational System" promulgated by the government two years earlier, but they are ignorant of its substance, no detailed syllabus of it having been distributed in the rural areas. Words like "economical" and "historical background," adopted from the Western language and long in use in the city, are not comprehensible to teachers in rural China.

The situation in Chengtu, the provincial capital of Szechuan, is even worse. Newspapers from Shanghai take two months to arrive. There is a 10 per cent surcharge on newspapers ordered from Shanghai and a 30 per cent surcharge on books. Remittances from Chengtu to Shanghai are subject to a discount of twenty cents on a dollar. The book agency refuses responsibility for damage caused by rain to books and newspapers in transit. From Shanghai to Chungking the Yangtze River is navigable. From Chungking to Chengtu transportation is by human labor at the rate of $15 per one hundred catties. Every load is damaged during the rainy seasons. Textbooks used in local schools are reproduced from the standard copies by a crude kind of printing and bear numerous misprints. The static way of life in Chengtu causes students to have little interest in new books published in Shanghai. Generally, a middle-school student does not spend more than five dollars per year on reference books. There is no demand for foreign books, and they are not carried by the bookshops.

In Po-tsu-chen, a rural town on the Chungking-Chengtu route, there is a primary school with six classes and two hundred students. A teacher draws a salary of $33 to $67 per year. A man's food costs $1.40 per month. Textbooks in use are five years out of date and are those that the Ministry of Education in Peking have declared "obsolete" and suppressed. Even the school itself cannot afford to buy the proper textbooks and so the old ones continue to be used. In places not on any main transportation route, conditions are even worse. School premises are often occupied by the militarists, and when this happens, the school ceases functioning for the duration. Families who have children studying in the city are judged rich on that criterion and are assessed heavier taxes.[112]

By modern standards rural China had become so primitive that men reared and educated in cities had no inclination to live in the countryside. Furthermore, the earnings of a man in the provinces would not be commensurate with the cost of his education. For this reason, men who had been abroad practically never returned to the interior, and even the ordinary college graduates returned only rarely.[113] Yet such severe urbanization materially limited their chances of employment, for while jobs were short in the cities, educated men were needed in rural areas.[114] It would seem that on a national basis primary and secondary teaching alone could have absorbed all of the college graduates. A study made in 1931 of the middle schools in Eastern China revealed a ratio of less than nine students per teacher.[115] In 1912 approximately 2,700,000 students were enrolled at the primary level, while about 100,000 were studying at the secondary level, and 40,000 at the college level. By 1929 the number of students had increased to 8,800,000 in primary schools and 300,000 in secondary schools, but had decreased to 30,000 in colleges. During the 1930's the number of students at all levels nearly tripled.[116] At a ratio of nine students per teacher, there should have been a shortage of college graduates for middle-school teaching. Moreover, there was no problem of unusable knowledge because nearly all Chinese schools concentrated on preparing students for further study[117] and thus the curriculum at the lower level was closely related to that at the succeeding one. The only difficulty was a geographical one: the colleges were located in a few metropolises; the middle schools were more dispersed across the country; and the grade schools were even more scattered. Consequently, to teach at a lower level meant in most cases relocation from more to less urbanized surroundings, a situation unappealing to college and middle-school graduates. In this way a shortage of teachers

112. SHC:CKT, 279-82.
113. CYTC (July, 1936), 58.
114. *Ibid.*
115. LAY, 416.
116. Compiled from WFC:CYS, 313-16; CHMKT, 308, 319, 324; EY (1924), 138. The totals do not include students under old-styled private tutors. There were in 1935 some 101,813 tutors teaching 1,757,014 students in China. Most of these were in less urbanized areas (CYTC [December, 1936], 136-37.)
117. Vocational training had little place in Chinese education. See YBE (1937), 580.

existed alongside widespread unemployment of potential teachers. Urbanization was consequently an important factor in the whole problem.

A third factor behind the poor adjustment of the foreign-educated was their inadequate training. As has already been indicated, the academic level of the Chinese students abroad was fairly low: until the 1930's, most of them were undergraduates. Furthermore, while in foreign countries, they received little guidance in their choice of fields. An important reason for this poor direction was the belief held by many Chinese that everything Western was worth emulating. A corollary was the notion that a student need not choose his field with an eye toward China's needs, since whatever he learned would be beneficial to himself as well as the country. Another reason was the lack of detailed factual knowledge—no one in China, government officials included, possessed much factual information. Government fellowships were generally administered by foreign-educated men who had little knowledge of rural China. Provincial scholarships probably could have been better geared to regional needs, but they were badly managed. Although the official policy was to promote technological training, the supervisors of students abroad in most cases did little counseling. It is not surprising that on their return the students were unable to put their training to practical use. Moreover, their inflated self-respect prevented them from adopting an experimental attitude, and their severely urban orientation helped matters not at all.[118]

The situation was succinctly described in 1919 in a letter, in English, addressed to Chinese students abroad by the Committee on National Industries:

> The boycott movement against the Japanese goods has been in full swing since it was started two months ago. But so long as we cannot produce the goods ourselves, such movements cannot last long. The most important thing is therefore to develop national industries. We depended on Japan for umbrellas, toilet articles, straw hats, toys, and numerous other useful things. Since the boycott, we have been using native-made goods, if available, and their prices have risen considerably, but the quality is poor. Besides, many Japanese goods cannot be substituted, and we have either to buy high-priced Western goods or go along without them. Such a state of affairs cannot last long. We must produce these goods ourselves. . . . The Western returned students should, at such a time, find great opportunities to serve the nation in industrial and commercial lines. But right here we find a few great faults in our

118. A few did undertake rural reconstruction work, notably Y. C. James Yen and T'ao Hsing-chih, but they were highly exceptional. In fact, their fame, richly deserved as it is, testifies not a little to their unusualness.

training which our students in America and Europe should know and correct.

First, our returned students generally specialized in big things such as civil engineering, mining, etc., neglecting those industries which are seemingly small and unimportant. The fault of this becomes very clear when we want to boycott the Japanese goods and make the goods ourselves. For example, one of the most pressing needs at present is to make umbrellas to take the place of the Japanese ones, yet we cannot find one returned student who is trained and skilled in making umbrellas. We want to have men who can make hats, toys, toilet articles, and other useful things. And again, the returned students cannot come to help. Here we have a great opportunity and a great duty to serve the nation, but we cannot take the opportunity nor perform the duty, as our training is at fault.

Second, regardless of what lines of specialization, generally speaking, the returned students had too little practical training while studying abroad. They came back too soon. What they should have done after graduating from the college was to acquire practical training, to learn some particular things really well so that when they came back they could start independent works. This has not been the case. The result is that we have so many returned students who are supposed to be specially trained in industrial, commercial, and practical lines, yet who can do nothing except teaching, talking, and joining the official institutions.

The faults of the returned students we have felt all the time, but they become very distinct and clear at the present when we want to boycott the Japanese goods and make the goods ourselves. . . .[119]

It may be said, then, that exaltation, urbanization, and inadequate training combined to make adjustments to Chinese conditions difficult. An aggravating factor was the belief, widely held among Chinese intellectuals, that the cause of the evil lay not in their education or attitude but in the lingering influences of the traditional order. In the intellectual atmosphere of the time, the fact that Western knowledge must be adapted to Chinese conditions, instead of the reverse, was not grasped. Many Western-trained men stubbornly refused to conform, and the situation did not begin to improve until the 1930's. By that time both the increasing competition from the Chinese college graduates[120] and the declining influence of the extended family

119. CSM, Vol. XV, No. 2, pp. 35-36. The poor phraseology is in the original English text.

120. In 1931 it was reported that a thousand men, including several returned students, were vying for twenty-four clerical positions in the provincial government at Canton. See Tsao Ch'u, "Social Conditions and the Direction of Chinese Education," CHCYC, Vol. XIX, No. 3, p. 90.

system induced a change in the attitudes of the Western-trained men. They were now more willing to work, a psychology that was helped further by the improvement in their own academic standards and by the greater industrialization of the country.[121] Had these factors continued to prevail, Western training would have been utilized to greater effect in the solution of Chinese problems.[122] Unfortunately, the war with Japan altered the whole process. During the eight years of China's struggle, the burden of war fell very unevenly on various segments of society. The intellectuals were among the hardest hit, and a sense of deep frustration developed among the largest group of Western-trained men in China, the college professors.[123] Under their influence, most of the college students turned increasingly against the regime. Once again, a vast destructive force was building up in the country's educational centers. In a few years it was to contribute powerfully to the end of the Kuomintang era.

EXPATRIATION

The large number of Chinese in the United States today is usually attributed to their reluctance to return to China while the Communists remain in power. In a number of cases this reason undoubtedly holds. But the tendency toward expatriation appeared at the very beginning of the movement to study abroad and has not always been linked with political changes at home. Long before the Communist take-over, sizable numbers of students began to forsake their Chinese origins and seek naturalization abroad. For example, among the 1,152 students listed in the Tsinghua Alumni Register of 1937, at least twenty-one maintained permanent residences in the United States. By that time most of them had been abroad for at least fourteen years and, as far as we know, most of them are still living in the United States. In the directory of Chinese students issued by the Chinese Students' Christian Association in 1936-37, fourteen Chinese were listed as being faculty members of American colleges and universities; of these at least five were known to be in the United States in 1956.[124]

A complicating factor in the desire of Chinese students to seek naturalization in the United States is the American immigration policy. The Sino-American treaty of 1868 specifically recognized the "inherent and inalienable right of man to change his home and allegiance" and sanctioned "migration . . . from the one country to the

121. For a brief description see D. K. Lieu, "Industry," CHY (1935-36), 1111.

122. In the mid-1930's even the long neglected rural areas attracted more public attention than before. See Li Tzu-hsiang, "The Theory and Practice of the Chinese Rural Reconstruction Movement," HCH, Vol. III, 18.

123. Statistics show that college professors in Kunming lost 98 per cent of their salary in terms of living cost from 1937 to 1943. See KC, Vol. I, No. 3, p. 7.

124. According to official Chinese sources, there were about 5,000 Chinese intellectuals in the United States in 1955, of whom approximately half were students and the rest were gainfully employed.

other, for the purposes of curiosity, of trade, or as permanent residents."[125] But United States policy was reversed twelve years later, and until 1943 the government always prohibited or discouraged Chinese immigration. Although the United States never officially barred Chinese students from studying in America, the word "student" was often interpreted with great stringency. On June 15, 1900, the solicitor of the Treasury defined a student as "a person who intends to pursue some of the higher branches of study, or one who seeks to be fitted for some particular profession or occupation for which facilities of study are not afforded in his own country; one for whose support and maintenance in this country, as a student, provision has been made, and who, upon completion of his studies, expects to return to China."[126] Subsequent rulings in 1906 and 1920 were more liberal, but the basic conditions of (1) guaranteed financial support while in the United States and (2) departure from the United States upon completion of study, were never waived.[127] In regard to students' working either for profit or experience, American interpretation has varied: several administrations tolerated the practice by bona fide students, while others maintained that the practice itself rendered a student fraudulent in his representation.[128] In the matter of citizenship, Chinese were declared ineligible for naturalization by the courts in 1878.[129]

The situation began to change only after Pearl Harbor. In April, 1942, the Department of State arranged with the Department of Justice to permit Chinese students, in case of need, to accept employment in America.[130] At the same time a number of grants were made by the State Department to Chinese students.[131] In October, 1943, the immigration law of 1924 was amended, and Chinese became eligible for American citizenship.[132] Both the Displaced Persons Act of 1948 and the Refugee Relief Act of 1953 contained provisions under which Chinese in America could apply for adjustment of immigration status. In 1955, nearly 1,050 Chinese took advantage of this provision. Of these, 747 did so under the Displaced Persons Act,[133] which in most cases allowed a permanent resident the opportunity of immediate naturalization.

American policy after 1942 contrasts very strikingly with that of the earlier period. If some Chinese managed to settle in the United States in spite of the earlier discriminatory measures, it may be assumed that more were now prepared to become Americans. Between

125. RFW:PC, 2.   126. MHF:CA, 251-52.
127. *Ibid.*, 254.   128. *Ibid.*, 258-62.
129. STC:WC, 42; KMR:AA, 80-88.   130. CIB (March-April, 1942), 1.
131. *Ibid.*   132. RFW:PC, 38-42.
133. Information furnished by the Immigration and Naturalization Service, U.S. Department of Justice, through the courtesy of Representative Barrett O'Hara.

1950 and 1951 a thousand Chinese students were estimated to have returned to the Chinese mainland.[134] Although the stream still continues, it has been reduced to a trickle. A great majority of the 2,500 Chinese employed in 1956 have probably settled permanently in the United States.

A similar situation prevails among Chinese students in France and Germany. Between four and five hundred of the student-workers in France remained after the movement collapsed in 1921.[135] A number of cases are known in which students who went to France at the beginning of the century passed their entire lives there.[136] A stay of twenty years was not too unusual among Chinese students in Paris.[137] Almost the same can be said of Chinese in Germany. A recent report from Formosa mentioned that most of the Chinese students in Western Germany were married to German girls.[138] On the other hand, very few Chinese students seem to have settled in Great Britain, even among those who came from British colonies and could claim British nationality. Perhaps the basic considerations are economic opportunity and social relationships. Expatriation tends to become widespread where it is easy to make a living and where social barriers are slight. A third factor is government policy, which can discourage immigration but which seldom eliminates the possibility— a determined man often finds the means to circumvent the regulations. Even in recent years, cases are known in which a Chinese student married an American or enlisted in the army for the sole purpose of seeking permanent residence or citizenship in the quickest possible way.

It should be noted that most Chinese students underwent a process of selection before they were sent abroad. In the course of their stay in America, they were subject to further testing in one form or another, until those who could compete on equal terms with American youth were identified. It was to this group that most expatriates belonged, at least in the period when American policy towards Asiatic immigration was extremely severe. The effect on China was, therefore, doubly serious, for it meant that after making a heavy investment, China lost many of her best men through study abroad.

A related phenomenon that has to do with expatriation is the inter-generational effect of study abroad. In the course of our study, the biographical data of several thousand returned students have

134. Wu Chün-sheng, *op. cit.*
135. Li Huang, "The Problem of Chinese Students in France," CHCYC, Vol. XV, No. 9; LPL:OY, 65.
136. See Hsü Chung-nien, "From Adieu to Eternity," EM, Vol. XLIII, No. 3. See also CPH:HW, a novel that describes in detail Chinese students in France in the 1920's.
137. CYYWH, Vol. X, No. 8, p. 16.   138. *Ibid.*, 14.

been examined. From this material there emerges a trend that shows that study abroad is a matter of family tradition—that is to say, a father who studied abroad tends to see that his son does also. The degree of alienation from Chinese culture seems to increase with time, and by the third generation expatriation is a distinct possibility. The ramifications of this pattern surely merit further study; and, to call attention to the matter, three sample cases are described in Appendix A.

[Part III]

FACETS OF THE
IMPACT ON CHINA

江山此地限華裔

[8] *The Political Thought*
of Yen Fu and Liang Ch'i-ch'ao:
A Prelude to Revolution

The aims of the Chinese movement to study abroad were, as indicated in Chapter 7, to beget political leadership, technological skill, and academic originality. A discussion of the impact of the new education might conceivably follow these lines, but to abide strictly by such a topical division would spoil the unity of the subject matter. Accordingly, the chapters that follow stress the logical sequence of the events discussed rather than their topical interests. Broadly, Chapters 8 through 10 deal with the collapse of the two time-honored institutions in China—the monarchy and the traditional moral code. Chapters 11 through 14 summarize the changing role of intellectuals in society and the economic and educational impact on China of men educated abroad.

In evaluating historical trends an author is faced with many difficulties. To begin with, the selection of data presupposes judgment, and the drawing of a conclusion invariably involves balancing one factor against another. A particular difficulty in Chinese history is the tendency of scholars to influence politics more by intellectual effort than by direct political action. The chain of reaction may be swift and obvious, but it may also be devious and obscure. Indeed, cases do not seem rare in which men's conscious efforts bring about totally unexpected results. The discernment of the underlying process depends as much on insight as on factual analysis.

In the intellectual upheaval that preceded the revolution of 1911, two individuals played unintentional but vitally important roles. The first, Yen Fu (1853-1921), was born near Foochow, the capital of Fukien province, to parents of limited means.[1] Yen's father practiced medicine, a profession not highly regarded in imperial China. His mother was the daughter of a "plain man," i.e., one who studied but never received a civil-service degree. Yen's great-grandfather and one of his uncles were *chü-jen*,[2] and the child therefore received a classical education. Begun in his sixth year, Yen's studies were completed some eight years later.[3] Of his tutors, the boy was especially devoted to a man named Huang Ch'ang-i, who was a "plain man" but an accomplished classicist and a strict teacher. After Huang's

1. WCC:YCT, 1.   2. *Ibid.*
3. *Ibid.*, 2-4.

death in 1865, Yen continued his studies under Huang's son.[4] Yen's classical education proved to have a bearing on his later thought.

Yen was married in 1866, and a short while later his father died. His mother's income as a seamstress was very meager, and Yen was attracted by the liberal stipends of the Foochow arsenal school—four taels of silver per month to each student and ten silver dollars to every top student in the tri-monthly tests.[5] Competing in the entrance examination, Yen wrote a touching essay on filial piety and was awarded the top place. He then entered the School of Navigation and studied English, geology, chemistry, astronomy, and mathematics, in addition to the more technical naval subjects.[6] Commissioned on his graduation in 1872, Yen accompanied Shen Pao-chen, head of the arsenal, to Formosa in 1874. Yen reportedly rendered outstanding technical and secretarial services.[7]

In 1876, Yen was selected to be among the first group of arsenal students to go to Europe. Of the twelve who went to England, three were placed directly on board warships, and the other nine, including Yen, were admitted to the Royal Naval College at Greenwich.[8] Because practical experience was then emphasized by Chinese officials, all of the twelve except Yen eventually spent much time on sea duty. The fact that Yen did not seems to indicate that his interests by then had broadened. During his stay of slightly more than two years in England, Yen not only read Darwin, Spencer, and other writers[9] but also developed an interest in British judicial procedure and municipal administration, which he found superior to the Chinese, and from which he believed Britain derived her strength.[10]

In 1877, Yen became acquainted with Kuo Sung-t'ao (1818-1891), the first Chinese minister to the Court of St. James. Despite differences in rank and age—Kuo was thirty-five years older—a lasting friendship developed between the two men. Kuo, who probably knew more about the West than any other Chinese official at the time, deeply admired the extent of Yen's knowledge. Kuo once wrote to a high dignitary in Peking: "How can I, who know no foreign language and am ignorant of world affairs, fulfill my post well? Only Mr. Yen can do that."[11]

On his return to China, Yen taught at the Foochow arsenal[12] and in 1880 was appointed dean of the new naval school at Tientsin. He remained there for twenty years, and became vice-president in 1889, and president in 1890.[13] His promotion was slow for a man known as an expert on the West, and this fact was probably due as much to

4. *Ibid.*, 4.
5. WS:YFC, 1.
6. WCC:YCT, 4-5.
7. *Ibid.*, 6.
8. *Ibid.*, 7.
9. WS:YFC, 8-10.
10. YIMCCK, V, 8.
11. WCC:YCT, 7.
12. WS:YFC, 11.
13. *Ibid.*, 13, 15.

his failure to court Li Hung-chang's favor as to his open criticism of government policy. Frustrated, he began his lifelong habit of smoking opium, although he continued to criticize the practice severely.[14]

Between 1884 and 1894 Yen searched for opportunities outside of Li Hung-chang's bailiwick. With a friend he made a modest investment in a coal mine in Honan. He also sought employment under Chang Chih-tung,[15] but for some reason established no rapport with Chang. Hoping to rise through the civil service, Yen purchased a title *(chien-sheng)*, and four times between 1885 and 1893 he unsuccessfully attended the provincial examination. Meanwhile, the situation in China rapidly approached a crisis as the war of 1894 ended in an ignominious defeat. The literati were stunned at first but soon began crying for the blood of the officials in charge. It was under these circumstances that Yen attracted much attention with four political essays published in a Tientsin newspaper owned by a German, C. von Hanneken.[16]

A distince feature of Yen's writings was their scholarly or semi-scholarly nature, their combination of political proposal with depth of reasoning. The first essay, entitled "The Perilous Changes in the World" *(Lun shih-pien chih-ch'i)*, embodied an analysis of Chinese and Western societies. Of the differences between them, Yen wrote, "none is greater than that while Chinese worship antiquity and belittle the contemporary, Westerners strive to make the present better than the past. Whereas Chinese accept the alternation of peace and chaos, prosperity and decay, as a natural course of the universe, Westerners assume progress . . . to be the goal of knowledge and statecraft."[17] Behind the Chinese attitude, Yen argued, lay the cherished desire to reduce strife and achieve social harmony. From time immemorial this goal had been pursued consistently. Thus the theory of Great Unity in *Spring and Autumn Annals* (*Ta-i-t'ung,* or the importance of all men to pledge allegiance to one reigning house) was to discourage the struggle for power; the burning of books and melting of metals by the Ch'in dynasty was to forestall the possibility of rebellions; and the civil-service examinations after the Sung were to render scholars politically harmless by sapping their energy and tantalizing them with a possible yet uncertain prize. Such a social system, Yen said, might continue indefinitely in a closed world but was now melting like ice in the face of Western penetration. Yet reality still escaped the Chinese, who viewed foreigners as barbarians and sneered at their compatriots who spoke the truth. Contrary to common belief, he argued, the quintessence of the West lay not in mechanical arts nor even in science but in "the pursuit of truth by

14. *Ibid.*, 14-15.   15. *Ibid.*, 15.
16. KKC:CKPHS, 73.   17. CCF:YFSWH, 3.

the scholars and the implementation of justice by the administrators."
Although these qualities were also valued in China, they were never
realized because the essential instrumentality—liberty—was lacking.[18]

Individual liberty, Yen asserted, was much feared by Chinese sages
and did not appear in their teachings. In the West, on the other
hand, all the laws were geared to its preservation; even the kings
could not encroach upon a man's liberty. The nearest Chinese concept was the principle of reciprocity; even this was a far cry from
liberty, for while the latter stressed the self, reciprocity emphasized
the other. This basic dissimilarity in turn led to other differences:
for example, while the Chinese valued economy, trusted in fate, and
differentiated between various sets of human relationships, Westerners
exalted the profit motive, tried to conquer Nature, and affirmed the
equality of all men. Of these two sets of values, Yen was uncertain
that the Chinese was superior.

He then cited concrete cases in Chinese diplomatic history to
stress the absurdity of the Chinese attitude toward foreigners. "If
we persist in this attitude, a collapse [of our society] will soon be
inevitable." Placing the blame squarely on the shoulders of officials
then in power, Yen drew a sharp distinction between them and the
xenophobes of earlier days, who, although unenlightened, acted in
good faith and were "righteous men": "Today only the blind do not
see the wealth and strength of the West. Only those out of their
minds can maintain that China does not need wealth and strength
or that she can have them without using the Western methods. . . .
Then why do the men in power go out of their way to resist the
inevitable? . . . Mr. Yao Nai once said: 'There are people who place
their momentary personal glory above the security of the country.'
Alas! How correct are his words."[19]

Yen's second essay, entitled "On Strength" (*Yüan ch'iang*), began
with a discussion of Darwin's *On the Origin of Species*. He stressed
the fact that the book took Darwin decades to write and was even
more important than Newtonian physics.

> According to the book, all species came from one origin but
> were gradually differentiated through surroundings and slight
> variations of physiology. . . . Two chapters of the book were
> particularly famous: . . . one is "Struggle for Existence" and
> one, "Natural Selection". . . . The idea is that because species
> . . . depend on natural resources for subsistence, they have to
> struggle for their existence. . . . The weak become the prey of
> the strong, and the clumsy submit to the crafty. . . . This is true
> not only of animals and plants but also of people. . . . The evi-
> dence is precise and strong. . . .[20]

18. Ibid., 4-5.   19. *Ibid.*, 6.
20. *Ibid.*, 14.

Passing on to Spencer, Yen stressed the philosopher's rigorous application of the evolutionary theory to social phenomena. He then described in particular the *First Principles* (which sought "a unified theory in all fields ranging from the study of insects and plants to that of men and celestial movements"), the *Study of Sociology,* and *Education: Intellectual, Moral, Physical.*

> The principal aim of this teaching is the development of intelligence, bodily vigor, and moral virtues. The reason why sociology has to be studied is that without it one cannot understand the causality of social phenomena. When a nation enforces a policy designed to benefit the people, not only may the desired effect fail to come about, but totally unexpected consequences may occur. Over a period of time the causes and effects act and react. No untrained mind can see through them.
>   In order to study sociology, it is necessary first to acquire other learning—mathematics and logic to give a sense of immutable laws, physics and chemistry to yield an awareness of causality . . . astronomy and geology to gain an idea of continuity, complexity, and contingency. . . . Because the group is an aggregate of individuals, it is also necessary to study biology . . . and psychology. Only then are we ready for sociology, to learn about the rise and fall of civilizations and to know the essence of statecraft.[21]

After stating that all development was from the homogeneous to the heterogeneous and that the differences became clear only after a more complex state is reached, Yen again compared China with Western nations:

> Western scholars interested in statecraft always judge a nation by the physique, intelligence, and morals of its people. If by such criteria the quality of the people is high, neither their livelihood nor their status as a nation can be bad. If, on the other hand, the people are slow, unenlightened, and selfish, the group cannot last and will be humiliated and annihilated when faced with stronger groups. The process does not need to take the form of armed conflicts but may come about through a gradual collapse as can be seen from many historical episodes. . . . Hence the West accepts the self-preservation urge of all living beings as the basic fact in politics and education . . . but extols the preservation of the species when it conflicts with the preservation of the individual. . . . In formulating a policy, the goal is always to improve the vigor, intelligence, and virtue of the people. . . .[22]

How did the Chinese fare by these criteria? In the war with Japan, he felt, one province showed no concern for the defense of another;

21. *Ibid.,* 16.   22. *Ibid.,* 17.

the service commanders were both corrupt and incompetent; the court officials, totally ignorant of national as well as world conditions, were interested only in staving off a crisis, and the worst ones even took advantage of the crisis to make personal fortunes. The outcome of one war might not be important, but the manifest lack of vigor, intelligence, and virtue certainly portended national annihilation.

Anticipating the skeptics in another way, Yen reminded them that the Westerners were completely different from the Inner Asians who used to invade China, for in addition to brute strength, the West also possessed fine systems.

> When everybody can say what he wants to say, there is no barrier in communication between the high and the low. The king is none too exalted and the people none too disdained. Because there are definite systems in government, military affairs, industry, and commerce, everybody knows his duty and carries it out without supervision. . . . As a consequence, the West is far richer than we in agriculture, industry, . . . transportation, and the art of government. . . .
>
> The way the Westerners act is completely guided by research, which is based on rigorous empirical testing. Consequently, there is nothing that can merely be talked about but not practiced. If the reason [of their superiority] is to be sought, then it clearly lies in their viewing liberty as the essence and democracy as the method. Because the [European] continent is divided into seven or eight [different countries], unity and progress result from diversity and competition. . . .
>
> When their system clashes with ours, theirs has the advantage. Why? A system is a means. Inefficiency is inevitable when improvement is long delayed. . . . This is precisely how natural selection is made through the struggle for existence.[23]

While the West was superior to China, it was by no means perfect,

> for none of the three criteria of an ideal society—material sufficiency enjoyed by all, moral excellence attained by many, and crimes committed by none—has been realized. Indeed, according to the sociologists, the West is heading toward the opposite direction. Why? Great peace in the world can be achieved only when wealth and rank do not differ too much among the people, for otherwise discontent will lead to fierce struggle, which often is the cause of chaos. In the last two hundred years technological progress . . . has indeed benefited the people, but it has also facilitated a monopoly by the unscrupulous. . . . The resultant great inequality of wealth has led to high incidence of crimes. The poor in a rich country fare no better than their counterparts in a poor country.[24]

23. *Ibid.*, 21-22.   24. *Ibid.*, 24.

The problem, Yen continued, did not escape the attention of Western sociologists and economists, but there was no easy solution because the root of unequal wealth lay in unequal intelligence, and unless the latter disappeared the former must also remain. Yen then generalized to say that the only way to launch an effective reform in China was to improve the caliber of the people. In support of his thesis he pointed to the indifferent results of all of the innovations in China since the Opium War—language institutes, arsenals, railroads, the navy, and so on. "Most of these were measures which had made the West strong. . . . Why were they so ineffectual when introduced in China?" The answer surely lay in the poor caliber of the Chinese people. Unless their qualifications could be improved, further reform might even lead to disaster: "If a democratic regime is established, and if more railroads are built, mines opened, armies trained, and hundreds of vessels constructed, in ten years I fear the result will be worse than poverty and weakness."[25] A nation, said Yen, was like a person; it could not stand strenuous exercises when in poor health.

In a basic program of development, bodily vigor was accorded first importance. "All of the academies in Greece and Rome had their gymnasiums, and Plato himself was known for his physical strength." More specifically, Yen named opium-smoking and foot-binding as China's worst evils and suggested that the government should refuse to employ or honor the offenders. In regard to the development of intelligence, he stated that before the fourteenth century there had been little difference between Western and Chinese scholarship, but that since that time the West had marched forward by extolling reason above rhetoric, encouraging creative thinking in education, and allowing doubt of ancient teachings. If China was to catch up, she would have to encourage empirical learning. The first prerequisite would be to abolish the civil-service examinations, because by rewarding only literary skill they, in effect, made other knowledge socially unattractive and impossible to pursue.[26]

In the development of virtue, the key difference between China and the West seemed to lie in religion: "Regardless of the inherent worth of the Christian faith, [the important feature is that] every seven days somebody gathers and teaches the people. God is exalted and the hope of eternal blessings kindled. By treating all, from prince to pauper, as children of God, the principle of equality is propagated. People are eager to do good because they have a sense of self-respect."[27] In China, on the other hand, moral excellence was expected only of the elite, and the masses were selfish because they had neither education nor religion. Actually, even the elite often proved deficient.

25. *Ibid.*, 25.   26. *Ibid.*, 29-30.
27. *Ibid.*, 30.

Thus, "in 1894 officials stealthily substituted scrap iron and dirt for torpedoes and shells. Their behavior prompted foreign newspapers to remark that the Chinese people would make a small profit even if this entailed the defeat of their nation. Considering such an observation, can China's present failure and future doom be attributed to fate?"[28]

A second factor, according to Yen, arose from China's social and political system. Since the days of the Ch'in, the masses had been treated and acted like slaves. As a result they felt no concern for public interest. In contrast, Westerners elected their officials and obeyed only laws made through parliament and were anxious to defend their nation because it was their own. The contrast thus indicated to Yen a general principle, that patriotism arose from a sense of possession, a concern for that which was one's own. The way to improve the morals of the Chinese therefore lay in making China the private possession of all. "As Ku Yen-wu said, men cannot but be selfish; the essence of statecraft is to turn self-interest into public interest." In order to accomplish this, Yen concluded, a parliament should be established and magistrates should be elected locally, at the county level.[29]

The third essay, entitled "Views on How to Save the Country" (Chiu-wang chüeh-lun), was a sweeping attack on Chinese learning. The "eight-legged essays" were said to have sapped the literati's intelligence, corrupted their morals, and made them parasites of society.[30] Even textual criticism and Neo-Confucian metaphysics were "enjoyable hobbies" at best and more likely "empty talks which had caused the country great harm."[31] China's urgent need was to put these away and achieve, as the Westerners had, the unity of theory and practice.

The fourth essay, entitled "In Refutation of Han Yü" (P'i Han), was a devastating attack on the institution of monarchy. Han Yü, the famous essayist of the T'ang, had asserted that men in ancient times had suffered from many evils. It was his theory that the sages chased away the wild animals and taught the people how to clothe and shelter themselves, and that as civil society developed, it became the duty of the sage-king to command, the minister to administer, and the masses to produce food for their superiors. Yen disagreed with this interpretation. If it was the sages who chased away the wild animals, he asked, how could the sages' ancestors have survived in the first place? Moreover, it was clear to him that all the emperors since the Ch'in had been tyrants and deceivers and that Lao Tzu was correct in saying that "he who steals a hook is executed, while he who steals a kingdom is enthroned." Why then should the masses toil to satisfy the whims of the ruler? To Yen's mind the institution of monarchy could be justified in only two ways. First, it modified the predatory struggle

28. *Ibid.,* 30-31.   29. *Ibid.,* 32.
30. *Ibid.,* 53-55.   31. *Ibid.,* 57-58.

among men, but even so it was a mere device and not a pillar of human relationships. The second justification was society's need for a division of labor. As the masses produced food, so the ruler attended to defense and administration. But then his only purpose was to pursue the welfare of the masses, and Mencius was correct in subordinating the ruler to the people and the country in the political hierarchy.[32]

On the question of the monarchy, Yen contended that it should temporarily be retained, for even in the good societies of the West "the people could attend to only seven-tenths of the state affairs and leave the other three-tenths—mainly defense and justice—in the hands of the court."[33] However, the Chinese emperor should in the meantime do his utmost to promote the vigor, intelligence, and virtue of his subjects so that eventually they could do without him. Yen had no doubt that under a good ruler China could improve within three decades and within six decades overtake the West, for after all, Western superiority was only a recent phenomenon. China needed only to follow an existing pattern of modernization instead of initiating it:

> Looking at the West, one should know that to be wealthy and strong was neither easy . . . nor difficult. . . . The secret is to eliminate the obstacles to wealth and strength and to share political power with the people. In trying to strengthen ourselves, we should not blindly follow the ancient teachings, much less the precedents accumulated since the Ch'in . . . most of which were designed by men who, having stolen the kingdom, wished to retain it by making the people ignorant, weak, and morally corrupt. . . . Alas! How could they know that trouble might come from an unexpected quarter? [The present situation is] just as Chuang Tzu described, a man locks his trunk to prevent theft, only to lose the whole thing through robbery.
>
> Whereas in the West the country belongs to the citizens and the officials are but public servants, in China the emperor supposedly owns the four seas and rules over millions of subjects. The people of the West are their own masters; those of China, slaves. . . . How can the slaves stand up to the master?[34]

Taken as a whole, these four essays revealed the basic trends of Yen's thought. He believed that social phenomena conform to invariable laws, that in the struggle for existence the fittest survive, and that human fitness is determined by vigor, intelligence, and virtue. Since the Chinese were inferior to Westerners in these qualities, they were doomed unless the basic causes of their inferiority could be removed. But the way to bring about this change was not by revolution, for the people were as yet unable to govern themselves. As in all improve-

32. *Ibid.*, 85-86.   33. *Ibid.*, 87.
34. *Ibid.*, 88.

ment, political restraints could be lifted only gradually in relation to the people's greater mastery of their surroundings, even though in the long run there would necessarily be less need for government.

In these conclusions the influence of Herbert Spencer was obvious. Yet Yen could not stop here, for his main aim was to advocate reform, through state action if necessary, and in no way could Spencer be stretched to support such a course. Clearly some other authority was needed; therefore Yen turned to Huxley's *Evolution and Ethics*. He probably started his translation of this work in 1894, and it was finished some two years later.[35] It included only the first two chapters of the original work. The translation was free and interspersed with comments that were often longer than the text. In the preface, Yen stressed the value of comparative studies and the universality of truth. He then discussed the importance of inductive and deductive methods and used many quotations to show that these were used in both the Chinese classics and Western works. It was only because her intellectual development had been stifled since the Ch'in that China had to learn from the West; and Huxley, by correcting the excessive *laissez-faire* in Spencer, indicated the way to preserve a nation.[36]

The last point is noteworthy, for there is nothing in Huxley's chapters to indicate a concern for national struggle. Yen obviously intended to use Huxley's work as a vehicle for his own teachings, an idea we can readily understand by reviewing Huxley's thought. According to Huxley, life is a process of change in which nothing is permanent except the rational order that pervades it. Furthermore, phenomena are often deceptive to human sight, so that what we call rest is often unperceived activity and what seems to be peace is a silent but strenuous battle. In the midst of change mankind evolved by the principle of selection through struggle. As civilization succeeded ages of barbarism, leisure and refinement appeared along with wealth and security. "To the struggle for bare existence . . . succeeded the struggle to make existence intelligible. . . ." Morals therefore are not inherent in the cosmic process but arise out of evolution and by reason of the two organic necessities peculiar to men— sympathy for and imitation of one another. The Stoic tendency to view the cosmos as beneficent is thus untenable. Nature is unfathomably unjust, and the microcosmic atom might well feel persecuted by the illimitable macrocosm. "Suffering is the badge of all the tribe of sentient things; . . . it is no accidental accompaniment, but an essential constituent of the cosmic process." Consistent with his basically cyclical view of nature, Huxley encourages no utopian anticipations: "If, for millions of years, our globe has taken the upward road, yet,

35. WS:YFC, 33.   36. CCF:YFSWH, 93-95.

sometime, the summit will be reached and the downward route will be commenced. The most daring imagination will hardly venture upon the suggestion that the power and the intelligence of man can ever arrest the procession of the great year."[37] But since doomsday has not yet arrived, men may reduce the essential evil of the cosmic process by subjecting it to the ethical process, which requires them to abandon their instinctual pursuit of pleasure and avoidance of pain.[38]

Huxley's cosmology is remarkably similar to Chinese Taoism, particularly that of the Lao Tzu school. According to the *Tao Te Ching*, the universe is a cosmic process in which being comes from non-being and is in turn differentiated into various beings. The principle behind this process is the *Tao* (way). Although it is profound and can hardly be described in words, one aspect is obvious, i.e., the idea that things exist by pairs of opposites; thus there is no beauty without ugliness and no virtue without depravity. Furthermore, there is a tendency for every condition to produce its opposite; strength leads to overgrowth, collapse, and impotency. In this eternal cycle of events, morality, which is man-made and artificial, has no place. "Heaven and earth are not humane: they treat the ten thousand things like [sacrificial] straw dogs." In the face of such a cosmic process, human endeavor is futile and self-defeating. But an intelligent man can master his destiny by knowing and following the cosmic process. This is called "practicing enlightenment" *(hsi-ming)*. He who does so "will not fail throughout his lifetime."[39]

In his writings Yen Fu repeatedly tells of his enchantment with Taoism. In one of his essays he states:[40] "Whether there is any difference between Taoism and Confucianism, or whether one is better than the other, I am not worthy enough to decide; but I know that even Confucius cannot improve upon Lao Tzu's theory of Nature." On another occasion Yen confided to his friends that "only Lao Tzu's doctrine is consistent with the concepts of Darwin, Montesquieu, and Spencer."[41] Had he imbibed Taoism first and then looked for similar ideas in the West and found these thinkers? Or was the reverse true? While available evidence remains inconclusive, there were indications that he had known of Taoism when he entered the Foochow arsenal school. At that time he changed his name from T'i-ch'ien (Knowing the Way of Heaven) to Tsung-kuang (Following the Path of Yen Kuang, a famous Taoist of the Later Han). Between 1879 and 1889 he once again changed his name, this time to Fu (Reversion, a Taoist term denoting the principle that when a thing moves to an extreme in one direction, a change must bring about an opposite result), and his

37. HTH:EE, 85.   38. *Ibid.*, 86.
39. FYL:HCP, I, 181-82.   40. CCF:YFSWH, 85.
41. WCC:YCT, 73.

courtesy name to Chi-tao (Approximating the Way) .[42] On the other hand, Yen himself dates his knowledge of Spencer's *Study of Sociology* from 1882,[43] and if his statement that the aim of Huxley is to curb the excesses of Spencer has any relevance here, it is possible that he learned of Huxley only after he had studied Spencer. At any rate he could not have known either of them before he went to the Foochow arsenal school.

Temporal sequence, however, is no measure of his convictions or their origin. There is little doubt that, in Yen, Taoism and evolutionism reinforced each other and that the latter, being far more specific, served to illuminate the former. But even if Spencer's *laissez-faire* resembles the non-activity of the Taoist philosophers, neither one is compatible with Yen's hopes of achieving an immediate political goal, namely, of saving China from destruction in the struggle of the nations. The method Yen prescribed can nevertheless be reconciled with the Taoist spirit since it does not start with the political process but works from intellectual enlightenment to national coherence and strength. However, there is still a gap between Taoist non-action and Spencer's repudiation of state control, on the one hand, and Yen's political goal of saving China through government action, on the other. It is here that Huxley fits in as a bridge.

In *Evolution and Ethics* Huxley affirms that the state of nature develops from relative uniformity to relative complexity. All plants and animals tend to vary and to multiply without limit. Because the means of support are limited, only the variations best adapted to the conditions of life survive. In this way the struggle for existence and the survival of the fittest become the two characteristics of the living world. However, in more advanced societies the struggle is not for the means of existence but for the means of enjoyment. Consequently social life differs both from the state of nature, in which the struggle is for bare existence, and from the state of art, in which selection can be made in the same way a gardener eliminates the weed and fosters the plant. From men's urges to imitate and sympathize with one another there arises an ethical process, which, if fostered and guided by moral and political philosophers, can create conditions favorable to the free expression of men's innate faculties. Here, and here only, is there even limited optimism on Huxley's part, for he affirms that the cosmic process is less in evidence in more advanced societies.[44]

In his translation Yen raises many criticisms of Huxley's ideas. Metaphysically, Yen accepts Descartes' *Cogito ergo sum* doctrine,[45] but he disagrees with Huxley that matter itself is unknowable because we can know only through our senses. He would rather say that the

42. *Ibid.*, 1.
43. *Ibid.*, 9.
44. HTH:EE, 35-36.
45. CCF:YF, 315.

ultimate is knowable but indescribable.[46] In sociology Yen believes with Spencer that evolution is identical with progress. He deletes a passage on retrogressive metamorphosis from Huxley's Prolegomena[47] and then comments in the second chapter:

> The position of Spencer, that by the natural process of evolution, society achieves progress and eventually the Good Life *(chih-chih)*, is solid and cannot be refuted. Why? . . . in zoology evolution has clearly resulted in the advance from insect to man. . . . Society is but an aggregate of individuals. . . . If an individual can advance through evolution, so can society. . . . Although Spencer concedes to Huxley that evil could result from evolution, it is difficult to see how that can happen . . . if the natural process is allowed positively to take its own course. According to Spencer, his sociology is like geometry. . . . All that it contains is based on reason *(yu-fa chih-hsing)*. . . . Students should not be alarmed by the fact that actual conditions are not always rational. They should separate the actual from the rational, which alone can form the basis of a theory. It is the failure to distinguish between the two that led Huxley to attack Spencer.[48]

Yen Fu's inclination toward scientism, i.e., the uncritical application of habits of thought to fields different from those in which these habits have been formed, is obvious. To his mind animal organisms and human societies are essentially similar, and by following principles that are scientifically determined, one sees progress as a necessity rather than an accident. In his effort to find a concrete basis for ethical notions, he also objects to Huxley's position that "the practice of self-restraint and renunciation is not happiness, although it may be something better." "This passage," he comments, "is erroneous. I do not know what is 'better' if it does not mean happiness." According to his beliefs, good necessarily yields pleasure, and evil, pain. To the question of whether labor is evil and indolence good, Yen replies:

> It is incorrect to view life from a limited point of view. . . . He who sacrifices himself to benefit the world does so because although he suffers, there are many who will obtain pleasure. Otherwise the deed of sacrifice becomes meaningless. . . . Good and evil can be defined by the quantity of pleasure and pain. However, the need that some one suffer in order that others may enjoy merely indicates the imperfection of society. In a

46. *Ibid.*, 318-19.
47. HTH:EE, 6. The sentence omitted reads: "Taken in its popular significa-tion it means progressive development, that is, gradual change from a condition of relative uniformity to one of relative complexity; but its connotation has been widened to include the phenomena of retrogressive metamorphosis, that is, of progress from a condition of relative complexity to one of relative uniformity."
48. YIMCCK, 1b.15.44-45.

Good Society every one will be self-sufficient; there will be no difference between good and pleasure and evil and pain.[49]

He also criticizes Huxley on several other points. Thus to Huxley's statement that sympathy and imitation are particular qualities of men, Yen replies that these organic necessities are functions of but not external to evolution, for without them, men cannot survive.[50] To Huxley's definition of the "fittest" as those best adapted to the conditions in any particular period, Yen adds that in addition to time there is also the element of space, that if new variations arrive from outside, they may well be fitter than the fittest so far.[51] To Huxley's assertion that peace leads to over-multiplication, which in turn makes peace impossible, Yen quotes Spencer's demonstration that men's procreative rate varies inversely with their intellectual capacity. The anxiety is thus unfounded except in regard to immature societies.[52]

Obviously, Yen Fu's views are closer to Spencer's than to Huxley's. Yet Huxley's book was vital to Yen's political ideas. It asserts that the cosmic process has no relation to moral ends; hence the weak are the prey of the strong. But once this principle is known, human effort can be made to counter the state of nature. Incorporated into Yen's scheme, it means that China should cease to confuse politics with morality, that she should pursue self-preservation according to the rules of the game, and that if properly guided, her efforts would be successful. The secret of Huxley's appeal was that although he began with evolution, he ended by stressing human endeavor.

Yen's translation was successful even before he published it in 1898. The manuscript was circulated among the reformers, and several unauthorized printings appeared. In the words of Wu Ju-lun, the well-known classicist, "There has never been a work of this caliber since China started to translate Western works. Not only is the theory of evolution epoch-making but the translation is superbly done and far surpasses all previous attempts in literary merit."[53] Yen's work was probably read by every eager student in China at the beginning of the century. Evolution became the talk of all school teachers; "natural selection" was a favorite topic in essay tests; many a father named his son "Fit," "Selection," or "Compete."[54] The enthusiastic response to Yen's work is not difficult to explain. Following the Sino-Japanese war of 1894, vociferous clamor for reform came from all quarters; yet no one knew precisely how to effect a change. The reformers were as inwardly paralyzed as they were outwardly agitated. But a new horizon appeared with the theory of evolution. The concept of natural selection not only explained China's plight but also indicated

49. *Ibid.*, 1a.18.47-48.
50. *Ibid.*, 1a.13.32-33.
51. *Ibid.*, 1a.4.13.
52. *Ibid.*, 1a.15.38-39.
53. WS:YFC, 33-34.
54. *Ibid.*, 37-38.

her possible fate in the future. The worst was known; even this con-clusion could not fail to afford some psychological relief. In addition, Huxley offered hope and indicated a formula. His emphasis on the struggle for existence and sympathy for one's kind could easily be interpreted to mean intra-group co-operation and inter-group struggle. The former might in turn indicate patriotism, something China had always lacked. All the symptoms Yen attacked in his essays—the indifference of one province to the needs of another, the substitution of dirt for shells, and so on—pointed to this defect. There is little doubt that in speaking of virtue, Yen, and for that matter, many others, really had in mind a public spirit. The message Huxley seemed to offer China was the need for national unity to resist foreigners. The scientific phrasing of the message gave it authority. For the first time in Chinese history social phenomena were not judged by moral values but explained in terms of inductively derived principles. The impact on the readers was unmistakable, even if the full ramifications were hardly understood.

Granted the principle of struggle without and coherence within, how was this course to be implemented? Yen's adherence to evolution-ism committed him to a certain type of program. "Successive genera-tions necessarily resemble that from which they come, but with enough differences to suit the conditions of survival."[55] Applied to politics, this statement meant that violent upheavals merely turned the clock back and that only gradual changes were warranted. "Human beings are infinitely malleable, but no fast amelioration can be expected."[56] Moreover, since political phenomena were but manifestations of the total conditions of survival, improvements could best be sought at the origin, i.e., beyond politics and in culture. Of the three factors that determined the strength of a nation, intellectual development was the most fundamental because knowledge alone could guide men to physical fitness and public-mindedness.

But these ideas were not immediately clear in Yen's writings. *Evolution and Ethics* appeared after "In Refutation of Han Yü," in which, it will be remembered, Yen attacked not only all of China's monarchs after the Ch'in, but also the monarchy as such. To be sure, he advocated the temporary retention of this institution, but the con-demnation loomed far larger than the reservation. Furthermore, in both his essays and the translation, the notion of progress was firmly established: the new was better than the old, and the West better than the East. Although the emphasis was cultural rather than political, the line between the two was extremely thin. Even Yen himself, partly indulging in hyperbole in order to shock, partly carried away by his emotion, and above all endeavoring to be concrete, proposed the

55. *Ibid.*, 35.   56. *Ibid.*, 59.

establishment of a parliament and the local election of officials.

However, if Yen actually meant what he said, he gave it little more than passing attention. Early in 1879, even before his *Evolution and Ethics* appeared, Yen cautioned Liang Ch'i-ch'ao against talking lightly of political reform.[57] Although still maintaining that China had been harmed by the monarchy and that Confucius should not be worshiped in any religious manner, Yen was already opposed to radical political changes. In an article written in that same year, he expressly reversed himself on the parliamentary issue and urged China to imitate Tzarist Russia.

> China today should not only ally with Russia but should imitate her, for in learning from others a necessary condition is a sufficient degree of similarity between the politics, culture, and customs of the imitator and the imitated. In the world today absolute monarchy exists only in China, Russia, and Turkey. In any country, the power of the throne must vary inversely with the level of intelligence of the people. Commentators love to talk about the reduction of the imperial prerogative and the establishment of a parliament in China. Alas! With the low intelligence of the Chinese people today, to emulate the good system of the West . . . is simply to court disaster.[58]

By early 1898, Yen had been convinced by his friend Wu Ju-lun that China was unprepared for local elections even on a limited scale. The second half of his "Petition of Ten Thousand Words to the Throne," which was to embody proposals of basic reform, never appeared. In the published first half, Yen merely suggested that the emperor make a tour abroad and at home in order to establish rapport with the foreigners and the masses.[59]

The seeming political retrogression has received much attention from critics, some of whom would see in Yen's life three distinct periods characterized by radicalism, compromise, and reaction.[60] But it is important to bear in mind the consistency as well as the inconsistency in Yen's views. In the four essays of 1895, there were a number of viewpoints which Yen continued to hold until at least his late years. The foundation of his thought was evolutionism. This theory in turn implied that the process of life, and for that matter history, was subject to a scientific law that was independent of human will. Only by knowing the law could men hope to influence their own destiny. In the pursuit of knowledge, a firm grasp of the scientific method was essential. Since mankind could evolve only by stages, there was no real possibility of any sudden transformation;

57. *Ibid.*, 42.
59. WCC:YCT, 47n.

58. *Ibid.*, 43.
60. CCF:YF, *passim.*

the most one could do was to promote favorable circumstances to quicken the pace of evolution. In so far as progress depended on total conditions of life, political means were of limited value, and when they were used, all measures had to be in harmony with the evolutionary position of society. As this position, or man's knowledge of it, changed, so should the prescription. Within such a framework it would seem that Yen would have no difficulty in justifying his stand on the questions of a parliament and the election of local officials. In his own terms he was too optimistic when he advocated them in 1895, and the mistake was indicated precisely by radicals like K'ang Yu-wei and Liang Ch'i-ch'ao. If they, the elite and the avant-garde, proved to be so immature, obviously China's evolutionary position was lower than it had appeared. A reassessment of the situation produced corresponding changes in the proposed reforms. Since China was not ready for a parliamentary regime, some form of paternalism was the only solution. Thus Yen's political inconsistency disappears in the light of his transcendent principles.

It is one thing, of course, to analyze Yen's thought in its own terms and another to trace the impact of his thought on society. There is little doubt that Yen's influence was at its height in 1898, after the publication of his four essays and *Evolution and Ethics*. Previously, in 1896, he had assisted another reformer, Chang Yüan-chi, who later became the chief editor of the Commercial Press in Shanghai, to establish a school in Peking. With the purpose of spreading new ideas among the educated class, the school recruited some forty to fifty students among the bureaucrats and included both English and mathematics in its curriculum.[61] In 1897 with two other friends Yen founded a journal called *Kuo Wen Pao (National News)* in Tientsin in order to facilitate communications "between the high and the low" in China. Many of his writings in this period appeared in it, including an unfinished "Petition of Ten Thousand Words" to the throne. Ranked on a par with *Shih Wu Pao (Current Affairs)*, which was then edited by Liang Ch'i-ch'ao in Shanghai, *Kuo Wen Pao* was the most influential journal in north China until it was discontinued in 1898.[62] Before this happened, Yen had been recommended to the throne as a "special talent" and was granted an audience of forty-five minutes.[63] He did not agree with the leaders of the reform clique, however, and for this and other reasons he suffered no severer punishment than the suspension of his journal when that movement failed.[64] It was not until 1900 that he left his post to go south.[65]

After his arrival at Shanghai, Yen continued his efforts to educate the public by delivering lectures on logic. He also participated in a

61. WS:YFC, 50-51.   62. *Ibid.*, 53.
63. *Ibid.*, 57.   64. *Ibid.*, 58-59; WCC:YCT, 48.
65. *Ibid.*, 55.

public forum on national affairs organized by T'ang Ts'ai-ch'ang, a member of K'ang Yu-wei's group, who was shortly to die in an abortive uprising in Hankow. In the autumn of 1900, Yen returned north to participate in relief work.[66] Meanwhile, he continued working on translations. The Chinese version of John Stuart Mill's *On Liberty* was undertaken in 1899; Spencer's *The Study of Sociology* between 1898 and 1902; Montesquieu's *The Spirit of the Laws* between 1900 and 1905; the first half of Mill's *System of Logic* between 1900 and 1902; and E. Jenk's *A History of Politics* in 1903.[67] In all of these works, Yen's professed aim was to achieve "accuracy," "comprehensibility," and "elegance."[68] In actual fact, he never hesitated to change the order of a passage or the illustrations of local color in the text. While his Chinese was elegant, it was not readily comprehensible because it had an archaic style and was filled with allusions. Thus, except in some transcendent sense, Fu cannot be said to have achieved his three aims. Rather his translations were attempts to assimilate the quintessence of Western European civilization into Chinese culture. Even the order of his translations was by his own account significant.[69] In the best tradition of Confucius, who was said to have tampered with the Six Classics extant in his time, Yen Fu innovated through translation.

When a bureau of translation was established under the University of Peking in 1902, Yen was invited to be its chief.[70] In 1903 his good friend Wu Ju-lun, who had in the previous year reluctantly accepted the deanship at the university, died. Wu had been extremely enthusiastic about Yen's work and had written a preface to each of his translations.[71] Probably influenced by the death of Wu, who with Kuo Sung-t'ao symbolized virtue and intelligence in Yen's mind, he resigned in 1904. At the invitation of Chang I, the Chinese director-general of the Kaiping mines that had fraudulently become a British concern in 1900, Yen went to London in 1905 to assist in the legal efforts to recover the mines.[72] Little resulted from his trip. The only event of interest to us here was Yen's interview with Sun Yat-sen, who had great respect for this well-known scholar but whose respect was not reciprocated. In fact, Yen had never had anything but contempt for Sun, whom he believed ignorant, boastful, and unscrupulous.[73] To his insistence that cultural improvement must precede political change and that rash effort would only result in disaster, Sun could

66. *Ibid.*, 55-57.   67. *Ibid.*, 74-75.
68. CCL:CPSL, II, 109-10.
69. *Ibid.*, 107-8. See also Yen's letter No. 51 in HH, XVI, 4.
70. See the biography of Chang Po-hsi in 1st CYNC, II, Sec. E, p. 423, and the biography of Wu Ju-lun in HA:ECCP, 871.
71. WCC:YCT, 69.   72. WTC:KLMK, 7-99.
73. CCF:YFSWH, 122; Yen's letters Nos. 28 and 42 in HH, XII, 7, and XV, 3-4.

only battle his way out by saying: "Mr. Yen, life is short. You are a thinker; I am a doer."[74]

After his return to China, Yen delivered eight public lectures on political science at the Y.M.C.A. in Shanghai. The notes were published in 1906 and became the first modern Chinese treatise in that field.[75] Between then and 1911, Yen Fu was engaged in educational and governmental work, serving successively as head of Futan College in Shanghai (1906), head of the Anhwei Normal College (1906-1907), examiner at the metropolitan examinations for the return students (1906), chief editor of a translation bureau under the Board of Education (1908-1911), and member of the National Assembly (1910), in addition to a number of honorary and advisory posts. In 1909 he published the Chinese version of W. S. Jevons' *Primer of Logic* and by a special edict was awarded, with eighteen others, the *chin-shih* degree. Although he had previously tried hard to obtain such a degree, the event did not seem to give him great satisfaction. He was now fifty-six years old and the degree, which he had wanted as a way of furthering his political influence, no longer served an important purpose.[76]

In 1912, Yen Fu was appointed by Yüan Shih-kai as president of Peking University. For some reason he stayed only a few months, but for the next four years he remained in the entourage of Yüan. The relationship between the two men sheds light on the characters of both. When Yüan was governor-general of Chihli and a rising power, he invited Yen to serve on his staff. Yen declined, and Yüan was offended. After Yüan's fall in 1910, however, Yen, in spite of his doubts about Yüan's moral probity, praised Yüan as a capable official who had been wronged.[77] Yen was possibly inclined to champion the unpopular cause, to view all public clamors with suspicion. Such a propensity seems to have underlain many of his attitudes in life, including his disapproval of Liang Ch'i-ch'ao and Sun Yat-sen.

Yüan's repeated attempts to have Yen on his staff went beyond the traditional pattern of a high official patronizing scholarship and scholars. Judging by Yüan's insistence in 1915 that Yen Fu be a sponsor of the Peace Planning Society,[78] an organ used by Yüan to further his monarchical ambitions, it would seem that Yüan was deeply impressed by Yen's prestige. But in actuality Yen had counted increasingly less with the youth after the turn of the century. There were two main reasons for his declining influence. In the first place he had little regard for the public. He himself admitted that he purposely wrote in an obscure style in order to limit his audience to the

74. WCC:YCT, 74-75.   75. YCTIC, 1-97: HKC:CKC, VI, 814.
76. WCC:YCT, 75-81; WS:YFC, 64-66; CCF:YFSWH, 227-29.
77. WS:YFC, 91.   78. *Ibid.*, 89-90.

learned.[79] Such an attitude was naturally unwelcome to the younger generation. An even more important factor was his political stand. He urged caution while Chinese intellectuals moved steadily toward radicalism. The march in opposite directions soon created a gulf between him and his readers. After 1900 his reputation was sustained only by his fame as a pioneer radical and by his renown as a translator, nor by his increasingly cautious views. As Yen himself remarked later: "In assessing the current critical situation of China, few reformers of years ago could escape responsibility. Having foreseen the danger, I followed up my work on *Evolution and Ethics* with the *Study of Sociology*, hoping to inspire the radicals with caution. Unfortunately, the fad had caught on. . . ."[80] Yüan, however, had not realized this. Surrounded by sycophants and looking toward the past, he mistakenly thought he could profit by Yen's prestige. On Yen's part, the assignment could hardly be refused without peril. Because of his age, his addiction to opium, and his dislike of a phantom republic in which the people had no voice, he decided to let his name be used without protesting actively.[81] His acquiescence led to the end of his influence over public opinion without any benefit to Yüan's cause.

Yen's only writing of importance after the revolution was a critical essay on Rousseau's *Social Contract*.[82] He lived in retirement after Yüan Shih-k'ai's death but managed to continue his correspondence with friends. In 1921 he died while visiting his birthplace, Foochow.[83]

Among the generation of intellectuals who owed a debt to Yen Fu was Liang Ch'i-ch'ao (1873-1929). A precocious child of a farmer-scholar family at Hsin-hui in Kwangtung province, Liang passed the provincial civil service examination at the age of sixteen. He failed the metropolitan examinations in 1890, but the trip north proved eventful for him. Passing through Shanghai, Liang was for the first time exposed to books on Western countries. With his interest in contemporary affairs thus kindled, Liang soon met and became a disciple of K'ang Yu-wei. In 1896, Liang began his journalistic activities by advocating political reform. After the *coup d'état* of 1898 he fled to Japan, where in addition to plotting against the Empress Dowager, he also propagated constitutional monarchism.[84] From about 1900, Liang clashed with the revolutionaries under Sun Yat-sen, who also had their headquarters in the Tokyo-Yokohama area in Japan, over the issues of strategy and political aim.[85]

After the establishment of the Republic, Liang returned to China and served intermittently as a high official until 1917 when his attention turned from politics to academic research and social reform.

79. CCF:YF, 304.
80. Yen's letter in HH, 16.51.4.
81. WS:YFC, 88.
82. CCF:YF, 339-42.
83. WS:YFC, 101-2.
84. LCC:YPSWC, 4.11.15-19.
85. LCN:PHC, 179-181; LJKHS, I, 139-41.

Although not a returned student in the ordinary sense of the term, Liang was deeply influenced by Western thought. His stay in Japan after 1898, his visit to the United States in 1903, and his tour of Europe at the end of World War I all marked important milestones in the development of his thought. He read widely in Japanese translations of Western works and made several attempts to learn European languages. His prolific writing—some fourteen million words in a relatively short life span—made him an important retailer of ideas.[86]

Before 1898, Liang was mainly under the spell of K'ang Yu-wei, who justified his political radicalism in terms of the "Modern Text" approach to Confucianism. Even then Liang was not immune to other influences. He avidly followed Yen Fu's writings and enthusiastically recommended his translation of Huxley to K'ang Yu-wei and others before the book was formally published.[87] Yen's ideas of evolution and political gradualism impressed Liang, whose thought was otherwise eclectic and extremely fluid. Both were ardent patriots, but otherwise they had little in common. One was as cautious as the other was impulsive. In politics Liang schemed and agitated while Yen discoursed from an Olympian height. By training Liang was a brilliant classicist while Yen prided himself on his knowledge of the West.[88] Perhaps these differences accounted for Yen's early disapproval of Liang's methods; in 1896 and 1897 just as Liang was achieving fame through his writings in *Current Affairs*, Yen cautioned him repeatedly against random talk that would "misguide youth and cause future regrets."[89] The irony was not that the advice fell on deaf ears, but that even Liang soon proved too conservative for the times and lost to Sun Yat-sen the leadership of the revolutionary movement.

At the time Liang was corresponding with Yen, he knew little about the West or about Japan, for he argued that "the Japanese had no less political right than the English or the Germans," and therefore it would be as feasible for China as Japan to pass immediately from autocracy to democracy.[90] But after his arrival in Japan in 1898, Liang began reading extensively and was able to produce in the following year a long and detailed bibliography of Japanese books—thirty-one on ethics, thirty-one on world history, thirteen on Chinese history, and eight on Japanese history.[91] Even more remarkably, he had developed a new emphasis on evidence and analysis in historical research. Declaring the new approach superior to the Chinese style of rendering judgment on the basis of scant facts, he produced between 1901 and 1902 a series of articles on Hobbes, Spinoza, Rousseau, and various Greek philosophers.[92] Although more

86. LJKHS, III, 782.
88. CCF:YFSWH, 181; YCTIC, 120.
90. CCF:YFSWH, 278.
92. *Ibid.*, 3.6.85-109, 5.12.61-77.

87. WS:YFC, 36.
89. WS:YFC, 42.
91. LCC:YPSWC, 2.4.82-102.

journalistic than scholarly, these studies bore unmistakable traces of Western influence. The moral overtones almost disappeared; a great deal of background information was inserted; and many terms were annotated with the English words. The appearance of these articles augured a new historiography in China.

Meanwhile, a metamorphosis was taking place in Liang's political attitude. With his broadened outlook came an independence of mind. Whereas he had maintained in 1897 that there were three stages of political evolution—disorder, approaching peace, and great unity—by 1901 and 1902 these had changed into a six-fold evolution, namely, kinship, tribe, theocracy, aristocracy, autocracy, and constitutionalism.[93] The ghost of the "Modern Text" school had thus given way to a spirit of ardent nationalism. In 1902, Liang started publishing a series of articles under the title "Discourses on the New People" (Hsin Min Shuo). National strength, he said, depended on the strength of the people. By "new" he did not mean the abandonment of the old heritage but rather the acquisition of additional qualities. The essence was to achieve a balance between conservatism and progressivism. Of all the peoples in the world, the Anglo-Saxons had best manifested this balance and should therefore be imitated.[94] Regarding the deficiencies in the Chinese character, none could be more serious than moral turpitude. Morality, said Liang, could be divided into two kinds, a "private" one dealing with relationships between individuals and a "public" one governing relationships between an individual and the whole group. Of the two, the latter was far more important because, ultimately, the purpose of morality was to benefit the group. Yet the Chinese were most deficient in this regard. Thus China's greatest need was to develop a new mentality that would place the well-being of the group above all other considerations.[95]

Of all the groups, he continued, the nation was the most nearly perfect, for only through it could men defend themselves in wars and share their lives in peace. The nation was higher than the government because the latter was only its agent. It was better than the world because civilization advanced through national competition. It was more important than the individual because without it man "would fare worse than the birds and beasts." Since time immemorial, Liang asserted, human beings had developed in different groups, each with its own language, customs, and spirit. Just as there were struggles among men, so there must be conflicts among nations. The existence of a nation depended on the willingness of each man to defend it to the last drop of his blood. Hence "the nation was the unit of self-love and the climax of human fraternity; anything less was uncivilized; and anything more was equally uncivilized."[96]

93. HKC:CKC, VI, 744.   94. LCC:YPSCC, 3.4.7-11.
95. Ibid., 3.4.15.   96. Ibid., 3.4.16-18.

Important as the concept of the nation was, it was yet undeveloped in China. One reason, according to Liang, was geographical. China had traditionally been surrounded by uncivilized countries and had therefore mistakenly considered herself the world. Another reason was ideological. All Chinese philosophies advocated great unity—i.e., one-worldism instead of nationalism—because at the time these views were proposed, in the pre-Ch'in feudal period, inter-state strife was the major evil. While conditions later changed, the doctrine of "great unity" was nevertheless retained because it enabled the reigning house to justify its monopoly of power. As ideology and the fact of unification continued to reinforce each other, the concept of one nation among many completely disappeared. As a result cultural conformity alone was required of a ruler, and no importance was attached to his ethnic origin. Gradually, moral values served merely as a cover for naked self-interest, and the Chinese were ready to serve virtually any master. Never had an alien dynasty been founded in China without important Chinese help, and even during the allied occupation of Peking (when the city had been ransacked by foreign troops for women and wealth), the people had acclaimed the benevolent government of the foreigners. Unless this shameful attitude was mended, Liang stressed, ethnic annihilation would be inevitable.[97]

Another idea unknown to Chinese thought was the concept of personal rights. The matter, said Liang, did not concern an individual alone, for the forfeiture of his rights fostered usurpation by default, which in turn spelled the doom of the group to which he belonged. Thus not even a minor infringement of one's rights should be tolerated. As an illustration, Liang compared China with Japan. Forty years ago, he said, a survey of the Japanese coast by foreigners aroused Japan and led to the Meiji Restoration; today, the Chinese were unmoved even by the allied occupation of Peking. One reason for this weakened sense of proprietorship was the Chinese exaltation of the benevolent government. "As benevolence was expected of others, the initiative was no longer my own. I became at best a ward and more likely a prey."[98] As an illustration Liang cited the Manchu policy of light taxation and no military conscription, which, although undeniably benevolent, had dire consequences for China.[99] Light taxation made the government impotent and incapable of launching innovations, while the hiring of mercenary troops inevitably dimmed the people's sense of patriotism. Moreover, if history taught anything, it was that representative government originated from tax problems. Thus England had its Magna Carta and France its revolution; but the Chinese had little or no sense of participation in their state because they had no tax problems. Thus only when the Chinese learned

97. *Ibid.,* 3.4.21-23.
98. *Ibid.,* 3.4.34-35.
99. *Ibid.,* 3.4.106.

to defend their individual interests would they be human in the fullest sense of the term. According to Roman law, which classified men without rights as no higher than animals, China had previously had four hundred million animals but not a single man.[100]

Turning next to freedom, Liang enumerated specific events in Western history since 1532 and asserted that all of these had been motivated by a struggle for freedom. It was this relentless search for liberty that had made the West what it was today. To the question whether the same aim could be pursued in China, Liang answered that liberty was a universal truth applicable to all nations. But as concrete circumstances differed, so specific goals must vary. Of the freedoms pursued by the West—political, religious, national, and economic—China had always had religions, and did not yet need economic freedom, which only became a problem as production reached a high plateau. Her urgent need was for national and political freedom. Actually, the two were basically one, because if the Manchu regime were replaced by a nation-state, political freedom would automatically result; but if the latter came about first, the fate of the Manchu monarchy would matter little. The problem, rather, was the popular misconception of liberty. The Chinese in general did not understand the restraints liberty imposed, and they took advantage of others whenever they could. Such licentious exercise weakened the group and rendered it prone to foreign aggression, with eventual harm to all individuals alike. The need was therefore to subordinate individual liberty to group liberty. In the second place, Liang urged that the Chinese needed spiritual freedom most of all, for they were slavishly bound to the ancients, to social conventions, to surroundings, and to desires. Unless they could be liberated from these restrictions, no liberty was worth the name.[101]

Still another deficiency was the lack of progress in China. In a colorful illustration, Liang compared the Chinese compass, unchanged through eight centuries, with Huang Tsün-hsien's well-known book on Japan, rendered obsolete by changes in Japan within two decades. Liang gave five reasons for China's stagnation: (1) lack of national competition under a unified monarchy, (2) geographical isolation, (3) the difficulty of the written language, (4) intellectual degeneration under despotism, (5) exaltation of one cult—Confucianism—since the Han dynasty.[102] Of the five factors, three were linked with the monarchy which was thus an obscurantism of the first order. (As an explanation for the long life of this institution, Liang suggested two interesting reasons in another essay. One was benevolent government, which by making despotism less intolerable, extended its life.[103] Another was the lack of an aristocracy in China—this had two effects:

100. *Ibid.*, 3.4.39.
101. *Ibid.*, 3.4.40-50.
102. *Ibid.*, 3.4.56-60.
103. *Ibid.*, 3.4.35-36.

one was a reduced burden on the masses, and the other, an absence of effective opposition to the monarchy. Thus, because the lot of the commoner was better in China than in the West, the evolution toward democracy was delayed—with serious consequences.[104] "For self-government is the basis of progress. . . . When the masses are treated like slaves and regarded as bandits and thieves, they inevitably become indolent and selfish . . . How then can deterioration be avoided?"[105]) The only remedy, Liang asserted, lay in destruction. The old had to go, whether through peaceful reform as in Japan or by violent means as in France.[106] Undesirable as revolution might become, it was a stage not all countries could avoid. Did the Japanese martyr of 1859, Yoshida Shōin, not say: "Destroy first and make plans later"? This was the spirit that had made Japan strong.[107]

Turning to economics, Liang believed that too many people in China were not engaged in productive work. He asserted that all of the Manchus in China proper lived idle lives[108] and that 60 to 70 per cent of all Chinese women did nothing.[109] The remedy should then consist of two steps: first, to stigmatize indolence in order to make lazy people feel ashamed, and then to devise means to absorb the idlers in production.[110]

Another topic Liang discussed was militarism. He compared China unfavorably with Sparta, Germany, Russia, Japan, and even Transvaal —which, although small, had valiantly resisted the mightiest nation on earth, England. Liang attributed China's weakness to four causes —long reigns of peace in an isolated world, excessive cosmopolitanism in the Confucian ideal, the willingness of despotic monarchs to maintain power by weakening the people, and the social attitude condemning violence. "Devoid of knowledge as well as physical strength, how can the Chinese survive in a competitive world?"[111]

As a final topic Liang described the political ineptitude of the Chinese. Numerous illustrations were used to indicate the connection between the fate of a nation and the political ability of its people. The Tong Hak of Korea had in 1894 the same aim as the Japanese samurai in 1868; South Americans sought their independence as the North Americans had a century earlier; and the French revolted in 1793 as the English had in 1649. Why in each case had a different result occurred? The reason, he answered, lay in the people's political ability.[112] As for the Chinese, their complete lack of such ability needed no stress. From government concerns to private enterprise, disorganization was a basic characteristic. Even the overseas com-

104. *Ibid.*, 4.9.80-82.
106. *Ibid.*, 3.4.65.
108. *Ibid.*, 3.4.93.
110. *Ibid.*, 3.4.96.
112. *Ibid.*, 3.4.149-50.

105. *Ibid.*, 3.4.58.
107. *Ibid.*, 3.4.67.
109. *Ibid.*, 3.4.87.
111. *Ibid.*, 3.4.109-118.

munities were no exception. While four thousand Britishers successfully established a government in Shanghai, thirty thousand Chinese
only fought *tong* wars in San Francisco.[113] If reasons for this ineptitude were to be sought, they could be found in China's despotic
tradition, her family system, her economy of scarcity, and her constant natural calamities, which either impaired personal initiative or
disrupted continuous development.[114] Given these conditions, improvement must start with the middle class (i.e., the intelligentsia),
through the two means of specialization and co-operation. In the
latter connection, Liang dwelt at length on the relationship between
the constitutionalists and the revolutionists. He argued that if constitutionalism succeeded, it would make the revolution unnecessary, and if
it failed, it would make the revolution inevitable. Thus the two causes
were mutually generative, and one faction had no reason to oppose the
other. Even more subtly, Liang argued that all innovations really
pointed in the same direction, for once a man started to see light,
he could no longer be contented with half-darkness. In this sense,
even the Manchu court played an important role. By launching
ineffectual reforms, it merely added fuel to the revolutionary fire.[115]

Such was the essence of Liang's theory of the New People. It
should be noted that Liang's abstract ideas bore a striking similarity
to Yen Fu's. His eulogy of the Anglo-Saxons as the people most
adapted to preserve the old and assimilate the new might have been
uttered by Yen himself. The assertion that the Chinese lacked public
spirit was a paraphrase of Yen's words in his four essays. The observation that Chinese lacked nationalism because of the early unification
of the country and the cosmopolitan ideals in Confucianism was also
a repetition of Yen's remarks.[116] Liang's emphasis upon personal
rights as a foundation of one's sense of duty toward the group echoed
Yen's conviction that "the essence of statecraft was to turn self-interest into public interest."[117] His condemnation of a slavish imitation of the ancients virtually repeated Yen's lament that "the Chinese
were too much confined by custom."[118] The attack on benevolent
government was derived from Yen's belief that "nothing corrupted
the people more in the long run than charity from above."[119] His
assertion that the Chinese people had been treated like slaves and
that self-government was the key to progress resembled Yen's words
except that Yen specified local self-government.[120] Liang's stress
on a new martial spirit seems to be related to Yen's exhortation
of bodily strength. Even the call for greater specialization of efforts
among the intellectuals probably came from Yen's advocacy of divi-

113. *Ibid.*, 3.4.151.
114. *Ibid.*, 3.4.152-56.
115. *Ibid.*, 3.4.159-60.
116. CCF:YFSWH, 4-5.
117. *Ibid.*, 32.
118. YIMCCK, 5.19.2.2.
119. *Ibid.*
120. CCF:YFSWH, 31, 32.

sion of labor in his version of the *Wealth of Nations*.[121] Finally, the bidding to destroy the old was almost a restatement of a view shared by Yen and Liang in 1895—in his second essay Yen approvingly quoted Liang as saying: "Change is inevitable, whether one wills it or not."[122] While the word used now was "destruction" rather than "change," this substitution could make little difference in implication. Precisely because all other channels of change had been obstructed, so reform could now come only through destruction. In spite of a shift in emphasis, Liang's view remained close to Yen's earlier utterances.

Elsewhere there were further evidences of Yen's early influence over Liang. The latter was so impressed with Yen's essays of 1895 that he had them reprinted in *Current Affairs* in the following autumn.[123] After Yen's translation of Huxley's work, the theory of evolution became a constant theme in Liang's writings. Even more striking, Yen's influence is clearly discernible in three other issues. One concerned the worship of Confucianism, a matter close to the heart of all Chinese scholars. Since Western impact became more intense in the nineteenth century and perhaps because of the numerous incidents connected with the missionary activities, many Chinese toyed with the idea of turning Confucianism into a religion. Liang had favored such an idea[124] but Yen opposed it. He cautioned Liang privately and wrote an article stressing the contradiction of treating Confucianism as a religion and thus negating its ideal of tolerance.[125] After some initial vacillation Liang was fully converted. By 1902 he was arguing against his mentor K'ang Yu-wei, who was organizing a Confucian Society and sponsoring the erection of Confucian temples.[126] Years later, Liang reminisced that this disagreement precipitated the break between him and K'ang.[127]

A second issue was devoted to a comparison between Chinese and Western civilizations, which had become a recurrent problem to Chinese intellectuals. Was the one better than the other and, if so, why? In 1895, Yen had said: "According to some commentators, the Chinese directed their thought to abstract ideas while Westerners put

121. LCC:YPSCC, 3.4.156-62; YIMCCK, 2.Chia.2.11.
122. CCF:YFSWH, 32.   123. YCTIC, 120-21.
124. LCC:YPSWC, 2.3.9-11. The letter Liang wrote to his friend advocating the establishment of a Confucian church is dated 1897 by the compiler of Liang's collected works, while his letter to Yen Fu agreeing that Confucian teachings could not and should not be turned into a religion is dated 1896. The chronology is probably wrong. Liang wrote in 1902 an article—"To Preserve the Confucian Teachings [by Turning it into a Religion] is not the way to Honor Confucius"—which almost repeated the arguments advanced by Yen. Hence it is probable that his personal letter to Yen was written after the letter he addressed to the other unnamed friend and before the article on how to honor Confucius. See also LJKHS, I, 42.
125. CCF:YFSWH, 133-37.   126. LJKHS, I, 151-54.
127. HICY:ITCP, 103.

their cleverness to concrete matters. This is incorrect. As I see it, Western thought is no less abstract than Chinese, and Chinese thought is no less concrete than Western. The difference simply does not lie there."[128] Two years later Liang argued that while a system could be good or bad, it could not in an abstract sense be either "Western" or "Chinese," for "all systems belonged to the world and were used by men." Thus the proper criterion was how to strengthen the nation with the most suitable means, regardless of whether they were "Western" or "Chinese."[129]

A third issue dealt with the Chinese attitude toward the scientific method. Yen always maintained that the pursuit of truth was a major Western achievement. In his writings he attached the greatest importance to the study of deductive and inductive logic, especially the establishing and testing of hypotheses relating to ascertainable facts.[130] However, either by a limitation of interest—Yen was ardently absorbed in the political rejuvenation of China—or by the natural circumspection of evolution, Yen did not produce works of an inductive nature. The void was to be filled by Liang. Even though his political essays were emotional in tone, as early as 1901 he adopted a new style of writing in his historical and philosophical essays. The best example was perhaps his *Biography of Li Hung-chang*, which, with its background data and objective analysis, was specifically declared by the author to have been modeled on Western works.[131] Later, after his return to China in 1912, and especially after his retirement from government service, Liang's style became increasingly detached. In his *Intellectual Trends in the Ch'ing Period*, written in 1920, he discussed at length the importance of the "scientific method," which he explained as (1) careful observation, (2) open-mindedness, (3) establishment of a hypothesis, (4) collection of evidence, (5) conclusion of the case, and (6) inference by applying the conclusions reached to other cases.[132] He stressed the lack of national boundaries in knowledge and the importance of pursuing knowledge as an end in itself.[133] In an important speech before the 1922 meetings of the China Science Society, Liang criticized both Chang Chih-tung, who thought of science as concrete and inferior to philosophy, and the New Culture leaders, who loudly proclaimed their faith in "Science." Neither side, in his opinion, even understood the term, for science was not confined to a single discipline such

128. CCF:YFSWH, 29.   129. LCC:YPSWC, 2.2.62.
130. YIMCCK, 6.8, 6.66; WCC:YCT, 55-56, 57-62, 78-79, 125.
131. LCC:YPSCC, 2.3.1.   132. *Ibid.*, 9.34.45.
133. *Ibid.*, 9.34.36; LCC:YPSWC, 14.39.16-18. Contrary to the claims of a recent writer, Liang does not seem to have been motivated successively by a desire to equate China with the West, to disparage the West, and to affirm the differences between Chinese and Western civilizations, all for the sake of easing his inner tension (LJR:LCC, 2-3).

as chemistry or engineering, nor could it be used as a political slogan. Rather it was the search for knowledge in all fields by open and systematic methods so that the results could easily be transmitted and accumulated.[134] In another speech delivered a year later, he differentiated between institutional studies (*wen-hsien-hsueh*) which could use the objective, scientific method of ascertaining and comparing facts, and ethical learning, which involved both intuition and the actual practicing of one's own convictions.[135]

Thus many of Liang's ideas ran parallel to Yen's or represented an effort to develop them further. But in spite of their spiritual affinity, Yen was extremely critical of Liang. Before discussing Yen's specific charges, however, we must examine Liang's political stand and his influences over Chinese intellectuals.

In his political thought, Liang seemed to waver constantly between two feelings, an anxiety to overthrow despotism on the one hand and a serious doubt of China's readiness for democracy on the other. While the first feeling prevailed, he advocated revolution against the Manchus; but as his less sanguinary mood returned, he appealed for enlightened paternalism, which in effect meant the strengthening of the political status quo. The alternation of these attitudes made Liang the most vacillating personality in modern Chinese politics. Broadly speaking, between the conclusion of the Sino-Japanese war in 1895 and the beginning of the abortive reform of 1898 he favored the overthrow of the Manchus. But his stand changed when the emperor took K'ang Yu-wei, who had concurred with Liang's views,[136] into his confidence. When the reform failed, Liang advocated constitutionalism—i.e., for the emperor but against the Empress Dowager, which in effect meant an anti-dynastic stand. After 1901, Liang's attitude further hardened. His increased knowledge of the West, his temporary entente with Sun Yat-sen, and, above all, his disappointment over the Manchus' failure to introduce real reforms turned him into a revolutionary.[137] In the "Discourses on the New People" he attacked specific Manchu emperors and urged the total destruction of the regime.[138]

Yet another change, this time back to conservatism, took place after his visit to America in 1903. He now argued that nationalism should mean not a struggle by Chinese against Manchus, but a unification of all of the ethnic groups in China against outsiders.[139] A revolution, he maintained, would only further the ambition of unscrupulous politicians. Even a constitutional monarchy was impractical, for the Chinese were much too immature for that. Only an en-

134. LJKHS, III, 612; LCC:YPSWC, 14.39.1-9.
135. *Ibid.*, 14-39.110-19.   136. LJKHS, I, 44.
137. *Ibid.*, I, 156-57.   138. LCC:YPSWC, 3.4.67, 3.4.129.
139. *Ibid.*, 5.13.75.76.

lightened autocracy could lead the way to these higher political forms. The essay advancing this argument ran to seventy pages, with quotations from both Chinese sages and Western figures from Lycurgus to Bismarck. According to Liang, it was logic alone that led him to this conclusion.[140]

Actually, of course, many factors contributed to this last change. One was a growing antagonism between him and Sun Yat-sen. As the latter favored republicanism, Liang quite naturally took a different stand.[141] Another factor was the pressure of K'ang Yu-wei, who disapproved of Liang's support for revolution. In 1903 he succeeded in making Liang promise to change his views.[142] Even though Liang at the time did not mean to keep his word, nevertheless this probably influenced him in some way. Still another reason was the influence of a Swiss political scientist, Bluntschli. In 1903 Liang was exposed to his writings and was deeply impressed by them. Adopting Bluntschli's definition of an ethnic group, Liang found that at least in terms of language, custom, and economic activities, there was little difference between Chinese and Manchus. On the question of a nation-state, the Swiss had postulated three essential conditions—a national awareness, the ability to form a state, and the determination to do so. Applying them to China, Liang found that while the first condition existed, the third was doubtful, and the second completely lacking. He concluded therefore that a revolution against the Manchus was premature. Furthermore, from his study of France, Switzerland, and the United States, Bluntschli had formed an unfavorable opinion of republican forms of government. Liang's visit to America convinced him that the Swiss was correct. In an essay entitled "The Theory of Bluntschli, a Great Political Scientist," Liang pointed out that Switzerland had very special surroundings and was hardly comparable to China. France had experienced political upheavals for eighty years between 1793 and 1870 and still lacked a stable political structure, even in the twentieth century. Although the United States had been favored by an English heritage, it too suffered from many political and moral defects, such as discrimination against Negroes, Indians, and Chinese, a lack of achievement in philosophy, literature, and arts, and a lack of continuity in administration. It was true, Liang asserted, that certain defects mentioned by Bluntschli—notably, America's military weakness and her lack of talented politicians and civil servants—had diminished under McKinley and Theodore Roosevelt, but only because the power of the federal government had expanded during these two administrations. "If the United States, which loves liberty the most, finds itself compelled to centralize political power, what is there left for other countries to do?"[143]

140. Ibid., 6.17.13-83.   141. LJKHS, I, 165.
142. Ibid., I, 181.   143. LCC:YPSWC, 5.13.77-89.

A factor that Liang did not mention in the essay, but that probably contributed to his drawing a negative lesson from American democracy was the corruption he found at the state level and the discrimination he experienced.[144] In 1900, Liang's efforts to come to the United States had failed because of a quarantine measure enforced against Asians.[145] During his visit in 1903, a Chinese consular employee committed suicide in San Francisco after being insulted by the police.[146] Liang viewed this incident as another national humiliation, which could only be avenged by a China strengthened through centralized reform but not weakened by a revolution.

Liang's stand underwent further changes in subsequent years. After the Manchu court had decreed a constitutional regime, he organized a political party in 1907 to advocate a parliamentary system.[147] When the republic became an accomplished fact in 1912, he declared his unswerving support and later fulfilled his pledge by doggedly opposing Yüan Shih-kai's attempt to become emperor.[148] A last change in his social thought took place following a tour of Europe at the end of World War I. Deeply touched by the ravages and devastations of the war, he no longer regarded the Anglo-Saxons as a superior race and the Western "materialistic" civilization as the best in the world. Rather, he preached for a syncretism of East and West through the medium of Taoism, which was then attracting much interest from Western scholars.[149] He seemed to retain this hope for the remaining years of his life.

Liang was well aware of his own inconsistency. He freely admitted his habit of "attacking the Liang of yesterday with the Liang of today."[150] While deploring his fickleness, he derived pleasure from what he believed to be his honesty and intellectual progress. The drawbacks were mainly of a political nature. Constant vacillation on his part shook his supporters' confidence and diminished their number. In spite of his strenuous efforts Liang achieved none of his more constructive political aims. Until his last years he agitated, organized, and schemed, but to little purpose. By the late 1910's his political failure had become so clear that he not only admitted it but also started to leave politics for academic and even business affairs.[151]

Nevertheless, he had wielded tremendous influence from the time he published his first essay at the age of twenty-three. Sought after by many high officials, he chose to teach at a new school in Hunan where he soon became so idolized that eleven students later joined him in exile in Japan.[152] By then Liang had become an international figure,

144. LCC:YPSCC, 5.22.140.   145. LJKHS, I, 111.
146. MHF:CA, 189; LJKHS, I, 187.   147. HTS:CK, III, 516-17, 527.
148. LCC:YPSCC, 9.33, *passim.*
149. *Ibid.,* 5.23.12, 15, 36; 10.35.15-18; LJR:LCC, p. 203, footnote 32.
150. LCC:YPSCC, 9.26.63.
151. *Ibid.,* 5.23.39; LJKHS, I, 6-7.   152. *Ibid.,* I, 92.

wanted by the Manchus and protected by the Japanese.[153] In the following years, his writings were avidly read in Japan and smuggled into China, where they were copied or reprinted.[154] Liang made no idle boast when he claimed to have influenced Chinese thinking for twenty years, as he is clearly borne out by the following testimonies.

> Every word [you write] is worth a thousand in gold. Nobody can write as you do, but everyone shares your thought. . . . I can think of no other writer, ancient or living, more effective than you.
>
> From Huang Tsün-hsien to Liang, 1902.[155]

> He attracted our abundantly curious mind . . . All of the sections in the "Discourse on the New People" opened up a new world for me.
>
> Hu Shih, 1931.[156]

> I think this great scholar did more than anyone else in his time to popularize modern knowledge among the rising generation. His was the fountain of wisdom from which every young man drew to quench his thirst for the new learning.
>
> Chiang Monlin, 1942.[157]

How can we reconcile his extensive influence with his failures? The question leads to an analysis of the nature and degree of his influence at different times.

One factor in Liang's popularity was his style of writing. Whereas other writers studiously avoided colloquialisms and vulgarisms, Liang purposely included such expressions in his writings in order to achieve an effect of unequaled lucidity and freedom. Liang himself often complained of his inability to stop once he started writing. At the same time, in contrast to the terse style of traditional writings, Liang's essays almost invariably conveyed much factual information. In his hands the Chinese language acquired a new character that was not much removed from the vernacular style advocated by Hu Shih years later. In a real sense Liang set the fashion and was imitated by a whole generation of writers.

A large part of his writings was devoted to the dissemination of knowledge of Western civilization. While perhaps little of it was profound, no other Chinese had done more than Liang in spreading this information. The *New People's Miscellany* he edited between 1902 and 1907 contained a wealth of information for the intellectually starved Chinese readers. For example, Number 9 of this semimonthly is composed of the following items: three pictures of Garibaldi, Cavour, and Mazzini; two pictures, with notations, of Chinese

---

153. LJKHS, I, 82; CPT:WHPF, II, 575.
154. LCC:YPSCC, 9.34.62.   155. LJKHS, I, 150.
156. HS: SSTS, 100.   157. CML:TFW, 51.

schools in Japan; selections from "Discourses on the New People," from a history of Western economic thought, a history of Chinese despotism, and a history of Chinese thought; biographies of Garibaldi, and Cavour, and Mazzini; an article on Chinese historical geography; a study of Chinese classics, penned by Chang Ping-lin, seeking partly to elucidate ancient Chinese usage by way of Japanese grammar; editorials on current world events; historical notes based on Gibbon's *Decline and Fall of the Roman Empire;* literary criticism dealing with Homer and Chinese poets; a Reader's Forum with replies to inquiries about Herbert Spencer and medieval Europe; current events, Chinese and Western; and a review of Japanese publications.

Many of the 120 pages of the periodical were thus devoted to Western civilization. Even the articles on China had a factual, analytical approach characteristic of Western scholarship. The journal also carried advertisements on books written by Chinese in Japan on such topics as world geography or foreign constitutional law. The *New People's Miscellany* consequently became a new intellectual horizon. Small wonder that it was smuggled into China and secretly, although widely, copied and reprinted. As the writer of most of these articles, Liang enjoyed a fame unequaled by any other at the time.

A third reason for Liang's influence was his bitter criticism of the Manchu regime, an attitude that suited the time and earned him much acclaim. The irony, however, was that Liang did not want to overthrow the Manchus. Yet, through a combination of circumstances, his writings consistently undermined the regime. One factor was his ambivalence—he sometimes favored revolution. Another reason was his persistent opposition to the Empress Dowager, who was, in effect, the government. By hammering at her debilities, Liang discredited the whole regime. Still another reason was Liang's attempt to present both sides of an argument. While arguing against revolution, he often made statements that brought about the opposite reaction. Thus he wrote: "I have no affection for the Manchus. Whenever I read the *Ten Days' Diary of Yang-chow* and the *Massacre of the City of Chia-ting* my eyes overflow with tears. . . . If there is a way that can save the nation and at the same time avenge us on the Manchus, I would certainly be delighted to follow it. . . . Unfortunately, the two are incompatible."[158] Liang's intention was to stress the importance of national survival over revenge and to urge the people to tolerate the Manchus for the time being, but he failed to realize that by dwelling on the past wrongs of the Manchus, he might unwittingly lend his own weight to the revolutionary cause he sought to combat. Because the wrongs he mentioned were accomplished facts while the

158. LCC:YPSWC, 7.19.43.

incompatibility between revolution and national survival was merely an opinion, the arguments were to his disadvantage from the beginning. When we further consider the rising contempt among Chinese intellectuals for the impotent Manchu court, it seems impossible that Liang's writing would not damage his own cause. Contemporary sources indicate that this was exactly what happened.[159]

Still another factor was his tactics. Liang held that to achieve a shocking effect, a writer should sound more radical than he really was, for "when a revolution is advocated, the people will not feel strange about reform and democracy."[160] Undoubtedly Liang himself followed this technique. But his forecast that the public would only go halfway with him proved inaccurate. The people surpassed his expectations and established a republic that Liang had not wanted.

Because it was his radicalism that attracted the youth, his influence reached its peak during his own most radical period, that is to say, around 1902. In that year the great majority of Chinese students in Japan belonged to the Emperor Protection Society.[161] Although the Manchu court had put a price on his head, individual officials continued to keep in touch with him and solicited his advice on various matters.[162] The procedure adopted by the Manchus in 1905 and 1906 for a constitutional reform strikingly resembled Liang's proposal of 1900.[163] Political assassination, which he had advocated since 1900,[164] appeared in China in 1904.[165] As Yen Fu noted, "Advocating assassination, he made people kill; recommending destruction, he made them deface and destroy."[166]

After 1903, as he turned conservative, Liang's political influence began to wane. The reform movement declined among the Chinese in Japan.[167] In 1905 most of them joined the T'ung Meng Hui organized by Sun Yat-sen.[168] A year later Liang himself admitted that the revolutionists had extended their influences to all parts of China.[169] Having lost the support of the rising generation, Liang shifted his emphasis to government officials and played a game of intrigue. He solicited Yüan Shih-kai's help in 1906 but plotted against him two years later.[170] In a dispute between the Board of Justice and the Supreme Court, he secretly wrote briefs for both sides.[171] Liang

159. LJKHS, I, 240; Yen Fu's letter in HH, 13.32.
160. LCC:YPSWC, 4.11.39.
161. Robert A. Scalapino and Harold Schiffrin, "Early Socialist Currents in the Chinese Revolutionary Movement: Sun Yat-sen Versus Liang Ch'i-ch'ao," JAS (May, 1959), 335.
162. LJKHS, II, 307.   163. HKC:CKC, VI, 748-49.
164. LCC:YPSCC, 2.2.70; LJKHS, I, 100.
165. CKCTSSC, 295.   166. HH, 12.25.2.
167. LJKHS, I, 186.
168. Scalapino and Schiffrin, op. cit., 335.
169. LJKHS, I, 217.   170. Ibid., I, 214, 217; II, 266-67.
171. Ibid., I, 223-24; II, 307.

also sought to organize and influence the members of the National Assembly.[172] When the revolution broke out, he hurriedly returned from Japan hoping to gain a political voice through the control of several army units.[173] But none of his efforts brought him the power he coveted.

By the time his "Enlightened Despotism" appeared in 1905, the Manchu regime had lost all public esteem; thus Liang's stand was directly contrary to the course of public opinion. The situation became even worse after the conclusion of the Treaty of Portsmouth. To the half-enlightened Chinese mind, the Russo-Japanese war conclusively proved the inferiority of autocracy to constitutionalism.[174] Even the Manchus themselves started making preparations for constitutional changes. Liang's advocacy of despotism therefore seemed to the public an obvious anachronism. His further shift to constitutionalism, after the Manchus had decreed it in 1906,[175] smacked of opportunism. By then Liang had been passed over by the main currents of Chinese thought. Basically, Liang probably never had succeeded in making the youth accept his thought. His influence before 1903 came partly from non-political factors and partly from the fact that his thought at the time happened to coincide with the rising tide. The moment this tide crested, Liang's seeming sway over the youth disappeared.

A related factor was the inherent infirmity of Liang's ideas. Endowed by nature with a quick intellect and an intense curiosity, Liang constantly absorbed new ideas without allowing adequate time for their digestion. Had he been content with purely intellectual pursuits, he might in time have developed more profound views. But events dictated otherwise. At the call of his social conscience, Liang expressed himself on national affairs; faced with an eager response, he was for many years unable to slacken the pace of his writing. Especially during his stay in Japan, most of his articles were published as soon as the first drafts were finished.[176] His response to the demand was so rapid that he never had time to reflect and polish. Although a little uneasy at first over his own inadequacy, he was soon overwhelmed by fame and glory and had no time for remorse.[177] Thus he composed essay after essay, marveled at their wide circulation, and shifted his stand almost whimsically, trusting in his own ability to

172. *Ibid.,* II, 307, 313-14. 173. *Ibid.,* II, 339-45.
174. See, for instance, Chang Ch'ien's letter to Yüan Shih-kai as quoted in LCN:PHC, 198-99.
175. LJKHS, I, 212.
176. LCC:YPSWC, 1.1.107. Also see the 1926 Chung Hua Book Company edition of Liang's *Collected Works,* Introduction, p. 1.
177. LCC:YPSWC, 1.1.107.

persuade his youthful followers in whatever he thought was right.[178] But in the long run his flamboyant rhetoric proved no substitute for consistent thinking, and his sway over the students steadily declined in the face of competition from other quarters.

Yen's rather severe censure of Liang was based on his negative role. To Yen's mind a man's position imposed corresponding obligations: Liang's ease in writing demanded that he be cautious.[179] Yet Liang turned all of his bizarre thought to revolution and assassination. It was all right, Yen remarked, for Liang to change his mind, but what about the men assassinated, the regime overthrown, and the institutions destroyed as a result of Liang's old influence?[180] Yen also scoffed at the defense Liang reportedly made of himself after the revolution in 1911. Unwilling to assume a large role in a fight that he had opposed, Liang maintained that he had merely attacked dynastic personalities and not the dynastic house; thus he had little to do with the fall of the monarchy. To this statement Yen's retort was merciless: "If Liang did not realize the difference between China and the West, that in China there was no distinction between the dynasty and the dynastic figures, then all of his learning was in vain."[181] The trouble, Yen continued, was that Liang's primary motive had not been to save China, but to seek fame for himself, and like Faust, he was unable to dismiss the devil he had conjured.[182]

178. One of Liang's friends, Huang Tsün-hsien, once told Liang that he was able to convince people of whatever views he happened to hold even though these views contradicted one another. See LJKHS, I, 203.

179. LCC:YPSWC, 1.1.107.

180. HH, 12.26.5.

181. Ibid., 8.18.6.

182. Ibid., 12.25.3.

[9] *Intellectuals*

and the Revolution of 1911

On October 10, 1911, a chance bomb explosion precipitated a revolutionary uprising in the mid-Yangtze cities of Wuhan. During the same night both the governor-general and the army commander fled. Twelve days later, two other provinces seceded, and within a month half of China's twenty-two provinces had declared their independence. Unable to cope with the rapidly deteriorating situation, the Manchu regent on November 9 yielded power to Yüan Shih-kai, who soon began using the crisis for his own ends. Largely because of his maneuvers, the dynasty fell on February 12, 1912, barely four months after the bomb exploded in Wuchang.

The Manchu abdication was a momentous event, for it marked the end not only of a dynasty but also of the whole imperial era since 221 B.C. Furthermore, it signified the quickening pace of change in China's social and political structure, the end of which is not yet in sight. How do we account for this important episode? At least in a superficial sense, this agitation began among the Chinese in Japan. Accordingly, in this chapter we shall examine the attitudes of these students, their attempts to form political organizations, the response of the Manchus to these popular movements, and, finally, the patterns of provincial secessions.

THE CHINESE IN JAPAN

The account begins with the school founded in the winter of 1897 by the Chinese merchants of Yokohama. With no suitable educators to run the school,[1] they asked Sun Yat-sen for his recommendations. Because he also lacked connections with the intellectuals, Sun referred these merchants to K'ang Yu-wei in Shanghai, who suggested one of his pupils, Hsü Ch'in, as principal and several others as teachers. Under Hsü's administration nationalism became one of the school's most pronounced characteristics. It is said that on every blackboard and textbook were written these words:

> Our national humiliations have not been avenged;
> The people's livelihood is extremely difficult.

1. CKCTSSC, 351-64. This school was first named by Sun Yat-sen as the T'ung-hsi School, which could be translated into English as the Miscellaneous School, obviously an inelegant name. It was K'ang Yu-wei who changed it to Ta-t'ung (Cosmopolitan). This is one of the instances which indicate Sun Yat-sen's lack of a good Chinese classical education. See HHKM, I, 46.

At no time should you forget this.
Try hard, young fellow!

Songs with a similar message were composed, and the students were required to chant them every day. In the curriculum Confucian teachings enjoyed a prominent place, and worship of the Master was conducted every Sunday. On Confucius' birthday in 1897, a special celebration was held with a number of well-known Japanese scholars in attendance. Its theme was Sino-Japanese solidarity against Western encroachment. As a result of Hsü's strenuous efforts, not only did a spirit of patriotism permeate the school but the students also thought of themselves as the future leaders of China.[2]

In 1898 Liang Ch'i-ch'ao arrived in Japan. Shortly afterwards he published a journal, *Public Opinion (Ch'ing I Pao)*, and began making efforts to organize the youth. On June 13, 1899, he and K'ang Yu-wei formed the Emperor Protection Society. Still later he founded a Chinese elementary school in Kobe and a Chinese high school in Tokyo with the help of local Chinese merchants. The school in Toyko opened with an enrollment of about twenty students, seven from Hsü's school at Yokohama and the rest from among Liang's students in Hunan who had chosen to follow him in exile. In addition to English and Japanese, the students were taught the history of Western revolutions, Greek philosophy, and the theories of Rousseau, Montesquieu, Darwin, and Spencer. Great enthusiasm soon developed, and each student aspired to be a Danton, Washington, or Robespierre.[3]

On December 19, 1899, Liang left Japan for the United States on a fund-raising mission. Because of a quarantine measure against Asians in San Francisco, he stopped at Honolulu and remained there for half a year. During this time he conducted propaganda among the Chinese settlers and joined the Triads in order to gain influence over the secret societies.[4] Meanwhile, a major plot was being laid by his friends and students in Tokyo. Under the leadership of T'ang Ts'ai-ch'ang, a former teacher in the Current Affairs Academy at Hunan, some twenty men left Japan to lead insurrections along the Yangtze. Their plan was to launch on August 9, 1900, simultaneous uprisings in five cities, with Hankow as the main center. Unforeseen difficulties soon developed; and, largely because the funds promised by K'ang and Liang were late as well as insufficient, the campaign failed completely. Only at Ta-t'ung did a revolt actually occur, while the campaign in Hankow was postponed twice and then discovered before it could be launched. Twenty men, including T'ang Ts'ai-ch'ang and ten Chinese students

2. FTY:KMIS, I, 47-48, 50-51.
3. *Ibid.*, II, 72. Some of Liang's students had come to Japan before the school opened; others were invited to Japan by the school.
4. LJKHS, I, 102.

from Japan, were ordered beheaded by Governor-General Chang Chih-tung.[5]

Although this failure severely hampered the Emperor Protection Society, the Chinese in Japan were aroused and student activities were spurred on. Before the end of 1900 a journal, *Translation Magazine (I Shu Hui Pien)*, appeared with the purpose of introducing Western writings to the Chinese students. The works of Rousseau, Montesquieu, Spencer, and John Stuart Mill were translated and popularized. In May, 1901, Ch'in Li-shan, a former student of Liang Ch'i-ch'ao, became associated with a new journal, the *Chinese National (Kuo Min Pao)*. Ch'in had led the Ta-t'ung rebellion and had miraculously escaped arrest and death. Blaming K'ang and Liang for T'ang's death, he deserted the royalist cause and openly advocated the overthrow of the Manchus.[6] In line with the practice of Chinese intellectuals of the time, he sought to justify his stand in terms of political philosophy. In an argument reminiscent of Yen Fu's, Ch'in asserted that the origin of monarchy lay in the popular need for a manager, but that as time advanced, the administrator had usurped the rights of the proprietors. Enslavement, Ch'in said, had deprived the Chinese of their vitality and public conscience, with the result that China could hardly survive as a nation. The corrective lay in making the people defend their rights, for the nation belonged to "all and yet none"; and in taxing the masses to pay for indemnities to foreigners, the emperor and his officials were no better than thieves and bandits. As to the specific cause China should follow, Ch'in wrote: "A Western proverb says that the cradle of revolution is France. China is twenty-five times larger than France, and our sufferings are also many times hers. Democracy has spread eastward across the Pacific [*sic*] and has bestowed some of its blessings on Japan. If China does not want to be aroused, that will be the end of the matter. If she should wake up from her sleep and do in the twentieth century what France did in the nineteenth [*sic*], I know the impact will be felt throughout the world."[7] This first open cry for revolution created quite a stir and was quickly emulated by other Chinese. In the spring of 1902, amid rumors that the Manchu regime was ceding Kwangtung to France, the students from that province agitated for secession.[8]

Significantly, the same suggestion was made by Ou Chü-chia, the editor of a Chinese newspaper in San Francisco. In a 26,000-word essay entitled "The New Kwangtung," Ou stressed China's urgent need for progress. He argued that since all men were selfish and placed their own provinces first, progress would be easier to obtain regionally

5. HHKM, I, 257; KTI:CTCK, II, 1097.
6. FTY:KMIS, I, 85-92.   7. HHCSN, 1st series, I, 71.
8. FTY:KMIS, I, 98.

than nationally. In his opinion, Kwangtung had adequate resources and was sufficiently Westernized to take such a step. As moral justification for such a move, he enumerated the wrongs committed by the Manchu regime—its discrimination against the Chinese, its subservience to foreigners, and its cowardice in ceding Hongkong, Macao, Kwangchow Bay, and Kowloon. Quoting Mencius' dictum that "when the king regards the people as grass, they [should] regard him as a robber and an enemy," Ou censured the Chinese for their failure to fight the Manchus. Remorsefully he depicted them as having no foresight and as being little better than animals, but he urged them to bear in mind the misery of the Formosans under Japanese rule as well as the shameful experience of Peking in 1900 when "wives of high officials were raped by Westerners in turn." Somewhat paradoxically, Ou also lauded the heroic quality of the people of Kwangtung, who, he believed, could have stopped the British from occupying Kowloon in 1898 had it not been for the treachery of Governor-General T'an Chung-lin. Since the Manchus preferred to capitulate to foreigners rather than to yield to the Chinese, he could see no alternative but for the people to seek independence by making good use of newspapers, schools, and secret societies.[9]

Ou Chü-chia, the author of this pamphlet, was one of K'ang Yu-wei's closest pupils. He had taught at the Current Affairs Academy in Hunan and had later served as an assistant editor of *Public Opinion* in Japan. In the latter capacity, he offended his mentor K'ang Yu-wei by publishing an essay entitled "An Outline History of Chinese Revolutions," in which he pointedly endorsed T'ang and Wu for overthrowing the Hsia and Yin dynasties. For this indiscretion K'ang ordered him to leave Japan and avoid the "contaminating influence of the Chinese revolutionists." Ou then went to San Francisco, where in 1902, with the help of his secret society brothers, he founded a Chinese newspaper, the *Cosmopolitan Daily (Ta-t'ung jih-pao).* "The New Kwangtung" first appeared in it serially and was later reprinted as a monograph by Liang Ch'i-ch'ao in Japan.[10]

The radicalist trend soon manifested itself in concrete actions. In April, 1902, with the endorsement of both Liang Ch'i-ch'ao and Sun Yat-sen, the two best-known men among the expatriates, the Chinese students proposed to commemorate the Manchu conquest of China 242 years before.[11] A special essay was composed for the occasion by the famous classicist Chang Ping-lin. Before the meeting was finally banned by the Japanese authorities, it had achieved its intended propaganda effect.[12] A few months later nine self-supporting students requested the Chinese minister to sponsor their entrance to the mili-

9. HHCSN, 1st series, I, 269-311.
10. FTY:KMIS, II, 119-121; HHCSN, 1st series, II, 969; LJKHS, II, 305-6.
11. FTY:KMIS, I, 59. 12. *Ibid.,* 57-60.

tary school Seijō Gakkō. When the minister demurred, over twenty students besieged the legation and had to be disbanded by the Japanese police.[13] Somewhat later, during the celebration of the Chinese New Year in 1903, a Hupeh student, Liu Ch'eng-yü, publicly urged his audience of a thousand persons to overthrow the Manchus. The Chinese minister himself was present, but he was unable to do more than cause Liu's expulsion from school.[14] At about the same time the first revolutionary organization came into being. Innocuously called the Young Men's Association, it was engaged both in compiling and distributing revolutionary literature and in planning direct action. In May, 1903, it sponsored a student volunteer corps ostensibly to resist Russian penetration of Manchuria. Daily military drills were held for the two hundred active members, and two representatives were sent to China to solicit the support of Yüan Shih-kai.[15] When the corps was barred by the Japanese government at China's request, several of its members formed a new secret organization called the Association for Universal Military Education. Each of its twenty members pledged to pursue the tasks of propaganda, assassination, and uprising on returning to his home province in China.[16]

By the second half of 1903 many other organizations had appeared. In August, Sun Yat-sen formed a secret military school at Aoyama with fourteen Chinese students. Directed by a Major Hino, this school was to give each entering class eight months of training, but the project foundered after Sun left Japan for Hawaii in September. Another type of organization was the Chinese provincial association. There were many such groups; each had at least one publication, and practically all were anti-Manchuist. They often described the Manchus as "bandits" (*man-tse*), and the Dowager Empress as "the lecherous Yehonala" (*na-la yin-fu*). Even though some of the students still opposed revolution in principle, none of them disputed the allegation that the Manchus were corrupt to the core. As the number of Chinese students in Tokyo steadily increased—from one hundred in 1900 to five hundred in 1902, thirteen hundred in 1904, and fifteen thousand in 1906[17]—the pitch of their political emotions rose correspondingly. By 1907 Yang Tu, a shrewd observer, was telling Liang Ch'i-ch'ao that anti-Manchuism had become "an irrational religion" with the Chinese, and that journals could attract readers only by heaping criticism on the government.[18]

But what were the causes of all of this animosity? The Manchus had treated these students well, and in the earlier years most of them were supported by government scholarships. Even in 1906 a full 53

13. *Supra,* Chapter 3. 14. FTY:KMIS, I, 153-54.
15. *Ibid.,* 106. 16. *Ibid.,* 112.
17. *Supra,* Chapter 8. 18. LJKHS, I, 237, 240.

per cent of them had such aid.[19] On their return to China, they enjoyed at least comparatively good opportunities. Yet many of them made frequent derogatory remarks about the court, and as a group they were the most vociferous people among the opposition. Why?

Perhaps the basic factor lay in the nature of the Chinese literati. For some two thousand years they had accepted Confucianism as absolute truth and assumed that China was the most advanced nation on earth. In the face of China's humiliating defeats in the nineteenth century an agonizing reappraisal became necessary. Broadly, only three attitudes were possible. One was adamant rejection of the West; the second was a mixed feeling of resentment against and admiration for the invaders; and the third was a complete reversal of traditional ethnocentrism and a willingness to admit Western superiority in every respect. Among these three major types, a person might of course make an infinite number of adjustments. He could move from one position to another as the sum total of his outlook and the external circumstances varied. He could experience all three types of reaction at different levels of consciousness, either at the same time or at different times. The first type of reaction—adamant rejection of the West—generally dominated Chinese thinking during the period 1840-60; the second—resentment and admiration—during the years 1870-85; and the third—remorse and self-deprecation—from 1895 to perhaps 1925. The trend in each period exercised an important influence over political events.

Furthermore, a common element behind all these attitudes was a resentment toward those in authority in China, since it was government failures that rendered such soul-searching necessary in the first place. But while resentment was probably present in all cases, its manifestation varied widely according to circumstances. A person who chose to reject the West might not vent his anger against the court because to do so would weaken his psychological basis—traditional virtues—for condemning the alien culture. Similarly, those who were anxious to express their dissatisfaction with the court might feel deterred by personal circumstances. In such cases they would hold back until conditions changed. This could occur in many ways, the quickest being through migration. Even an emigrant of a short term might indulge in an outburst to relieve his long suppressed frustration.

In the case of Chinese students in Japan, the situation was also affected by the problems of communication. In all societies the expression of opinion is limited by such institutional factors as the linguistic structure, the accepted ways of discourse, and the channels through which opinions are communicated to others. In such a tra-

19. J. A. Wallace, "Chinese Students in Tokio and the Revolution," NAS (June 1913), 171.

dition-laden society as China's, all of these factors tended to hinder the expression of radical thought. A notable example was the tutorial system in which most Chinese received their education. The teacher-pupil relationship and the content of the textbooks were such that there was normally little possibility for airing new ideas. A further difficulty lay in the lack of effective channels of communication. In China the usual impersonal medium was through the publication of poems, essays, and couplets, most of which were inadequate and unsuitable for subversive political propaganda.

But the historical and institutional circumstances were altered by Western impact. As the dynasty visibly grew weaker, its ban on political discourse lost force. As part of its reform program the regime itself instituted new channels of communication through the press and the schools. In the first place, it sponsored a full-fledged political journal, *The Chinese and Foreign Record* (*Chung-wai chi-wen*) in 1895. Even though the enterprise failed to withstand conservative pressure and was reorganized within a few months, it yielded two permanent results. First, it stimulated the growth of many reformist clubs in the provinces, each with a publication of its own.[20] Thus it popularized the cause and turned it into a national trend. Second, it was with the *Chinese and Foreign Record* that Liang Ch'i-ch'ao made his debut as a journalist, and his success pointed the way to a new profession. Many young radicals could now achieve national fame within a matter of months. Using a new, more lucid, style of writing they were able to reach a far wider public than had hitherto been possible. As a result, an entirely new situation existed in the formation of Chinese public opinion.

The second major change in the realm of communications stemmed from the schools. Before 1895 modern training in China had only a technical meaning. In that year Sheng Hsüan-huai established a Sino-Western Academy (*Chung-hsi hsueh-t'ang*) in Tientsin with C. D. Tenny as president.[21] A year later Sheng founded a second school in Shanghai with another American, John C. Ferguson, as head.[22] Unlike the earlier government colleges, these schools aimed at giving the students a general education. But more significant was the all-Chinese institution founded in 1897 by Governor Ch'en Pao-chen of Hunan—the Current Affairs Academy (*Shih-Wu hsueh-t'ang*). It had a student body of forty and a faculty of eight, including Liang Ch'i-ch'ao, T'ang Ts'ai-ch'ang (1867-1900), T'an Ssu-t'ung (1865-1898), Ou Chü-chia, and Han Wen-chü, all of whom later became famous either as reformists or as martyrs.[23] Liang, then only twenty-four years old, was the academic head. He led a cloistered life with the students, discoursing on politics and writing copiously on the students'

20. KKC:CKPHS, 123.
21. FA:CEI, 69.
22. *Ibid.*, 70.
23. YTF:TST, 104-5; LJKHS, I, 45.

book reports. In these comments he maintained that all past emperors were enemies of the people, that a prolonged dynasty was an evil, and that his anger "made his hair stand on end" whenever he read about the Manchu massacre of the Chinese in 1645. Because the students lived apart in a dormitory, Liang's methods and opinions were not known to the public until after the New Year's vacation. Then a storm of protest broke, but the students, all between fourteen and twenty years old, were enthralled. In spite of the shortness of Liang's stay, they felt deeply attached to him. After he fled to Japan in 1898, eleven of them braved all difficulties to follow him there.[24]

The Current Affairs Academy was not alone in serving as a channel of revolutionary propaganda. After 1902 many schools were established, and became primary vehicles for the spread of radical ideas. From the point of view of communications, these institutions differed from the old tutorial system in several respects. In the first place their larger student bodies and new dormitory facilities made possible intimate contact and political discussion in an atmosphere charged with emotionalism. Moreover, the teachers were no longer the same. By their nature the schools attracted radicals who were eager to inspire the students with new ideas. Even the locations of these schools are different. For the most part they were in larger cities where the general environment was far more cosmopolitan. In the context of political crisis and nascent nationalism, they soon became a hotbed of revolution.

We saw in Chapter 3 how officials like Chang Chih-tung promoted the movement to study in Japan. In their anxiety to re-educate the intellectuals, they failed to understand that resulting changes would have an inherently radical bias. Away from his usual surroundings, a student in Japan no longer needed to fear the consequences of political unorthodoxy, either for himself or for his family. Indeed, the pressure was now operating in the other direction. On their arrival thousands of Chinese congregated in a single district of Tokyo, with little to occupy their time except political discussion with their fellow expatriates.[25] Predisposed to compare all things by a national measuring rod, they saw in every one of their experiences a reminder of China's debility, from the personal prejudices they encountered to the impressions they gained of Japan's striking progress.[26] Added to

24. LJKHS, I, 92.

25. See, for instance, Sung Chiao-jen's and Ching Mei-chiu's diaries in HHKM, II, 209-16, 242-56.

26. Significantly, the outward appearance of a modern city never failed to impress the Chinese intellectuals. Thus, Yen Fu, K'ang Yu-wei, Liang Ch'i-ch'ao, and Sun Yat-sen all noted the contrast between the clean, paved roads of a foreign city and the extreme untidiness of a Chinese one. As early as 1897 Liang wrote an essay entitled "Good Roads are the Beginning of Good Government" (LCC: YPSWC, 2.2.17-19).

these changes in social environment was a broadening of their intellectual horizon. Japan offered a flourishing press and ample translations of Western works. While a cursory glance at these might not enable the sojourners to gain any profound knowledge, it was sufficient to reinforce their feeling that China must change, by violence if necessary. As this belief became the dominant trend, even the more hesitant persons in the Chinese student colony felt a pressure to conform.

Just as in China, journalism became an important means of propaganda. Several factors contributed to the rise of a powerful press among the Chinese in Japan. One was the similarity between Japanese and Chinese, which facilitated the printing of Chinese works in Japan. Another was the slight distance between the two countries, which enabled the expatriates to maintain contacts and develop the home audience necessary to the success of an overseas press. Still another was the personal talent of Liang Ch'i-ch'ao, whose lucid style and emotional appeal popularized the cause and set the pattern for practically all of the publicists.

TSOU JUNG AND THE KIANGSU JOURNAL CASE

Repercussions were soon felt in China, as can be seen from the life of Tsou Jung (1885-1905). A precocious child of a mercantile family in Szechuan, Tsou had a good command of the classics but he refused to attend the civil-service examinations. Instead, he went to Japan in 1902 and joined the student volunteer corps when it was formed. Angered by its forced dissolution, Tsou sought revenge in an impetuous way. He caught a Chinese supervisor of military students in an improper act by rushing into the man's bedroom unexpectedly. He then slapped the supervisor's face and cut off his queue. Having made a mortal enemy and having jeopardized his stay in Japan, Tsou returned to Shanghai and joined a local revolutionary group, the Patriotic Society.[27] He then published a 20,000-word pamphlet entitled "The Revolutionary Army" ("Ke Ming Chün"), in which he discussed the meaning of "race," the need for revolution, the importance of nurturing a revolutionary spirit, and the basic principles of a revolutionary program.[28] Although it lacked disciplined thought, Tsou's pamphlet was effective propaganda. Written in a lucid, almost colloquial style similar to Liang Ch'i-ch'ao's, it offered interesting information on the government's exploitation of the masses and on its discrimination against Chinese civil servants. It challenged many accepted judgments of society: it accused the emperors K'ang-hsi and Ch'ien-lung of leading the most decadent lives, and it criticized Tseng Kuo-fan and Li Hung-chang for their subservience to the Manchus. Coming at a time when existing institutions were being discredited,

27. HHKM, I, 365-66.   28. SC:SHS, 626-661.

Tsou's denunciation aroused his readers and stimulated their thought. Moreover, his pamphlet presented the comforting argument that except for Manchu misrule, China would have played a glorious role in world politics, possibly even replacing the Western powers in the conquest of India, Poland, Egypt, and Turkey.[29] As to the way of saving the country, Tsou blamed the subservient behavior of the Chinese on the traditional stress of loyalty to the prince. In a sentence that foreshadowed the stand of many later intellectuals, he called on the Chinese to free themselves from such basic causes of evil. Only then, he said, could China have a revolution similar to the French and the American. In phrasing that indicated an imperfect knowledge of Yen Fu's theme, Tsou predicted that unless a revolution occurred, the iron law of evolution would work in reverse and China would degenerate into a primeval world.[30]

Shortly after the appearance of this pamphlet, the Patriotic Society to which Tsou belonged became involved in a legal suit. Previously the society had operated a school for the benefit of students expelled or withdrawn from government institutes. In order to raise funds, members of the society undertook to write editorials for a newspaper, the Kiangsu Journal (Su Pao). When this paper prospered, its owner Ch'en Fan entrusted the editorship to a member of the group, Chang Shih-chao, who initiated a sustained attack on the Manchu regime.[31] The emperor was insultingly called by his personal name and described as "an idiot who could not distinguish one kind of grain from another." The Manchus were described as "thieves," "stupid pigs," and no better than the "foreign devils."[32] By such extreme defiance the paper finally forced the government to take action. Late in June of 1903 the governor-general at Nanking dispatched a circuit intendant to Shanghai, who in a conciliatory gesture divulged his mission to a member of the Patriotic Society. The aim undoubtedly was to forewarn the revolutionaries and to urge them to flee.[33] What transpired between this member, Wu Chih-hui, and the others is in dispute, but it is likely that he withheld the information from several members with whom he was on poor terms.[34] At any rate Tsou Jung, Chang Ping-lin, and four others were arrested by the settlement police between June 29 and July 1, 1903.[35] But the foreign authorities refused the Chinese demand for extradition and allowed the regime only to sue the writers within the bounds of international settlement. On May 21, 1904, the foreign-Chinese court announced its verdict. Only two defendants were found guilty; for

29. Ibid., 644.
31. HHHIL, I, 276-77.
33. Ibid., 373.
35. KTI:CTCK, II, 1183.

30. Ibid., 629, 644.
32. Ibid., I, 374-75.
34. Ibid., 398-407.

sedition Chang Ping-lin was condemned to three years' imprisonment, and Tsou Jung, to two.[36] The *Kiangsu Journal* case proved to be a serious setback for the Manchus. While Chinese publications abroad had long abused the court with impunity, it was the first time such an attack had taken place in China. Consequently, much of the regime's prestige was at stake. Once the arrests were made, the government tried in every possible way to obtain the extradition of the defendants, but it failed and had to sue them in a foreign court. For a government operating on the principle of paternalism, such a procedure was highly humiliating. Moreover, the regime incurred a further reverse in its attempt to inflict heavy sentences on the accused. For ten months it pressured the foreign diplomats in Peking to accede to its request. The governor-general at Wuchang was in constant communication with his colleagues at Nanking, and Grand Secretary Chang Chih-tung was informed of all the consultations. A number of officials were sent to Shanghai, and among those who sided with the government was the noted Sinologue John C. Ferguson. Yet the government's efforts backfired.[37] Under the scorching limelight every setback was a fresh blow to the regime's dwindling prestige. The image of an inviolable government was quickly replaced by the sorrowful spectacle of an impotent state. The opposition press mushroomed, and its criticism was less restrained than ever. All the ablest officials could do was to procure a few mouthpieces of their own, whose enunciations were generally ignored by the reading public.[38]

Of the two prisoners only Chang Ping-lin served out his terms. Plagued by poor health, Tsou Jung died in confinement on April 3, 1905. The rumors of foul play, coupled with the previous publicity of his trial and a government ban on his book, turned *The Revolutionary Army* into one of the best sellers of the time. It went through more than twenty printings, with a single copy occasionally selling for ten taels of silver.[39] For his outstanding contributions to the cause, Tsou Jung was remembered by all his comrades. During the short administration of Sun Yat-sen in 1912, he was posthumously honored with the title of Grand Marshall (*Ta-chiang-chün*).[40]

According to contemporary sources, the *Kiangsu Journal* case also led indirectly to a series of uprisings in Chekiang and Anhwei between 1906 and 1907. Because Chang was a native of Chekiang, the trial aroused strong feelings in that province. To take advantage of this situation, T'ao Ch'eng-chang (1877-1912), another Chekiang student in Japan, sailed for home early in 1904. Concentrating his

---

36. HHKM, I, 384. According to Kuo T'ing-i, the date should be May 22, 1904. See KTI:CTCK, II, 1204.

37. HHKM, I, 380-84.   38. KKC:CKPHS, 140.
39. HHKM, I, 366.   40. *Ibid.*

attention on the six southeastern prefectures, he spent the next ten months crisscrossing the country to contact secret societies, spread revolutionary ideals, and organize converts.[41] With the backing of some local merchants, he formed revolutionary centers at Hangchow and Shaoshing under the guise of prefectural associations and schools for physical education. On the grounds that the youth needed preparation for the conscription system, T'ao petitioned for and obtained official endorsement of his school at Shaoshing. He made it a habit to have the local prefect present at commencement exercises. In this way he received permission to purchase arms and operated his school for three years without outside interference.[42]

Meanwhile, T'ao traveled widely and kept up with his other activities. On one of his trips to Japan, he became acquainted with Chiu Chin, a girl from Chekiang who had been separated from her husband and wished to dedicate herself to the revolutionary cause. During the summer of 1905 Chiu Chin made a trip home. Through T'ao's introduction she joined the Restoration Society in Shanghai, which had been formed by several members of the Association for Universal Military Education to carry out political assassination. Chiu Chin then went home to secure funds from her mother. On her return to Japan, she found the Chinese students divided on the issue of recent regulative measures taken by the Japanese government, some favoring and some opposed to a mass withdrawal from Japan. Chiu naturally sided with the radical view, and when this stand failed to gain enough support, she returned to China on her own.[43]

In December, 1906, uprisings occurred in several places in Hunan, partly because of a local famine and partly in protest to the execution of a secret society leader by the Ch'ing officials. Although these revolts came as a surprise to the revolutionaries, the Restoration Society in Shanghai decided to launch a responsive campaign. Chiu Chin was made head of the Ta-t'ung School in her native Shaoshing. In her plan of action, members of the affiliated secret societies were divided into eight groups and comrades of the Restoration Society into sixteen. They were to rise simultaneously in several counties on July 6, 1907.[44]

Earlier, the resourceful T'ao Ch'eng-chang had extended the range of his activities. In 1903 he met in Japan a school teacher named Hsü Hsi-lin, whom he converted to the revolutionary cause. Upon his return to Shaoshing, Hsü founded two schools and a bookshop to spread the revolutionary ideal. A great enthusiast for marksmanship, he carried a pistol and often practiced on a dummy representing a Russian. Between 1904 and 1905 Hsü made a trip to Shanghai, met T'ao there, and through him joined the Restoration Society. T'ao

41. *Ibid.*, III, 12. 42. *Ibid.*, 26.
43. *Ibid.*, 61. 44. *Ibid.*, 62-63.

Ch'eng-chang had always believed in "revolution from within" (*chung-yang ke-ming*), which meant, among other things, joining officialdom and sabotaging the regime from a position of authority. Agreeing with T'ao, Hsü obtained the backing of a Shaoshing merchant and with fifty thousand silver dollars purchased the title of circuit intendant. Believing that he now needed more military knowledge, Hsü went to Japan to seek admission to a military school, but he failed the physical examination on account of myopia. Before he could decide on his next step, a rumor reached him that the Manchus intended to murder Chang Ping-lin in prison. He hastened to Shanghai in the hope of securing Chang's freedom, but when he was not able to do so, he returned again to Japan. His intention was now to study military logistics. After another futile effort, he departed for China in the summer of 1906.[45]

In his purchase of the official title, Hsü was sponsored by his cousin Yü Lien-san, a former provincial governor. In 1906 Yü's Manchu pupil En Ming became governor of Anhwei. Seizing this opportunity Hsü went to Anhwei and was by the spring of 1907 placed in charge of the police school at Anking. From this strategic position Hsü conspired with Chiu Chin. The plan was to launch uprisings in Anhwei and Chekiang toward the end of the fifth lunar month. But as the date approached, their scheme suffered several setbacks. In the first place, a member of their group, Yeh Yang-kao, implicated them after he was arrested in Shanghai. When the governor-general at Nanking cabled the names to En Ming, the latter handed the list to Hsü Hsi-lin for action, unaware that Hsü's alias was on it. Feeling that time was running out, Hsü decided to advance the date of the uprising. At the same time things also went wrong in Chekiang. In line with a common tendency among the revolutionaries, Chiu Chin had relied on secret society leaders who were tougher than they were intelligent. In one county the insurrection broke out prematurely; in another, the plan leaked out so that the conspirators were surrounded by government troops before they could make a move; in yet another the ringleader carelessly revealed his plan when arrested on other charges.[46] As the situation got out of hand, Hsü decided to gamble on assassination. At the graduation exercise of the police school on the twenty-sixth of the fifth month (July 6, 1905), he shot and wounded the governor. With the aid of two accomplices, Hsü had intended to kill all the high officials at once and to declare himself governor. But he had not calculated on how the rules of etiquette might affect his marksmanship. According to Chinese custom, a man could not wear glasses in the presence of men of equal or superior status. Hsü took his glasses off after the governor arrived and did not have an opportunity to replace them when he started shooting. Through rapid

45. *Ibid.*, 57.   46. *Ibid.*, 34-36.

firing he injured En Ming, but the other officials escaped. When Hsü ordered the students to march to the armory, a number managed to elude him; those who went found that the ammunition stored there did not fit their guns.[47] The whole plot collapsed, and Hsü was caught and executed on the same day. A strenuous effort was then made to capture all the co-conspirators. Arrested at Kiukiang, Hsü's brother, who was not an active revolutionary, revealed Hsü's relations with Chiu Chin. On the basis of this and other information gathered in Chekiang, government troops beseiged the Ta-t'ung School. Chiu Chin was forewarned by her friends at the provincial capital, but she was paralyzed by indecision. On July 15, 1907, she too was executed at Hangchow.[48]

According to T'ao Ch'eng-chang, the Chekiang uprisings had an important influence on subsequent events. In the first place, local revolts continued until April, 1908, killing "thousands of government troops" and creating a tension that seriously jeopardized the regime.[49] Furthermore, the fear of assassination materially affected the behavior of many high officials. Some of them placed spies among the Chinese students in Tokyo; others sought to obtain good will through money gifts and other kindnesses.[50] Their constant concern for their personal safety lowered their morale and contributed to the success of the revolution of 1911.

SUN YAT-SEN AND THE ANTI-MANCHU STRUGGLES

Before going further in the account of conditions in China, we must take another look at the Chinese students in Japan. A major event between 1900 and 1905 was the increasing prominence of Sun Yat-sen. Sun was born in 1866 to a very poor family at Hsiang-shan near Macao. His father was a hired farm hand who could not afford even to buy shoes.[51] Extreme poverty forced him to marry late, and when the children were born, he had hardly the means of giving them a proper education. At the age of seventeen Yat-sen's elder brother emigrated as a laborer to Hawaii, while Yat-sen himself, only five years old, helped his two sisters chop wood and do other chores. Contrary to the claims of his admirers in later years, Sun Yat-sen probably did not begin his schooling until he was nine, and then only on a

47. *Ibid.*, 39. I have not seen any other source mention that Hsü took his spectacles off and did not put them on again. But in his narrative T'ao Ch'eng-chang in one place describes Hsü as an excellent marksman and in another place dwells at length on how Hsü suffered from myopia and could not aim at his victims (HHKM, III, 39, 56). This discrepancy would be an inexplicable riddle if we did not know the custom at that time. The interesting thing is that this custom has completely disappeared under Western impact. Not too many Chinese know that there was such a custom.

48. HHKM, III, 42, 63.   49. *Ibid.*, 73.
50. *Ibid.*, 48; KMWH, 225-26.   51. CHC:TMH, 6.

part-time basis.[52] In 1879 his brother, who had done well in Hawaii, brought him to Honolulu, where for three years he studied at a British missionary school, learning, among other things, Chinese. He then went to an American school and spent a year there. Returning to Hongkong in 1883, he had still another year of basic education in two different schools. Between 1886 and 1892 he pursued six years of medical training in Canton and Hongkong, which completed his formal instruction.[53] Neither the length (a total of eleven years) nor the quality of his education was impressive. In this respect his background differed from that of Yen Fu and Liang Ch'i-ch'ao, who had sound classical educations.

Although he studied medicine, Sun always had political ambitions. In 1890 he sought the patronage of a fellow native of Hsiang-shan, Cheng Tsao-ju, minister to the United States between 1881 and 1885. In a letter Sun told Cheng of his long cherished desire "to be of service to society" (*yung-shih*). He modestly hoped that he could "practice his statecraft within a county" and then be allowed to write down proven truths for the world's benefit.[54] How Cheng reacted to Sun's hopes is unknown; at that time he received no appointment, either as a county magistrate or in any other capacity.

After graduating from the Medical College for Chinese, Sun briefly practiced medicine in Macao. But his career was cut short by colonial discrimination late in 1892, when his license was withdrawn because "he was not a resident."[55] After a short stay in Canton he went north in 1894 to seek the patronage of Li Hung-chang. While in Shanghai he met Wang T'ao, a famous radical who had helped James Legge in his translations of Chinese classics. At Sun's request, Wang polished the phrasing of Sun's memorandum to Li Hung-chang.[56] But Li was either unimpressed with Sun's ideas or more concerned with the critical situation in Korea. At any rate Sun received only a perfunctory endorsement of his scheme for an agricultural-sericultural association, and with this scant reference he went to Hawaii in October, 1894. A month later, he founded a secret revolutionary organization called the Revive China Society (*Hsing Chung Hui*).[57]

A look at the social composition of this society reveals the milieu in which Sun moved. Practically all of the 112 persons who joined between November, 1894, and September, 1895, worked as cooks, tailors, farmers, laborers, and low-echelon employees of the colonial services. Of the 500 persons who joined the society between 1894 and 1905, only 316 names can be traced. Of these only about 30 were educated; most of the rest were Chinese settlers—cooks, laborers, and the

52. *Ibid.*, p. 9, footnote 5.   53. KFNP, I, 21, 24-28, 31, 34, 38, 45.
54. CHC:TMH, 24.   55. KFNP, I, 46.
56. SYL:HTCC, 23; HHKM, I, 28.   57. KFNP, 51.

like.[58] Few intellectuals became members, and this deficiency seriously impaired the work of the organization. For a time the party was unable to do any propagandizing beyond the distribution of some seventeenth century anti-Manchu pamphlets.[59] Indeed, the Revive China Society, although well known in later years for historical reasons, was undistinguished during its existence from 1894 to 1905. In this period, only two small uprisings were organized, one in Canton in 1895 and one at Hui-chou in 1900.[60] With the exception of Sun Yat-sen, none of the members of the society became national figures.

Why did the literati shun Sun's group? For one thing, they were unprepared for revolutionary ideas; for another, they were deeply suspicious of Sun, whose background differed so much from theirs. As Sun recalled in his autobiography, they regarded him as "a bandit, an unprincipled man guilty of treason . . . [who was] as untouchable as a poisonous snake or a wild animal."[61]

But the intellectual climate began to change between 1895 and 1900. First, there was Yen Fu's attack on the monarchy as such; then came Liang Ch'i-ch'ao's censure of the Dowager Empress and his cry for an end to the status quo. Whatever their intentions might have been, Yen and Liang virtually destroyed the sanctity of the existing order. Revolution therefore became at least conceptually respectable, and Sun Yat-sen was not a snake but a man after all.

Politically, the Manchus had made many suicidal moves. The imprisonment of the emperor in 1898 was followed by an incredible resort to witchcraft in 1900, and when this proved unavailing, the policy was shifted to the other extreme of appeasing the foreigners at all costs. In official terms the strategy was now to "gain the good will of other nations through a proper evaluation of China's own strength" (*liang chung-kuo chih wu-li, chieh ke-kuo chih huan-hsin*).[62] Apart from the euphemistic phrasing, this meant that the court would purchase its own tranquillity at the expense of China's national interests. To those who still cherished some illusion of the dynasty, this idea was a revelation of the first order, for it meant that if China was to resist the foreigners, leadership must come from other quarters. Revolution was thus the sole means of achieving national salvation.

Accordingly the years 1903 and 1904 saw a great acceleration of student activities. Both at home and in Japan, Chinese publications mushroomed, as did organizations for direct military action. Significantly, most of the groups in China were not connected with one another even though the influence of several Japanese-educated individuals was in every case unmistakable. The role they played created an image and in turn made all Chinese radicals anxious to

58. HCT:HH, 45.   59. FTY:KMIS, I, 10-11.
60. HCT:HH, 31, 33; KFNP, I, 98-101.
61. KFCC, I, 38.   62. HHKM, I, 343.

secure guidance from Tokyo. As revolutionary activities sprouted in China, the need for a consolidated central organization was increasingly felt by the Chinese in Japan.

Among the expatriates, one of the most prominent was Sun Yat-sen. While the Revive China Society had been dormant since 1900, Sun had become famous for other reasons. In 1896 he had been kidnapped by the Chinese legation in London. After his release through the intervention of the British Foreign Office, he became an international figure.[63] In August, 1897, he returned to Japan and quickly developed friendships with several Japanese, especially Miyazaki Torazō, an associate of Inukai Ki, later a premier of Japan. Wishing to extend their influence over future Chinese leaders, these Japanese went out of their way to help the expatriates, and Sun was probably the most favored of all.[64] Through a combination of circumstances he was similarly successful in developing Western connections. He was able to rely on Sir James Cantlie in the kidnapping incident of 1896, and he derived much help from Governor Doumer and the French government between 1903 and 1908.[65] All of these connections stood him in good stead with the Chinese, who were only too mindful of the crucial importance of foreign aid.

An additional but related factor was Sun's understanding of the West. He was one of a very few among the expatriates in Tokyo with a firsthand knowledge of Europe and America, a factor that powerfully strengthened his claims of good connections with the West. Conscious of his advantages, Sun developed a habit of dwelling on world conditions in all his talks and speeches. Some of his remarks were accurate and even perspicacious, others were undiscerning and incorrect, but all were revelations to the eager and uninformed Chinese intellectuals of the time. A further advantage was Sun's own personality. By all contemporary accounts he had a magnetic quality; people found him amiable and even genteel.[66] Perhaps the year 1901 saw a decisive change in Sun's relationship with the students. Before that time he was regarded as an unsavory character, whereas afterwards he increasingly became one of them. It was in 1901 that he joined, or was asked to join, the Kwangtung Independence Association,[67] and in 1902 that he sponsored the commemoration of the 242nd anniversary of the Manchu conquest of China.[68] By the time he organized the secret military school in 1903, his home in Yokohama was frequented by many students.[69] Thus, through the

63. KFNP, I, 67-72.
64. JMB:JSYS, *passim,* especially pages 202-205.
65. *Ibid.,* 115, 125.
66. WCH:CC, Vol. V, Book IX, pp. 46-49. Also see Chang Ping-lin's remarks quoted in HHHIL, I, 271.
67. FTY:KMIS, I, 98.   68. *Ibid.,* 59.
69. *Ibid.,* 133.

turn of external circumstances, Sun's standing among the revolutionaries improved while his direct role in revolutionary activities declined.

Seeking to strengthen the image of his foreign connections, Sun made frequent trips abroad. Between October, 1895, and December, 1911, he was practically never in China. From 1895 to March, 1907, he in effect used Japan as a home base, but was there less than half of the time.[70] During this period he made two extensive tours of America and Europe, the first from 1895 through 1897 and the second from 1903 through 1905. On the latter occasion he spent five months in Hawaii and almost a year in America. Arriving in England on December 12, 1904, he visited Brussels, Berlin, and Paris in the following spring and administered in each city a revolutionary oath to the Chinese students there. On June 11, 1905, he left Marseilles for Japan.[71] When he reached Yokohama on July 19, he was welcomed by over a hundred Chinese student representatives.[72]

On July 28, Sun met Huang Hsing (1874-1916) through their mutual friends Miyazaki Torazō[73] and Yang Tu, a student leader from Hunan.[74] Huang was from the same province as Yang and went to Japan as a government scholar in 1902. Like many other Chinese students he rapidly developed revolutionary tendencies. With seven others he founded the *Translations by Students Abroad (Yu-hsueh i-pien)*, and a year later he joined the Association for Universal Military Education. On June 4, 1903, after graduating from the Kōbun Institute, a school established especially for Chinese students, Huang left Tokyo for Hunan.[75] As he passed through Shanghai, he met Hu Yüan-t'an, a fellow provincial who had been in Japan and who was now principal of the Ming-te School in Changsha. At Hu's invitation Huang joined his faculty, but in addition he founded a Japanese language institute of his own. True to his pledge to the Association for Universal Military Training, Huang used every opportunity to spread revolutionary ideas. According to contemporary sources, he succeeded so well that youths not supporting the revolution were condemned by their fellow students, and among Hunan's young revolutionaries, Ming-te graduates formed the great majority.[76] But Huang also sought to influence the military men. To accomplish this end he relied mainly on the pamphlets written by Chinese students in Japan. It was said that on one journey to Wuhan, Huang distributed no less than four thousand copies of Tsou Jung's *The Revolutionary Army* and Ch'en T'ien-hua's *Awake! (Meng hui-t'ou,* a pamphlet in rime which was then as popular as Tsou's work). Such activities naturally attracted attention, and the governor of Hunan soon ordered an in-

70. KFNP, I, 63-176.
72. HHKM, II, 4.
74. YSK, 12; HHHIL, II, 141.
76. HHKM, IV, 276.

71. *Ibid.,* 145.
73. HCT:HH, 40.
75. HCT:HH, 12.

vestigation. But neither he nor his assistants really wanted to perse-
cute the revolutionaries. All they wanted was to prevent a too obvious
violation of the law. On the recommendation of Huang's gentry
friends, the case against him was dismissed.[77]

Huang's larger aim was of course military action. In December,
1903, he formed a secret organization by the name of China Rise
Society *(Hua Hsing Hui)*. This was affiliated with another called the
Common Front Society *(T'ung Ch'ou Hui)*, whose purpose was to rally
the secret societies under a revolutionary banner. For a time the latter
organization did well; it reportedly controlled an underground force
of a hundred thousand men.[78] After raising a substantial sum of
money through contributions from his gentry friends, Huang decided
to launch an insurrection on the birthday of the Dowager Empress,
which fell on the tenth day of the tenth month, or November 16,
1904.[79] But the scheme miscarried after vital information leaked out
either through espionage or indiscretion. On October 24, a warrant for
Huang's arrest was issued. As usual, Huang was forewarned and was
able to hide in a former official's home. Later, a pastor helped him
leave Changsha.[80] After a short stay in Shanghai, Huang reached
Japan toward the end of 1904. Hearing that his underground cohorts
in Hunan were ready for another coup, he hastened home in the
spring of 1905. But even before he arrived, the leader of the group
was arrested and executed. For the third time Huang sought refuge in
Japan. It was then that he met Sun Yat-sen.[81]

In their meeting the two quickly agreed on a unified organization
for all revolutionaries. After some discussion among Huang's followers,
a formal meeting with Sun took place on July 30, 1905, at the office of
the Japanese Black Dragon Society. Between sixty and seventy persons
attended, and in spite of the small number of Sun's own followers
present, he was made president of the Alliance Society *(T'ung Meng
Hui)*, which was organized to pursue the four aims of "overthrowing
the Manchus, restoring China, establishing democracy, and equalizing
the land rights." On August 13, a student meeting was held at the
Fuji View Restaurant, with more than thirteen hundred men attending.[82] In his speech Sun declared that for many years he had been
associated exclusively with the secret societies and that this new support from the student class was a sign of China's progress. Discussing
his recent tour of America, England, Germany, and France, he
expressed his conviction that Chinese civilization was superior to
Western and that with some modernization China could match or
even surpass the West within ten to twenty years.[83] While his speech

77. HCT:HH, 17.
79. *Ibid.*, 19.
81. HCT:HH, 40.
83. KFCC, III, 1-8.

78. *Ibid.*, 21.
80. HHKM, IX, 279.
82. HHKM, II, 4.

was fairly short, it provided a typical example of his approach. He had faith in Chinese culture and was confident of its future. Both the conviction and the optimism must have deeply moved his anxious listeners.

After its formation, the first task of the society was propaganda. By agreement with Huang Hsing's group, the Alliance Society took over its magazine, *Twentieth-Century China,* and renamed it the *People's Journal (Min Pao).*[84] The first issue appeared on November 26, 1905. In an editorial signed by Sun three basic revolutionary concepts— nationalism, democracy, and socialism—were advanced. Significantly, he attributed each term to a Western origin: thus, nationalism developed after the fall of Rome; democracy was generated by the eclipse of European absolutism; and socialism appeared as the after- math of the Industrial Revolution.[85] In his view these three principles constituted a proper ideological basis for the new China. While his followers developed this theme in subsequent issues of the journal, Liang Ch'i-ch'ao bitterly contested it through the columns of the *New People's Miscellany.* It was his view that nationalism should be broadened to include the Manchus in a struggle against the foreign "races," that only enlightened despotism could achieve the supreme goal of strengthening China, and that economic progress in China depended far more upon industrial than agricultural productivity. Liang was particularly disdainful of Sun's land program, which he held to be confusing and irrelevant to China's problems. In its stead, Liang favored the development of private capital under state control—a kind of "social reformism" characterized by public owner- ship of utilities, factory laws, regulation of monopolies, progressive income taxes, and similar measures.[86]

Although Liang's criticism of Sun's land program was not un- justified, he missed the point by failing to realize that the burning issue of the day was not socialism but anti-Manchuism. There is no question that on this point the great majority of the Chinese in Tokyo agreed with Sun. Liang's valiant struggle merely spread Sun's reputa- tion and increased his following. On the first anniversary of the *People's Journal* in December, 1906, no less than six thousand joined in the celebration.[87] The journal was now being smuggled into China while the *New People's Miscellany* was rapidly losing ground. In the seventh month of 1907 it ceased publication altogether.[88]

However, certain difficulties confronted the revolutionists.[89] To

---

84. HCT:HH, 48; KFNP, I, 152-53.   85. HHKM, II, 259.
86. Robert A. Scalapino and Harold Schiffrin, "Early Socialist Currents in the Chinese Revolutionary Movement: Sun Yat-sen Versus Liang Ch'i-ch'ao," JAS (May, 1959), 321-42; HIS:CTTS, IV, 2425-35.
87. KFNP, I, 165.   88. LJKHS, I, 227.
89. Because many, perhaps most, intellectuals at the time wavered between

begin with, not all Japanese officials favored aiding the Chinese radicals. The Japanese Foreign Office in particular had misgivings about Sun and his Japanese cohorts. In February, 1907, it decided to heed the Manchus' protest and ask Sun to leave Japan. To soften the blow, it presented him with a sizable sum of money, supplemented by personal gifts from sympathetic individuals.[90] Ironically, this new affluence precipitated a feud within the revolutionary ranks. Because Sun left only a small sum with the *People's Journal*, then faced with a financial crisis, its editor, Chang Ping-lin, loudly condemned him in party circles.[91] Meanwhile, four uprisings occurred in China between May and December of 1907. These were largely the work of Huang Hsing, but because they failed, the members soon became dissatisfied with their peregrinating leader, Sun Yat-sen. T'ao Ch'eng-chang, the head of the Chekiang clique, attempted to have Sun ousted from the presidency, and only Huang Hsing's unswerving support saved him from this embarrassment.[92]

The four uprisings of 1907 took place in the southern provinces of Kwangtung, Kwangsi, and Yunnan. The first two were small local revolts, one lasting six days and the other, ten.[93] The third revolt, which began on September 1, 1907, in the Ch'in-chou prefecture, was led by the local secret societies. At its height the rebels were said to possess some four hundred guns. They succeeded in capturing a county seat, Fang-ch'eng, and in killing the magistrate. But the expected mutiny of government troops did not occur, and the movement collapsed after seventeen days.[94]

The fourth campaign took place on November 30, 1907, at a border mountain pass between Kwangsi and French Indo-China. The plot was established by Sun's emissaries and several local bandits. Mainly because the government forces were extremely weak, one hundred rebels succeeded in holding a fort for eight days. During that time Sun, Huang, a Japanese, and an opium-smoking Frenchman visited the fort for a night.[95] This was the only time after 1895 that Sun himself was near a battle scene.

Between March and May of 1908 two more uprisings occurred.

---

reform and revolution and because most self-professed constitutionists did in fact participate in the revolution, it is considered better to use the word "revolutionaries" to describe both the revolutionists and the constitutionalists who did revolutionary work.

90. Reports on the exact amount Sun received vary from 13,000 dollars (SYL: HTCC, 30) to 80,000 yen (JMB:JSYS, 123). Official Kuomintang sources choose the figure 15,000 dollars, 10,000 from the Japanese government and 5,000 from the stockbroker. See KFNP, I, 176.

91. *Ibid.*; HCT:HH, 53.   92. HCT:HH, 54.

93. KFCC, VI, 367-68.   94. KFNP, I, 188-91.

95. KFCC, VI, 370-71; KFNP, I, 193-95. The latter source contains two misprints of dates on page 193. See also HCT:HH, 67.

Both were based in French Indo-China and were in many ways a continuation of the earlier attempt at the mountain pass. In the first of these Huang Hsing marched into southwestern Kwangtung at the head of two hundred men. For forty-three days they battled their way through two provinces, hoping that government troops would rise and join them. When this hope failed, the venture collapsed.[96] In the second campaign, the leader of one of the secret societies raised a force of four hundred men and captured the city of Hokow across the river from his base at Laokai in French Indo-China. After advancing northward to Mengtzu, the rebels were defeated by the larger government forces. This effort lasted from April 30 to May 26, or for twenty-six days.[97]

For almost two years the Alliance Society was unable to organize further military action. A mood of frustration and distress descended upon the members. Seeing no future in armed rebellion, they were increasingly attracted to the idea of assassination. This trend was fully reflected by editorials in the People's Journal, one of which read: "That which I respect in the Indian civilization [sic] is the spirit of the warrior. . . . Why do I wish to extol this spirit? It is that I prefer to substitute military action by assassination and group exercise by personal labor. While we still retain a common goal, our action will be on an individual basis. This is the proper way to initiate a new era."[98] It is important to note that although assassination had been practiced since 1900, it had hardly proved to be an effective method of securing political change. Out of the more than six attempts between 1900 and 1907 only one official was killed, with no discernible political impact.[99] The words of the journal therefore reflected the feeling of desperation within the Alliance group at this time.

In the absence of a more effective method, the revolutionaries made at least six attempts on the lives of high officials between 1910 and 1911.[100] The most sensational case was Wang Ching-wei's effort to assassinate the Manchu regent. Wang (1883-1944) had gone to Japan in 1903 as a governmental scholar from Kwangtung. After he graduated from a two-year law college in 1906, he joined the Alliance Society and participated in both the polemics with Liang Ch'i-ch'ao and the campaigns of Kwangtung and Kwangsi.[101] When these failed, he returned to Japan in a mood of despondency, only to find this feeling shared by his comrades. After some thought he decided that only a sensational act could restore the morale of the party. With this plan in mind, he left Tokyo for China probably during the summer of 1909. Wang's first intention was to assassinate the governor-general

96. KFNP, I, 199-203.
97. Ibid., 201-6.
98. HHKM, II, 444.
99. KFCC, VI, 351, 358, 362, 368.
100. Ibid., 379-87; CKCTSSC, 347.
101. WCW:CPTS, xii-xiv; HCT:HH, p. 199, footnote 20.

at Canton, but he then considered the situation in Hankow and finally decided on a coup at the capital. During the several months occupied by the journey between Japan, Canton, and Hankow, Wang's funds dwindled, and he was forced to return to Tokyo while Ch'en Pi-chün, an accomplice who later became his wife, went to her home at Penang to raise additional funds.[102]

During his short stay in Tokyo, Wang resumed the publication of the *People's Journal*, which had been banned by the Japanese authorities since October 19, 1908.[103] Using a Paris address, Wang published two more issues (January and February, 1910) under the pretense that they had been printed in France. He then left for Peking, taking copies of the journal along with explosives furnished by Nicholai Russel, a Russian refugee at Nagasaki. When he reached his destination, Wang was met by Ch'en Pi-chün and three other comrades who had come earlier. At first the conspirators intended to throw a bomb at the regent, but since they had no chance to approach him, they decided to place explosives under a bridge used by the Manchu every day. For three nights Wang and his accomplices worked at their task, unaware of the incident that would foil their plan. On the third night, March 28, as they completed their project and waited for the regent to pass overhead, one of them inadvertently hit a sleeping dog, which started barking and caused the other dogs in the vicinity to issue a chorus of howls.[104] The police became suspicious and quickly discovered the plot. No one was arrested, however, and on the following morning three of the revolutionaries returned to Japan, Wang himself remained in hiding and another comrade, Huang Fu-sheng, stayed behind to keep him company. Through his own carelessness Huang was recognized and followed by the police. On April 16, 1910, both he and Wang were seized. In an extraordinary gesture of leniency the Manchu regime sentenced them only to life imprisonment.[105]

Meanwhile, an unsuccessful revolt was launched in Canton on February 13, 1910. A notable feature of this campaign was the role assigned to the foreign-style army. For the first time it was the troops, and not the secret societies, who were expected to initiate the insurrection. In the fall of 1909 there were three regiments in Canton. Chao Sheng, a Japanese-educated graduate of the military academy in Nanking, had been regimental commander in Kiangsu. Discharged by

102. WCW:CPTS, xiv-xv.
103. HHKM, II, 443-44; KTI:CTCK, II, 1315-16.
104. The date of Wang's attempted assassination varies in different sources. One has it on March 31 (CKCTSSC, 335); another, April 2 (KTI:CTCK, II, 1353). March 28 is the date given in a biographical sketch by T'ang Leang-li in Wang Ching-wei's book *China's Problems and Their Solutions* (p. xvi). For a different account of Wang's attempt, see FTY:CHMK, II, 230-52.
105. WCW:CPST, xvi-xviii.

Governor-General Tuan Fang for his revolutionary activities, he went to Canton and secured a similar post, which he held until his past was discovered. He then went to Hongkong and worked with other revolutionists in planning a *putsch*.[106] The head of the revolutionary cell in Canton was Ni Ying-tien, who was at one time a platoon leader in the Canton army. Although dismissed for questionable loyalty, he remained near the barracks to recruit members for the Alliance Society. By the end of 1909 two thousand men were said to have joined, and it was with this force that the revolutionists hoped to launch an uprising in late February, 1910, after the Chinese New Year. But the plan was wrecked on February 9, New Year's Eve, when a petty quarrel between a soldier and a constable developed into a conflict between the army and the police. The situation soon got out of hand, and on February 12, Ni Ying-tien shot down a battalion commander in order to start the revolt. With a thousand men he made an assault on the city wall, but the campaign was doomed because in the midst of the confusion the army authorities took the precaution of impounding the ammunition. Ni was killed, and the rebellion ended within two days.[107]

After this failure, only one more unsuccessful attempt was made in Canton. This was the Three Twenty-Ninth Revolution, named for its date, the twenty-ninth day of the third lunar month in 1911. Preparations for it had been started during the previous year. In May, Huang Hsing wrote a long letter to Sun in which he outlined the plans to capture Canton through the use of sympathetic government forces.[108] In November a meeting was held at Penang between Sun and the other revolutionary leaders. It was decided to raise a large sum of money for a major campaign. Emissaries were sent to various Chinese communities abroad to persuade them to make donations. By January, 1911, a total of 187,000 Hongkong dollars had been raised.[109] The headquarters of the movement were then established in Hongkong, and Huang Hsing was placed in charge. Weapons were purchased abroad, and more than forty secret cells were organized in Canton. To provide the conspirators with references needed for many local transactions, the party set up two rice shops in the city. It also looked for possible sympathizers among the students of the military school.[110] In the final plan of action the individual leaders were instructed to recruit from among their fellow-provincials a special "Dare-to-Die" corps of eight hundred men, which would initiate the attack and then be joined by government forces.[111]

The target date was set for April 26, 1911. In spite of the elaborate preparations, the campaign did not fare any better than previous ones.

106. HHKM, IV, 312-14.
107. *Ibid.*, III, 347-354.
108. HCT:HH, 79.
109. *Ibid.*, 86.
110. HHKM, IV, 195-96.
111. *Ibid.*, 198.

Difficulties continued to crop up, and on the eve of the insurrection a postponement became necessary because the arms purchased from Japan and French Indo-China had not arrived.[112] Meanwhile, the campaign was no longer a guarded secret. At the time the revolutionists were soliciting funds, they eagerly divulged much of their plan to all contributors. The information soon reached the officials and enabled them to make elaborate preparations. Three days before the target date the governor-general in Canton had assured the capital that he had taken all necessary precautionary measures.[113]

On the other hand, the rebel leaders committed a number of errors. A key agent at Hui-chou absconded with thousands of dollars. The "Dare-to-Die" corps was kept, oddly enough, in Hongkong, waiting to be ferried 110 miles to Canton just in time for the outbreak.[114] Indecision frequently characterized the rebels' most important moves. On April 24, Huang Hsing wired from Canton to Hongkong and ordered a halt to the flow of men and arms. But two days later, he wired that the attack was set for the following day and that all men and arms should be sent immediately to Canton. Unfortunately, by then no means of transportation were available.[115] As a result, few of the resources were actually used. Thus, instead of the planned 800 men, only 170 took part in the insurrection.[116] The ten-route offensive was reduced first to a four-route and then to a single raid on the governor-general's office.[117] Those who participated fought heroically, for no less than eighty-six men sacrificed their lives,[118] but militarily it was a worse blunder than the previous campaigns.

After this unsuccessful attempt, the difficulties faced by the revolutionists seemed insurmountable. Neither assassination nor armed revolt had produced any results. For a time many of the comrades must have doubted whether the Manchu regime would ever be overthrown. But they did not realize the extreme weakness of the traditional order which that regime represented. As Li Hung-chang and others had observed, China was faced in the nineteenth century with a situation unprecedented in her three thousand years of history. Having long been set in their habits and ideas, the Chinese literati were slow in grasping the significance of the new situation. Procrastination necessitated drastic action, and by the time an all-out reform was launched after 1900, it had to be introduced at breakneck speed. But the very reasons that dictated such a course also ensured its failure. Almost all the measures undertaken yielded results contrary to their goals. Yet as long as the basic cause of her troubles—Western impact— continued to exist, the Manchu dynasty had no alternative but to

112. *Ibid.*, 228-29.
113. *Ibid.*, 233; HCT:HH, 89.
114. HHKM, IV, 227-28.
115. *Ibid.*, 168-69, 198.
116. *Ibid.*, 207.
117. *Ibid.*, 208.
118. *Ibid.*, 200-201, 207-208; HCT:HH, 91-92.

continue the reforms, until by its own efforts it would be ready to collapse and disappear.

THE CONSTITUTIONAL REFORM, 1905-1911

A decisive event in modern Chinese history took place in 1905 when Japan emerged victorious from her war with Russia. In the mistaken belief that the war had proved the superiority of Japanese constitutionalism over Russian despotism, the Chinese officials led the popular clamor for a parliamentary regime. The pressure became too great to resist, and in the summer of 1905 the Dowager Empress appointed a five-member mission to investigate the constitutional systems abroad. When the officials were about to depart on September 24, a bomb was thrown at them by Wu Yueh, a self-appointed revolutionary who had been influenced by Liang Ch'i-ch'ao and other writers. Two of the envoys were slightly injured while Wu sacrificed himself. As a consequence the mission was delayed until December, and two of the original members were replaced.[119] On their return in 1906, the envoys enthusiastically endorsed the principle of constitutional government and urged that it be adopted by China.[120]

On September 1 the court consented to this suggestion but stipulated a number of measures that had to be taken first, including reorganization of the central and provincial governments, codification of the laws, promotion of education, improvement of the fiscal system, and establishment of new armed services. While this work was progressing, the throne authorized in September of 1907 the establishment of national and provincial assemblies.[121] On August 27, 1908, it further decreed the basic constitutional principles and the preparatory work to be accomplished in each of the following nine years, at the end of which a constitutional system would come into being.[122]

Before this edict could take effect, an event occurred that drastically altered the political scene. On November 14 and 15, 1908, the Emperor and the Empress Dowager died. The removal of the Empress' firm hand from the helm of the state was a serious blow to the dynasty. To make matters worse, the successor to the throne was a boy of three, whose father, as regent, was anxious to reassert Manchu power. In this attempt he was influenced by the examples of two newly risen powers. While on a mission to Germany in 1901, he learned from Prince Heinrich of Prussia the importance of exercising direct control over the armed forces.[123] Later, the imperial envoys of 1905 concluded that centralization was the essence of the Meiji

119. KFCC, VI, 383.
120. CKCTSSC, 300, 301, 304; KTI:CTCK, II, 1239, 1241, 1243, 1244.
121. HHKM, IV, 24-47.   122. CKCTSSC, 309, 317.
123. KTI:CTCK, II, 1312.

Restoration in Japan.[124] This example led the Manchus to undertake a reorganization of provincial government, to transfer the two most powerful governor-generals—Chang Chih-tung and Yüan Shih-kai—to Peking, and to reduce provincial autonomy in general. The Prussian example led the regent to place one of his brothers in charge of the army and another in charge of the navy. Since they were no more competent than the regent himself, the new policy weakened rather than strengthened the dynastic position.

But the most damaging innovation was the provincial councils. According to the initiating regulations drafted by two men educated in Japan and promulgated by the court on July 8, 1908, members of the council were to be elected by males of no less than twenty-five years of age, on meeting one of the following requirements: completion of three years of service in educational or other work conducive to the public good, graduation from a middle school or better, possession of a literary degree under the old system of examinations, past government service above a certain rank, or ownership of property worth five thousand silver dollars. Candidates were to be males above the age of thirty who were qualified to vote. Certain employments debarred men from voting or serving, among them being public office, military and police service, priesthood in any religious order, and enrollment as a student in any school. Teachers in primary schools were entitled to vote but not to serve.[125] The number of councilors in a province varied from 30 to 140 according to a formula generally based on the old civil-service examination quotas. Each council was to be headed by a chairman and two vice-chairmen elected by the councilors themselves. The more important functions of the council were as follows: (1) to make suggestions concerning policy and administrative matters to the provincial authorities; (2) to authorize the provincial budget and approve the final accounts; (3) to approve tax laws and issuance of bonds; (4) to elect from among themselves delegates to the National Assembly; (5) to render upon request advisory opinions to provincial heads and individual councilors; (6) to arbitrate disputes between various self-governing agencies within the province. But these extensive powers were offset by the power granted to provincial heads to supervise the councils and veto their resolutions when it was deemed necessary. The provincial heads also received authority to suspend the councils and to request an imperial sanction for dissolving them.[126] In short, the councils were meant to be conservative in tone and to serve as channels of communication between the government and the populace, rather than as instruments of democracy.

Actually, a wide discrepancy developed between intention and

124. LCN:CKCP, I, 280.   125. HTS:CK, III, 517.
126. *Ibid.*, 537-38.

practice. According to contemporary sources, two main features characterized the provincial councils of this period. In the first place, within their narrow confines they functioned remarkably well. While the number of votes cast was small in proportion to the electorate, the elections were honest and free from outside interference. Once elected, the councilors, who were generally men of ability and integrity, conducted their proceedings in a serious but calm manner. The "excellent good sense" they demonstrated earned them praise from all quarters, including the *North China Herald*, which was the mouthpiece of the British community in Shanghai.[127]

On the other hand, these councilors were in no mood to be puppets of the government. Disputes soon arose between them and the provincial officials. Generally these disagreements were of a procedural or jurisdictional nature, with the councils claiming more rights than the officials were willing to concede. Thus, early in its proceedings the Szechuan council, which was especially noted for the large percentage of Japanese-educated men among its members and for its criticisms of the authorities, became involved in a constitutional struggle with the governor-general over its rights and privileges. The council won the day and thereby increased its prestige.[128] In Kwangsi, the councilors were compelled to make an early protest "against the attempted encroachment on their privileges" by the governor.[129] In Canton there was friction over the forms of address to be used by the council and the provincial authorities.[130] In these disputes the advantage was generally with the councilors because many of them came from the less radical segment of the Japanese-trained group who knew far more about parliamentary procedure than the mandarins.

By comparison, the first year of the provincial councils was much less stormy than the second. One reason was the councilors' primary concern at first to press the court for a full-fledged parliamentary system. Early in its session the Kiangsu council passed a resolution urging concerted action by all the provinces. Its chairman, Chang Ch'ien, sent out emissaries to contact the various assemblies. As a result, fifty-one councilors representing sixteen provinces met in Shanghai from November 18 through November 25 in 1909. On the twenty-seventh an Association of Provincial Councils was formed with the first order of business that of sending a deputation to Peking.[131] By January 16, 1910, thirty-two representatives had arrived at the capital. In a petition to the government they argued that the National Assembly scheduled for that year would serve little purpose because it

127. *Ibid.*, 538; HHKM, IV, 68-69.

128. NCH (October 16, 1909), 123-24; (December 11, 1909), 573-74; (February 18, 1910), 358-59.

129. NCH (February 18, 1910), 359.   130. *Ibid.*

131. Li shou-kung, "The Association of Provincial Councils and the Revolution of 1911," CKHTS, III, 330.

had no power to control the executive. Rather, they suggested that the nine-year program be telescoped and that a full-fledged parliamentary system be realized within one year. When the Censorate-General, to which the petition was first submitted, refused to accept it, the representatives built up pressure by interviewing individual officials and announcing that they were seeking joint action with other civic groups throughout the nation. The Censorate-General then yielded and accepted the petition, but in an edict of January 30, 1910, the court politely turned down this appeal, insisting that only deliberate steps could secure worthwhile results and that nine years of preparation were necessary for this gigantic task.[132] Undaunted, the representatives then organized a permanent Association of Petitioning for the Immediate Establishment of a Parliament (*Ch'ing-yuan chi-k'ai kuo-hui t'ung-chih hui*), with headquarters in Peking and branches throughout the country. At its inaugural meeting the delegates indicated their determination to continue the struggle by providing for a plenary conference every summer, to be attended by representatives of all the provinces.[133] Meanwhile, the councilors conducted a vigorous campaign. In Peking they contacted their influential fellow-provincials and solicited their personal support.[134] The movement soon assumed a mass nature. In February, 1910, a few hundred intellectuals organized a Society in Expectation of a Parliament (*Kuo-hui ch'i-ch'eng-hui*) and invited the participation of other civic groups.[135] At a rally in Peking during the same month, all of the representatives of the provincial councils then present pledged to continue their fight for constitutionalism; and one was especially applauded when he said, clearly with Western precedents in mind, that "the government should halt the sale of bonds until a parliament came into being." As tension mounted, one man cut off his finger, and another his arm, to indicate their determination to continue the fight.[136] After returning to their provinces, the councilors spoke to students and distributed copies of petitions to be presented to the court, some of which were written in human blood. At their invitation, the public flocked to add their names to a new mass petition. In Shantung alone over sixty thousand signatures were obtained in this way.[137]

By May, 1910, deputations in Peking represented not only the provincial councils but educators and businessmen, as well as overseas Chinese. The provincial representatives, with their usual vigor, then began to finance a united society called The Petitioners for the Establishment of a Parliament (*Kuo-hui ch'ing-yuan tai-piao-t'uan*), and to publish a newspaper as its organ. Meanwhile, ten separate petitions, including one from the Manchu bannermen of Chihli, were

132. *Ibid.*, 332.
133. *Ibid.*
134. HTS:CK, III, 543.
135. Li shou-kung, *op. cit.*, 333.
136. *Ibid.*
137. *Ibid.*, 337.

presented to the throne on July 16, 1910, through the Censorate-General. After consulting the high court officials, the regent refused these appeals and again maintained that nine years of preparation were necessary for the proper implementation of a parliamentary system.[138]

Upon hearing this, the delegates met and discussed the measures to be adopted. They agreed to present a third petition to the court early in the following year with at least a million signatures from each province. In addition, each county in the realm was to send one or two delegates to Peking for the presentation. Third, the Petitioners and the councils would be instructed to appeal to the provincial heads and the National Assembly, which would soon come into existence. While these resolutions were being conveyed to the provinces, the delegates were flooded with messages of support. The council of Heilungkiang, for instance, declared that previous campaigns had already awakened the masses and taught them the meaning of constitutionalism. Heartened by this response, the delegates resolved on August 15 to advance the date of the third petition to October, and to request the provincial councils (1) to advocate boycotting all taxes, (2) to confine their proceedings during the coming session to the discussion of the parliamentary issue, and (3) to dissolve themselves if this course of action was violated. In Shanghai the Association of Provincial Councils passed a series of important resolutions during its July meetings. In addition to stressing China's need for a parliament, the association specifically opposed any attempt by the government to nationalize China's railroads before a parliament came into existence.[139]

On October 7, 1910, the delegates presented their third petition to the court. Just as they were on their way to the regent's palace, seventeen students arrived to bid them farewell. After expressing the conviction that only a parliament could save China but that some violence was needed to arouse the court, two students attempted to take their own lives. Although held back by onlookers, they still succeeded in cutting their own flesh and writing with their blood that they wanted a parliament.[140] When the delegates reached the palace, the guards—probably on orders from the regent—refused to accept the petition. The deputations persisted and finally succeeded in presenting it to Prince Su, Minister of the Interior. On the following day the delegates were received by Prince Ch'ing and several other officials. They also presented a copy of the petition to the National Assembly.

The assembly had been convened on October 3, 1910. According to the amended regulations of August 23, 1909, it consisted of two hundred members, half of whom were elected by the provincial

138. *Ibid.*, 338.   139. *Ibid.*, 339-40.
140. *Ibid.*, 342-43.

councils from among their members, and the other half appointed by the throne from among the nobles, officials, scholars, and men paying the heaviest taxes.[141] The functions of the assembly were similar to those of the provincial councils, but its president and vice-president were appointed by the throne rather than elected by the members. Actually, the appointed members were mainly junior officials, while those elected included a number of top provincial leaders.[142] Consequently, they had a larger voice in the work of the assembly.

When the third petition for a parliament was presented to the assembly, many delegates were present as assemblymen. On October 22, 1910, the matter came up for discussion, and the members unanimously endorsed the immediate convocation of a parliament.[143] Meanwhile, the gentry outside of Peking continued to sponsor mass demonstrations. In Tientsin well over a thousand men demanded that Governor-General Ch'en K'ui-lung petition the court on their behalf. In Kaifeng three thousand persons held a rally and sent a ten-member deputation to the governor. In Foochow four thousand men, including delegates from Chinese settlers abroad, held a similar rally at the prefectural school. The provincial council of Shensi announced that unless a parliament were convened, it would not recognize the foreign debts incurred by the government. Pressured by the gentry and piqued by the court's persistent attempts to reduce their power, eighteen provincial officials wired the Grand Council on October 25 and urged the establishment of a parliament and a responsible cabinet. Faced by such united opposition, the regent weakened and on November 4 altered the date for the establishment of a parliament from 1917 to 1913.

An important group in all of this agitation was the constitutionalists headed by Liang Ch'-i-ch'ao. Although he had forsaken constitutionalism in favor of enlightened despotism in 1903, Liang changed his mind after the Manchu court declared itself for constitutional principles on September 1, 1906. In July, 1907, he organized the Political Learning Society *(Cheng Wen She)* to further the cause.[144] As its influence spread, the court decided to ban the society,[145] but the indefatigable Liang was undeterred. Through his followers and friends he maintained close contact with the councilors and assemblymen. To provide them with urgently needed knowledge of parliamentary issues and current events, he founded a journal called *The National Trend (Kuo Feng Pao)* in February, 1910.[146] At first mild in

141. HTS:CK, III, 539-40; HHKM, IV, 68. For an exact count of the various categories of National Assemblymen, see KTI:CTCK, II, 1356-69.

142. HTS:CK, III, 541.   143. Li Shou-kung, *op. cit.,* 343.

144. LJKHS, I, 215-18; HHKM, IV, 105-126. For a discussion of the date of the founding of this organ, see HIS:CTTS, IV, 2440.

145. LJKHS, II, 273-74, 284-88.   146. *Ibid.,* 309-10.

his attitude toward the Manchus, Liang began to lose patience as the establishment of a parliament drew no closer. When the regent advanced the date for parliamentary government from 1917 to 1913, he bluntly warned that unless the dynasty made a radical change in its policy, it would not last another three years.[147]

To a large extent Liang maintained his contacts with the assemblymen through Hsü Fo-su (1880-?), a native of Changsha, Hunan, and a former collaborator of Huang Hsing in the China Rise Society.[148] After the debacle of 1904, Hsü fled to Shanghai and then to Japan, where he became known to Liang through his writings in the *New People's Miscellany*. When the Political Learning Society was formed, Hsü became a resident member (*ch'ang-wu-yüan*).[149] In 1909 he went to Peking as an unofficial representative of Liang's group and was active among the provincial delegates. In the autumn of 1910 he became editor of their journal, *The Chinese Public (Kuo-min kung-pao)*, which quickly became a key organ in the parliamentary movement. On the night it became known, the delegates discussed the regent's reply to the third petition at the office of the *Chinese Public*. They regarded the outcome as unsatisfactory and the intention of the throne insincere.[150] They saw no further hope in the dynasty and agreed secretly to overthrow it by force; they then issued a farewell address and announced the dissolution of the society of Petitioners but the continuation of the Association of Provincial Councils.[151]

Before the delegates had time to leave, the popular reaction to the court's decision had become obvious. The provincial councils of Honan, Hupeh, Fukien, Kiangsi, Chihli, and Shansi all wired to urge the delegates to stay in Peking and to continue the struggle. The council of Kwangsi approached its counterpart in Chihli for a joint statement opposing the government's attempts to contract foreign loans. Protests were made by other civic groups, and the shops in Peking ignored the police order to celebrate the granting of a parliament by 1913. The national assembly, sharing Liang Ch'i-ch'ao's gloomy view of the dynastic future, presented a memorial to the throne on November 10, urging it to reconsider its decision.[152] Except for the few papers controlled directly by high government officials, the press was unanimous in its condemnation. One comment read: "To the government's thinking the people are no better than snakes and bandits. Even at such a perilous time as the present one, those on high have apparently no intention of dealing sincerely and openly with those below. With such a government in power, one can easily

147. LJKHS, II, 310. The article appeared in the seventeenth issue of the *Kuo Feng Pao* and is reprinted in LCC:YPSWC, 9.25a.106-130.
148. *Ibid.*, I, 207, 236, 250.   149. *Ibid.*, 344-45.
150. *Ibid.*, II, 265.   151. Li Shou-kung, *op. cit.*, 346.
152. *Ibid.*, 345, 346.

imagine the kind of . . . constitution, the caliber of cabinet ministers, and the degree of governmental despotism that lie ahead of us. Alas! From now on our attention should no longer be directed to the date set for the opening of the parliament, but to the problems outlined above."[153]

Outcries and defiance brought forth government repression. On November 22, 1910, the governor-general of Chihli used troops to disperse students who had gathered to discuss the launching of another constitutional campaign. On December 22, several delegates who had arrived at the capital to present another petition to the court were banished to their home provinces to live under the surveillance of the governor-general. Censorship was imposed on the mails of all provincial delegates who remained in Peking. On January 8, 1911, Wen Shih-lin, a native of Tientsin, was banished to Sinkiang for his attempt to organize a nation-wide student strike.[154]

Such highhanded measures only engendered more hostility. When the second session of the provincial councils opened in 1910, conflict with the government became the dominant feature. In Chekiang it centered around the dismissal of a railroad director who was popular with the shareholders. In Kwangtung the issue was focused on the prohibition of gambling. In Kwangsi it revolved around the date that the suppression of opium began. In all three provinces the councilors either resigned in mass protest or suspended their deliberations until the government capitulated. After the national assembly was established, it was often asked by the provincial councils to intercede. In one case it was informed that the governor of Hunan had issued bonds without the council's approval. When it addressed inquiries to the court, it was told that the government had indeed been delinquent, but because prior approval had been granted by the throne, the bond issue must continue. The dissatisfied assembly then moved to interpellate the Grand Councilors in person. When they refused to appear, the assembly sought to determine to what extent the Councilors were responsible for their policies.[155]

Before this matter could be settled, other issues arose. The Yunnan council complained that the government had increased the price of salt without its approval. The Kwangsi body disagreed with government restrictions on non-native students in local schools. In both cases the national assembly, following normal procedure, drafted its replies and submitted them for imperial sanction. When it learned that the regent had referred them to the ministries for consideration, it impeached the Grand Councilors on the grounds that the executive had encroached upon the legislative. The regent then approved the proposals without change, but this gesture no longer satisfied the

153. *Ibid.,* 347.   154. *Ibid.,* 347-48.
155. HHKM, IV, 69-70.

assemblymen. Instead of dropping their impeachment charges, they added inconsistency and irresponsibility to them. Faced with such hostility the chief Councilor, Prince Ch'ing, tendered his resignation, but the regent refused to accept it. Instead, he rebuked the assemblymen for interfering with the royal prerogative of appointment.[156]

On January 11, 1911, the National Assembly adjourned amid feelings of frustration and discord. On March 22 the Peking branch of the Association of Provincial Councils extended an invitation to all council chairmen to come to the capital immediately for a conference. On May 12 the meeting opened with delegates from twelve provinces in attendance.[157] Four days earlier, the court had reorganized the Grand Council into a cabinet. On May 9 it had also nationalized the Szechuan-Hankow and the Canton-Hankow railway lines. Both of these issues came up for discussion. Strikingly, it was the government reorganization rather than the railway issue that claimed the attention of the delegates. While few opposed nationalization of the railways, feelings against the new cabinet were strong because it remained responsible only to the throne and included fewer Chinese members than before: of the thirteen ministers, four were Manchus, four were high Manchu noblemen, one was Mongolian, and only four were Chinese.[158] For this reason the delegates regarded the reorganization as a deception and doubted the sincerity of the court. Accordingly, they agreed on the use of force as a basic solution to the political impasse, but for the time being they decided to oppose the new cabinet by all available means, including a warning to foreign countries that the Chinese would not be responsible for any loans contracted by the government. To achieve greater unity the delegates decided to form a political party. Known as Friends of the Constitution (Hsien Yu Hui), the group was organized to pursue the three-fold aim of hastening the establishment of a parliament, spreading knowledge among the people, and seeking political power by constitutional means.[159] Broadly, it represented the more enlightened members of the gentry and the less radical elements of the intelligentsia. In particular it had the support of Liang Ch'i-ch'ao and a number of the chairmen of provincial councils—e.g., P'u Tien-chün of Szechuan, T'an Yen-kai of Hunan, T'ang Hua-lung of Hupeh, Liang Shan-chi of Shansi, and Yüan Chin-kai of Mukden.[160]

In June, 1911, Chang Ch'ien, the chairman of the Kiangsu council, came north. Because of his literary fame and entrepreneurial skill, he

156. Ibid., 70-71.   157. Li Shou-kung, op. cit., 353-54.
158. KTI:CTCK, II, 1385-86; HTS:CK, III, 546-47.
159. This was the real aim as told by Hsü Fo-su in an essay in commemoration of Liang Ch'i-ch'ao (LJKHS, II, 315). For its formal platform, see Li Shou-kung, op. cit., 354.
160. HTS:CK, III, 541; HHKM, IV, 73-74.

was treated with respect by the Manchus, who went as far as to offer him a position at court. But the feeling was not reciprocated. In fact, Chang considered both the regent and Prince Ch'ing incompetent, for while they asked for and appreciated his opinion, they totally lacked the energy to take any action.[161] The only man who impressed Chang was Yüan Shih-kai. Meeting him at Changteh on the way north, Chang found his erstwhile *bête noire* "improved beyond measure" and the most likely person to lead China.[162] According to several sources, Chang's esteem materially aided Yüan's rise after the Wuchang uprising of October, 1911, for Chang had a large following among the constitutionalists in the revolutionary camp.[163]

Meanwhile the battle of words continued. On June 10, 1911, the Association of Provincial Councils requested the court to appoint someone other than Prince Ch'ing as prime minister. When no reply was made, it presented a second appeal on July 5 and argued that a cabinet of noblemen was in violation of basic constitutional principles. This time the regent responded with a sharp rebuttal. He reminded the petitioners that according to principles laid down during the previous reign, they had no business interfering with official policy. Knowing that the opposition remained unplacated, the court further decided to amend the organizational laws of both the assembly and the councils. The assembly was now allowed one president and one vice-president instead of two, and the councils were required to make all public announcements through the governors. Inevitably, these changes aroused public indignation, for if the organizational laws could be revised, why should the royal prerogative of appointment remain unaltered? Increasingly the public attributed a complete lack of sincerity to the court.[164]

THE RAILWAY DISPUTE

The issue that precipitated armed conflict was the railway dispute. On May 9, 1911, the court approved the suggestion of Sheng Hsüan-huai, Minister of Posts and Communications, to nationalize all of the trunk railway lines. On May 20, Sheng signed an agreement with a four-power banking consortium that provided China with a loan of £6,000,000 for the construction of the Canton-Hankow and the Szechuan-Hankow railways.[165] Immediately a storm of protest arose in those provinces.

A brief historical sketch helps to explain the popular reaction. In 1896 the Manchu regime established an Imperial Railway Administration and appointed Sheng Hsüan-huai as its head. At first his plan was to utilize both native and foreign capital, but since neither the

161. *Ibid.*, VIII, 38-39.   162. CKHTS, I, 8.
163. *Ibid.*, 8-9.   164. Li Shou-kung, *op. cit.*, 358.
165. CKHTS, I, 227-28.

government nor the people provided sufficient funds, Sheng was forced to rely on foreign resources.[166] During the next ten years he constructed some 3,000 miles of railroads with nearly 300,000,000 silver dollars borrowed from the Western powers.[167] But the loans did not always work to China's advantage or satisfaction. From one of the loans stemmed the notorious case of the American China Development Company, which had secured the right to construct the Canton-Hankow line. Signed in 1898, the agreement with the Chinese government specifically forbade the company to transfer its rights to other nationals. But by 1903 it had sold its controlling interest to a Belgian group. This was precisely what the Chinese had feared because the Belgians, with the Russians behind them, already dominated the Peking-Hankow line. When China protested, she was told that the company was still legally American. Only after protracted negotiations did the government succeed in canceling the whole agreement, but in so doing it was compelled to pay 6,750,000 dollars for thirty miles of track laid on level ground.[168] This and other unpleasant experiences prompted the Chinese gentry to launch a "rights recovery movement." While the effort to replace foreign enterprises with Chinese was largely unsuccessful, a general distrust of foreign capital developed after 1904.

Behind this reaction to Western imperialism there was strong economic motivation. Even before 1900 the gentry members had learned of the possible profits of modern entrepreneurship. Like many other things, this awareness came from Western inspiration, with several discernible stages of development. The first step was for the gentry members to serve as middlemen for foreign interests. Broadly this pattern existed between 1895 and 1903. In a rescript of October, 1898, Governor-General Chang Chih-tung observed that "Since railroads appeared in China, eager and covetous gentry-merchants have not ceased to initiate some projects. Despite their claim of affluence what they actually have is often nothing but an intention to cheat. When they say that they have contracted foreign loans, it often means that they are in the employ of foreigners. Their only purpose is to make a fortune for themselves through obtaining a concession."[169]

When the "rights recovery movement" was launched, the gentry were no longer satisfied to serve as middlemen but aspired rather to run their own enterprises. Between 1904 and 1910 at least thirteen railroad companies were founded, of which the Szechuan-Hankow line was one of the larger ones.[170] According to its regulations of January, 1905, the shareholders were limited to Chinese nationals, and the capital was expected to come from four sources: (1) voluntary subscriptions, (2) government funds, (3) profits from enterprises

166. YWYT, VIII, 59.
168. FEQ (February, 1952), 147-65.
170. CKHTS, I, 210.
167. FA:CEI, 68.
169. CWHK, 118.33.106-11a.

managed by the company, (4) a 3 per cent levy on the harvests of all farm families in Szechuan whose annual crops exceeded ten piculs of rice paddy.[171] As the company paid little attention to accounting procedures, its financial condition is difficult to analyze;[172] but broadly speaking, as of June, 1911, the "shares by officials and people" amounted to 2,600,000 taels; the accrued interests and miscellaneous income to 3,300,000 taels; the 3 per cent levy to 9,500,000 taels; and miscellaneous levies to 1,200,000 taels—making a total of 16,600,000 taels.[173] Out of this, 4,000,000 taels had been spent on the construction of seventy miles of roadbed; 6,000,000 taels had been dissipated in various ways, including embezzlement by the company's representative in Shanghai; and between six and seven million taels were held in cash.[174]

Shortly after the railroads were nationalized in May, 1911, the Ministry of Posts and Communications announced that it would buy out the provincial interests, but that the terms would vary from one province to another according to circumstances.[175] On June 22, 1911, an edict was issued stipulating that in Hunan and Hupeh the capital subscribed by "merchants" was to be reimbursed in cash, while the amount raised through various levies was to be repaid in bonds carrying 6 per cent interest per year; that in Kwangtung, the shares, whose market value had depreciated by more than 50 per cent, were to be fully reimbursed, 60 per cent in cash and 40 per cent in bonds carrying no interest; and that in Szechuan, interest-bearing bonds were to be issued in exchange for the cash then held and in payment of the amount actually spent on construction. Interest-free bonds were to be issued in settlement of a specified amount of administrative expenses, but no reimbursement was to be made for wasted funds.[176] In formulating this plan the Ministry relied mainly on two criteria— the nature and the amount of the funds involved. The claims of "merchants," or private capitalists, were more respected than those of peasant tax-payers, and smaller sums were paid more readily than larger ones. Since Hupeh had raised only 960,000 taels (with no breakdown available) and Hunan had procured one million taels through merchant subscriptions as well as four million taels through levies, they received the most equitable treatment.[177] Because Kwangtung had secured all its 14,000,000 taels through subscription,[178] it was awarded more funds for reimbursement than Szechuan, which had raised most of its 16,600,000 taels through taxation. Thus, in fairness to the ministry it may be said that the scheme embodied realistic thinking and was partial but not altogether arbitrary.

171. SPL, 33.
172. *Ibid.*, 171.
173. CKHTS, I, 214-15.
174. *Ibid.*, 218-20.
175. *Ibid.*, 225-26.
176. *Ibid.*
177. *Ibid.*, 215.
178. *Ibid.*, p. 221, footnote 7.

The over-all circumstances were, however, extremely unfavorable. When nationalization was announced, the Three Twenty-Ninth Revolution had just occurred, and the agitation for a parliament was still continuing. Although the provincial delegates who were meeting in Peking did not particularly object to the government's economic policy, they were leaving no stone unturned to embarrass the new cabinet headed by Prince Ch'ing. Political considerations combined once again with vested interests to cause an explosion. Almost immediately campaigns for the protection of railway rights broke out in all of the four provinces concerned. In Hunan handbills and circulars appeared denouncing the government; a deputation was sent to Peking opposing the railway policy;[179] and on May 31, 1911, Governor Yang Wen-ting informed the court of the provincial council's refusal to accept foreign funds for railway construction.[180] On June 5, the Kwangtung shareholders of the Canton-Hankow line met and reaffirmed their determination to remain a private enterprise. Ten days later the people began boycotting the paper currency issued by the governmental bank.[181] But the most violent reaction came understandably from Szechuan. As soon as the news of nationalization reached Chengtu, the provincial council and the directors of the railway agreed on joint action. They decided, first of all, to convene a shareholders' meeting, which in effect meant a mass meeting, since most of the taxpayers were shareholders.[182] Later, they also agreed to establish newspapers using colloquial language, to send deputations to Peking and other cities, and to rely on secret societies for armed support.[183] While P'u Tien-chün, the Japanese-educated chairman of the council, personally went to the capital, Wang Jen-wen, the acting governorgeneral, strongly urged the court to reconsider its policy.[184] But, as usual, the regime refused to yield while there was still time. Rather than come to terms with the gentry, it severely reprimanded Wang and deported P'u from Peking. On his departure P'u informed the delegates of the other provinces that Szechuan was at the point of an uprising.[185]

Meanwhile, events occurred in swift succession at Chengtu. First, at the shareholders' meeting held on June 17, 1911, Lo Lun and Teng Hsiao-k'o, two followers of K'ang Yu-wei and Liang Ch'i-ch'ao, moved an audience of two thousand to tears by their emotional call to action.[186] The shareholders then resolved to form a League for the Protection of Railroads with P'u Tien-chün and Lo Lun, the chairman and vice-chairman of the provincial council, as its head. Finally,

179. CKCTSSC, 344-45; CKHTS, III, 356.
180. CKHTS, I, 230, 236, footnote 1.
181. *Ibid.*, 230.   182. HHKM, IV, 332.
183. CKHTS, III, 357, footnote 93.   184. SPL, 158-59.
185. CKHTS, III, 356.   186. HHKM, IV, 450.

the participants demonstrated in front of the office of the acting gov-ernor-general, Wang Jen-wen. After speaking to the crowd, Wang presented another memorial to the throne, impeaching Sheng Hsüan-huai and urging the abrogation of the loan agreement.[187] Although the move resulted only in Wang's downfall, it encouraged the League and prompted it to energetic action. Symbolic of its close affiliation with K'ang and Liang, the League chose for slogans two sentences taken directly from Emperor Kuang-hsü's edicts: "Government is sub-ject to public criticism" (*shu-cheng kung-chu yü-lun*), and "The Sze-chuan railroad shall be a commercial enterprise" (*tieh-lu chün-kui shang-pan*). Under the League's direction all households at Chengtu burned incense to the deceased sovereign's tablet, with scrolls bearing these slogans hanging on the sides. Since the edicts of a departed em-peror were by tradition inviolate, this maneuver made it impossible for the officials to press charges against the agitators. Furthermore, the slogans provided good summaries of the issues and had great emo-tional appeal because they came from a man whose anxiety for China and whose personal tragedy had been made well known by Liang Ch'i-ch'ao's writings.[188]

The League had a great financial advantage because it had access to the railway funds. With these, it was able to issue pamphlets and newspapers, to send agents to other provinces, and to erect wooden platforms in the streets of Chengtu to display Kuang-hsü's tablet and scrolls, thus forcing the mandarins to dismount from their sedan-chairs and walk on foot.[189] On August 24, 1911, the merchants at Chengtu struck and declared that they would refuse to pay taxes. When the government denied the League telegraph service, it utilized the excellent waterways of the province by sending its messages down-stream painted on lumber.[190]

The exact purpose of the League is less clear. Despite their angry denunciations, the leaders had no plan to topple the dynasty. Basically, what they desired was political reform that would place them in the saddle. On the railway issue they wavered at the beginning be-tween two alternatives, seeking adequate compensation from the gov-ernment or insisting on provincial ownership of the railway.[191] The more conservative elements in the League favored the former course, but as Peking flatly refused to make any adjustment, the issue became academic. From that time the League's stand hardened, but the focus was blurred. The campaign took on an increasingly political char-acter, until both the government and the League lost control of events to the revolutionists.

A crucial factor was the attitude of the officials. Unfortunately

187. *Ibid.*, 452; CKHTS, I, 233; SPL, 199-203.
188. HHKM, IV, 453-54.   189. *Ibid.*, 454.
190. *Ibid.*, 456.   191. SPL, 151-55.

for the Manchus there was a serious split of opinion among members of the bureaucracy, largely along the lines dividing the court officials from provincial ones. A key figure in Peking was Sheng Hsüan-huai (1844-1916), who initiated the nationalization plan. To understand his role, it is necessary to give a brief sketch of his career. Sheng was born at Ch'ang-chou, 150 miles from Shanghai, to a family of gentry noted for its keen interest in foreign affairs. In 1870 he joined the entourage of Li Hung-chang, first in a secretarial capacity and then as a deputy in economic matters. By 1893 he had secured control over the China Merchants' Steamship Company, the Telegraph Administration, and the Hua Sheng Cotton Mill, to which he later added the newly formed Imperial Railway Administration and the Hanyang Ironworks.[192] By far the most important official-entrepreneur in the empire, Sheng also amassed a large personal fortune through manipulation of official funds and sharp financial dealings. Naturally he acquired an unsavory reputation and was repeatedly impeached by the censors.[193] But through patronage and political machinations, he maintained his interests and continued to prosper. This experience probably made him disdainful of public criticism and overconscious of support from above. Furthermore, by the nature of his activities, Sheng had extensive contacts with foreigners and was deeply impressed by them. Even in 1899, when conservative influences were strong at court, he unhesitatingly told the throne that foreign management was the only way to develop China's economic potential.[194] These two features—admiration of the West and contempt for Chinese popular feeling—describe Shen's attitude in 1911.

Unmindful of broad political currents, Sheng instituted nationalization when the Manchu regime was in no position to impose its will on the country.[195] Even after the Szechuan opposition had broken into the open, he refused to accept the advice of the provincial heads. Instead, he continued to deny the gentry telegraphic service and sought to exchange government bonds, which were distrusted by the people, for hard cash held by the railway company.[196] Worse still, when the gentry dispatched one of the company's officers, Li Chi-hsün, to Peking, Sheng made a deal with him behind their backs. Li agreed to persuade the Szechuan shareholders to subscribe to the proposed government concern or, in other words, to let Sheng have immediate control of the company's cash funds.[197] This scheme was soon exposed, and the gentry secured Li's dismissal from office. Sheng then had him reappointed to the same job by a government decree.[198] Criticizing

192. FA:CEI, 65-67.   193. YWYT, VIII, 57.
194. FA:CEI, 94.
195. See the comments by Sheng's political opponents in LYSNP, I, 97-98.
196. SPL, 166; CKHTS, I, 226.
197. SPL, 225, 227.   198. Ibid., 263, 271.

Governor-General Chao Erh-feng for accepting Li's dismissal and coddling the gentry, Sheng had an edict issued holding Chao responsible for all future incidents.[199]

Sheng's high-handedness led to a general strike at Chengtu on August 24, 1911. During the same night handbills appeared urging the people not to pay taxes.[200] Alarmed by the rising tide of discontent, the high officials of Szechuan urged the court on August 28 to shelve the nationalization plan and submit the loan agreement to the national assembly for ratification.[201] This proposal was flatly rejected by the cabinet, but on the pretext of clarification Sheng announced several important concessions on August 30. According to them, the Szechuan company was allowed to keep its liquid capital, and the government agreed to repay all of its past expenditures except those funds lost through bank failures. Furthermore, if for any reason the accounts of the company could not be audited, the Ministry would be willing to forego this procedure, but would then limit its reimbursements to ascertainable past expenditures. In addition, the Ministry would set aside government bonds to the value of a million dollars and use the interest accruing from them to establish a railway school in Szechuan.[202] If these proposals had been made earlier, they would probably have satisfied the Szechuan gentry, but the compromise came too late. With the support of Wang and Chao, the popular demands had been raised, and the gentry refused to give any consideration to Sheng's proposals.

Among the most important factors in the Szechuan dispute were the intrigues and open feuds among the officials. Perhaps the five most influential men in Peking at the time were the regent, his two brothers, the Minister of Finance Duke Tsai Tse, and the Prime Minister Prince Ch'ing. Of these, Prince Ch'ing (1836-1917)[203] was by far the oldest and most experienced. He had headed the Foreign Office since 1884 and had enjoyed great power under the Dowager Empress Tz'u Hsi. Forty years senior to the regent and immeasurably more experienced in affairs of state, he naturally expected a greater share of power under the new sovereign, but events soon dashed all his hopes. Genealogically he was only distantly related to the imperial line, and his notorious reputation for corruption did not endear him to his royal kinsmen. Even more important, he was closely allied with Yüan Shih-kai, a man whom the regent both feared and hated because of his political influence and his role in causing the downfall of Emperor Kuang-hsü.[204] For these reasons, the regent excluded

199. *Ibid.*, 287.   200. CKHTS, I, 235.
201. SPL 28-82.   202. *Ibid.*, 289-90.
203. The date 1917 is based on the account given in P'u I's autobiography (PI:WTC, I, 68). This date is deemed more accurate than the 1916 given in HA: ECCP, II, 964.
204. PI:WTC, I, 21-23.

Prince Ch'ing from participation in the making of policy decisions and appointments, thus depriving him of the fees and gifts tendered by hopeful office-seekers.[205] On their part the nobles showed no respect for the Prime Minister and often openly contested his leadership. The elder man retaliated by repeatedly tendering his resignation, knowing that none of his rivals had enough confidence to assume his post. He declared in private that if he could not retain power, neither would he allow his rivals to exercise it.[206]

It was against such a background that the Szechuan incident occurred. In all probability Prince Ch'ing had neither known about nor favored the railway policy promoted by Sheng Hsüan-huai with the support of Duke Tsai Tse.[207] As opposition mounted in Szechuan, Prince Ch'ing suggested bowing to the local interests, but his advice was ignored.[208] On September 29, 1911, after once again tendering his resignation, he simply absented himself from office, leaving unanswered urgent telegrams from the governor-general of Szechuan.[209] Such was the administrative decay that destroyed the Manchu regime from within.

At a lower level similar conditions existed. A key figure was Tuan Fang (1861-1911), commonly regarded as the ablest Manchu of his day. He had been one of the five envoys appointed in 1905 to study foreign constitutional systems, but was removed as governor-general of Chihli in November, 1909, on the flimsy charge that he had taken photographs on his way to the imperial mausoleum and had "moved about in his sedan chair with undue freedom." Grieved by the political intrigues against him, he reportedly bribed his way to a new appointment in May, 1911, as emperial commissioner for the Canton-Hankow-Chengtu Railways.[210] There is little doubt that Tuan viewed this post as a stepping stone to a more substantial provincial post and that he saw in the Szechuan dispute an opportunity for himself. On August 29, with Sheng's prior knowledge, Tuan impeached Chao Erh-feng for his weakness and incompetence. In a personal telegram he advised Sheng to appoint Jui Cheng, the governor-general at Wuchang, to head an investigating mission to Szechuan.[211] Although he did not say so, it is quite clear that he hoped to be Jui's successor in the Wuchang post. Aware of Tuan's ambition, Jui joined the

205. HHKM, IV, 333; HTS:CK, III, 555. Compare also the version in PI:WTC, 22-23.
206. HTS:CK, III, 555.
207. HHKM, IV, 332, 335. Interestingly, an edict of October 26, 1911, blamed Sheng for his failure to seek Prince Ch'ing's prior approval of the nationalization policy; at the same time it rebuked the prince for having failed to be more vigilant (SPL, 470-471).
208. HTS:CK, III, 551.
209. SPL, 352, 380; HHKM, IV, 335, 336, 337-78.
210. HA:ECCP, II, 781; CM:TRM, 119; HHKM, IV, 333.
211. SPL, 283-84, 285-86, 295.

chorus against Chao in order to make sure that Tuan and not himself would be Chao's successor at Chengtu.[212] A fierce jockeying for position followed, and, as a result, Sheng informed Tuan, on September 1, that he had been appointed to Szechuan. Even at this point Tuan argued that it was wrong for an accuser to investigate the accused,[213] but his pleas went unheeded.

All of these moves did not escape the attention of Chao Erh-feng, whose brother was also a governor-general and had influence at the court. On September 1, 1911, a telegram was sent to the cabinet by the ranking officials in Szechuan, including the Tartar-General Yü K'un, who was very close to Prince Ch'ing. In it the signers repeated their suggestion of August 28 that the loan agreement be submitted to the National Assembly for ratification and that the Szechuan railway remain for the time being as a private enterprise. Furthermore, they censored Sheng Hsüan-huai and asked for his immediate dismissal.[214] At this juncture Chao's sympathy for the people of Szechuan reached a peak. In taking such a resolute stand, he undoubtedly counted on the support of Prince Ch'ing; but the prime minister, vexed by the "arrogance and disrespect" of both high and low, chose to remain aloof from the struggle. His attitude radically changed the power position and perhaps even affected the future of the dynasty. On September 4 the court sharply rebuked the Szechuan officials for their telegrams and specifically warned Chao of his impending punishment.[215] Two days later it appointed Tuan Fang to command the armed forces in Szechuan.[216] Clearly, Chao was in imperial disfavor. He was confronted with the choice of following his convictions and jeopardizing his official career, or of seeking to regain royal grace through a radical change in attitude. He chose the latter course.

An excuse or contributary cause to Chao's about-face was the appearance in Chengtu on September 5, 1911, of an unsigned letter urging the people to seek "self-protection"—i.e., to end all connections with the Manchu regime. Like Ou Chü-chia's "The New Kwangtung" of a few years earlier, the letter began by listing China's sufferings at the hands of foreigners and suggesting that Szechuan take immediate steps to protect herself.[217] This startling and dangerous development prompted Peking to order Chao to take the most energetic countermeasures and to execute those whose crimes were "beyond doubt."[218] But even before this telegram arrived, Chao had taken the opportunity to rebuild his political fortunes. On September 7 he arrested P'u

212. *Ibid.*, 286, 291-92.
213. *Ibid.*, 296, 299, 300-1, 302-3. One factor in Jui Cheng's favor was his relationship with Tsai Tse. The two were related by marriage. See CKK:HH, 80.
214. *Ibid.*, 292-94.   215. *Ibid.*, 294.
216. *Ibid.*, 310.   217. *Ibid.*, 304-8.
218. *Ibid.*, 309.

Tien-chün, Lo Lun, and seven others, for treason. According to one source, Chao fully intended to have these men executed, and he was deterred only by the Tartar-General Yü K'un, who shared Prince Ch'ing's opposition to the railway policy.[219]

The governor-general's repressive measures sparked immediate mass demonstrations. On the same afternoon he arrested the nine men, thousands of persons assembled in front of his office to demand the release of their leaders. Who was responsible for the bloodshed that followed is in dispute. Chao claimed a premeditated plan to revolt, and one eyewitness records that Chao's guards opened fire after repeated warnings failed to halt the advancing masses. But others maintain that the shooting was a totally unjustified attack on innocent people. Accounts differ even about the number of casualties; the best estimate is that between thirty and forty demonstrators lost their lives.[220]

As a result of the riot, the railway issue faded into the background. Henceforth the campaign assumed the nature of a spontaneous revolt against existing authority. Because of the imprisonment of their leaders, neither the provincial council nor the League for the Protection of Railroads provided effective direction. Nor did other groups such as the Alliance Society take over the helm at this stage. Rather, it was the local gentry who led the battle. Aided by special circumstances, they were able to organize a highly effective campaign. One factor that redounded to their advantage was the sense of unity among the people, who resented foreign encroachments on provincial interests. Second, unlike most provinces, Szechuan had a large number of secret societies that were connected with the gentry. When the rebellion broke out, these societies joined the insurgents and became the nucleus of their forces. Although poorly equipped, the militia knew the surrounding terrain and could move about swiftly. The rebel forces had a numerical advantage and a will to fight, whereas many of the government troops were natives of Szechuan and secretly sympathized with the rebel cause.[221] A decisive victory, which the government needed to reassert its influence, was thus impossible to obtain. In one of his dispatches, Chao rather boastfully reported: "Since the sixteenth (September 8, 1911) our forces have been in action for seven days . . . . Manifesting invincibility, they have captured and killed many enemies. They have seized no less than two thousand guns, rifles, swords, and flags. However, as one group of bandits disperses, another cluster is formed. The situation is like

219. HHKM, IV, 335. Actually, eleven persons were arrested (Ibid., IV, 335), but only nine were mentioned in official correspondences. One possibility is that two were released ahead of the others. See also HIS:CTTS, IV, 2554.

220. HHKM, IV, 336; CKHTS, I, 240-44.

221. SPL, 357, 366; CKHTS, I, 254.

a prairie fire."[222] Actually, the situation was far worse than Chao conceded. After September 8 Chengtu was besieged and lost its telegraph connections with Peking.[223] Outside the provincial capital scores of counties fell into rebel hands.[224] While the insurgents were unable to capture the provincial authority, the confusion itself embarrassed the dynasty and encouraged uprisings elsewhere.

Belatedly the seriousness of the situation dawned on the court. On September 15, 1911, Ts'en Ch'un-hsuan was recalled from retirement and placed in charge of government forces in Szechuan. A ludicrous spectacle followed as three officials appointed to the same province without a clear division of authority made conflicting statements on policy.[225] Of the three, Ts'en's prestige was highest. He was often mentioned with Yüan Shih-kai as the ablest of all provincial officials, but he was a sworn enemy of Prince Ch'ing. He had tried unsuccessfully to oust the prince in 1907, and as a result had been dismissed from office.[226] Even during a time of crisis, old wounds failed to heal, and word soon spread that Prince Ch'ing was again seeking Ts'en's scalp.[227] What influence the rumor had on Ts'en is unknown, but his stand on the railway dispute took a strange turn. On September 20 he wired the court, suggesting that it (1) issue a penitential edict, (2) order the release of the imprisoned Szechuan leaders, and (3) reimburse in full the railway capital raised in Szechuan. Obviously, he was less interested in defending the regime than in courting public favor and embarrassing his rivals.

While Ts'en was playing politics, the other parties to the dispute were not remaining idle. On September 10 the Szechuan natives in Peking assembled before the Prime Minister's house and got down on their knees in prayer, only to be kicked and chased away by the guards.[228] Frustrated, the demonstrators then sent telegrams to Tuan Fang, denouncing him in vehement terms.[229] At their instigation the censors also impeached Chao Erh-feng and demanded his execution.[230] Only Ts'en remained free of criticism. On his part, Tuan Fang halted his journey when Ts'en's appointment was announced. He asked Peking for a clarification of his position, and because a satisfactory answer was not given, he devoted more time to political maneuvers than to the railway dispute. Two days after Ts'en made his proposal to the court, Tuan professed shock that capitulation should have become a hero's hallmark. In a personal telegram to Sheng Hsüan-huai and Tsai Tse, he prophetically warned that if

222. *Ibid.*, 348.   223. *Ibid.*, 350.
224. HHKM, IV, 456; VI, 5.
225. SPL, 363-64, 371, 374, 378, 385; HHKM, IV, 364.
226. SYL:HTCC, 126, 135-39.
227. HIS:CTTS, IV, 2556; SPH:JY, 2.21a-b, 3.4b.
228. HIS:CTTS, IV, 2553-54; SPL, 313-14.
229. HHKM, IV, 406.   230. SPL, 390.

Ts'en's advice was followed, their own positions would be seriously jeopardized.[231]

Nevertheless, the court equivocated. In response to Ts'en's proposal, it authorized the Ministry of Posts and Communications to reimburse in full the railway capital raised in Szechuan, Kwangtung, Hunan, and Hupeh, but would not accept Ts'en's other suggestions.[232] In a confidential message Sheng urged Tuan Fang to proceed to Szechuan as quickly as possible.[233] On his part, Chao Erh-feng sought to eliminate the need of Ts'en's mission by announcing on September 20 and 29 his victories over the rebels.[234] While the people in Peking at first accepted Chao's reports, Ts'en knew only too well their real meaning. From his temporary quarters in Wuhan, he asked for and obtained a brief sick leave.[235] Thus the only effect of Ts'en's appointment was to damage even further the court's prestige. By his maneuvers Ts'en secured financial concessions for the shareholders, but because of the court's ineptitude, he was unable to end the insurrection in Szechuan.

When the Wuchang revolution broke out on October 10, 1911, the apprehensive regime turned once again to Yüan Shih-kai and Ts'en Ch'un-hsuan. On the fourteenth it appointed Yüan as governor-general of Hunan and Hupeh, and Ts'en as governor-general of Szechuan. But the situation was in all respects worse than before, and Ts'en had no wish to be buried along with the tottering regime. From Wuhan he escaped to the foreign settlements in Shanghai, where he remained unavailable to imperial calls.[236]

On October 26, four days after two more provinces—Hunan and Shensi—had seceded, the National Assembly met and impeached Sheng Hsüan-huai. With a characteristically late burst of energy the regent dismissed Sheng from his offices and stipulated that he was never to be employed again.[237] But nothing else was changed. Even the feud between Tuan and Chao continued. Instead of drawing them together, the deepening crisis only caused them to drop their masks. They incriminated each other not only in their memorials but also in their talks with visitors.[238] As if this were not enough, each girded himself for an armed showdown. Before Tuan left Wuchang on September 8, 1911, he asked for and obtained two (undersized) regiments as guards. Because of the political situation, he proceeded slowly, reaching Chungking only on October 13.[239] The fall of Wuchang three days earlier had placed him in a bind, for he could no longer retreat to Hupeh or advance to Chengtu, which was controlled

231. *Ibid.*, 385.
232. *Ibid.*, 376.
233. *Ibid.*, 377.
234. *Ibid.*, 375, 380, 398.
235. *Ibid.*, 412.
236. CCH:LCM, 18-19.
237. SPL, 470.
238. HHHIL, III, 167-68.
239. HHKM, IV, 517.

by his enemy Chao, "the Butcher."[240] To cope with the situation, Tuan decided he must increase his military strength. He charged Li K'an-yang, a former police intendant of Canton, with the task of expanding and modernizing the Szechuan Defense and Patrol troops. Though a conscientious man, Li unknowingly recruited many revolutionaries, giving them for the first time a foothold in the local armed forces.[241] Feeling uncertain of their strength, these men launched experimental revolts in Yu-yang, Ho-chiang, and other counties to the south of Chungking. The situation became more critical after Tuan and his Hupeh forces left between November 2 and 18. On the twenty-second, several units of the Defense and Patrol troops returned from Chien-yang to Chungking, where they established the first autonomous regime in Szechuan.[242]

Before Tuan Fang left Chungking, the turn of events had changed his opinion on many issues. At his request the court, on October 26, ordered Chao Erh-feng to release the imprisoned gentry leaders.[243] As Tuan reached Tzu-chou, approximately halfway between Chungking and Chengtu, he decided to ingratiate himself with his guards and the Szechuan people in general. Among other things he made his own brother a "sworn brother" of key regimental officers. He also announced that since his family had been Chinese only four generations earlier, he was reverting to his Chinese surname, T'ao.[244] In the hope of establishing himself in Szechuan, he dispatched two agents to Chengtu to spearhead an independence movement with himself as leader, but in this he failed, largely because Chao Erh-feng had forewarned the gentry of Tuan's unsavory character.[245]

Even at this late date (November 18 to 22, 1911), Tuan could probably have escaped with his life. But he ambitiously decided to march with his troops to Shensi, where he could establish contact with the powerful Yüan Shih-kai, one of whose sons had married his daughter.[246] But this imaginative plan backfired, for in spite of Tuan's efforts the troops felt no loyalty to a Manchu nor had any desire to march with him to an unknown country. They were anxious to return to their home province of Hupeh and decided that Tuan's head might prove an excellent gift to the revolutionaries there. On November 27, 1911, Tuan was slain by the very men whom he had brought along to protect him.[247]

Meanwhile Chao Erh-feng ignored the court order to release the nine gentry members. Just as Tuan Fang had objected to Ts'en's

240. *Ibid.*, 454.
242. *Ibid.*, 8.
244. HHHIL, II, 101.

241. *Ibid.*, VI, 6.
243. SPL, 471-72.
245. HHKM, IV, 337.

246. HHHIL, II, 101. For a list of the families to which the Yüans were related by marriage, see YSK, 196.
247. *Ibid.*, 98, 101-2. A number of the Hupeh forces Tuan brought with him were members of revolutionist societies.

proposal in September, Chao presented a memorial to the throne on November 2 in which he argued that Tuan Fang was wrong and that the men should be tried for treason by the Supreme Court.[248] But like Tuan, Chao soon changed his mind. One reason for his new attitude was an impeachment charge by the National Assembly and an edict of November 10 instructing the Supreme Court to try him for dereliction of duty.[249] An even more pressing reason was Tuan's effort to establish an autonomous regime in Szechuan, which, if successful, would probably mean Chao's ouster or death. Faced with such a crisis, Chao had no alternative but to attempt a *rapprochement* with the local gentry. Luckily for him, this was accomplished through the release of the nine men on November 14 and through a series of meetings at which Chao blamed everything in the past on Tuan Fang by showing copies of Tuan's memorials and correspondence.[250] As to the future of Szechuan, all agreed on the necessity of restoring peace. To this end the governor-general issued a penitential decree abolishing many of the taxes and ordering a reorganization of the armed forces.[251] On their part, the gentry leaders urgently appealed to the populace to lay down their arms. On the grounds that the aims of the League for the Protection of Railroads had been realized, they called for the dissolution of the organization.[252]

Behind the nine men's appeal was a strong aversion to prolonged and needless destruction. True to the spirit of constitutionalism they believed that when substantial reforms were in sight, opposition to existing authority must cease. But unfortunately this approach was based more on their natural inclination than on logic or facts. In a way reminiscent of Liang Ch'i-ch'ao, P'u Tien-chün had consistently undermined the *status quo;* yet he was ready to lay down his arms the moment his demands were seemingly accepted. In spite of his naïveté, the imperial regime would not spare him if it succeeded in securing itself; and if it could not, the existing government machinery would hardly serve as an effective vehicle for reform. Furthermore, the leadership of the nine men was based on their opposition to railway nationalization. Their conciliatory attitude and the disbandment of the League materially lessened their claims to power. Had the nine men been more shrewd, they would in November, 1911, have declared themselves in favor of the revolution. By coming to terms with Chao Erh-feng and publicly urging peace, they acknowledged their lack of ideas and yielded the leadership by default.

But all this was not clear to them at the time. As they came to terms, P'u and Chao proceeded to negotiate for a peaceful change of

---

248. SPL, 472-74. By this time Tuan had publicly announced the imperial order to release the nine men.
249. SPL, 484-85.   250. HHKM, IV, 364, 429-31.
251. SPL, 486-88.   252. *Ibid.,* 489-91.

government. On November 27, 1911, P'u became the new governor and Chu Ch'ing-lan, commander of the New Army in Szechuan, the vice-governor. Chao was appointed to serve as their advisor until he could leave for the Szechuan-Yunnan region to engage in "border affairs" (i.e., colonial administration).[253] Outwardly smooth, this arrangement lasted for only eleven days. A key to its failure was the lack of popular response. Politically, the new order had no aim other than preserving peace. Militarily, because no previous governor-general of Szechuan had stressed reform, the New Army was little more than a token force. When independence was declared, the militia under the old League for the Protection of Railroads was established in the city along with a number of other forces. They quarreled with one another but shared the common vice of plundering the populace. On December 8 a mutiny occurred. Chu Ch'ing-lan fled, and P'u resigned in favor of a Japanese-educated revolutionary, Yin Ch'ang-heng, who had been principal of a military primary school under the Manchu dynasty. Lo Lun became the new vice-governor. During the mutiny Chao Erh-feng issued proclamations from the governor-general's residence and acted as if he were still in power. When Yin discovered that Chao was sending for outside troops, he had him arrested and executed on December 22, 1911.[254]

This description of the Szechuan incident is relevant to our study of the revolution of 1911 in several ways. To begin with, the ineffectiveness of the government, both at the provincial level and at the central, policy-making level, must be noted. At a time of extreme dynastic weakness it was clearly a mistake to decree the nationalization of the railways. The government made further errors through its habit of first maintaining a rigid stand and then giving way before mounting pressure. Moreover, the court demonstrated extremely poor judgment by appointing three officials with conflicting authority to the same province. All of these factors demonstrate the lack of government leadership, which was complicated by factional struggles at almost all levels of the bureaucracy. Without such extreme administrative decay, the Szechuan dispute could hardly have developed into an open rebellion.

A second feature of the episode that needs consideration is the concurrent strength and weakness of the gentry. It was they who organized the League for the Protection of Railroads and led the armed struggle against the government. Their widespread support among the masses vividly depicts an important aspect of the traditional Chinese political order. On the other hand, the gentry's role indicates the uncertainty of the elite on the eve of the revolution, for

253. SPL, 506.

254. HHKM, IV, 365-66; SPL, 516-17. Significantly, even Yin Ch'ang-heng was not a member of the Alliance Society (HHHIL, III, 138).

the Szechuan dispute neither arose from well-defined motives nor unfolded according to a well-planned strategy on either side of the struggle. In this respect the gentry merits only slightly less censure than the incompetent government leaders. It was through the confusion and ambivalence of both sides that what might have remained a mere quarrel over the method of settling a railway claim drifted into an open rebellion against existing authority.

Of course, vacillation and ambivalence are by their very nature reflections of more basic factors. Besides pointing out government ineffectiveness, little need be said about the general decline of the Manchu regime. Rather, our attention should be directed toward the gentry. To begin with, all of the active leaders in the railway dispute seem to have belonged to the constitutionalist group led by K'ang Yu-wei and Liang Ch'i-ch'ao. Socially they were members of a well-to-do class whose fortunes were dependent on the maintenance of the *status quo* and who had a deep aversion to violence and bloodshed. At the same time they were imbued with a sense of personal mission toward society and humanity. These basic features of their attitude, the pursuit of self-interest and the leaning toward altruism, were in fundamental opposition to each other but had reached some kind of equilibrium within the traditional social framework. Forces arising from Western impact, however, rudely disrupted this balance. Politically, China's defeats at the hands of foreigners weighed heavily on the consciences of the gentry and drove them to persistent demands for reform. Yet their training did not include knowledge that could guide them in such difficult and unprecedented tasks. Moreover, accustomed as they were to the traditional political order, they lacked the resolution to act decisively against it. They were hampered by many types of contradictions. They urgently desired reform, yet they had no precise ideas about how to accomplish what they wanted. They were opposed to the government, but their outlook was very similar to that of the officials in power. Consequently, the gentry, especially the upper layer of it, was as inwardly perplexed as it was outwardly agitated. The conflicting feelings of the Szechuan leaders— their ill-defined attitudes toward the dynasty, their half-hearted call for an independence movement, and their readiness to come to terms with the government—can be explained only in terms of their feelings of anxiety and confusion. Against this background the government's challenge to those with interests in the railways became the immediate cause of the explosion.

A further question that must be considered is the connection between the Szechuan dispute and the revolution of 1911. There seems to be no evidence of a direct link between the Szechuan leaders and subsequent uprisings elsewhere in China. In light of the known indecision of these leaders, such a connection seems highly improbable.

But in point of time, the Szechuan dispute preceded the uprising at Wuchang, and it is likely that the government's manifest inability to cope with open defiance in Szechuan had a psychological effect on the restless intellectuals in other provinces who subsequently engineered the revolution. Probably it was because of similar reasoning that Kuo Mo-jo declared "the prime credit for the revolution of 1911 must go to the shareholders of the Szechuan Railroad Company."[255] On purely logical grounds, there is no reason to doubt that under gentry leadership, the shareholders, or tax-payers, of Szechuan did make a contribution to the revolutionary cause.

THE WUCHANG UPRISING

Three months after the railway dispute arose in Szechuan a revolution broke out at Wuchang. According to Yang Yü-ju, an eyewitness who belonged to the Alliance Society, the revolutionary history of Wuchang began in 1900 when some twenty reformists died in an unsuccessful coup, rousing the public to a new political awareness.[256] In 1902 the students from Hupeh founded a journal, the *Hupeh Students' Circle,* in Tokyo, and in the following year they organized an agency, the Ch'ang Ming Company, to distribute the revolutionary publications, to assist the Hupeh students in Japan, and to further their contacts with the home province. Raising two thousand silver dollars from among their meager stipends, the students purchased a slide projector and sent it to Wuhan, where it became a popular attraction in meetings on world events. As the Hupeh students in Japan frequently returned home, several of them were always on hand to operate the machine and give comments, in which nationalism always loomed as a topic. In response to the public enthusiasm for education, several reading rooms were established. These became the meeting place for men interested in the revolutionary cause.[257]

In the spring of 1904 a number of Japanese-trained students at Wuchang met and discussed the strategy of revolution. After a review of past failures, the participants agreed to discard the tactics of assassination and reliance on secret societies, but to seek to infiltrate the armed forces. In line with this decision, a number of them enlisted in the army.[258] In the late spring the Remedial Science Study Group *(K'e-hsueh pu-hsi so)* was formed to serve as a front.[259] When Huang Hsing passed through Hankow in the summer, he met with the group and revealed his plan for an uprising in Changsha on the birthday of the Empress Dowager. His audience in turn pledged to undertake concerted action in Hupeh. When the Changsha plot failed in

255. HHKM, IV, 449.
256. YYJ:HH, 8-9.
257. *Ibid.,* 10-11.
258. *Ibid.,* 11.
259. *Ibid.,* 11-12, 39.

October, the governor of Hunan learned about the nature of the Remedial Science Study Group and informed his colleague in Hupeh. Fortunately, the group had been warned in time and had destroyed all incriminating evidence before the police arrived. Unwilling to pursue the matter, the authorities merely expelled two of the students from their schools.[260]

Before the case was dropped, one of the members, Liu Ching-an, went into hiding at the Episcopal church in Wuchang. After taking care of the reading room for sometime, he received permission to use it as a revolutionary center. A new group was organized under the old name of the Society for the Daily Increase of Knowledge. With a hundred men at its first meeting in February, 1906, the society held weekly forums and distributed revolutionary pamphlets among students and soldiers.[261] Through arrangements made by Sun Yat-sen in Japan, a French officer addressed the society on June 29, 1906.[262] This gesture of sympathy had a cheering effect on the members, but it also attracted the notice of the provincial authorities. When revolts broke out at P'ing-hsiang, Li-ling, and Liu-yang in December, the society was banned by the government.[263]

After the Alliance Society was formed in 1905, its leadership paid exclusive attention to activities in southern China. This apparent bias caused discontent among the members from other parts of China. Without leaving the party these men formed a separate organization in the fall of 1907. Known as the Common Advancement Society, this group maintained branches in various cities but was particularly active in Wuhan.[264] Its strategy was to infiltrate the new army and turn it against the government. Coincidentally, under the influence of widespread revolutionary propaganda, another group, the Army Alliance Society (Chün-tui t'ung-meng-hui), also emerged in the summer of 1908. Composed mainly of army privates who had never been abroad, the group underwent several changes and finally became the Literary Society (Wen-hsueh-she). Less than a month after its formation on January 30, 1911, it had a membership of four hundred persons, including several commissioned officers. The strategy of this group was to expand its influence in the army until it could muster a force of a battalion or more; then it would launch an insurrection. Operating on this principle of "army-lifting" (t'ai-ying), the men did not welcome civilian participants. But their exclusiveness was ended when the Common Advancement Society began recruiting members from the army. To preserve harmony within the revolutionary camp, the two groups met and agreed in principle to co-operate with each other. This understanding was reached on May 11, 1911.[265]

260. *Ibid.*, 12.
262. *Ibid.*, 13.
264. YYJ:HH, 14-17.

261. *Ibid.*
263. KFNP, I, 166-68.
265. *Ibid.*, 39-41.

When the railway dispute in Szechuan developed into a protracted armed struggle, the men at Wuchang felt that their opportunity had arrived; but neither the Literary Society nor the Common Advancement group had adequate resources. The former group depended on dues paid by its members, while the latter had only eight hundred dollars which it had received as a gift from Huang Hsing.[266] In their desperate attempt to obtain money, the men stopped at nothing. Once a member volunteered to drug and rob his aunt. He procured the anaesthetic from an army physician, and arranged for three comrades to relieve the sleeping woman of her jewels. But the scheme failed when the drug had no effect.[267] On another occasion several members made an elaborate plan to rob a buddha of its gold plating. They sneaked into the temple but proved poor chiselers. When dawn came, they had severed no more than two limbs of the huge body and had to abandon those when they were detected and chased away by angry farmers.[268]

Finally, the revolutionary fortune improved. A comrade who had just received 5,000 taels from his family donated the entire sum to the cause. On September 14, 1911, the Common Advancement and Literary groups decided to merge and take immediate action.[269] As a preliminary step, they invited Huang Hsing and Sung Chiao-jen to come to Wuhan and be their leaders. Two men, Chü Cheng and Yang Yü-ju, were sent to Shanghai to issue the offer and procure ammunition. Huang was in Hongkong, and Sung was skeptical of the possibilities at Wuchang. Ch'en Ch'i-mei, an important leader in Shanghai, undertook the task of purchasing arms, but even this promise remained unfulfilled.[270]

Meanwhile, preparations in Wuhan moved ahead. Several hiding places were established in Wuchang and the foreign settlements of Hankow for the making of bombs and banners.[271] On September 24, sixty comrades decided that since neither Huang nor Sung had sent any definite word, they should continue on their own. October 6 was chosen as the date of insurrection, and plans were laid for its execution. Unfortunately, even while the members were still assembled, an incident occurred in the barracks. Several soldiers of the Eighth Regiment were making merry and becoming boisterous. When their platoon chief intervened, the men, rebellious and drunk, mutinied. But because they had been suspicious of the men's loyalty, the officers had removed the firing pins from their rifles and reduced the supply of

266. *Ibid.*, 43.   267. *Ibid.*
268. FTY:KMIS, II, 303-4. According to another account, the men succeeded in chiseling some gold off the buddha but were in turn robbed by some soldiers on patrol. See WCSI, 243.
269. YYJ:HH, 45-47.   270. *Ibid.*, 48, 52-53.
271. *Ibid.*, 48.

shells. These difficulties and the lack of spontaneous support from the other units quickly extinguished any spark of rebellion. When the revolutionists learned of the incident, they sent word for the men to surrender and throw all the blame on one person, who was to flee. The authorities, on their part, were fearful of opening a Pandora's box. Instead of a thorough investigation, they merely ordered severe precautionary measures. With the police patrolling the streets and searching suspect houses, the revolutionists were forced to postpone their insurrection.[272]

On October 9, 1911, while bombs were being made at the revolutionary headquarters in the Russian concession at Hankow, a careless onlooker caused an explosion by dropping cigarette ashes into a vat of chemicals. The noise immediately brought the police to the scene. After a quick search they arrested a number of suspects and seized many documents, including the group's membership list. As these were handed over to the Chinese, tension mounted throughout the tri-city. Although he had been aware of the revolutionary activities, the governor-general was alarmed at the large number of men involved. He called in regular troops from other areas, had the city gates of Wuchang closed, and ordered the arrest of all the rebels. Rumors circulated that these men would be executed by being drowned in the Yangtze.[273]

Clearly, the revolutionists had no choice but to gamble on an immediate uprising. Instructions were sent out for the various units to rise that night, but because of road blocks, these messages failed to arrive in time.[274] Meanwhile, another hiding place at Wuchang was discovered; three men were caught and executed, while several others escaped and dispersed. The campaign was now virtually leaderless. In desperation several soldiers in the Eight Engineering Battalion struck on the night of October 10, 1911. After shooting down four officers, they marched to the armory and stormed it.[275] By this time an infantry battalion from the Twenty-First Mixed Brigade had joined them, as well as eighty students from a surveying school nearby. Outside the city wall an artillery company of the Eighth Regiment and the engineering and transportation companies of the Twenty-First Mixed Brigade also revolted, and shortly afterwards the 1,000 students of the military middle school joined in. Pitted against this rebel force of 3,850 men were nine battalions of the new army and two battalions of the governor-general's guards, totaling 5,500 men, in addition to 3,000 water police and Defense and Patrol troops.[276] If Jui Cheng, who boasted on the ninth of October of his calmness in dealing with a crisis,[277] had retained his composure on the tenth, he could at least

272. *Ibid.*, 53-54.
274. YYJ:HH, 56-57.
276. CKK:HH, 69-70.

273. WCSI, 234, 248-251.
275. *Ibid.*, 60-61.
277. HHKM, V, 289.

have given the insurgents a hard fight. But he fled to a warship as soon as shells began falling within earshot.[278] Nor did the army commander, Chang Piao, show much courage. Throughout the night he remained at home, surrounded by guards but making no contact with his forces. Only the next morning did he emerge, when a battalion commander came to assure him that he was safe. After sending his favorite concubine to the Japanese settlement of Hankow, Chang moved his troops away from the insurgents to eliminate the possibility of surprise. He then consulted his Japanese adviser, but refused either to lead a counterattack or flee to Japan as the latter suggested. After some hesitation he decided to await reinforcements from the north.[279] While he waited, four more battalions went over to the rebels because they had not heard from Chang and were short of provisions.[280]

In 1911 the New Army of Hupeh consisted of one division and one mixed brigade. The latter was commanded by Li Yüan-hung, who was popular with the rank and file because he was honest and considerate of others. On the night of the outbreak he was with his forces and personally killed a saboteur sent by the rebels.[281] But as the bombardment increased, he, too, attempted to hide himself in the home of his aide-de-camp. On the morning of October 11 he was discovered by the rebels, and in the afternoon was taken to the provincial council for a conference with the councilors and revolutionists.[282] Because the rebels considered it important to have a well-known military man as their head, Li was forced to become the new governor while T'ang Hua-lung, the Japanese-educated chairman of the provincial council, served as the civil chief. A military government was established, and all orders were henceforth issued in the name of the governor.[283]

Haphazard as the uprising of October 10 was, the fall of Wuchang proved to be a disaster for the Manchu regime. At the time the city was captured, there were no less than 40,000,000 silver dollars in the treasury and tens of thousands of guns as well as millions of rounds of ammunition at the armory.[284] This enormous wealth powerfully boosted the revolutionary cause and overcame many of the disadvantages of the inexperienced rebels. Because of the continued inaction of Jui Cheng and Chang Piao, on October 11 and 12 the rebels captured Hankow and Hanyang, the two towns which formed with Wuchang the tri-city of Wuhan. During the next few days the court dismissed Chang Piao from office and ordered Yin Ch'ang, the Minister

278. *Ibid.,* 112-13.   279. *Ibid.,* 113, 116, 134-35.
280. *Ibid.,* 134-135; CKK:HH, 78-79.
281. *Ibid.,* 113. According to another source, Li killed two revolutionaries. See WCSI, 350.
282. CKK:HH, 81-83.
283. *Ibid.,* 119, 121, 131, 132, 137, 141, 142.
284. YYJ:HH, 61, 79.

of War, to head an expeditionary force composed of two armies, or four (undersized) divisions.[285] On October 17 three warships commanded by Sa Chen-ping, a Foochow arsenal graduate who had studied in England, arrived to help subdue the rebels.[286] Reinforcements also came from such neighboring provinces as Hunan and Honan.[287] Yet little was accomplished. In a telegram to the court Jui Cheng complained that the reinforcements were too small, poorly equipped, and unresponsive to his commands. On the pretext that the naval vessels must be kept from falling into the enemies' hands, Jui left Hankow for Kiukiang on October 18. From there he quickly made his way to Shanghai, where the foreigners could protect him from both the revolutionaries and the Manchus.[288]

The new commander-in-chief, Yin Ch'ang, was a general who had never seen action. On October 22 he arrived at the front but immediately had difficulty in enforcing his orders. At Prince Ch'ing's suggestion, the court then decided to place more power in the hands of Yüan Shih-kai. Previously, Yüan had been appointed governor-general of Hunan and Hupeh, but he was in no haste to accept this post. His aim now was to create a military stalemate between the rebels and the Manchus so that he could hold the balance of power. As part of the strategy he obtained the court's approval to send his two close followers, Feng Kuo-chang and Tuan Ch'i-jui, to the Hankow front.[289] Meanwhile, Yüan himself remained at home and pleaded illness. When pressed by the court, he asked for unrestricted power over the armed forces, ample financing, and an undertaking by the Manchus to establish a parliament and pardon the rebels.[290] Ordinarily, the court would not have considered such terms, but the situation was fast deteriorating. On October 22, Hunan and Shensi seceded, and on the following day Kiukiang also declared its independence.[291] On the twenty-fourth, the new Tartar-General of Canton was assassinated by the revolutionaries.[292] This succession of disasters forced the court to yield to Yüan. On October 27 he was appointed imperial commissioner in charge of all forces at the Hankow front. Five days later Feng Kuo-chang recovered Hankow from the hands of the revolutionaries.[293]

Until October 26 the rebels held up fairly well against the government forces, but this was owing rather to the latter's weakness than to their own strength. In spite of the military origin of the revolt, few rebel leaders knew how to conduct a battle, and there was an almost

---

285. CKK:HH, 105.
286. *Ibid.*, 127; WCSI, 595; KTI:CTCK, II, 1409.
287. CKK:HH, 117.   288. YYJ:HH, 129-30; HHKM, V, 299.
289. CKK:HH, 107.   290. LCN:CKCP, I, 308-9.
291. CKK:HH, 4.   292. KTI:CTCK, II, 1412.
293. CKK:HH, 107, 140, 145.

daily shuffle in the commanding position. Evidence indicates a gross lack of discipline. One man nearly executed for his pro-dynastic stand was appointed field commander the following day because no one else wanted the job.[294] Another man, ordered to lead his forces to the front, got drunk and lost his way.[295] Still another officer who was to participate in a concerted attack on the government forces stayed behind to exchange nuptial vows with his sweetheart.[296] All this was relatively harmless as long as the government forces practically refused to fight. But on October 27 the Manchus replaced Yin Ch'ang with Feng Kuo-chang. An attack was launched on Hankow, and panic began to spread through the ranks of the revolutionary army. To cope with the situation, the rebels made a great deal of Huang's arrival on October 28.[297] They appointed him commander-in-chief and circulated signs through the streets reading "Huang Hsing has arrived in Hupeh."[298]

The propaganda failed to work, however. Neither Huang nor the rebel forces proved equal to their enemies,[299] and Hankow fell on November 2. In the absence of any other alternative, the members of the Alliance Society in Hupeh continued to believe in the strength that Huang's name carried. They considered appointing him to succeed Li Yüan-hung as head of the revolutionary regime, and when this idea failed to gain unanimous support, they sought to boost Huang's prestige by a special ceremony marking his appointment as commander-in-chief.

Luckily for them, several events occurred at this time to favor their cause. On November 1, three warships in the mid-Yangtze waters declared their allegiance to the revolutionaries, and the naval forces in Shanghai and Chinkiang followed suit on November 4 and 10.[300] Second, several Japanese *ronin* joined the anti-Manchu cause and helped in the intelligence and staff work, to the great delight of the revolutionaries.[301] Third, two brigades arrived from newly independent Hunan between November 3 and 6, and their senior officers insisted on an immediate offensive against the Manchus.[302] Finally, and significantly, Yüan Shih-kai, for his own purposes, induced the court to decree on November 4 a halt to the army's advance against the insurgents.[303]

294. WCSI, 442, 476.
295. *Ibid.*, 502.
296. *Ibid.*, 507.
297. HCT:HH, 110; WCSI, 474.
298. HCH:HH, 110.
299. One reason why the rebel forces were weak was their rapid expansion. The revolutionary regime had increased its army from one division to nine after October 10. As a result, these troops were an undisciplined mob rather than an organized army. See CKK:HH, 94-98.
300. CKCTSSC, 354; WCSI, 604-5; CKK:HH, 190-91.
301. WCSI, 496.
302. CKK:HH, 152-53.
303. KTI:CTCK, II, 1420.

Thus emboldened, Huang Hsing launched a counterattack against Hankow on November 16, but his efforts met with dismal failure. Four days later, the government forces began attacking the strategic town of Hanyang. When it fell on the twenty-seventh, Wuchang became indefensible. Huang Hsing resigned and left for Shanghai on the same day, while arguments raged among the lesser revolutionaries over the necessity of a general withdrawal. Finally, it was decided to make a further stand at Wuchang but to move all the noncombatants, Li Yüan-hung included, five miles to the rear.[304] On its part, the elated Manchu court bestowed a baronage on Feng Kuo-chang on November 28.[305] Feng would certainly have taken Wuchang if Yüan Shih-kai had not personally telephoned him to forbid any further advance.[306] On December 9, Feng was made commandant of the Imperial Guards. After a vain protest he yielded his battle command to Tuan Ch'i-jui, whom Yüan had sent to the Hankow front on October 23 and who had been made governor-general on November 17.[307] Tuan apparently understood Yüan better than Feng did. Under him all military activities on the Wuchang front ceased.

OTHER PROVINCIAL CAMPAIGNS

While the situation in Wuhan favored the Manchus, this was not the case in other places. On October 22, 1911, the same day that Shensi and Hunan seceded, the National Assembly convened for its second session. Almost immediately it resolved to present the court with four demands: (1) abolition of the noblemen's cabinet, (2) participation by the people's representatives in the constitution-making process, (3) amnesty to all political offenders, and (4) establishment of a parliament.[308] Before the throne had sufficient time to consider them, the New Army at Luanchow, only 140 miles east of Peking, made a dramatic move. On October 29, Chang Shao-tseng, commander of the Twentieth Division, and Lan T'ien-wei, commander of the Second Mixed Brigade, presented the court with twelve demands which, if accepted, would lead to the establishment of a parliamentary government with the crown serving only as a figurehead.[309] As this telegram reached Peking, Chang detained at Luanchow several train-loads of munitions en route from Mukden to the Hankow front.[310] Faced with such a show of force the regent had no choice but to accede to the petition of the National Assembly and to praise the generals for their patriotism. To retrieve some semblance of dignity he followed the

304. CKK:HH, 185.
306. KTI:CTCK, II, 1435.
308. LCN:CKCP, I, 310.
310. HHKM, VI, 340-42.

305. HHKM, V, 351.
307. Ibid., 345; HHKM, V, 345.
309. Ibid., 310-11.

tradition of issuing a penitential edict, in which he especially criticized his earlier appointments and railway policy.[311]

On the same day Chang and Lan made their stand known, Shansi seceded under the combined leadership of Yen Hsi-shan, a Japanese-trained New Army officer, and Liang Shan-chi, the chairman of the provincial council. As a protective measure Peking ordered the commander of the Sixth Division, Wu Lu-chen (1879-1911), to move his headquarters from Paoting to Shihchiachuang near the border of Shansi. Because he had been a schoolmate of Chang and Lan when they were in Japan, Wu was further directed on November 2 to go to Luanchow on a mission of good will.[312] But this move again demonstrated the Manchus' poor judgment, for Wu was as politically unreliable as the other two. A native of Hupeh, he had been sent by Chang Chih-tung to Japan in 1896. He joined the Japanese Cadets' School and with Chang and Lan became known among the Chinese as the "three bright men" of that institution *(Shih-kuan san-chieh)*.[313] In 1900 he returned to China to participate in T'ang Ts'ai-ch'ang's campaign at Hankow. When this failed, Wu went back to Japan after robbing a *likin* bureau to raise enough money to pay off his followers. Probably in 1903 he returned to Hankow and became a teacher in the School for Military Officers and Sub-Officers. After a trip to Hunan during Huang Hsing's abortive campaign of 1904, Wu went to Peking and became a staff member of the Commission for Army Reorganization. In 1906 he volunteered to go to Yen-chi in Kirin and made a name for himself by repulsing the encroachments of the Japanese army. For this action he was promoted as Deputy Tartar-General of the Mongol Border Red Banner and was sent to Germany and France as an observer of their army maneuvers. On the recommendation of his Manchu friend Liang Pi, Wu replaced Tuan Ch'i-jui as commander of the Sixth Division in 1910.[314]

Like Chang and Lan, Wu was appointed to his command during Yüan Shih-kai's retirement. In their anxiety to reduce Yüan's influence, the Manchus often replaced his followers with men whom they did not really know. Politically Wu was one of those men who insisted on radical reform but who preferred not to have a racial or anti-Manchu revolution. This ideological stand drew him close to Liang Ch'i-ch'ao and permitted him to befriend Liang Pi.[315] On the other hand, because the reform he envisaged involved a change of government leadership, his program was actually undistinguishable from a revolution. Consequently, Wu felt a strong urge to co-operate with the

311. HTS:CK, III, 554-56; For the text of this pathetic edict, see CM:TRM, 130-31.

312. HHKM, VI, 371.   313. *Ibid.*, 362.

314. *Ibid.*, 329, 368-69.

315. *Ibid.*, 370; HSW:LCM, p. 50, footnote 1.

revolutionaries. When he reached Luanchow on November 2, 1911, he did not seek to pacify Chang and Lan but rather to persuade them to march on Peking with him. On the third, Wu arranged a meeting with Yen Hsi-shan at Niang-tze Pass on the Shansi border. On the fourth, he detained several train-loads of munitions passing through Shihchiachuang to Hankow.[316] At the same time he impeached Yin Ch'ang for atrocities committed by his troops and demanded an immediate truce between the court and the rebels.[317]

The situation was extremely critical for the Manchus, for Wu's forces were then only 175 miles southwest of Peking. If he marched on Peking and had the Luanchow troops close in from the east, the regime would be doomed within hours.[318] Fortunately for the Manchus, the telegram Wu sent to Luanchow asking for Chang's aid did not reach its destination for some reason.[319] This mishap caused Wu to delay his plan for two days and during that time to lose his life. Previously, in the midst of the Luanchow mutiny and the secessions of Shansi and Yunnan (October 30, 1911), Yüan Shih-kai had replaced Prince Ch'ing as prime minister on November 1. On the same day Yüan had left his home in Honan to make a tour of the battle front at Hankow. Wu's moves on the third and fourth effectively cut the Peking-Hankow railroad in half and prevented Yüan from reaching Peking. Furthermore, if the regime collapsed before Yüan was ready, he would be shut off from power. Faced with such a challenge, Yüan acted decisively. On November 5, Chang Shao-tseng was promoted to a non-military post and forced to yield his command.[320] In the early hours of November 7, Wu Lu-chen was assassinated by his own subordinates.[321] On the eighth, Tuan Ch'i-jui, who had secretly traveled north from Hankow, arrived at Shihchiachuang with part of the Luanchow forces. Within a few days the Sixth Division had been reorganized and returned to the fold of the Pei-yang clique.[322] On the fourteenth, Lan T'ien-wei, then at Mukden, was cashiered from office.[323] Thus, through a combination of force and strategem Yüan turned a severe crisis into an excellent stepping stone for his own ascent.

His success, of course, added nothing to the Manchus' strength. On November 4 the revolution spread to Kweichow, Shanghai, and Chekiang. The case of Kweichow is noteworthy for the role played by the officials. According to contemporary sources, three men were responsible for the intellectual awakening of that distant province. It was Yen Hsiu (1861-1929) who, as provincial director of education in 1894, established the School of Practical Learning (*Ching-shih hsueh-*

316. HHKM, VI, 330, 371.   317. CKK:HH, 204.
318. LCN:CKCP, I, 313.   319. HHKM, VI, 330.
320. CKK:HH, 327.   321. *Ibid.,* 205.
322. HHKM, VI, 331.
323. CKCTSSC, 357. For a description of the episode, see HHHIL, VI, 564, 600.

t'ang). At his invitation Lei T'ing-chen, a native *chü-jen,* came to teach history, classics, mathematics, and current events. When Yen left after his tour of duty was up, Lei, whose attempt to harmonize modern science with Chinese etymology had lent itself to attack, also resigned. The pioneering role then fell to Wu Chia-jui, a constitutionalist from Changsha who was outspoken on politics and the need for a revolution.[324] Under the influence of these men a number of students formed a Science Club *(K'e-hsueh-hui)* for the typical purposes of learning science and saving the country. As the members became increasingly radical and began to cut their queues, the government intervened. Through the mediation of gentry members, the students were sent to Japan to study, and the Science Club was dissolved.[325]

In 1902 the Manchu court decreed a new educational system for the country. Like many other provinces Kweichow established a university before it had other schools. In a few years the university underwent several reorganizations, becoming first a high school and then a preparatory academy. In spite of such mistakes, enthusiasm spread. By 1907 at least fifteen private schools had come into existence at Kweiyang, the capital.[326]

When the "rights recovery" movement swept China between 1904 and 1905, Kweichow established a bureau for railroads and mines under the leadership of Li Tuan-fen, a brother-in-law of Liang Ch'i-ch'ao, and Yü Te-k'ai, a member of the gentry.[327] Because of Kweichow's poverty, it accomplished even less than some of the other provinces. But in keeping with the current emphasis on education, Li and Yü attributed their difficulties to public apathy and ignorance. In the summer of 1907 they were persuaded by an intellectual, Chou P'ei-i, to establish a bookshop and a newspaper.[328]

By then the constitutional movement was in full swing throughout China. In September and October, 1907, the court decreed the establishment of national and provincial assemblies. The move promptly led to an upsurge of political activities throughout the country and among the Chinese in Japan. Toward the end of the year a Self-Government Society was organized at Kweiyang by Chou P'ei-i and his friends with a membership consisting largely of students. Like all other groups of that time, it had nationalistic aims. At first adopting the name of an unrelated organization in Tientsin in order to secure government approval, Chou and his friends soon discovered more virtue in the word than they had thought. Accordingly their theme was to develop national strength (self-government for China) through

324. HHKM, VI, 407-8. For a brief biography of Yen Hsiu, see 1st CYNC, Wu.422.
325. HHKM, VI, 408.   326. *Ibid.,* 411.
327. *Ibid.* Li was not Liang's father-in-law as J. R. Levenson believes (LJR:LCC, 30).
328. HHKM, VI, 412.

a stress on civic duties and regional improvement (personal and provincial self-government).[329]

Within this general principle, the society was apparently fairly flexible in its strategy. Through the Kweichow students in Japan it became affiliated with the Alliance Society, but this association did not prevent it from pursuing activities more in keeping with a constitutionalist group. With the help of individual gentry members and officials, it established schools, a journal, a newspaper, a home for slave girls, and a rehabilitation center for beggars. It also had control over the educational society, the agricultural association, and the chamber of commerce. A decisive factor in the rise of the self-government group was the protective attitude of the Governor, P'eng Hung-shu. When Ch'en K'ui-lung, governor-general of Szechuan, returned to Kweichow in 1907, Chou P'ei-i published an editorial warning him not to become a Chia Ssu-tao, the notorious Sung official who had gained fame and lived in ease while the dynasty tottered. In revenge Ch'en accused Chou of political subversion, and it was only P'eng Hung-shu's resolute stand that saved him. In 1909 Chou's group openly stated that all corrupt officials should be slaughtered. This intemperate and imprudent remark led a rival clique to accuse them of treason. Stressing that "Kweichow had no talents to spare," Peng again refused to pursue the matter.[330]

Thus protected, the Self-Government Society was able to derive much benefit from the imperial rescript of August, 1908, requiring all provinces to establish local self-government according to a nine-year timetable. Having no clear idea of the meaning of self-government, the officials of Kweichow felt compelled to consult the Self-Government Society. As a result, the group not only dominated the provincial council but also held positions in all government agencies. Because of its prestige, the society attained a membership of 100,000 between 1910 and 1911.[331]

In May, 1911, P'eng Hung-shu was replaced by Shen Yü-ch'ing, the son of the famous reformer Pao-chen. As he arrived, the Szechuan dispute broke into the open. In the fall the prolonged crisis tempted the Self-Government group to launch a coup. With this in mind the leaders sought the support of the armed forces, especially the two brigades and two battalions that made up the New Army of Kweichow. Faced with a virtually certain revolt, Governor Shen adopted four measures. He withheld ammunition from the foreign-modeled army, ordered frequent drills in order to deplete the existing supplies, and as often as he could justify his reasons, he moved the troops away from the capital. In addition, he summoned Liu Hsien-shih, a gentry member from a remote area, to the capital with his old-fashioned

329. *Ibid.*, 414-16.   330. *Ibid.*, 425-26, 440.
331. *Ibid.*, 429, 432-36.

private army. When Chairman T'an Hsi-keng heard of these measures, he used the council's funds to purchase ammunition and conspired to have more stolen from the armory. A successful uprising on November 4, 1911, ended in Shen's flight and the accession of Yang Ching-ch'eng, the Japanese-educated brigadier commander, to the governorship.[332]

Like that of Kweichow, the campaign in Shanghai was the work of both the constitutionalists and the revolutionists, the former led by Li P'ing-shu, the head of the Chinese self-government council (*Tzu-chih kung-so*) and the latter by the Restoration Society. The two unique factors in Shanghai were the foreign settlements, which afforded the insurgents a sanctuary, and the Merchant Volunteer Corps, the Chinese unit of which was under Li P'ing-shu's control.[333] Previously, after the Wuchang uprising had broken out, Li Hsieh-ho, a leader of the Restoration Society, had come to Shanghai in the hope of engineering a coup. He was able to establish contact with the local troops because most of them were Huanaese—they had been so since Tseng Kuo-fan's time—and were Li's fellow-provincials.[334] Finding his task relatively easy because a number of these troops had been deployed to the Hankow front,[335] Li scheduled an uprising for November 5, 1911.[336] Unfortunately for him, he divulged the plan to Ch'en Ch'i-mei, who, though a personal friend, was politically for Sun Yat-sen and against the Restoration clique.[337] Moreover, Ch'en had reached an understanding with Li P'ing-shu on the use of the Merchant Volunteer Corps.[338] To forestall Li Hsieh-ho, Ch'en attacked the armory on the afternoon of November 3. At first his efforts failed and he was captured, but when Li P'ing-shu followed with his forces, little resistance was encountered. Shanghai became autonomous in the early hours of November 4, 1911.[339]

Because of the city's importance, the impact was felt throughout China. As its secession became probable on the evening of November 3, the New Army in Hangchow revolted. The Manchu Banner forces put up a fight at first, but this ceased after T'ang Shou-ch'ien, the former president of the provincial railway company and a popular constitutionalist leader, was elected governor.[340] On November 5, the governor of Kiangsu, Ch'eng Te-ch'üan, also seceded and formed a new

332. *Ibid.*, 425, 446-47.   333. *Ibid.*, VII, 86-89.
334. *Ibid.*, 38, 41-47.   335. *Ibid.*, 40.
336. CKK:HH, 227.

337. It was common knowledge that there was no love lost between Sun Yat-sen and T'ao Cheng-chang. A contemporary source went so far as to state that Sun tried to have T'ao killed in 1909 (HHKM, I, 525). It seems to be a fact that T'ao was assassinated in 1912 by men dispatched by Ch'en Ch'i-mei (HHKM, I, 520).

338. HHHIL, IV, 48.   339. CKK:HH, 227.
340. *Ibid.*, 239.

regime. Chairman Chang Ch'ien of the provincial council then dispatched a circular telegram urging similar action by all provinces.[341] Within the next eight days, five more provinces—Kwangsi, Anhwei, Fukien, Kwangtung, and Shantung—seceded.[342] The only resistance on behalf of the dynasty was made at Nanking, significantly by the old-fashioned troops commanded by Chang Hsün. Hostilities broke out between the New Army and Chang's forces on November 7. At first the rebels were repulsed, but as reinforcements arrived from Soochow, Hangchow, and other cities, Nanking fell on December 2.[343]

By this time all of the provinces south of the Yangtze had declared their independence. As these were by far the richer regions of China, their loss raised extreme financial difficulties for the dynasty. Even more serious was the psychological effect. The Manchu regime became paralyzed with fear. Bent on placating the opposition, the regent accepted on November 3 nineteen constitutional principles submitted by the National Assembly. Three days later he took an oath at the imperial ancestral temple, and on November 8 the Assembly elected Yüan Shih-kai prime minister. On the thirteenth, Yüan arrived in the capital and, on the sixteenth, he completed his cabinet.[344] There was little doubt that he had the military means to crush the insurgents, but he insisted on negotiation. Because of the resulting stalemate, seven more provinces seceded in November. On December 2, Nanking fell; and on the sixth the regent resigned. The only possible obstacle in Yüan's path was the single division of imperial guards under Tsai T'ao's command. Calculating that nothing would frighten the nobleman more than actual fighting, Yüan hinted that the guards and their commander were needed at the front. Tsai T'ao yielded.[345] On December 8 he was replaced by Feng Kuo-chang (whose departure from Hankow thus served a double purpose).[346] After this shuffle the Manchus were completely at Yüan's mercy.

THE PEACE TALKS AND YÜAN'S MANEUVERS

Previously, on November 11, 1911, the military governors of Kiangsu, Chekiang, and Shanghai had invited all insurgent provinces to send delegates to a meeting in Shanghai "in emulation of the Continental Congress of America."[347] On the twelfth, the four delegates of Kiangsu and Chekiang suggested in a circular telegram that Wu T'ing-fang and Wen Tsung-yao be appointed as the diplomatic representatives of the regime that would shortly be estab-

341. CKHTS, III, 368.   342. CKK:HH, 5.
343. HHKM, VII, 77-79.
344. LCN:CKCP, I, 313-14; LYSNP, I, 103.
345. Ibid., 315.   346. CKCTSSC, 360.
347. KKKM, 15.

lished.[348] On the fifteenth, delegates from eleven provinces met and agreed to recognize the Wuchang regime as the central government. At the invitation of that regime, the delegates then moved their meeting to Hankow, where on December 2 they enacted an Outline for the Organization of a Provisional Government of China.[349] Meanwhile, through intermediaries—notably Wang Ching-wei, who had been released from prison on November 6, and Sir John Jordan, the British minister to China—Yüan had made known his three propositions to the revolutionaries: an immediate cease-fire, Manchu abdication, and election of Yüan as president of the republic.[350] These were accepted by the provincial delegates meeting in the British settlement of Hankow.[351] On December 7 Yüan appointed T'ang Shao-i as his representative, and on the eighteenth a peace conference opened in the British-controlled International Settlement at Shanghai. Since the two sides had secretly agreed on their goal,[352] the problems centered around Yüan's formal ascension to the leadership of the republic. One aspect of this problem was the need to cow the Manchus into submission. Here Yüan was helped by his enemies. On January 16, 1912, several revolutionists, acting against the party police, made an unsuccessful attempt on his life.[353] Ten days later, a lone assassin killed Liang Pi, the nobleman noted for his strenuous efforts against the republican cause. These acts of terror unnerved the Manchus and silenced their opposition.[354]

But, unwilling to trust his luck, Yüan had made his own plans. Of the measures he had adopted, two were especially effective. On the grounds that the imperial treasury was empty, an edict of January 3 directed all nobles and officials to donate as much as they could to a campaign fund.[355] This measure silenced those who were parsimonious[356] and weakened those who were liberal. An even more effective means of intimidation was the stand taken by the army. The most articulate officer was Tuan Ch'i-jui, who between January 23 and February 5 dispatched no less than five messages to Peking, first announcing his support for republicanism,[357] then specifically attacking Princes P'u Wei and Tsai Tse for obstructing the peace,[358] and finally stating that he was marching on Peking to "explain the situation to certain depraved noblemen."[359] As other generals—and Chinese envoys abroad—added their voices to Tuan's,[360] the court swiftly capitulated.

But this did not end Yüan's problems, for he still had to deal with the revolutionaries. Once again he used the same tactics. The most

348. *Ibid.*, 16.
349. *Ibid.*, 17.
350. CKHTS, I, 9-10; HHKM, VI, 298, VIII, 117-18, 314; KMWH, 427.
351. KKKM, 17.
352. HHKM, VIII, 118.
353. *Ibid.*, VI, 309.
354. YYJ:HH, 272, 275.
355. CKCTSSC, 362.
356. CKK:HH, 299.
357. HHKM, VIII, 171.
358. *Ibid.*, 172.
359. *Ibid.*, 178-79.
360. *Ibid.*, 179-83.

notable example was his reaction to Sun Yat-sen's assumption of the provisional presidency in January, 1912. Previously, Sun had been on a world tour and was at Denver, Colorado, when the revolution broke out at Wuchang. Returning to China by way of Europe, he arrived at Shanghai on December 25, 1911, amid rumors spread by his followers that he had brought back large sums of money.[361] Because of his supposed funds, and because of his wide foreign connections and seniority as a revolutionary leader, he was elected to the presidency on December 29 by the representatives of seventeen provinces.[362] Sun's election naturally angered Yüan. On January 2, 1912, the day after Sun assumed office, T'ang Shao-i resigned as Yüan's representative at the peace conference.[363] Sixteen generals led by Feng Kuo-chang announced their firm opposition to republicanism.[364] Clearly, Sun must yield or there would be no presidency at all.

Strenuous maneuvers were made by both sides during the next two weeks. Realizing his slim chances, Sun was quite willing to resign, but he insisted that Yüan receive his authority from the republic rather than from the Manchus. To secure this concession from Yüan, he announced to the newspapers on January 23 that he would step down after the abdication and that Yüan would be elected as his successor.[365] Although this candid and direct approach was somewhat embarrassing, Yüan was nonetheless pleased. At his bidding, the northern militarists once again raised their voice; but the ringleader this time was Tuan Ch'i-jui instead of Feng Kuo-chang, and the target was the "depraved" Manchus instead of the infant republic.

Even though Sun's words sounded sincere to Yüan, he was still taking no chances. In the abdication edict, Yüan on his own initiative added a sentence specifically instructing himself "to organize a provisional regime and to confer with the people's army."[366] In this way, if Sun refused to yield the presidency after all, Yüan could remain in power as the Manchu's successor. The south was shocked by this move on Yüan's part, but it was helpless to take any corrective action.[367] Once again the revolutionaries were outmaneuvered by an enemy of superior resources.

THE NEW ARMY

Obviously, the key factor in the last days of the Manchu regime was the attitude and strength of the armed forces. It was the lack of firm military support that forced the hands of the Manchus and the revolutionaries alike. An important question then is what made Yüan so strong. A striking feature of the revolution was the division of the

361. *Ibid.*, I, 528; KKKM, 525.   362. KKKM, 55.
363. *Ibid.*, 528. T'ang's resignation was tendered on December 31, 1911, and accepted on January 2, 1912.
364. HHKM, V, 317-18.   365. KKKM, 602-3.
366. *Ibid.*, 615.   367. HHKM, VIII, 46.

Chinese New Army into two segments. The forces trained and controlled by Yüan were non-revolutionaries and good fighters, while the other units were weak, divided, and anti-dynastic. To understand how this situation came about, we must trace the growth of the foreign-style army in China, which can best be done through a sketch of its two founders—Chang Chih-tung and Yüan Shih-kai.

In 1895 Chang, as acting governor-general at Nanking, began training a new army with the aid of German instructors. Designated as the Self-Strengthening Army, this force consisted of eight battalions of infantry, two squadrons of cavalry, two battalions of artillery, and one battalion of engineers. The soldiers were selected with care from among the peasants. They were required to enlist for no less than ten years, during which they were taught to read and write. By contemporary Chinese standards, their pay was generous.[368] As organization of the new army proceeded, Chang announced on December 27, 1895 that he would eventually expand its strength to 10,000 men. But he was transferred to Wuchang on January 2, 1896, and had no opportunity to realize his plan. By order of the court, Chang left in Nanking a force of some 2,880 men. Before his transfer he had also founded a military academy of 150 cadets and a railway school of 90 students.[369] In Hupeh Chang continued his goal of modernizing the army. Two new battalions were formed in 1896. By 1902 these had been expanded into a force of 7,750 men and were rated by Western observers as the best in China.[370] Meanwhile, as the Empress Dowager initiated reforms in the post-Boxer period, she too became interested in army reorganization. At her order the Board of War prepared a comprehensive report in 1904, which envisaged the establishment by 1922 of a standing army of thirty-six divisions for all of China, of which Hupeh was to have three divisions and Hunan, one (12,500 men).[371] But because of financial and other difficulties, neither Chang nor his successors expanded the New Army at Hupeh to more than one division and one mixed brigade, which in 1911 totaled 13,000 men, not counting a thousand or more military cadets.[372]

Before we deal with Yüan's activities, we should briefly describe his background, which was unusual and had an important bearing on his military career. Yüan was born in 1859 to a family of officials at Changteh, Hanan. Because his mother was a concubine of little status in an old-fashioned household, Yüan had a rather unhappy childhood and was in fact known as a delinquent.[373] By the standards of the Chi-

368. PRL:RCM, 63.   369. *Ibid.*, 61-62, 67.
370. *Ibid.*, 148-49.   371. *Ibid.*, 172, 179-80.
372. HHKM, III, 330; CKK:HH, 69.
373. SYL:HTCC, p. 43. This source, though short of giving a complete account of Yüan's life, is far more reliable than some of the other works. The belief voiced by one author (PRL:RCM, 73) that Yüan had a sound classical education is un-

nese scholar-official class, his education was poor—a fact that might have contributed to Yüan's insensitivity to traditional moral values. In 1866 he acquired the honorific title of Secretary of the Imperial Patent Office *(Chung-shu)* through a privilege inherited from his uncle Pao-heng (canonized Wen-ch'eng), which entitled him to compete at the provincial civil-service examinations.[374] This he did in the autumn of 1879, but he failed and became convinced that he should give up the life of "brush and ink" in favor of military pursuits.[375] Joining the staff of General Wu Ch'ang-ch'ing in 1880, a family friend of long standing, he took part in an expedition to Korea in 1882. Partly through Wu's patronage and partly because of his own ability, Yüan rapidly ascended the nine-rung mandarin's ladder. He earned his Peacock Feather in 1882[376] and was the *de facto* Chinese resident in Korea between 1885 and 1894.[377] Through adroit maneuvers in Peking Yüan secured his recall from Korea on the eve of the war with Japan.[378] On his return in July, 1894, he was appointed, through the influence of Grand Councilors Weng T'ung-ho and Li Hung-tsao, intendant of a circuit in Chekiang,[379] but he went instead to Manchuria to help in sending supplies to troops fighting the Japanese.[380] After the war he was directed by the court to train a foreign-style army, a task that had been begun under Hu Yü-fen and von Hanneken, a German military advisor of Li Hung-chang. Starting with the ten battalions already formed, Yüan moved the training site from Tientsin to Hsiao-chan, twenty miles south, and started his work in earnest in mid-December, 1895. He soon expanded the corps to seven thousand men and impressed all observers with their efficiency and discipline.[381] The reputation of the Peiyang forces earned Yüan the notice of the reformist faction headed by Emperor Kuang-hsü, who in 1898 made him an expectant Vice-President of the Board in the hope of using his forces to protect himself from the Dowager Empress. But Yüan threw in his lot with the enemy and thus brought about the disgrace of the emperor as well as the collapse of the reform movement.[382]

By gaining the confidence of the Queen Mother, Yüan rose rapidly in officialdom. In 1899 he became governor of Shantung. Taking his division with him, he remained on the sidelines during the Boxer troubles but seized the opportunity of expanding his forces from 7,400 to 10,000 or more.[383] After Li Hung-chang's death in 1901, Yüan was

founded, and the statement by another that Yüan sat for the first level civil-service examinations (CJ:YSK, 14) is even more erroneous.

374. SYL:HTCC, 42-43; HA:ECCP, II, 950.
375. STH:JATT, 7.   376. *Ibid.*, 12.
377. HA:ECCP, II, 951.   378. SYL:HTCC, 47.
379. *Ibid.*, 48.   380. HA:ECCP, II, 951.
381. PRL:RCM, 76-77, 105.
382. TSS:CTS, 159-66; SYL:HTCC, 54.
383. PRL:RCM, 124-25.

moved to Chihli as the premier governor-general of China. During the following six years he sponsored many reform programs, but his main interest was still the new army. In July, 1901, he took over the troops first organized by Chang Chih-tung in Nanking. Between 1902 and 1905 he increased his forces to six divisions and made them the best drilled and best equipped in China.[384]

Chang and Yüan set the pace for all China. In September, 1901, the court directed all provinces to establish military academies and to train their forces according to foreign methods.[385] In December of the following year, to strengthen this program, the court directed one group of provinces to send their men to Chihli for training, and another group to send their men to Hupeh.[386] In 1903, at the suggestion of Yüan Shih-kai, the throne approved the establishment of a Committee for Army Reorganization. In conjunction with the Board of War this committee drew up in 1904 a scheme providing for a standing army of thirty-six divisions with a peace-time strength of 450,000 men. This proposal was approved,[387] but owing to financial and other reasons, it was never implemented. The actual strength of the armies in existence on the eve of the revolution is unknown, but some estimates placed the total number of troops at 600,000 and the New Army at between 150,000 and 190,000, of which about 80,000 were under the influence of Yüan Shih-kai.[388] In addition, there were in October, 1911, some seventy military educational institutions scattered throughout the country with a total enrollment of at least 10,000 students.[389]

While Yüan and Chang were co-founders of the new army, they made strikingly different contributions to it. Yüan was particularly noted for the close personal attention he paid to his army. From 1895 to 1899 he was stationed at Hsiao-chan and took direct charge of the training. Because the corps was not then a part of the regular forces, Yüan was free to choose his own officers.[390] For both political and geographical reasons, nearly all of his officers were graduates of the Tientsin military academy founded by Li Hung-chang in 1885.[391] Even after Yüan became governor-general of Chihli, he continued to take a personal interest in the army. Unlike the other provincial heads he was not forced to rely on men trained in Japan, and as a matter of policy he excluded them from his military entourage. This procedure was in contrast to the training and organization of units controlled by Chang Chih-tung and the others, who, as scholars or indolent aristocrats, were either unwilling or un-

384. *Ibid.*, 205-9.   385. KTI:CTCK, II, 1147.
386. *Ibid.*, II, 1171.   387. BHS:PDPO, 139, 285-89.
388. PRL:RCM, 288-89, 296-97: CM:TRM, 91.
389. PRL:RCM, 299.   390. *Ibid.*, 211-12.
391. HHKM, III, 324, 325.

able to share the hardships of a soldier's life. Invariably they assigned the supervisory duties to some other officers. Because some technical knowledge was needed and few Western-trained Chinese were available, persons who had studied in Japan were the logical choice for officers and instructors.[392] As practically all of them had been exposed to radical thought, they lost no time in spreading revolutionary ideals within their units.

Related to this difference in approach were many other factors that separated Yüan from the other officials. Chang Chih-tung, for instance, was in his late fifties when he began organizing the new army in Nanking. He had achieved great prestige and was known throughout China as a Confucian scholar. It is most unlikely that he ever entertained thoughts of usurping the throne. His primary motivation in undertaking military reform was presumably to help in the strengthening of his country. He felt no need to build a personal following among his troops, nor would circumstances have favored him if he had wished to do so. Yüan, on the other hand, was born in a period of rapid dynastic decline. He was only twenty-three years old when he earned his Peacock Feather, and thirty-six when he launched the training program at Hsiao-chan. By all contemporary accounts he was both able and unscrupulous. He attached little importance to moral standards and chose his subordinates on the basis of ability rather than character. Unlike Chang he had no claims to fame and authority. Therefore he gave his greatest attention to the army and always contrived to move his forces with him when he was transferred from one post to another. To develop a large personal following, he dispensed patronage liberally among his lieutenants. As a recent writer points out, no less than five future presidents or chief executives, a premier, and most of the warlords of northern China came from among the officers of a single brigade that Yüan trained at Hsiao-chan in 1895.[393] Even his civilian aides received unusually rapid promotions; thus, Hsü Shih-ch'ang rose from an expectant circuit intendant to Grand Councilor in five years while T'ang Shao-i, one of Yung Wing's C.E.M. boys, was promoted from a customs intendant to provincial governor in as short a time.[394] But it should be noted that Yüan's success in taking care of his friends depended as much on his scheming as on his luck. Had it not been for the abortive reform of 1908 he could hardly have obtained so much support from the Empress Dowager. He would then have been unable to dispense patronage and retain his command. Even Chang Chih-tung lost thir-

392. WCSI, 445.
393. PRL:RCM, 79-80. Actually, there were two future premiers among these officers instead of one, for Chia Te-yao, who was a regimental commander under Yüan (WCSI, 472), acted as premier from February to April in 1926 (KYT:CTSC, 201, 209).
394. PRL:RCM, 213.

teen battalions to Liu K'un-i in 1895 and eight more to Ts'en Ch'un-hsuan in 1903.[395] By contrast, Yüan's first setback did not come until 1906 when he lost four of his six divisions to the Board of War.[396] By then the bond between him and the officers had become so firm that the transfer made little difference.

Because the circumstances of his career were unique, Yüan was inimitable. Other provincial officials either emulated Chang Chih-tung or kept aloof from the reform movement. When the revolution broke out, none of them could rally the foreign-style troops under the Manchu banner. Yüan was the only exception, and the Manchus had no choice but to recall him. Their mistake lay not so much in making this move as in drifting into a position that allowed no alternative.

AN INTERPRETATION

In the most basic sense this revolution seems to have resulted from the inability of the traditional order to adjust to the new situation that developed after the Opium War of 1839-42. By that time the basic institutions in China, such as the monarchy and the bureaucracy, had existed for two thousand years. They had acquired a rigidity that prevented modification. As a result, while attempts at reform were repeatedly made, they failed to relieve China's troubles but rather compounded them by creating more tension within the educated class. Each successive wave of innovation brought about a sharper division within it and a greater degree of hostility toward the regime. Thus it was the reform of the seventies that produced the writings of Yen Fu and the effort of the nineties that initiated Liang Ch'i-ch'ao's activities in Japan. Both of these men were the most outspoken critics of the regime during their times. By 1905 the Russo-Japanese War had brought about a third wave of innovation in China. This resulted in a great exodus of Chinese intellectuals to Japan, which directly led to the mushrooming of revolutionary activities and the subsequent fall'of the Manchus from power.

More specifically, the prelude to the revolution of 1911 consisted of two phases: a period of intellectual fermentation from 1895 to 1905 and a period of action from 1905 to 1911. The first could again be divided into two sub-phases, of which the earlier witnessed the impact of Yen Fu's thought and the later, that of Liang's. It would seem that these two together furnished all of the intellectual ingredients necessary for a revolutionary movement. The fact that neither Yen nor Liang wanted to overthrow the Manchus was quite immaterial, as was the effort by many revolutionists to deny them a place in their midst. Indeed, the best testimonials of Yen's and Liang's revolutionary roles are found in the writings of their critics.

395. *Ibid.*, 156.   396. *Ibid.*, 216.

Thus, according to Sun Ch'uan-yüan, a member of the Alliance Society, "Toward the end of the Ch'ing dynasty, two different schools of thought stirred the mind of the nation. One was nationalism with its anti-Manchu, revolutionary stand, and the other was constitutional monarchism. Bearing in mind the evolutionary principle of the survival of the fittest, the idealistic youth knew that China would perish without a revolution. Hence they all rallied under the revolutionary banner."[397] Since Yen Fu was the first and foremost exponent of evolutionism in China, Sun's statement unwittingly indicates Yen's contribution to China's revolutionary thought.

Similarly, Liang's impact can be deduced from writings whose purpose was to deny it. Thus Wu Yueh wrote:

> [When I was twenty-four years old], a friend lent me a copy of *The Revolutionary Army*. I read it three times and was much moved. It so happened that Russia was then occupying Mukden, and the newspapers were filled with alarming reports. [The book and this crisis] opened my eyes to the emergency faced by the country . . . but still I did not pay attention to the alien origin of the reigning house. A little later somebody lent me his copies of *Public Opinion* (*Ch'ing I Pao*). Before I finished reading it, the writer's thought had become mine. Thereafter I constantly talked about constitutionalism and hoped to see the establishment of a constitutional government. I told everybody that the Dowager Empress had let the country down, and that the Emperor was a most sagacious person. [At this time] whoever criticized K'ang Yu-wei and Liang Ch'i ch'ao incurred my animosity. . . . Some time later I became exposed to *The New Kwangtung*, *The New Hunan*, *The Alarm to Arouse the Age* . . . [and other pamphlets], and my thought again changed.[398]

Even though Wu continued by denouncing Liang's complaisance toward the Manchus, his words revealed two things of that he himself did not fully realize. One was that his anti-Manchuism was initiated by Liang's merciless attack on the Empress Dowager, and the other that not a few of the books Wu mentioned as sources of his revolutionism were actually written by men in or near the constitutionalist camp. *The New Kwangtung*, it will be recalled, was written by Ou Chü-chia, and *The Alarm to Arouse the Age* was penned by Ch'en T'ien-hua, who at least in early 1905 was close to Liang and his group.[399] Thus, not only was Liang responsible for Wu's metamorphosis but he also influenced him through these other writers.

By contrast the impetus in the final phase of the revolution stemmed from a variety of sources. A primary contribution came

397. HHKM, VII, 181.   398. SC:SHS, 760-61.

399. Ernest P. Young, "Ch'en T'ien-hua (1875-1905): A Chinese Nationalist," HPC (December, 1959), 130.

from the unwitting officials. Many were demonstrably inept, except perhaps in the conduct of intrigues. Ironically, the abler and more conscientious officials caused the regime only additional trouble in the long run, for it was they who inaugurated the press, sent students abroad, trained an army, and founded pseudo-representative bodies. While it is true that these innovations followed rather than preceded the dynastic decline, they nevertheless doomed the regime. In this sense the ablest officials contributed most heavily to the revolution, whatever their intentions may have been.

A look at the provincial campaigns clearly reveals the connection between reform and revolution. While disturbances occurred in all of the provinces, they were far worse in the "progressive" than in the "backward" ones. Thus, Wuchang, where Chang Chih-tung practically ruled from 1889 to 1907, was the scene of the first outbreak, but Kansu, the only province which by 1905 had not sent any students to Japan,[400] experienced the least turmoil. If it is argued that the difference was due to Hupeh's richness and Kansu's poverty, then we could use Kweichow to show that with official encouragement even the poorest region could still develop political radicalism.

An even more significant case is Singkiang, where two regimes, a republican one at Ili and a loyalist one at Tihua, existed between January and June of 1912. Basically, the whole province was economically undeveloped and was the only one in China without a provincial council. But Ch'ang Keng, Tartar-General of Ili from 1905 to 1909, favored reform. During his administration he opened schools, built roads, constructed factories, and inaugurated public utilities. Using several hundred soldiers from Hupeh as a nucleus, he had a training camp, the Model Battalion, set up. In the process many positions were created and offered to the incoming Japanese-trained men. Ch'ang Keng was replaced in the autumn of 1909 by Kuang Fu, an illiterate but "progressive" official who continued his predecessor's policy. Two years later, he was in turn replaced by Chih Jui, who on arrival disbanded the foreign-style troops, but without immediately paying them their parting travel allowance. This provided the revolutionaries with an issue, and an insurrection occurred on January 7, 1912. Chih Jui was killed, and Ili seceded with Kuang Fu acting as its head.[401]

In contrast, Tihua remained loyal. Although Yüan Ta-hua had been governor only since the summer of 1911, he was able to maintain order. On December 28, 1911, a Japanese-trained revolutionary from Hunan, Liu Hsien-chün, organized an outbreak with the support of secret society members and some of the regular troops, but the movement was crushed by Yüan Ta-hua within two days.[402]

400. HHKM, II, 7.   401. *Ibid.,* VII, 428-30.
402. *Ibid.,* 442-44.

After Ili's secession, Yüan launched a punitive expedition and kept it going until he, refusing to be a Republican official, resigned in June, 1912.[403] It was then four months after the Manchu emperor had abdicated. Tihua thus stood out as a bastion of strength for the decaying Manchu regime. While this situation might have resulted from Yüan's ability, a more basic reason probably lay in Tihua's isolation from the reform stream. It is from instances like this that the correlation between innovation and revolution stands out at its clearest.

Next to the officials an important group was the provincial councilors, whose authority stemmed from the newly established representative bodies. The councilers were generally the enlightened members of the gentry, who bore the stamp of their status and background. As avowed moralists and humanitarians, they could lash out mercilessly at the men in power or take it upon themselves to protect worthy fugitives at great risk to themselves. But as a rule they abhorred violent upheaval and distrusted the masses. Some reorientation took place as the national crisis deepened and many members of the higher gentry traveled or studied in Japan. Convinced of the need for change, they criticized and organized. Some even went as far as to plot against the regime. But the majority contented themselves with talk. Had it not been for the national and provincial assemblies, they would have been much less active in the final phase of the revolution.

The situation, however, was radically altered by the appearance of these bodies. In spite of their inherent passivity the higher gentry had come into its own, for reasons not difficult to determine. Although the gentry had always played an important role in the Chinese political process, they had done so informally and on the sufferance of the court. As officials these men became members of the gentry, but as gentry they had no claims on the government. They were, in a word, tools of the throne rather than watchdogs of the people. The constitutional reform of 1909 reversed this process. Not only were the councilors recognized by the government, but they also had an open forum in which to express their opinion. Furthermore, circumstances were in their favor. The tottering court was in no position to impose its will, and both a press and political parties had developed. By exercising group pressure and utilizing the press, the councilors could achieve their ends more effectively than a traditional censor. The situation improved even further after the convocation of the National Assembly, for pressure could now be brought on the throne, which by tradition never favored an official in trouble with the people. A compelling need arose for the governors to in-

403. *Ibid.*, 438.

gratiate themselves with the gentry, who could now effectively challenge the existing power structure. Thus, in Shensi the head of the provincial army staff (*Tu-lien kung-so tsung-pan*) was replaced in 1910 after being persistently attacked by the councilors. According to contemporary sources, this was the first step toward the revolution in that province.[404]

A further strength of the provincial council lay in the fact that it was often the only group that could aid an official when he lost contact with Peking. In the last months of 1911, many governors were uncertain of the fate of the regime. Never born in the province in which they held office, provincial heads were helpless once their official status was in doubt. The only way they could ensure their personal safety was to establish rapport with local interests. This was why Chao Erh-feng, in spite of his earlier insistence on their guilt, dealt with the nine gentry members and made one of them governor.

The importance of the councils naturally meant that they played crucial roles in the final struggle. In some provinces they directly organized the revolution; in others they served as middlemen and arranged for the peaceful transfer of power. As far as we know, in all of the provinces at least some of the councilors became key members of the revolutionary movement. In addition to P'u Tien-chün, both T'an Yen-kai and T'ang Shou-ch'ien became governors.[405] Chang Ch'ien was of course even more important. He not only encouraged Chang Shao-tseng's anti-dynastic moves at Luanchow but was probably the first to support Yüan Shih-kai for the presidency.[406] As minister of industries in Sun Yat-sen's provisional government, he raised 300,000 silver dollars for the hard-pressed regime by mortgaging the cotton mill he personally controlled.[407]

No account of the revolution of 1911 should overlook the Alliance Society. Most of the New Army officers outside the Peiyang clique were affiliated with this group, and in every provincial campaign several key individuals belonged to it. However, to what extent credit for the revolution should be attributed to the Alliance Society as such is open to question. To begin with, the members shared no common belief beyond anti-Manchuism; as Sun Yat-sen repeatedly pointed out, few of them understood his basic principles.[408] Nor did they have a common strategy beyond the use of violence. Indeed, the outstanding feature of the 1911 uprisings was their spontaneity. Of the earliest and perhaps most important campaigns, the Szechuan dispute was until the very last waged by the gentry at large, while the Wuchang revolt had no prior guidance from any of the top

404. *Ibid.*, VI, 61-62.
405. For a list of the revolutionary provincial governors, see KKKM, 13-14.
406. CKHTS, I, 8-9.   407. HHKM, VIII, 51.
408. KFCC, I, 206, II, 1; SCSHC, II, 797.

Alliance Society leaders. Sun Yat-sen was on a world tour, and Huang Hsing had virtually ignored the possibilities. Although Huang went to Wuhan after the uprising began, he soon fled in accordance with his pattern of "fighting, failing, and fleeing."[409] In almost all of the campaigns there was confusion and poor leadership; it was for this reason that the insurgents often forced the old officials to remain at their posts.

A powerful factor behind the impotence of the Alliance Society was internal dissension, which raged before, during, and after the revolution of 1911. The acute antagonism between T'ao Ch'eng-chang and Sun Yat-sen culminated in T'ao's assassination in 1911.[410] Even as Sun assumed the provisional presidency, key leaders quarreled on such basic issues as the proper political structure and the choice of a capital. Chang Ping-lin, who favored Peking as opposed to Sun's selection of Nanking, openly called his colleagues "pilfering rats and dogs" (shu-ch-ieh kou-t'ou).[411] Sung Chiao-jen differed from Sun even more. He disliked not only Sun's choice of a capital but also his principle of livelihood and his insistence on the presidential form of government.[412] Largely through Sung's efforts, the Alliance Society was reorganized into the Kuomintang in August, 1912, and one of the first things it did was to delete from its platform the provision for "equalization of landownership."[413]

Such basic disagreements necessarily weakened the society's military position. According to Hu Han-min's memoirs, although there were seventeen divisions under the revolutionary banner, the Nanking regime actually controlled less than a few thousand men, and even for these it could not provide adequate resources.[414] The only solution was to come to terms with Yüan Shih-kai, and it was no accident that Yüan was elected by the provincial delegates with one more vote than Sun Yat-sen.[415]

Contrary to popular belief the Alliance Society did not launch the revolution of 1911. Indeed, no one did, if by launching we mean conscious aims and fairly precise planning. On the other hand, if the revolution was the inevitable outcome of change, it was promoted by everyone, including the Manchus themselves. In short, the events of 1911 resulted from the interactions of many persons, all of whom desired change but none of whom knew what was happening, an altogether reasonable phenomenon if we regard the upheaval as a cataclysm arising out of Western impact.

Within this general interpretation the significant role of the Chinese in Japan should be noted, for it was in their midst that

409. HHKM, VIII, 104.
411. SYL:HTCC, 35.
413. KFNP, I, 336.
415. KKKM, 56, 631.

410. Ibid., I, 520.
412. LS:HH, 56.
414. KMWH, 433.

anti-Manchu propaganda first flourished and influential revolutionary organizations appeared. Subsequently, it was these men who in an immediate sense secured the overthrow of the dynasty. Perhaps the surest evidence of their distinction was a negative one: whenever these men were absent—whether at Tihua or among Yüan Shih-kai's forces—there was correspondingly less impetus toward change. This conclusion does not identify them as masters of China's destiny, but only as unconscious tools of history.

The years immediately after 1919 are known in China as the May Fourth period.[1] The name is derived from a student demonstration in Peking on May 4, 1919, the immediate cause of which was China's failure to regain her lost interests in Shantung at the Paris Peace Conference. Previously, by a treaty concluded in 1898, China had leased Kiaochow in Shantung to Germany. In 1914, Japan declared war on Germany and occupied the leased territory over China's protest. A few months later, Japan presented the Twenty-one Demands to China, which, among other things, sought to legitimize Japanese interests in Shantung. When the peace conference opened in Paris, China, encouraged by President Wilson's fourteen points, entertained high hopes of regaining her rights from Japan. But these hopes were shattered by a series of secret treaties in which England, France, and Italy pledged their support to Japan.[2] Another obstacle in China's path was an agreement made with Japan in September, 1918, in which she had granted Japan the right to station troops in Shantung in return for a sizable loan. In an official note, the Chinese government declared that China "gladly agrees to these terms."[3] This document is said to have seriously weakened China's case at the peace conference.[4]

Internally, the Chinese government was also in a weak condition. Since the turn of the century and particularly during the last years of the Manchu regime, the intelligentsia had become extremely restless. Student strikes, petitions, and demonstrations had become a regular feature of Chinese educational life.[5] The death of Yüan Shih-kai in 1916 left China without a strong leader and intensified the difficulties of the government. The chronic financial situation inherited from previous regimes was further weakened by the burden of armaments, and the Peking government looked longingly for foreign loans. In the winter of 1916, Japan adopted a new policy which stressed economic and financial encroachment. During the next two years, a series of loans were made to the Peking government—mainly through a Japanese intermediary named Nishihara, who was a close friend of Japanese Prime Minister Terauchi—totaling some 150,000,000

1. CTT:TMM, 1; LCC:YCC, 14-52. 2. CTT:TMM, 86
3. WYS:LSN, VI, 184-87. 4. CTT:TMM, 87-89.
5. WCSJ (January-February, 1908), 39; *ibid.* (November, 1908), 170; CM:TRM, 87.

Japanese yen.[6] In May, 1918, a mutual military defense agreement was concluded between China and Japan. All of these developments appeared highly suspicious to the students.

In addition, several very influential intellectual leaders were daily condemning the old order and extolling the virtues of revolution. The chancellor of Peking University, Ts'ai Yüan-p'ei, an old Han-lin scholar turned revolutionary, who had gone to Europe to study and who commanded an immense following among the younger intellectuals, was hostile to the Peking authorities and encouraged the students to defy them.[7] During March and April of 1919, when feverish diplomatic activities were taking place in Paris, rumors began spreading in China that the Peking government had imposed restrictions on the Chinese delegates to the conference in the interests of Japan, a rumor supported by an unusual telegram to the Shanghai newspapers by one of the delegates, C. T. Wang, who represented the Southern government in Canton.[8] When the news reached Peking of China's diplomatic failure in Paris, a huge student demonstration broke out in the city, one that has since become a landmark in modern Chinese history.

On the afternoon of May 4, 1919, some three thousand students from thirteen schools in Peking staged a demonstration in which they carried white flags bearing such inscriptions as "International Justice," "Return Our Tsingtao," "Abolish the Twenty-One Demands," and "Down with the Traitors." Three officials in the government were specifically denounced: Ts'ao Ju-lin, a principal negotiator of the treaties relating to the Twenty-One Demands and the Nishihara loans; Lu Tsung-yu, Chinese Minister to Japan at the time of the Twenty-One Demands and currently president of the Sino-Japanese Exchange Bank, which handled the Nishihara loans; and Chang Tsung-hsiang, Chinese Minister to Tokyo on leave in Peking. All three were Japanese-educated and appeared to the public as Japanophiles. Despite police protection, the demonstrators stormed Ts'ao's residence, severely assaulted Chang Tsung-hsiang who by chance happened to be there, and set fire to the house after Ts'ao himself narrowly escaped through a back door. Some thirty-two students were subsequently arrested, but the public was solidly behind the students. Elder politicians petitioned the government to release the students.[9] Both Ts'ai Yüan-p'ei and Fu Tseng-hsiang, the Minister of Education, resigned. Throughout the country there were strikes, and many merchants shut up their shops. A month later,

6. LYSNP, I, 414.

7. PTP:CKC, II, 26; CML:TFW, 123. Ts'ai's manifest sympathy for the rebellious students naturally exasperated the Peking authorities. For a rumored scheme to oust Ts'ai, see DJA:LCJ, 296.

8. CTST, 43.   9. *Ibid.*, 55-56.

the government capitulated, and all three "traitors" were dismissed from office.[10]

The May Fourth incident was the focus of a series of intellectual upheavals which took place after 1915. In that year Ch'en Tu-hsiu (1879-1942), a native of Huai-ning, Anhwei, who had studied in Japan and France, founded a magazine, *Youth (Ch'ing Nien)*, in Shanghai.[11] Almost from the beginning the journal declared war on Confucianism. According to Ch'en, the destruction of the old cultural values embodied in Confucianism was a prerequisite to the modernization of China.

> If we think . . . the Confucian way can enable [China] to survive in this competitive world, then all the reform of the last decade . . . is superfluous . . . and should be undone. If . . . we expect to establish a Western type of modern nation . . . then the most basic step is to import the foundation of modern Western society—the faith in the equality of men. In regard to Confucianism, which is incompatible with a new society, a new nation, a new faith, we must have a complete awakening and determination. Unless the [old] one is demolished, the [new] one will not arise.[12]

The fight against tradition was carried on by Ch'en and a few contributors to the magazine until 1917, when Ch'en was invited by Ts'ai Yüan-p'ei (1876-1940), the new president of National Peking University, to be dean of the School of Letters. With Ts'ai as protector and Ch'en as key administrator, a new group of intellectuals soon joined the faculty. A little earlier, Hu Shih (1891-1962), then still a student at Columbia, had communicated with Ch'en in regard to a proposed literary reform. At Ch'en's suggestion, he submitted an article entitled "Some Tentative Suggestions for the Reform of Chinese Literature," which Ch'en published in the January issue of the journal (now renamed *New Youth*). In the very next issue Ch'en himself supported Hu in a leading article boldly designated "On the Literary Revolution." These writings fired the imagination of many others, among whom was Ch'ien Hsuan-t'ung (1887-1939), a well-known Japanese-educated philologist then teaching at the University. Ch'ien joined the New Youth group and persuaded Lu Hsün (1891-1934), another Japanese-trained writer, to become a contributor.[13] In his first short story, "The Diary of a Madman," which appeared in *New Youth* in May, 1918, Lu Hsün maintained that: "I looked at a book of Chinese history . . . On every page are

10. *Ibid.*, 39-107.

11. CTT:TMM, 42*n*, 44. The magazine was renamed *New Youth* with a French title *La Jeunesse* in September, 1916.

12. LJ, Vol. II, No. 3.   13. CTT:TMM, 53*n*, 308.

written such words as 'righteousness' and 'moral virtues'. . . . . After reading carefully for half the night, I found other words in between the columns; everywhere in the book are the two words 'man-eating.' "

In a series of articles on Confucianism, Wu Yü, another writer trained in Japan, concluded that China's ethical system had impeded her intellectual development and furthered the cause of autocracy.[14] This indictment was highly praised by Hu Shih, who wrote: "I want to introduce to the youth of the nation this great hero, Mr. Wu Yü, the great anti-Confucianist from Szechuan."[15] Hu joined the faculty of Peking University in 1917 while Wu Yü and Lu Hsün did so in 1919 and 1920 respectively.[16] The university now became the center of radical agitation. To attract the attention of the public, the *New Youth* group published a planted letter to the editor and then refuted the absurd charges it leveled against the magazine.[17] Meanwhile, the group benefited from an attack by a real opponent, Lin Shu (1852-1924), who was a strict Confucian moralist in his personal life but who was widely known for having translated some 180 Western novels without knowing a foreign language.[18] Lin particularly objected to the use of the university by Ch'en's group as a forum to spread their anti-traditional ideas. In an open letter he listed his charges and urged President Ts'ai to be mindful of his duty as a guardian of public morality. In a reply the latter, whom Lin rather sarcastically addressed by the old Manchu title of *han-lin*, denied the charges.[19] Both letters received widespread attention. At about the same time Lin satirized Ts'ai, Ch'en, Hu, and their group in several of his short stories, thus providing them with further publicity.[20]

But most of all, it was the May Fourth incident that greatly boosted the anti-Confucian campaign. In the following months *New Youth* achieved a circulation unprecedented for a journal of its nature in China.[21] Over four hundred new magazines soon appeared, each concentrating its fire on tradition and the old ethics. The idea of "dumping the national heritage" was enthusiastically embraced by the youth, who revolted against all existing institutions. Among other things, they launched a "Family Revolution," a "Theatre Revolution," and a "Freedom and Equality Between Father and Son Revolution."[22] A number of these people went as far as to change their family names either to some arbitrary symbols such as "You-

14. Quoted in KCP:CWS, 283.   15. HS:WT (1953) I, 797.
16. CTT:TMM, 53.   17. *Ibid.*, 66.
18. *Ibid.*, 64n.   19. CKHWH, I, 193-99.
20. *Ibid.*, 202-3.
21. WTC:TYM, 77. A reliable source estimates the circulation of *New Youth* at fifteen thousand copies. See TCJ:WTWS, 98.
22. WTC:TYM, 81.

I-He" or to tendentious words such as "Doubting-Antiquity."[23] After May, 1919, discipline largely disappeared in Chinese schools. Students went on strike for trifles and claimed the right to engage and dismiss teachers. They refused to take examinations, boycotted newly-appointed school principals or university presidents, and demanded changes in the curriculum to suit their tastes.[24] An immense destructive force was released which profoundly influenced contemporary Chinese history.

The movement, spectacular as it was, had a logical explanation. The same forces that had discredited Chinese practices before Chang Chih-tung's time now operated to discredit Confucian values. The prime mover behind all agitation for change since 1860 was the agonizing concern of the literati with China's international and internal debilitation. As long as the situation remained unimproved, experimenting with new ways, reformist or revolutionary, would continue. From 1860 to 1911 the scope of change increasingly widened; it ranged from the acquisition of linguistic skill to education and politics. Then the Manchu regime was overthrown. At every stage people saw the millennium ahead; yet time brought only disillusion, and the process repeated itself on a larger scale.

By 1915 the only major institution that had not been called into question was Confucianism. Its turn was not long in coming. A sign of this was the shrinking place the Confucian classics occupied in the school curriculum. According to the 1904 regulations, there was in Peking University a faculty of Chinese classics consisting of eleven departments. In the middle school, classics occupied nine hours per week or one quarter of the total class hours; in the higher primary school, twelve hours or one third of the total; in the lower primary school, twelve hours or two-fifths of the total.[25] By 1909 and 1910 protests were heard against teaching the classics in elementary schools. As a consequence, such teaching was eliminated from the first two grades and reduced to five hours in the third and fourth grades, to eleven in the fifth through the seventh, and to ten in the eighth.[26] Yet opposition continued, and in May, 1912, the course was entirely eliminated in the primary schools. Meanwhile, in Peking University, the faculty of Chinese classics was incorporated in the faculty of literature. In 1915, Yüan Shih-kai personally ordered the reinstatement of three hours of Chinese classics in the higher grades of the primary schools, but he died and the order was ignored.[27] Thus it is clear that the tendency to turn away from Confucianism

23. CTT:TMM, 316n.   24. WTC:TYM, 192-95.
25. WFC:CYS, 293-94.
26. Ibid., 295-96; "Thirty Five Years of Chinese Primary Education," SSWN, 11-20.
27. Ibid., 300.

had started before Ch'en Tu-hsiu appeared on the scene. However, the influence exercised by Ch'en's group turned a gradual process into a spectacular demise. Henceforth Confucianism was so thoroughly discredited that to youthful minds the mere name connoted musty obscurantism.

Yet this "transvaluation of values" raised more problems than it settled. China had long been accustomed to a comprehensive explicit system of beliefs, and the repudiation of Confucianism left a serious void to be filled. In January, 1919, Ch'en wrote: "In order to foster Democracy, we must oppose Confucianism, chastity, old ethics, and old politics. In order to foster Science, we must oppose the old arts and religion. In order to foster both Democracy and Science, we must oppose our national heritage and our old literature."[28] The antithesis pointed naturally to the replacement of Confucianism by Science and Democracy, which as symbols of Western strength were much cherished by Chinese intellectuals. But Ch'en used these terms as little more than rhetorical expressions. What precisely did they mean, and how could they be realized? When the need for clarification arose, as it did after May 4, 1919, Ch'en had to seek out a new source of inspiration. He soon found it in John Dewey, who was then lecturing in China.

Speaking of American democracy, Dewey dwelled on four basic principles: (1) political democracy as practiced through constitutionalism and the parliamentary system; (2) democracy in people's rights such as freedom of speech, press, belief, residence, and the like; (3) social democracy or the abolition of social inequality; (4) economic democracy or a more equitable redistribution of wealth. Throughout his talks he stressed the importance of local self-government at the village level in America and suggested that China might utilize its old guild system in building a democracy.[29] Taking the cue, Ch'en published an article (December, 1919) entitled "The Basis for the Realization of Democracy in China," in which he suggested two programs: local self-government and a new guild system. The two were possible, he believed, because under the traditional *laissez-faire* policy there had been many self-governing bodies in the Chinese body politic. Democracy needed only to develop from this historical basis. The guilds should be joined by both the employers and employees because "except in a few big factories, railroads, and mines . . . the status of employers and employees differs little in China." He then laid down five general principles for the organization of these self-governing bodies: (1) the unit should be as small as possible, (2) everybody, male and female, should participate directly in group affairs, (3) executives should be elected at frequent

---

28. "In Defense of the Crimes Committed by This Magazine," LJ, Vol. VI, No. 1.
29. CTT:TMM, 228, 229, 231.

intervals with strictly limited tenure, (4) stress should be given to the practical needs of the group concerned rather than to broad problems facing the nation, and (5) these self-governing bodies should entertain no connection with militarists, bureaucrats, or politicians.[30]

Two articles on science appeared in New Youth in 1919 and 1920, before the journal became an organ of the Communists. Both were written by Wang Hsin-kung, an English-educated man who later became president of Wuhan University. In the first, entitled "The Origin and Consequences of Science," Wang attributed the growth of science to man's curiosity, his aesthetic taste, his inclination to seek truth, and his urge to summarize through abstraction.[31] In the second, entitled "What is the Scientific Method?" Wang described the five steps of a correct procedure to gain knowledge. These were: (1) observing the relevant facts, (2) analyzing the results, (3) selecting data for closer study, (4) drawing inferences, and (5) testing the conclusions by the empirical method.[32] In the same period the journal also featured two articles on American municipal government by Chang Wei-tz'u (who had a Ph.D. from Iowa State University), a series of reports on social and labor conditions in China, and another article by Ch'en Tu-hsiu urging the Chinese to study Christianity and to incorporate "the loftiness and greatness of Jesus Christ into their blood."[33] All of these were presumably part of Ch'en's efforts to introduce new knowledge in order to implement his Science and Democracy program.

But the attempt fell far short of the goal. In the first article by Wang Hsin-kung, the word "science" was undefined; no distinction was made between the sciences or between them and the scientific method, and there was no reference to the history of science. His second article, though broadly correct, was unsophisticated and excluded far more than it included. Ch'en's own suggestion of local self-government and a new guild system was vague, and the reports on labor conditions were impressionistic. While admiring science, Ch'en and his cohorts seldom demonstrated any real objectivity in their reasoning. An instance was the controversy between them and Mu Hsiang-yueh, one of the few modern Chinese entrepreneurs. In 1919, Mu's cotton mill in Shanghai decided to recruit fifty female workers from Hunan. This rather unusual gesture attracted considerable journalistic attention. There were some complaints that the wages were low and the hours long, the posting of bond by the workers humiliating, sanitary conditions in the factory poor, and

30. LJ, Vol. VII, No. 1.   31. Ibid., 22-24.
32. Ibid., No. 5, pp. 3-4.   33. LJ, Vol. VII, Nos. 1, 2, 3, 5, 6.

medical facilities lacking.[34] In his reply, Mu pointed out that the wage rates in his mill were equal to the general market level, that the posting of bond was a time-honored Chinese business practice, that twelve working hours were shorter than the average in Chinese mills, that the sanitary conditions in his mill had been judged by experts as adequate within the general circumstances, and that free medical care was provided to all workers. Although factually correct, Mu's answers failed to placate the critics. Ch'en, in particular, published a sarcastic rejoinder (May, 1920), stating that the labor movement had in the twentieth century advanced beyond seeking better wages to seeking the right of management; that he deigned to discuss Mu's answer only because Mu was probably not yet qualified as a capitalist; that the wage rates could not be just because Mu's profit depended on surplus value; that twelve working hours were prejudicial to health; and that only a socialized economy could solve China's problem.[35]

A significant feature of these utterances was their extremely hostile tone, which contrasted strikingly with Ch'en's earlier conciliatory stand for a new guild system. Had he been insincere in the first instance, or had he changed his mind in the meantime? It is true that between the appearance of these articles, Ch'en switched his belief from democracy to Marxism-Leninism. Yet he had hardly mastered the tortuous reasoning of this latter credo in June, 1920,[36] and was unlikely to have been influenced solely by the anti-capitalist stand of this belief. A weightier factor was probably the anti-mercantile bias common among Chinese intellectuals which Ch'en shared even though he had consciously repudiated the tradition of which this bias was a part. In other words, his hostility toward Mu was in all probability the Confucian conscience emerging through a Marxist body—by his own behavior Ch'en had demonstrated the impossibility of disowning one's own cultural heritage. But far more important than his psychology was his ignorance of commercial conditions in China, which he clearly demonstrated in his writings. Perhaps this lapse was the key to the weakness of his earlier program of Science and Democracy for China, because implicit in that program was a key role to be played by intellectuals in initiating local self-government and a new guild system. Not knowing the conditions of Chinese business, and being equally detached from the rural masses, Ch'en was hardly able to play a useful role in his own program. Furthermore, the intellectuals inclined toward such a goal were few while the masses to be initiated were many. Even if all circumstances had been favorable, a program like Ch'en's would still fail to yield any

34. Ch'en Tu-hsiu, "The Female Workers of Hou Shen Cotton Textile Mill," LJ, Vol. VII, No. 6, pp. 1-19.

35. *Ibid.,* 19-37.   36. SBI:CCRM, 31.

appreciable result within a foreseeable time. The only way it might be expedited was through central direction by the government, but then the problem would be one of political reform or revolution rather than local self-government.

Ch'en's basic fault was his intellectual superficiality. Indeed, it is doubtful that he understood his own motivation. He had consciously repudiated nationalism, but his burning desire to see China rejuvenated could hardly be explained in other terms. Although the same desire had motivated all of the reformers since 1860 and nearly all of the intellectuals since 1895, it is important to note that the feeling was largely confined to the elite. The masses, if they felt a similar concern, lacked the ability to give it a constructive expression. Consequently, every reform not only had to work from the top down but also had to promise immediate relief to a steadily worsening situation. Dewey's approach hardly fitted the circumstances. Throughout his lectures Dewey had assumed that China could and should evolve into industrialism and democracy more or less in accordance with the Anglo-American pattern. Such an assumption obviously neglected to account for a number of important factors—the overwhelming pressure from abroad, the crushing burden of tradition, and the vastness of a thickly populated territory—which completely differentiated contemporary China from Britain or the United States of an earlier era. In hastily borrowing from Dewey, Ch'en merely indicated his own lack of reflection.

Still another flaw in his effort to replace Confucianism with Science and Democracy was the basic dissimilarity of these three concepts. Whereas Confucianism had grown into a very concrete pattern of life, science, however defined, could hardly govern all human relationships. Nor could democracy, which results from an essentially evolutionary process, be imposed from above. Hence neither the one nor the other fitted the frame vacated by Confucianism. As Ch'en wrote "The Basis for the Realization of Democracy in China," these difficulties presumably became clear to him, with the result that he forsook liberalism for Marxism-Leninism. The very short interval between his writing of this article and his acceptance of the latter faith suggests a direct link between these two events.

In tracing the origins of Marxism-Leninism in China, we may first of all note that modern Chinese intellectuals all disliked the inequality of wealth, and to that extent they were predisposed to socialist ideas. On the other hand, it is equally striking that until 1919, none of them looked upon any socialist doctrine as a possible panacea for China's evils. Even Sun Yat-sen, who advocated some sort of socialism as early as 1906, felt that it was applicable to China's future problems rather than to those of the present.[37] A perusal of the pages of *New Youth* between 1915 and 1918 will reveal much discussion of Adam Smith, John Stuart Mill, Darwin, and a host of others but none of Marx. This inattention was deliberate and striking. How can it be explained?

One possible reason, of course, was the stress by Marx that socialism necessarily followed capitalism in historical evolution. Since China had not reached the capitalist stage, socialism became rather irrelevant by Marx's own terms.[38] However, this explanation is inadequate because it presupposes an understanding of Marx by Chinese intellectuals which their inattention seems to refute. A more likely factor lay in the fact that the aim of these intellectuals was always to save China. Since China was to be saved from the West, it was thought necessary that the remedial measures should incorporate the strong points of the West. This tactic was referred to in Chinese official circles as "using the barbarians' methods to subdue the barbarians." Consistent with this principle, the Chinese had since 1860 imitated the West in one field after another; they had found interest even in Christianity, which in its basic tenets—the doctrine of original sin, for instance—was incompatible with traditional Chinese thought. But until the early 1920's, Marxism never received much attention, for a basically simple reason. This credo was not the professed faith of China's invaders and thus not a "barbarian method" that China needed to emulate. Furthermore, there was really no room in the Chinese mind for any political ideal other than democracy. From the time Yen Fu's essays appeared in 1895, the Chinese intellectuals tended to accept the virtue of liberty and democracy without question even if they did not really understand the deeper implications of these concepts. It was not until the extreme difficulty of introducing democracy to China became clear that these intellectuals began to think about possible alternatives. In Ch'en Tu-hsiu's case this stage was reached in 1920. By then, Russia had not only turned socialist but had also weathered and survived an Allied intervention. This latter feat was bound to be impressive to the Chinese, since it was exactly what they had attempted but failed to perform. Henceforth, socialism rather than liberalism became the main stream of Chinese thought.

In emulating the West, the Chinese had repeatedly shifted their point of emphasis. In the 1860's it was mainly the gunboat that impressed the Chinese; by the nineties liberty and scholarship were taken by Chinese thinkers as the essence of Western virtue. But this latter view did not replace the earlier one: it merely supplemented it.

37. TSC:SMCI, 52; KFCC, I, 206-7; Harold Schiffrin, "Sun Yat-sen's Early Land Policy," JAS (August, 1957), 552.
38. See SBI:CCRM, 7-8.

Out of this merger gradually arose the phrase "Science and Democracy" as a characterization of the West in the Chinese mind, a more accurate abstraction but one that added little to the earlier understanding of the West. Thus Ch'en Tu-hsiu's adoption of this phrase in itself demonstrated little originality on his part. When he later abandoned democracy, after his attempt to define it in a more concrete manner, it became obvious that his particular belief had been shallow and had risen more out of environment than out of understanding.

In tracing the origins of Marxism-Leninism in China, several writers have accepted a Japanese source for the establishment in 1918 of the Society for the Study of Marxism at Peking University.[39] If this source is correct, it means that Ch'en and the others of the same group had known about Marxism before they gave their blessings to Science and Democracy in January, 1919, and that they therefore made a deliberate choice on that occasion. Such a possibility does not contradict my thesis that Ch'en hardly understood the meaning of democracy; on the contrary it perhaps strengthens my contention that Science and Democracy as symbols of Western strength were welcome to Chinese intellectuals. But the important point is that in all likelihood no such society existed at Peking University in 1918.[40] Rather Ch'en's interest in Marxism developed in 1919. At any rate, in May of that year New Youth devoted a special issue to that topic. Significantly, the spirit that pervaded the issue was one of disapprobation. While there is no way to prove a direct relationship, it will be recalled that at the time Ch'en had not written "The Basis for the Realization of Democracy in China" and was probably still optimistic about the future of science and democracy in China. But by May, 1920, his stand had completely changed. The New Youth of that month was devoted to Labor Day, and the tone was now one of enthusiasm for the Marxist cause. By June, Ch'en had progressed enough to write: "I recognize the existence of only two nations, that of the capitalists and that of the workers."[41] In August of the same year, he organized the Chinese Socialist Youth Corps and was on his way to founding the Chinese Communist Party.[42] Thus, the decisive change in Ch'en's attitude clearly took place between December, 1919, when he still called for Science and Democracy, and June, 1920, when he committed himself to Marxism. It is difficult to account for the change except in terms of Ch'en's frustrated attempt to implement Science and Democracy in China. Having disowned Confucianism and the "national heritage," he was under severe mental pressure to find a constructive cause. After the shocking discovery that, in spite of his hopes and

39. Ibid., 16.   40. CTT:TMM, 244n.
41. "My Views on the Current Situation," LJ, Vol. VIII, No. 1.
42. CTT:TMM, 249.

efforts, Science and Democracy were poorly suited to the Confucian frame, Ch'en was able to derive much comfort from an equally unexpected quarter, the credo of Marx and Lenin.

On closer examination none of the debilities suffered by Ch'en's original program applied to Marxism-Leninism. Here was a creed that through "scientific" reasoning pointed to the mission of the elite to make history without their having to know the tedious details of peasant or merchant life. The program was to be realized through the charismatic leadership of a few rather than through the self-effacing toil of many. Like Confucianism, the Leninist credo was not only comprehensive and explicit but also rationalistic and a priori. Under both systems a single body of doctrines, which extolled the group far above the individual, was assumed to be the truth, transcending all political and ethnic barriers. The exaltation of this truth had in turn two consequences. In the first place, it meant that all political actions must be justified in terms of the theory; and in the second, the justification was to be accomplished by men whose claim to power rested on their position as knowers of the truth and who almost always developed a penchant for excessively fine reasoning and a habit of waging political struggles in the name of sacred crusades. It was these similarities that made Marxism-Leninism a viable substitute for the defunct Confucianism.

There were, of course, differences between these two faiths. But in the context of China at the time, all of their differences redounded to the advantage of Marxism-Leninism. Thus, the Confucian theory of harmony among all men became unrealistic when China had to struggle continually for national survival; the moral restraints stressed by the Chinese sage hardly seemed the foundation of society when that which China most needed was technology and production; and a golden era in the past was less appealing than a utopia in the future when a nation was threatened with extinction here and now. The fact that Lenin's theory of imperialism fitted the Chinese scene even though it was undesigned for her amply demonstrated to the Chinese mind the correctness of that doctrine. After all, had not the foreign onslaught on China since 1839 been primarily motivated by economic considerations? Was not imperialism then demonstrably the last stage of capitalism?

If Lenin's theory proved prophetic in regard to Western policy, it augured equally well for Russia's behavior in the future. The offer by Leo P. Karakhan in July, 1919, to relinquish all the privileges wrested from China by the Tsar put to shame the West's treatment of China at Versailles a bare two months earlier.[43] It was thus not only in word but also in deed that Lenin had proved himself to be a "superior man." Here at last were the wisdom and justice that

43. *Ibid.*, 210.

Chinese intellectuals had sought in vain from the West. Whereas Western democracy, with its implicit ideology, its cult of the individual, its economic free enterprise, and its religious belief, could find no room in the Confucian frame, Marxism-Leninism was perfectly at home in China because it was sufficiently similar to Confucianism to satisfy the subconscious habits of the intellectuals and yet different enough from it to rouse new hopes.

But once Ch'en was committed to Communism, disadvantages appeared and weighed increasingly more. He was harassed by the Kremlin throughout his association with the Party. In spite of his long disagreement with the Kuomintang,[44] he was forced to ally with it and submit to its authority. Repeated appeals by Ch'en for the Communists to withdraw from the other party were ignored by the Comintern. In 1926, when an open break between the two parties was clearly in the making, Ch'en was ordered to perform the impossible task of retaining a good standing in the Kuomintang and of gaining a "proletarian hegemony" from within. After the alliance finally broke down, Ch'en became the scapegoat and was relieved of his position as the secretary-general of the party. In November, 1929, he was expelled from the party. Some thirteen months later, he organized a separate Communist leadership in Shanghai under the influence of Trotsky.[45] But by then the power base of the party had shifted to the Soviet areas in the interior, and there was little Ch'en could do. In October, 1932, he was arrested by the Kuomintang and sentenced to imprisonment. A bare five years were left to him after his release in 1937. These he spent in quietude, having freed himself from all party affiliations. The views he uttered in private correspondence were, however, not without some significance. As an individual, he once again turned away from Communism and back toward Western democracy. In 1940, he wrote: "The National Socialism and the G.P.U. politics of Germany and Russia are the 'religious courts' of our times. They are worse than the 'religious courts' of the medieval age and must be overthrown if humanity is to march forward."[46] Referring to the war situation, Ch'en said: "If Germany and Russia are to emerge victorious, humanity will face a dark age for at least half a century. Only if the capitalistic democracy can be preserved through a victory by England, France, and America can there be a path to proletarian democracy."[47] The implied view that "proletarian democracy" could evolve only out of "capitalistic democracy" apparently led to a storm of protest among Ch'en's friends. In reply, the erstwhile patriarch of the Chinese Communist Party stated:

> Your mistake is the same as that made by Lenin, Trotsky, and others. It lies first and foremost in not knowing the real value

44. CTH:CTH, 178 ff; NR:KCC, 25.   45. BC:DHCC, 35-36.
46. CTH, 2.   47. Ibid.

of capitalistic democracy and taking it to be a sham, deceptive device of the capitalist class. You do not know that in substance, democratic government means (1) no seizure of persons except by legal authority, (2) no taxation without representation, (3) no taxation except through proper parliamentary sanction, (4) freedom of organization, speech, and press on the part of the opposition, (5) right to strike by the workers, (6) right to cultivate by the farmers, (7) freedom of thought, religion, etc. All of these are needed by the masses and secured by them after over seven hundred years of struggle since the thirteenth century. Taken together, these constitute the so-called capitalistic democracy. The difference between the so-called proletarian democracy and the capitalistic democracy is only one of scope. There does not exist a proletarian democracy with a different content.

After the October Revolution, efforts were made to destroy the substance of capitalistic democracy. It was replaced by a mere abstract term: proletarian democracy. The result is the Stalinist regime in Russia today, which is in turn imitated by Italy and Germany.[48]

In another letter, Ch'en emphasized that he had come to these conclusions after "six or seven years of deep reflection on the Russian experience of the last twenty years."[49]

Viewing Ch'en's life as a whole, it is difficult to detect any profound conviction on his part. He embraced Democracy and Science in 1919, when he was already forty years old. A bare few months later he forsook them for Communism. As leader of the party, he could not agree with the Comintern line, but yet lived by it for "disciplinary reasons."[50] These, however, disappeared as soon as he lost the secretary-generalship, for contrary to the Communist practice of Democratic Centralism, of which Ch'en doubtless had full knowledge, he started to criticize the policy of the Politburo.[51] For this he was expelled, and the setback immediately turned his thought to the formation of a Trotskyist faction. After his release from prison in 1937, his attitude once again changed. Trotsky and Lenin now in turn yielded the place of honor to Western democracy. In a span of twenty years Ch'en's thought had turned a full circle. What were the factors that underlay his volatility?

One reason clearly was his intellectual shallowness. At no time did Ch'en really understand the causes that he either supported or opposed. Discrediting Confucianism, he showed no awareness of the disrupting effects this attack would have on social continuity. Espousing Democracy and Science, he was yet unable even to define the terms. A year was to elapse between his declaration for democracy

48. *Ibid.*, 3-4.
50. SBI:CCRM, 41-45.
49. *Ibid.*, 19.
51. *Ibid.*, 146.

and his attempt to elaborate on it. When it did appear, the elaboration was no more than an adaption of Dewey's lectures with some shallow observations on China's guild system and village democracy. As a recent writer has shown, even when Ch'en had become totally committed to Marxism-Leninism, he was blissfully unaware of the myriad theoretical difficulties confronting Lenin and other Marxists.[52] While anxious to lead, Ch'en possessed little of the training, temperament, and intelligence needed for the task. As a Communist, he failed to play the expected role of implementing a Comintern policy and then taking the blame upon himself when that policy misfired. As a strategist, he was oblivious of the importance of the peasantry as a political force. While there is no way to isolate and measure the effect of environmental influence in the shaping of Ch'en's personality, it might be noted that his refusal to play a modest role and his detachment from the rural masses were unmistakably characteristic of the foreign-educated in China. Perhaps what differentiated him from the rest of that group was mainly his unusual restlessness that, coupled with his propensity to declare himself on issues, turned him into a "permanent opposition," as he called himself in his last years.[53] Through a combination of circumstances, this readiness to oppose makes Ch'en an important historical figure, instrumental both in destroying the old Confucian order and in launching its substitute, the Communist movement of China.

A different attempt to fill the ideological vacuum in the post-May Fourth period was made by Sun Yat-sen, who delivered a series of weekly lectures on his Three Principles of the People in 1924. An examination of these doctrines will illuminate Sun's individuality as well as his similarities to the other intellectuals thus far discussed.

In his series Sun had intended to deliver eighteen lectures, six to each of his three principles. But the plan was interrupted after he had delivered only sixteen, thus falling two short on his last principle, that of livelihood. In his first lecture on the principle of nationalism, Sun defined "race" in terms of blood affinity and common language, livelihood, religion, and habits. He then argued that the Chinese "race" was faced with three dangers—a declining or stagnant population, foreign political domination, and foreign economic encroachment. Citing an unspecified source for the Ch'ien-lung period (1736-1795) and an estimate made by W. W. Rockhill (1854-1914), he observed that the figure for Chinese population was 400,000,000 in the earlier reference and 300,000,000 in the latter. Allowing for all possible errors, China obviously had not increased her population during that period, whereas within the last hundred years alone population increased ten times in America, three times in Great Britain and Japan, and four times in Russia. Hence, in another century the Chinese

52. *Ibid.*, 13-27.   53. CTH, 30.

would be such a minority in the world that they would lose their identity through assimilation.[54]

Turning to foreign domination, Sun dwelled on China's military as well as diplomatic vulnerability. In a broad discussion of conditions abroad, he quoted many unsubstantiated figures to show that militarily Japan could conquer China in ten days, while the United States and Great Britain could do so in one and two months respectively. Even swifter would be China's downfall through the diplomatic channels. If the Powers should agree among themselves, Sun said, they needed no more than a pen and a piece of paper to partition China.[55]

Third, Sun enumerated many of the economic advantages enjoyed by the foreigners in China. He stressed that the native industries in China were not only unprotected by tariffs but also paid far higher taxes to the Chinese government than foreign industries in China; that through note-issues the foreign banks in China made millions of dollars at no cost or risk; that the same banks held huge Chinese deposit accounts and controlled both the foreign exchange market and the rates of exchange between one Chinese seaport and another; that foreign carriers earned more than one hundred million dollars annually from ocean shipping and inland navigation in China; that foreigners further gained from four to five hundred million dollars per year from real estate and the general administration of concessions and settlements in Chinese seaports; and that they also made huge profits in unsavory commercial and speculative enterprises.[56]

According to Sun the key factor responsible for China's sorrowful state was the lack of national awareness among her people. This in turn had resulted from the Manchu control of China in the last few hundred years. Because the dynasty had concentrated on purging the anti-foreign thought of the literati, nationalistic feeling survived only among members of the lower classes who belonged to the secret societies founded by the Ming loyalists. Unfortunately, Sun continued, these naïve lower classes did not know how to take advantage of the ideas.[57] In his customary way of reinforcing his argument with hearsay evidence, Sun then accused the anti-Taiping scholar-general Tso Tsung-t'ang of destroying the nationalism of these secret societies. Tso allegedly learned about these societies during his campaign in Sinkiang, joined one of them, and succeeded in making them tools of the Manchu government, with the consequence that when Sun rose to oppose the Manchus, there was no organized body for him to utilize.[58]

Another factor that to Sun's mind had hampered Chinese national-

54. KFCC, I, 1-14.   55. *Ibid.*, 51-54.
56. *Ibid.*, 20-27.   57. *Ibid.*, 30.
58. *Ibid.*, 31.

ism was the one-world ideal in Chinese tradition. While he saw nothing intrinsically wrong with this ideal, he nevertheless had two objections. On the one hand, the ideal might make the people who accepted it less resistant to foreign domination; on the other, it was too often a mere camouflage for imperialism. Sun believed that a country advocates the one-world ideal only when it is seeking imperial control over other nations, and that this was as true of China, Russia, and Germany in earlier periods as it was of Great Britain in a later period. But unlike other countries, China had come to believe in this ideal and had thus made herself vulnerable to foreign domination. The remedy for this situation was to preserve the essence of the ideal, which was the love of peace, but to combine it with nationalism. Only in this way could the interminable wars among imperialistic nations be averted.

Following his tendency to emulate and criticize the West at the same time, Sun then pointed to the First World War as a typical example of incessant strife among a group of equally imperialistic powers. The only ray of hope had stemmed from Wilson's Fourteen Points—the sole reason, according to Sun, why the smaller nations had sided with the Allies—but this hope had been shattered by the Treaty of Versailles. On the other hand, by triggering the revolution in Russia, the war had accidentally kindled a new hope for mankind. Sun believed that the Russian struggle against imperialism marked the beginning of a new era for the world, for in spite of the Allied effort to destroy Lenin's government, "the people had their eyes opened and would not be deceived again."[59]

In order for the Chinese to regain their national consciousness, Sun thought that first they should be educated and alerted to the danger of not having such consciousness. After this had been done, the social units of the family and the clan should be strengthened so that the 400,000,000 Chinese could be grouped into between 100 and 400 clans, and these were in turn to be welded into a strong single unit—the nation-state. Once such a unification was achieved, there would be no difficulty in facing foreign pressure, be it military, economic, or demographic; the Gandhian kind of economic boycott would alone solve all of China's short-run problems with foreign powers.[60]

In the long run, however, the only way for China to regain her past greatness was to advocate the Confucian virtues of loyalty, filial piety, benevolence, love, integrity, righteousness, peace, and equitableness (*chung-hsiao, jen-ai, hsin-i, ho-p'ing*). Although a nation might rise through military prowess, she could maintain her stature only by practicing sound morals. Sun did not doubt that the old Chinese morality was superior to that of the other nations, even though in

59. *Ibid.*, 33-43.   60. *Ibid.*, 56-59.

some respects it needed to be readjusted to modern conditions—thus, loyalty to the nation should replace loyalty to a throne that no longer existed. The solution therefore lay in preserving and strengthening these virtues and not in discarding them as some misguided men would have the people do.[61]

> As for China's old moral standards, they are not yet lost sight of by the people of China. . . . But since our domination by alien races and since the proliferation of foreign culture in China, a group intoxicated with the new ideas have begun to reject the old morality, saying that the former makes the latter unnecessary. They do not understand that we ought to preserve that which is good in our past and throw away only the bad. China now is in a period of conflict between old and new currents and a large number of our people have nothing to follow after.[62]

In addition to morals, there was, according to Sun, another area in which China was superior to all Western nations. The political philosophy propounded in *Great Learning*—that if a ruler wished to pacify the world, he must start by rectifying his own mind—was a unique treasury of wisdom that had unfortunately been neglected by the Chinese. As an illustration Sun undertook a discussion of how the Chinese "in the last few hundred years" had violated teachings on personal cultivation by neglecting hygiene and table manners. Here Chinese youth would have to learn from the West in order to regain the traditional wisdom of China, but once they acquired a good character, technological ability would come easily. For "the newest and most formidable skill is to pilot an airplane. If even this had been easy for us to learn, what else can we not learn?"[63] With his characteristic optimism Sun maintained that it would take China only a short time to learn and to overtake the West, because she could benefit by the latter's experience. The only thing the Chinese needed to remember, he added, was to be good to smaller nations after China had become the foremost power on earth.[64]

In his second group of six lectures on democracy, Sun began with his own interpretation of history. There were, he said, four broad stages of human evolution: the "Great Wilderness" *(hung huang)* during which men struggled with beasts; theocracy, during which men struggled with nature; autocracy, during which nations fought with one another; and democracy, during which the people fought with monarchs. The distinguishing characteristic of each stage was a matter of human intelligence: thus, theocracy arose because men then believed only in divine power, and autocracy developed from intel-

---

61. *Ibid.*, 61-63.
63. *Ibid.*, 70.
62. *Ibid.*, 61-63.
64. *Ibid.*, 65-72.

lectual inequality between rulers and subjects. While Sun thought that autocracy had been a successful political system in China, he believed that China would make further progress by entering the stage of democracy. His subsequent arguments revolved around two points: that China was ready for such a change because democratic thought had long ago been propounded by Confucius and Mencius, and that democracy was good because world history had proved it so. The latter topic afforded him an opportunity to consider the history of revolution in England, America, and France. From revolution in France he quite characteristically passed on to Rousseau and indulged in some gratuitous criticism. The Swiss-French thinker, he said, had been widely censured for imputing a false historical origin to his theory of social contract; in actual fact, the critics erred as much as Rousseau, for although the latter's historical view was a falsehood, the error was small compared to his contributions to French history. In fact, Rousseau's theories had generated the French Revolution; and as long as a doctrine espoused the rising cause of popular sovereignty, technical faults in its exposition need not be taken too seriously. After establishing democracy as a universal trend, Sun tried to show that such a system would confer great benefits on China. He observed that all of the past, and many of the current, internal struggles in China had a single, common origin, the desire of various claimants to ascend the throne. Only by firmly establishing democracy could this evil be permanently eradicated.[65]

In his second lecture Sun dwelled at length on the importance attached to liberty in the West. For more than two hundred years, he maintained, Europeans and Americans had struggled to gain liberty, and it was as a result of this struggle that democracy had developed. Democracy was thus only a means to preserve an end. Why was liberty so important? Because, he answered, the Europeans had been so oppressed under the feudal and monarchical systems. While he did not know the details, he thought that life under a European autocracy had probably been worse than that of an ill-treated Chinese settler in contemporary French Indochina or the Dutch East Indies, for, unlike the Chinese, the earlier Europeans had not even had the right of free worship. But it was such extreme restraints that drove the Europeans to battle for their liberty, and after they had won it through toil and bloodshed, they naturally set great store by it.[66]

Sun could see no parallel situation in China, for in spite of the shortcomings of the old regime, it left the people virtually alone after they paid the annual grain tax. Indeed, freedom was taken so much for granted by the Chinese that they failed even to have a name for it. Foreigners, Sun contended, often berated the Chinese for knowing neither liberty nor unity, but they failed to realize that these charges

65. *Ibid.*, 73-90.   66. *Ibid.*, 90-94.

were mutually contradictory. If the people attached little importance to the group, it was because they indulged in too much personal freedom; thus a lack of unity indicated an abundance of liberty.[67] As for those Chinese who clamored for liberty, as if there had been none in China, Sun had great contempt. Obviously referring to the May Fourth movement and its leaders, he declared:

> As the revolutionary ferment of the West has lately spread to China, the new students and many earnest scholars have risen up to proclaim liberty. They think that because European revolutions, like the French Revolution, were struggles for liberty, we, too, should fight for liberty. This is nothing but parroting. . . .
> The watchword of the French Revolution was "Liberty"; the watchword of the American Revolution was "Independence"; the watchword of our revolution is the "Three Principles of the People." This is formulated after much thought and work. It is not mere parroting. . . . In declaring for an objective and asking the masses to struggle with us, it is imperative that the goal be intimately related to their lives. . . . To advocate liberty when the people suffered no despotism is hardly the way to arouse response. . . .[68]
> The action of modern Chinese scholars in preaching liberty to the masses is like exhorting the aboriginal Yao tribes (who have only a barter economy) to make money. . . . It is truly an impertinence. . . . Even in advanced countries like France and the United States, students, service men, bureaucrats, and minors enjoy no freedom of action.[69]

In actual fact, Sun argued, China's problem was the reverse of Europe's. Because each individual had too much liberty, society lacked the cohesiveness needed to resist foreign aggression, and as society was crippled, individual liberty was in turn impaired. The corrective therefore lay in an initial curtailment of individual liberty so that the national strength could be increased and individual liberty indirectly but permanently secured. There was, according to Sun, no difference between East and West in the pursuit of liberty as a goal, but the paths to be followed should differ according to concrete conditions.[70] In his third lecture Sun examined the issue of equality. He first observed that the physical universe is characterized by unlikeness and inequality. "In the world of Nature we do not find any two things level, except the surface of water. On level ground there is no place truly level. . . . This shows that nothing produced in the world is just like anything else, and since all things are different, they naturally

67. *Ibid.*, 94-97.
68. *Ibid.*, 96.
69. *Ibid.*, 99.
70. *Ibid.*, 100-1.

cannot be called equal. If there is no equality in the natural world, how can there be such a thing as human equality?"[71] Sun then proceeded to develop his ideas on the origins of various political theories. According to him, as feudalism evolved into monarchism in Europe, the inequality among men grew cumulatively worse, and when the lot of the oppressed became truly intolerable, a corrective process occurred in the form of revolution. To protect their own interests the monarchs claimed that their authority was of divine origin. This theory so successfully convinced the ignorant masses that the scholars were eventually forced to combat it with another theory. "As the idea that men are all born free gained currency . . . the kings of Europe fell one by one without struggle."[72] But the masses then began to take this theory too seriously; they continued trying to make all men equal, not knowing that such a thing was impossible. Only recently, in the light of scientific advances, had men begun to realize that no natural equality exists.[73]

Comparing China with Europe, Sun observed that the latter had experienced far greater inequality than China because it had practiced a hereditary system on a much wider scale. Even the United States had suffered more inequality than China because of discrimination, first against the colonists and then against the Negroes. It was not that Western scholars had not tried to combat these evils. The American War of Independence was fought to secure equality for whites and the Civil War to secure benefits for Negroes. Then there were the French and Russian revolutions. All these were glorious pages in human history, and Sun was especially impressed by the Russian attempt to abolish all class distinctions.[74] But even here he was not entirely satisfied. He seemed to have doubts about the proletarian dictatorship and was certain that no basic solution to the problem of equality had been found in any country.[75] Nor was he surprised by this failure, for, contrary to the general belief of the Chinese people, Westerners did not excel in everything and were in fact very weak in all non-material fields. Those who wished to imitate the West even in politics merely indicated their complete lack of self-confidence. To Sun's mind it was definitely harmful to imitate the West without knowing the special conditions in China.[76]

How then could China resolve the problem of equality? A correct answer, Sun maintained, must come from a study of all relevant factors including the past experience of the West and the newest concepts advanced by its scholars. From a discussion of a wide range of topics, varying from the terror of the French Revolution to the disputes between the Federalists and the Jeffersonian Republicans,

71. *Ibid.*, 103.   72. *Ibid.*, 104-5.
73. *Ibid.*, 105.   74. *Ibid.*, 107-8.
75. *Ibid.*, 133-39.   76. *Ibid.*, 140.

Bismarck's national socialism, and the failure of the labor movements in Europe and China, he concluded that the real issue was how to avoid mob rule on the one hand and arbitrary government on the other. In other words, he believed that the masses should be given political power, but that because they were invariably inferior in intellect, they should also be provided with proper guidance. The aim was therefore to have an all powerful government that would voluntarily submit to popular control. This, Sun said, was the "newest concept" advanced by an American scholar, but whereas the latter had only found the proper goal, Sun's own principle of democracy would furnish a concrete solution.[77]

The key factor lay, he insisted, in the people's attitude toward the government. Whereas the Chinese in the past had virtually worshipped the legendary sage-kings Yao, Shun, Yü, and others, they had under Western impact become scornful of all despots including these sages. Sun believed such an attitude was biased and unconducive to good government. He urged a change and quoted as his authority an unnamed Swiss scholar, but characteristically he added that no Westerner had ever devised the necessary tools to bring about such a change. With a great deal of pride Sun then stressed the need to distinguish the sovereignty of the people from the ability or power of the government. Once the people were made clearly aware of this difference and its implications, they would have no more reason to fear a strong government.[78]

To Sun's mind this distinction between sovereignty and ability represented a major contribution on his part.[79] Citing Chinese legends he proved to his own satisfaction that from the earliest times political power had always come from ability, or the kind of knowledge most needed by society at that particular time: thus, Shen Nung (the Divine Husbandman) became king because of his knowledge of medicinal herbs, and Sui Jen (the man who bored a hole) mounted the throne because he knew how to produce fire and could thus satisfy the gastronomic urges of man.[80] By their ability men could be divided into three groups: those who were the first to perceive, those who perceived somewhat later, and those who did not perceive at all but simply acted. While all men should have an equal share in sovereignty, each of these groups should play its respective role in government, for only with the correct allocation of functions—the first group as policymakers, the second as administrators, and the third as followers—could the best results be secured. On the other hand, since one role was as necessary as another to the accomplishment of the over-all task, no one should feel unequal in striving to do his utmost for the group. This duty to society Sun euphemistically called

77. *Ibid.*, 141.
79. *Ibid.*, 142, 153.
78. *Ibid.*, 142-54.
80. *Ibid.*, 148.

a "moral equality," which should be shared by everyone.[81]

Once the distinction between sovereignty and power was understood to be an allocation of duty according to ability, there would be no more ground for men to fear authority. The only remaining consideration was to devise the machinery through which ability and sovereignty could best be exercised. This Sun found in the four political powers—suffrage, recall, initiative, and referendum. These would be used by the people, and the five governing powers—legislative, judicial, executive, civil examination, and censoring—would be deposited in the various departments of the government. The separation of the five governing powers was to Sun another of his great contributions to political theory.[82] He believed that under such a system the government would have enough power to be efficient while still remaining amenable to popular control. Such a system in conjunction with China's vast resources (which "exceeded America's") would make the country in no time as strong as the United States.[83]

Sun's third principle was the principle of livelihood. He stressed that livelihood involved new problems as machinery began to replace labor in the productive process. The ensuing difficulties stimulated socialist thought, and of all of the socialist thinkers the most outstanding was Karl Marx. According to Sun, he was the first to pursue such studies scientifically by "reading and comparing all the relevant works available at the British Museum." The outcome was his theory of historical materialism, which postulates that human behavior was ultimately determined by the material environment, especially by the relationships of production, and that social progress took place through a class struggle between capitalists and laborers.[84]

Sun did not find Marx's analysis entirely satisfactory. Summarizing recent Western economic progress under four heads—labor and industrial legislation, public ownership of means of communications, direct taxation, and "socialized distribution of wealth," i.e., voluntary improvement of the workers' lot by the capitalists—Sun asserted that all of these resulted from class co-operation rather than class struggle. Marx was therefore a social pathologist instead of a social physiologist. Furthermore, Sun denied the validity of the theory of surplus value and maintained that profits result from the functioning of total social forces to which the workers have no exclusive claims. At this point he made one of his familiar digressions into a wide range of topics varying from foreign income tax systems to disputes between the First and Second Communist Internationales, labor legislation in Bismarckian Germany, Henry Ford, the Standard Oil Company, and the sale of the Han-yeh-p'ing products abroad, from all of which he concluded that production was governed by the needs of

81. *Ibid.*, 117-18, 143-44.   82. *Ibid.*, 174-75.
83. *Ibid.*, 167.   84. *Ibid.*, 176-184.

consumers. Since these had grown out of man's desire to live decently, it was in that desire that the key to history lay—not, as Marx claimed, in the material forces. According to Sun, the essence of statecraft consisted in the ability to provide all men with a livelihood, and by thus addressing himself directly to the central issue, he thought he had demonstrably improved upon Marx. Probably as a gesture to his Communist allies, Sun condescendingly added: "Let me now define the relationship between Communism and the Principle of Livelihood. The former is the goal of the latter, and the latter is the method of the former. There is no essential difference between the two except in their approaches."[85]

After laying the groundwork, he proceeded to discuss the means by which the problem of livelihood was to be solved. He once again ruled out the possibility of a solution through imitation of the West, including the adoption of Marxist methods. He noted that the Marxists disagreed among themselves, that many of them disliked violence, and that by common recognition the Russian experiment in Marxism had failed. The apologists for Russia, he said, attributed this failure to Russia's backward economy, but if so, how could China, which was even less developed, benefit from Marxism? Clearly, the solution did not lie there.[86]

According to Sun, the basic feature of Chinese economy was its lack of radical change in the past. For two thousand years industry and commerce had remained largely undeveloped, landholding had been small, and the relationship between the landowners and the populace had been good over most parts of the country. But under Western impact merchants began speculating in land, and their activities were now driving the price of real estate to phenomenal heights— for instance, the value of a site on the Bund in Shanghai had risen ten thousand times in a mere eighty years. The net result was a growing inequality of wealth which, if unchecked, would create serious economic problems and thwart the road to Good Society. This assertion led to his proposal to "equalize the landownership," according to which each owner would declare the value of his land, leaving the government with the choice of buying or taxing it according to its declared value. If it was high, the owner would suffer through the taxes; if it was low, he might lose by being required to sell the land. Once a fair price was established, all future unearned increments, exclusive of the profits resulting from the owner's efforts to improve the land, would be taxed away by the government. In Sun's opinion this scheme was ideal for China because it would arouse little or no opposition from the landowners since their past and present gains would be untouched. Yet at the same time it would materially reduce the formation of large private fortunes that

85. *Ibid.*, 187-202.   86. *Ibid.*, 200, 213.

Sun disliked. Furthermore, in his opinion, the scheme would provide the government with such a large revenue that no other taxes would be needed.[87] Thus, if the scheme could be implemented before the rising price of land became too widespread, many of China's economic problems would be painlessly solved.[88]

Another idea that Sun discussed under the principle of livelihood was the "regulation of capital." On the negative side, this involved governmental control of private enterprise—presumably by the four methods of restriction of fields, limitation of scope, heavy taxation, and governmental protection of labor;[89] and, on the positive side, it advocated the expansion of state industries. "In accordance with the American pattern of industrialization," he urged the development of communications, manufacturing, and mining with the use of foreign capital. "If we use existing foreign capital to build up a future Communistic society in China, 'half the work will bring double the results.' "[90] Optimistically, he seemed to anticipate little reluctance on the parts of the foreigners, who, he wrote elsewhere, could always be induced to invest in China by means of the profit motive.[91]

In his third lecture on livelihood Sun finally discussed agriculture. As usual he started with a discussion of conditions abroad and supported his arguments with numerous unsubstantiated figures. On the basis of "accurate foreign reports" he now declared that the population of China had declined by ninety million in the previous decade.[92] He attributed the causes of this decline to low agricultural production and to China's forced export of foodstuffs in payment for foreign exactions. As a solution, he advocated—without spelling out the details—a "land to the tillers" program which would somehow be accomplished through the "equalization of landownership." He then turned to a discussion of technical methods of increasing production. Seven possible ways were mentioned, namely, mechanized farming, use of fertilizers, rotation of crops, eradication of pests, food processing, more control over food supply through better transportation, and prevention of natural disasters. For such technological improvements Sun unhesitatingly urged China to learn from the West.[93]

The fourth and last lecture was a discussion of another one of man's needs that Sun aimed to satisfy, namely, clothing. He talked at length on the supply and manufacture of silk, hemp, cotton, and wool. In his opinion the problem of the Chinese silk industry was technological whereas that of the Chinese cotton industry was political, for all of its foreign competitors in China were protected by "unequal treaties" and paid far less taxes to the Chinese government.

87. *Ibid.*, 203-4, 209.   88. *Ibid.*, 212.
89. TSC:SMCI, 334-36.   90. KFCC, I, 215.
91. *Ibid.*, III, 24.   92. *Ibid.*, I, 218.
93. *Ibid.*, 222-31.

Contradicting his earlier stand that economic boycott could work political wonders, he now maintained that China's economic problems awaited a political answer, for unless Chinese cloth could sell cheaper than foreign cloth, "no patriotic feeling could long defy economic principles."[94] From a rapid excursion into the economic conditions of Japan, Britain, and America, Sun concluded that it was imperative for China to abrogate the "unequal treaties" and adopt a protective tariff. Looking still further into the future, Sun thought that the state should first develop agricultural and manufacturing industries in connection with silk, hemp, cotton, and wool, and then establish clothing factories throughout the nation to provide for the needs of the people.[95]

Several features of the Three Principles of the People are immediately recognizable. The first is Sun's intense nationalism. This can be seen from the purposes of his second and third principles, which are respectively to strengthen the nation by strengthening the government, and to make China rich so that all Chinese can live in affluence. It would seem that, like the first, these two were also principles of nationalism.

A second noticeable feature is Sun's attachment to China's cultural tradition. Unlike many other intellectuals during this period, Sun consistently idealized China's past. In 1918 he wrote: "By the time of the Chou dynasty (1122-249 B.C.) Chinese civilization had reached a high plateau; the political system, morality, literature, scholarship, and technology then were almost as good as those of the modern West."[96] In 1922 he praised the Three Dynasties (2205?-249 B.C.) as having done more than any other regime to nurture and educate the people.[97] Although a revolutionary himself, Sun insisted that the monarchy had been successful in China and that there would have been no reason to replace it had democracy not been so superior.[98] In his interpretations of history, Sun always tended to cast China in a favorable light. Thus, instead of agreeing with Yen and Liang that the theory of Great Unity had hindered intellectual development through its discouragement of diversity of thought, Sun maintained that all of the world's imperial powers had preached one-worldism to further their control over other nations, and that China's only fault was her willingness to practice the ideal she preached.[99] By attributing China's political weakness to her moral superiority, Sun cleverly changed the perspective. Similarly, when he traced China's lack of national strength to an abundance of personal liberty, he implied that China's weakness was not a sign of inferiority.

94. *Ibid.,* 234-48.
96. *Ibid.,* II, 48.
98. *Ibid.,* I, 81, 107.

95. *Ibid.,* 247-50.
97. *Ibid.,* VI, 142.
99. *Ibid.,* 33-34.

A corollary of his cultural nationalism was his antagonism toward the New Culture leaders who believed that China was inferior and that the Confucian virtues in particular were "man-eating" forces. To Sun's argument that China's spiritual heritage was the finest in the world and that all she needed was new institutions and technology,[100] this group replied that the spiritual and the material could not be separated and that China's inferiority in science and technology proved her inferiority in all other matters.[101] As a corollary this group insisted that China must search abroad for the prescription to cure her evils. Although a violent quarrel soon occurred among the New Culture leaders over the exact course they were to pursue, this disagreement should not obscure the basic difference that remained between them and Sun. In contrast to their stand, Sun believed that China must find her own solution and, moreover, that he was the one most likely to find it. Thus, not only was Sun more nationalistic but he also had a greater sense of mission. Although not a member of the literati, Sun was in this respect much nearer to them than the New Culture leaders.

Another ramification of Sun's conservatism was his literary taste. He was opposed to Hu Shih's campaign for a literary revolution. In 1918, Sun wrote:

During the past centuries China was often occupied by foreign invaders but never once was she enslaved . . . . On the contrary the conquerers were often assimilated by the Chinese. This could only be due to the exceptional quality of the Chinese language. Some modern Chinese writers agitate for the abolition of Chinese writing, but this author holds that it should definitely not be abolished.

. . . Language has the function to further the intellectual progress of mankind. . . . If we compare modern Chinese civilization with the Western, we shall see that, while we fall behind the West in the material respect, yet in the moral and intellectual field we have many achievements equal or superior to those of the West. People who reject Chinese civilization *in toto* merely indicate their own lack of thought. Furthermore, the mode of thought and the ideals of the Chinese today were all shaped by their forefathers. . . . If we abolish Chinese writing, how shall we understand and study the ancient mode of thought? Since the beginning of history, Chinese writing is the only language that has recorded, exactly and continuously, all events during four or five thousand years. . . . Western scholars are not afraid of the dead languages of Egypt and Babylon even though these countries perished long ago. . . . How then can Chinese writing be abolished?

100. *Ibid.*, 48, 163.   101. HS:WT (1953), III, 1-5.

In China the spoken and written languages are not identical. . . . Since the Han dynasty, there were changes in conversational Chinese, but no progress. In the written language, on the other hand, although the characters were inherited from former times, the technique of their use was improved. The Chinese spoken language is the most awkward in the world. It is often unable to express what the written language can. . . . The reason is that only the writing can be handed down from the remote ages. The old classics can be imitated. But speech . . . could not be recorded and was thus lost through time. Hence our writing is progressive while our speech is regressive. . . . The compositions of gifted writers in Chinese history excel those of foreign writers—this is universally recognized.[102]

In spite of the considerable amount of ambiguity in Sun's argument, his position was broadly clear; he was vehemently opposed to both the Latinization of Chinese and the discarding of its literary style.

Since the May Fourth movement in a sense paved the way for both the Kuomintang and the Chinese Communist Party, these groups tend to hail it as the beginning of the revolution. Because Sun's memory is respected by both parties, he is often said to have endorsed this movement. The documents generally cited are a telegraphic protest which Sun and six others sent to the Peking government in May, 1919, and a message Sun wrote to his overseas followers in January, 1920. Actually, the intent of both documents seems to have been misconstrued.

To begin with, Sun's letter to his followers was intended only as an appeal for financial contributions to a publishing house and a journal in English which he planned to establish. It was only to justify these efforts that he referred to contemporary intellectual developments, and, as an example, he pointed to the May Fourth movement. Comprising only one-tenth of the whole letter, the relevant part reads:

Since the students of Peking University launched the May Fourth movement, the youthful patriots in China have been adopting new ideas in preparation for practical reform activities. Consequently, with the support of public opinion, there has been a rapid growth of expressions of views. The new publications that have been sponsored by the enthusiastic young people have one after another made their appearance to meet the needs of the times. They have had so much influence on society that even the corrupt [Peking] regime has not dared to oppose them.

This kind of new culture movement is a clear indication

102. KFCC, II, 27-29.

of the unprecedented ideological upheaval which is taking place today. Actually it owed its inception to a handful of men in the publishing world. Gradually we see that throughout the length and breadth of the country the brilliance of their pens has been radiating; the student strikes have been spreading; and the conscience of the people has been awakened to such a degree that a number of patriotic activities were undertaken even at the risk of one's own life.

If efforts along these lines could continue to develop, the achievements are bound to be imposing, enduring, and far-reaching. The success of the revolution which our party desires to see accomplished will have to depend upon a general reorientation of thought. This is why military strategy stresses the tactics of "attacking the mind" while "transforming the thought" is likewise a popular watchword. Indeed, it is this new culture movement to which I am attaching the highest value.[103]

If this passage is considered in relation to the whole body of Sun's writings, it becomes obvious that Sun's concern was only to derive political benefit from the existing agitation. For a time he withheld comment on the merit of the May Fourth movement, but his lectures in 1924 clearly revealed his hearty disapproval.

Two observations should be made concerning the telegraphic protest to Peking. While Sun's name was first on the list of signatures, he had actually been absent from Canton for almost a year and was not on good terms with any of the other men. Thus his signature did not necessarily indicate his personal feelings. Furthermore, the message itself was marked more by its hostility to Peking than by any respect for the students: "The youthful students . . . should be excused . . . . If the authorities of Peking do not seek a basic solution in their policies but instead oppress the people by brutal force, the people will not be afraid of death. A careless start might result in a serious catastrophe. . . . Accordingly, we hope you will handle the matter reasonably in order to satisfy the public sentiment of the whole country. . . ."[104] This language was mild in comparison with the remarks he made on student strikes in 1924. A passage in the second lecture on democracy read: "Having absorbed the idea of liberty, the students can find no place to practice it except in their schools. Insurrections and strikes followed, under the dignified guise of fighting for 'liberty.' The liberty which Westerners talk about has its strict limitations and cannot be described as belonging to everyone. When young Chinese students talk about liberty, they break down all restraints. Because no one welcomes their theory in the society outside, they can only bring it back into their schools, and constant

103. *Ibid.*, V, 384-89.
104. CTT:TMM, 126, and footnote j on the same page.

disorders result. This is abuse of freedom."[105] Thus, there is no doubt that apart from political tactics Sun's ideas differed fundamentally from those of the New Culture leaders.

Paradoxically, however, Sun's deep attachment to China's past did not prevent him from being indebted to the West. To begin with, nearly all of the illustrations in his lectures came from Western society or Westernized city life in China and not from traditional Chinese rural life. Then, too, he was anxious to draw parallels between Western ideas and his own. Thus, he identified his principle of nationalism with Woodrow Wilson's "self-determination by all nations";[106] and he saw an analogy between his three principles and Lincoln's famous phrase "government of the people, by the people, and for the people."[107] He also argued that since his first principle dealt with "national liberty," his second with political equality, and his third with the welfare of all Chinese, they corresponded respectively to the three watchwords of the French Revolution—liberty, equality, and fraternity.[108]

There was, moreover, a Western root to many of Sun's ideas. He himself admitted that he owed his distinction between sovereignty and ability to an American who had commented on the fear of governmental power in a democracy and to a Swiss who had urged a change in this attitude.[109] From these two ideas, Sun developed his four sovereign rights and five political powers, most of which were copied directly from the West. Of the sovereign rights, referendum and initiative had long been practiced in Switzerland. In the United States they were adopted by Nebraska in 1897 and by twenty more states before 1918.[110] In 1919 four works on popular government by J. D. Barnett, D. F. Wilcox, A. L. Lowell, and W. A. Rappard were translated and published by a Kuomintang journal, and they clearly served as the sources of Sun's inspiration.[111] Of the five political powers, three—legislative, judiciary, and executive—were Western, and only two—examination and censorship—were Chinese.

Sun has received lavish praise for achieving this synthesis. Leaving aside its intrinsic worth, Sun's scheme throws important light on his personality. The very fact that he incorporated traditional institutions into his program differentiates him sharply from Yen, Liang, or Ch'en Tu-hsiu, none of whom during the height of their influence had any use for such institutions. But while Sun was attached to the past, it is clear that the attachment was not sustained by any real understanding. He had no new ideas to offer on these Chinese institutions and relied on Western authorities to justify their incorporaton in his

105. KFCC, I, 99-100.
107. KFCC, III, 192, 211, 215.
109. *Ibid.*, 141-42.
111. *Ibid.*, 189n.

106. TSC:SMCI, 8-9.
108. *Ibid.*, I, 102.
110. TSC:SCMI, 181.

scheme. Thus, he quoted W. A. P. Martin as saying that "had the United States used the examination method, the defects of popular election would have been less";[112] and he noted that "Professor Cecil of Columbia University" had suggested in his book, *Liberty*, that the censorial function should be separated from the legislative.[113] Furthermore, John W. Burgess had stated that the Chinese censorial device would make it possible to reconcile individual liberty with governmental authority.[114] Regardless of the accuracy of these quotations, it is clear that the Chinese part of Sun's synthesis reached him through Western sources.

Sun's emotional attachment to China coupled with his Western orientation indicate a marginal personality in both Chinese and Western societies. Possibly because of this ambiguity, Sun was deficient in his knowledge of both the East and the West. In the examples cited above, Lord Hugh Cecil never taught at Columbia, and the professor Sun had in mind was probably John W. Burgess. In his book *Liberty and Authority* (London, 1912), Lord Cecil dwelt on the conflict between liberty and equality, but he did not discuss the separation of powers. In fact, his contention that equality is detrimental to liberty was probably Sun's source for maintaining that "to make all men equal" would yield a "false equality." By coupling this idea to his own observation that the West had indeed tried to make all men equal, he quite logically argued that Western societies had known only false equality and that under his own guidance true equality would one day prevail in China.

Aside from these misquotations and incorrect deductions, Sun revealed little understanding of Western history. Throughout his discussion of the American Civil War he maintained that the war was fought purely for the benefit of the Negroes.[115] Some of his other statements were even more bizarre. For example, he seriously claimed that the automatic reverse action of the piston was invented by a child laborer in a cotton mill who was too lazy to manipulate the piston by hand.[116] In his discussion of democracy, Sun argued that the Westerners had enjoyed only limited political rights,[117] but that with the use of suffrage, recall, referendum, and initiative, the Chinese would soon achieve full liberty.[118] Since these were the same devices Sun had copied from the West, it is difficult to understand how, even according to Sun's logic, the less literate Chinese could do better than the Westerners.

The clearest example of Sun's limited knowledge of China is his fear of under-population. Quoting figures that had no basis, he was

112. *Ibid.*, 200.
113. SCSHC, II, 573-74.
114. TSC:SMCI, 200.
115. KFCC, I, 108-11.
116. *Ibid.*, 156-57.
117. *Ibid.*, 153, 162-63.
118. *Ibid.*, 174.

apparently unaware that Hung Liang-chi had in the eighteenth century called attention to China's surplus population,[119] and that among the causes of the Taiping Rebellion population pressure was one of the most important.[120] Even during Sun's own time there was no sign that the Chinese population had declined. Furthermore, if there were such signs, then Sun could hardly be justified in devising a tax program based solely on a general rise of land value in China. Thus, Sun not only committed factual errors but demonstrated poor reasoning as well.

Only two further instances need to be cited. In his autobiography of 1896 Sun professed a taste for the "literature of Three Dynasties and the two Han."[121] Historically one of the Three Dynasties was the Hsia, a legendary period, and another was the Shang, from which no authenticated literature, save words carved on oracle bones, have survived. Even if the few short documents traditionally attributed to that period are accepted as genuine, they are still unlikely objects for literary appreciation.

The second instance was Sun's attempt to ridicule the Chinese anarchists in 1921. Following the May Fourth movement, every conceivable type of "advanced" doctrine from the West found support in China, and anarchism was no exception. Disagreeing with its Chinese proponents, Sun pointed out that this philosophy had existed in China "before the Three Dynasties" (traditionally dated as starting from 2205 B.C.). As evidence he cited the theories of Huang-ti and Lao Tzu and passages from the book *Lieh Tzu*,[122] unaware that none of these could have dated earlier than the sixth century B.C.

Thus, Sun was emotionally attached to China but intellectually alienated from her. One probable factor in this paradox is his family background. As indicated in the last chapter, he came from a poor family near Macao, and his brother was actually an emigrant to Hawaii. In 1879, at the age of thirteen Sun went to Honolulu to see his brother, and from then until 1895 he was in China (not including Hongkong) less than two complete years.[123] After he became a revolutionary in 1895, he remained abroad until the end of 1911, spending most of these years among the Chinese settlers in foreign countries. His background was thus far more similar to theirs than to that of a Chinese scholar, old or new style. Moreover, the division between these social classes was severe in Sun's days. Broadly, the settlers came from low social groups, had no family tradition of learning, and did not pursue any education after their arrival in a foreign country. Perhaps for this reason they tended to cling to Chinese traditions and usually had a vague but idealized view of Chinese

119. THM (October, 1935), 248-50.   120. LCN:PHC, 47-49; HPT:PC, 64.
121. TLNP, 10.   122. SCSHC, II, 581.
123. KFCC, VI, 329-36.

history. Meanwhile, their minority status in their new homes, and the discriminatory practices they experienced, invariably lent them a strong nationalistic feeling (which helps explain their readiness to part with their hard-earned cash in support of reform or revolutionary campaigns in China).

Like them, Sun felt a deep attachment to China's past, but unlike most people, he was extremely ambitious and self-confident. Evidences of both abound in his biographies. At the age of twenty-four, he expressed a desire to "pursue a career higher than that of an emperor."[124] For displays of egotism like this he earned the sobriquet of *Sun Wu K'ung*, a Chinese play on words capable of several interpretations. First, it is the name of the famous monkey in a sixteenth century novel who had unbounded energy and an endless repertoire of magic. *Wu K'ung* also means "aware of vacuity," which in Chinese would be an appropriate designation for any person who boasts a great deal but achieves very little. In a speech of 1923 Sun himself acknowledged that the people of Kwangtung nicknamed him *Ta P'ao,* or the "Big Mouth,"[125] and if my own childhood recollections are correct, Sun was known by this sobriquet throughout China before 1927.

But Sun's educational limitations were a severe obstacle to the achievement of his goals. His entire training consisted of a few years of attending classes in several scattered schools in Hawaii and Hongkong, plus five more years of instruction in a newly founded colonial medical college.[126] Although he received high marks in his medical courses,[127] it is doubtful that they contributed very much to his general knowledge. Probably because of this handicap, Sun persevered in self-education. He is recorded to have studied every day in his life,[128] and his speeches and writings reveal an acquaintance with an astonishingly large range of topics. But practically all his works are marred by inaccuracies, misconceptions, and shallowness of thought, probably because he had no academic foundation and was therefore unable to conduct fruitful self-study.

From the extensive references in his writings it becomes obvious that his reading was largely limited to contemporary literature—especially newspapers and semi-scholarly writings. While his relentless search for knowledge sometimes led him to obscure sources, such as the political writings of the American dentist, Maurice William, he was singularly unacquainted with the classical works in political philosophy. With such a limited intellectual horizon, his wide reading and his usual conceit made him ready in all cases to claim improvements on other people's concepts. While the intellectual result

124. LHL:KFTH, 30-31.   125. KFCC, III, 258.
126. *Ibid.,* VI, 329-34.   127. LHL:KFTH, 43-57.
128. *Ibid.,* 95.

was seldom satisfactory, this approach served his main purpose, which was to secure mass support partly by a display of intellectual leadership. It is well known that among his followers Sun had a reputation for wide erudition. By comparing his public statements with his sources, we will be able to understand how he achieved such a reputation while making so many errors.

A basic point in Sun's view of history is the idea that Chinese history falls into two periods, the pre-Chou which was progressive and the post-Chou which was regressive.[129] It was in this context that Sun compared the Chou to the modern West in political institutions, morality, and technology. As far as objective evaluation is possible, Sun's statement is patently false. But on what authorities did he base this opinion? The likely sources were Yen Fu and Liang Ch'i-ch'ao. The former had declared in his fourth essay of 1895 that "all those who became emperors since the Ch'in (221-206 B.C.) did so because they were the most tyrannical and crafty and could cheat and plunder more than others could." In a preface to an anthology on Western politics Liang wrote in 1897 that: "Apart from the good Three Dynasties, all the emperors after the Ch'in and Han secured their throne by force. The laws and regulations they promulgated were designed for their own protection rather than for the welfare of the people."[130] Sun seems to have modified these statements in two steps. He first deduced from them that the emperors before the Ch'in were good,[131] and after reaching this conclusion, he exaggerated slightly by arguing that the Chou (that is, the dynasty before the Ch'in) was almost as progressive as the modern West.

Many of Sun's other opinions bear traces of Yen's and Liang's influences. In his first lecture on nationalism Sun praised Great Britain as the foremost power and the Anglo-Saxons as the foremost race on earth. This remark had a striking resemblance to Liang's earlier statement that "the Teutons are the best race in the world and the Anglo-Saxons the best of the Teutons."[132] While Yen's remarks were more circumspect, they were no less enthusiastic. Thus, he eulogized the British naval strength,[133] praised her judicial and monetary systems,[134] and as early as 1914 predicted her ultimate victory in the First World War.[135] Perhaps it is relevant to note that at the time Sun delivered his lectures in 1924 he was feuding bitterly with Great Britain over the latter's refusal to allow him access to the surplus customs recipts at Canton. Moreover, the British were rendering active support to Sun's opponents, notably the warlord Wu P'ei-fu and the comprador of the Hongkong and Shanghai Banking

129. SCSHC, I, 145.
131. KFCC, III, 272.
133. YIMCCK, 5.21.7.13.
135. WCC:YCT, 89.

130. LCC:YPSWC, 2.2.62-63.
132. LCC:YPSCC, 3.4.8.
134. *Ibid.*, 5.18.15.14; WCC:YCT, 7.

Corporation Ch'en Lien-po, who was the commander of the Canton Merchant Volunteer Corps.[136] Indeed, Sun was so indignant that he publicly accused Great Britain of interfering in China's internal affairs.[137] While resentment is not incompatible with admiration in certain circumstances, it is strange that Sun, with all his convictions of China's greatness, should hail Britain's "racial" superiority, at a time when he bitterly complained of her injustice. A plausible explanation is that he had long ago accepted Liang's theme of Anglo-Saxon grandeur and that the idea persisted even when it was no longer consistent with his other notions. As we shall later see in regard to his theory of the distribution of wealth, inconsistency arising from intellectual indigestion was a characteristic of Sun's thought.

In his second lecture on nationalism, Sun called China a "hypocolony" because she was "subject to many powers and hence inferior to a colony." This remark almost repeated Yen's words that "China is the common slave of all powers."[138] In his sixth lecture Sun expressed his belief that China could modernize quickly because the West had pointed the way. This again echoed Yen's thought that "our task is easy because they [the West] have done the difficult part."[139]

Using slightly different expressions, Yen, Liang, and Sun all believed that the Chinese suffered from a lack of national conscience. In his analysis of Western and Chinese societies, Yen stressed that the basic Chinese goal had been to eliminate strife. It was for this reason, he said, that Chinese philosophers called for all men to pledge allegiance to one reigning house. But as political unity was achieved, other evils appeared, notably a lack of stimulating influences from other nations and the determination of the reigning house to keep the masses unenlightened. As a result the Chinese had lost their strength of character and had come to have no public virtue at all.[140] Like Yen, Liang stressed the corrupting effect of the traditional ideal of great unity, which he said was first preached by philosophers to combat political strife but which was later used by the monarch to perpetuate his power. Because the ideal of unity necessarily implied a de-emphasis on ethnic differences, Liang detected in it a cause of China's subservience to alien masters.[141] In Sun's version, the ideal of unity was first used by China to facilitate her domination of the known world, but as the Chinese came genuinely to believe in this ideal, they lost their hostility to the foreigners and became easy prey to alien conquest. The thought of Yen, Liang, and Sun bears interesting comparison. All three saw in ideology an important reason for

136. CY (1924), 849-57; KFCC, IV, 126-27.
137. Ibid., 527, 531, 533.   138. YIMCCK, 5.15.16.19.
139. CCF:YFSWH, 88.   140. Ibid., 3-4.
141. LCC:YPSCC, 3.4.56, 58-59.

China's failure to develop a national consciousness. In point of time Yen was the one who initiated this argument, and in view of his prominence, it may be assumed that Liang and Sun followed him. Yet their reactions were not identical. In a nutshell, Yen maintained that the one-world ideal was originated by philosophers and perpetuated by despots. In other words, there was much in the Chinese tradition that was undesirable. This covert criticism was turned into an open call for destruction by Liang Ch'i-ch'ao. Sun, on the other hand, associated the one-world ideal with China's imperial splendor and its perpetuation with Chinese idealism and sincerity. The root of the argument remained, but the evaluation changed. Sun could see no tarnish upon China's heritage.

One of Sun's major concerns in his lectures on democracy was to elucidate the concepts of liberty and equality. He criticized Rousseau's theory of natural rights as lacking in historical foundation and "conflicting with the principle of historical evolution."[142] This remark clearly indicates his unfamiliarity with Rousseau's work, for in his second *Discours* the philosopher explicitly stated that he was "putting aside the facts."[143] Sun's knowledge of the French-Swiss moralist probably came from secondary sources, among which the writings of Yen and Liang were the most likely ones. Although Liang's first essay on Rousseau was not written until 1901, and Yen's only in 1914, their interest in Rousseau had developed earlier. In 1895 Yen had attributed Western strength to liberty and had assailed the Chinese for their lack of public spirit. Since all these remarks were intended to help solve China's immediate crisis, Yen did not at that time dwell on the possible conflict between group unity and individual liberty; if he had been pressed on this point, he would probably have said that there was no conflict between the two because both would result from the same source, intellectual enlightenment. But Liang in the following years developed a more sophisticated notion. Taking Yen as his authority, he expressed a concern for liberty, but with a politician's mind he also realized that unity necessarily involved restraints on individuals. The problem boiled down to how China could have both—liberty to emulate the West in the long run and unity to tide her over the immediate crisis. For a solution, Liang turned to Rousseau and published in 1901 a detailed summary of the *Social Contract* as well as a biographical sketch of the author.[144] In an article written in 1903 he stated that: "Rousseau's theory of social contract has often been attacked by modern scholars. While we may possibly maintain that his theory does not account for the historical origin of the state, we cannot argue that he fails to describe the reason

142. KFCC, I, 83. 143. VCE:JJR, 141.
144. LCC:YPSWC, 3.6.97-110.

for which the state is formed. Even Rousseau's enemies cannot maintain that."[145]

Yen's article on Rousseau was written in 1914. Bearing the title "A Critique of the *Social Contract*," it was written in response to Liang's request for contribution to a journal.[146] In his article Yen stressed that liberty did not stem from Nature but resulted from convention, that equality in the sense of universal manhood suffrage presupposed a level of mass intelligence which the Chinese did not have, and that to make China strong, every Chinese should sacrifice his liberty instead of seeking more. He considered Rousseau's theory harmful because it created a mistaken image of liberty and contributed to its abuse. While aware of Rousseau's statement in the second *Discours* he nevertheless deplored the philosopher's unhistorical approach. The appearance of Yen's article brought a rebuttal from Chang Shih-chao (1886——), a Scottish-educated writer especially known for his prose style. With considerable logic, Chang argued that Yen's criticism of Rousseau rested mainly on a confusion between nature in an abstract sense as used by Rousseau and nature in a historical and biological sense as Yen understood from Huxley. Chang also stated that since liberty and equality were the bases on which convention stood, they had obviously existed prior to it.[147] This polemic between Yen and Chang was well publicized, and it was probably from his knowledge of these articles that Sun made his comments on Rousseau. The similarity between his views and Liang's is especially noticeable. The only difference was that while Yen and Liang merely discussed a theoretical objection to Rousseau's method of approach, Sun flatly and erroneously condemned the philosopher's historical knowledge.

In arguing that liberty and equality loomed large to Westerners because they had had neither, Sun repeated almost verbatim a passage written by Liang in 1902: "The two classes of aristocracy and commoners in the Far West had vastly different rights and obligations. . . . Because they were extremely unequal, so they eagerly sought equality. . . . The situation in China was the opposite. . . ."[148] But when Sun continued by arguing that the Chinese had too much liberty, he distorted Liang, who had written in 1900:

> Is there no liberty in China? . . . In actuality we have all the freedoms guaranteed by the constitutions of other nations to their people. However, I would not call our freedoms liberty because they lack one essential quality, which is [the assurance] that what I have and enjoy cannot be [arbitrarily] taken away by any other men. . . . In China . . . we luckily have our liberty when the officials do not prohibit it. Once they do, it evap-

145. *Ibid.*, 4.10.1.   146. CCF:YF, 272, 339.
147. *Ibid.*, 339.   148. LCC:YPSWC, 4.9.80-81.

orates. The reason that they usually don't is not because they respect human rights but because they are inept administrators and too occupied to bother. . . . A liberty that can be lost instantly is no more than a slave's freedom.[149]

In 1902, Liang further stated that the essence of liberty was to restrain a government from overstepping its authority and doing evil, and that a government based on liberty was superior to one exercising benevolence because the latter depended on the rulers' will and was therefore uncertain.[150] In saying this he clearly had in mind the differences between such Western institutions as habeas corpus and trial by jury and the Chinese practice of little actual intervention in people's lives.

Liang's opinion changed after the First World War. In a book on Chinese philosophy published in 1922, he advanced the belief that the Chinese had enjoyed more freedom in the pre-Ch'in times than had the Europeans before the French Revolution.[151] Although the point of emphasis had definitely shifted, his statement could still be defended. Sun, however, went one step farther and maintained that the Chinese had too much liberty. Thus, he distorted Liang's thought into an invalid statement.

In arguing that only by curtailing their liberty could the Chinese save China and ultimately enhance their freedom, Sun again repeated what Yen and Liang had already said. Yen had advanced a similar argument in his "Critique of the *Social Contract*," and Liang had stated in 1902: "No man can exist apart from the group. If the group cannot preserve its freedom of action, other groups will come and oppress it. Then the freedom of the individuals in that group will be lost."[152] To forestall such an eventuality, Liang urged the Chinese to be more public-minded and to exercise more self-control in pursuing their interests. But Sun made the enhancement of "national liberty" the central aim of an elaborate political scheme. After intriguing his audience with the paradox that liberty must be curtailed in order to be expanded, he proposed a system of four sovereign rights and five administrative powers, claiming that such a system would make the government democratic but would allow it enough power to solve all of China's problems. While seven of these nine functions were clearly Western in origin, the goal of Sun's scheme revealed obvious traces of Liang's influence.

When Liang turned conservative in 1903, he declared that China was not yet ready for democracy. To support his view, Liang based his arguments on the experiences of the United States and France,

149. *Ibid.*, 2.5.45. 150. *Ibid.*, 4.10.5.
151. LCC:YPSCC, 13.50.3-4. Note also the connection between Liang's argument and Sun's contention that pre-Ch'in China was as progressive as the modern West.
152. *Ibid.*, 3.4.46. For similar statements, see 3.4.14.

which he believed had both made a deplorable shambles of the democratic system. France had experienced eighty years of political chaos before she was able to erect an even partially stable regime, the Third Republic;[153] America, in spite of a fine democratic tradition inherited from England, also demonstrated many infirmities, including discrimination against Negroes, Chinese, and Indians, and the "world-renowned" system of corruption exemplified by such weaknesses as the "spoils system."[154] Liang's views in this regard were fully reflected in Sun's thought. In a speech of 1906 he said:

> In [American] elections those who are eloquent can flatter the public and be returned to office while those who are learned and righteous often receive no attention. Hence in the Assemblies sit many stupid and ignorant men. The [American electoral] history is indeed a farce. Furthermore, in their appointive system, all the officials shift with the president, who is either a Democrat or a Republican. As a consequence, every change in the presidency means a change of some sixty to seventy thousand officials from cabinet ministers to postmasters. Hence the corruption and inefficiency of American politics is unparalleled in the whole world.[155]

In his lectures of 1924, Sun stressed that during the French Revolution even men like Danton lost their lives and that the extreme cruelty in turn gave rise to the dictatorship of Napoleon. He complained that in the United States Jefferson and his disciples were equally unsuccessful in their attempt to win more rights for the people.[156] It was on the basis of the alleged Western failures that Sun erected his own political system.

In his discussion of equality, Sun first distinguished between "true equality," in which the mediocre should follow the sage, and "false equality," in which the foolish and the wise were treated alike. After a lengthy review of Western struggles for equality, especially the French and American revolutions and the American Civil War, Sun concluded that equality had been abused in the West[157] and that only by following his program could China secure "true equality." This was his second paradox—that equality was to be achieved through inequality—and the basis for his paternalistic political structure.

It seems probable that in this argument Sun was influenced by both Yen Fu and Liang Ch'i-ch'ao. Yen had once said:

> Democracy is the highest form of government. However, it is a system extremely difficult to adopt because the quality

153. LCC:YPSWC, 5.13.78, 85.
154. *Ibid.*, 5.13.79; LCC:YPSCC, 5.22.140-41.
155. SCSHC, I, 80.
156. KFCC, I, 124-26. See also TSC:SMCI, 123.
157. KFCC, I, 108-13.

of the people is often not up to it. A chief ingredient of democracy is equality . . . [but this] cannot be achieved by arbitrary means. Only when the people's bodily strength, intelligence, and moral capacity are equal can democracy be realized. If equality is enforced among people who have not reached this stage, then the foolish will not submit to the wise, the stupid will not listen to the intelligent, and the weak will not follow the strong.[158]

If true equality was so difficult to attain, and if, as Liang said, neither France nor the United States was a political success, would it not be logical to deduce that only "false equality" had prevailed in these countries? In spite of the somewhat startling nature of this conclusion, Sun probably thought that he was only improving upon views already expressed by others.

This seems even more likely when we note the parallels between his discussions of liberty and of equality. In both cases his contention was strikingly similar to either Yen's or Liang's, but on both occasions he distorted their views by overlooking certain nuances and reservations. For example, they both made important distinctions between Chinese and Western "liberty," and only with this understood would they agree that the Chinese had too much "liberty." Sun, however, accepted this conclusion without their vital qualification. Again, Liang commented unfavorably on the conditions in France and the United States, but his remarks were part of a careful and reasoned analysis. In Sun's hands, they were turned into a sweeping assertion that in these lands man's potential was limited by arbitrary restrictions. This argument was patently false, but its very absurdity deserves attention. In both his discussions of liberty and of equality he twisted Yen's and Liang's thought in the same direction, that is, to assert China's, and his own, superiority over the West and its thinkers. Thus, according to Sun, China had too much liberty while the West had none, and his scheme would realize the true equality denied to all Westerners. Besides Sun's obvious ethnocentrism and egotism, the neat pattern of his arguments suggests a conscious effort to borrow and modify Yen's and Liang's concepts.

The same tendency becomes even clearer at the next stage of his argument, when he advocates equal opportunity for all people to realize their unequal potentialities. Here two points may usefully be distinguished: the emphasis on intelligence as the basic criterion of ability and the more concrete scheme of a hierarchical political order. The former had always been a characteristic of Chinese thought. Besides finding expression through such institutions as the civil-service examinations, it was fully endorsed by modern thinkers.

158. YIMCCK, 5.8.2.3.

When Yen Fu spoke of the struggle for human existence, he argued in particular that only the most intelligent could survive. On his part, Liang always viewed intellectual development as a key to modernization. In 1898 he specifically linked intelligence to political power. He stated: "The consensus in China today is that she should have democracy. While this is undoubtedly true, democracy yet cannot be realized overnight, for people can only have power when they have intelligence. A little intelligence will yield a little power; much of it will yield much power."[159] On the classification of men by intelligence, Liang said in 1899: "There are three kinds of men, those who are servile to old customs, those who are capable of ignoring them, and and those who can initiate new trends. The progress of the world depends on the last group. Oftentimes the behavior of one or two pioneers, who a mere ten years ago were viewed as eccentrics by the whole world, is imitated by all at the end of that time."[160] Apart from the rather prophetic nature of the last sentence when it is applied to Sun's career, Liang's method of rating men was strikingly similar to the tripartite division Sun suggested in 1924, the only difference being that Sun reversed Liang's order and enumerated the highest class first. This similarity persisted in Sun's theory of revolution by stages. In his opinion the most able men should be able to direct and complete the revolution in three stages—a military stage to pacify the country, a tutelary one to educate the people, and a final one to confer sovereign rights on the people. In defending his tutelary concept, which was the heart of his idea, Sun repeated almost verbatim the arguments in Liang's "Enlightened Despotism" of 1903. Comparing the United States with France, Sun attributed France's "eighty years of chaos" to her unreadiness for democracy. Since the Chinese were even less mature than the French, he argued that a transitional period of tutelage was the only practical path. Aware of the plagiarism, Sun sought to cover it up by a direct denial. Referring to Liang as "the twisted scholar" (ch'ü-hsueh-che), he peremptorily stated that because Liang's purpose was to further autocracy while his was to promote democracy, the difference between them was as wide as "heaven and earth."[161] In actual fact Liang also advocated democracy as an ultimate goal, and they both agreed on the need for a period of tutelage and on the reasons for it. The fact that Liang wanted a tutelage under an enlightened despot while Sun preferred a dictatorship by the party seems to be of little consequence. Thus Sun's categorical denial merely confirmed his imitation.

While Sun's principle of livelihood had little in common with Liang's ideas, traces of Yen's influence were evident. Perhaps the most noticeable was Sun's insistence that the West had not solved its

159. LCC:YPSWC, 2.3.41.   160. Ibid., 2.3.63.
161. SCSHC, I, 153-56.

"social problems," a view that Yen had advanced in 1895. For Sun this was an important point because his claim that the principle of livelihood was the only correct path for China was based on his rejection of both Marxism and capitalism. His reasons for dismissing Marxism, to be discussed later, were largely taken from Maurice William, but his sharp criticisim of capitalism came mainly from Yen, although for political reasons he never acknowledged his debt. As pointed out earlier, Yen in 1895 idealized the West in all respects except for the gross inequality of wealth among its people. This, too, was Sun's concern. Not only did he repeatedly deplore economic inequality but on many occasions he also used the attainment of economic equality as a means of evaluating political measures.[162] Indeed, this goal was so natural to him that he never attempted to justify it.

Yen's influence over Sun becomes more apparent as we move on to other points in Sun's principle of livelihood. In 1895, Yen argued that economic inequality would lead to luxurious living among the rich, frequent cases of mental disturbance in society, and discontent and strife among the people. While conditions in the West had not deteriorated to such an extent, he thought that the only saving condition was the Western tradition of liberty and equality, which compelled the rich to refrain from overburdening the poor. Nevertheless, he was convinced that economic inequality was an irreversible process; once it occurred, no correction was possible.[163]

Yen seems to have been the only Chinese writer who maintained this point of view. It profoundly influenced Sun and prompted him to study the means by which economic inequality could be forestalled. Under the influence of Henry George, he devised an "equalization of landownership" formula, and by 1902 or 1903 this slogan was added to the three-point oath taken by members of his secret organization, the Revive China Society.[164] After this time he consistently maintained that the only way to solve economic inequality was to prevent it from occurring.

In 1924 he repeated this view in his lectures, but there it conflicted with his observation that through class co-operation Western societies had recently achieved progress by levying heavy income and inheritance taxes. If, as Sun maintained, the receipts in Germany from such levies amounted to between 60 and 80 per cent of the annual revenue,[165] then economic inequality obviously was no longer an irreversible process. Yet Sun did not attempt to resolve this contradiction. Possibly he had taken Yen's idea so much for granted that

162. TSC:SMCI, 271. 163. CCF:YFSWH, 23-24.
164. Harold Schiffrin, "Sun Yat-sen's Early Land Policy," JAS (August, 1957), 549-60.
165. KFCC, I, 188.

he no longer questioned it in the light of his newer notions. (Another possible factor was the peculiar position of the land tax program in his whole scheme. There is no doubt that this device had an air of ingenuity that Sun greatly valued. Yet it could not merit special attention in a land where production was admittedly a far more important problem than distribution, unless it could be shown that economic inequality was an irreversible process and that preventive measures were therefore essential from the beginning.)

Several other similarities can be noted between Sun and Yen. In 1895, Yen had stated that "the basic assumption in both Western philosophy and politics is that all living beings aim to preserve their lives" *(ke-pao ch'i-sheng)*.[166] An obvious reference to the instinct of self-preservation, his phrase probably inspired Sun to maintain that the struggle for existence *(jen-lei ch'iu sheng-ts'un)* was the central force in history. Sun also agreed with Yen that poverty was no problem in China and that foreign capital should be used to develop China.[167] A brief historical sketch will indicate how unusual these views seemed at the time. The two basic ideas in traditional Chinese economic thought were that wealth was a fixed stock and that as little as possible should be exacted from the people. Consequently, even in good times the literati emphasized the crushing burdens of the masses. When China was forced to pay out huge indemnities and was on the verge of breaking up in the late nineteenth century, all commentators dreaded an imminent economic collapse. Yen was one of the very few who believed otherwise. He specifically noted the growing importance of the Customs receipts and forecast a great increase of government revenue with the expansion of the railroads.[168] Significantly, a few years later Sun also stressed these possibilities.[169] Being an optimist by nature, he went one step farther and stated in 1912 that once her mines and railways were developed, China would be so rich that she would have difficulty spending all her revenue.[170]

In urging the use of foreign capital and technical knowledge for China's development, Yen was taking an extremely unpopular stand. Since 1876 foreigners had sought Chinese railway concessions, but the government had resisted such attempts, at first because it disliked innovation but later because it detected political motives behind these demands. After the "scramble for concessions" began in 1895, the Chinese became increasingly suspicious of all foreign activities. Widespread attempts were made around 1904 to recover, through negotiation and purchase, all economic rights previously granted to foreigners. Yen was almost alone in voicing dissent. While he denounced political encroachments such as extraterritoriality and

166. CCF:YFSWH, 17.　　167. CCF:YF, 157.
168. YIMCCK, 2.Wu.1.723-24, Wu.2.858.
169. SCSHC, I, 89.　　170. KFCC, III, 25.

foreign management of the Chinese Customs, he strongly favored using foreign capital and know-how in the development of China.[171] This stand foreshadowed Sun's attitude in later years.

Controversies have been waged since Sun's death on the nature and extent of Western influence in his principle of livelihood. To facilitate discussion we will distinguish the four concepts involved, namely, that the search for livelihood was the central force in history, that landownership should be "equalized," that the state should play a dominant economic role, and that the land should belong to the tillers. Under the first concept we may also conveniently discuss Sun's attitude toward Marxism-Leninism. In his book *Sun Yat-Sen Versus Communism* Maurice William claimed not only that Sun's Principle of Livelihood was based on his own theory but also that his work must have come to Sun's attention between April and August of 1924 and thereby caused a reversal in his views on Marxism, with all its consequences on subsequent Chinese politics.[172] But as a recent Chinese writer points out, Sun actually knew about William's earlier work, *The Social Interpretation of History,* and recommended it to the party delegates in January, 1924, before he delivered his first lecture on the principle of nationalism.[173] Thus any discrepancies in those lectures can not be attributed to reading William's book at that particular time. This, of course, is not to deny that Sun was influenced by William. As the latter meticulously shows in some one hundred pages, most of the materials in Sun's first two lectures on livelihood bear striking resemblances to passages in William's book. But contrary to William's conclusion, which was natural under the circumstances, the similarity does not necessarily prove the origin of Sun's thought. Rather, the crucial point is whether Sun had made parallel statements before William's book appeared. In a speech in 1912 Sun said: "How would we go about working for the welfare of mankind? Here we have to know the causes of human sufferings. The main determinant of man's position in society, of whether he is to be happy or miserable, is his means of subsistence *(sheng-chi)*. Even the physical existence of men is limited by their mode of livelihood. Only when the problem of livelihood is solved can men exist at all."[174] It seems that at least in a rudimentary form Sun had, then, already entertained the thought that man's struggle for subsistence is the central force in history.

William's claim that Sun turned against Marxism only after reading his book is also untenable. Sun had long known about Marxism

171. CCF:YF, 138, 168. For a discussion of the personal relationships among Yen, Liang, and Sun, see my article "The Influence of Yen Fu and Liang Ch'i-ch'ao on the *San Min Chu I*," PHR (May, 1965), 163-84.
172. WM:SYS, XVI-XVII. 173. TSC:SCS, 153-54.
174. TSC:SMCI, 284-85.

and had on many occasions indicated his disagreement. Thus, in 1912 he said: "After the Industrial Revolution socialist doctrines arose. Only then did the scholars become aware of the injustice involved in the old system of distribution. . . . The correct way to allocate profit is to distribute it according to the work performed, both mental and physical, with the remaining part going to society."[175] On class relationships his position was even more specific. In the same year he expressed the hope that: "Chinese industries would in the future be placed on a co-operative basis so that both politics and industry would be democratized and every social class would depend on and live with another in a spirit of love."[176] Seven years later, in 1919, he declared that: "In this International Development Scheme, I venture to present a practical solution for the three great world problems which are the International War, the Commercial War, and the Class War. As it has been discovered by post-Darwin philosophers that the primary force of human evolution is co-operation and not struggle as that of the animal world, so the fighting nature, a residue of the animal instinct in man, must be eliminated from man, the sooner the better."[177] In 1922 he explained the relationship between mind and matter by saying that while the former was dependent on the latter, the latter could not function by itself.[178] Clearly, Sun's views were at variance with Marx's.

On the other hand, in his 1924 lectures Sun praised Marx before refuting him. The reason for this inconsistency was probably a political one. Somewhat earlier Sun had concluded an alliance with Russia which he hoped would help him achieve power in China. Yet this move had encountered severe opposition within his own party.[179] Convinced of his persuasive powers, he then delivered a series of lectures in order to justify the alliance and to assert his own supremacy short of offending the Communists. This purpose required him to praise Marx and Lenin in general terms, to stress their similarities to him, but to reject their faith at some vital point. By sheer coincidence, the order of Sun's principles lent itself admirably to his task. Sun had always thought his first principle was the simplest, and his last, the principle of livelihood, the most important.[180] Hence one would expect Sun to praise Marx and Lenin in his early lectures but to reject them toward the end. An analysis of Sun's lectures indicates that this is exactly what he did. Thus, in nationalism, he called the Russian revolution a new hope of mankind and Lenin a man who led the world in vision and foresight. In his lectures on democracy, Sun described Russia as a foremost world power, her revolution as the most successful of all revolutions, and the

175. *Ibid.*, 88-89.
177. KFCC, II, 261.
179. MFTG, 386.

176. *Ibid.*, 291.
178. TSC:SCMI, 284.
180. TSC:SCMI, 52; SCSHC, II, 796-97.

"people's dictatorship *(jen-ming tu-ts'ai)*" as a great improvement on the parliamentary system. It is important to notice that these comments were unaccompanied by any specific references; their purely complimentary nature was clarified by Sun's own remark that he knew little about the Russian system.[181] Even as he began his lectures on livelihood, he still found Marx's approach "scientific" and his aim correct, but from this point on he refuted Marx's main tenets one by one, from surplus value to historical materialism. We may then conclude that Sun devised his plan of battle with infinite care and skill, and that instead of being radically influenced by William, he was merely using American ammunition to good advantage.

A conspicuous feature of Sun's lectures was his failure to mention Lenin's theories. This omission is striking for two reasons: Sun was anxious to praise Lenin, and he could profit from Lenin's theory of imperialism in his tirade against the Western powers. In all probability this brilliant piece of argument was unknown to Sun. Several reasons can be advanced to account for his ignorance. In the first place, he was a genuine politician to whom reading was a means but not an end in itself. Since he had rejected Marxism, no work which aimed to reinforce it was likely to arouse his curiosity. Nor would he be interested in Russia as such because after 1905 she was, to the Chinese mind, no longer a part of the powerful West which the Chinese resented and admired. Naturally Russia's stature grew after she agreed to give Sun aid; but then only two years remained of his life. He was far more intrigued by Lenin's "political achievement," that is to say, his organizational talent, than by his abstract theory. The reason for this attraction is also clear. The evils of imperialism were too obvious to a Chinese to need any elaboration, while a sternly disciplined party organization remained Sun's fervent aspiration. Blaming his followers for his political setbacks, he vainly tried after 1914 to impose strict discipline upon them;[182] his failure naturally drew his attention to Lenin's success in the same objective. In the absence of other knowledge about Russia, this was the only real ground for his eulogy of Russia and the "people's dictatorship."

The major influence on Sun's land program was, as he himself admitted, Henry George.[183] Basically, both men were concerned with land that had situation value, mainly urban sites and not agricultural land. Furthermore, they agreed that social progress and population increases were responsible for the appreciation of land value; that the unearned increment was the cause of social injustice; and that the tax on land would channel wealth into productive investment.[184] But beyond these points, their views differed considerably. While

181. KFCC, I, 133.
182. HCT:HH, 162-68; KFCC, III, 180-81, 183; SCSHC, I, 96-97.
183. Schiffrin, *op. cit.*, 550.   184. *Ibid.*, 559-60.

George aimed at taxing away all unearned increments, past and future, Sun would leave the past portion intact in the hands of the landowners. The reasons he gave for this position are characteristic. He believed that land values would rise throughout China as they had in the port cities,[185] that these increases would be infinitely larger than past ones, and that by promising the landowners their present incomes, he was obtaining their support without making any real concessions. His argument was thus based on a rosy estimate and an eagerness to secure support.

Sun also disagreed with George on the single-tax issue and on the method of collection. His views on the former had fluctuated until 1922, when he finally decided that a single tax was inadequate under present conditions.[186] In this regard his ideas were derived from many sources. The cities and countries specifically mentioned in his speeches included London, New York, Canada, Britain, the United States, Germany, the Netherlands, and Australia.[187] But it was Kiaochow that convinced him to tax future increase in land value, and New Zealand that taught him the method of self-assessment by the landowner with possible government purchases of land as a check.[188]

For his ideas on state socialism, Sun was probably most indebted to Bismarck. As a symbol of Germany's unification and rapid rise to world power, Bismarck had long been admired by the Chinese, and Sun's respect for him clearly indicates that he placed nationalism above democracy. On many occasions Sun quoted Bismarck to support his principle of livelihood, which he often defined as a "method to develop by governmental action the natural resources of China." In 1912 he stated that:

> England and America are now suffering the consequences of not having followed this policy [state socialism] from the beginning. The United States has recently attempted to nationalize all the railroads, but because [the government] does not have enough funds to purchase them, there is no way to change the status quo. Germany is the only country which had adopted preventive measures in time. She owns all her railways precisely because she industrialized late and could foresee the drawbacks of industrialization [from the examples of other countries]. China should imitate Germany.[189]

185. In 1912 Sun told some reporters that levying a tax on land titles alone would yield ten times the current annual government revenue. This obviously presupposed an increase of land value throughout China. See KFCC, IV, 462; also TSC:SCMI, 308.

186. *Ibid.*, 309.

188. Schiffrin, *op. cit.*, 561.

187. KFCC, III, 13, 14, 23, 39, 47.

189. KFCC, III, 25.

A few months later he declared in another speech: "In opposing socialism by state socialism, Bismarck has had a worldwide following in the last ten years. . . . We can therefore feel sure that this principle is correct. . . . To promote it is the only way by which we can avoid economic injustice in the future."[190] Sun's belief in this regard was not shaken by Germany's defeat in the first World War. Next to Germany, Russia drew considerable praise. The New Economic Policy was described as a kind of state socialism under which major resources were nationalized.[191] From the examples of these two countries Sun concluded that state ownership of the means of production was "a practical and reliable system," and on this premise he drafted an ambitious industrial plan for China.

While "land to the tillers" was supposedly one of the key programs of the Kuomintang, Sun's references to it were extremely vague; actually, no more than a single slogan (*"keng-che yu ch'i-t'ien"*) was advanced.[192] This reticence should be contrasted with Sun's lengthy treatment of such problems as the separation of powers and the collection of a land tax. A probable factor in his treatment of these problems was the availability of Western materials: where they were plentiful, Sun's discussion was extensive; but where they were not, he had little to offer beyond general ideas, which in this particular case were probably derived from the Chinese dynastic practice of alloting land to peasants.

One of Sun's intellectual drawbacks was his almost complete concern with practical objectives. To him theory was only a tool to further political aims. A good example is his doctrine of knowledge and action, which held that to know is more difficult than to do. In a preface he frankly explained why he held this view. Blaming his political setbacks on the inertia of his followers, he insisted that if they would only follow his leadership less hesitantly, there would be nothing to prevent his rise to power.[193] He then sought to inspire them by establishing that to do was easy, once the knowledge for doing was obtained. He attempted to prove his proposal by giving ten illustrations. Men, he said, eat without a knowledge of cooking, nutrition, physiology, and other related subjects, just as they write, spend money, and so on without knowing the ramifications of their actions; to do is therefore easier than to know, contrary to the old Chinese saying that to know is easier than to do, which, besides being untrue, has the harmful effect of making people do nothing.[194]

In spite of the acclaim given it by Sun's followers, this argument actually rests on a false premise. The old saying in question refers primarily to ethical behavior; it is easy to know the ideal but difficult

190. *Ibid.*, 69.
191. *Ibid.*, 295.
192. TSC:SCMI, 318-21.
193. KFCC, II, 2-3.
194. *Ibid.*, 5-79.

to live up to it. Attempting to prove the reverse, Sun took all of his illustrations from the physical side of life. Obviously to know how to build a bridge is more difficult than to pour the concrete, but this is hardly the concern of the proverb, which deals with different types of actions. Sun's claim to have improved upon traditional Chinese thought thus rested on confusion. But this claim enhanced his reputation as a "knower," which, if we judge by the implication of his words, was his primary objective.

Because Sun's theories were intended to inspire his followers, they were seldom well reasoned statements. In the principle of nationalism, he asserted that the way to strengthen the nation was by strengthening the family and the clan.[195] Just how the one would lead to the other was not explained. A similar ambiguity existed in the problem of ethnic minorities. Before 1920 he favored a "republic of five races" composed of Chinese, Manchus, Mongolians, Moslems, and Tibetans,[196] but in the same year he stated that there were more than five "races" in China and that assimilation was better than separate identity anyway.[197] He did not mention this problem in the 1924 lectures, but earlier in that year, through the manifesto of the first Kuomintang congress, he advocated equality for all ethnic groups and promised them self-determination, but without defining the term.[198] Because Sun's nationalism meant only the strengthening of China, he probably had no consistent ideas on the minority problem.

Nor did Sun give a consistent description of the organization of his five-power government. He contradicted himself on whether the president was to be elected directly by the people or indirectly by the national assembly.[199] He stressed co-ordination among the five governmental branches but prescribed no way to attain it.[200] Nor did he have any consistent ideas on the relationship between the central and the provincial governments.[201] By 1924 he seems to have finally decided on the principle of an "equal distribution of power" (chün-ch'uan), whose meaning he never clarified.[202] In 1912 he considered political parties essential for the democratic process;[203] but by 1914 his political setback had led him to advocate a single-party system with all members pledging allegiance to him.[204]

Although the principle of livelihood was the most important of his theories, it suffered just as much from vagueness and inconsistency. Sun's method of assessing land values included no provision for price changes through purely monetary forces, nor was it capable of dealing with cases involving declining land values. Even less can be said for

195. KFCC, I, 57-58.
196. Ibid., III, 19, 66-67.
197. Ibid., 182, 184.
198. SCSHC, II, 526.
199. TSC:SCMI, 202.
200. Ibid., 201, 204.
201. Ibid., 210-12.
202. SCSHC, II, 571.
203. KFCC, III, 111-12, 129-32.
204. TSC:SMCI, 225.

the six grandiose plans that he singlehandedly drafted for China's industrialization, which called for the construction of 200,000 miles of railroads, 1,000,000 miles of highways, a vast communications network, and three harbors as large as the port of New York.[205]

A comparison of Sun with Yen and Liang reveals similarities as well as differences. To begin with, they differed in their educational backgrounds. Of the three Yen received the most Western-oriented education and was particularly confident of his attainments in social philosophy. On the other hand, he made little claim to competence in Chinese studies, in spite of his reputation as an essayist of the classical school.[206] This self-evaluation appears to have been correct, for although he demonstrated an interest in Taoist philosophy and some skill in Chinese poetry, his major strength lay in his thorough knowledge of such Western thinkers as Montesquieu, J. S. Mill, Spencer, and Huxley. It was from these men's writings that he acquired an insight into modern Western civilization. He was the first and perhaps the keenest Chinese observer of Western society. He correctly analyzed individual liberty in terms of the profit motive and marketing processes. This insight enabled him to compare the underlying principles of Chinese and Western societies with an impartiality notably absent from the writings of other Chinese, whether such cultural conservatives as Sun Yat-sen, or such ardent Westernizers as Hu Shih. Even Yen's mistakes reflected his understanding of the West; both his evolutionism and his belief that social phenomena could be studied by methods of physical science were attitudes shared by many European thinkers.

Unlike Yen, Liang Ch'i-ch'ao had an excellent training in Chinese, but he was not exposed to Western thought until 1895. Moreover, it was only in 1898 that he began studying it on his own, but by then he was too busy with politics to undertake a concentrated program, a fact demonstrated by his several unsuccessful attempts to acquire a working knowledge of English and other foreign languages.[207] But his native intelligence and mastery of Chinese historiography helped him to acquire a general knowledge of many Western works, which profoundly influenced him by their method. In a style that was almost colloquial, he produced many studies on Chinese topics which were notable for their factual content as well as their critical observations. In this limited respect Liang was even more Westernized than Yen, who not only wrote less extensively but, perhaps limited by his knowledge of China, never contributed an empirical study.

205. KFCC, II, 101-265. In a preface Sun acknowledged the editorial assistance of five persons (SYS:IDC, p. vi). In addition he had some help from Dr. P. W. Kuo. But none of these men was an engineer.
206. CCF:YFSWH, 153-54.
207. YCTIC, 120; LJKHS, III, 555, 565.

As indicated earlier, Sun Yat-sen had neither a scholarly family background nor a systematic liberal education. His own extensive reading was marred by poor selection and inadequate understanding. Although political philosophy was his main concern, he had little acquaintance with the basic works in the field. In his 1924 lectures, which contained many illustrations taken from Western society, he mentioned only four Western thinkers, and of these four, he erred on no less than three. He misunderstood Rousseau and described J. S. Mill as the first Westerner to set limits on liberty. He viewed the continued interest of Western scholars in Plato as a sign of their intellectual stagnation.[208] Marx was the only one Sun understood in any real degree.

In all of his discussions on political authority, Sun showed no awareness that the basic problem was the corrupting effect of power and that this evil was particularly serious in China because institutional checks and balances had never been stressed. His ill-defined proposal to establish a government of five branches scarcely touched the problem; on the contrary, his stress on the intellectual inequality of men and his advocacy of a party tutelage over the nation would necessarily aggravate it. Possibly he himself sensed something amiss, for toward the end of his third lecture on democracy, he spoke about a "moral equality" or the duty of all men to be altruistic.[209] The meaning of this passage is obscure, but it may indicate that Sun felt corruption would pose no problem in his system because the "knowers" would demonstrate so much moral excellence that they would inspire altruism. But if this were Sun's view, it would raise fresh difficulties in his concept. For if, as he maintained, the search for livelihood is actually the central force in history, men must be motivated by feelings of pleasure and pain. Can they be altruistic at the same time? Sun's failure to consider this question suggests his unawareness of both the problem and the contradiction.

Actually, it seems that Sun was heavily influenced by the traditional Chinese ideal of benevolent government, but being unable, and perhaps also unwilling, to express his thoughts in purely Chinese terms, he clothed them in all of the Western paraphanalia known to him. Basically, his principle of democracy was a modified version of the old idea of elitist government, complete with all the assumptions of benevolence from above and the spreading of virtue through the power of example. Similarly, his principle of livelihood was very nearly a resurrection of the ideals of governmental paternalism, economic egalitarianism, and social justice. The only addition to these time-honored values was the quest for affluence, which Sun inherited from the earlier Chinese reformers of the nineteenth century. Unlike

208. KFCC, I, 138.   209. Ibid., 117-18.

Yen and Liang, neither of whom discussed civilization in terms of its spiritual essence or a separate technological "practice," Sun clearly stated that China should revive Confucian values while assimilating Western technology.[210] In this respect he agreed with Chang Chih-tung. But while the latter spoke only generally about Western institutions, Sun derived his basic knowledge from the West and applied his understanding of its institutions to Chinese conditions. In this sense it might be said that Sun used "Western learning as the essence and Chinese knowledge as the practice."

But intellectual caliber alone is no measure of political success. In this regard Sun enjoyed many advantages over Yen and Liang. Both of the latter emphasized the scientific method, and in his later years even Liang wrote with a certain objectivity; but they never pretended, like Sun, to be the knower of knowers. While this lack of pretension both aided and reflected their intellectual achievement, it also caused them to be politically hesitant. Yen was never a man of action, and Liang pursued his intellectual endeavors to the point of political inconsistency. In contrast, Sun never doubted his position and demonstrated neither intellectual nor moral scruples. A few examples will illustrate his *modus operandi*. In order to obtain American protection, he falsely swore in Hawaii in February, 1904, that he had been born there.[211] To court the favor of Japan in 1907, he publicly declared in that country that it was justified in annexing all Chinese territories north of Ch'ang-ch'un.[212] As soon as he became provisional president in 1912, he mortgaged the Han-yeh-p'ing mines to Japan over the strenuous opposition of his minister of industries, Chang Ch'ien, an old fashioned scholar-official.[213] In 1915 Sun accused Yüan Shih-kai of betraying China to Japan for his personal benefit. Actually, Sun himself had solicited, and was still soliciting, political aid from Japan, in return for which he was perfectly willing to co-operate with Japanese exploitation of China.[214] In fact, there was little Sun would not do to obtain power. At one point he agreed to cede Manchuria to Japan in return for military aid and twenty million yen;[215] on another occasion he plotted with a Mr. Dietrick of San Francisco to raise funds among American businessmen on the pretext of forming a "department store trust" in China.[216] While Liang also engaged in cloak and dagger politics, there is no evidence that he ever conducted himself in Sun's manner.

210. *Ibid.*, I, 48, 163; II, 27; III, 416.
211. FTY:KMIS, II, 110. See also SSAS, 129. The dates given in this source are, however, wrong.
212. JMB:JSYS, 122.
213. Ch'uan Han-sheng, "A Historical Study of Han Yeh P'ing Co.," in CKHTS, II, 301-5. See also SYL:HTCC, 182.
214. JMB:JSYS, 188-89, 191-94.   215. *Ibid.*, 165-66.
216. *Ibid.*, 172-73.

In their attitudes toward the masses, the three men revealed striking differences. Yen hardly thought the public was fit to read his writings,[217] while Liang looked primarily to the official class for support. Sun, however, was far more at home among the lower classes of Chinese society. In fact, one might say that his whole program was devised for them. His encyclopedic knowledge of the world, his detection of flaws in all theories and institutions, his readiness to suggest improvements, his reasoned claims of Chinese superiority, his air of authority, and his promise of an affluent society in China within five decades, with free lodging and food for all, free education, free medical care, free retirement benefits, and so on—all of these could not fail to impress an audience in a land of scarcity.[218] Even though Sun's boastfulness was well known, any skepticism on the part of his audience was likely to change into enthusiastic expectation when he succeeded in obtaining Soviet aid. At any rate, rudimentary as his principles were, they were still more coherent and understandable to the masses than the words of any of his rivals at the time.

Of the similarities among Yen, Liang, and Sun, the most noticeable was their nationalism. All Yen's writings, even his poetry, expressed his patriotism. He first published his essays in the midst of a national crisis. He translated Western classics to provide a theoretical basis for his political stand. Even his works on logic were meant to serve the nation by fostering correct habits of thought. As late as 1917, when he bade farewell to the departing British minister to China, Sir John Jordan, he wept bitterly over the sad state of China.[219] He was then sixty-four years old. For a man of his age, such a display of emotion amply testified to the intensity of his feelings.

Liang's ardent nationalism was equally apparent in his writings, notably the "Discourses on the New People" discussed in Chapter 8. While Sun was less emotional in this particular respect, all of his doctrines were nonetheless nationalistic. Of China's political radicals Sun had the most unadulterated pride in the national culture. He spoke of a utopia, but it was a utopia based on traditional Chinese morality.[220] Most of his ideas came from the West; yet he never consciously adopted a Western concept except to serve a specific Chinese need. To obtain foreign aid, he was prepared to pay any price, but he undoubtedly justified this attitude by maintaining that only his accession to power could solve China's problems.

This basic stand on the part of Yen, Liang, and Sun distinguished them sharply from later intellectuals like Ch'en Tu-hsiu, who consciously rejected nationalism on principle. Even during the Manchu rule Ch'en refused to join the revolutionists because he resented

217. CCF:YFSWH, 154.
218. KFCC, III, 25, 398-99, 409-10; TSC:SCMI, 388-93.
219. WS:YFC, 101.   220. KFCC, I, 72.

their nationalist banner.[221] Later, as secretary-general of the Chinese Communist Party, Ch'en submitted meekly to the authority of the Comintern.[222] While his submission might have been prompted by a quest for power, it was more likely justified by cosmopolitanism. Thus, in a sense he was the first to break away from the intense patriotism that increasingly dominated the Chinese elite in the latter part of the nineteenth century. On the other hand, Ch'en was in many ways squarely within the scholar-moralist tradition: his agonizing concern for China's fate, his life-long political struggle, and his endurance of hardships and personal tragedies—all these were faintly reminiscent of the life of Ku Yen-wu three centuries earlier. After Ch'en's time the attitude of foreign-educated Chinese became more individualistic, and none of them aspired to a messianic role. In this limited sense Sun, and to a lesser extent, Ch'en, were the last of a disappearing breed. As Sun described himself in 1921, with usual exaggeration but some justice, he was a successor to Confucius in the upholding of this tradition.[223]

One result of the rising nationalism among the early radicals was their unanimous emphasis on group solidarity. While individual rights had never been stressed in China, the people had actually enjoyed considerable freedom, mainly because the idea of an omnipotent state had also been undeveloped. As all traditional institutions came under the searching examination of the new patriots, this *de facto* personal freedom was held as the cause of China's national weakness. This condemnation was shared not only by cultural conservatives like Sun Yat-sen but also by Westernizers like Yen Fu. The tortuous path that Yen's reasoning took is striking. After tracing Western strength to an abundance of personal liberty, he did not advocate such a system for China. Rather, he thought that individuals should yield more to the state.[224] The same view was held by Liang Ch'i-ch'ao, who defended his position by arguing that only as the level of civilization advanced could the power of the state be reduced.[225] Actually, all of this was a kind of intellectual subterfuge. The truth is, at the beginning of the twentieth century all Chinese intellectuals had only one goal in mind, the strengthening of China within the shortest possible period. Since their aim was the same, so also was the method they proposed. None really valued liberty above national salvation. In this regard there was no difference between conservatives and radicals.

Significantly, this trend toward statism persisted among later intellectuals. Even Hu Shih, who was widely known as a liberal, was no exception. The pattern of his thought was a familiar one—a pro-

---

221. CTH:CTH, 178-79.   222. SBI:CCRM, 55-56.
223. TCT:SW, 36.   224. CCF:YF, 272.
225. LCC:YPSWC, 4.10.2.

fession of love for liberty, especially during his early mature life, and a subtle reversion to statism somewhat later. Thus Hu loudly proclaimed in 1918 that "nothing in the world is as important as yourself,"[226] but by 1932 he was lamenting the absence of a social and political rallying force—i.e., a strong and well supported government— in China. Among other things, he attributed this failure to "too much equality among the social classes."[227] A year later, he declared in the newspapers that all governments had a right to suppress subversive activities.[228] Such persistent ambivalence toward liberty on the part of Chinese intellectuals was not the result of accident. It was symbolic of a larger issue confronting them, China's relationship with the West in general. Their own intense admiration for the West led them to hope that China could be Westernized so that they could live like their Western counterparts, but the only remote chance for this to happen was for a strong government to appear in China. Thus a strong undercurrent of statism persisted underneath the professed love for liberty.

Another feature which Yen, Liang, and Sun shared with the later intellectuals was their urban outlook. None of the three gave much consideration to agriculture. Yen merely noted that Adam Smith had advocated small-scale farming, but that since it was incompatible with mechanization, much depended on the concrete circumstances.[229] While Liang claimed special competence in economics, few of his fourteen million published words were concerned with farming. When he was drawn into debate with Sun's followers in 1905 over the land problem, one of his theses was that China's progress depended far more on industrial than agrarian productivity, and that the correct emphasis was on the factories, not on the land.[230]

If Liang said little about agriculture, Sun was positively wrong in his views. He maintained that China was far richer than the United States in natural resources,[231] and he feared that China's declining population would spell national doom. He saw no land problem at all prior to the period of Western impact, and he assumed that land values would rise throughout China as they had in port cities. All of these attitudes revealed Sun's ignorance. China's basic problem was a scarcity of land in relation to population. Even if land rights could have been "equalized," which is doubtful, this measure would scarcely have affected the great majority of the population, the farmers. To the latter, Sun could offer only a vague promise of government aid

226. HS:WT (1953), IV, 612.   227. Ibid., 453-56.
228. HSSHPP, III, 90.   229. YIMCCK, 2.ping.4.414.
230. Robert A. Scalapino and Harold Schiffrin, "Early Socialist Currents in the Chinese Revolutionary Movement," JAS (May, 1959), 339.
231. SCSHC, I, 163.

and general suggestions on scientific farming and distribution, all compressed into a single lecture on food.[232]

We must attempt to reconcile this striking neglect of the peasantry by China's leading intellectuals with their nationalism and their professed paternalism. The answer to this problem seems to lie in the limiting influences of these men's environments, which stand out very clearly when they are compared with the situation surrounding the old literati. As I discussed in Chapter 1, a close rapport was maintained between the official class and the peasants, through the family institution, the attachment to the ancestral seat, and the close bond between persons of the same district. These factors no longer held for the men whose lives and thoughts I have delineated in this chapter. Although Yen Fu, Liang Ch'i-ch'ao, and Sun Yat-sen were born in rural surroundings, they left their native districts relatively early. Liang and Sun spent many years abroad as political fugitives. During their exiles they had virtually no contact with the ordinary folk in their home districts. Most of Liang's later years were spent in Tientsin while Sun's were split between Shanghai and Canton. Of the three, Yen maintained the closest connections with his native province. He visited it a few times and eventually died there, but even in his case the relationship fell far short of the traditional pattern. One result was their limited knowledge of peasant conditions.

In addition to these environmental changes, there was an important intellectual consideration. As Western influence increased in China, the attention of Chinese intellectuals was drawn to advantages that China did not possess. At first their concern was mainly with military weapons and technology, but by the 1890's philosophy and social thought were also being investigated. Still, little attention was given to agriculture, first because none of her assailants was as dependent upon agriculture as China, whose soil had been so productive for many centuries. Furthermore, in order to speak with authority on the agrarian problem, a man needed special training as well as practical experience in the field. This combination of knowledge was unlikely under the circumstances of China's contact with the West. Accordingly, all of the early reformers neglected agriculture.

232. KFCC, I, 216-34.

[11] *Some Features*
of Chinese Education

Historically the main factor in modern Chinese education was its failure to develop spontaneously in answer to popular needs for enlightenment. Rather, it occurred as an accelerated, even forced, adaptation of Western practices imposed from above. Partly because of this the foreign-educated, the group best acquainted with the contents of foreign education, came to dominate the field shortly after their return from abroad. The downfall of the Manchus in 1911 afforded them more opportunities as it caused the removal of many officials at the top. After 1920, and particularly after 1927, top administrative posts, ranging from Minister of Education to directors of provincial education and college presidents, were always held by men trained in the West. College faculties were equally dominated by this group. In evaluating the impact of the foreign-educated, we can see that education was a field in which their influence was quite pronounced. Of course, these men did not operate independently of historical trends, but rather there was an interplay between their role and circumstances. However, with such influence over several decades, even the continuation of trends became in a sense their responsibility, unless the extreme view is taken that man's behavior is strictly molded by society without any free will on his part.

This chapter is not a general evaluation of modern Chinese education but an analysis of several of its features that seem to have particularly affected the social order.

An interesting phenomenon of the Chinese educational system was its frequent revision more or less in accordance with the background of the educators. Men reared in the classical tradition set the spirit of the first comprehensive regulations, drawn in 1902 and revised in 1904. But from 1906, with the establishment of the Board of Education, Japanese-trained men began to influence educational policy. They introduced a number of changes along Japanese lines, notably in regard to the education of women, the length and curriculum of the primary school, and the establishment of two departments—arts and sciences—in the middle school. The same trend continued under the Republic.[1] In 1904 the official aim of education had been "to foster loyalty to the emperor and veneration for Confucianism, and to promote public-spirit, martial spirit, and practical (in contrast to book-

1. WFC:CYS, 294-96.

ish) learning."[2] In 1912, it was changed to "fostering moral education, and supplementing it with utilitarian, military, and aesthetic education." The last aspect was added at the insistence of Ts'ai Yüan-p'ei, the Minister of Education who had been trained in France and Germany, but the provision received little public support and attention.[3] The moral, military, and utilitarian aspects were virtually paraphrases of Arinori Mori's program of education in Japan.[4] Another similarity was the multi-track system with separate schools for academic, normal, vocational, and technical education. In 1914 it was further decided to divide the country into seven university zones on the model of the Japanese imperial universities, but this scheme was not realized.[5]

As more American-trained men returned and their influence grew, a complete overhauling of the educational system took place in 1922. The official aim was now "to foster the formation of healthy character and to promote the democratic spirit."[6] As a manifestation of this spirit, individual schools were given extensive freedom to organize their own curricula, and all single-faculty colleges were granted the option of renaming themselves universities. In the recommended curriculum for the middle schools, social studies replaced ethics and citizenship, and electives were introduced. The credit system was adopted, as well as the American system then in vogue of six years for primary education, three years for junior high, three years for senior high, and four years for college. In place of the multi-track system, separate disciplines were established within the same school.[7]

After the Kuomintang came to power in 1927, the influence of foreign-educated men became even more complete than before, but at the same time they deferred to the basically Russian orientation of the Party. All activities were in principle subject to government control, and education specifically became a weapon in the hands of the regime. Consequently, two trends can be discerned. On the one hand, there was the introduction of compulsory military training and "Party Doctrine" as a required course, the standardization of curricula, the abolition of electives in the middle schools, and the curbing of single-faculty colleges—in short, a much tighter control over education by the government. On the other hand, some important features of Chinese education, which had their origin in the circumstances surrounding China's modernization, simply continued and even became more pronounced under the Kuomintang. One of these was the emphasis on higher education at the expense of lower education.

2. *Ibid.*, 359.
4. ARS:JTME, 11.
6. 1st CYNC, 5, 9-10.

3. *Ibid.*, 303, 359-60.
5. *Ibid.*, 125-26; WFC:CYS, 300-2.
7. WFC:CYS, 303-10.

Between 1862 and 1895 about a dozen professional schools were established for the study of foreign languages, military science, shipbuilding, and navigation.[8] But the first institution that approached the modern primary school was not established until 1897.[9] The first suggestion of a systematic educational system, with primary schools in the counties and prefectures, middle schools in the provincial capitals, and a university in Peking, was made in the same year by Li Tuan-fen, a high court official, but it was not carried out.[10] Early in 1902 a high commissioner of education was appointed by the court and charged with the mission of establishing a university. Only then was it realized that since there had been no primary and secondary schools, the university lacked prospective students.[11] The defect was gradually corrected but the inattention to the needs of lower education persisted. In 1931, for instance, the proportion of the yearly expenses per pupil in Chinese primary schools to that in Chinese universities was about 1:200 as compared with about 1:8 in European countries.[12] In 1936 the expenditure on higher education was ten times larger than in 1912, with almost the same number of students; the expenditure on secondary education increased by less than ten times during that period, with a 500 per cent increase in the student body; the expenditure on primary education increased six times, with a 600 per cent increase in the student body.[13] Thus the stress on higher education continued.

Many factors seem to have contributed to this situation, not the least of which was tradition. In China, learning had always been associated with political leadership. The hierarchical concept of society encompassed two broad strata of people—the leaders and the masses—of which the latter were not expected to play an active role in politics or even communal affairs. There had never been a system of public instruction for the development of individual personality. At its most concrete level, education was a means of advancement within the narrow bounds of personal and family interests; and only in the course of acquiring knowledge was there a sense of *noblesse oblige,* of a mission toward the mass and humanity, implanted and awakened, usually but not necessarily, in the students. While learning was respected by society, it was essentially a matter of private concern. From the personal viewpoint of the educated, the purpose was ful-

8. See the years between 1862 and 1895 in TCP:CKC: also Ho Ping-sung, "The Last Thirty-Five Years of Chinese College Education," SSWN, 61.

9. *Ibid.,* 1; CC:CYS, 573.

10. Li Tuan-fen's memorial, reportedly written by Liang Ch'i-ch'ao, is reprinted in SHC:CKCY, I, 1-5.

11. Ho Ping-sung, *op. cit.,* 78-79.   12. TRE, 51.

13. WFC:CYS, 320.

filled only when they attained a recognized status of advanced learning and were thereby able to enter officialdom. Lower education was necessary as a ladder to that final aim but had no meaning apart from it. In fact, men who studied throughout their lifetimes but who failed to pass the official civil service examinations were often the most frustrated members of the traditional order. Even under changed conditions, the continuity of social outlook—the "cultural lag"—helped bolster an educational structure that assigned little weight to lower education.

Another consideration was the circumstances in which modern education developed in China and the immediate political purposes behind it. In the period after 1895, China's main concern was national survival, and it was to achieve this end that modern education was recognized as necessary. The aim was not to derive long-range benefits but to give the existing elite sufficient knowledge to deal with foreigners. Needless to say, in such a scheme adult and higher education were given first place.

But in time the situation changed. As industry and commerce gradually developed, new channels of employment were opened to the educated class, which was no longer concerned exclusively with politics or the well-being of its fellow men. On the contrary, it tended to develop an individualized attitude toward life based essentially on profit motives. At the same time, political democracy, which could only thrive on the foundation of general enlightenment through education, became the avowed goal of all intellectuals. Under the circumstances, one would expect the topsy-turvy structure of the school system, under the charge of men educated abroad, to be gradually corrected. Yet evidence indicates the contrary. According to well-informed observers, the emphasis on higher education was sustained by the pressure of Western-educated men who had vested interests in college teaching, which because it was commonly associated with erudition, commanded far more social prestige than teaching at the elementary level. The monopoly of educational administrative posts in the government by Western-trained men, according to the same source, had a similar effect. Because the administrators were mostly specialists in disciplines other than pedagogy, their policy reflected little interest in lower education.[14]

Another feature of Chinese higher education was the heavy concentration of colleges in a few of the cities, particularly Shanghai and Peking. In 1922 the latter accounted for 30 per cent of the country's colleges, and over 41 per cent of all the college students; in 1932 Shanghai accounted for 24 per cent of the colleges and students, not

14. Wu Yen-yin and Weng Chih-ta, "Chinese Primary Education in the Last Thirty-five Years," in SSWN, 35-36.

including those in the adjacent cities along the Nanking-Shanghai-Hangchow railways. A third area of concentration was Canton in Kwangtung, which in 1932 claimed 8 out of 108 institutions and almost 9 per cent of the total student population in higher education. The vast territory to the west of Nanking, stretching to the farther end of Szechuan and including Honan, Hupeh, and Hunan, had only fifteen institutions with some 6 per cent of the total number of college students. Several provinces, including Shensi, Sikang, and Chinghai, had no institutions of higher education.[15] In the words of Shih-chieh Wang, Minister of Education from 1933 to 1937, "a picture of more grotesque inequality cannot be imagined."[16] This inequality seems to have had a far-reaching social impact, but before we consider it, we must investigate the causes that produced this inequality.

Table 8 shows clearly that the uneven geographical distribution of Chinese higher education did not take place before 1909 but became increasingly pronounced after 1922. The number of colleges in Shanghai was large under the Manchus but not excessive in relation to the rest of the country. Most of the colleges disappeared in 1911, and those listed under 1916 in Table 8 were mainly new ones. Thus the uneven distribution of Chinese colleges had little to do with historical factors. Nor can it be explained by socio-economic circumstances in the general sense of the term. It is true that between 1922 and 1931 the population of Greater Shanghai increased from 1.5 million to 3.2 million,[17] but rapid urbanization characterized many other cities as well. In the same period Peking and the twin city of Wuchang and Hankow gained proportionately as much in population;[18] yet both suffered a decline in the number of colleges and students. Economically, the years from 1922 to 1931 were on the whole much less prosperous for Shanghai than previous years—the boycotts of foreign goods in 1925 and 1926 were particularly injurious to the economy.[19] Yet the number of colleges in Shanghai increased from thirteen to twenty-five during the period between 1927 and 1932, when the total number of colleges in China decreased as a result of tighter controls by the Kuomintang government. The city remained the leading educational center until 1949, although during World War II a vast educational expansion in the interior reduced its proportionate advantage. Because of Shanghai, Kiangsu province had a far greater share of China's college students than its population warranted.[20]

15. KYC:GHE, Tables 23-27.   16. YBE (1937), 572.
17. CGB:CGF, 300.   18. *Ibid.*, 174, 300.
19. Dorothy J. Orchard, "China's Use of the Boycott as a Political Weapon," AN (November, 1930), 252-61.
20. KYC:GHE, Table 96-99.

TABLE 8. *Geographical Distribution of Chinese Colleges and College Students*[a]

	1909		1916		1922		1932		1947	
Hopeh	26	(4,399)	24	(7,908)	48	(18,932)	25	(15,058)	25	(22,306)
Peking	10	(2,115)	17	(6,534)	40	(15,440)	17	(13,238)	13	(17,354)
Tientsin	16	(2,284)[b]	7	(1,374)[b]	5	(1,291)	5	(1,467)	8	(4,046)
Other cities					3	(2,201)	3	(353)	4	(906)
Kiangsu	21	(2,295)	16	(2,016)	20	(5,616)	34	(14,224)	57	(45,070)
Shanghai			12	(1,583)	13	(3,643)	25	(10,520)	34	(28,777)
Nanking area[d]	21	(2,295)[c]	4	(433)	7	(1,973)	8	(3,365)	18	(14,141)
Other cities							1	(339)	5	(2,152)
Chekiang	8	(1,197)	5	(500)	4	(1,041)	4	(1,201)	5	(4,771)
Kwangtung	9	(2,291)	8	(961)	6	(1,814)	8	(3,998)	17	(14,330)
Hupeh	7	(1,346)	5	(1,197)	7	(1,980)	6	(1,831)	9	(5,439)
Hunan	9	(1,607)	7	(1,313)	9	(1,822)	3	(575)	6	(3,513)
Fukien	3	(1,286)	5	(546)	6	(842)	4	(792)	7	(4,510)
Szechuan	10	(2,238)	2	(385)	2	(1,814)	2	(1,814)	23	(19,531)
Rest of China	68	(13,169)	29	(5,753)	30	(2,640)	22	(4,035)	58	(35,566)
Total	161	(29,828)	101	(20,579)	132	(36,501)	108	(43,528)	207	(155,036)

a. Compiled from KYC:GHE, Appendix B, Tables 23-27. The figures in parentheses are numbers of students.
b. The figures refer to Tientsin and Paoting, the old provincial co-capital.
c. These figures refer to Shanghai and Nanking.
d. Nanking area includes Nanking and one or two other cities along the Nanking-Shanghai railway.

	Per cent of Kiangsu in China's population	Per cent of college students in Kiangsu	Difference
1916	7.95	9.80	1.85
1922	7.60	15.34	7.74
1932	9.11	35.26	26.15
1947	9.04	29.07	20.03

The factor most responsible for the concentration of colleges in Shanghai seems to have been the presence of a large number of Western-trained men there. As quoted earlier, the 1925 survey of 584 American-educated men indicated that 34 per cent lived in Shanghai, and the 1937 data on 1,152 American-trained showed that 28 per cent resided there. Although these surveys were insufficient in scope and detail to prove anything conclusive, it is likely that many Western-trained men came to Shanghai in the late 1920's after the national capital was moved to Nanking. At any rate the number of these men increased with time, and a large proportion of them lived in Shanghai. Because it was not unusual for a new institution to open without elaborate physical equipment, the only thing a college needed, besides faculty and administrators, was students; and these Shanghai, with a large urban population, had in abundance.

The important position of Western-educated men can be demonstrated by still another fact. A classification of the colleges in Shanghai by their supporting bodies shows that the number of mission institutions, under the charge of Westerners, changed little during these years, while the number of government and private colleges, both of which were controlled by Western-educated Chinese, increased rapidly after 1922 (Table 9).

TABLE 9. *Colleges in Shanghai Classified by Supporting Bodies*[a]

	Government		Private	(Chinese)	Missionary	
	No.	Per Cent of National Total of Its Kind	No.	Per Cent of National Total	No.	Per Cent of National Total
1909	18	12	—	—	3	25
1916	2	3	8	35	2	10
1922	3	4	7	23	3	11
1932	9	16	12	43	4	16
1947	12	10	19	31	3	16

a. KYC:GHE, Tables 96-99.

Significantly, while colleges abounded in Shanghai, the city had a reputation for being an "intellectual desert." Except for a very fine library of Chinese books owned by the Commercial Press, which was largely destroyed during the Sino-Japanese conflict in 1932, Shanghai had no library worthy of the name. Writing in 1947, Chiang Monlin, a Ph.D. from Columbia and an eminent educator, made two telling points in regard to Shanghai. One was that Shanghai was endowed with a "settlement mind"—meaning the worship of power and admiration of superficiality and vulgarity. The other point was that "Shanghai was a financial sea but an intellectual desert."[21] That so many colleges could have been founded with so little cultural effect is difficult to understand unless we realize that these institutions were established by an urbanized self-seeking elite primarily for its own material needs and for the needs of students who wanted academic certification but not necessarily academic knowledge.

Generally speaking, the colleges in Peking, the second area of concentration, were recognized as better. But there were also many colleges that catered to various kinds of special student needs. In both cases, the availability of choice—knowledge, a mere diploma, or a combination of both in whatever proportions—attracted students from the less urbanized areas. A significant fact is that once they came and became exposed to urban influences, these students seldom returned to rural areas. The process was familiar to most observers.

21. CML:TFW, 183-84.

In 1926, John H. Reisner remarked:[22] "I do not know of a single graduate of a college of agriculture returned from the United States who has gone back to a strictly rural community. . . . I know of no graduate of agricultural colleges in China who has done it. I do know of a few middle school graduates, but not many, who are beginning to make themselves felt in the life of the community and will become indispensable to its welfare." In 1946, Fei Hsiao-t'ung observed that nearly all college graduates who had come from the rural areas chose to remain in the city even when they were unemployed and had to live on borrowed funds. One cause was the lack of economic opportunity in rural areas, but more important was the students' reluctance or inability to readjust themselves to rural living.[23] In this respect the college graduates differed from the returned students only in degree: whereas the latter congregated in the largest cities, the former tended to be more dispersed, but neither the one nor the other re-established themselves in rural areas. The only exceptions seem to have been the few rural reconstruction workers led by Y. C. James Yen and T'ao Hsing-chih. Yen was a Yale graduate who began his career in social work among the Chinese laborers in France during World War I, and who later led the famous project at Ting-hsien in northern China.[24] T'ao studied under John Dewey at Columbia and was a prominent figure in the Chinese mass education movement after 1920.[25] Both men became famous for their work, partly because of its unusual nature.

One effect of the urban concentration of schools was the increasing denial of educational opportunity to the rural masses and people of limited means. This reversed a time-honored tradition in China. Before the period of Western impact, to pursue a life of study was by no means easy, but not because of immediate financial reasons. The books needed were relatively few and the tuition fees highly elastic. For a tutor to bargain over the fees of his pupils was against all known rules of decorum. While the well-paying ones probably received more supervision than those who paid less, rarely was a pupil turned away on financial grounds. In the communal life of the village or the clan, instruction was often free for those of limited means. At a more advanced stage, a promising student could do even better. In the private colleges (*shu-yüan*), cash prizes were nearly always awarded to the winners of essay contests, and a man with a felicitous pen usually had little difficulty even in supporting his family on his income.[26]

This situation persisted after the establishment of modern schools

22. CSM (February, 1926), 11-12. 23. FHT:HTCC, 70-73.
24. BPS:TP, *passim*. 25. THCC, *passim*.
26. Evidences abound in personal memoirs. See, for instance, SHC:WHCY, 45.

in the 1860's; stipends, for instance, were paid to the students at the Foochow arsenal. But circumstances began to change when major educational efforts were undertaken by the government around the turn of the century. Precisely because education was now planned on a large scale, free schooling could not be provided, and the students, instead of receiving stipends, had to pay for instruction. As early as 1898, Chang Chih-tung in his *Exhortation to Learning* attacked the traditional practice of subsidizing the students and approvingly noted the Western example of making them pay.[27] He wrote, "The colleges of China mistakenly identified education with relief. As a result, students often came for the exclusive purpose of money. Being thus wrong in their aim, they counted pennies, attacked one another, plagiarized others' writings, and generally so conducted themselves that not a trace of decorum remained. Even if we could not now immediately adopt the Western system of tuition payment, we must still mend the old ways and provide in the school free meals but grant no stipends."

In the same essay Chang asserted that tuition charges offered three advantages. "A paying student would not fall victim to indolence; not aiming at pecuniary gains, he would not feud with his fellow students; freed from the financial burden, the government could expand the schools."[28] When a school system was established in Hupeh in 1903, Chang put his ideas into practice by announcing that the primary schools would be free to the natives of the province, that other schools would be free for two years, but that a fee must be paid by all students from other provinces.[29] The 1904 educational regulations provided for four years of compulsory education and for free tuition at all normal schools, but established fees for others.

After that time, education became increasingly expensive for a number of reasons. Unlike the old learning with its heavy emphasis on intensive reading, modern education required expensive physical equipment and reference materials. Its costly nature was aggravated by the inability of the declining communal organs to render their former degree of support to individual students. The government, which was to play a major role in education, suffered from political paralysis. High officials no longer had an interest in education. Consequently, private institutions, which in China depended exclusively on fees, became more important, and education as a whole became a luxury enjoyed by a few. The situation was further complicated by the uneven development of urban and rural China. In lower education, the academic standards of the rural schools lagged far behind. In higher, only those who were favored financially as well as geographically could attend college. Under the changed circumstances,

27. CWHK, 203.10b.   28. *Ibid.*, 203.4.13a.
29. *Ibid.*, 57.10b-11a.

even the examination system, traditionally an instrument in the attainment of social equity, worked to the disadvantage of the socially less fortunate, for the severe entrance tests of the better schools were far more difficult for them than for those who were better prepared because they came from urban centers and wealthy families.[30]

Another feature of Chinese education was the large use made of foreign materials in the curriculum. The practice of mechanical imitation went so far at one time that a publisher not only plagiarized the contents of a Japanese book but also retained the Japanese flag on the cover, where a Chinese flag should have been.[31] In December, 1924, a student in Nankai University published an article entitled "The Revolving Education," which read in part:[32]

> The educators love to say: "The aim of education is to save the country." We like to ask, how? Can the present educational system save the country? If we know the thought and ambitions of the students . . . and inquire into the careers of past students . . . perhaps we dare not . . . say it can . . . . Students of literature have become teachers; students of sciences have become teachers; students of commerce likewise have become teachers. You are teachers and we are teachers. . . . We ask what a middle school teacher does, and the answer is to teach the students English, mathematics, and other knowledge to prepare them for university education. Why university education? The answer is to get a diploma. Why a diploma? The answer is to become a middle school teacher. Thus men revolve around education, generation after generation. Can such a merry-go-round save the country?
>
> The university teachers teach American politics, American economy, American commerce, American railways, American this, American that. They praise the United States in the same way old scholars praised the sages Yao, Shun, Yü, T'ang, and the like. The student, when he graduates, also goes to the United States and somehow manages to secure a master's or doctoral degree. After he returns to China, he steps into the shoes of his teachers and perpetuates the revolving educational system. Only this revolving is one stage higher than the first kind. The difference between the two is that the middle school teacher plays a Chinese-American hoax, while the university teacher bluffs through his Americanism.

This article aroused much resentment among the faculty members at Nankai. At the same time it received widespread public attention.

30. Ho Ping-sung, *op. cit.*, SSWN, 55.
31. Yi-yi, "Problems of Study Abroad," CHCYC, Vol. XIII, No. 10.
32. "The Revolving Education," as quoted in SHC:CKT, 286-95.

According to some commentators, it succinctly depicted educational conditions in China before 1924.[33]

Conditions changed little in subsequent years. In 1929 a noted Chinese educator wrote:[34] "America, the home of the scientific study of education! The scientific construction of the curriculum, the intelligence test, the achievement norm, the Dalton Plan, the Platoon system, and so on. Look over our educational magazines of the last ten years, and one will find that every time one of these plans or movements was produced in the United States, the Chinese educational magazines responded like an echo." In 1931 a mission of educational experts sent by the League of Nations to China commented:[35]

> Not only are the majority of books studied by students in a foreign tongue, but . . . the examples employed to illustrate a principle, and the subjects to which the students' thought is directed by their teachers, are, to a surprising extent, of Western origin. A visitor who examines the plan of work in History, Political Science, or Economics in some universities in China may be pardoned if he feels uncertain whether it is for Western students who are studying China, or for Chinese students who are studying the West. In the Natural Sciences, the exotic character of much of the teaching is even more noticeable.

In many Chinese universities, the large number of courses on foreign subjects contrasted strikingly with the paucity of lectures on Chinese studies. Under the leadership of Hu Shih and others, a movement to apply Western methodology to the study of Chinese history was launched in the mid-1920's. For a time the spirit of skepticism prevailed, and nearly all traditions and legends were called into question. Eventually much was accomplished; yet the movement was limited to a narrow group and had no immediate effect upon Chinese studies in the schools. For instance, not a single textbook was made available on Chinese economic history, and as late as 1950 many universities in China did not offer courses on that subject because no faculty members were capable of teaching it.

A consistent tendency amid the changes in the educational system after 1904 was that classics and ethics received a smaller place in the curriculum. Under the 1902 and 1904 educational regulations the study of Chinese classics was emphasized at all levels.[36] After

33. Shu Hsin-ch'eng, "Preface to the Special Issue on the Future of Chinese Education," CHCYC, Vol. XIX, No. 3.

34. Theodore Hsi-en Chen, "Is American Education Good for China?" ER (1929), 260.

35. TRE, 165.   36. CC:CYS, 609.

the establishment of the Republic in 1912, classics were eliminated from all schools below the college level, and in the colleges the classics no longer retained their separate faculties.[37] In 1915, Yüan Shih-kai in vain tried to restore classical studies to the curriculum.[38] In the next two decades similar attempts were made by several provincial heads—war lords—but, powerful as they were, none of them succeeded.[39] It appeared that among the educators Confucianism had definitely fallen into disrepute and that any effort to re-introduce it was deemed reactionary and intolerable. This attitude was unfortunate because day-to-day life in rural China had not changed radically and conformed largely to the basic ideals of Confucianism. Unfamiliarity with the classics therefore diminished the students' understanding of the traditional social order. Furthermore, because a universal church or system of belief did not exist in China, the rejection of Confucianism meant the absence of all moral teachings outside the family, which was also in the process of disintegration.

Supposedly a new social ideal—public spiritedness—was to be instilled in the minds of the youth through the citizenship curriculum at the primary and secondary levels, but the frequent changes made in such courses nullified their possible beneficial effects. Even nationalistic feeling, unwittingly fostered by foreign powers through a century of encroachment on Chinese rights, failed to become the pivotal point of a new culture. After 1928 the course in Party Doctrine, which supposedly embodied the Principle of Nationalism, became increasingly perfunctory and aroused little enthusiasm among the students.

In the face of mounting political pressure from Japan, China steadily looked to the West for support. In actual policy the Kuomintang government maintained friendly relations not only with England and America but also with Germany and Italy. There was widespread hatred of Japan but hardly a wholesome national spirit based on pride in Chinese culture. Furthermore, since its establishment, the Kuomintang regime had never been free from troubles with the students. Fearing the influence of the Left under the guise of patriotism against Japan, the government sought to discourage all political activities, including discussion of current events. While this policy failed to block the steady rise of Marxist influences, it probably did stifle the nascent civic spirit among the people.

Perhaps partly to curb the political zeal of the students, great emphasis was placed by the government on science and engineering. Drastic measures were adopted to increase the enrollment in these disciplines. Beginning in 1933, the faculties of arts and social sciences were not allowed to have more students than the faculties of science

---

37. *Ibid.*, 670.   38. *Ibid.*, 652.
39. "Miscellaneous," CHCYC, Vol. XXI, No. 2.

and engineering.[40] And after April, 1935, new students in the arts and humanities were limited to thirty per department per year, except in girls' colleges and colleges of outstanding record.[41]

The strenuous promotion of science and technology seems to have achieved results. On the credit side, it probably had much to do with the world renown enjoyed by many Chinese in these fields today. Among those currently teaching in the United States, there are two Nobel-prize winners, a leading authority on endocrinology, several mathematicians of fame, and men of recognized standing in many scientific disciplines. All of these men had their initial college training between the late 1920's and the mid-1940's. Even students from Formosa in recent years feel that they have an edge in mathematics over most Americans at a comparable academic level, and it seems to be true that most Chinese engineers rely more on their mathematical tools than on their ability to handle the more practical aspects of designing, testing, and so on, which circumstances did not permit them to learn in China. Clearly, the creditable performance of Chinese scientists today is partly a result of the policy of the Kuomintang.

Yet the enthusiasm for science and technology is not without some adverse effect on the social order in China. By historical coincidence, all the factors I have analyzed so far—the emphasis on higher education, the congregation of colleges in large cities, the high financial cost of modern education, the use of foreign materials, and the stress of science and technology—served to produce an elite unconnected with the life surrounding them and who were not really aware of actual conditions in the country at large. A striking proof is that even in central government service college graduates were often found to be misfits. This defect was widely recognized, and in 1936 the Kuomintang government launched a training program for several hundred college graduates, with a curriculum devoted almost entirely to the study of Chinese conditions and government administration. At the inauguration of the program, a number of high government dignitaries spoke. Representing President Chiang Kai-shek, Dr. Weng Wen-hao stressed the anomaly of college graduates suffering from unemployment while jobs went unfilled for lack of qualified men. He conceded that the educational system had been at fault, and urged the trainees to (1) improve their practical ability, (2) change their ideas of employment, (3) increase their usefulness to society, (4) change their habits of living, (5) have more faith in the revolution, and (6) manifest a spirit of self-reliance.[42] Weng's speech indicated an acute awareness of a thorny problem—the unemployment and unemployability of Chinese intellectuals.

40. 1st CYNC, Sec. C, pp. 191-92, 540.   41. YE (1937), 570.
42. Reported in CYTC (December, 1936), 125-26.

How far did this influence, which tended to alienate educated men from society, spread downward in the Chinese educational system? Available evidence indicates that it was much less pronounced at the middle-school level. Geographically, the junior middle schools were often located in the old county (*hsien*) seat, and the senior middle schools, in the prefectural city,[43] but there was no pronounced concentration in any one region. The number of middle-school students was more in proportion to the population of the various provinces.[44] A survey of 210 secondary schools in twelve provinces in 1936 revealed that 51.45 per cent of the students enrolled came from rural towns of 5,000 inhabitants or less,[45] compared to 21.03 per cent of college students who came from agricultural families in 1934-35,[46] and to 11.5 per cent of Chinese students in America in 1947 who claimed to have come from families of landlords and farmers. Equally revealing were the employment patterns of the various groups of students. We have seen that the two major sources of employment for the American-trained in China were government service and college teaching. From a group of some 1,150 men, these fields accounted in 1937 for some 25 to 30 per cent each, with commerce and industry in third place, taking another 15 per cent.[47] Statistics on the employment of Chinese college graduates are not available, but some idea may be gained from a report made in 1929 by nine mission colleges on 4,664 of their graduates.[48]

	Percentage
Religious work	13
Government service	14
Teaching	24
Medicine, law, engineering	13
Business	15
In further study	6
Unknown	9
Other occupations	6
Total	100

Except in two respects, this pattern of employment may be assumed to apply to all Chinese college men. In all probability, among the non-mission school graduates, unemployment was higher and religious workers were much fewer, the former because most students attending mission colleges came from well-to-do families and had less difficulty in finding employment. Percentage-wise, these two factors—

43. SHC:CKT, 204-13.   44. CKCC (1935), Sec. B, pp. 44-45.
45. T'ung Jun-chih, "A Survey of the Degree of Ruralization of Chinese Secondary Schools," CYTC, Vol. XXVI, No. 10, pp. 33-44.
46. 23d CKTC, 37.   47. See Appendix C, Table 13.
48. LAY, 370, 399.

fewer religious workers and more unemployment—might well cancel each other out and leave the broad pattern unchanged. On this assumption it would appear that Chinese college graduates pursued essentially the same careers as the Western-educated, namely, teaching, government service, professions, and business. The major difference lay in their prestige and standing. With rare exceptions the Chinese-trained taught in middle schools and the Western-educated in colleges. Similar differentiation existed in government service and business concerns, but neither group engaged in rural occupations.

By contrast, the middle-school graduates had rural outlets. According to Shu Hsin-ch'eng, there were in the 1920's five major outlets for the middle-school graduates: (1) to do further study in college; (2) to teach in primary schools; (3) to become junior staff members in government service, publishing houses, or business concerns; (4) to become gentry members; (5) to become mercenaries or soldiers of fortune.[49] The actual distribution among these five outlets varied from one locality to another. The proportion of students going on to further study was higher in urban than in rural areas. The publishing houses and business concerns existed only in large cities. Primary school teaching was available in all regions, but government service was usually in rural areas because government clerks enjoyed higher prestige there than in the cities, and because government agencies in the latter usually required of their employees more than a middle-school education. The other outlets—army, gentry, and lackeys of militarists—were confined to rural regions. There was little difference, Shu noted, between a gentryman and a lackey: both could do great harm to the people and both were in a sense unemployed. A student could become a gentry member if his family had some influence in the district; otherwise he might become a lackey of a local militarist. All students hated soldiery in principle, but some were lured into it when, after trying other outlets, they found in a military career the only possibility of advancement.[50]

Statistically, Shu made a sample study of the graduates of the Tenth Middle School at Hsü-chou, a fairly important railway junction in northern Kiangsu. He found that 28 per cent attended college; 35 per cent became educational workers, mainly primary school teachers; and 27 per cent were distributed among the other three outlets, including 4 per cent that became militarists of one kind or another.[51]

In brief, the two elements of the Chinese tradition—education as a matter of private concern and study as the main way of entering

49. SHC:CKT, 131-41, 204-13.
50. Cf. NR:KCC, 55, 59, where a confirmatory conclusion is reached from different materials.
51. SHC:CKT, loc. cit.

officialdom—were greatly enhanced by modern educational developments in China. The severe emphasis on higher education had several consequences, not the least of which were the values attached to study abroad and the slight attention given to lower education. Secondary and grade schools became mere appendages to the colleges and had hardly any importance of their own. Partly because of this, social ideals and citizenship training were manifestly undeveloped within the school system. Higher education was controlled by men educated abroad, and because these people congregated in a few metropolises, so did the colleges. The cost of living in these cities was often many times higher than in the interior, mainly because Western influences bore unevenly upon the urban and rural areas of China. The increased cost of higher education meant that only the rich could afford it. For the few who came to the cities from rural areas, education was a process of urbanization, for once exposed, the students never returned to their native places. The large use of foreign materials in the curriculum, a necessity at the initial stage of modern education in China, perpetuated and further contributed to the alienation of the students from their native culture and surrounding life. There were almost no forces to counteract this tendency; even the strenuous promotion of science and technology served to reinforce it, for such knowledge had no immediate relevance to the Chinese rural scene. Consequently, there was a deep gulf between the higher intellectuals—the foreign-educated and the college graduates—and the mass of the Chinese people. Only from the middle-school students down was the gap narrowed. That the intellectuals nearest to the people were also the least educated is one of the supreme ironies in the modernization of China.

[1 2] *The Changing*
Intelligentsia

As indicated in the first chapter, the scholar in pre-nineteenth-century China held a particular place in the political and intellectual structure of society. One stabilizing factor of this remarkably lasting structure was the educational system. Through its heavy emphasis on Confucian precepts, Chinese classical education homogenized the outlook of the scholar class. Another sustaining element was the fact that the educated man had little possibility for employment outside of politics and a few closely related fields. His interest was hence confined within a narrow range, and this limitation on his endeavors reduced the possibility of change from within the system.

However, both the educational system and the economic system started to crumble in the 1870's under Western impact. Men were sent abroad to study technology, and within the country steamship companies, railroads, mines, telegraph services, and textile mills appeared. Other new professions had come into being even earlier. The first Chinese Christian convert became a clergyman in 1827.[1] The first newspaper in Chinese appeared in Hongkong in 1858[2] and in Shanghai in 1862.[3] The largest of Chinese publishing firms started in 1897.[4] Only shortly thereafter Liang Ch'i-ch'ao became so successful as a writer that he financed his political activities partly with money he made from his publications.[5] Several Chinese women qualified abroad as physicians before 1900, having been taken by missionary friends to the United States and educated there.[6] The first Chinese Chamber of Commerce was formed in 1903, and official regulations pertaining to such organs were enacted in 1911.[7] By that same year some one thousand novels had appeared on the market.[8] A year later the first Chinese Bar Association was formed in Peking.[9] By 1932, there were some 5,685 lawyers, 3,679 Catholic clergymen, and 5,000 Protestant clergymen in China.[10] While these figures may seem small, they nevertheless indicate the rise of important

1. KKC:CKPHS, 65.   2. *Ibid.*, 73.
3. *Ibid.*
4. SSWN, C 1-3, WCY:CKKYS, II, 982.
5. LJKHS, I, 225.
6. See under Shih Mei-yu in PM:WW; WKCWLT, 620.
7. TCKNC, 1539.   8. CCL:CPSL, I, 184.
9. IYLJ:KT, 3.4b.   10. SPNC (1934), 356-57, 1146-47.

new professions that affected the attitudes of the educated Chinese. The interests of this group were no longer confined to politics or morality; with the emergence of a new professional spirit, interest in occupational excellence over-shadowed or replaced concern with public affairs.

While a comprehensive study of the rise of professional occupations and their subsequent social implications lies outside the scope of this book, certain changes that took place within the educated class as a result of this metamorphosis will be noted here. The present chapter will treat the academic and literary groups, while the engineers, entrepreneurs, and bankers will be discussed later. The academic group under consideration consisted of two sub-groups —the scientists, physical and biological, and the social scientists— while the literary group included mainly essayists and novelists. As we shall see, the Western-educated men predominated in the academic group, while the Japanese-educated stood out in the literary company.

The first scientific discipline to reach some kind of maturity in China was geology. In 1914 the Chinese Geological Survey was established and headed by V. K. Ting (Ting Wen-chiang, 1887-1936), who is probably still the most outstanding man in this field. Ting was born to a gentry family in northern Kiangsu. He had a good classical training and because of his precocity became known to the county magistrate, who in 1902 persuaded Ting's father to send Ting to Japan to study.[11] During his stay of nearly two years, he followed the current vogue of writing political essays directed against the Manchus.[12] In 1904, as a result of information received indirectly from Wu Chih-hui in Scotland, Ting and a friend decided to pursue further study in Edinburgh. They had little money with them, but since enthusiasm for education ran high at the time, they received donations from all sources, including K'ang Yu-wei and Boon-keng Lim, an educator among overseas Chinese in Malaya, neither of whom had personally known Ting and his friend before. After his arrival in England, Ting received financial assistance from his home county, Tai-hsing, in China.

During a stay of seven years, he finished high school, spent half a year at Cambridge, and graduated from the University of Glasgow with two degrees, one in zoology and geology and one in geology and geography.[13] After his return to China in 1911, he purposely landed at Haiphong and traveled overland from there to Hunan and Kiangsu, as part of his geographical training. After a year during which he taught in a middle school, wrote a Chinese textbook on zoology, and started a survey of the geology of Yangtze Valley below Wu-hu, Ting

11. HS:TWC, 5.   12. *Ibid.*, 6.
13. *Ibid.*, 11.

went to Peking and became chief of the geology section in the Ministry of Industry and Commerce.[14] In spite of an acute shortage of funds, he gave a geological training course, from which emerged most of China's younger geologists. In 1914, the new Ministry of Agriculture and Commerce, under Chang Ch'ien, raised enough funds to inaugurate a Geological Survey and appointed Ting as its head. In 1919 he published and received much praise for his paper on the sedimentation problem of the Yangtze Delta region.

It was through Ting's initiative that the Chinese Geological Society was founded in 1922 and the Chinese Paleontological Society in 1929. The journals of both societies soon attracted international attention for the papers they published.[15] Starting from 1924 the Survey undertook a geologic study of China and by 1949 had finished about a third of the planned geological mapping. Because of political chaos as well as difficulties in communications, field work was hazardous and several geologists lost their lives.[16] Considering the universal desire among the Chinese to industrialize their country, the Survey's search for ores was a most important task. Several reports were published which gave the first systematic and factual information about the mineral reserves and the mining industry in China. Ting did some prospecting himself, and his associates discovered several coal deposits and, during the Second World War, an oil basin.[17]

The greatest achievement of the Chinese Geological Survey was in research. At Ting's invitation, A. W. Grabau left Columbia University in 1919 to come to Peking University (Peita) and become at the same time the chief paleontologist of the Chinese Geological Survey. This move marked a decisive point in the development of Chinese paleontology. Though severely afflicted with arthritis, Grabau led an extremely active life until his death in 1946. His most important contribution to paleontology was the pulsation theory, published in the *Chinese Geological Journal* of 1936, which cast a new light on stratigraphic studies not only of China but of the world.[18] Another outstanding geologist who in 1920 joined the faculty of Peking University at Ting's recommendation was J. S. Lee (Li Ssu-kuang, 1889-   ). A native of Huang-kang, Hupeh, Lee first studied engineering in Japan but later went to England and received a doctorate in geology from the University of Birmingham. He became famous for his work on the classification of millipedes of the myriapod group and on continental glaciation.[19] Still another outstanding achievement of the Chinese Geological Survey was the

14. *Ibid.*, 15.   15. *Ibid.*, 27-32.
16. Juan Wei-chou, "Chinese Geology in the Past Fifty Years," CHMKHC, II, 12.
17. *Ibid.*, 13; HS:TWC, 19-20, 71.
18. *Ibid.*, 28. Also see biography of Grabau in the *Encyclopedia Britannica.*
19. HCKJWC, II, 69.

discovery of the Peking Man in 1929. Previously, several Western scholars—J. G. Anderson, W. Granger, and O. Zdansky—had made small excavations at Chou-k'ou-tien near Peking. In 1927 the work was taken over by a team organized by the Survey and the Peking Union Medical College with the financial support of the Rockefeller Foundation. In 1929 a near-complete skull of the Peking Man was discovered by Pei Wen-chung (1898-   ), a graduate of Peking University.[20] This and other finds shed important light on the early stages of human evolution. As a recent writer said, geology in pre-Communist China was "not considered far behind the West," even though the number of geologists was small.[21] The credit for this remarkable achievement was largely Ting's. Up to 1949 there was scarcely any Chinese geologist who had not received encouragement from him. A large proportion of this small group of scientists were actually Ting's students.

Promotion of science did not, however, claim Ting's whole attention. He took a great deal of interest in politics, and in his non-scientific writings he often used the pen-name "Chung-yen" to signify his approval of Fan Chung-yen's dictum that a scholar should "worry about the world before the world worries about itself, and feel happy only after all mankind has achieved happiness." Between 1918 and 1920 he accompanied Liang Ch'i-ch'ao on a tour of Europe.[22] In 1922 he and Hu Shih founded a political journal called *Endeavor* (*Nu Li*), which took the stand that political reform was a prerequisite to all reforms, that politics is primarily the duty of a small elite, and that the path to constitutional government in China lay in a more active political role of men of integrity (*hao jen*) who had other occupations and means of living. In the same year Ting published a number of articles on the military situation in China, and in 1926 he wrote a book, based on these articles, on the military history of the Chinese Republic.[23]

In 1923, Ting became a leading participant in a polemic on science versus metaphysics. The controversy started with a speech at Tsinghua College by Carson Chang (Chang Chün-man, 1886-   ), a German-trained philosopher-jurist who was a friend of Liang Ch'i-ch'ao. Influenced by Liang's view that the First World War had indicated the "bankruptcy of Western materialistic civilization," Chang sought to minimize the importance of science. According to him the central problem of life is "I" which stands in opposition to "not-I." The relationship between "I" and "not-I" is not governed by any scientific principle or laws. A philosophy of life is subjective, intuitive, synthetic, undetermined, and unique, whereas science is objective, logical, analytical, causative, and uniform. "Hence," said

20. Juan Wei-Chou, *op. cit.*, 21-23. 21. GSH:SCC, 50.
22. LJKHS, I, 1, 6-7; III, 551 ff. 23. HS:TWC, 35-41.

Chang, "no matter how far science develops, it is not able to solve the problems of life." Furthermore, he maintained that modern civilization was a "material civilization" achieved by science and that "Since the end of World War I, many Westerners had expressed their detestation of it."[24]

Chang's views aroused Ting and others who believed in the omnipotence of science and the superiority of Western culture. In an article titled "Metaphysics and Science," Ting accused Chang of being possessed by "Ghost Metaphysics" and asserted that a philosophy of life, even if not determined by science, is yet subject to "scientific methods." Furthermore, "while science and views of life are not unified at present, this does not mean that they will not be unified in the future."[25] Second, "science is omnipotent in the field of knowledge," and "nothing that cannot be logically studied constitutes real knowledge." Even the purest psychological phenomena cannot be outside the law of causality.[26] Third, "if European civilization is bankrupt, science is not responsible for it . . . for the people most responsible for the outbreak of the war are politicians and educators, most of whom are unscientific."[27] Fourth, Eastern and Western civilizations cannot be distinguished as spiritual and material.[28]

The controversy between science and metaphysics was a major issue among Chinese intellectuals in this period. The debate lasted a year and led to the publication of some 300,000 words on both sides. The last article from the camp of the scientists, as Ting's group called themselves, was written by Wu Chih-hui. In an essay of 70,000 words Wu first postulated a universe which is a "dark and chaotic whole" with no god or soul.[29] Man is an animal with two hands and a brain which enable him to make tools and create civilization to satisfy his desires and better his living. The means by which he achieves these ends is science and its application. Man's morality is improved by means of material progress. Wu described his own view of life as threefold: eating, mating, and having the companionship of friends, which are, according to Wu, the three basic physical desires of man. "The metaphysical spectre and the religious deity are alien invaders of humanity."[30] From his mechanistic view of the universe and an analysis of love and morality in terms of physical desire, Wu concluded that the whole universe and life can be expressed by science.

Wu's thesis was acclaimed by the scientists as a successful unification of science and a philosophy of life, founded upon "the gen-

24. KHYSK, I, 9-11.   25. Ibid., I, 3.
26. Ibid., I, 7-16.   27. Ibid., I, 22.
28. Ibid., 27-28.   29. WCH:HSLC, 11-31.
30. Ibid., 46, 62, 70-71.

erally accepted scientific knowledge of the last two or three hundred years."[31] With this tour de force, the scientists proclaimed victory, which, significantly, was conceded to them by the reading public.[32] Actually, their writings suggest that the scientists had only a vague concept of science and the West. Key terms were not defined or used consistently; arguments were not confined to well-defined issues; and value judgments were mingled liberally with objective facts. It is striking that Ting, an eminent scientist in his own right, failed to exhibit rigorous reasoning in his non-scientific writings.

In 1921, Ting resigned from the directorship of the geological survey and became an executive of a coal mine in Jehol. He held this position until 1926 when he became a member of an advisory body to the British government in connection with the Boxer indemnity refunds. His reason for joining the coal company was his heavy family burden, including the expenses of a brother whom he had sent to Germany to study and who was not on a government scholarship merely because Ting wanted the stipends to go to poorer students. Though in perfect accordance with the traditional Chinese code of justice and self-denial, Ting's attitude caused him severe hardship.[33]

In May, 1926, he was appointed commissioner for the Special Municipality of Woosung and Shanghai. A year earlier, he had participated in political intrigue by members of Kiangsu gentry to rid their province of the army under the Manchurian warlord Chang Tso-lin.[34] The move succeeded, and Ting was appointed commissioner by Sun Ch'uan-fang, the new overlord of five southern provinces. According to Ting's late biographer, Hu Shih, the purpose of establishing a special municipality in Shanghai was first to turn the area into a model city and then to negotiate for the surrender of Western-held enclaves within that territory. Because of the fluid political situation, Ting remained in his post only eight months. During this short period, an agreement was reached between Kiangsu Province and the foreign powers to establish a new court system in Shanghai which made Chinese laws applicable and which gave the Chinese judges more power in making decisions.[35]

In 1928, after a short stay in Dairen, Ting conducted a geological survey in Kwangsi. During the next two years he took charge of a large-scale study of southwestern China sponsored by the Chinese Geological Survey. In 1931, Chiang Monlin became president of Peking University and obtained, through Hu Shih, grants from the foundation that controlled the American Boxer indemnity remissions. Fifteen research professorships were established at the University, and

31. HS:WT (1953), II, 137. 32. KCP:CWS, 320-28.
33. HS:TWC, 32-34. 34. *Ibid.*, 61.
35. *Ibid.*, 65-69.

Ting was appointed to one of them.[36] He remained at this post until he was appointed secretary-general of the Academia Sinica in 1934.

In spite of his diverse activities after 1921, Ting intermittently continued his scholarly pursuits. In 1923 he published an article describing his effort in reprinting from a Japanese edition a seventeenth-century Chinese work on technology, titled *Exploitation of the Works of Nature (Tien Kung Kai Wu)*, by Sung Ying-hsin;[37] in 1928 he compiled a chronological biography of the seventeenth-century Chinese geographer Hsu Hsia-k'e.[38] In 1929 he was elected president of the Chinese Geological Society, and on his inauguration he delivered an address on the orogenic movements in China.[39] In 1932 he wrote a paper entitled "A Statistical Study of the Difference between the Width-Height Ratio of *Spirifer tingi* and That of *Spirifer hsiehi*."[40] The following year he, with Grabau, read two other papers at the sixteenth International Geological Congress, one on the Permian of China and its bearing on Permian classification and the other on the Carboniferous of China and its bearing on the classification of the Mississippian and Pennsylvanian.[41] Until his death in 1936 he remained editor of the *Chinese Paleontological Journal*.

As the Kuomintang became stabilized in China and as the Japanese occupied Manchuria in 1931, Ting renewed his interest in politics. In 1932, he, Hu Shih, and a handful of other Western-educated men founded a journal of opinion, *The Independent Review (Tu Li P'ing Lun)*. During the three years and seven months' existence of that journal, Ting contributed no less than sixty-four articles.[42] A number of these dealt with Sino-Japanese diplomacy, a burning issue at the time. Ting made specific suggestions on China's defense plan, advocated that China should seek a settlement through direct negotiation with Japan, and even personally contacted Chiang Kai-shek to urge his views upon the latter. In other articles he clarified his basic political stand. Stressing the intellectual inequality of men, he spoke disdainfully of parliamentary government and urged a new kind of dictatorship for China, one that was headed by a man who "thoroughly understood the nature of a modern nation," who had only China's interests in his mind, who could unite under him all Chinese qualified to participate in politics, and who knew how to utilize all the available specialists of China.[43] On another critical topic in China at the time, economic planning, Ting emphasized that unless China had a unified and efficient government and was freed from the shackles of unequal treaties, a planned economic

36. *Ibid.*, 76-77.
38. *Ibid.*, 27.
40. *Ibid.*, 22.
42. HS:TWC, 85.

37. *Ibid.*, 71.
39. *Ibid.*, 73.
41. YTL:CWL, 538.
43. *Ibid.*, 106.

order was unrealizable.[44] By implication he was in favor of planning but regretted that the conditions for it had not yet existed.

In 1933, after attending an international geological conference in Washington, D.C., Ting made a trip of some forty days to Soviet Russia. In his published reports, he deplored the absence of personal liberty in Russia but endorsed the principle of economic equality. He fervently hoped that Soviet Russia would succeed lest equality become more than ever unrealizable and that "all those who had been executed, exiled, and starved in the previous fifteen years would have been sacrificed for nothing." Significantly, he stated he would prefer the life of a factory worker in England or America to that of an intellectual in Russia, but he would choose the lot of a geologist in Soviet Russia rather than that of a White Russian refugee in Paris. Ting's stand is considered self-contradictory by his otherwise sympathetic biographer, Hu Shih. According to Hu, Ting himself admitted that liberty was a condition of equality; he knew that there was no liberty in Russia, yet he assumed that Russia's success would indicate a path to human equality.[45]

In 1935, as war between China and Japan drew nearer, the Chinese government redoubled its effort to complete the Canton-Hankow railway and planned to explore the coal mines along the line. Ting participated in the planning and volunteered personally to make a survey tour. It was during this journey that Ting fell victim of poisoning from gas heat while he slept. He died on January 5, 1936.[46]

Ting's life illustrates a transitional type between the scholar-moralist of old and the specialist of modern society. A competent scientist and the founder of Chinese geology, he yet had a passion for politics. He accepted an important appointment from a warlord, and when this was cut short by political changes, he retired only temporarily. By the early 1930's he had already established personal connections with the leading figures in the Kuomintang government. If death had not intervened, he would have become a member of that regime,[47] and if he were alive today, he would probably be working under the Communists since he preferred to be a "Russian geologist in Soviet Russia rather than a Russian refugee in Paris." This apparent readiness to co-operate indicates, on the one hand, Ting's eagerness to help China and, on the other, his lack of firm political convictions.

The latter characteristic probably resulted from his earlier environment. His experience in the West inspired him with the value of liberty and equality and the importance of amateurism in politics—he insisted that all politicians should have their own occupations and incomes. But his Chinese background made him keenly conscious

44. *Ibid.,* 103-4.
46. *Ibid.,* 119.
45. *Ibid.,* 99.
47. HSSHPP, III, 62.

of the Chinese nation and the importance of the group over that of the individual. Similarly, it was his Chinese heritage that made him value economic equality as a goal but stress men's intellectual inequality as a fact. Influenced by these rather incongruent views, he hoped to see the rise of a dictator in China who was altruistic in spirit and efficient in operation, who could rally the elite and use the specialists to develop China. In other words, liberty was an enticing prospect for Ting, but national rejuvenation through industrialization was even more important; if they could not both be had, liberty must yield to national strength. The pattern of Ting's thought was broadly similar to that of Yen, Liang, and Sun; the only differences were his belief in political amateurism and his emphatic respect for technical expertise. In these ways he typified a stage in the metamorphosis of Chinese intellectuals from a total political man to a specialist unconcerned with politics.

The second scientific field to reach a high level of development was chemistry. One of the earlier and better known men in this field was the biochemist Hsien Wu (1893-1959). Wu was born to a scholarly family in Foochow.[48] At eleven he participated, at the county level, in the civil-service examinations, and was later enrolled in the Foochow provincial high school. Influenced by some of his teachers who were graduates of the Foochow arsenal, Wu at the time aspired to a reconstruction of the Chinese Navy. In 1910 he passed the American Boxer indemnity scholarship examination, and when he arrived in the United States a year later, he went to study naval architecture at the Massachusetts Institute of Technology. However, during the summer of 1912, on a farm in Center Harbor, New Hampshire, Wu read and was influenced by Thomas Huxley's essays, especially "The Physical Basis of Life." Shortly thereafter he changed to a major in chemistry and a minor in biology. After receiving his B.S. degree in 1916, he went on to graduate work, first at M.I.T. and later at Harvard under Professor Otto Folin. His Ph.D. dissertation, completed in 1919, suggested a new method of blood analysis and represented an important contribution to chemical research in medicine. Instead of requiring several hundred milliliters of blood sample to determine one chemical constituent, it took, by Wu's method, only ten cubic centimeters or less to ascertain all the important constituents. While serving as a research fellow from 1919 to 1920, Wu co-authored with Folin a number of publications which further advanced the Folin-Wu methods.[49]

In 1920 he returned to China and joined the staff of the newly organized Peking Union Medical College, under the China Medical Board of the Rockefeller Foundation. He continued to publish his

48. WDY:HW, 1.   49. Ibid., 1-3.

writings and in 1924 became head of biochemistry and in 1928 one of the first three Chinese to attain full professorial rank at that college (the other two being Robert K. S. Lim and J. Heng Liu).[50] Another notable event was Wu's marriage in 1924 to Daisy Yen, his assistant, who had studied food chemistry and nutrition at Columbia. Wu had previously married a girl in his native city but had left her behind when he went abroad in 1911. After long exposure to different environments, he became acutely unhappy with his wife, and insisted upon a divorce. After his second marriage, Wu went with his bride to the United States and spent a year there, during which time he pursued research with Donald D. Van Slyke.

On his return to China, Wu further expanded his activities. He continued to serve in the chemistry division of the National Committee on the Standardization of Scientific Terminology (1921-1927), helped to organize the Chinese Physiological Society in 1926, was elected its president, and was on the editorial board of the well-known *Chinese Journal of Physiology*.[51] In 1924 Wu began a long program of investigation into protein denaturation. Many of his experiments, such as molecular weight determinations before and after denaturation, are quoted in standard Western works. Most interesting is his recognition, in 1931, that some proteins are composed of strands associated by forces which can be disrupted by heat, acid, and alkali. This conclusion is recognized as a significant advance in the theory of protein structure.[52] During this period, Wu also studied the nutritive value of vegetarian diets as judged by growth, reproduction, basal metabolism, spontaneous activity, and life span of rats. These studies led to the conclusion that the smaller stature and the generally poor health statistics of the average Chinese as compared with those of the Westerners are due to the fact that the largely vegetarian Chinese diet contains proteins of low biological value and less calcium and fat soluble vitamins.[53] In 1929, Wu published a treatise in Chinese on nutrition, and in 1934 he wrote a textbook in English on physical biochemistry. From 1937 on he and his collaborators published a series of studies on immunochemistry. Using an antigen with a colored group such as hemoglobin, or iodinated albumin which can be quantitatively determined in the presence of other proteins, they made quantitative analyses of the antigen-antibody precipitate. Their methods of isolating and purifying antibodies are said to have represented a significant improvement upon the older practices.[54]

Scientific pursuits did not monopolize Wu's interests, however.

50. *Ibid.*, 48.   51. *Ibid.*, 3-4.

52. Thomas H. Bergeman, "The Origins of Modern Science in China; Research in Chemistry and Mathematics Before 1938," unpublished paper read at the 1962 meetings of the Association for Asian Studies, Boston, pp. 9-10.

53. WDY:HW, 16.   54. *Ibid.*, 17; WHCC, 37-38.

For hobbies he collected Chinese porcelain and recited "favorite Chinese poems on appropriate occasions."[55] In 1934, he purchased for his residence an old ducal palace at Fang Chia Yüan in Peking; for almost ten years he acted as his own architect in remodeling and expanding his property. In 1932 he and nine others, including V. K. Ting and Hu Shih, established *The Independent Review* to express their political opinion. While Wu was less active than some of the others, he nevertheless contributed thirteen articles during the five year existence of the journal, writing on popular scientific topics as well as political and economic ones. During the Sino-Japanese war he remained in Peking until 1944. In that year he was summoned to Chunking by the Chinese government there to organize a Nutrition Institute, of which he was appointed the first director. In July of that year he went to the United States as China's nutrition expert on a commission to study postwar problems of rehabilitation and reconstruction. He returned to China after the war ended and resumed charge of the Nutrition Institute. In 1947 he again went abroad, first to England to participate in the International Physiological Congress, and then to New York to learn the technique of running the mass spectrometer, and to familiarize himself with isotope research at Columbia University.[56]

Because of the worsening political situation in China, Wu's return was postponed several times. Instead, his family joined him in the United States, where they eventually settled down and became citizens. Wu himself obtained a visiting professorship in biochemistry at the University of Alabama, resigning in 1953 following an attack of coronary thrombosis. He then retired to Boston, but even in his last years he did not forsake his interest in research. A series of three papers on the excretion pattern of N^{15}-labeled amino acids in man appeared in the *Journal of Applied Physiology* in 1959. Meanwhile, he continued to dabble in various non-scientific topics, finishing a draft of a book entitled *A Guide to Scientific Living* and starting on several manuscripts on the evolution of Chinese calligraphy, Chinese phonetics, and world peace. After a second attack in April, 1958, his health steadily declined and the end came on August 8, 1959.[57] As Wu had always planned, all of his five children completed their education in this country. Both of his sons hold a Ph.D., one of his three daughters is an M.D., and two have master's degrees.[58]

Wu was not the only notable chemist in that period. Another was K. K. Chen, a Tsinghua alumnus who specialized in pharmaceutical chemistry. In 1923 he succeeded in isolating ephedrine from the Chinese medicinal herb Ma Huang, the results of which led to the use of the drug for bronchial asthma, hay fever, sinusitis, and in

55. WDY:HW, 13, 65.   56. *Ibid.*, 5-9.
57. *Ibid.*, 10-14.   58. *Ibid.*, 67-73.

spinal anesthesia. He returned to America in 1925 and has since become one of the foremost authorities in pharmacology and its related fields.[59] From 1930, the work of a third Chinese chemist, Sa Pen-t'ieh, began to appear in American, British, and Chinese journals, ultimately appearing in annual reviews and standard reference works. The sort of thing he did was to prepare and characterize a series of esters, or to test a long list of reagents for separating aldehydes and ketones. His use of styphnic acid for the identification of alkaloids was a novel and useful idea.[60]

In 1933 the Chinese Chemical Society was formed. Starting with twenty-four papers the first year, its journal expanded to seventy-two in the third, with the summaries appearing in *Chemical Abstracts* published in America. During this period a number of Chinese became internationally known in their respective fields: Tseng Chao-lun, grandson of Tseng Kuo-fan, in organic analysis, Yüan Han-ch'ing in stereoisomerism, Chou Hou-fu in theoretical organic reactions, and so on. In the opinion of a recent writer, organic chemistry was the only field before 1938 in which one could be prepared for individual scientific investigation by an entirely Chinese education.[61]

Physics, like chemistry, developed in China along lines begun by the scientists who received their graduate education in the West. The first full-fledged physicist was probably John Yiu-bong Lee (1884-   ), a Ph.D. of Chicago, 1915, whose dissertation concerned the investigation of the electron by Millikan's method. However, on his return to China, Lee devoted himself to Y.M.C.A. work and had little to do with physics. Between 1920 and 1925 half a dozen men, mostly Tsinghua alumni who had held Boxer indemnity scholarships, returned with their doctorates. Hu Kang-fu (1893-   ) taught at Southeastern University, Yen Jen-kuang and Li Shu-hua at Peking University, Yao Yü-tai at Nankai University, and Yeh Chi-sun at Tsinghua College. Their work at this stage was mainly to replace the foreigners who alone had taught physics in China, and to augment the courses and laboratory equipment within the limits of the rather meager resources available.[62]

Only after 1926 did Chinese research really begin. The direct influence of individual Western scientists is illustrated by the case of Woo Yu-hsün (1896-   ), who as a student of A. H. Compton at Chicago, calculated scattering intensity at long wave-lengths in the Compton effect. After his return to China, Woo formulated scattering form factors for atoms and later for molecules. His results are

59. "We Salute . . . K. K. Chen, Ph.D., M.D.," *Anesthesia and Analgesia,* XXXVII (July-Aug., 1958), p. [24].

60. Bergeman, *op. cit.,* 7.

61. *Ibid.,* 14.

62. I am indebted to Dr. Shu-hua Li of the Academia Sinica for this information.

part of the standard literature on the subject. Until the application of quantum mechanical considerations by Heisenberg in 1934, Woo was a recognized leader in this field.[63]

Another physicist, Ny Tsi-ze (Yen Chi-tz'u, 1900-   ), who had studied at Paris, made notable contributions to spectroscopy, contributing some twenty papers to French journals. A further name worth mentioning is that of Chao Chung-yao, who in 1931 at California Institute of Technology obtained some gamma-ray scattering results that deviated from prediction by the Klein-Nishina formula. Had he continued in this investigation instead of going back to China, Chao might have discovered the cause of this anomaly—namely the creation of the first known particle of anti-matter, the positron—and earned the Nobel Prize which went to Carl Anderson. Another Caltech man, Chou P'ei-yüan, who was a student of H. P. Robertson, published after 1932 some studies in relativistic cosmology in the new *Chinese Journal of Physics*. The work was impressive enough to earn him a position at the Princeton Institute for Advanced Study in 1937, and it is listed in the bibliographies of standard works on general relativity.

Lastly, a Chicago man, Wu Ta-yu (1907-   ), after several years of study with George E. Uhlenbeck and Samuel A. Goudsmit, presented an extended study of molecular vibrational frequencies and the effect of isotope substitution.[64] It is interesting to note that Wu was in turn the teacher of the Chinese Nobel Prize winner Tsung-dao Lee and was responsible for his coming to the United States, while Chen-ning Yang, who shared the Nobel Prize with Lee, had been a student of Chao Chung-yao and Yeh Chi-sun at Kunming.[65] Thus one can clearly see the cumulative effect of scientific learning in China. The founding of the Chinese Physical Society in 1932 reflected this expansion and provided further impetus for research.

In point of time, the fourth field to reach maturity was mathematics. Although this discipline had received much attention from scholars in the past, modern Chinese mathematicians owed their achievements completely to the West and to Japan. There were few mathematics teachers during the early Republic; the two best known were Feng Tsu-hsün (1880-   ), a graduate of Kyoto Imperial University, who taught at National Peking University, and Ho Lu (1895-   ), a *licencié* of the University of Lyon, who taught at Southeast University. Their work was limited to teaching what they had been taught abroad. By the early thirties, a number of others who had studied in France and Japan returned to China and not merely staffed the teaching positions but also published: Su Pu-ch'ing in geometry, Chen Chien-kung in orthogonal functions and infinite

63. Bergeman, *op. cit.*, 10-11.   64. *Ibid.*, 12-13.
65. I am indebted to Dr. Shu-hua Li for this information.

series, Hsiung Ch'ing-lai in theory of functions, Yang Wu-chih in theory of numbers, and Sun Kuang-yüan in projective differential geometry.[66]

Furthermore, it was at this time that a number of eminent mathematicians visited Chinese campuses from abroad, notably W. Blaschke, G. Birkhoff, N. Wiener, W. F. Osgood, and J. Hadamard. Through their influence the Chinese Mathematical Society was founded in 1935, and a journal appeared the next year.[67] By then several men who subsequently achieved international standing in their fields broke into print. One was Shiing-shen Chern (Ch'en Hsing-shen, 1911-   ), who was born at Chia-hsing, Chekiang, graduated from Nankai University in 1930, and received his M.S. from Tsinghua in 1934 and his doctorate from Hamburg in 1936. He taught at Tsinghua from 1937 to 1947 and was a research associate at Academia Sinica from 1942 to 1947.[68] While visiting the Institute for Advanced Study at Princeton in 1943, he published a series of papers on fibre spaces which attracted international attention. In 1949 he came to this country, teaching first at Chicago and more recently at Berkeley. A past editor of both the *Transactions* and the *Proceedings of the American Mathematical Society*, he is most noted for his work on differential geometry, differentiable manifolds, and fibre spaces. His work has had important recent applications in the transcendental theory of algebraic varieties.[69]

A man of comparable caliber is Chow Wei-liang (Chou Wei-liang, 1911-   ), a great-grandson of former governor-general Chou Fu and a grand-nephew of the government official and industrialist Chou Hsueh-hsi. Wei-liang received his B.A. and his M.A. from Chicago in 1931 and 1932 and obtained his doctorate from Leipzig in 1936.[70] He is, along with B. L. van der Waerden, Zariski, and Weil, one of the four pioneers of modern algebraic geometry. While van der Waerden's interest later shifted to other topics, Chow has continued to be in the forefront of this field. His most recent work has dealt with Jacobian varieties, complex manifolds, and equivalence relations on algebraic varieties.[71] Chow is at Johns Hopkins and has been chairman of the mathematics department there since 1955.

Mathematics is probably the most highly developed of all sciences in China. The achievements of Chern and Chow have been equaled by some of their younger countrymen. One of these is Chung Kai-lai (1917-   ), who received his Ph.D. from Princeton in 1947 and is very well known in probability and the stochastic processes. Another

66. I am indebted to Dr. Shiing-shen Chern for this information.
67. Chou Hung-ching, "Mathematics," CHMKHC, I-II, 1.
68. CYYCY, 3.
69. I am indebted to Dr. W. E. Jenner of Chapel Hill for this information.
70. I am indebted to Dr. Shiing-shen Chern for this information.
71. Information received from Dr. W. E. Jenner.

is Wang Hao (1921-   ) in mathematical logic. Wang received his undergraduate training in China and his doctorate from Harvard. He belonged to the Harvard Society of Fellows (1948-51), was a reader in philosophy of mathematics at Oxford (1957-60), and holds the Gordon Kay chair of Mathematical Logic at Harvard (1961). There are a number of noted mathematicians in Communist China, of whom perhaps Hua Lo-keng (1911-   ), in theory of numbers, is the best known. The high level of mathematical knowledge in China can be seen in other ways. One indication is that mathematics has served as a foundation for achievement in other sciences; in addition to those already mentioned, Professor Y. H. Koo (1901-   ) of the University of Pennsylvania is famous for his mathematical work in electrical engineering, and Tsien Hsüeh-shen (1909-   ) in China, a pupil of von Karman, is noted for his contribution to aerodynamics. Another indication is the high standards in mathematics in Chinese schools both on the mainland and in Formosa. All middle-school graduates are required to have considerable knowledge of higher algebra, analytic geometry, and often solid geometry, as well as calculus. A recent report in the *American Mathematical Monthly* on the 1956-57 mathematical competitions for middle-school students astonished many people.[72] The tests were so difficult that some mathematicians doubted their authenticity. In view of the resolute emphasis on mathematics in Chinese schools, these tests appears to have been within reason.

Thus, there were clearly stages in the development of science in China. Pioneers like V. K. Ting devoted themselves more to organizing and teaching than to research, not because of their own limitations but because it was difficult to conduct research in isolation. As a result of their efforts, the universities were adequately staffed and undergraduate training in most cases was available by the early 1930's. This broadened curriculum provided a foundation for higher achievement, and today many Chinese are recognized authorities in their own fields. None of these men, however, was educated exclusively in China. A few did their graduate training in Germany, but a majority received their doctorates from American universities. Furthermore, most of the Chinese scientists in America agree that they have to remain here to be intellectually productive, either because they need elaborate equipment for their work or because contact with their professional colleagues is essential. Thus it could be said that science in China has never become truly self-sufficient.

From the point of view of our study perhaps the most significant phenomenon is the emergence of an elite group whose interest was exclusively scientific, as distinguished from social and political. This metamorphosis of the Chinese elite can clearly be seen if we compare

72. AMM, Vol. 67 (1960), p. 756.

V. K. Ting, Hsien Wu, Shiing-shen Chern, and Wei-liang Chow with one another. Ting, the oldest, was also the most politically oriented. Although he was an excellent scientist and could have made significant contributions, his time was largely consumed by politics. By contrast, Hsien Wu, who was six years younger than Ting and had a more specialized training, showed only a mild interest in national affairs. He participated in *The Independent Review* and became head of a government institute, but he wrote 159 scientific papers and only 13 journalistic articles.[73] This trend toward specialization reached its peak in Chern, who is a prolific writer of mathematical papers but who has produced no political works. He had no connection with the government beyond taking charge at one time of the mathematical institute. The same is generally true of Wei-liang Chow, who came from a politically prominent family, but whose only venture outside mathematics was some business activities during the Second World War when his scientific efforts were interrupted. Thus, with the rise of science as a profession came a new intellectual orientation among the Chinese elite, which in turn led to a change in the role of intellectuals in society.

Among the humanists and social scientists a similar metamorphosis took place, as can be seen from the career of Hu Shih (1891-1962). Hu was born in Shanghai, of a family whose ancestral seat was at Chi-hsi of Anhwei and which, like many others in the district, had both commercial interests and connections with the official world. After the death of Hu's father in 1895, the family finances deteriorated, and Hu Shih at one time earned his living in Shanghai by teaching English. In 1910 he went north to participate in the examinations for the American Boxer indemnity scholarships. The tests were divided into two parts: the languages, Chinese and English; and the sciences. Hu received 100 per cent on his Chinese, 60 per cent on his English, but placed rather low in sciences, being the fifty-fifth of seventy qualified candidates. Late in that year he arrived in the United States and entered Cornell. First enrolled in agriculture, he soon switched to the humanities and graduated in 1914. In 1915 he went to Columbia and two years later he finished his doctoral dissertation on the development of logical methods in ancient China.[74] Upon his return he joined the faculty of Peking University and remained connected with that institution, at least in a spiritual sense, all his life.

An examination of Hu's influence might well start with his views on culture. At the time Confucianism was attacked in 1917, there was a discussion among Chinese intellectuals on the nature of and

73. WDY:HW, 33.
74. Li Shu-hua, "Hu Shih's Life and His Contributions," TLTC (May 31, 1962), 1-3.

differences between Chinese and Western civilizations. In 1915, Ch'en Tu-hsiu published an article entitled "The Basic Differences in Thought of the Eastern and Western Nations," in which he made the following comparisons:[75]

Characteristics of

Eastern Races	Western Races
Complacency	Struggle
Family as the pole of life	Individualism
Personal relations based upon emotion and conventionality	Personal relations based upon utilitarian considerations and governed by the rule of law

The conclusion Ch'en reached was that Chinese culture was inferior to Western, and that, in order to survive in the present world order, China must embrace the two highest accomplishments of Western civilization—Democracy and Science.

Following Ch'en's lead a number of others contributed to the discussion of the problem. Some, notably Li Ta-chao, a returned student from Japan and later a founder and martyr of the Chinese Communist Party, and Ts'ang Fu, editor of a leading magazine, *The Eastern Miscellany*, advanced the theme that Chinese culture is quietistic while Western culture is dynamic.[76] Others, notably Liang Ch'i-ch'ao, believed that Chinese culture was idealistic while Western culture was materialistic.[77] Still others, notably Hu Shih, maintained that the Easterners are characterized by their contentment with intellectual ignorance and material scarcity while the Westerners are motivated by "divine discontent" and an incessant urge to conquer nature.[78] In spite of the variety of arguments, the great majority of writers favored a rapid adoption of the Western way of life for China. The intellectual trend in China reached a point where disparagement of traditional Chinese culture and the national heritage became the predominant thought of the generation. This attitude was most succinctly stated in a passage by Hu Shih.

> I unreservedly condemn our Eastern civilization and warmly praise the modern civilization of the West. It has often been said that Eastern civilization is idealistic while that of the West is materialistic. This is an untruth manufactured by people suffering from ethnocentric delusions. . . . There are half-wits . . . who wish you to believe that the old Chinese culture and moral values are superior to all others. There are also fools who, having never been abroad, shouted: "To the East! To the East! The Western tricks no longer work now." I want to say to you, don't be fooled. We must admit . . . that

75. LJ, Vol. 1, No. 4.   76. CWJ:SCC, 43-44.
77. *Ibid.*, 47.   78. HS:WT (1953), III, 1-14.

we are inferior to others not only in technology and political institutions but also in moral values, knowledge, literature, music, fine arts and body physique.[79]

Consistent with this stand, Hu favored individualism and believed in science and expertise.[80] In an article published in 1918, he described the spirit of the New Tide as the transvaluation of all values and its aim as the rejuvenation of China through gradual evolution and piecemeal reform.[81] He deprecated the efforts of others to replace Confucianism with another "ism" and advocated the study of particular problems: "To study a particular problem is most difficult. . . . It needs much time and thought. Data have to be collected; opinions sought; actual conditions surveyed. Only by taking risk and enduring hardship can one reach a conclusion that may serve to solve a problem."[82] General theory, according to Hu, is useful only as an aid in the study of a specific problem, and one must have an exhaustive understanding of the historical background as well as the influence of the theory before one may rely on it.[83]

Consistent with his belief in expertise, Hu promoted rigorous reasoning in historical research and advocated writing in the colloquial style in order to express thoughts more precisely. In a sense the use of the vernacular was not an innovation in China; popular novels and folksongs had always been written in the colloquial language. In the second half of the nineteenth century, Protestant missionaries translated the Bible into various Chinese spoken languages.[84] In 1911, *The Eastern Miscellany* (*T'ung Fang Tsa Chih*), a leading semi-academic magazine in China, urged that the vernacular language be used in all primary schools in the interest of unifying all Chinese dialects.[85] Nevertheless, it was Hu Shih, then a student at Columbia University, who first entertained the idea of replacing the literary language with the vernacular. The idea was first propounded by Hu in June, 1916, when he stated that the Chinese literary language was a dead language and that the spoken words were not vulgar, as they were traditionally thought to be.[86] Having aroused little sympathy among his fellow students in America,[87] Hu later wrote to Ch'en Tu-hsiu in Peking criticizing the classical school in Chinese literature and suggesting an eight-point program of reform:

1. Avoid classical allusions.
2. Avoid stale, time-worn phrases.

79. *Ibid.* (1930), 14-16.
80. *Ibid.* (1953), IV, 612.
81. *Ibid.*, I, 736.
82. *Ibid.*, II, 345.
83. *Ibid.*, II, 374-78.
84. KWH:TCS, 29.
85. "Editorial," EM, Vol. VIII, No. 3, p. 1.
86. CSM (June, 1916), 567-68.
87. HS:LHJC, XIV, 981.

3. Avoid parallel construction of sentences and abolish the established rules of rhymes, tones, and antitheses in poems.
4. Do not avoid vulgar words and phrases.
5. Seek and follow grammatical rules.
6. Avoid pretending to be sad and worried.
7. Show your own personality, do not imitate the ancients.
8. What you write should have real substance.[88]

Ch'en endorsed this program, in general, but characteristically went one step farther than Hu in condemning not only the classical school but also classical literature, stating that "measured by the level of Western literature, how can the works of Tu, Yüan, Po, and Liu (traditionally the greatest poets in China) be considered free from errors and stupidity?"[89]

At Ch'en Tu-hsiu's suggestion, Hu's eight points were expanded into an article entitled "Some Tentative Suggestions for the Reform of Chinese Literature," which appeared in *New Youth* in January, 1917. In the next issue of the same journal, Ch'en followed with an article called "Literary Revolution," in which he asserted that the "glorious modern Europe" was a product of revolution and that revolutions, ethical and literary as well as political, were needed in China.[90] The views of Hu and Ch'en immediately attracted attention and were supported by a number of intellectuals, particularly Ch'ien Hsuen-t'ung, Li Ta-chao, and Chou Tso-jen, all professors at Peking University.[91] Ch'ien was particularly enthusiastic. Hitherto Hu had merely urged writers "not to avoid vulgar words." He chiefly opposed the heavy use of allusions and the consequent obscurity of meaning. Even here Hu had some reservations—for instance, he acknowledged the skill of some writers of the old school.[92] Ch'ien Hsuen-t'ung took Hu to task for his lack of firmness. In a letter to Hu, Ch'en Tu-hsiu also declared that since the colloquial was so obviously superior to the literary, further discussion would serve little purpose; he would not tolerate any opposition to this cause.[93]

Prodded by such energetic assertions, Hu, in April, 1918, reformulated his stand in an article entitled "A Constructive View of Literary Revolution." Besides repeating his eight earlier points, he advanced four positive rules stressing the use of expressions current at the time of writing. He condemned Chinese literature of the last two thousand years and traced its poverty to the use of "a dead language as the medium." A living literature, according to Hu, has to be based on a current language; by the same token, extensive literary effort would lead to the development of a standard dialect for all the country,

88. HS:WT (1953), I, 5.   89. LJ, Vol. II, No. 2, pp. 1-3.
90. *Ibid.*, Vol. II, No. 6, p. 1.
91. Li Ta-chao and Chou Tso-jen were both educated in Japan. Chou was a brother of Lu Hsün and a well-known writer himself.
92. HS:WT (1953), I, 12-13.   93. *Ibid.*, 32, 52.

as could be seen from the effects of the work of Dante, Chaucer, and Wycliff. Hence the proper route was to proceed from "vernacular literature to literary vernacular." In this phrase, ironically enough, Hu was unconsciously resorting to a parallelism more characteristic of the old literature than of the colloquial which he advocated.[94]

The novel and seemingly revolutionary nature of Hu's thesis aroused the youth, and soon the movement flourished. In 1918 all of the articles in *New Youth* appeared in the vernacular, as did Hu's own *History of Chinese Philosophy* (1919), essentially based on his doctoral dissertation at Columbia and widely acclaimed as the first treatise on the subject using the rigorous, analytical approach borrowed from the West. New poetry composed in the vernacular was also experimented with,[95] though with less success. The May Fourth Incident of 1919 created great commotion in China and by association popularized the cause of the new literary movement. Over four hundred tabloid newspapers appeared in the vernacular,[96] and even the supplements of established newspapers switched to that medium. In 1920 the Ministry of Education decreed that books used in primary schools must, within a specific time limit, be changed to the colloquial language.[97]

To be sure there was some opposition, first from a few conservatives, notably Lin Shu,[98] then from a group of Western-educated men connected with Southeast University in Nanking, who established a high-caliber journal using exclusively the literary medium;[99] and finally from a few local warlords who attempted to make classical studies compulsory in primary schools.[100] None of these efforts could retard the steady increase in the use of the vernacular. Since the 1930's most books and nearly all magazine articles, including scholarly works, have been in the colloquial style.

Hu and the literary movement he espoused were strongly influenced by the West. The first letter from Hu to Ch'en Tu-hsiu in 1916 deals primarily with poetry and appears to have been written under the influence of the American literary movement of the second decade of this century.[101] With the publication of Harriet Monroe's *Poetry: A Magazine of Verse* in 1912, the "new poetry" movement had become a potent force in American literature. By 1917, the new poetry was

94. *Ibid.*, 55-73.   95. CTT:TMM, 586.
96. Li Chin-hsi, "The Kuo Yü Movement in the Last Thirty-five Years," SSWN, 101.
97. *Ibid.*, 112.
98. Lin Shu knew no foreign language but translated Western novels into literary Chinese by writing down the stories told him by his translators. See CKHWH, I, 199-204.
99. *Ibid.*, II, 119-54.
100. HS:WT (1953), IV, 530, 537; Li Chin-hsi, *op. cit.*, 125, 126.
101. CTT:TMM, 29.

considered by some as "America's first national art."[102] One of the most distinct characteristics of the poetry was its freedom from the traditionally stilted "poetic diction" and its effort to introduce the syntax of plain speech into verse. There is little doubt that this movement provided some of the inspiration for Hu Shih's proposal to reform Chinese poetry. In fact, when he made his first experimental composition of a Chinese poem somewhat in the vernacular, one of his critics in America charged that Hu was pirating the "worthless European and American New Tide."[103] Still another reflection of Western influence can be seen in the name Hu gave to the May Fourth movement—the "Chinese Renaissance." In so far as the movement was anti-traditional, this name is obviously inappropriate. Its use merely reflects Hu's efforts to justify his role in Western terms.

An even more significant contribution on Hu's part was his advocacy of better methods in literary and historical research. His early interest in this area is shown by the topic of his doctoral dissertation. Later, in the same article in which he announced the formula "from a vernacular literature to literary vernacular," he also dwelled lengthily on literary technique. In the first place, he said, a writer should collect materials not merely from the bureaucratic life or the lives of prostitutes, as Chinese novelists tended to do, but also from family tragedies and actual living conditions of the masses. A writer should have both keen powers of observation and a fertile imagination. He should seek the best structure and organization for his projected work. Hu then put forth general rules on the technique of description and characteristically concluded that Chinese literature was far behind Western literature in technique. "Even the Greek drama is ten times better than the Yüan drama, and Shakespeare and Molière, being more modern, are of course better still."[104] While Hu's penchant for the modern way may be more symptomatic than rational, his discussion of methods was among the first of its kind in China. Art in itself had not been highly regarded, and novels had been particularly disreputable. For this reason the few amateur novelists that emerged chose to remain anonymous. Although they must have thought about plot and organization, they never openly discussed them. Hu's discourse not only marked a step forward in literary education but also signified a change in the attitude of Chinese intellectuals toward literary art.

From 1918 on Hu devoted a large part of his writings to the study of methods of literary and historical research. His aim was to instill a habit of rigorous reasoning, and he chose to do it primarily by applying this process to well-known Chinese classical novels. In 1920, through Hu's effort, the Ya T'ung Book Company of Shanghai

102. UL:MAP, 12-13. 103. HS:LHJC, XIV, 981.
104. HS:WT (1953), I, 67-73.

published a new edition of *Shui Hu Chuan* (variously translated as *Water Margin, All Men are Brothers,* or *Robbers and Soldiers*) with unprecedented Western-styled punctuation. In a long introduction, Hu first disputed the old marginal comments by Chin Sheng-t'an, a seventeenth-century intellectual rebel, mainly on the grounds that Chin had not taken a pure literary viewpoint but was still encumbered, even if unconsciously, with traditional ethical values. Rating the novel as more important than either the *Historical Records (Shih Chi)* or the *Commentaries* by Tso Ch'iu-ming, Hu then launched into a comprehensive study of the historical origin of the novel and the various editions of it. He compared the work with versions appearing in the Yüan drama and concluded, by way of hypothesis and a process of elimination, that the author was an unknown person of the Ming dynasty, who for political reasons used the pseudonym of Shih Nai-an. The introduction ran to some twenty-three thousand words,[105] but was only the beginning of his work on that novel. In subsequent years he also did studies on other Chinese novels, and became known especially for his success in ascertaining that *Dream of the Red Chamber* was based on the life of Ts'ao Hsueh-ch'in.[106] Such scholarly studies of popular novels were unprecedented in China. As Hu himself declared, his aim was not primarily to further literary or textual criticism but to teach a method of reasoning.[107]

There is no doubt that Hu powerfully influenced subsequent scholarship in China. Writing in 1926, Ku Chieh-kang, who has since become an authority on ancient Chinese history, freely attributed his achievements in research to Hu's influence. Said he: "I had not known that the authorship and editions of a novel could become such a complex problem involving so many twists. The appearance of Hu's long introduction to the *Shui Hu* in 1920 gave me a powerful hint that a similar method could be applied to the study of many other problems. In the same year Hu also published polemical essays on the Well-Field System in the journal *Chien She.* The method he used was the same."[108] Ku was by no means alone in his indebtedness. Lo Erh-kang, an authority on the Taiping Rebellion, said in 1943:

When I was in college I felt nothing but woe toward textual research. After my graduation in 1930 I became an assistant to Mr. Hu in his editing of his late father's collected works. Having to copy the minute characters which filled the pages of the draft, I learned to be patient. In 1931 Mr. Hu did a study on *Hsing-shih yin-yüan chuan (A Warning to the Generations Regarding the Destined Sequences of Marriage,* a novel of the seventeenth century). I had to copy three different editions and to separate the spurious passages contained in the lithographic

105. *Ibid.,* 500-47.
107. HS:WT (1953), IV, 623.

106. Li Shu-hua, *op. cit.,* 7.
108. KCK:KSP, I, 40.

edition. In this way I learned the technique of collation. In the autumn of that year I returned to my native district, Kui-hsien, in Kwangsi. There I read the local gazetteer and discovered a great discrepancy between that and Hsueh Fu-ch'eng's writing on Chang Chung-wu-kung. This made me suspicious of all records on the Taiping Kingdom. In 1934 I again went to Peking, living with Mr. Hu but had no work other than study. I wrote two articles on Chu Chiu-t'ao and Huang Wan, both of which were examined by Hu.[109]

In Hu's own writings on methodology, he consistently advocated the rule "Be bold in making hypotheses but cautious in seeking the proof." In an article of 1921 he characterized this as the method used by the early Ch'ing scholars in attaining their towering height of philological and historical studies.[110] Later, he stated that while the method of Ch'ing scholars resembled that of Galileo, Newton, Darwin, and Pasteur, the Chinese achieved less than the Europeans because they confined their investigation to documentary materials.[111] The corrective hence was not to change the method but to extend it to all fields. It is a credit to Hu that he kept on repeating his words until the concept of hypothesis and testing has become widely known in China.

He also influenced the Chinese intellectuals through his philosophy of life. Mention has already been made of his belief in individualism. In a famous essay introducing his own thought, Hu urged upon the youth of China the supreme importance of the individual. Quoting Ibsen, he wrote: "All that I expect from you is a kind of true, pure individualism. I want you to feel that in all the world only matters concerning yourself are the most important. Compared to them, other things mean little."[112] Although it was a radical departure from orthodox Chinese thought, Hu's stand was shared by a large number of Western-educated men in China. For example, Hsü Chih-mo (1896-1931), a famous poet of the new school, once wrote: "I only know and believe in myself. To my mind, democracy is only individualism universalized. The spirit of real democracy lies in an individual's self-awareness and self-improvement."[113] In his personal life, Hsü seems to have fully carried out his belief. The only son of an affluent industrialist of Chekiang, Hsü graduated from Peking University in 1916 and two years later went to the United States. In the fall of 1920 he left Columbia and went to Cambridge and London in England. Much against the wish of his father, Hsü gave up banking and sociology in favor of poetry. Having divorced his first wife, Hsü married in 1926 a Chinese socialite with whom he had become infatuated while she was still married to

109. LEK:TPTK, 2.
111. *Ibid.*, III, 111-22.
113. WY:CKHWH, 74.
110. HS:WT (1953), I, 409.
112. HS:WT (1953), IV, 612.

another man.[114] "The memory of beauty," Hsü once mused, "is the most valuable possession of man; the instinct to appreciate beauty is the key to heaven."[115] An ardent admirer of Katherine Mansfield, he strove for perfection of form, laying emphasis on the correct number of words and lines in a poem, on the use of meters, and on the structure of the verses. One of the very first in China to write poems in the vernacular but Westernized style, Hsü achieved great fame as a poet.

In addition to individualism and the great emphasis on technical competency, Hu also stressed sanity and dignity. When he, Hsü Chih-mo, and a few others founded the *Crescent Monthly* (*Hsin Yüeh*) in 1928, these two words became the basic principles of their editorial policy.[116] Even though the journal was founded to combat the leftist influence in the Chinese literary world, the Crescentists carefully refrained from making personal attacks on writers whom they opposed. In an article titled "Literature and Revolution," Liang Shih-ch'iu, a Tsinghua-Harvard-trained Crescentist, argued that literary appreciation, like revolutionary leadership, would always lie beyond the capacity of the masses, and that the criterion of literature was its quality, not its topic.[117] Another academician, the Hongkong- and Edinburgh-educated Chu Kuang-ch'ien, wrote a pamphlet titled *The Crisis in Chinese Thought,* in which he criticized, without mentioning names, the attempt to hold the mind of youth by shallow slogans and narrow concepts, to substitute belief for thought, and to accept one theory as true to the exclusion of all others. Chu advocated, in lieu of all this, scientific training and "a correct habit of thought."[118]

Still another trend that Hu did much to promote was the study of narrow, non-political topics. This tendency followed naturally from the insistence on mastery of details and was already discernible in the works of Liang Ch'i-ch'ao. But Hu gave it fresh impetus by demonstrating through his literary researches the fruitfulness of the narrow approach. By association he also promoted other kinds of non-political writings. In the early 1930's leisurely essays became very popular. The short, humorous articles by Lin Yutang (1895-   ) were particularly famous. A Harvard M.A. and Leipzig Ph.D., Lin taught in many universities but was essentially a writer of light prose. In his essays he advocated a more or less Epicurean philosophy. Life, he said, does not consist of achievement, in the mental sallies of philosophers or the imaginative flights of poets; rather it consists in the enjoyment of ourselves, "in having a haircut once in two weeks, or watering a potted flower, or watching a neighbor falling off his

114. LJKHS, III, 710; BHL:MPMC, 59-62.
115. WCF:CKHW, 109.   116. TY:SHMC, 50.
117. LHL:CECN, 223-26, 230-33.   118. HKC:CCY, 215-26.

roof."[119] In 1932 he published *Analects* (*Lun Yü*) and in the following year *Human World* (*Jen Chien Shih*), both of which were given exclusively to humorous articles for leisurely reading. Lin said: "The short essays of today embrace all kinds of topics—as big as the universe and as small as a fly."[120] Though leisurely writings had existed in China for centuries, they had not been considered as worthy of serious attention. Lin's effort to promote them was hence an innovation, well liked by some but violently upbraided by leftist writers, who thought of these writings as the "opium of the people."[121]

The influence of Hu Shih was not all pervading, however. Paradoxically, it was very weak among the novelists. As Kuo Mo-jo, a writer who has become a high Communist official, said: "The Chinese world of letters to a large extent is built by students returned from Japan. All the important writers of the Creation Society studied in Japan. So did those of the Yu-ssü School. . . . Although there are some Western-educated men struggling and rising like meteors, their efforts and accomplishments fall far behind those of the two groups mentioned above. Furthermore, the new men are mostly under the influence of these two groups."[122] A preliminary question is why did only the Japanese-educated excel in this field? Historically, one motive for sending Chinese students abroad was to train men who could translate foreign books. Some provincial authorities made the award of scholarships contingent upon the student's undertaking translation work at additional pay.[123] This and other factors, primarily the large number of Chinese students in Japan and the use of Chinese characters in Japanese writings, led to thousands of Japanese books being translated into Chinese, including Western writings which had been translated into Japanese.[124] Many Chinese men of letters achieved their positions through translation.

Another factor lay in the Japanese educational system, where great emphasis in the curriculum was placed on foreign languages. In Japanese government high schools of the 1910's, foreign language courses often accounted for twenty-two to twenty-three hours per week of the students' class work.[125] A large number of works in Western languages had Japanese translations, which broadened the literary outlook of the students in Japan and afforded them an opportunity to re-translate these works into Chinese.

Other favorable conditions existed, too. As compared to their compatriots in the West, the Chinese students in Japan, on an average, had a far better command of Chinese[126] and showed more

119. Quoted on the jacket blurb, LYT:IL.
120. Quoted in TY:SHMC, 57.   121. TY:SHMC, 57-58.
122. Quoted in CMS:JPWH, 33.   123. EM, Vol. I, No. 7, p. 163.
124. T. H. Tsien, "Western Impact on China Through Translation," FEQ (May, 1954), 325.
125. KMJ:KMCC, 47.
126. WCSJ (December, 1906), 8; RPS:IPC, 211.

interest in the socio-political development of China. Both factors were conducive to a literary career. The frequent trips home of a Chinese student in Japan enabled him to maintain contact with Chinese publishing houses. Finally, the mental agony and physical hardships occasioned by the frequent mass withdrawals of Chinese students from Japan probably helped rather than hindered their literary endeavors.

Perhaps the most influential man of letters in modern China was Lu Hsün (1881-1936), who studied in Japan between 1902 and 1909 as a Chinese government student. At first enrolled in medicine, he switched to literature in 1904 and started to write in 1907. But his work attracted little attention, and he became a school teacher upon his return to China. During the New Tide of 1918, Lu Hsün published "The Diary of a Madman," which by its biting indictment of the national heritage won him great popularity with the students. When in 1921 a group of writers organized a literary society, Lu Hsün became the main contributor to its publications. The Literary Research Club, as the society was called, was founded for the purpose of opposing the old literature, advocating literary writing as a full career instead of as an avocation, promoting realistic description of actual life, and making art a means to the improvement of life.[127] The membership soon comprised nearly all the ranking writers of the new literature, but the loose organization of the club permitted its members to have more intimate units of their own. Late in 1924, Lu Hsün and his brother Chou Tso-jen, also educated in Japan, formed a Yu-ssü (Thread of Talk) Society for the purpose of "hastening the birth of a new order." Exactly what this new order was and how it was to be produced, however, were not clear. "When hard pressed [on these points]," Lu Hsün later admitted, "We had to be purposely ambiguous."[128] The leftist tendency lay dormant in him at this time.

In 1922, Kuo Mo-jo appeared. Kuo was born in 1892 in a village in Szechuan. His grandfather was a member of a secret society; his father traded in opium. In his youth, Kuo had led a decadent life.[129] In 1913 he went north to enroll in an army medical school but changed his mind and proceeded to Japan. An unusually bright young man, he succeeded in entering a Japanese government high school in 1914, and four years later he enrolled in the Imperial University at Fukuoka as a medical student.[130] However, the strong curriculum in foreign languages and literature in Japanese government schools had aroused in Kuo a deep interest in literature, and

127. WCF:CKHW, 293-95; WY:CKHWH, 40-42.
128. TCJ:WTWS, 100. 129. SC:KMJ, 16, 17, 19, 23-44.
130. KMJ:KMCC, 33.

he began to write in 1919. He read a great deal of Tagore and translated a part of *Faust* in 1920. In that year he organized with a few of his friends in Japan a literary group called the Creation Society. In May, 1922, the first issue of the *Creation Quarterly* appeared in Shanghai. As the name implies, the group emphasized creative writing rather than translation, "art for art's sake" rather than "art for life's sake."[131] They violently attacked Lu Hsün and others for their vulgarity, opportunitism, and incompetency in translation.[132] The members of the Creation Society in this period were essentially romanticists. In 1921, Kuo wrote of himself as "a proletarian" and as "willing to be a Communist." Yet he later described this declaration as "a game of words." "Actually I had not yet understood the conceptions of the proletariat or Communism."[133]

However a change was taking place. In the autumn of 1924, Kuo translated a book entitled *Social Organization and Social Revolution* by the Japanese Marxist, Kawakami Hajime. This book profoundly influenced Kuo's thought: "The benefit I derived from the book is substantial. Hitherto I only vaguely detested individualistic capitalism. Now I have a rational basis for my faith in social revolution. The translation of this book marks a transition in my life; it awakened me from my half-sleep; it guided me out of my conflicting thoughts; it saved me from the dark shadow of death."[134]

Shortly after Kuo wrote the foregoing passage, student incidents flared up in China. First, there were agitations in Peking in May, 1925, in commemoration of the Twenty-One Demands and the May Fourth movement. Later in the month, a Chinese worker of a Japanese cotton mill in Shanghai was shot to death by a Japanese guard. When students demonstrated in protest, the police under British control opened fire and killed some fifteen of them. Thereupon all China was roused and strikes were organized everywhere against the "Imperialists," not only by students but by merchants as well. The prestige of the Peking government sank to a new low, and on July 9, 1926, Chiang Kai-shek launched the northern expedition to crush the warlords. A few months earlier, Kuo Mo-jo had gone to Canton, where he soon became a political commissar in the army, directly under Teng Yen-ta, a famous leftist. It was under these earlier circumstances that Kuo published in 1926 an essay entitled *Revolution and Literature,* in which he says: "O, Youth! O, Youth! Substantiate your lives. Acknowledge the main current of literature. Go among the soldiers, the people, the workers, the whirlpools of revolution. You should know that the literature we need is a socialistic

131. WCF:CKHW, 61.
132. WY:CKHWH, 61; KMJ:KMCC, 22.
133. *Ibid.,* 140.   134. *Ibid.,* 192.

literature that is sympathetic toward the proletariat. . . ."[135] This essay is considered by many as the main landmark in the transition from the literary revolution to the revolutionary literature in China. Under the banner of the latter, a revived Creation Society renewed its attack upon Lu Hsün and his friends in 1928. For about a year Lu Hsün was the target of much abuse and was referred to as "a man of leisure," "a Fascist out of power," "a spokesman of the petty bourgeoisie," and "remnant of the feudal forces."[136] By way of response, Lu Hsün resorted to reading and translating the literary theories of the left. From Japanese, he translated Katagami Shin's *Proletarian Literature in Theory and Practice;* from Russian, but through Japanese, he introduced the writings of Plehanov and Lunacharski, and official documents from the literature of the Communist Party in Russia.[137] Furthermore, Lu Hsün familiarized himself with Russian literature in general, and in an essay entitled *Congratulations on the Establishment of Linguistic Relationships between China and Soviet Russia,* he commented at some length on the works of L. Andreev, M. Artsybashev, V. Korolenko, and Maxim Gorky.[138] In 1931, he translated A. A. Fadeev's *Razgrom*, again from a Japanese version.[139]

The groups led by Lu Hsün and Kuo Mo-jo were probably the most influential in the Chinese literary world. Lu Hsün in particular was the idol of a large section of the reading public. According to Communist sources, his effort was mainly responsible for the formation in 1930 of the Federation of Leftist Writers, which united all previously quarreling sects, battled the few non-leftist writers, and served as a powerful auxiliary force to the Communist Party.[140] When Lu Hsün died in 1936, he was at the height of his glory. The funeral committee was made up of such national figures as Ts'ai Yüan-p'ei and Sung Ch'ing-ling (Madam Sun Yat-sen); tens of thousands of people went to pay their last respects. In Mao Tse-tung's *New Democracy,* written in 1940, Lu Hsün is called "the greatest bannerman in the cultural forces of the Communist Party."[141]

The episodes of Lu Hsün and Kuo Mo-jo are illustrations of the metamorphosis of an important type of Chinese intellectual. Both had fairly good training in Chinese classics but were ardent anti-traditionalists. Both belonged to the new profession of literary writer, itself a significant innovation in Chinese society in that men of letters no longer had to be particularly concerned with morals and politics. Indeed, for a time the political urge was dormant in both Kuo and Lu Hsün. Nevertheless, undiminished by the influence of Western

135. Quoted in WY:CKHWH, 54.
136. LHL:CECN, 121-22.
137. CPH:ST, 203-8.
138. LH:CC, V, 56.
139. TTH:WIC, 206-7.
140. WY:CKHWH, 156 ff.
141. *Ibid.,* 186-89.

individualism, their social consciences eventually led them to a modified but active role in political and social movements. Although both consciously denied Confucianism, by force of habit they felt the need for a comprehensive, explicit ideology to guide and justify their actions. Personally repugnant to each other, they nevertheless channeled their rivalry into an emulation of political radicalism.

Both Lu Hsün and Kuo detested the group led by Hu Shih. Criticisms of Hu abound in Lu Hsün's writings. To cite only a few examples, he once recalled his experience as a member of the editorial board of *New Youth* and said that even in those days he had doubts of Hu's sincerity. Of Hu's scholarship, he had this to say: "[It is true that] Dewey has his pragmatism and Babbitt his humanism, [but could] any one who has learned only a wee bit from them thereby become a top scholar in China?"[142] Of Hu's method of literary research, Lu Hsün was equally disdainful: "To impress people, [he] often relies on rare editions and materials to which he alone has access. . . . My way is slightly different. I read only books commonly available; hence I am no 'scholar.' "[143] Nor was the stricture limited to Hu. Liang Shih-ch'iu was to the leftists an "inferior running dog of the capitalists,"[144] and Lin Yutang, besides "discussing the flies and forgetting about the universe," advocated humor only "to make people laugh away the cruelty of a butcher [i.e., Chiang Kai-shek]."[145]

Thus a sharp division existed between two groups of intellectuals. There were, on the one hand, the refined, erudite specialists who generally also taught in the better colleges of China; and, on the other, the crude, often abusive men of letters with little expert knowledge but much political fervor. It is significant that the division was almost entirely along educational lines: the Japanese-trained, and to a lesser extent, the Chinese-trained, versus the Anglo-American-trained. In fact, some members of the latter group, especially Liang Shih-ch'iu and Wen I-to, had published in radical journals such as the *Creation Quarterly* before they went to study in America, but once the pilgrimage had been made, the parting of ways seemed inevitable.[146]

The position of Hu Shih was a curious one. He was the one who promoted the vernacular medium in which all of the leftists wrote, and he was also the one who through his research succeeded in raising the stature of both novels and novelists in public esteem. Yet he was regarded by the novelists as an antagonist. This was partly because he was inclined toward historical rather than literary research; however, a more important factor was the factionalism among in-

---

142. HSSHPP, III, 83.
143. *Ibid.*, 86.
144. *Ibid.*, 88.
145. TY:SHMC, 58.
146. WCF:CKHW, 66.

tellectuals of different educational backgrounds, which endowed them with incompatible personal traits. As the commonly acknowledged leader of the Western-educated group, Hu could hardly escape the wrath of the leftist group.

In politics, the influence of Hu and his group was equally ambiguous. At the time Hu returned to China from the United States he believed that the rejuvenation of China had to come about gradually through moral and literary reform. Politics was not to him a basic issue and merited no special attention.[147] By 1919, however, the collapse of Confucianism had led to an agitated search for its replacement. Hu's one-time allies, Ch'en Tu-hsiu and many others now talked exclusively in terms of "isms," which Hu defined as abstractions extracted from concrete proposals at one time, but applied indiscriminately to all occasions in later times.[148] The tendency seemed to Hu to be highly "unscientific" and even dangerous. Hence in an article he publicly urged "more study of concrete problems and less talk of 'isms' " (not realizing that his own advocacy of "total Westernization" also came dangerously close to being a sweeping generality). At any rate, the article marked the beginning of Hu's participation in the discussion of political problems. From 1922 to 1923, Hu, with his friend V. K. Ting, and others, edited the political journal *Endeavor.*

In May, 1922, sixteen well-known intellectuals, including Ts'ai Yüan-p'ei, Wang Ch'ung-hui, Lo Wen-kan, V. K. Ting, and Hu, published a statement of their political beliefs. Basically, they urged a "good" government that would eradicate corruption, further public welfare, and foster individual freedom. More specifically, they advocated a constitutional regime that would have an open financial and personnel system, a definite program, and functionaries who "believed in their own goodness and integrity."[149] In a subsequent article, Ting described a good man as doing four basic things: practicing what he expected of others, having a professional status and seeking to improve it (so that he would have independent means of living), avoiding a lavish personal life, and organizing a small group of from four to nine like-minded persons in preparation for political activities.[150]

During the seventeen-month existence of *Endeavor,* Hu was politically active. He maintained close contact with the leading members of the Peking regime and sought to convince them of a plan he had for the future of China, namely, to amalgamate the northern and southern governments, to accept financial assistance from the consortium composed of British, French, American, and Japanese

---

147. HS:WT (1953), I, 58.
149. HS:TWC, 37.
148. *Ibid.,* III, 343.
150. *Ibid.,* 38.

financiers, and to establish a federal political structure for China.[151] Since three of the sixteen men who urged a "good government" for China had become cabinet ministers—Wang Ch'ung-hui as premier, Lo Wen-kan as minister of finance, and T'ang Erh-ho as minister of education—Hu entertained high hopes for his own plan. To enlist the backing of a powerful warlord, Wu P'ei-fu, Hu contacted his aides Pai Chien-wu, Sun Tan-lin, and Kao En-hung.[152] To secure American support, Hu kept in close contact with Paul Reinsch, a former American envoy to China then visiting Peking.[153] To sound out public opinion, Hu published on September 14, 1922, an article titled "If We Were the Prime Minister." On October 1 he published another, titled "International China," in which he vigorously defended the West, arguing that the beneficial influence resulting from American participation in the four-power consortium had amply demonstrated American capitalists' good will toward China, that foreign investors were as anxious as the Chinese to see China unified and peaceful, and that the Chinese should work for this goal instead of imagining foreign aggressions.[154] Coming as it did after the Second Congress of the Chinese Communist Party had called on all Chinese to oppose imperialism, Hu's article was interpreted by the leftists as a challenge to them.[155]

Another man Hu defied at this time was Sun Yat-sen, who had vowed to crush the Peking regime by force. Hu warmly praised Ch'en Chiung-ming when he revolted against Sun in June, 1922.[156] While declining Ch'en's invitation to join him in Canton, Hu continued to urge him to be a second Yen Hsi-shan (a warlord entrenched in his native province Shansi).[157] One reason for Hu's refusal was probably the uncertain situation in the south, but another was his hope for a genuine "good" government in the north. Unfortunately, Wang Ch'ung-hui's cabinet fell in November, 1922, and *Endeavor* ceased publication in October, 1923.[158]

Hu's third attempt to participate in politics began with the appearance of the *Crescent Monthly* in 1928. For a time he was critical of the new Kuomintang regime. He censored the government for denying the people their basic rights and demanded the promulgation of a constitution.[159] He also sneered at the "revolutionary regime's policy of preserving the old tradition and resisting cultural

151. HSSHPP, III, 49, 53; VII, 147.   152. *Ibid.*, III, 51.
153. *Ibid.*, III, 51-52.   154. *Ibid.*, I, 60-61; III, 51-52.
155. *Ibid.*, VII, 150; NL (October 21, 1923), 1-2.
156. NL (June 25, 1922), 1.   157. HSSHPP, III, 50.
158. *Ibid.*, III, 52.
159. HSSHPP, VI, 150-51; Hu Shih, "Human Rights and the Kuomintang," HY (April 10, 1929), 1-7; Hu Shih, "The New Culture Movement and the Kuomintang," HY (September 10, 1929), 1-15.

influences from abroad."[160] In April, 1930, he set forth his own political views in an article titled "Which Route Should We Take."
Stressing that China's enemies were not capitalism, feudalism, or
imperialism, but poverty, disease, ignorance, corruption, and internal
disturbances, he argued that these evils could be conquered gradually
with the aid of science, but not through armed conflicts among political factions. In subsequent open letters to Liang Shu-ming, who
commented on his article, Hu repeated his view that neither China's
poverty nor her civil wars could be blamed on imperialism because
China had been poor long before the Westerners arrived and because
most of China's civil wars involved no foreigners. In his opinion,
rather, it was the intellectuals who had always stirred up disturbances
—for instance, the Communist insurrections.[161]

The same stand characterized Hu's article of November, 1930,
titled "An Introduction to My Own Thought." In this piece he
pointedly remarked: "Some Ch'an (Zen) monk of centuries ago said
that Budhidharma came all the way to China to search for a man who
would not be deceived by men. In these essays, I too wish to present
a method of how not to be deceived by men. To be led by the nose
by a Confucius or a Chu Hsi is not highly commendable. But to be
led by the nose by a Marx, a Lenin, or a Stalin is also not quite becoming a man."[162] Perhaps it was on this anti-Communist stand
that a relationship developed between Hu and the Kuomintang
leaders. Toward the second half of the year 1930 we find him writing
to Chiang Kai-shek's personal secretary, Ch'en Pu-lei, saying that
"since mutual understanding was prerequisite to a sharing of views,"
he hoped that Ch'en and Chiang would look at the *Crescent Monthly*
he enclosed.[163]

Apparently, things went well. By the time the Manchurian incident occurred in September, 1931, Hu was busily corresponding with
high officials in Nanking. Some time later, he received the offer of a
cabinet post. Declining, he wrote to Wang Ching-wei: "After mature
consideration I feel that I can contribute more by staying outside
the government than inside it . . . for then at some critical moment
I may be able to utter impartial views which would benefit the
country. . . . Directly or indirectly, this would also benefit the Government."[164] The impartial opinion Hu later propounded centered
around two points, supporting the Nanking regime against internal
dissenters and advocating concessions to Japan in the Sino-Japanese
dispute. Both were controversial views. Ever since Chiang Kai-shek's
advance to power, he had been faced with armed opposition. The

160. *Ibid.*, VII, 157.   161. HS:WT (1953), IV, 429-46.
162. *Ibid.*, 623-24. See also Hu's article "John Dewey in China (1919-21)," in
AS (September 26, 1959), 5.
163. HSSHPP, III, 60.   164. *Ibid.*, 62.

Kwangsi generals revolted in 1929; a large number of Chiang's opponents rallied in an "Enlarged Conference" at Peking in 1930; the Canton warlords seceded in 1931; the Communists withstood five campaigns of annihilation from 1930 to 1934. Moreover, student opposition became widespread after Japan occupied Manchuria. They commandeered free passage to the capital by lying on the railway tracks to prevent the movement of trains. They attacked government offices and assaulted high officials. Yet Chiang was determined to wipe out the Communists before he would fight external foes. To promote unity within the party he made Wang Ching-wei head of the Executive Yüan in January, 1932, but this in no way satisfied his critics. They unceasingly berated him for his inaction toward foreign aggressors, and the Communists made political capital by appealing for resistance to Japan. Both Chiang and Wang were embarrassed, and it was under these circumstances that Hu launched *The Independent Review* to influence public opinion.

In the inaugural number Hu stressed an editorial policy of political independence and intellectual tolerance. From May 22, 1932, to July 28, 1937, he personally wrote over a hundred articles.[165] Basically, he favored a new elite of intellectuals, merchants, and technicians to serve as the central political force of China: political unification through some measure of decentralization; and a drastic curtailment of governmental power—i.e., a voluntary restraint by Chiang Kai-shek in imposing his own will. With Ting, Hu believed that China lacked the conditions for a planned economy and that attempts toward that goal should cease. He praised Chiang's leadership but urged him to delegate more power to others.[166]

On the more pressing issue of political freedom, Hu and his group were at one with the government. They missed no opportunity to berate the radicals. Even before the review appeared, Hu had made speeches stressing that every government had a right to suppress subversive activities, and his views had been reported in the influential English newspaper of Shanghai, the *North China Daily News*.[167] Later, when the League for the Protection of Human Rights led by Lu Hsün, Yang Ch'üan, and Mme Sun Yat-sen demanded the government to release all political prisoners, Hu dissented by saying that this was tantamount to asking immunity for subversive activities.[168] In 1933, when a secessionist move was made by Fukien, Hu roundly denounced the leaders. And when the Kwangsi generals plotted to set up a separate regime in 1936, Hu personally cabled the leaders urging them to avoid a crisis. He also wrote a Sunday editorial for the influential *Ta Kung Pao* asserting that public opinion would not tolerate any splinter move and that dire consequences would befall

165. Li Shu-hua, *op. cit.*, 10.   166. HSSHPP, III, 66-67.
167. *Ibid.*, 90.   168. *Ibid.*, VII, 158-59.

the southern generals if they went through with their intentions. This article was published simultaneously in Shanghai and Tientsin. Chiang was informed in advance of its contents.[169] By 1937 relations between the two men were so smooth that Hu wrote: "Mr. Chiang Kai-shek's courage and ability are truly extraordinary. Some of his policies have already yielded results. We cannot but be convinced. His achievement has inspired men to trust in their leader."[170]

On the crucial issue of Sino-Japanese relations, Hu advocated negotiation and compromise. Shortly after Japan occupied Mukden, he organized a discussion group that he called Society for the Study of Possible Concessions to Japan (*Tui-jih jang-pu yen-chiu-hui*).[171] In September, 1932, the report of the Lytton Commission was published. While many Chinese found its views of China and its suggestion for an autonomous Manchuria humiliating, Hu gave these his emphatic endorsement. He warmly praised the commission for its industry, impartiality, and love of peace.[172] When the report was rejected by Japan, and the League of Nations failed to offer any solution to the conflict, Hu counseled the Chinese people to be patient and to allow fifty years for the recovery of the lost territory.[173] As Japan penetrated farther into China, Hu suggested to Chiang Kai-shek the idea of demilitarizing the two provinces of Charhar and Hopeh.[174] When the Ho-Umetsu agreement was signed in June, 1935, providing for the withdrawal of all Kuomintang agencies and troops from Hopeh and Charhar, Hu endorsed the move in the face of intense public animosity. According to him, the ability to suffer aggression in silence and dignity indicated a new strength and a new hope for China.[175]

On January 21, 1936, foreign minister Hirota announced three principles on which Japan would conduct her relations with China: (1) China should forsake the policy of playing one foreign nation against another, (2) China should recognize the *fait accompli* in Manchuria, (3) China should join a common cause with Japan against Communism. Fearing the unfavorable reaction of the Chinese public, the Kuomintang government immediately dissociated itself from these principles.[176] In February, Hu Han-min, a prominent party leader who had bitterly opposed Chiang since 1931, granted an interview to a Japanese and took the opportunity to rebuke Hirota.[177] Undaunted by these gestures, Hu wrote an article on

169. *Ibid.*, III, 70; Hu Shih, "Looking Toward 1937," in *Ta Kung Pao*, as quoted in HSSHPP, II, 337.
170. *Ibid.*, II, 337.
171. *Ibid.*, III, 62; TLPL (October 9, 1932), 2-6.
172. *Ibid.*, 68-69.   173. *Ibid.*, VI, 115.
174. *Ibid.*, II, 68; TLPL (June 16, 1935), 2-3.
175. *Ibid.*, I, 65.   176. KYT:CTSC, 415.
177. *Ibid.*, 417; TLPL (April 19, 1936), 3-5; (May 15, 1936), 2-5.

April 12 in which he dwelled lengthily on Hirota's third principle. In a nutshell, he maintained that an anti-Communist front under Japanese domination would serve little purpose because it would only arouse the Chinese and increase their sympathy for the Communists.[178] The meaning of this article was a subtle one. By leaving out the first two principles, he implied their feasibility; by arguing against the third one, he was appealing for concessions by Japan. Meanwhile, the article was an effort to sound out public opinion in both countries. This trial balloon got nowhere, however. The Chinese press denounced Hu with vehemence.

Even after the Sino-Japanese conflict broke out in Peking in July, 1937, Hu continued to maneuver for peace. He and several others, including Chou Fo-hai, and Ch'en kung-po, formed a "Low Tune Club" (*Ti-tiao chü-lo-pu*) to counteract the prevailing heroic talk and to advocate negotiation with Japan.[179] Efforts in this direction claimed Hu's attention throughout July and August. The August 6 entry in his diary in part reads:

> . . . Returning home I received word that Mr. Chiang wanted to talk to me. I thereupon prepared a long letter, to be used if our talk should prove inadequate. In it I stressed that before declaring war we must make the utmost effort for peace. There are three reasons for this: (1) negotiation with Konoe's cabinet is possible. This opportunity should be grasped, (2) Japan's financial conditions are bad; hence peace has hope, (3) the hope of China today is built on the modern army controlled by the central government. This should not be lightly thrown away. Peace will be more unlikely if [this basic strength of] the nation is shattered.
>
> We have two goals in negotiating for peace. First, bargaining from our ability to fight, we should try to protect our present territory and to recover the recently lost ones. Second, we should seek fifty years of peace through a thorough readjustment of Sino-Japanese relations.
>
> This negotiation should have two stages: first, a truce to recover the conditions prior to July 7; second, formal talks to start within two to three months for the readjustment of Sino-Japanese relations.[180]

While Hu's efforts failed to halt the war, he had plainly tried to prevent it.

Consistent with his support for Chiang and his belief in negotiation with Japan, Hu disapproved of all the student demonstrations and made no secret of his position. Meanwhile, the students came increasingly under Communist influence. In 1932, they opposed

178. HSSHPP, VI, 117.   179. *Ibid.*, VII, 167.
180. *Ibid.*, III, 71-72; TLPL (July 10, 1932), 14-15.

the heavier academic load decreed by the government and called it a "Fascist" measure. In a special article Hu challenged this label and bluntly stated that the whole movement was "a game played by students who had no intention to learn but every wish to create disturbance."[181] On December 9, 1935, the students in Peking demonstrated against the autonomous regime in east Hopeh and the Japanese-inspired movements for self-government in northern China. The demonstrators urged a united front by all Chinese, Nationalists as well as Communists, to fight Japan. In the ensuing melee with the police scores of students were arrested and hundreds were wounded. More demonstrations occurred on December 16 when the semi-autonomous Political Council of Hopeh and Charhar was inaugurated. The strikes spread to other cities, and the government had a hard time maintaining order. Speaking as a teacher, Hu Shih promptly rebuked the students. Writing three days after the first demonstration he stressed that they should differentiate between proper and improper goals, should learn that demagoguery could not prevail, should develop intellectual independence and law-abiding habits, and should remember that social progress could come only through piecemeal achievements by individuals.[182] Ten days later he again emphasized that society would not condone strikes and that the only correct path was for the students to go back to school and make up for the time lost by studying through the winter vacation.[183]

While the extent of Hu's influence is difficult to measure, several things may yet be pointed out. His stand, that China should compromise with Japan while seeking internal unification, was the same as Chiang Kai-shek's except that Hu could advocate it openly while Chiang, because of his official position, could not. He was thus handicapped in the seeking of public support. A factor in his favor was that Manchuria had been in the charge of Chang Hsueh-liang, and when it was lost to Japan, public opinion in China initially held Chang responsible. However, Chiang could not shirk his responsibility indefinitely. His position was weakened by two factors. One was Japan's unceasing aggression, which kept on arousing nationalistic feelings in China, and the other was Chiang's determined campaign against the Communists, which raised a question in the minds of the Chinese as to why Chiang's forces could not be deployed against the external foes. Mounting opposition seriously damaged Chiang's prestige, and he desperately needed a public relations man. Hu's reputation as a progressive and his eminence in scholarship and teaching made him the ideal choice. His cogent reasoning powerfully boosted Chiang's cause.

Small wonder that a number of Hu's cohorts at the *Review* soon

181. *Ibid.*, II, 327; TLPL (December 12, 1935), 4-7.
182. *Ibid.*, VI, 120-21.   183. *Ibid.*, 122.

embarked on colorful official careers. Weng Wen-hao was secretary-general of the Executive Yüan in 1935, minister of economics in 1938, and head of the Executive Yüan in 1945. T. F. Tsiang was ambassador to Russia in 1936, and for many years after World War II China's chief delegate to the United Nations. Ch'en Chih-mai became a councilor of the Executive Yüan in 1938 and later ambassador to Australia. Wu Ching-ch'ao was a senior secretary at the Executive Yüan in 1936 and remained in the civil service for more than ten years.[184] Hsien Wu was appointed head of the Nutrition Institute in 1944. Fu Ssu-nien was a member of the People's Political Council during the war and president of Taiwan University in 1948. A seventh man, V. K. Ting, would certainly have entered the officialdom had death not entervened.

In the midst of all these activities Hu himself pursued a more varied career. In 1925 he had become a trustee of the China Foundation, which dispensed the American Boxer indemnity remissions for educational purposes in China. In 1932 he was appointed to several government commissions, including the board for the administration of the British Boxer indemnity refunds.[185] By the following year he was freely discussing with Wang Ching-wei suitable candidates for the cabinet portfolios of foreign affairs and education.[186] Evidence indicates that he was behind the entrance of a number of his friends into officialdom.[187] In 1938 he was appointed ambassador to the United States with his mission that of influencing American public opinion in favor of China. How well he succeeded was attested both by America's growing sympathy for China and by honors bestowed on Hu himself; between 1939 and 1945 he received no less than twenty-six honorary degrees.[188]

Hu relinquished his office in 1942, but continued to live in America until 1946 when he was appointed president of National Peking University. During his tenure in this office, he sought to discourage student demonstrations through both moral suasion and material inducement in the form of food subsidies.[189] In December, 1946, anti-American demonstrations occurred in many Chinese cities. Initially concerned with a rape charge against an American marine in Peking, the protest soon included a demand for the withdrawals of all American forces from China. In his announcements Hu stressed the isolated nature of the assault case and urged that the matter be kept apart from the political issues. In an interview with a reporter he expressed the view that the basic difficulty was a cultural one:

184. *Ibid.*, III, 111.
186. *Ibid.*, III, 63.
188. YTL:GDD, 225-26.
189. *Ta Kung Pao, Shanghai* (December 30, 1946), as quoted in HSSHPP, VII, 168-69.
185. *Ibid.*, VI, 113.
187. *Ibid.*, III, 62, 68, 111.

"The Americans did not attach as much importance to chastity as did the Chinese." However, he was confident that justice would prevail in the court-martial then being organized.[190]

The focus of Hu's writings in this period was on international politics. In a number of articles he dwelt at length on the growing tension between the United States and Russia. He observed that the conflict came from a basic incompatibility of the two ways of life. Recalling the Western largess toward Russia during the war, he regretted that the Soviet Union should have become within a short while "a frightening aggressive influence" in the world. He admitted that he would have to give up his "past sympathy for Russia," but he had no doubt about the ultimate victory of "democracy and liberty."[191] When the students in China protested against the United States policy toward Japan, he asserted that the U. S. would never tolerate a resurgence of militarism in Japan, and that the Soviet Union was the only power which would not let Japan and Germany live in peace.[192]

Hu's partisanship was obvious concerning China's internal politics. He belittled the assassination of two leftist college professors, Wen I-to and Li Kung-p'u, as a "small incident in the midst of general progress toward democracy."[193] In 1946 he was made a member of the presidium of the National Assembly which adopted a constitution. Afterward Hu compared the meeting to the Continental Congress of 1776. "While fifty-five persons drafted a constitution [*sic*] in America," he said, "China accomplished a similar task with over a thousand delegates."[194] Under the constitution, the first presidential election took place in March, 1948. Feigning reluctance, Chiang Kai-shek spoke of the qualifications of an ideal president, obviously with Hu in mind.[195] His talk started a rumor that Hu was slated for the presidency, but nothing materialized. Chiang was probably less than sincere in his words, and Hu was too clever to be taken in.

On the eve of the Communist takeover in 1948, Hu left Peking in a special airplane sent by Chiang Kai-shek. Shortly thereafter Hu came to the United States. It was known that he would like to be associated with a university, but his wish went unfulfilled except for a short tenure of curatorship at the Gest Oriental Library at Princeton. In 1958 he was recalled to Taipeh to head the Academia Sinica. He died of heart failure on February 24, 1962, while still holding this post.

190. *Ibid.*, 168-69.   191. *Ibid.*, III, 76.
192. Hu's statement at a press conference originally reported in *Ta Kung Pao* (July 20, 1946), as quoted in HSSHPP, III, 74.
193. *Ibid.*, III, 74.   194. *Ibid.*, VII, 171.
195. HSP (April 5, 1948), 2; NYT (April 5, 1948), 1:4; (April 6, 1948), 22:3

In spite of his professed faith in democracy, Hu's political activities demonstrated more opportunism than conviction. In the end he was a mere hanger-on to the Kuomintang regime, respected but not influential. As he aptly stated in a poem, he was a "pawn [in Chinese chess] who could only go forward."[196] An episode in 1959 vividly illustrated his position. As Chiang's second term as president approached its end, a debate waged among his supporters as to whether he should retire or whether the constitution should be amended to permit him a third term. Hu favored Chiang's retirement, but when a third term materialized, he dutifully served in a congratulatory mission from the Assembly to the president. He had indeed become a "pawn" whose only course was to go forward.

Why did a man of Hu's stature have so little political influence? Perhaps the question can best be answered if we first analyze the factors behind Hu's fame. He had a remarkable knowledge of the Chinese classics and an especially lucid style of writing. But the most important element was his American connections. In the first place, when he returned to China in 1917, the prestige of American education was at its highest in China. The combination of his doctorate, his youth, and his facility with the pen marked him out as a man of great promise. These were the qualities that enabled him to reap full advantage of the literary reform campaign, and the path was thus paved for his future.

Secondly, his American training also influenced his thought. As he was fond of saying: "My thought is mostly influenced by two men. . . . Huxley taught me how to doubt and to reject all things for which adequate evidence does not exist; Mr. Dewey taught me how to think, how to deal with problems facing me, how to treat all theories and ideas as hypotheses awaiting test, and how to observe the practical consequences of a thought."[197] While the philosophical worth of Hu's view is debatable, his insistence on correct methods of study performed a most timely service to the Chinese learned world. It was here that Hu's position in history is the least controversial.

It should be noted that Hu's experience in the United States developed in him an enthusiasm for Western civilization. Throughout his life Hu kept up his praise for the West, especially America. Partly by doing so he achieved a unique position. To the Chinese he was a renowned scholar of the West; to the Westerners he was the best and the most agreeable of new China. He prepared himself well for this position. Even during his student days in the United States he cultivated relations with Dewey, Taft, and other well-known personalities. By 1925 he became a trustee of the China Foundation and was in a position to exercise influence on many Chinese learned

196. HSSHPP, II, 355.   197. HS:WT (1953), IV, 608.

institutions. The British government consulted him in the following year concerning its remission of Boxer indemnity funds.[198] As Western acknowledgment of his position grew, his stature in China correspondingly increased. Thus, in a cumulative way he became a Chinese ambassador to the United States, and while there, as a symbol of China's heroic struggle, he was honored by a large number of American universities. This in turn probably led Chiang to remark, however halfheartedly, that an ideal president should be an internationally renowned scholar.[199]

Hu's strength also constituted his weakness, however. In the first place, his commitment to Western culture necessarily limited his audience to men who had some knowledge of the West, i.e., to middle-school students or above in fairly large cities. He could scarcely communicate with the peasants in any meaningful way. Although he always wrote in a vernacular medium, it was in reality only a lengthened form of the literary language and very far removed from the true colloquial. He engaged in political pamphleteering, but in his writings he addressed himself more to the men in power than to the man in the street. This was not necessarily because he wished to enter officialdom or sympathized with any particular group of politicians, but rather because he believed in gradualism and in seeking political accomplishment through existing leadership. As a logical consequence, he was ready to support a strong government and to defend it against opposition, but unwilling to form a political party of his own. A further characteristic was his coolness toward all mass political movements. Unlike Liang Ch'i-ch'ao or Ch'en Tu-hsiu, he never tried to stir up the people, but he almost always opposed the popular cause. Indeed, one suspects that his exaltation of expert knowledge originated from his inner aversion to mass ignorance. Thus, in contrast to Sun Yat-sen, Hu may well be described as a cultural radical who was politically conservative.

But Hu's approach had its own limitations. For one thing, the men in power might not share Hu's enthusiasm for the West. Thus, throughout the twenties he was little appreciated by the warlords. His political star rose only after Chiang Kai-shek decided to fight the Communists with all possible Western support. Secondly, the goal of serving the powers that be necessitated a frequent shift of views. Over the years Hu's opinion was noticeably variable. In 1922 he severely criticized Sun Yat-sen for his talk of a northern expedition. He warmly praised the Kuomintang rebel Ch'en Chiung-ming for his endeavor to curb Sun's "perverse schemes."[200] Seeking rapport with the warlord Wu P'ei-fu, he advocated federalism as the best means to

198. HS:TWC, 59-61.
199. NL (December 31, 1922), 2; HT (March 14, 1925), 883-84.
200. HSSHPP, I, 40.

counter the tendency toward the breakup of China into satrapies.[201]
He denied the possibility of an imminent revolution and spoke of a
government by good men—i.e., his own group.[202]

Nearly all of these ideas changed after Chiang Kai-shek had consolidated his power. Hu was now opposed to secessionist moves, and
the members of the *Review* variously advocated the military unification of China under "a new dictatorship," which would make full
use of the available experts and which would practice "*laissez-faire*"
by delegating power to others. Even Hu's diplomatic views varied.
In 1933 he echoed the Stimson Doctrine of non-recognition and
urged the Chinese to wait fifty years for the recovery of Manchuria.
By 1936, as Japan penetrated further into China, Hu's goal was only
to recover "the newly lost territories."[203] In reviewing Hu's thought,
the only two consistent points seem to have been his willingness to
compromise with the *status quo* and his belief in Western superiority.

Yet these two traits conflicted in implications. For there is no
doubt that Hu's willingness to compromise with the *status quo* came
from his belief in gradualism, while his esteem for the West led him
to decry the Chinese culture. But gradualism is incompatible with
the rejection of tradition. If China is inferior to the West in every
respect, as Hu insisted, then only drastic social engineering can save
China. On the other hand, if true amelioration could only be piecemeal, as Hu also asserted, then the cultural heritage has to be respected. By combining gradualism with a rejection of tradition Hu
put himself in an untenable position. He was in this respect far less
consistent than either Ch'en Tu-hsiu, who favored revolution, or
Yen Fu, who wanted change through stability. It is interesting to
speculate on the reasons why Hu failed to achieve some synthesis out
of his two strains of thought. Possibly he was a gradualist by inclination and a Westernizer by design. Having gained fame through
his condemnation of Chinese culture, he felt that he had to advocate
Westernization, while co-operation with existing leadership represented his pragmatic approach to politics.

As we have seen, Hu was not entirely typical of the Western-
educated intellectuals. Nevertheless, there are perhaps some common
features. Our study of the scientists and writers indicates that during
the past five decades the role of intellectuals in Chinese society has
changed. So has their outlook. Instead of a homogeneous group
selected on the basis of literary excellence, administrative ability, and
conformity to Confucian virtues, the top Chinese elite now had their
specialized fields. Among other things, this caused them to move
away from politics. Even those who participated in politics did so
with an entirely different spirit from that of the old scholar-official.

201. *Ibid.*, VII, 148-49.   202. *Ibid.*, I, 40.
203. *Ibid.*, VII, 182.

Men like Shiing-shen Chern had no particular interest in politics; Hsien Wu had only a little; even Ting and Hu were only amateurs. They were proud of their own professions, believing that a politician who has his own means of support is encumbered with less vested interests. But they failed to see that an amateur politician is also limited in his potential achievement. He is unlikely to be a revolutionary but tends to be on somebody else's bandwagon. The change from the old role to the new has weakened the voice of the intellectuals by weakening this political attachment.

Of the forces underlying the change, the new education was one of the most powerful. In contrast to the old Chinese education, modern specialized training deals with the means but not the ends of life. In the course of such training, a man is taught to exclude rigorously his own value judgment in order to become more objective. A scholar is usually detached from politics, and if he joins the government for want of any other suitable outlet, he does so in the capacity of an expert, that is to say, he has a trade but no mission to perform. He will carry out to the best of his capacity decisions reached by others, which are of course always couched in respectable terms as being in the best interests of the country. Even if he wishes to look behind the phrases and question the implications of a policy, he would be deterred by the inherent limitations of his own knowledge, for the more specialized man is, the narrower is his field of competence. Consequently, the best-trained man is often the most helpless in judging the merits of political leadership. Only after the situation has deteriorated beyond repair, or only when acute personal hardship is experienced, does a scholar descend from his ivory tower into the realm of politics.

An illustration of this is the case of the late Wen I-to, a distinguished American-trained poet who persisted in his literary romanticism until 1944, when the combination of personal poverty and awakened social conscience led to an outburst of political activity for the Left. He was assassinated soon afterwards.[204] While in this case Wen might be said to have died for a political cause, the haphazard nature of his behavior rather indicates another feature of the political life of top scholars in China: instead of leading the lower intellectuals and the masses, they trailed them in political sentiment. Every major student movement from 1919 to 1949 seems to have demonstrated this truism. English- and American-educated academicians might have added fuel to the fire by their passively critical attitude toward the government, but they had exercised little positive leadership in these movements. Rather it was the leftists and Communists who infiltrated the colleges and continually harassed the government by organizing student strikes and demonstrations.

204. K. Y. Hsü, "The Life and Poetry of Wen I-to," HJAS, 1958.

Another ramification of the new education was its influence on scholars' writing habits. Previously the pattern of a learned man was to write voluminously on morals and related subjects, to compose poems, to keep up correspondence with a large circle of friends, and to save all of his manuscripts for his "collected works." It was mainly through this means that a scholar became known to his peers and beyond them to a public, who, though less sophisticated, were conditioned by custom to appreciate his performance. This pattern of social action broke down under Western impact. Few Anglo-American-trained specialists wrote. Most of them had little facility with their language. Chinese was rarely emphasized at school; the increasing tempo of life tended to restrict attempts at literary proficiency; and prolonged periods abroad without using the language made it even less usable. Thus most of the Western-educated elite did not write and had no rapport with the public.

Among those who did write, the nature of their efforts had changed. Their topics were often specialized, and the substance unintelligible to the public. When Hu Shih exalted expertise and devoted himself to historical research, he was not seeking communication with the masses. The same tendency was more pronounced among the scientists. Not only were their interests little related to the more urgent needs of the time but they also made no attempt to communicate their findings in simplified versions to the public. According to a record of the Academia Sinica, the 53 academicians in the physical and biological science divisions had up to 1948 written 42 books and 1,815 papers, of which no less than 16 books and 1,707 papers were in foreign languages, mostly English.[205] As some of these men recently admitted, it was common at the time to emulate Western authorities, to have one's works published in international journals, and to consider the task of popularizing science unscholarly.[206] In this way communications between the Western-educated and the public, including the lower intellectuals, were disrupted.

One can clearly see the political significance of this metamorphosis. Prior to Western impact the pen of a scholar was his best protection. By using it he could vent his feelings, enlist public sympathy, and indict a despot before the bar of history. Now the intellectual was a voiceless man. If he worked in the government, he was unprotected by either public support or civil service regulations that had broken down after the fall of the Manchus. Unless he had factional affiliations, his only source of power was the patronage of the man who had appointed him, for which the price was often unquestioned obedience on his part. Thus one result of the metamorphosis was the diminution of the bureaucrat from a high priest to a tool of powerful men.

205. Compiled from CYYCY.   206. SHKT, 39.

Furthermore, the lack of mass support and the absence of coherent political ideas made political organization impossible. In every Chinese regime since 1912 there have been Western-educated men occupying policy-making positions. Some of them have been prominent for half a century. Yet none of them has headed a party, and all have probably gained longevity at the expense of their beliefs. A second group of less active intellectuals did try to organize, but the units they formed, notably the China Youth and Social Democratic parties, were without exception impotent. Even the Democratic League, formed in 1941 by a long list of prominent academicians, soon degenerated into a satellite of the Communist Party and has never had a voice in any regime.

The whole Western-educated elite was, then, politically weak. Among other things, this situation meant that moral and political leadership, so important to people accustomed to the collective and paternal way of life, had to come from men other than the most Westernized and democratically-inclined group. Neither the detachedness of the scientists nor the upward orientation of Hu and Ting could satisfy the political hunger of the lower intellectuals. Through the inaction of the top elite, the field was left wide open to popular writers of the Left whose inflammatory words in time penetrated the minds of Chinese youth. Although there is no way to demonstrate a causal relationship in concrete terms, it is possible that the trend toward specialization and individualization diminished the chances for democracy in China and thus left the way open for the opposite cause.

If we look at the history of the Kuomintang regime, war was the dominant feature of the whole period from 1926 to 1949. The campaigns began with the Northern Expedition and continued in the conflicts among various cliques inside the Kuomintang. Thus, Chiang Kai-shek fought against the Kwangsi generals from March through June, 1929; against Feng Yü-hsiang from May through October of the same year; against Chang Fa-k'ui and T'ang Sheng-chih from the fall of 1929 to the spring of 1930; against a coalition formed by Wang Ching-wei, Feng Yü-hsiang, Yen Hsi-shan, and others from April through September, 1930. This last campaign lasted six months and reportedly had a quarter of a million casualties. Between May and October, 1931, two rival governments existed in Nanking and Canton. In January, 1934, Ch'en Ming-shu and Ts'ai T'ing-k'ai organized a People's Government in Fukien, and in the summer of 1936, a major rebellion was also brewing in Kwangtung and Kwangsi.[1] In addition, Chiang Kai-shek relentlessly pursued the Communists from 1930 to 1934. Five major campaigns were conducted, and in the last one a million men were deployed on Chiang's side alone.[2] On top of all this, there were external troubles. Japan occupied Manchuria in 1931, launched a local war in Shanghai in 1932, and attempted to conquer all of China in 1937. Shortly after this war ended in 1945, the government renewed its struggle against the Communists. Thus, fighting hardly ceased during the two decades of Kuomintang rule. The only difference was in the regime's adversaries. It is by this criterion that the Kuomintang decades are usually divided into three periods, with the Sino-Japanese war of 1937-45 as the middle phase.

Actually, the initial period from 1928 to 1937 was probably the most important, for in that time Chiang Kai-shek's authority was constantly challenged, and a slight shift of power might have resulted in a change not only of the government but also of the subsequent events. The problem is, therefore, how best to study the Kuomintang regime during the period from 1928 to 1937. We have seen that the dominant feature was war. One of the most crucial factors in any war is its financing; and the study of Kuomintang finances is particularly pertinent to this work because through the ten years between 1928 and 1937, and even beyond that, the Kuomintang's fiscal policy was in the charge of only two men—T. V. Soong and H. H. Kung.

1. LSK:CKH, 171.   2. HH:CKH, 141.

Both of these men were American-educated. While we cannot say that their policies were entirely a result of their educational backgrounds, their situation provides a clear-cut study of the impact of American-educated men on Chinese finances. Only two men were involved; their responsibility was almost all inclusive; and the policies they pursued bore clear marks of Western influences.

The first minister of finance in the Nanking government, T. V. Soong, was born in 1894 in Shanghai. His father, Sung Yao-ju (1866-1918), migrated as a child from his native village on Hainan Island, first to East India and then to Boston.[3] Unhappy as an apprentice in a Chinese tea and silk shop, Sung ran away to join the Coast Guard. Through the influence of one of his officers, he decided to become a Christian, and, when his ship touched Wilmington, N.C., Sung was baptized at the Fifth Street Church and given the name Charles Jones Soon. Through the instrumentality of a Colonel Moore, Soon was released from government service. A Confederate veteran, General Carr, then decided to invest in the boy, sending him first to Trinity College and later to Vanderbilt University. In 1885, Charles Jones Soon graduated in theology from Vanderbilt and was promptly ordained and appointed a missionary to China by the Methodist Episcopal Church, South. Unfortunately, after Soon's arrival at Shanghai, he was unable to work easily with his superintendent, Young J. Allen, who admired Chinese culture and took a dim view of Soon's unscholarly background. On his part, the young man, having "felt the easy chair" while in the United States, resented being treated as a native preacher at fifteen dollars a month. He decided to leave the Mission and establish himself in business. Within a few years he had founded a printing house which published Bibles. Some wealthy men recognized the value of his American background and made him the manager of a flour mill in Shanghai and an industrialist in a modest way. Like many others of the new middle class, Soon became disillusioned with the Manchu government and associated himself with the revolutionaries. It is not clear how he became a friend of Sun Yat-sen; but in 1910, when Soon was a political refugee in Japan, his eldest daughter, Eling, was Sun's English secretary. In that year Eling married H. H. Kung and let her younger sister Chingling take over her job with Sun. Later, Sun left his wife and married his secretary, a girl twenty-four years his junior.[4]

While Charles Jones was in America, he had encountered S. C. New, one of the C.E.M. boys. In 1887 the two met again in Shanghai, and New's efforts resulted in Charles Jones's marriage to Ni Kwei-tseng, a descendant of the famous Catholic official, Hsü Kuang-ch'i of the Ming. There were six children from this marriage. Tse-vung, or T. V., Soong was the third. He was preceded by two sisters, who were

3. CET:CC, 13 ff.   4. YL:KHH, 28.

later destined to marry Kung and Sun Yat-sen. In accordance with their father's wishes, the two girls entered the missionary McTyeire School when they were barely five and seven years old. Because the Methodists had no school for boys in Shanghai, T. V. was sent to the Episcopal St. John's College, which had special classes for wealthy young students with church connections.[5]

In 1912 the government sent T. V. Soong to America with a number of other "revolutionary workers." After spending some time at Vanderbilt, he went to Harvard as a second-semester sophomore. Upon graduation in 1915, he found a job with the International Banking Corporation, at the same time taking graduate courses in economics at Columbia. In 1923 he went to Canton, where a year later his brother-in-law, Sun Yat-sen, made him general manager of the new Central Bank. During the Northern Expedition, Soong was reportedly one of the men who persuaded the Shanghai bankers to throw their support to Chiang Kai-shek. For this signal service he was appointed to the portfolio of finance, where he raised huge sums to finance Chiang's campaigns.[6]

Yet true to his business experience in America, Soong strenuously advocated economy in military expenditure and recommended sound government credit management and strict budgetary control. It was at least partly this approach that drew the new business leaders to him and made them his personal friends. Indeed, one of Soong's first acts as the minister of finance was to convene a National Economic Conference among the nation's leading merchants, industrialists, bankers, and financial experts. The meeting was held in Shanghai from June 20 to 30, 1928. In his opening address, Soong stressed the unprecedented nature of such a conference in China and expressed his hope that the "people" would share in making economic plans with the government.

During the following ten days, five groups of resolutions were passed by the conference. The first group urged the reduction of the army from more than eighty to fifty divisions and the curtailment of annual military expenditure from an estimated C$360 million to C$192 million. The second advocated the promotion of commerce through the recovery of tariff autonomy, currency reforms, restoration of privately owned means of transportation to their owners, the settlement of industrial disputes by enacting labor laws, and the abolition of injurious internal levies. The third suggested methods for more effective control of government indebtedness, such as the creation of a sinking fund and the establishment of a committee to renegotiate inadequately secured loans. The fourth recommended proper demarcation between national and local finances, adoption of a national budget, and tighter central control over provincial administrations.

5. CET:CC, 44.   6. CB (1941), 808.

The fifth, and last, group of resolutions called for the establishment of a powerful central bank, the promulgation of regulations governing private banks, and the introduction of a standard national currency.[7]
Undoubtedly these five resolutions embodied the major policies of T. V. Soong. With a few important exceptions, they also became the basic financial program pursued by the Nanking regime. During the next five years a number of steps were taken to achieve these goals. First, immediately upon the close of the Economic Conference, another conference was held for the provincial and central financial administrators. In addition to endorsing the programs suggested by the business leaders, the conferees made a number of additional recommendations, one of which suggested the assignment of land tax to the provinces in order to help demarcate national and local finances.[8] To facilitate the implementation of economic reforms, the Ministry of Finance invited many American experts to China; E. W. Kemmerer, A. N. Young, O. C. Lockhart, F. A. Cleveland, F. B. Lynch, B. W. Wallace, William Watson, Clifford Hewitt, and R. J. Grant were prominent among those who came. Kemmerer, head of a commission of over ten experts, urged China to adopt a gold standard currency. Although this recommendation was not adopted, the Nanking government did replace the tael, an artificial unit of account used by customs, with a new Gold Unit. Two years later, the regime further banned all forms of the tael and introduced a standard national dollar. On January 1, 1931, it also abolished the *likin,* an obnoxious transit tax which merchants had long resented and all commentators had condemned.[9]

Even more significant progress was made in the realm of regaining tariff autonomy. Throughout the Nanking period, the most important source of revenue was the customs' receipts, but earlier governments had allowed control of that revenue source to fall into foreign hands. As early as 1843, China was forced to concede to Britain a customs rate of 5 per cent for both exports and imports. In Article X of the same treaty, China also agreed to exempt British goods from internal dues once a transit tax of 2.5 per cent had been paid.[10] In 1862, China granted Russia the reduced rate of 3.5 per cent on merchandise shipped across land frontiers,[11] and because of the most favored nation clause, the privileges granted Britain and Russia were shared by other treaty nations. Furthermore, beginning with 1853, China gradually lost her control over the customs administration itself. By an agreement of 1898, the actual head of the service, the inspector-general, was required to be a British subject for at least as long as

7. CHY (1935-36), 1171-74. 8. *Ibid.,* 1175.
9. *Ibid.,* 1272-73. 10. *Ibid.,* 1256-57.
11. *Ibid.,* 1257. All rates were ad valorem unless otherwise specified.

British trade exceeded that of any other state.[12] When the revolution of 1911 interrupted the repayment of certain foreign loans secured on custom receipts, the foreign Diplomatic Corps obtained from the Manchu regime an agreement whereby all customs funds would be deposited with the inspector-general.[13] This meant that without the latter's consent, the Chinese government had no access to its own revenues.

The whole system was odious to the Chinese. They resented as much their inability to change the 5 per cent tariff rate as their failure to collect even that modest sum. During the eighty-three years from 1843 to 1926, only four adjustments were sanctioned by the powers. The first revision in 1858 was actually a reduction of duties because commodity prices had been declining. The other three revisions were increases, but they were all placebos granted for special political reasons. The 1902 adjustment was to enable China to pay the huge Boxer indemnity; the one in 1918 constituted a rather meager reward for China's role during the First World War; and the 1922 revision was an offshoot of the Washington Conference, from which China had expected far more than she obtained.[14] Furthermore, even with these revisions, China never really collected an effective 5 per cent from her imports and exports. Because of the continual rise in commodity prices, the actual amount of duties quickly fell below the supposed percentage after each readjustment.

It was not until the 1920's that conditions began to change. In October, 1926, the Kuomintang government in Canton unilaterally levied a surtax of 2.5 per cent on all articles of import and 5 per cent on luxuries.[15] Soon after the conclusion of the Northern Expedition, the regime obtained tariff autonomy from the powers. New rates were announced on December 7, 1928, and went into effect on February 1, 1929. Between that time and 1937, Nanking changed the import tariff five times, in January, 1931, in August, 1932, in May and December, 1933, and in July, 1934.[16] In the tariff of February, 1929, the rates ranged from 7.5 to 27.5 per cent.[17] Though nominally remaining in force until 1932, this schedule was actually changed through the introduction in February, 1930, of the Customs Gold Unit, a theoretical token having a gold content of 60.1866 centigrams whose daily exchange value was fixed by the Central Bank of China. By requiring the merchants to pay their duties on a gold basis, the Ministry of Finance actually achieved a 25 per cent increase on import levies.[18] In January, 1931, an import tariff readjustment led to increases ranging from 5 to over 60 per cent. In August, 1932, the Chinese customs

12. CT:CKP, 78.
13. CHY (1935-36), 1258.
14. Ibid., 1260-61; MHFLDF, 180-81.
15. CHY (1935-36), 1262.
16. Ibid., 1265-66.
17. Ibid. 1263.
18. WSF:CSTA, 652.

were ousted from Manchuria. The loss in revenue amounted to some forty million Chinese dollars a year. To compensate for this loss, the government decreed an immediate increase in the import tariffs. Thirty-four groups of commodities were affected, and the average increase was 60.65 per cent.[19] In May, 1933, steep increases were further decreed, especially on cotton goods. The rise on imitation poplins was roughly 800 per cent; on certain types of woolen goods, 200 per cent; and on various grades of paper, from 8 to 280 per cent.[20] A new tariff was introduced in June, 1931, on China's exports, with rates changed from 5 to 7.5 per cent ad valorem.[21]

Meanwhile, Minister Soong took a series of steps to improve and Sinify the customs administration. Before 1928 the Chinese organ in nominal charge of customs was the Shui Wu Ch'u, an office independent of the Ministry of Finance. In June of that year, this office was renamed Kuan Wu Shu (Bureau of Customs Affairs) and placed under the Ministry of Finance. In September the inspector-general of customs was notified that he was immediately responsible to the bureau chief in the ministry, and in November he was further ordered to move the inspectorate from Peking to Nanking (and later to Shanghai).[22] At the same time, the inspector-general was directed to deposit all import duties in excess of that collectable under the Import Tariff of 1922, with the Central Bank of China. On February 28, 1929, the ministry instructed the inspector-general not to engage additional foreign staff members and to accord equal opportunities to Chinese and foreign staff members.[23] Now the ministry, upon the recommendation of the inspector-general, might appoint any Chinese to the highest rank within the service. In April, 1929, the ministry required that Chinese be the official language of the customs service, and for the first time two Chinese were appointed as commissioners of customs at Hangchow and Soochow.[24] In December of that year, the ministry succeeded in removing A. H. F. Edwards from his position as the inspector-general and appointed in his stead Frederick Maze.[25] With a view to improving the caliber of the Chinese staff members, the ministry sent the most promising men to study in England and America. Moreover, Chinese graduates of universities abroad were recruited, and advanced courses were offered at the Customs College.[26]

Some of the other numerous changes instituted by Soong deserve mention. In April, 1931, the obnoxious system of "drawbacks" was abolished. This was the practice whereby traders could claim refunds of duties when they re-exported their imports abroad. This originally

19. *Ibid.*, 676-77.
20. *Ibid.*, 677.
21. CHY (1935-36), 1266.
22. *Ibid.*, 1263-64.
23. H. D. Fong, "Toward Economic Control in China," NSEQ (July, 1936), 344.
24. PDS:CPF, 175.
25. CHY (1935-36), 1264.
26. *Ibid.*, 1196; WSF:CSTA, 669.

was a privilege exacted from the Chinese Taotai at Shanghai by the British Consul Rutherford Alcock in 1847, but by 1858 it had hardened into a treaty right shared by all the powers. Like many other Western-imposed institutions, the practice soon gave rise to the most flagrant abuses. Certificates were often altered illegally so that they might be used a second or third time. In this way, traders secured drawbacks on goods which they did not re-export. Sometimes import certificates, after having been approved for drawback and entered in the register of one broker, would be surreptitiously removed from the customs' office. Then the name of another broker would be substituted, and the goods in question would be entered again for drawback in the register of the second broker. Even more often, expensive goods were replaced by broken bricks, stones, and rubbish packed in cases with similar marks and of like weight, for re-export and the right of drawback.[27] Soong's abolition of this practice on April 1, 1931, was in accord with the rising public demand to end all Western abuses in China.

The directive of March 1, 1932, provided another major innovation by its decree that all customs revenues, except the part reserved for the pension funds of foreign personnel, were to be deposited with the Central Bank. Thus ended the practice that began in 1911 of entrusting the important customs receipts to the care of a foreign inspector-general. The significance of this measure was both political and financial. The ability of a foreign employee to withhold vital sources of revenue from a government could not avoid having the most sinister political implications, and the custody of funds to the magnitude of an average C$100 million spelled economic power.[28] It was no accident that the Hongkong and Shanghai Banking Corporation, which had held the lion's share of this deposit, was the most powerful financial concern in China. The shift from this firm to the Central Bank signified both the decline of British influence and the rise of Chinese state power.

Soong also dealt with the problem of smuggling, which became rampant after China had achieved tariff autonomy and increased duties. Partly because of her extended coast line, but more significantly because of her loss of control over such key areas as Hongkong and North China (during the mid-1930's), smuggling often became a large-scale, highly organized venture against which the Chinese government could do little. Soong did do all that he could. In November, 1930, the ministry ordered all anti-smuggling forces to carry arms and use them when needed. Early in 1931 it established a preventive department and created a fleet, which by 1934 consisted of twenty-six main seagoing vessels and thirty-three launches.[29]

27. *Ibid.*, 664-65.   28. TF:BFC, 100.
29. WSF:CSTA, 661-62.

As a result of the tariff changes and administrative improvements, the customs revenue increased from C$179 million in 1928-29 to C$369 million in 1931-32.[30] Throughout T. V. Soong's tenure as the finance minister, the customs revenue was the leading source of all tax receipts, accounting for 56 to 68 per cent of the total. Territorially, Shanghai was by far the most important port, and in 1933 it collected 51.9 per cent of the revenue.[31] Among the receipts the most important were the import duties which in 1934 accounted for 77.76 per cent of the total customs duties.[32]

Another field in which T. V. Soong's ability found remarkable expression was in the administration of the salt tax. Government control of salt began early in China when Kuan Chung in the seventh century B.C. supposedly explained to his prince the profits that could be derived from a monopoly system. Although the authenticity of this account is doubtful, it is certain that for some two millenniums salt was an essential item in Chinese public finance. Because fiscal income was the only purpose of this taxation, there was a natural tendency to adapt the details of administration to local circumstances. The result was an extraordinarily heterogeneous and cumbersome machinery, which varied from one locality to another. Vested interests developed, and every attempt at reform increased the patchwork nature of the machinery and afforded more room for future entrenched interests. Broadly speaking, state control extended over the manufacture, transportation, and sale of salt. Following a tradition set in the Sung period, the country was divided into eleven salt producing and consumption districts,[33] but rates, regulations, and even the administrative structures varied not only from one district to another but often from one section to another within the same district.[34] The inevitable result was that both the government and the consumers suffered—the former because of loss in revenue and the latter because of their inability to know where they stood. To give one illustration, consumption of illegitimate salt was an offense, but legitimate salt became illegitimate as soon as it moved out of the local administrative boundary; so the people were in constant danger of eating the wrong salt![35] Furthermore, because taxes were many times higher than the cost of the salt, smuggling was rampant throughout the country. According to qualified observers, a full one-third of the salt consumed in the late 1920's escaped taxation.[36]

Like all the other taxes, the salt revenue was collected by the

30. CHY (1935-36), 1194, 1213.   31. *Ibid.*, 1290.
32. Compiled from Table 7, CHY (1936-37), 605.
33. CSI:MKT, 2d series, 2d *pien*, pp. 207-10.
34. TYF:CKY, 131-33.
35. CSI:MKT, 2d series, 2d *pien*, p. 292.
36. *Ibid.*, 262.

provincial governments during the Manchu dynasty. When the constitutional movement began in 1906, the Board of Revenue was reorganized into the Ministry of Finance with a new department to supervise the excise on salt and other taxable commodities. In line with the centralization policy pursued at the time, an Office of Controller-General of the Salt Gabelle was created in December 1909.[37] More administrative reorganization was undertaken in 1911, but the goal of centralizing financial resources remained unfulfilled. At the beginning of the republic, the central government had little income and depended largely on loans to meet its expenditures. In order to use the salt revenue as security, further reform was undertaken. An inspectorate was established within the Ministry of Finance for the purpose of auditing reports from the provinces.[38] In January, 1913, a presidential order required that all salt revenue be placed in a special account, and not be retained by provincial authorities. In April, 1913, the government contracted a loan of £25,000,000 from a five-power consortium. The salt revenue formed a part of the securities. Article V of this Loan Agreement provided for the establishment of a Chief Inspectorate of Salt Revenues with a foreign associate chief-inspector in Peking and with foreign inspectors in the salt-producing districts. These inspectors were to superintend the issue of licenses, to collect all fees and salt dues, and to deposit such proceeds with the Consortium banks.[39]

This system of foreign controlled debt collection aroused deep resentment in China. The provision was viewed as implying a receivership, and it was also felt that economic control would lead to political interference. That the fear was not entirely groundless was shown by the Gold Franc controversy of 1924, when a French bank withheld the salt revenues lodged with it in order to force China to come to terms with France.[40] On the other hand, the foreign-dominated inspectorate undoubtedly performed useful functions. Though largely supervisory in function, it was able to check many abuses and to increase the gross revenue from C$19 million in 1913 to C$98 million in 1922. From the fiscal point of view the problem was not that the inspectorate had too much power; but rather that it had too little. Because it was not an executive agency like the customs service, it was unable to eradicate corrupt practices and was powerless to deal with the local authorities who retained the salt proceeds by force. After 1923, the inspectorate could no longer function effectively because the warlords in various provinces had fallen into the habit of issuing direct orders to Chinese salt officials. As a consequence, the total national collection dropped to C$88 million in 1924 and C$86 million in 1926, while the surplus over the amounts required for the service of loans shrank to

37. BHS:PDPO, 122.   38. TYF:CKY, 126.
39. CHY (1935-36), 1297.   40. WSF:CCR, 216-22.

C$64 million and C$56 million between those two years. The net amounts received by the central government decreased from C$47 million in 1922 to C$31 million in 1924 and to less than C$9 million in 1926. When the Kuomintang army assumed control of Central China in 1927, the salt inspectorate had largely broken down. Its offices in several districts had not been open for years, the charges on the loans had been taken over by the customs administration, and the status of the salt service itself was in doubt.[41]

After an initial period of indecision and experimentation, the new Kuomintang regime decided in November, 1928, to reinstate the Inspectorate Service. Three months later Minister Soong announced the names and stations of the foreign collectors, but made it clear that they were to serve as the subordinate employees of the ministry. He specifically stressed that they would not be in charge of earmarking funds for the repayment of foreign loans. That task, he asserted, was strictly a function of the ministry or its designated representatives. In other words, foreign personnel were now to contribute their expertise without exercising any political power. This of course violated the loan agreement of 1913, but to the joint protest delivered by British, French, and Japanese envoys, Soong merely replied that he was restoring China's inherent rights. As the regime consolidated, and as the salt collection improved, Soong got his way. The powers acquiesced.[42]

A great deal of reform was carried through in the next three years. There had been, previously, two main units in the Chinese salt administration: namely the Salt Commissioner (*Yen-yun-shih*), who was in charge of the producing districts, and the Director of Transportation (*Chüeh-yun-chü-chang*), who was in charge of the shipment and consumption areas. These men were almost always appointed by the regional strong men rather than by the central government. Inevitably much confusion resulted. Each commissariat and directorate had its own anti-smuggling force and was a system in itself.[43] They co-operated little among themselves and clashed even more with the inspectorate. Under Soong, the trend was toward an enlargement of the inspectorate at the expense of the other two units.

In January, 1929, the salt inspectorate was ordered to move its headquarters from Peking to Nanking. In July the director of accounts in the ministry (*k'uai-chi ssu-chang*) was appointed the Chinese chief inspector. During the following month, all the salt commissioners and directors of transportation were ordered to hand over their tax collection to the inspectorate. Meanwhile, as the Kuomintang regime extended its power to new areas, the inspectorate correspondingly enlarged its jurisdiction. Between 1928 and 1929, the ministry's

41. CHY (1935-36), 1299.   42. *Ibid.*, 1301.
43. PDS:CPF, 182-83.

authority reached Hopei, Shantung, Kiangsi, Hupeh, and Honan. In the middle of 1930, the Kwangtung inspectorate was reopened, and by March, 1931, the minister of finance reported that all the inspectorates within the country had been restored.[44] The impact on tax collection was immediate. Gross revenue jumped to C$85 million in 1929, C$129 million in 1930, and C$155 million in 1931.[45]

To achieve a more basic reform, the government instituted a new law on salt on May 30, 1931. Article 1 of this law provided that the duty on salt should be collected at the place of production and that the purchase and sale of salt should not be subject to monopoly. Articles 24 through 26 stipulated that alimentary salt was to be taxed at C$5 and fishery salt at 30 cents per 100 kilograms, that industrial and agricultural salt was to be exempted from duty, and that no surtax or extra charge of any description would be levied. Article 36 decreed that all offices not established in accordance with the law were to be abolished.[46]

Obviously, had the law been enforced, it would have done away with abuses that had existed for centuries in Chinese salt administration. But, mainly because of the pressing fiscal needs, the minister of finance felt unable to enforce any law which, however desirable and productive of revenues in the long run, would cause a temporary decrease in the tax yield. So instead of putting the law into effect, Soong merely prepared for its implementation by more administrative reforms. Aware of both the need for efficiency and the danger of arousing unified opposition among the vested interests, he cleverly retained the salt commissariats and directorates in name but placed the inspectorate officers in concurrent charge of them as the opportunity arose. By 1932, when this process was completed in Honan, Anhwei, Fukien, Shantung, Chekiang, and the four Yangtze areas, two million dollars had been saved in salaries and a great deal had been gained in efficiency.[47] In a similar move toward unification Soong gradually placed all the anti-smuggling forces under the inspectorate.[48] Later, these forces were greatly strengthened.

This administrative revamping yielded substantial gains. Generally speaking, the basic trouble in the old salt system had been too much government control, resulting in cumbersome organization and immense opportunity for graft. Before the inspectorate came into being in 1913, it was customary for the trader to move salt out of the producing area before he paid the taxes. Consequently, he often connived with the officials to cheat the government. The weights used were inaccurate, and the traders claimed excessive allowances of waste. The inspectors stopped many such abuses,[49] but not until the reorga-

44. CHY (1935-36), 1304.
46. TYF:CKY, 286-95.
48. *Ibid.*, 279-80, 285.

45. *Ibid.*, 1308.
47. *Ibid.*, 275.
49. *Ibid.*, 268-70.

nization of 1929 were they able to introduce more positive improvements. By the construction of more depots and a better use of the anti-smuggling forces, the government was able to reduce drastically the illicit trade in salt. It then turned its attention to the tax rates.

Soong realized that a uniform rate for the whole country could not be achieved immediately. One of his reasons was that the rates had varied from twenty cents to twelve dollars per picul of 140 pounds, with no duties levied in areas around some of the producing centers.[50] Even a rate of three dollars would have required of the areas of twenty cents the impossible task of raising their taxation fifteen times. Therefore the only practical method, he believed, was one of gradual improvement. As a preliminary step, the ministry ordered the inspectorate to take over all the surtaxes levied by local authorities. In 1932 it succeeded in simplifying the rate structure, leaving about twenty different rates prevailing throughout the country. A year later the ministry increased the rates in low-tax areas in anticipation of decreasing the rates in high-tax areas. While the work was not completed during the Nanking period, there is little reason to doubt that substantial progress had been made toward a more efficient salt tax structure.[51]

With the reforms in force, gross salt revenue increased from C$59 million in 1927 to C$155 million in 1931. In spite of a slight decline in 1932 because of the Japanese seizure of Manchuria, the receipts in 1933 amounted to C$159 million.[52] Although higher taxes were undoubtedly a factor, administrative improvements in tax collection probably contributed even more to this remarkable increase in revenue. Moreover, as the Kuomintang extended its authority, the amount retained or transferred to local governments declined—for example, it was no more than C$37 million in 1932-33.[53] Consequently, the salt revenue became an important item in the Kuomintang finance. It furnished 26 to 30 per cent of the net total tax revenue in 1931-33.[54]

Payments began as early as March, 1929, in the salt-loan service. By September the minister of finance announced plans for the payment of interest and principal in arrears. Between 1930 and 1934, payment was completed on the arrears of interest of the 1912 Crisp Loan and all arrears of the Hukwang (1911) and of the Anglo-French (1908) loans. Thus the government not only met its own obligations but gradually cleared the defaults of its predecessors.[55]

The third tax matter that Soong tackled successfully was the excise tax. Upon its establishment in April, 1927, the Kuomintang regime

50. CHY (1935-36), 1307. The sums are stated in Chinese currency.
51. *Ibid.*, 1307-8.   52. *Ibid.*, 1308.
53. *Ibid.*, 1309.
54. Calculated from the official financial reports (*ibid.*, 1212-13, 1222-23).
55. *Ibid.*, 1303.

found itself saddled with a motley collection of taxes, surtaxes, and levies collected by innumerable bureaus. Among these were many duplicate taxes, for each of which a different collecting agency was maintained. In 1928, Shanghai alone had 130 national and local tax offices. The Ministry of Finance itself had ten tax units, each with a loosely connected chain of national, provincial, and local offices.[56] As soon as he assumed the portfolio of finance, Soong announced his readiness to consolidate taxes and reduce the number of tax organs, to decree uniform tax rates, and to develop a sound civil service to implement these changes. But the outlook for such reforms was bleak. The central government was poorly consolidated, and the militarists refused to bow to civilian authority. The public, although dissatisfied with the old ways, were little inclined toward innovation. They were only too willing to split profits with the corrupt tax collectors. Those bureaucrats who wished to do a good job suffered either from a lack of familiarity with the cumbersome tax machinery or from an excessive zeal which quickly turned into discouragement when severe difficulties arose.[57] Formidable foreign complications compounded these internal difficulties. Because most industries within the Kuomintang-controlled territory were located in the foreign settlements of Shanghai, the government was unable to collect any excise without the close co-operation of Western authorities. It was necessary therefore to use both diplomatic and administrative skill to bring about a workable tax system.

One of the first steps Soong took was to consolidate the various tax offices. Early in 1928, all of the organs in charge of levies on cigars and cigarettes were merged into the Rolled Tobacco Consolidated Tax Bureaus under the jurisdiction of a special department in the ministry. A little later the Opium Suppression Department and its provincial bureaus were abolished. In July of the same year, the consolidated tax units were placed in charge of the new flour tax, which had been instituted to supersede the numerous *likin* levies on wheat. In February, 1931, the Rolled Tobacco Consolidated Tax Department took over the newly instituted excise taxes on cotton yarn, cement, and matches, and it was then renamed the Consolidated Tax Administration. Meanwhile, two other departments in charge of the tobacco and wine tax and the stamp tax were merged into one department, and in July, 1932, they were amalgamated with the Consolidated Tax Administration to become the Internal Tax Administration.[58] With these mergers and other minor changes, every one of which required much skill and patience to accomplish, all national taxes were finally consolidated into three major services: namely, the Customs, Salt, and Internal Revenue Administrations. In 1932-33, under the new system,

56. *Ibid.*, 1326.   57. *Ibid.*, 1327.
58. *Ibid.*, 1328-29.

the customs yielded 52 per cent of the gross tax revenues, the salt receipts, 26 per cent, and the seven taxes under the internal revenue service, 15 per cent. Among the consolidated taxes, rolled tobacco and cotton yarn levies were by far the most important, contributing respectively 9 and 2.5 per cent to the gross government tax revenues in that year.[59]

Unlike the customs and salt services, the consolidated tax system was largely Minister Soong's own brainchild, and its features are indicative of the man's thinking. First, this tax was enforced on the basis of a single rate for all localities. For example, no local authorities were allowed to levy any surcharges. If this rule was violated, a merchant was permitted to apply to the ministry for refund. Also, if a merchant shipped his goods outside the consolidated tax areas to an area where local taxes were levied on them, he was able to get a ministry refund. Second, all manufacturers of goods liable to the consolidated taxes were required to register with the Internal Revenue Administration. The taxes were collected at the places of registry or, in the case of imported goods, at the point where the goods entered the tax area. By special arrangement with the foreign authorities, an inspection squad was maintained for the prevention of tax evasion in the settlements in Shanghai. In return, the minister of finance pledged himself to the principle of equal treatment for all goods regardless of national origin.

Third, the consolidated tax system was marked by a rapid rate of growth in both the number of commodities and the size of the area of enforcement. Beginning with rolled tobacco in 1928, the consolidated system had incorporated eight other commodities by 1935: namely, cotton yarn, flour, matches, cement, flue-cured leaf tobacco, beer, mineral products, and alcohol. In addition, the same tax office also took charge of the documentary stamp and the native wine and tobacco tax, which, unlike the consolidated taxes, were collected at points of distribution or consumption. Geographically, the consolidated taxes were first introduced in Kiangsu, Chekiang, Anhwei, Fukien, and Kiangsi, but by 1936 the system was operating in sixteen provinces including Szechuan. Apart from Manchuria, the only areas where the taxes were not enforced were the border provinces in which there was little or no manufacture of taxable products.[60] The able management of the consolidated system was reflected both in low collection expenses—4 per cent of the revenue as against 20 per cent in the case of the older wine and tobacco tax—and in its increasing importance in national finance.[61] In 1933-34 it contributed 15.3 per cent of the net government revenues.[62]

59. Calculated on the basis of the financial report (*ibid.*, 1222-23).
60. *Ibid.*, 1332.   61. *Ibid.*, 1329.
62. *Ibid.*, 1224.

As a result of rapid increases in all three main tax revenues, current government receipts increased from C$260 million in 1928-29 to C$559 million in 1932-33, with no substantial change in the value of the dollar.[63] But in spite of such improvements, the Kuomintang continued to incur large deficits. To some extent, this was due to the burden of the indemnity payments and foreign loan obligations contracted by its predecessors. In 1932 such payments required C$122 million or 22 per cent of net total revenue.[64] But by far the most serious drain was the military outlay incurred in civil wars. According to official returns, this item rose steadily from C$131 million in 1928 to C$321 million in 1933.[65] On a percentage basis it claimed some 44 per cent of the total government expenditures.[66]

Furthermore, this figure did not adequately represent the amount spent, because large subsidies to the provinces were often made directly from the tax proceeds, and not in the name of military outlays.[67] Excessive spending naturally led to increasing deficits. In 1931, 30 per cent of the regime's net total payments, or C$217 million in concrete figures, had to be met by borrowing.[68] The exact methods Soong used in floating internal debt were never divulged. According to one contemporary source, he first relied on direct bank advances but later resorted to short-term treasury bills. These were sold sometimes through the Chinese stock exchange, but more often directly to banks at prices below the market quotations.[69] While this information does not tally exactly with other contemporary sources on the subject, all writers seem to agree that the government received no more than 50 to 60 per cent of the face value of its securities.[70] Between 1927 and 1931, the ministry of finance alone issued C$1,058 million of bonds and treasury bills, and cumulative government deficits ending June, 1931, came to C$491 million.[71]

Perhaps more than anybody else in the government, Soong was anxious to put an end to limitless spending on military campaigns. He was aware that as long as large sums were squandered on destructive goals and government finance was run on a haphazard, hand-to-mouth basis, economic development was impossible. Accordingly, he made strong pleas for the disbandment of all troops beyond a fixed number and for the establishment of an effective budget system. Largely at his insistence, a conference was convened among the nation's top military leaders in January, 1929. After agreeing that

63. *Ibid.*, 1194, 1223.   64. *Ibid.*, 1271.
65. *Ibid.*, 1167, 1235.
66. Douglas S. Paauw, "Chinese National Expenditures During the Nanking Period," FEQ (November, 1952), 22.
67. CHY (1935-36), 1201-2.   68. *Ibid.*, 1212.
69. YL:KHH, 49.
70. Ch'ien Chia-chü, "A Historical Study of Government Bonds in Old China," LSYC (1955), 126.
71. *Ibid.;* CHY (1935-36), 1244.

total military expenditures should be limited to C$192 million and that the Ministry of Finance should have unified control over national finances, the conferees proceeded to a discussion of the concrete methods of disbandment.[72] This was a much more delicate issue because it affected the balance of military power. Generals hostile to Chiang Kai-shek quickly discovered his plan to dispossess them under the guise of disarmament.[73] The conference broke up and civil wars ensued. For the remainder of 1929, government troops battered the units under Feng Yü-hsiang, Li Tsung-jen, Chang Fa-k'ui, and T'ang Sheng-chih. Although a second disbandment conference was called in December and agreed to an annual military expenditure of C$216 million, the plan was never implemented.[74] Antagonism and deep distrust had poisoned the relationship among the leading generals. Ironically, Soong's effort to initiate an era of peace precipitated war and led to more military outlay.

A little earlier, in August, 1928, the Central Executive Committee of the Kuomintang met in its fifth plenary session, and Soong again pressed for the adoption of a national budget. As a step toward this goal, the government appointed a national budget committee with six military and three civilian leaders as its members. For several months the committee tried to prepare a national budget, but the deterioration in military conditions prevented it from accomplishing anything. Undaunted, Soong continued to seek better financial co-ordination among government organs. In September, 1928, a Central Financial Reorganization Committee was formed for the purpose of achieving financial unification of the country. After the central government adopted the "five-power" political structure in April, 1929, a National Finance Committee was organized among the high functionaries of the party, the legislature, and the auditing and finance ministries.[75] The aim once again was to control the revenue and expenditure of the government. In November, 1930, a Comptroller General's Office was created. It was divided into three departments: the first was in charge of budgeting; the second, the accounting personnel in government offices; the third, statistics. In actual fact, the immediate emphasis was on budgeting, and to enable the office to carry out its functions more effectively, it was given the prestige of being directly under the national government.[76]

Even before all this happened, the Ministry of Finance had compiled estimates for the coming financial year. For 1927 and 1928 the formats of these trial budgets followed closely those used by the defunct Peking regime. In 1929 new forms were devised which used the Arabic numerals and followed the Western way of writing from

72. *Ibid.*, 1178-79.
74. CHY (1935-36), 1248.
76. Fong, "Toward Economic Control," NSEQ (July, 1936), 341.
73. FYH:WSJS, 12.
75. *Ibid.*, 1180.

left to right, but as a concession to the old-fashioned accountants then employed by many government offices, the ministry permitted the use of Chinese forms with their right-to-left vertical columns for another year. In February, 1930, a new set of regulations was drawn up to govern the trial budget for 1930-31. Owing to the time lag, the budget for that year was not formulated according to these regulations, but the next one, for the year 1931-32, was. By this time, the Comptroller-General's Office had come into being. It co-operated with the Ministry of Finance to produce the first comprehensive budget in the history of the republic, on the basis of the ministerial regulations of February, 1930.[77]

In April, 1931, the Comptroller General's Office was enlarged into the Directorate of Budget, Accounts, and Statistics. In November of that year, a new set of regulations governing budget-making was promulgated. Besides designating the directorate as the body in charge of the budget, these regulations modified those of 1930 by prescribing the procedures more fully. In September, 1932, a new budget law consisting of ninety-six articles and eleven appendices was passed by the Legislative Yüan, but this was not approved by the government.[78] In April, 1937, another budget law, considerably simpler than the 1932 version and more in line with the 1931 regulations, was approved and issued by the government.[79] Since none of the budgets compiled after 1931 was executed, the writing of budget laws was more indicative of intentions than of actual changes. From our point of view the significance of these measures is their indication of T. V. Soong's strenuous efforts to establish budgetary control.

The basic cause underlying Soong's failure was the unceasing military campaigning that Chiang Kai-shek insisted on conducting. As the wars continued, the drain on the economy increased and all hopes of ending the deficits vanished. From the fiscal point of view, it is remarkable that in spite of the mounting deficits, the government was able to raise the funds with relatively little use of inflationary credit. The secret appears to have lain in the regime's ability to control the large modern banks that were centered in Shanghai, and in this very important matter, T. V. Soong played a key role.

As we have previously indicated, Soong had contacted the bankers in Shanghai even before the Kuomintang forces reached there. As quickly as the city had been taken, Soong created a sinking fund for domestic loans out of the customs' 2.5 per cent surtax, employing a number of businessmen as trustees.[80] Among those invited to the National Economic Conference, bankers were accorded particular honors. As a result of such kid-glove tactics, Soong was able to win

77. CSI:MKT, 2d series, 5th *pien*, pp. 47-49.
78. CHY (1935-36), 1250.   79. CSI:MKT, 3d series, p. 481.
80. WSF:CCR, 350-51.

their support in the floating of internal debt. This support not only solved the regime's economic difficulties but also strengthened the regime's control over the business world, for as the banks filled their portfolios with government bonds, they became politically committed to that regime. By the end of 1931, the government had issued C$1,058 million in internal loans, and the banks, which had absorbed most of these, had tied themselves irretrievably to the Kuomintang cause.[81]

Meanwhile, conditions in the country were deteriorating. In 1931 there was a disastrous flood in the Yangtze Valley and a famine of unprecedented proportions. In September of the same year, the Japanese seized Manchuria. Four months later, they carried the war into Shanghai. At that time the Nanking government was faced with acute financial difficulties. The total annual revenue was about C$500 million. The military expenditure amounted to C$300 million, and the service of internal debt cost C$210 million.[82] There was serious doubt about the government's ability to meet the interest payments and the amortization of the domestic loans. Previously, an intra-Kuomintang feud had resulted in Chiang Kai-shek's resignation in December, 1931. T. V. Soong had resigned with Chiang, but the January, 1932, financial and military crisis brought both back into office.[83] Shortly thereafter, Soong maneuvered the bondholders (i.e., the banks) into agreeing to a consolidation scheme.

Briefly, the interest rates on all domestic loans were reduced to a flat 6 per cent per annum from the previous average rate of 8.57 per cent (or 8.28 per cent if domestic loans incurred by the Peking regime were included). More important, current payments for amortization of principal were halved through doubling the term of repayment of the loans. The resulting reduction in service charges amounted to over C$107 million.[84] In return, more than half of the old Peking issues of C$202 million were recognized and incorporated into the reorganization scheme. A new sinking fund commission was established to replace the old one, and the foreign inspector-general of customs was made a member with a monthly allotment of C$8.6 million authorized from the customs receipts. Moreover, the government declared that it would assign a single revenue as security for all loans and that, for four years, it would supply no more than C$8.6 million monthly for loan service. On these assurances, the bondholders were led to believe that the government would refrain from internal borrowing within that period.[85] Finally, in a public state-

81. CKN:IS, 118-19. According to this source, the Nanking government had by the end of 1931 issued twenty-five internal loans to the face value of C$1,108 million, of which the outstanding balance was then C$753 million.

82. WSF:CCR, 380; CHY (1935-36), 1244.

83. LSK:CKH, 175-76; WSF:CCR, 380.

84. PDS:CPF, 314-15.   85. *Ibid.*, 320; CKN:IS, 119.

ment voicing their support of the regime, the bondholders reiterated their fervent hopes that the government would practice economy, enforce budgetary control, abide by the terms of the reorganization scheme, and raise no loans for current and military expenses.[86]

All of these hopes were dashed, however, when early in 1933 the Nanking regime again resorted to internal borrowing. In spite of their efforts, Soong and the bankers were unable to contain the action of the man in power, Chiang Kai-shek. Just as a previous law passed by the legislature in April, 1929, forbidding the issuing of loans for non-productive purposes had proved completely futile, so the pledge given by Chiang, through Soong, to the bankers was kept only for a year. By early 1933, Chiang Kai-shek was making plans to launch a final campaign to crush the Communists, and he would not be deterred by financial obstacles. In that year another C$124 million in bonds was floated, and a cotton and wheat loan was contracted with the United States.[87] Soong acquiesced in all of this, but he was nevertheless opposed to Chiang's policy. To him, war was strictly a means to an end. The Northern Expedition had deserved support because it was a civil war to end all civil wars. As this campaign drew to a successful end, the task of economic reconstruction should have begun. Government credit had to be maintained and bottomless spending on destructive goals avoided at all cost. When internecine wars started again in 1929, Soong resigned in protest. He was persuaded to stay only by Chiang's promise to curtail military expenditure and institute strict budgetary control.[88] But by 1933 these pledges had proved worthless, and the wars continued. In October the national treasury was reportedly empty except for C$27 million of unsold treasury notes.[89] Tired of eternally wrangling with Chiang over financial solvency, Soong resigned. After a short interval, he was succeeded by his brother-in-law, H. H. Kung.

What were the outstanding features of Soong's personality? Perhaps more than any other Chinese official of his time, he was able to impress Western observers. A British public figure who knew China well described Soong in these words:

> Of middle height, powerful and graceful in build, with a face of great oriental beauty, an expression now of brooding meditation and now of vivid animation, he combines as few have done much of the best of the East and the West. . . . His English enables him to speak and write, not only easily and well, but with brilliance. . . . He is temperamental and sensitive, moods of black depression alternating with gay courage; he has great personal charm and a genius in personal relations, reflected

86. Ch'ien Chia-chü, *op. cit.*, 124, 127.   87. *Ibid.*, 123; CY (1935), 491.
88. PDS:CPF, 118.   89. YL:KHH, 44.

in intimate friendships not only with those of his own race but with such Westerners as Frederick Whyte, Tony Keswick and, perhaps above all, L. Rajchmen.[90]

In short, according to Sir Arthur Salter, Soong's standing with Western statesmen and capitalists was "unequalled and unchallengeable."[91]

Such unreserved praise from a man of Salter's stature testifies amply to Soong's talents. However, his ability to absorb foreign knowledge was much greater at the technical than the imaginative level. He apparently used his knowledge of Western economics efficiently in China. His insistence on issuing financial reports, his management of internal debt, his attempt to institute budgetary control, and his succesful reorganization of the tax administration—all of these were unprecedented in China and indicative of Western capitalistic influences. It also is known that he was more at ease with English than with Chinese: his speeches were written in English and then translated for delivery, and important documents requiring his personal attention had to be translated into English first.[92] All of this tended to impair his rapport with other Chinese, except a type of Chinese businessman in Shanghai who lived and operated on the fringe of Chinese culture. But such non-Chinese characteristics did not completely Westernize Soong, even in the intellectual sense. In many respects, he was undoubtedly quite Chinese, as can be seen from his insistence that Chinese, and not English, be the official language of the customs service. It was he who established the regulation that Western employees of the salt inspectorate could exercise no policy-making powers. In other words, we have a typical example of an amorphous mixture of Chinese and Western influences. This marginal quality in Soong may also have had policy implications. While a genuine Chinese or a shrewd Westerner would readily have seen the importance of the land tax to Chinese finances, Soong apparently found dealing with the rustic peasants far more complex and difficult than grappling with bond promotions. It is perhaps in this light that we should interpret his decision to assign the land tax to the provinces in 1928.

A further indication of Soong's blended personality was his relationship with Chiang Kai-shek. In a strict sense, the two men differed greatly. Chiang was primarily militarily inclined; he always identified his own destiny with that of China, and most probably held a rather low opinion of Western politics and politicians. Soong, on the other hand, typified the rising *bourgeoisie* of China, whose fortunes had

90. SA:PP, 219.   91. *Ibid.*, 220.

92. Hsueh Kuan-lan, who was Soong's secretary after World War II, disputes this. See CC (March 16, 1958), 4. My own belief is that Soong continuously sought to improve his Chinese and that by the mid-1940's he used less English than he had before.

been founded on connections with the West. While members of this class might have reservations about certain aspects of the Western way of life (for instance, the Western tendency to discriminate against non-Caucasians), they generally had unbounded admiration for the principles of Western democracy and for its key institutions, especially the commercial ones. All of Soong's policies reflected this basic penchant. Although dependent on Chiang for political support, he was quite logically opposed to Chiang's military policies.

Chiang himself probably had little regard for such pedantic principles as sound finance, but he needed Western support and knew that Soong was the one most likely to gain it for him. There was thus a base for common interests between the two, and understanding was made still easier since both Chiang and Soong were almost natives of the foreign enclaves in Shanghai. Undoubtedly, the political attractions of a Chiang-Soong alliance led also to Chiang's decision to divorce his wife and marry Mayling Soong in 1927. This family tie introduced, however, a complicating as well as a stabilizing factor into their relations, for Chiang was now related not only to Soong but also to H. H. Kung and his able and ambitious wife, Eling Soong. In competing for the fickle favors of Chiang, T. V. could count only occasionally on his younger sister Mayling, while Kung always had Eling on his side.[93] Thus, the relationship between T. V. Soong and Chiang Kai-shek was complicated by policy differences and personality clashes as well as family jealousies and feminine influences.

But if family bonds did not satisfy all of Soong's ambitions, they at least provided him with minimum support. After his resignation in 1933, Soong continued to be a member of the Kuomintang's inner circle. He was successively head of the Bank of China and other important government enterprises, Minister of Foreign Affairs, President of the Executive Yüan, and Chairman of Kwangtung province. By and large, his relationship with Chiang fitted the norms of neither Chinese nor Western societies. To begin with, Chiang's marriage in 1927 was highly unusual. Yet once the family tie was formed, it was unethical as well as bad form in traditional China to compete with one's relatives, as Soong and Kung did in wooing Chiang Kai-shek's favors. On the other hand, a Westerner probably would not have resigned over a political issue and then take advantage of his family status to serve in other key posts. Thus, Soong's personality and career showed cross currents of East and West but conformed to neither culture.

The man who succeeded Soong at the finance ministry, H. H. Kung, was born in 1881 to a mercantile family at Taiku, Shansi. Very few facts are known about Kung's childhood, except that his mother died early, that he had only one sister, and that for some reason the two

93. SA:PP, 220.

were not close. Around 1895, he went to T'ung-chou to enroll in the missionary-run North China College, and in 1901 he went to the United States under Christian sponsorship, having been previously converted. He first studied at Oberlin and then did graduate work in science at Yale. After receiving his master's degree at the latter institution, he returned to China around 1908. It is said that at this time he founded the Ming Hsien School at his native Taiku. Because of his anti-Manchu activities, he was soon forced to flee to Japan. In 1910 he married Eling Soong in Tokyo.[94] Again few details are known. According to one source, Kung had been married before, but supposedly his first wife had died.[95]

During the next decade, Kung did not seem to hold any important position. In the United States he had met and become the "sworn brother" of C. T. Wang and K. P. Chen. When Japan agreed to return Kiaochow to China in 1923, Wang was appointed by the government as head of the Tsingtao municipality, and Kung became a department chief under him. Later, he made a world tour and was in Peking when Sun died in 1925.[96]

During the Northern Campaign, one Kuomintang faction established itself in Wuhan, while another, headed by Chiang Kai-shek, made Nanking its base. Kung sided with Chiang and was sent north to secure the support of Feng Yü-hsiang and Yen Hsi-shan.[97] He succeeded and, as a result, became Minister of Industry and Commerce in 1928. Four years later he was sent to Europe on a mission to purchase munitions from Germany and Italy. On his return in 1933, he was made the governor of the central bank, and when Soong resigned from the finance ministry, Kung was appointed to that portfolio. From then until April, 1945, he remained in that post, although during this period he undertook several missions abroad and was also head of the Executive Yüan for some time.[98]

Before we start to discuss Kung's policies, a word should be said about his personality. In contrast to Soong's transparent brilliance in speech and action, Kung appeared to be a *bonhomme* of Chinese politics. He tried to be as amiable as possible with all politicians and warlords. He often bestowed gifts on men who were out of favor with the Generalissimo. In many ways he was undoubtedly more Chinese than Soong. He loved to stress his descendance from Confucius, and he relished telling about the drug firm and the native banks his family supposedly had owned, and about the British Petroleum Company for which his family acted as the Shansi agent. In both private conversations and public speeches, Kung was almost colorless, dwelling on moral themes without depth or subtlety. His study in the United

94. YL:KHH, 26.
96. YL:KHH, 31-32.
98. *Ibid.*, 156-80, 187-94.

95. CET:CC, 55.
97. *Ibid.*, 33.

States did train him to speak English fluently, but in contrast to Soong's acquired Boston accent, Kung had "an accent derived from the least cultivated of American circles and a tone to match the accent."[99] At least outwardly Kung's personality was far more subdued than Soong's, and for that reason is more difficult to delineate, especially in regard to showing how East and West merged in his character. But as Sir Arthur Salter pointed out, his qualities were more complex than a casual observer could discern.[100] As we shall see, Kung achieved far more as a financial expert than any of his predecessors including Soong. Since the game of high finance was hardly an outstanding feature of Chinese tradition, Kung's career presumably had much Western influence behind it.

After his induction as the minister of finance, Kung largely continued his predecessor's policy in fiscal matters. He strengthened the preventive fleet and repeatedly changed the import tariff in order to obtain larger revenues. In December, 1933, the rates on wheat were increased. In July of the following year, a more comprehensive revision was introduced. Because of pressure by Japan, fifty-six items of special interest to her, including cotton piece goods, woolen manufactures, and sea products, were granted reductions varying from 2 to 48 per cent.[101] On the other hand, the rates on certain articles of import from the West, especially the United States, were heavily increased. Thus the rates on raw cotton went up 43 per cent; on oils, including kerosene, about 38 per cent; on certain kinds of machinery and tools, 100 per cent; on chemicals and pharmaceuticals, 14 to 100 per cent. Moreover, certain duties were made ad valorem, while others were put on a specific per quantity basis.[102]

The government was clearly seeking to realize several objectives through one action. Raising more revenues had first priority, but the tariff changes also aimed at coping with diplomatic pressures, protecting home industries, and restricting imports of luxury goods. The same multiple motivation underlay the export tariff revisions of 1934 and 1935. On the first occasion, certain goods whose export the government desired to encourage were exempted from duties. But at the same time the rates on other goods were shifted from the ad valorem to per quantity basis.[103] This resulted in many hidden increases which the government apparently thought could compensate for the incurred losses. The June, 1935, revision signified an intention to introduce genuine reductions. According to the new schedule, 138 out of 278 items were reduced or exempted from duty. But for fiscal reasons, this well-intended scheme was never put into effect.[104]

From a technical point of view, the policy of the Nanking regime

99. SA:PP, 219.   100. Ibid.
101. WSF:CSTA, 678.   102. Ibid.
103. CHY (1935-36), 1268.   104. Ibid., 1269.

was eminently successful. Gross customs revenue increased from C$113 million in 1927 to C$387 million in 1931.[105] Subsequently, the Manchurian provinces were lost, and the effect of the world depression spread to China. Yet the customs revenue remained at a high level— C$339 million in 1933 and C$342 million in 1937.[106] In 1934-35, which was the last year that the Kuomintang regime issued any general financial statement, the customs revenue accounted for as much as 47 per cent of the current revenue.[107]

In salt collection, Kung continued to stress simplification of procedures and increase of government control through the strengthening of the salt inspectorate. In January, 1934, the standard metric weights were introduced, and age-old abuses practiced by tax collectors through the manipulation of varying standards were done away with.[108] At the same time, the Ministry of Finance ordered that in cases where the aggregate of the national and local taxes amounted to more than C$10 per picul of salt, the aggregate rate should be uniformly collected at C$10. No uniform rate for aggregate rates less than C$10 was fixed, but the goal was to move cautiously toward abolishing all inter-area duty differentials.[109] In November, 1933, all salt administration in the Ch'ang-lu (Hopeh) region was assigned exclusively to the inspectorate, and in April, 1935, the Szechuan region was similarly absorbed.[110] By 1937 the central authority had extended to all corners of the nation except Manchuria, Kwangtung, Kwangsi, Yunnan, and Shansi, and gross salt revenue had increased to C$219 million, from C$54 million in 1928 and C$155 million in 1931.[111] Thus, although not completely successful, the Nanking regime made very notable progress in the unification of the salt administration.

Meanwhile, efforts to unify the excise-collecting agencies were continued. Beginning in July, 1936, the plan was to combine the regional offices in charge of the consolidated taxes with those in charge of the stamp tax and the tobacco and wine tax. Although this plan does not seem to have been put into effect, the administration of the consolidated and related taxes during the Nanking period was remarkably successful. From a modest sum of C$2 million collected from the rolled tobacco tax in 1928-29, the receipt grew to C$123 million in 1932-33 and to C$198 million in 1936-37, collected from some fourteen kinds of taxes, most of which were inaugurated between 1928 and 1935.[112] One unusual feature of the history of the Internal

105. *Ibid.*, 1283.
106. CHY (1938-39), 400.
107. CHY (1936-37), 551.
108. CHY (1935-36), 1306.
109. *Ibid.*
110. TYF:CKY, 285.
111. CHY (1935-36), 1298, 1308.
112. CHY (1938-39), 416-17, 420. The figure 2 million, however, seems too low. Possibly it is a misprint for 21 million, which figure is used both in the *Chinese Yearbook* of 1935-36 (p. 1345) and of 1936-37 (p. 647). Whichever is correct, the basic fact about the consolidated tax remains to be one of phenomenal growth.

Revenue Administration was the continual extension of its jurisdiction. First introduced in 1928 in the five provinces of Kiangsu, Chekiang, Anhwei, Fukien, and Kiangsi, the taxes were by 1936 levied in sixteen provinces, including Szechuan.[113] This geographical extension, coupled with higher rates and improved administration, led to a phenomenal growth in the tax receipts.

A notable innovation toward the end of the Nanking period was the introduction of the income tax. This particular form of taxation had been considered repeatedly by the Manchu and Peking regimes, but no concrete plan was advanced until Kung made his proposal in July, 1935, to the Central Political Council, the highest ruling organ of the Kuomintang.[114] An income tax law was passed by the legislature in 1936 and put into effect in its entirety in January, 1938.[115] Only three kinds of income—business profits, salaries and remunerations above a certain amount, and income accruing from stocks—were subject to taxation; the rates were modest, ranging from 5 to 20 per cent. Actual receipts amounted to C$6 million in the fiscal year ending June, 1937, and to C$19 million in the year following. The tax was administered by a special bureau, and great emphasis was placed on the training of personnel.[116] Had it not been for the Sino-Japanese war and the resultant inflation, the tax could have developed into an important item of government revenues.

Further innovations were embodied in Kung's attempts to introduce order into local finance. In May, 1934, he convened a Second Financial Conference for the specific purpose of abolishing exorbitant local taxes, reducing farm surtaxes, instituting local budgetary systems, and encouraging land registration.[117] According to Kung's reports to the Kuomintang, all the key programs charted by the Conference were successfully implemented. As of August 31, 1935, more than five thousand levies involving a revenue of C$49 million had been canceled by twenty-three provinces and municipalities, seven provincial governments had reviewed and sanctioned the budget of every county within their jurisdiction, and land registration had been carried out in eight counties situated in Anhwei, Kiangsu, and Honan.[118] These changes resulted in greater revenues at lower tax rates. In a later account Kung even claimed that the improvements made during 1935-37 paved the way for the collection of a land tax in kind during the war with Japan.[119]

To what extent these claims were true is, of course, doubtful. Not

113. CHY (1936-37), 639.   114. *Ibid.*, 666.
115. CHY (1938-39), 423.   116. *Ibid.*, 422.
117. CHY (1935-36), 1186-89, 1378-79.
118. CHY (1936-37), 692-93. According to Chia Shih-i, local levies totaling C$67 million and farm surtaxes totaling C$39 million had been abolished by 1937 (CSI: MKT, 3d series, pp. 960, 964).
119. YL:KHH, 82.

only may Kung have been too optimistic but the reports he received may also have been unreliable. From materials furnished by Kung himself, it seems probable that the Second Financial Conference was intended to serve a political purpose, namely, to strengthen the central government's control over the provinces. Apparently one of Chiang Kai-shek's trusted advisors had suggested to him that the best way to control the provincial governors was not to disband their armies but to deprive them of their financial resources.[120] Kung's first aim therefore was to persuade the provinces to yield their power of taxation and to accept in its place more aid from the central government.[121] Since all of this was done in the name of relieving the masses, and since the aid was in some measure granted in proportion to the local taxes abolished, it would not be surprising if the local authorities made rather extravagant claims. While we have no basis for any firm evaluation, the effects of Kung's reform were probably less than he asserted.

The expansion of the central bank was another major development during Kung's administration. Before the Kuomintang's rise to national power, two attempts had been made to develop central banking. In August, 1924, a "baby" central bank was established in Canton with Soong as the manager. As the Kuomintang army advanced into central China, the head office of this bank was moved to Hankow, where the issuing of inadequately backed notes soon placed it in difficulty.[122] Yet the experience had taught the Kuomintang authorities the immense advantages they could derive from a central bank, and the lesson was never forgotten. As early as October, 1927, the Nanking regime issued a set of regulations concerning central banking. Both the economic and the financial conferences held in 1928 voiced the need to establish a central bank to act as the government treasury. In October of that year, the Central Bank of China was founded with a capital of C$20 million and a board of nine directors chosen by the government, three of whom were businessmen of prominence.[123] T. V. Soong was the governor from 1928 to 1933. Although the bank shared the privilege of note-issuing with a score of other concerns and conducted its operations little differently from the ordinary banks, it thrived on official backing.

Beginning in 1928 it shared custody of the customs and salt revenues, which had an average balance of C$100 million.[124] In 1930, the regime introduced the Customs Gold Unit and authorized the central bank to determine the exchange rates between this unit and other currencies.[125] In addition, the bank reportedly made huge profits by engaging in speculative activities and by shipping gold bars

120. *Ibid.,* 58.
121. CHY (1935-36), 1378-79.
122. TF:BFC, 50.
123. *Ibid.,* 122.
124. *Ibid.,* 100.
125. *Ibid.,* 102n.

abroad at a time when such practices were officially forbidden.[126] If the bank's total assets are counted as 100 in 1928, the index would then be 765 for 1933 and 2,594 for 1936. On the same basis, its deposits would be 1,581 and 4,912, and its note-issue 607 and 2,906 for 1933 and 1936. Its profits in 1933 were C$11 million or 45 times larger than in 1928.[127] Although the official returns indicated a substantial decline in the profits of 1936—only half as much as 1933—these figures were disputed by contemporary private sources, some of which put the true figure at 71 times that of 1928.[128] Whichever the case, there is no doubt that in the latter part of the Nanking period banking operations became an extremely important part of public finance. One indication was the note issue, which after 1935 was no longer directly linked to silver reserve. In June, 1937, the central bank alone had C$376 million in notes outstanding, while the other three government banks had another C$1,032 million.[129] The combined total thus exceeded the total government expenditure of C$1,195 million for 1936-37.[130]

The rapid expansion of the central bank was largely due to Kung's policy. To understand this we have to go back to the broad economic situation in China. Because of a variety of factors, especially her use of silver, China did not feel the effect of the world depression until late in 1931, when both the United Kingdom and Japan devaluated their currencies. The deflationary effect this had on the Chinese dollar precipitated a crisis, which was later aggravated by the American silver policy of 1933.[131] In December of that year, President Roosevelt by proclamation ordered the Treasury to purchase 24,000,000 ounces of silver at $1.29 an ounce. Minus the charges, this amounted to 64.5 cents, which was well above the market price of about 45 cents. Furthermore, the Silver Purchase Act of June, 1934, authorized the President to buy silver until the world price rose to $1.29 and to take several other actions to increase the value of silver.[132] As a result, a huge amount of silver was shipped from China for sale abroad, and the commodity prices plunged downward. With 1926 as the base, the index number of wholesale prices in Shanghai went from 126.7 in 1931 to 98.4 in December, 1933, to 94.6 in April, 1934, and to 92.1 in June, 1935.[133]

To prevent the situation from further deterioration, the Ministry of Finance, on October 15, 1934, imposed a duty and a variable equalization charge on the export of silver. On the same day it made public its communications with the American government concerning

126. CYL:CK, 106.   127. CHY (1935-36), 1232.
128. CPT:CKST, 22.   129. TF:BFC, 144.
130. Paauw, "Chinese National Expenditures," FEQ (November, 1952), 5.
131. SA:CAD, 8; YAN:CHH, 10n.   132. BAC:RAEL, 623.
133. CHY (1935-36), 1046.

the possibilities of minimizing fluctuations in silver price and exchange of gold and silver between China and the United States.[134] On October 16, the Chinese government placed more restrictions on speculative transactions in gold bar and foreign exchange. But these measures proved ineffective. Instead of being exported openly, silver was now smuggled abroad.[135] The illicit traffic was extremely difficult to stop because, among other reasons, foreigners enjoyed extraterritoriality and thus were not accountable to Chinese law. As the effect of depression spread, bank failures occurred in many parts of the country. An incomplete survey indicated that between January and November, 1935, twenty banks and one hundred native banks failed.[136]

Using the crisis as a reason, the government issued C$100 million in Currency Bonds of the Twenty-Fourth Year of the Republic, a small part of which was set aside for relief to banks in need of funds. The principal purpose of this measure was to increase the capital of the central bank from C$20 million to C$100 million, and to augment the government shares in the Bank of China and Bank of Communications, the two largest Chinese banks in which the government had had no controlling influence.[137] By the simple device of ordering these concerns to accept bond certificates as capital, the government gained absolute control because it became the majority shareholder. The capital of the Bank of China was raised from C$25 million to C$40 million, and the government share in it went from C$5 million to C$20 million.[138] The capital of the Bank of Communications was raised from C$10 million to C$20 million, and the government share went from C$2 million to C$12 million.[139] These actions, which Kung took in March, 1935, were exceedingly important because the two banks had long been leaders in their field and had commanded more resources than the central bank. The shift of control from the hands of a small group of bankers to those of the government represented a basic change in the power structure of urban China. Managers of the large Chinese banks had been the only business group that had important political influence, and their eclipse therefore signified not only complete government domination over the Chinese financial world but also the end of the entrepreneurs as an independent pressure group.

134. TLL:CNC, 66-69.
135. *Ibid.*, 70; Fong, "Toward Economic Control," NSEQ (July, 1936), 355; YYP: CKCY, 303.
136. CHY (1936-37), 805.
137. *Ibid.*, 808-9. According to Tamagna, the capital of the central bank was raised from C$20 million to C$100 million in the latter part of 1934 (TF:BFC, 123).
138. Ch'ien Chia-chü, *op. cit.*, 127-28.
139. TF:BFC, 128.

Of course Kung did not bring about such a coup without careful planning. Although the details are unknown, several points seem to be certain. First, Kung had the full backing of Chiang, who may even have initiated the idea. Second, the plan was kept a secret until the last moment. Most probably, only Chiang, Kung, Soong, and a very few others knew in advance what was going to happen. The bankers were literally caught unawares and, although enraged, found themselves helpless. Belatedly they sought the intervention of Wang Ching-wei, then president of the Executive Yüan. Piqued by not having been consulted, Wang argued forcefully against the impropriety of the seizure.[140] But the die had been cast, and in any case he could not have prevailed against Chiang in measures as important as this. The banks were reorganized as Kung had planned. Soong, who had not always agreed with Kung, was nevertheless offered the chairmanship of the reorganized Bank of China. Chang Kia-ngau, the former general manager, was deprived of all power by being made the deputy governor of the central bank. Because the top executives of the Bank of Communications had been elected in 1933 according to government wishes, they remained unchanged in 1935.[141] In July, Wang Ching-wei went on sick leave, and Kung became the acting head of the Executive Yüan.[142]

As a result of the reorganization, the Nanking regime acquired a dominating influence over Chinese banking. In 1928 the regime had control only over the central bank. In 1936 it had direct control over five banks—the fourth one being the Farmers Bank of China established by Chiang Kai-shek in 1933, and the fifth being the Postal Remittances and Savings Bank formed in 1930. In addition, the regime had various degrees of influence over a number of other commercial banks. Whereas the earning assets of the central bank amounted to only C\$14.5 million in 1928, those of the five government banks alone consisted of C\$1,889.9 million in 1936.[143] The enormous financial power wielded by the Kuomintang regime equipped it to launch a currency reform in 1935 and to fight the war against Japan in 1937.

On November 3, 1935, the government issued a decree with these four features: (1) silver was nationalized; (2) the notes of the three (later four) government banks were made full legal tender; (3)

140. YL:KHH, 53-54, 249. Cf. Chang Kia-ngau's interesting letter to Mrs. Huang Fu (CKHTS, IV, 33), in which Chang tells of his attempt to contact Chiang Kai-shek through Huang Fu. Apparently, Chang acted in the hope that Chiang Kai-shek either had not committed himself fully to Kung's plans or could be persuaded to countermand Kung's action. Even Huang Fu, who was a "sworn brother" of Chiang, supported the bankers, but Chiang was not to be dissuaded.
141. Ch'ien Chia-chü, *op. cit.*, 127-28.
142. YL:KHH, 54.
143. TF:BFC, 134, 174.

foreign exchange was to be stabilized through market operations by the government banks; (4) a Currency Reserve Board was to be established to control note-issuing and to keep custody of reserves. At the same time the regime committed itself to a program of balancing the budget within eighteen months and of reorganizing the central bank into an independent bankers' bank.[144] Although neither goal was realized, the currency reform was a success. Some C$300,000,000 in silver were turned in by the people; government bank notes circulated without question; the price level remained stable; and for the first time since the days of the Canton trade, the external value of the Chinese dollar was stabilized between 1 shilling 2½ pence and 1 shilling 2¾ pence.[145]

An important feature of the currency reform was the role played by Western powers. In September, 1935, Great Britain, which had been concerned for some time with strengthening its declining position in China's foreign trade, sent its chief economic advisor, Sir Frederick W. Leith-Ross, on a special mission to China. During his stay until June, 1936, Leith-Ross maintained close contact with Kung and rendered him invaluable help. As soon as the Chinese announced the currency reform, the British ambassador issued an Order-in-Council prohibiting all British subjects in China from making payment in silver. At the same time, the government of Hongkong also withdrew silver money from circulation and imposed control over foreign exchange.[146] By January, 1936, the British banks in China had agreed to turn in their silver holdings to the Chinese government. An arrangement was made whereby they could deposit with the central bank an amount made up of 60 per cent of silver and 40 per cent of acceptable securities—i.e., Chinese government bonds whose face values were above their market prices—in exchange for a deposit of like amount by the central bank with them. The central bank's deposit was made up of legal tender notes. Although interest was allowed by both parties, the difference in interest rates favored the banks turning over their silver.[147] This arrangement was of vital importance to the Nanking regime because in spite of their decline after the First World War, British firms maintained extensive interests in China.[148] Protected by extraterritorial rights, they could well have blocked the currency reform by ignoring it. Their willingness to surrender the silver was thus a signal success for the Kuomintang authorities.

The key role played by Great Britain led many to believe that Leith-Ross initiated the currency reform. This assertion, however,

144. CKN:IS, 8; CHY (1936-37), 812. 145. CSH:CI, 118.
146. TLL:CNC, 92. 147. *Ibid.*, 95.
148. In 1930, Great Britain was still the largest foreign investor in China. See RCF:FIC, 333, 397, 505.

was denied by both Leith-Ross and several other sources.[149] Furthermore, even if Leith-Ross played a key role in the currency reform, he certainly had nothing to do either with the reorganization of the Bank of China and the Bank of Communications or with American purchase of Chinese silver between November, 1935, and July, 1937, both of which contributed greatly to the success of the currency reform. At China's urging, the American government in December, 1935, lowered its buying price for silver, reduced its purchases in London, and started buying from China. In February, 1936, Secretary Morgenthau revealed that total silver purchases from China had amounted to fifty million ounces.[150] In May of that year, K. P. Chen, a "sworn brother" of Kung, headed a Chinese mission to the United States and succeeded in augmenting China's dollar reserves through the sale of silver.[151] In July, 1937, Kung himself visited Washington to negotiate for Sino-American monetary co-operation. Although no official figures were released, the proceeds of sales of silver by China probably amounted to C$270 million.[152] This, coupled with a smaller holding of gold, formed the financial basis on which China began her war against Japan in 1937.[153]

In a recent work, Kung claims, through the mouth of an anonymous author, that the most successful of all of the Kuomintang policies during the years from 1928 to 1949 was the currency reform of 1935.[154] There is no doubt that the measure fulfilled its purpose and greatly strengthened the government. Without the managed paper standard it would have been impossible for the regime to prosecute the war against Japan, and if the war is thought desirable, due credit must be given Kung and those who worked with him. But this is not to imply that when Kung introduced the reform, he had the war in mind. Whatever the Kuomintang government may claim, all of the evidence indicates that it did not make up its mind to fight Japan until the very last.[155] The major purpose behind the currency reform was merely to strengthen the government against its internal foes. Because of its determination to crush the Communists, the regime spent 39 per cent or more of its total expenditures on military outlay in the years 1935 through 1937.[156] According to recent estimates, current government revenue amounted to only 40 per cent of the expenditures in 1935-36 and only 65.81 per cent in 1936-37.[157] Consequently, even before the Sino-Japanese conflict broke out in July, 1937, the government had already resorted to inflation through the printing press. The total note-issue of the four government banks increased from

149. YL:KHH, 70-74.   150. TLL:CNC, 91.
151. CHY (1938-39), 377.   152. CKN:IS, 284.
153. Ibid.   154. YL:KHH, 68.
155. See Hu Shih's diary as quoted in HSSHPP, III, 71-72.
156. Paauw, "Chinese National Expenditures," FEQ (November, 1952), 22.
157. CSH:CI, 40.

C$453 million in 1935 to C$1,477 million in 1937, but only half of the increase was covered by silver surrendered.[158] Thus within two years of the currency reform the fiduciary issue had expanded by more than C$500 million. The Currency Reserve Board, headed by H. H. Kung as the chairman and T. V. Soong as chairman of the standing committee, had acquiesced in this expansion, in spite of its solemn promises to the contrary.

The fear of divulging this large increase in note-issue was undoubtedly the main reason behind Kung's decision to suspend the annual financial reports after 1935. By means of market operations through the central bank, he even succeeded in maintaining the external value of the Chinese dollar at the November, 1935, level. But he was unable to eliminate the effect of increased money supply on internal prices. Between 1935 and 1937 the wholesale price index in Shanghai rose by 24 per cent.[159] Realizing the seriousness of the situation, Kung and Soong refrained from resorting further to the press. Instead, they turned once more to internal borrowing.

When the Chinese bonds were consolidated in 1932, the Nanking regime had promised not to contract internal loans for four years. But the promise was kept for less than one year. Between 1933 and 1935, a total of C$826 million of government bonds was issued, not including £1,500,000 of railway bonds secured on the British portion of the Boxer indemnity and US$26,318,211 of the American Cotton and Wheat Loan.[160] By early 1936 the annual service of the domestic loans required C$186 million.[161] This amount could not be covered by the sinking fund created in 1932, which was itself operating at a deficit, because the customs receipts had been less than expected.[162] Thus the situation once again became critical for the Kuomintang regime. Fortunately, with its domination over Chinese banking, the government had no difficulty in securing the consent of the bondholders to another consolidation.

According to this scheme, thirty-three issues of bonds and treasury notes were merged into a new Twenty-Fifth Year Consolidation Loan comprising five classes of bonds, which carried the same interest rate of 6 per cent per annum but matured at more distant dates. Instead of repaying 70 per cent of the domestic obligations in the six-year period from 1936 through 1941, the regime would reimburse 76 per cent of the loans in eighteen to twenty-one years and would amortize the other 24 per cent in another twelve to twenty-four years.[163] By this process the government succeeded in reducing annual service payments by C$85 million.[164] Moreover, the Consolidation Loan involved

158. CKN:IS, 8.
159. *Ibid.*, 10.
160. Ch'ien Chia-chü, *op. cit.*, 123; CY (1939), 500, 502.
161. PDS:CPF, 326.
162. CHY (1936-37), 721.
163. MYC:CCL, 66-70.
164. PDS:CPF, 327.

a new issue of C$183 million because its total amount exceeded the old debts by that much.[165] On top of all this the regime further floated a Twenty-Fifth Year Recovery loan to the amount of C$340 million, at 6 per cent annual interest and repayable by semi-annual drawings over a twenty-four year period.[166] Both the consolidation and the recovery issues were secured on customs receipts.

The Nanking government's debt policy was as audacious as it was skillful. No opportunity was lost to make the loan services more efficient. Before the 1936 consolidation, bonds were usually redeemed by drawing, while notes were by fixed monthly payment.[167] The Ministry of Finance had made little differentiation between bonds and treasury notes. It used both forms to cover current deficits, but because all bonds had to be approved by the legislature, it tended to prefer treasury notes. As the number of both kinds of issues increased, their management became a complex process. Through consolidation, thirty-three issues were merged into five, and all were now serviced by semi-annual drawings.[168] Another improvement was the creation of a fund designed to stabilize the internal bond market. From March, 1936, to the outbreak of the Sino-Japanese conflict in mid-1937, the internal bond prices remained firm.[169]

No other domestic loans for general purposes were floated between 1936 and 1937. However, a Szechuan Rehabilitation Loan of C$15 million, a Kwangtung Currency Readjustment Loan of C$120 million, and two railway loans totaling C$67 million were raised.[170] The Szechuan issue was directly connected with the anti-Communist campaigns. In his fifth attempt to annihilate the Communists, Chiang Kai-shek adopted the slogan of "30 per cent military measures and 70 per cent political action." In regard to the latter, he strengthened thought control in the Kuomintang controlled areas, floated more loans, and appointed military men to provincial posts. The strategy worked. In October, 1934, the Communists rushed the siege and began their Long March. By the summer of 1935 the battle had spread to Szechuan, and the government seized the opportunity to extend its authority in that province. In that year it floated two loans totaling C$100 million for the rehabilitation of Szechuan,[171] and a third loan of C$15 million in 1936 represented a follow-up in that program.

Since 1929 a number of Kuomintang politicians opposed to

165. The excess of the new issue over the unpaid portion of the old debt was C$340 million, according to Ma Yin-ch'u (MYC:CCL, 75), and C$190 million, according to Yang Yin-p'u (YYP:CKCY, 209). Actually, the outstanding balance of the old debt amounted to C$1,277,429,690 (CSI:MKT, 3d series, p. 581). The new issue therefore exceeded the old by C$183 million.

166. CHY (1936-37), 725.
167. MYC:CCL, 63-64.
168. CHY (1936-37), 721.
169. YAN:CHH, 10n.
170. CHY (1936-37), 699; CY (1938), 510.
171. CHY (1936-37), 556, 694-96.

Chiang Kai-shek had rallied around General Ch'en Chi-t'ang in Kwangtung. Several times a separatist movement was on foot. In June, 1936, Ch'en again planned to rise against Chiang, but just as he was about to strike, Chiang managed to turn Ch'en's air force pilots and his key army officers against him.[172] After Ch'en's collapse, the Nanking government sent T. V.'s brother, T. L. Soong, to Kwangtung as the provincial financial commissioner. Mainly to strengthen Nanking's hold on the province, T. L. Soong undertook a thorough reorganization of the provincial finance, starting with the replacement of the Kwangtung currency with national currency. For T. L.'s initial operating fund, Minister Kung issued a Kwangtung Currency Reorganization Loan of C$120 million.[173]

These episodes of provincial politics, especially the Kwangtung incident, clearly reveal the design of Chiang Kai-shek's strategy. He achieved military victory mainly by fomenting defections in the enemy camp. While the means he used to achieve such an end are not too clear, circumstantial evidence points to inducements by monetary gifts and official promotions. In fact, most of Chiang's campaigns conformed to a pattern. When a battle reached its critical stage, one or more of key enemy generals would defect to the government side, thus causing the opposition to collapse. For their contribution the defectors would be promoted, often to the posts formerly held by their fallen chief. The situation would then develop in a variety of ways according to circumstances. In some cases the defectors would remain in Chiang's camp, either willingly in military capacities or unwillingly in sinecurist positions. In other cases the men became disenchanted with Chiang and revolted against him. At the same time effective government authority over the areas in dispute varied a great deal. Generally, Chiang was satisfied with nominal supremacy in the distant and poverty-stricken provinces, but in areas important to him—as, for example, Kwangtung and Szechuan—he would seek a thorough reorganization of the provincial administration and finance. To the extent that such efforts were successful, the government would have more political power and larger tax receipts.

While this strategy worked reasonably well, it had certain limitations. In the first place, it could not prevail against enemies who were well organized and who feared no defections. (Such would seem to have been the case with the Communists.) Another drawback was the financial cost. Defections were expensive to purchase, and the triumphs that resulted were frequently all too transitory. In spite of the façade of power that Chiang enjoyed, the hard fact was that his policy caused huge government deficits without achieving internal unification. The whole situation seems to boil down to one fact: Chiang's persistent refusal to weigh his political gains in economic

172. KYT:CTST, 420-21.   173. CHY (1936-37), 696-700.

terms. By making funds readily available, it was probably the Kuomintang financiers who promoted this tendency on Chiang's part. At any rate, it was they who made it possible for him to spend lavishly on internal campaigns.

Before we proceed to examine the exact impact of the Kuomintang's internal debt policy, it is interesting to note that foreign indebtedness was handled quite differently from internal indebtedness. Whereas the latter increased seven times between 1927 and 1937, total foreign loans decreased from C$1,500 million to C$924 million.[174] The actual decrease would have been much greater if the Chinese currency had not depreciated severely in terms of foreign currencies. Broadly speaking, most of the foreign loans were serviced regularly during the Nanking period. Either because of a sense of national pride or because of their hopes for loans, both Soong and Kung were deeply concerned with maintaining good credit abroad. They were eager to make up for past defaults on foreign debts. The salt loans were paid first, and four railway loans, some in default since 1917, were settled in 1936. To be sure, the terms offered were quite severe, involving cancellation of most of the interest in arrears, reduction of interest rate, and postponement of amortization.[175] Yet the Kuomintang was technically meticulous in fulfilling its foreign obligations, and it carefully avoided the appearance of soliciting foreign assistance. As a result, prices of Chinese external bonds rose steadily after 1933, reaching a level of only 5 per cent annual yield in mid-1937.[176] Thus, in spite of the huge deficits it incurred, the Nanking regime enjoyed an excellent reputation abroad.

The broad picture of Kuomintang finance can be summarized quite clearly. Between 1928 and 1937, tax revenues increased from C$78 million to C$865 million, but the expenditures expanded even more—from C$151 million to C$1,894 million.[177] Up to 1935, the resultant deficits were largely covered by borrowing, but after that year a considerable part was met through note-issue. On the expenditure side, the two most important items were military expenses and debt service charges; the former averaged 44 per cent of the total expenditures, and the latter averaged 35 per cent with the indemnity payments and 31 per cent without.[178] Expenditures for civil purposes, including funds spent on education and economic development, were comparatively small, although attempts were made during Kung's administration to increase them. On the revenue side, the three major items were the customs revenue, salt tax, and commodity tax. They

174. PDS:CPF, 334-36.   175. CHY (1936-37), 712-16.
176. YAN:CHH, 10n.   177. CHY (1935-36), 1166; CKN:IS, 16.
178. Paauw, "Chinese National Expenditures," FEQ (November, 1952), 16; CRYS:FPC, 180.

contributed 53, 21, and 12 per cent respectively of the total current revenues in the years from 1928 through 1935.[179]

From several points of view, the management of Kuomintang finance was remarkably successful. During the Nanking period, Soong and Kung were able to finance the huge military expenditures with relatively little use of inflationary credit. They strengthened the tax administration, gained control over the major banks, deprived foreigners of much of their political and financial power in China, and at the same time improved the regime's credit abroad. Of the two, Kung was even more successful than Soong. He not only remained longer at the helm of the finance ministry but also achieved more. In addition to increasing revenues and floating debts, he built from scratch for Chiang's regime a reserve of US$900 million and six million ounces of gold.[180] Although the feat was largely accomplished during the Second World War, Kung's ability as a financier is hardly open to question.

But it is one thing to manage the purse well and quite another to bring about improvements in the economy. In any broad evaluation of the two men's efforts, this latter objective must be taken into account. Presumably, the economic platform of the Kuomintang was based on Sun Yat-sen's teachings. While Sun's writings are admittedly ambiguous, his economic program obviously included scientific farming, reclamation, improvement of tea and silk production, "equalization of land ownership," "land to the tillers," promotion of co-operatives, labor legislation, and development of state capitalism (especially with regard to the construction of harbors and railways).[181] In spite of the claims made by the Kuomintang, practically none of these programs was seriously attempted.

Under T. V. Soong's leadership a National Economic Council was established in 1933. This organization eventually became the National Resources Commission and controlled a large number of industrial plants. But during the Nanking period, the Council's most notable achievements were road construction and railway development. In 1934 a full one-third of the National Economic Council's financial provisions was devoted to road construction and related activities. Yet, according to Sir Arthur Salter, the whole program yielded no economic benefit commensurate with the cost in cash and in human misery, because land was confiscated from the people without compensation. The roads almost exclusively served the needs of the authorities for the movement of troops, stores, and police forces. There was little goods transport. Worst of all, the peasants often lost their only means of transportation when rickshaws and wheelbarrows

179. CSH:CI, 40-41.   180. YL:KHH, 287.
181. See TSC:SMCI, Chapters 21-24; SYS:IDC, *passim*.

were taxed off the roads that had been built out of the old paths.[182] In short, the Kuomintang's economic program, if we can call it that, suffered from two main defects. In the first place, there was a certain amount of bad planning, arising largely from a lack of acquaintance, or concern, with the peasants' immediate surroundings and problems. More importantly, all of the Kuomintang programs were geared primarily to military objectives. To a large extent, the economic factor was stressed only for propaganda purposes.

This general apathy toward civilian and especially rural issues also caused the regime to make an even more serious error, that is, the neglect of the farm problem that confronted 75 per cent of the Chinese population. In spite of their known abject poverty, the government made no real efforts to alleviate it. The only time the Kuomintang ever attempted a direct assault on this problem was in October, 1926, when the party was contending for national power. In that month it launched a movement to reduce the farm rent from the usual 50 per cent to 37.5 per cent of the main crop. This movement was started in Kwangtung: it spread to Hunan, Kiangsu, and Chekiang in 1927 and to Hupeh in 1929. But only in parts of Chekiang was the program seriously enforced, and even there the results were extremely unsatisfactory. According to contemporary sources, the tenants failed to reap the full benefit, while the government and the landlords suffered. Land values fell. The provincial government had difficulties in collecting the land tax. In some cases tenants were evicted by their landlords. In others the benefit of reduction accrued to the middlemen that stood between the tenant and the landlord.[183] Although the statute remained in force, the rent-reduction movement for all practical purposes collapsed after 1929.

Perhaps the key factor underlying the failure was administrative incompetency. In no province was there adequate machinery to enforce the law and to adjudicate the disputes that arose between landlords and tenants. The only hope of success lay therefore in the central government's providing the necessary impetus through planning, legislation, and exhortation. By its attitude of complete indifference, the Nanking regime made the collapse of the rent-reduction movement inevitable.

Other facts equally testify to Nanking's refusal to involve itself in peasant problems. In 1934, Kung proudly proclaimed the abolition of numerous local levies, but he had relied solely on reports of provincial governments, whose optimistic tone was not borne out by independent contemporary sources. Another example of the government's indifference to the masses was the case of the Farmers Bank of China. Estab-

182. SA:CAD, 79, 122, 124.

183. Franklin L. Ho, "Rural Economic Reconstruction in China," NSEQ (July, 1936), 519.

lished in 1933 by Chiang Kai-shek to cope with farm problems in areas of anti-Communist warfare, the bank was reorganized in 1935, only shortly after the Communists were forced out of their stronghold in Kiangsi. From then on the bank ceased to be specially concerned with farm economics. Instead, it became just another government bank, operating little differently from any profit-making concern.[184] To be sure, Kung and Soong were not directly responsible for these short-comings, but it is hard to relieve them of all indirect responsibilities. For the most basic cause of these failures was the regime's relentless pursuit of military conquests, and by making these campaigns financially possible, Kung and Soong contributed to the symptoms that resulted from such an unbalanced program.

Ironically, neither of them evinced any enthusiasm for the bottomless military spending. Both attempted to establish budgetary controls, but their achievement in this direction was just as feeble as their contribution to Chiang's coffers was successful. Indeed, under their administration the entire tax system was geared to the purpose of raising more funds. Immediately after tariff autonomy was achieved, the customs duties were repeatedly raised. Even export rates, which had been maintained at 5 per cent ad valorem during the decades of foreign domination, were increased to 7.5 per cent in 1931, and additional hidden raises were brought about through the change from a purely ad valorem basis to a mixed system of value and quantity assessment.[185] A second tariff adjustment in 1934 fell heavily on beans and cotton textiles, the two leading items in the export list. The same striving for revenue affected the import tariff even more strongly. Between 1931 and 1934 rates were increased five times. In a few cases, notably cotton cloth after 1933,[186] imports were discouraged, but such coincidences between economic and fiscal goals were extremely rare. The general situation was that imports of luxuries increased while the government loudly proclaimed its sumptuary intentions.[187] It is probably unfair to argue that the authorities were insincere in their pronouncements or that they were unaware of the consequences of their policies. The central factor, rather, was their scale of preference. Without the will or ability to contain military spending, they had to subordinate all other aims to the fiscal one.

Of the other two leading tax revenues, the salt levies were severely regressive. Under the Kuomintang, the rates were raised until they were thirty to seventy times the producing cost.[188] As usual, the authorities protested their intention of lowering the rates, but never succeeded in doing so. For the sake of revenue, they were impelled to

184. TF:BFC, 137, 169. 185. WSF:CSTA, 679; PDS:CPF, 154.
186. YCP:CKMFC, 233. 187. PDS:CPF, 164.
188. MYC:CCL, 59; CSI:MKT, 2d series, 2d *pien*, pp. 229-35, and 3d series, p. 376.

pursue a course in clear opposition to Sun Yat-sen's goal of providing the people with all the necessities of life.

The consolidated taxes, which ranked next to the customs and salt taxes in importance, were initiated during Soong's administration. Though efficiently managed, these excise taxes served little economic function. This fact can be seen from the examples of the cotton yarn and rolled tobacco excises, the two leading items which in 1934 accounted for 50 per cent of all commodity tax receipts.[189] When the excise was first introduced in February, 1931, the Chinese textile mills strenuously opposed the two-fold classification of (1) C$3.75 per picule of cotton yarn above 23 counts, and (2) C$2.75 per picul of yarn 23 counts or below. Their opposition rested mainly on two grounds. First, such a division placed a lighter burden on the Japanese mills in China, which specialized in yarns of higher counts. The Chinese merchants estimated that the tax amounted to 4.27 per cent ad valorem when applied to a bale of yarn of 10 counts but only 2.41 per cent when applied to a bale of yarn of 42 counts. Hence they urged that a classification parallel to the one used in the Customs Import Tariff of December, 1930, be employed. This classification divided cotton yarn into five groups, with a graduating scale of tax rates, from 5.30 gold units per picul for counts up to and including 17 to 7.5 per cent ad valorem for counts above 45. Furthermore, the merchants pointed out that the new tax rate, being uniform all over the nation, placed a heavier burden on the interior mills than on those along the coastal ports. (Under the old arrangement some of the interior mills had been wholly exempted from taxation, while others had been taxed lightly, on the grounds that machinery, supplies, and fuel were more expensive for the interior mills than for mills in the seaports.[190])

The government, however, refused to heed these appeals. While agreeing that China's infant industries should be protected, the authorities still placed the fiscal consideration above the economic. For the remainder of the Nanking period the broad structure of the consolidated taxes remained unchanged. According to a detailed study by Yen Chung-p'ing, the tax burden and the interest charges were nearly five times as heavy for the Chinese mills as for the Japanese mills in China. During the period from 1931 through 1937 more than thirty Chinese mills went into bankruptcy.[191] Although many other forces were at work, government policy certainly did not help these mills.

Strikingly, similar situations also existed in the rolled tobacco field. In July, 1927, T. V. Soong imposed a 50 per cent ad valorem tax on cigarettes. But only the Chinese firms paid it because the foreign

189. CHY (1935-36), 1224.
190. FHD:CIT, I, 101-2.
191. YCP:CKMFC, 248-49.

firms in China refused to do so. This anomaly was corrected in 1928, when by mutual agreement Soong lowered the impost to 22.5 per cent and the foreign firms agreed to pay it.[192] Later, as the regime grew in strength, Soong again raised the tax rates. Between February, 1929, and May, 1933, the cigarette excise was increased four times. In February, 1931, a new method of tax computation was introduced. Instead of dividing cigarettes into seven categories according to quality, the new method recognized only three categories. The trend was now toward a regressive system. Whereas in 1928 cigarettes valued at C\$1,000 per 50,000 were taxed 17.89 per cent and those valued at C\$138 per 50,000, 14.67 per cent, from 1933 through 1937 the same cigarettes were taxed 16.00 per cent and 57.97 per cent respectively.[193] The change was extremely unfavorable to Chinese manufacturers because they specialized in less expensive merchandise. Furthermore, by reason of their size, foreign firms in China were able to win special concessions from the Chinese government. A clear example was the giant British-American Tobacco Company, which in 1936 paid 61 per cent of the entire Chinese cigarette excise.[194] By offering to pay their tax in advance, the company obtained a 25 per cent rebate on its tax payment.[195] The Chinese firms were unable to secure the same privilege because their tax payments were too small to earn special consideration. It is improbable that the Kuomintang regime discriminated against the Chinese firms on purpose. The decisive factor was rather of fiscal origin. Having committed itself to a military program, the regime naturally attached utmost importance to the raising of funds. On the premise that only its consolidation could guarantee China's future, the government felt little compunction in placing impediments on Chinese industries.

As we have seen, the flotation of internal debt was a major feature of Kuomintang finance. Among the factors that made such practice possible was the concentration of wealth in seaports, especially Shanghai. According to the best trade estimates, China had in the early 1930's a total silver stock of C\$2,200 million. Of this amount, no more than C\$600 million could be called liquid funds, of which sum more than one-half was to be found in Shanghai.[196] Normally such a concentration of funds would lead to easier credit and greater industrial activities, but because the government tapped a large part of the funds for military purposes, very little was available for entrepreneurial use. One criterion was the prevailing interest rate. Because the yield on government bonds was in excess of 10 per cent per annum,[197] the rate on industrial loans rose correspondingly. This trend had extremely serious consequences for Chinese textile mills

192. NYHT, 383; CHY (1935-36), 1334.   193. NYHT, 385.
194. *Ibid.*, 421.   195. *Ibid.*, 420.
196. Ch'ien Chia-chü, *op. cit.*, 129. 197. TF:BFC, 217.

because most of them relied on borrowed funds not only for their working capital but for their fixed capital as well. According to a trade report of 1935, interest charges constituted a third of the total cost of Chinese yarn manufacture.[198] As a result, the industry constantly operated under a shadow of crisis. At least partly for monetary reasons, mills with 37 per cent of Chinese-owned spindles were possessed by creditors between 1931 and 1937.[199]

The unfavorable impact of government spending on economic development can be seen from yet another angle. A very large share of the tax burden fell on an extremely small sector of the economy. About 42 per cent of the current central government revenue came from import duties; yet in no year did imports exceed 5 per cent of the gross national product.[200] Modern industry accounted for a small percentage of the national income; yet it contributed the entirety of the consolidated taxes, which from 1928 through 1935 averaged 12 per cent of the current government revenue.[201] In combination, the customs and the excise taxes raised about 85 per cent of the total tax revenues, but the value of output taxed did not represent more than 10 or 15 per cent of the national income.[202] On the other hand, agriculture, which contributed more than 60 per cent of the gross national product for every year between 1931 and 1936,[203] was untapped as a tax source. The situation was consequently highly anomalous. Government spending was much too large in terms of revenue, but extremely small in terms of the gross national product—only 3.5 per cent of it from 1931 through 1936.[204] Most of the revenues came from the embryonic industrial sector, with the inevitable result that the small government spending was sufficient to stifle industrial development.

The question is then, what caused the Kuomintang authorities, Kung and Soong in particular, to confine the tax collection to the modern business sector located in the coastal region? To some extent, the reason lay in the geography of military control. The regime was most entrenched in Kiangsu and Chekiang, but it lacked unquestioned authority in some of the other provinces. Yet this explanation is not entirely satisfactory, because if military authority was the only factor, the regime could certainly have tapped the tax potential of rural Kiangsu, traditionally the area that produced the most land tax revenue. For an adequate explanation we must also study the personal characteristics of Soong and Kung.

198. H. D. Fong, "China's Cotton Industry," NSEQ (July, 1936), 407.
199. YCP:CKMFC, 248-59.   200. CSH:CI, 72.
201. *Ibid.*, 41.
202. Douglas S. Paauw, "The Kuomintang and Economic Stagnation, 1928-37," JAS (February, 1957), 217.
203. LTC:CNI, 13.
204. Paauw, "Chinese National Expenditures," FEQ (November, 1952), 14.

An important factor seems to be their lack of any rural ties. Soong was practically a native of the foreign enclaves in Shanghai, and Kung, while born in more rural surroundings, left his native district early and spent most of his life either abroad or in large Chinese cities. To them, the industrial and commercial wealth of Shanghai loomed far larger than the remote, dispersed agricultural resources of the interior. Once such an image took shape, they could rationalize their neglect of rural tax sources in many ways. For one thing, adequate machinery for land tax collection was lacking, and the need for revenues could hardly have been satisfied until such a machinery was established. By comparison, existing institutions were available for both the customs and the salt collections. As for the consolidated excise, it could be levied at a few centers of production and was therefore administratively convenient. As a result, the central government retained and developed these three tax sources, while the less-wanted land tax was assigned to the provinces. Although undoubtedly more expedient in the short-run, this policy eventually weakened the tax structure to the point of defeating the fiscal objective.

Thus we see that there were two sides to the management of the Nanking finances. On the one hand, Soong and Kung showed remarkable skill in increasing the revenues, meeting the deficits, and building up the financial strength of the regime. On the other, they were unable to tap the rural tax potential, and their policies undoubtedly had adverse effects on Chinese economic development. To draw a balance of debits and credits is always a subjective matter, for which no writer can claim any special competence. Perhaps the ultimate criterion in this case is a political one: to what extent were the military expenditures incurred by Nanking justified as a necessary condition for the restoration of order and the establishment of nation-wide authority? The answer to this question in turn depends upon one's evaluation of Chiang Kai-shek. Was his leadership indispensable to China's well-being? If it was, then all financial means to assure his consolidation of power were legitimate, and whatever shortcomings Kung and Soong demonstrated should not outweigh their remarkable achievements. On the other hand, if Chiang's leadership was not necessary and if there were equally good alternatives, then the huge military spending had no meaning; and those who made it possible must be censured, regardless of their technical competence.

There seem to be three possible answers to this question. One could say, as many did, that Chiang was China's only hope, and that it was indeed the duty of every patriot to rally around him. Such a position, however, would pose a number of problems. To begin with, Chiang's enemies included not only warlords and Communists but also many veterans of the Kuomintang party. In fact, a great majority of the party's elders had at one point or another denounced Chiang with vehemence. Even T. V. Soong himself once resigned his finance portfolio in protest against Chiang's policies. The very fact that so many military campaigns were needed to keep Chiang in power also casts strong doubt on his indispensability. Furthermore, it is beyond dispute that Chiang's behavior was occasionally erratic. In addition to the widely accepted reports of his frequent resort to bribery and assassination, there were such undeniable errors as his imprisonment of Hu Han-min, then head of the Legislative Yüan, in 1931, a move which tended to deprive him of any claim to statesmanship.[205] It seems unlikely that either Kung or Soong truly believed in Chiang's indispensability.

On the other hand, to deny completely Chiang's weight in Chinese politics is an equally untenable position. One need only remember the popular enthusiasm that greeted Chiang on his release from captivity in December, 1936.[206] Perhaps the only logical position was one which suggested that although Chiang had his faults, he nonetheless deserved conditional support as the most likely person to give China progress.

If such was the attitude of Soong and Kung, they should certainly have judged each of Chiang's efforts on its own merit. If so, they might have refused to execute policies that were obviously illegal and detrimental to China's interests. However, neither Soong nor Kung adhered to such a standard of action. While Soong did once resign in protest, his subsequent role in the seizure of banks, expansion of the note-issue, and numerous other matters do not indicate an independence of mind on his part. Kung is not known to have opposed Chiang in any way.

Thus we have in the two leading financial experts of the Kuomintang regime the types of personalities delineated in an earlier chapter. Both were highly skilled in their specialized field, urban-oriented, and not morally too fastidious. As I have indicated before, such characteristics would seem to result naturally from the circumstances in which Chinese intellectuals became Westernized. To begin with, the discredit of Confucianism had created a moral vacuum that Sun Yat-senism was unable to fill; second, the new education put tremendous stress on technology and expertise; and finally, both economic and educational changes contributed to an urbanization movement. All educated men flocked to the cities and stayed there. They were so removed from the peasant masses that they did not bother even to tax them. Politically, these educated men occupied high positions, but they were not policy-makers in any real sense. They were willing to follow a strong man and to execute his policy as expediently as possible, regardless of the broader political and economic implications.

205. CKHTS, III, 295-97; FYH:WSJS, 17.
206. CTC:HPC, 61.

Although economic reconstruction was a major goal behind the movement to study abroad, the early reformers did not understand the complex nature of an industrial society. Limited in their perspective to the economically undifferentiated Confucian society, they did not foresee that economic development would produce a number of distinct occupational fields, such as technology, management, and finance. For one thing, they did not realize that a short training period of a few years would not adequately equip a student for a highly specialized field. Neither did they recognize the fact that no individual could hope to master all of these fields. Thus China's economic development did not proceed according to the expectations of these early reformers.

The students trained abroad who entered economic fields upon their return to China fell into three basic groups: the technicians, the entrepreneurs, and the financiers. The technicians, serving mainly as engineers, were the largest group, while the entrepreneurs were extremely few. The financiers, although not numerous, played a particularly important role. The following pages trace the impact of the returned students on Chinese economy through the careers of certain pioneers who in most cases set the pace for those who followed them.

Perhaps the earliest and best-known Chinese engineer was Jeme Tien Yau (Chan Tien-yu, 1861-1919), who was one of the C.E.M. boys. The eldest son of a small tea merchant, Jeme was born at Namhai near Canton.[1] In 1872 he went with a group of thirty to study in the United States, and was one of eleven in the group to declare their intention to study technology. In 1881, just before the C.E.M. was recalled, Jeme received a Ph.B. in civil engineering and two awards in mathematics from Yale. When he returned to China, he was assigned to the Foochow arsenal school to study navigation. As a naval officer in 1884, he showed great valor in the battle of Ma-wei. Later that year, he accepted an invitation from Chang Chih-tung to go to Canton to survey and map the coast of southern China.[2]

In 1888, through another C.E.M. boy, Kwong Kin Yang, Jeme became acquainted with Wu T'ing-fang, the director of the New China Railway Company. Wu offered Jeme a position in railway construction and administration in northern China. Jeme accepted and became in 1894 the first Chinese member of the English Institute of Civil Engineers.[3] His first major opportunity came in 1902, when the government decided to construct a line between Kao-pei-tien and Liang-ke-chuang for a planned trip of the Empress Dowager. The regime had intended to employ a British engineer, C. W. Kinder, but the French objected because the new line was to be connected with the Peking-Hankow Railroad, which they had financed. Caught between the Anglo-French rivalry, the Chinese government decided to risk using a native engineer, and Jeme received the appointment. By then it was winter, an unfavorable season for construction, and the Empress Dowager's trip was only four months away. By borrowing available stock from other lines and working fifteen hours a day, Jeme succeeded in finishing the construction on time. Although the new line was only forty kilometers long, its satisfactory completion made Jeme well known in official circles.[4]

In 1904 the government decided to build a line between Peking and Kalgan. Again the construction became a bone of contention between two Western powers, this time Britain and Russia. The British insisted on the appointment of a British engineer on the grounds that the construction was to be financed by funds from other lines in which British stockholders had important interests. The Russians objected because the line was to be built north of Peking, within the Russian sphere of influence. After prolonged negotiations, the Chinese decided not to employ a foreign engineer. The British and the Russians accepted this decision, believing that the Chinese would be unable to build a railroad across such a mountainous region. Even Yüan Shih-kai, the official in charge, had grave doubts, and was barely persuaded by his associate, Liang Tun-yen, another C.E.M. boy, to let Jeme undertake the job.[5]

Jeme pursued his new assignment with confidence and perseverance. He personally surveyed the route twice before construction began on September 4, 1905. While the railroad was being constructed, Jeme faced social problems as well as technical difficulties. A powerful Manchu family, believing in geomancy, refused to let the railroad pass near its ancestral tomb. Only after Jeme conducted a ritual sacrifice to the ancestors of the family and created a creek between the tomb and the track were their fears allayed and Jeme granted permission to proceed according to his plans. In spite of such hindrances, the work was completed on May 17, 1909.[6] All of Chinese officialdom was elated by the feat. The government had scarcely dared

3. *Ibid.*, 30. Jeme was also the first Chinese to become a member of the American Society of Civil Engineers in 1909.
4. *Ibid.*, 37-38.   5. *Ibid.*, 41, 100.
6. HY:CTY, 43.

to believe that it could construct a railroad without foreign funds and technical assistance.

The importance of Jeme's accomplishment was made doubly significant by the technical difficulties that he had faced. Steep grades marked the entire route, their number reaching as high as one in thirty.[7] Jeme solved this problem by constructing a series of zig-zag tracks onto which the trains switched in reverse at every other junction. Two special locomotives, one pulling and one pushing, shunted the trains from one track to another. Four tunnels had to be dug, the longest one some 1,091 meters in length. Because most of the digging was by hand, only two meters per day were completed at first. To speed up the work, Jeme sank shafts from the tops of the hills to the beds of the tunnels. Horizontal galleries were then extended from the bottoms of the shafts. By sinking two such shafts, work could proceed from six different points at the same time. Jeme's solution to this problem raised other difficulties, such as ventilation, shoring, and leveling, which he solved not by imitating Western experience but largely through his own ingenuity.[8]

The undeveloped, extremely rugged terrain of the region caused great difficulties in securing supplies and recruiting skilled labor. Trained engineers were nowhere to be found. Therefore, Jeme recruited youths of intelligence and gave them on-the-job training in construction engineering with generous pay. From apprentices he promoted them to assistants and then to engineers. Most of China's earliest railway technicians were trained in this way.[9] Another difficulty stemmed from the problem of technical nomenclature. Until this time there were no standard railway engineering terms in Chinese. When necessary, engineers improvised their own terms or transliterated foreign words. During the construction of the Peking-Kalgan line, Jeme used only the Chinese language, and thereafter a standard terminology slowly began to appear. Under Jeme's auspices, a Chinese dictionary of engineering terms was later published.[10]

Perhaps the most important result of Jeme's achievement was its psychological effect on the Chinese people. It was widely known that the Peking-Kalgan line was more difficult to construct than any other line in China. Yet the 250-kilometer track, including a branch line from Peking to Men-t'ou-kou, was finished four months ahead of schedule and was completed at a cost much lower than that of the foreign-supervised lines. Whereas the average per kilometer cost was C\$94,600 for the Peking-Mukden line and C\$122,900 for the Shanghai-

7. LHH:CTY, 52. For an elucidation of the engineering problems involved and for their correct expression, I owe much to Messrs. Harold L. Meyer and Frank Chen of Chicago.

8. *Ibid.*, 47, 51, 56-57, 60, 64-65.   9. *Ibid.*, 52.

10. *Ibid.*, 54.

Nanking line, the average cost of the Peking-Kalgan line was only C$48,600. Similarly, the average cost per foot of tunnel was C$400 for the Canton-Hankow line, C$358 for the Peking-Hankow line, but only C$319 for the Peking-Kalgan line. The difference in administrative expenses was even greater. On a per kilometer basis, the administrative cost of the Tientsin-Pukow line was C$10,000; of the Peking-Hankow line, C$8,500; of the Peking-Kalgan line, only C$3,100.[11] Among the factors that kept the costs of the Peking-Kalgan line so low were Jeme's personal honesty and integrity, which his staff emulated; the elimination of "financial charges" paid to foreign creditors, and the omission of middlemen, on whom foreign engineers necessarily relied for the purchase of materials and the recruiting of workers.[12]

Jeme's success exceeded all expectations and inspired the Chinese people with confidence in the future of their country. In the words of Hsü Shih-ch'ang, then President of the Board of Posts and Communications: "When this line was first constructed, foreign observers all forecast a failure because they thought that Chinese engineers were inferior to Western engineers. This opinion was so prevalent that it was accepted as a fact. Yet, within a short period this difficult and great project . . . has been accomplished. . . . This not only brings honor to Chinese engineers of today but it will inspire those of the future. In this sense the Peking-Kalgan line sets the example for many more lines to come. This is certainly no small matter."[13]

A secondary result of Jeme's success was the heightened status it gave to engineers in China. Jeme himself was showered with honors from all sides. With eighteen others, including Yen Fu, he was created a *chin-shih*,[14] and his services were sought by the major Chinese railroads. In 1912 he became deputy director-general of the Hankow-Kwangtung-Szechuan Railway, a line involving British, German, and American interests. While serving in this capacity, Jeme persuaded the British chief engineer of the Hunan-Hupeh section to give his subordinates equal pay for equal work, regardless of nationality. A year later, Linow, the German chief engineer of the Kwangshui-Ichang section accused Chinese engineers of incompetence and demanded that they be replaced by Germans. The matter was turned over to Jeme, at his own request, for settlement. He summoned Linow to his office and asked him if the wording of his accusation was correct. After being assured that it was, Jeme demanded to know the specific charges. When he heard them, he carefully pointed out that the charges pertained only to certain individuals and that they should not

11. *Ibid.*, 96-98.   12. *Ibid.*, 96.
13. *Ibid.*, 62-63.
14. WCC:YCT, 79. The number of *chin-shih* is erroneously stated as twelve in LHH:CTY, 67.

be extended indiscriminately to Chinese engineers in general. Jeme replaced the men involved, but with other Chinese instead of Germans, a clever maneuver that was hardly characteristic of Chinese diplomacy during this period.[15] Such a firm stand on Jeme's part naturally received enthusiastic praise from his countrymen who were accustomed to seeing Chinese rights surrendered to foreign powers.

In 1912, Jeme played an important part in the founding of the Chinese Society of Engineers. Under his sponsorship, the society established its own headquarters in Peking, where Jeme chose to live on all his visits to that city. Before he died in April, 1919, he mentioned in his will the importance of the Society for China, and he urged the government to do its utmost to foster its development.[16] The society later united with two similar bodies and became an important professional organization, with over twenty thousand members by the early 1940's.[17]

For the purposes of this brief study, the most significant feature of Jeme's life was his career as a pioneer technician. When he returned from studying in the United States, few opportunities were open to Chinese railway engineers. He had to spend seven years working in other fields before he finally turned to his own. By the time Jeme began his career in railway construction and administration, American education had become popular, and many of the C.E.M. boys had gained prominence. Although Jeme undoubtedly benefited from his friendship with the other C.E.M. boys, he never sought a political position through them. Convinced of the importance of technology for China, Jeme always took his job seriously and placed his duty to his country above personal considerations. During the revolution of 1911, for example, all of China's railways suffered considerable damage except the southern section of the Hankow-Canton line, which Jeme kept open by staying at his post at considerable danger to himself.[18] While devotion to duty was certainly not a new virtue in China, Jeme added to the concept of duty toward human beings a new responsibility toward the maintenance of property and the performance of services. His career exemplifies the rise of a new professional spirit in China.

But typical of the period of transition from old to new vocational standards, Jeme's career was not purely technical. In spite of his reluctance, administrative positions were heaped upon him once his technical ingenuity became known. When the Peking-Kalgan line was completed, Jeme was appointed chief of that line. Three years later, in 1910, he was persuaded by his associates to become the director of the commercial Canton-Hankow Railroad Company.[19]

15. LHH:CTY, 72, 75-76. 16. *Ibid.,* 85.
17. See the membership list in CKKCJML.
18. LHH:CTY, 70-71. 19. *Ibid.,* 68.

And in 1914 the government appointed him director-general of the Hankow-Kwangtung-Szechuan Railways.[20] When China decided in 1918 to participate in the Siberian campaign, Jeme was chosen by the government to serve on the joint allied commission on Siberian railways. At first reluctant on account of poor health, he finally accepted the appointment because the mission concerned Chinese railways in Manchuria. He left Peking for Vladivostok in late February, 1919, and divided his time thereafter between the conference table and inspection tours of Manchurian railway centers. He was soon worn out by heavy work and continual traveling in bitter weather. Leaving Harbin for a warmer climate, he reached Hankow on April 20 and died of dysentery four days later.[21]

While Jeme's technical abilities earned him fame and inspired national pride, competent observers agree that administrative support played a large role in his success. A recent biographer, Lin Hung-hsün, himself an engineer-administrator, points out that while Jeme was constructing the Peking-Kalgan line, he had the Manchu government's complete support and never suffered from a lack of funds. Moreover, the government allowed him undivided leadership. Even in his dealings with local officials, he served as a circuit intendant and hence as their superior. He was therefore able to complete the line within four years in spite of its great technical difficulties. During his later career under the Republic, however, Jeme served as an overseer with no direct voice in construction and financial policy. Because China's railways had been built as separate units from one another, differences in equipment and methods of operation rendered unification extremely difficult. According to Lin, the problems of diversity and Jeme's lack of direct control over local magistrates seriously hampered his achievements.[22]

Since Jeme's time, technicians in China have generally enjoyed great prestige and assumed high administrative posts. A rule of the Kuomintang made it mandatory for all railroads under construction to be directly supervised by their chief engineers.[23] A similar pattern existed in other government industries. In 1935 the government established the National Resources Commission to supervise industrialization. By 1942 this commission had become a mammoth concern operating ninety-eight industrial plants in various fields.[24] After the Second World War, the commission acquired control of the gigantic Japanese textile industry in China. A large number of American-trained engineers worked as administrators,[25] but compared to Jeme they accomplished little. They had to operate within a government framework that became less efficient as the scope of its activity

20. *Ibid.*, 78.   21. *Ibid.*, 84-85.
22. *Ibid.*, 82.   23. *Ibid.*, p. 57.
24. CH (1937-1945), 365.   25. CTT:TMM, 334.

widened. Moreover, the civil strife of the 1930's, the Sino-Japanese war, and the Kuomintang-Communist struggle gave the engineers little opportunity to progress in their field. After 1945 their function was largely limited to the repair of industrial facilities that had been purposely wrecked by the warring forces. No matter how competent the individual technicians, technological and economic development cannot take place without favorable political conditions.

Although the number of engineers was large, none emerged as an entrepreneur in his own right. There were few industrialists at all in China during this period. Capital was scarce, the political atmosphere was unfavorable, and there had never been a strong business class in society. A survey of the few industrial concerns in China reveals two types of entrepreneurs—those who had been high officials and those who had risen from their trade. A prominent example of the former was Sheng Hsüan-huai (1849-1916), who founded, for the most part with official funds, mining companies, telegraph services, shipping lines, railroads, and banks, and who became a very rich man himself.[26] Another great industrialist was Chang Ch'ien (1853-1926), a *chuang-yüan* (first in rank) in the palace examinations of 1894,[27] who gave up a promising official career to devote himself to industrial development in his native district, Nantung. After encountering great difficulties, he succeeded in making the Dah Sun Cotton Mill a financial success and developed it into an industrial complex including flour and oil mills, shipping lines, a distillery, a silk filature, and a machine shop.[28] Through these and through various educational and philanthropic activities, Chang made Nantung a model Chinese town during his own lifetime.

Besides Sheng and Chang, several younger officials pioneered in industry. Sun To-sen (1868-1927?), a grandnephew of Grand Secretary Sun Chia-nai, first followed his father in the salt business.[29] In 1898, sensing the growing importance of the West, he sent his brother To-hsin to the United States to purchase machinery for a flour mill from Allis Chalmers. Since To-hsin did not speak a word of English, he was guided by Yen Tzu-ching, a brother of the diplomat W. W. Yen, whose father had studied at Kenyon College under missionary sponsorship. The mill was established at Shanghai in 1899 and subsequently developed into one of the largest in China. Meanwhile, Sun To-sen himself became a government official both under the Manchus and in the Republic. A bank was formed in 1916 and added to the thriving family business,[30] one of very few such combines in the modern Chinese business world. A similar case, though probably on a larger

26. FA:CEI, 58-95.   27. BHL:MPMC, 8.
28. *Ibid.*, 9. See also TTP:MKMJ, 151-58, and LHS:CCCC, *passim.*
29. I am indebted to Mr. Chao-hsiang Sze of New York for this information.
30. YHNC (1934), B 70.

scale, was the enterprise founded by Chou Hsueh-hsi (1865-1947), the fourth son of Governor-General Chou Fu (1837-1921) and a minister of finance under Yüan Shih-kai.[31] In 1907, with Yüan's backing, Chou founded the Luan Chou mines to compete with the British-dominated Kaiping mines. Later, he used the profit to establish or to buy into other concerns, notably the Chi Hsin Cement Company, the largest in China, four textile mills, and a number of auxiliary concerns.[32] Like the Suns, the Chou interest benefited from official connections but studiously maintained control within the family circle.

From the compradore class came a different type of entrepreneur, namely T'ang Ching-hsing (Tong King-sing, 1832-1889?) of Jardine, Matheson and Company, who contributed to the establishment of the Kaiping mines, China Merchants' Steam Navigation Company, Tang-shan railway, and Chi Hsin Cement Company.[33] Another prominent member of the same class was Hsü Jun (1838-1911), a native of Chung-shan in Kwangtung who came to Shanghai when he was four-teen years old and worked as an apprentice in the American firm Dent and Company. Gradually he was promoted to assistant compra-dore. He also participated in the trade between Shanghai and Nagasaki.[34] Commissioned by Li Hung-chang to organize the China Merchants' Steam Navigation Company in 1872, he organized the first two Chinese insurance companies to underwrite all the business of China Merchants' ships. Later, he established a publishing com-pany, bought property in Shanghai, and after many vicissitudes became a very wealthy man.[35] Known for his ability and familiarity with Western business practices, he participated in most of the eco-nomic enterprises launched by Li Hung-chang and Sheng Hsüan-huai.

Another closely related group consisted of men who had learned their trade from foreigners either in Shanghai or abroad and who established their own businesses without having been compradores. For example, we may mention Hsia Jui-fang (1872-1914), a student of a mission school in Shanghai who later learned type-setting in an American newspaper, the *Shanghai Mercury*. He and several others founded the Commercial Press in 1897, which became the largest book publishing company in China.[36] Two other names that might be noted are Chien Chao-nan, a Cantonese who dealt in import-export trade with Siam and Japan and who founded the largest Chinese cigarette manufacturing firm, the Nanyang Brothers Tobacco Com-pany,[37] and Kuo Lo (James Gocklock), an overseas Chinese from

31. CSC:CCA, *passim.*   32. CKCTKS, 2nd Ser., II, 931-33.
33. Kwang-ching Liu, "T'ang T'ing-shu as a Compradore," THP (June, 1961), 143-80; CKCTKS, 2nd Ser., II, 972-74.
34. YWYT, VIII, 95.   35. *Ibid.*, 122-29.
36. CKCTKS, 2nd Ser., II, 982; TKL:CT, I, 640-41.
37. Y. C. Wang, "Free Enterprise in China," PHR (November, 1960), 395-414.

Australia who controlled the Wing On Company, the largest modern department store in China.[38] Neither the compradores nor the former apprentices had higher education abroad, but all of them sent their children abroad to study after they themselves succeeded in business. In many cases, their sons were able to step into their shoes and keep the family businesses going. However, these men could hardly be called pioneers; one of the very few American-trained Chinese who established a name for himself as a great entrepreneur was Mu Hsiang-yueh (1876-1943). For its rarity, his case merits further attention.

Mu was born in the family of a cotton merchant in Shanghai.[39] At the age of thirteen he became an apprentice under a cotton dealer while his elder brother Shu-tsai attempted the first-level civil service examinations. Three years later his father died, and the duty of supporting their mother fell upon the two brothers. When China was defeated by Japan in 1895, Hsiang-yueh shared the national humiliation deeply felt by all Chinese. He noted in his memoirs that from that time on he was determined to acquire Western knowledge. In 1897 he started to learn English in an evening school and two years later took private lessons from a Mr. Brown, a half-caste of a British father and a Chinese mother who had had "evil habits" and lived in dire poverty until he joined the Chinese customs service.[40] With this preparation Mu himself joined that service and remained with it for six years. During this period he increased his knowledge of the West, but he also became disturbed by the severe discrimination against the Chinese in the matter of rank and salary. In 1905, Mu participated in the boycott against American goods, and having thus incurred the displeasure of his superior, the American deputy commissioner, Mu resigned.[41] After a short time as an English teacher and as Police Chief of the Kiangsu Railway Company, Mu borrowed two thousand dollars from his relatives and sailed to study in the United States.[42]

Having no previous formal education, Mu entered the University of Wisconsin as a special student with the understanding that should his average grade go above 80 per cent, he would be accepted as a regular student in agriculture. Hard work temporarily injured Mu's health, but he succeeded in adjusting himself and was able to fulfil the 80 per cent requirement.[43] In 1910, through the effort of his brother Shu-tsai, who was now a *chü-jen,* Mu received a Kiangsu provincial scholarship under which he received his B.S. from the University of Illinois and his M.S. from Texas A. and M. College, returning to China in 1914. With an eye to his future career, he had also spent

38. WOC, 1-14.
40. *Ibid.,* 7.
42. *Ibid.,* 13-14.
39. MOC:WSTS, 1, 4-5.
41. *Ibid.,* 12.
43. *Ibid.,* 20.

the summer of 1913 studying soap manufacturing at the Armour Institute.[44]

On his return Mu considered establishing a soap factory but was deterred by the tight control over the supply of caustic soda by "a foreign firm"—probably the Imperial Chemical Industries.[45] Instead, he raised a capital of 200,000 taels through his brother Shu-tsai, with which he organized a cotton textile mill. A year later the success of this mill brought Mu several offers of financial support. Mu wished to use the offered resources to enlarge his existing mill, but he found that the major sponsors preferred to invest in their own separate concerns.[46] In 1918 a second mill, capitalized at 1,200,000 taels, came into being with Mu as the manager. Both mills became prosperous almost at once. The first increased its assets in a few years from 200,000 to 1,500,000 taels. It was the first among Chinese manufactures to produce fine cotton yarns of 42 counts.[47] The second mill had an accumulated profit of over a million taels in a mere three years. This phenomenal success encouraged Mu to expand further. In 1919 he organized a third mill in Chengchow, Honan, with a capital of 500,000 taels. According to Mu's memoirs, he chose this site because he wished to utilize the raw cotton produced in the two provinces of Shansi and Shensi.[48] The tendency to expand beyond Shanghai into the interior was a general characteristic of Chinese industries at the time.[49] The First World War had spurred rapid development of native enterprises, and the keen competition in Shanghai and the general optimism among Chinese entrepreneurs led them to look beyond the confines of that port city.

Mu's business success led him to other activities. He organized a cotton seed improvement society and was instrumental in donating some C$60,000 to the University of Nanking for agricultural research.[50] In 1920 he himself donated 50,000 taels to form a scholarship fund to send students to Europe and America to study. The fund, managed by the eminent educator Ts'ai Yüan-p'ei, was open to students regardless of native origins or fields of interest. The only provision was that the grantee should show promise of leadership.[51] Later, Mu sent a number of students abroad on his own. A number of these students, including the economist Hsien-t'ing Fang (H. D. Fong), became quite prominent after returning to China.[52]

In 1920, Mu was appointed an honorary industrial advisor to the government in Peking. A year later, he led in a campaign to raise 80,000 taels to send two "people's representatives"—David Yui and

44. Ibid., 29, 42, 45, 47.   45. Ibid., 47.
46. Ibid., 54.   47. YCL:MKMJ, Sec. 8, p. 178.
48. MOC:WSTS, 66.   49. CKCTKM, 311.
50. MOC:WSTS, 48, 64.   51. Ibid., 68.
52. I am indebted to Dr. C. M. Chang of New York for this information.

Chiang Monlin—to assist official Chinese delegates at the Washington Conference.[53] He traveled to Honan to work for famine relief there. Shortly thereafter he organized in Shanghai a bank for the long-term development of Chinese industry and a cotton exchange that made possible forward transactions in cotton yarns.[54] By then Mu became generally known as "the cotton king" of China. He was also a member of the executive committee of the Shanghai Chamber of Commerce and an advisor to the Western-controlled Shanghai Municipal Council.

Even at the beginning of his career, Mu was faced with certain difficulties, some stemming from the peculiar conditions in Shanghai, others originating in the unequal competitive positions of Chinese and foreign industries in China. Two incidents in Mu's career will serve as examples of the former. When he decided to purchase land for the premises of his first mill, he commissioned a real estate agent to do the buying in order to avoid public knowledge. The agreement was almost completed when an acquaintance, a village director *(hsiang-tung)* of the area in which Mu's mill was to be located, called on Mu and learned of the situation. Obstacles soon cropped up. A tiny piece in the middle of the land Mu was to acquire was held back, apparently in an attempt to extort more money from him, and the bargain nearly fell through. How exactly he solved the problem is not recorded, but in his memoirs Mu commented bitterly on the difference between American and Chinese societies. A chamber of commerce in America, he said, would welcome new business with open arms, while a Chinese local leader would stop at nothing to make a few dollars.[55] In making this observation, Mu obviously failed to understand the exceptional nature of Shanghai where there was little feeling of local loyalty, but his words do point out accurately the difficult position of a Chinese entrepreneur.

Another problem Mu had concerned his shareholders. Since there were only four shareholders in the second mill they each wielded much personal influence on the daily operations of the corporation. The officers they supported tended to quarrel with one another. This mattered little while the mill was making a healthy profit, but misunderstandings arose as soon as business conditions took a turn for the worse. In one instance two important officers had to be fired simultaneously because of their mutual antagonism. The shareholders, motivated more by immediate profit than by long-range goals, gave Mu their unqualified support while the firm prospered but turned against him when times were bad.[56]

The years from 1917 to 1921 had been the golden era of Chinese native industry. Before 1914, Western influence had long dominated the modern sector of the Chinese economy. Following the outbreak

53. MOC:WSTS, 80.
54. *Ibid.*, 77.
55. *Ibid.*, 49.
56. *Ibid.*, 66-67, 88-90.

of the World War, imports to China radically declined while exports increased. If we take the 1913 level as 100 per cent, the imports from Britain dropped to 51.5 per cent by 1918, those from Germany ceased after 1917, and those from France dropped to 29.6 per cent by 1918. China's purchases from the United States increased, but the increase was less than the decline suffered by Britain.[57] Japan's position in China was strengthened, but from 1915 to 1919 there were repeated boycotts of Japanese goods in China because of political tension. Thus, between 1917 and 1921, like the rest of Chinese industry, textile mills enjoyed windfall profits. For instance, the Shen Hsin First Mill under Jung Tsung-ching (1873-193?), another important Chinese entrepreneur who rose from apprenticeship, increased its profit from 20,000 dollars in 1915 to 800,000 dollars in 1918; the Chen-hsin Mill at Wuhsi, which had not fared too well from 1905 to 1918, was able to distribute a dividend in 1919-20 which amounted to 60 per cent of its capital.[58] As a consequence, rapid expansion took place; the spindlage of Chinese concerns in China increased by 125 per cent between 1914 and 1921.[59] It was in those circumstances that Mu's mill prospered.

By 1921, however, the situation changed. While Chinese mills continued to expand because of previously made plans, renewed foreign competition began to drive them into bankruptcy. The most severe threat came from the Japanese mills in China, which increased their spindlage from 111,926 in 1913 to 621,828 in 1922 and 1,268,176 in 1925.[60] This enormous expansion is attributable to the economic and political advantages of the Japanese over the Chinese. For one thing, they were affiliated with large concerns in Japan and had access to a more developed capital market. Hence their financial position was far stronger. The capital investment per spindle of Japanese mills in China was 80 per cent higher than that of the Chinese.[61] Furthermore, the Japanese mills were able to borrow from the Japanese banks at an interest of 3 per cent per annum, while the Chinese had to pay 10 per cent or more.[62] Through special arrangement with the shipping lines, the Japanese paid 30 per cent less on freight when they imported raw cotton from India.[63] Even in taxation the Japanese fared better: they were exempt from local Chinese levies, including the onerous *likin*, which fell heavily upon the Chinese merchants. In the early 1930's it was estimated that the cost of production per bale of 20-count cotton yarn was more than 114 per cent higher for the Chinese than for their Japanese competitors in China.[64]

57. HPY:FTC, 55-57; CHL:TIT, 12-13.
58. YCP:CKMFC, 185.   59. CKCTKM, 310.
60. YCP:CKMFC, 368-69.
61. FHD:CIT, I, 208, 210; RCF:FIC, 433, 495.
62. YCP:CKMFC, 218, 244.   63. *Ibid.*, 182.
64. *Ibid.*, 217.

Mu's mills, as had many other Chinese concerns, had fallen into difficulty long before this stage was reached. In 1923, Mu urgently appealed to his shareholders for an increase of capital. The shareholders agreed to this proposal but were hesitant to carry it out. When they appointed an assistant manager without Mu's prior knowledge, he felt compelled to sever his relationship with this mill.[65] His third mill, located in the interior of China, had fallen under the shadow of civil wars after 1920 and was taken over by its American creditor, Anderson Meyer and Company, in 1923. Two years later Mu's first mill was sold to another Chinese industrialist.[66] While he continued to be active in public affairs, his days as an entrepreneur were over. Instead, he became a bureaucrat, accepting posts as a vice-minister of finance in 1929 and managing director of the Cotton and Cotton Yarn Administration in 1941.

To place Mu's career in proper perspective, it must be pointed out that it was atypical of Western-educated Chinese, among whom there were many technologists but very few entrepreneurs. Most of the latter had enterprises founded by their fathers and grandfathers who had not studied abroad. Thus they owed their careers in industry more to their inheritance than to their training and ability. Mu was one of very few men who studied abroad with a business career in mind who eventually did build his own empire, short-lived as it was.

Several unusual features of Mu's life are noteworthy. He had no formal education, but started his career as an apprentice in an old-fashioned Chinese cotton shop. However, he learned English well enough to teach it in the well-known Lung-men Normal School in Shanghai for a time. Most unusually, at a time when the majority of Chinese students in the United States were in their teens, Mu was thirty-five years old when he arrived and thirty-nine when he left. These were probably the decisive factors which gave Mu his business knowledge and enabled him to be a successful entrepreneur immediately after his return. In his memoirs Mu attributed his early success to his knowledge of "scientific factory management."[67] The fact is that all Chinese mills made good profit at the time, and Mu's achievement was hardly exceptional. Both of his mills in Shanghai were eventually absorbed by Jung Tsung-ching's interests, which, in spite of changes of fortune, were able to survive and grow until the Communist takeover in 1949. Neither Jung Tsung-ching nor his brother Te-sheng had any formal education at all; thus Mu's American training helped him little in the long-run over his competitors. His great fame in the early 1920's probably came from his generosity as a philanthropist rather than from his business ability. The extraneousness of a Western education to Mu's business fortune is further

65. MOC:WSTS, 88-90. 66. YCP:CKMFC, 197, 352.
67. MOC:WSTS, 51-52, 57, 79.

borne out by the absence of other American-trained men among China's pioneer entrepreneurs.

In the field of banking, those who had studied abroad, especially those who returned from Japan, played an important role. The first Chinese modern bank, the Imperial Bank of China, was established in 1897 by Sheng Hsüan-huai along the lines of the Hongkong and Shanghai Banking Corporation, the dominant British bank in China. The new concern was capitalized at five million taels, had the right to issue notes, and was headed by a Britisher, A. M. Maitland.[68] For a time the new bank did well, but Sheng's hope to secure a monopoly for it did not materialize. In 1905 another government bank, later known as the Bank of China, came into being under the auspices of the Board of Revenue, with a former compradore of the Hongkong and Shanghai Banking Corporation as its first manager.[69] Two years later a third government bank, the Bank of Communications, was chartered under the jurisdiction of the Board of Posts and Communications.[70] After the revolution of 1911, Sheng lost his political influence. Although struggling to adapt to the new conditions by changing its name and converting to a commercial status, the Imperial Bank of China gradually lost ground and nearly went into bankruptcy in 1935.[71] By contrast, both the Bank of China and the Bank of Communications thrived and became the two largest banks in the country.

The guiding force behind the Bank of Communications was Liang Shih-i, a Han-lin scholar who became an intimate associate of Yüan Shih-kai. Liang founded the Bank of Communications, and used it to further his political activities under the Republic. Capable as well as munificent, Liang afforded support to most of the budding talents in Chinese banking. With his help, and with funds provided by a cousin of Yüan Shih-kai, Wu Ting-ch'ang founded the Yen Yieh Bank, which was to deal primarily in financing salt merchants.[72] Wu was a 1909 graduate of the Japanese Commercial High School who had worked under the Manchu regime. As the Yen Yieh prospered, Wu's fortune steadily rose. He was a delegate of the Peking government to negotiate peace with the South at Shanghai in 1919, a vice-minister of finance in 1919, president of the influential newspaper *Ta Kung Pao* from 1926 to 1939, minister of industry in 1935-37, governor of Kweichow province in 1937-45, and secretary-general of the national government from 1945 to 1949.[73]

Another protégé of Liang Shih-i who later rose to eminence was Chou Tso-min. Educated in Japan, Chou had been a junior officer in

68. TYT:CKCY, 15.   69. TF:BFC, 36.
70. *Ibid.*, 37.   71. TYT:CKCY, 19.
72. I am indebted to Mr. M. P. Fu of New York for this information. Mr. Fu was a banker in China.
73. YCL:MKMJ, sec. 8, p. 94; PM:WW, 240.

the Bank of Communications before he founded the Kincheng Banking Corporation with capital provided partly by the warlord Ni Ssu-ch'ung and partly by the Bank of Communications itself.[74] Unlike many other bankers, Chou accepted no official appointments from either the Peking or the Kuomintang regime, but his bank benefited from its close connections with the current administration and grew to be one of the largest in China. A third beneficiary of Liang Shih-i was T'an Li-sun, who founded the Continental Bank in 1919, reportedly with the assistance of both the Bank of Communications and the Bank of China. T'an, also a returned student from Japan, was succeeded after his death by Hsü Fu-ping, an associate who had risen through the ranks of the Bank of China.[75] A fourth member of Liang's group of protégés, Hu Chün, started from apprenticeship in a native bank, rose to be a manager in the Bank of Communications, and eventually became chief executive of the China and South Sea Bank, founded in 1921 by a Chinese settler in the Dutch East Indies.[76] Until Hu's accidental death during the Sino-Japanese War, he not only controlled the China and South Sea but extended his activities to include, after 1933, the chairmanship of the Bank of Communications. Known as the Northern Four, these banks—Yen Yieh, Kincheng, Continental, and China and South Sea—co-operated closely. For instance, in 1923 they established a joint reserve fund and a joint savings society. The combined resources of the four equaled about half the total resources of all Chinese commercial banks in the mid-1930's.[77]

Three other important commercial banks originated in the South. Both the Chekiang Industrial Bank and the National Commercial Bank had started in 1907-1908 as semi-provincial institutions but were later transferred to private ownership.[78] The former came under the control of Li Ming, a graduate of Yamaguchi Commercial High School in Japan, while the latter became dominated by Yeh Ching-k'ui, a member of the old Chekiang gentry. Li had served as a compradore in some Shanghai firms after his graduation, and also made money by dealing in foreign stocks.[79] He was active both in banking and in related political maneuvers. Yeh, on the other hand, came from a wealthy family and usually preferred to stay behind the scene, using his two top assistants, Hsü Hsin-liu and Hsü Chi-ch'ing, as business and political contacts. Educated at Birmingham and Manchester, Hsin-liu had close personal relations with Liang Ch'i-ch'ao and was a former councilor of the Peking Ministry of Finance.[80] He became general manager of the National Commercial Bank in 1926 and a

74. I am indebted to Mr. M. P. Fu for this information.
75. YCL:MKMJ, Sec. 2, p. 122.   76. TCKNC, 802; SYCT, II, 254.
77. TF:BFC, 160.   78. *Ibid.*, 37.
79. I am indebted to Mr. Fu for this information.
80. CY (1924), p. 1003; LJKHS, III, 551-52.

councilor of Shanghai Municipal Council, a highly coveted position, in 1929. In the mid-thirties he held as many as sixteen concurrent posts in fields that varied from journalism to education.[81] After Hsin-liu's accidental death in 1938, Yeh Ching-k'ui increasingly relied on Hsü Chi-ch'ing and in the mid-forties made him his successor.[82] Chi-ch'ing, educated in Japan, was somewhat less glamorous than Hsin-liu, but he was equally active in government circles and in the civic activities of Shanghai. As will become clear presently, these were the most vital fields for a Chinese banker.

The last of the seven leading commercial banks, the Shanghai Commercial and Savings Bank, was founded by K. P. Chen in 1915. The concern started modestly with a capital of only C$100,000—of which one part was reportedly raised by Chen personally, another part provided by the Bank of China, and the remainder furnished by H. H. Kung, a sworn brother of Chen from the days of their study in the United States.[83] In his business methods, Chen resorted to a practice then considered highly disreputable among Chinese bankers: he attracted small depositors through widespread advertisement. He also drew customers by inaugurating in 1923 a travel service department. The first of its kind in China, it was an immediate success and soon became a separate concern. By 1935 it operated forty-three branches and a chain of hotels, while the resources of the bank rose to C$212,000,000.[84]

The list of foremost Chinese bankers would not be complete without two other names. The first, Chang Kia-ngau, occupied a key position in the Bank of China between 1917 and 1935, and was later a high government official. Educated at Keio University in Japan, Chang had been at one time a senior clerk in the Board of Posts and Communications. He joined the revolutionary forces in 1912 and became the chief-secretary of the new Senate in 1913. Probably through the political connection between his brother Carson and Liang Ch'i-ch'ao, Kia-ngau obtained a position with the Bank of China and became an assistant manager in its Shanghai branch. On April 12, 1916, the Peking government, under Tuan Ch'i-jui, ordered both the Bank of China and the Bank of Communications to suspend conversion of their C$70,000,000 notes in circulation so that the reserve could be pre-empted for government use. All the branches of the Bank of Communications obeyed this decree, but at the suggestion of Chang Kia-ngau, who reportedly had the backing of military figures opposed to Peking, the Shanghai branch of the Bank of China refused.[85] Instead, it maintained the convertibility of its notes by

81. YCL:MKMJ, sec. 9, p. 61.   82. PM:WW, 83.
83. I am indebted to Mr. Fu for this information.
84. CR (July-September, 1935), 22; TF:BFC, 160.
85. LYSNP, I, 338-39.

placing the reserves with foreign lawyers out of the reach of Peking. The action won the branch much popular support and made Chang Kia-ngau an outstanding figure. Before that time the top executives of the Bank of China had been directly appointed by Peking and hence changed as frequently as the minister of finance. In November, 1917, during Liang Ch'i-ch'ao's brief charge of government finance, the regulations were amended to free the bank from political influence. Its governor and deputy governor were henceforth to be chosen by the government from among the directors, whose position did not depend on the government.[86] This meant that the bank administration was no longer tied to political changes but became in effect a self-perpetuating body. Chang Kia-ngau dominated the bank until 1935 when it was once again taken over by the government—this time, the Kuomintang. Meanwhile, the bank had expanded rapidly: in 1928 it issued some 68 per cent of all notes issued by Chinese banks and held over one-third of the deposits of all Chinese banks.[87]

A man of considerable influence in the Bank of Communications was Ch'ien Yung-ming. Educated in the Kobe Commercial High School in Japan, he managed the Shanghai branch of the Bank of Communications in 1920 and was transferred to the head office as vice-president in 1922. Three years later he became vice-president of the Joint Savings Society under Wu Ting-ch'ang. When the Kuomintang reached Shanghai, Ch'ien was one of the first bankers to align himself with it,[88] and he became very prominent in that administration, holding at various times the positions of vice-minister of finance, provincial commissioner of finance, minister to France, and director in numerous enterprises. He succeeded Hu Chün as chairman of the Bank of Communications and remained in that post until 1949.[89]

Before the rise of the Central Bank of China, both the Bank of China and the Bank of Communications had the status of government banks. In actual fact, however, there was little difference between them and the private banks, since both of these banks transacted ordinary business, while the seven commercial banks also acted as government agents. As a group, these nine banks dominated the entire Chinese modern banking sector, which means that this sector was virtually controlled by the twelve men who ran these banks. Although it has been impossible to study each of these men in detail, it is clear that they held certain characteristics and business practices in common, and that they can be considered representative of the Chinese banking world in general. Of these twelve men, six were educated in Japan,

86. TYT:CKCY, 170-71; LJKHS, III, 522-23, 538-40; I:MKT, 2d series, 3d *pien*, Ch. 6, pp. 35-36.

87. TYT:CKCY, 172; CYL:CK, 108.   88. IHR:FY, 82-92.

89. TYT:CKCY, 254, 256, 260, 263.

one in America, one in England, and four in China. The similarities
between them were therefore not entirely due to their educational
backgrounds. But since there is no way to isolate the effects of each
factor, we shall analyze this group and speculate on its impact as a
whole.

Among the other features of Chinese modern banking, perhaps
the most important was its total dependence on the government. Like
so many other institutions in China, the modern bank was established
by high government officials as part of the modernization movement,
rather than as a response to existing commercial needs. For decades
after its inception the modern bank had relatively little to do with
the masses or even with the merchants. On the one hand, it did not
replace the native banks, which even in the late period from 1933 to
1938 had four times greater inter-bank clearings than those among
Chinese modern banks.[90] On the other hand, in the modern sector
the Chinese concerns were in many ways completely at the mercy of
foreign banks in China, which had numerous political advantages in
addition to their far greater capitalization. For instance, up to 1928,
the Hongkong and Shanghai Banking Corporation held China's
customs and salt receipts.[91] In addition it had the accounts of foreign
governments, which spent about C$100,000,000 in China during a
normal pre-1937 year; foreign-controlled municipalities in China,
which had an annual income of C$80,000,000;[92] and wealthy Chinese
who saw in the Western idea of sanctity of private property an excellent protection for their sometimes ill-gotten money. Moreover, it
issued notes and financed China's international trade. Up to the end
of the twenties, it controlled the exchange rates between Chinese and
foreign currencies.[93]

Between the giant foreign concerns which dominated the modern
economic sector and the native banks which served the traditional
sector, often with funds obtained from the foreign banks on a call loan
basis, the modern Chinese banks had little outlet other than to serve
the needs of the government. Their dependence on the regime can be
seen in numerous ways. Liang Shih-i, who until 1928 had absolute
control over the Bank of Communications and much influence over
the other banks, was a high government official to whom banking was
but a means to political ends. In 1914 the Bank of China and the
Bank of Communications obtained 35 and 22 per cent respectively of
two loans to the government totaling C$48,000,000.[94] In 1916, accord-
ing to Liang himself, notes issued by the same two banks totaled
C$70,000,000, out of which no less than C$40,000,000 had been spent

90. CHY (1935-36), 1483; CKCCNC, D 79; TF:BFC, 235.
91. *Ibid.*, 100, 131.   92. *Ibid.*, 99.
93. *Ibid.*, 113.   94. *Ibid.*, 44.

by the government to meet its regular expenditures.[95] In 1918 out-standing claims of these two banks on the government increased further to C$93,000,000, while their notes were depreciated to 60 per cent of face value.[96] Alarmed at the prospect of a banking crisis that would deprive the government of further financing, the regime then decided to redeem these depreciated notes at par by offering two loans in 1918 and 1920 totaling C$153,000,000 which were subscribed at heavy discount by the banks themselves.[97] The process was mutually satisfactory to the government and the bankers, since without it the regime, which received little revenue from the provinces, could not survive, and with it the bankers reaped large profits by manipulating the discounts and by speculating on government bonds in the open market. The close contact they had with government officials also yielded other benefits to the bankers. For instance, Kincheng Bank, nominally a commercial bank, acted as the cashier of the Peking-Hankow and Peking-Kalgan Railroads after 1918 and in this way not only secured a large deposit account but also handled a monthly outpayment of some ten million Chinese dollars, mostly in notes issued by Kincheng itself. Experience had shown that over a period of ten years not more than 20 per cent of one-dollar bills issued, and not more than 60 per cent of larger ones, would turn up for redemption; thus the profit on note-issuing was very large.[98] Often much of the profit was again invested in government loans, making a bank an increasingly larger creditor of the regime.

Under the Kuomintang, relations between the government and the bankers became even closer. This trend started during the famous Northern Expedition, before the Kuomintang army reached Shanghai in March, 1927. Previously, there had been acute conflict within the Kuomintang regarding the alliance with the Communists. Chiang Kai-shek had maintained a noncommital attitude in this conflict until March, 1926, when he took action against some Communist officers as well as Russian advisers in a coup named after the gunboat *Chung-shan*.[99] Even after the incident, however, Chiang continued to pay lip service to Russia and the idea of world revolution, delaying the final break until he reached Shanghai and the wealth centered there. By November, 1926, Chiang's army reached Nanchang, not far away from the Yangtze port of Kiukiang. By then there were intense political maneuvers in the foreign settlements of Shanghai among the bankers-compradores, right-wing Kuomintang politicians, and Chinese underworld leaders who were used as police officers by settlement authorities.[100] The two common objectives of these groups were to

95. LYSNP, I, 338.   96. TF:BFC, 44.
97. CSI:MKT, 2d series, 2d pien, Ch. 4, pp. 12-13, 15-16.
98. I am indebted to Mr. Fu for this information.
99. IHR:TCR, 95.   100. *Ibid.*, 151, 175.

oust the northern army from Shanghai and Kiangsu and to purge the Kuomintang of the Communists. Chiang Kai-shek was to command both campaigns, the bankers were to finance them, and the underworld was to help with its police power over the foreign-administered enclaves from which Chinese armed forces were barred.

On March 26, 1927, Chiang himself arrived at Shanghai and the next day T. V. Soong was summoned there to take charge of finance.[101] On the twenty-ninth a delegation representing more than fifty leading banks and commercial firms called on Chiang to assure him of their support, which in the following week materialized into a sum of ten million Chinese dollars.[102] From then on Shanghai banks became a regular source of government income, subscribing to no less than 2,600 million Chinese dollars' worth of bonds by the end of 1935,[103] when the total resources of all Chinese banks in China were 5,512 million.[104] The magnitude of this support can also be shown by comparing it with the 872 million Chinese dollars in bonds issued by the Peking government between 1912 and 1927[105] and with the regular revenue of the Kuomintang government itself, which in 1934 amounted to 622 million Chinese dollars.[106] Did the banks co-operate willingly with the Kuomintang regime? Contemporary sources indicate that many cross forces were at work. On the one hand, the banks obviously preferred to diversify their investments. Shortly after the purge of the Communists on April 12, 1927, for instance, the banks tried to ignore Chiang's demand for a levy of twenty-two million dollars.[107] But the pressure proved too strong for them. The immediate hinterland of Shanghai was now under the complete control of the Kuomintang army. With State Socialism its basic ideology, the regime had no scruples about crushing private businessmen if the need arose; and, with Soong at the financial helm, the government could no longer be outmaneuvered by the shrewd bankers.

Furthermore, under the Kuomintang regime Chinese businessmen could no longer find sanctuary in the foreign settlements because Chiang's influence had penetrated the underworld gangs that controlled the police power over the Chinese in those enclaves. Well-known newspapers, including the *New York Times*, reported the plight of Chinese merchants who procrastinated in subscribing to government loans.[108] Many were arrested and had to buy their freedom with cash. Thus they were intimidated with bodily harm and at the same time were lured by handsome profits. Through working with the regime, the banks received large benefits from both the interest

101. KYT:CTSC, 251.   102. IH:TCR, 151.
103. CYL:CK, 81.   104. CHY (1936-37), 784-87.
105. *Ibid.*, 62.   106. CHY (1935-36), 1235.
107. CYL:CK, 101-2.
108. *New York Times*, May 4, 1927, as quoted in IH:TCR, 181-82.

yield of the bonds and the heavy discount of their face value. The latter averaged 45 per cent between 1927 and 1934, with the yield on government bonds varying between 10 and 20 per cent per annum.[109] Moreover, their intimate connection with government circles ensured the bankers of enormous opportunity for speculation on these bonds. A further attraction was the participation by the banks in the management of bond issues. A committee was organized in 1927 and enlarged in 1932 to take charge of all servicing, amortization, and redemption of bonds. The normal practice was for the Ministry of Finance to consult the committee before new bonds were issued and to give it the responsibility of allocating the bonds among the banks after they were issued.[110] Largely made up of bankers and merchants, the committee also included the British inspector-general of customs. In the company of a man who controlled the revenue on which the bonds were secured, the bankers derived a reasonable sense of safety in regard to their investment.

As government bonds accumulated in their portfolios, however, the bankers became increasingly tied to the regime. The continued existence of their enterprises was now predicated upon the rule of Chiang Kai-shek, who consequently felt more ready to ask the banks to shoulder the expenses of the military unification campaign. To remove any vestiges of private ownership of the Bank of China and Bank of Communications, both were reorganized in March, 1935.[111] In both cases, executive control was vested in the chairman of the board, an appointee of the Minister of Finance.[112] Chang Kia-ngau was replaced by T. V. Soong as head of the Bank of China. Hu Chün, who had been chairman of the Bank of Communications since 1933, continued in his post, but was given new power over the general manager. Hu was succeeded after his death in 1938 by Ch'ien Yung-ming, while the Bank of China post passed from T. V. Soong to H. H. Kung in 1944,[113] with no change in over-all government policy.

After the rise of the Kuomintang in 1928, a number of other government banks were established. The Central Bank of China came into being in 1928, the Postal Remittances and Savings Bank in 1930, the Farmers Bank in 1933, and the Central Trust Company in 1935.[114] In addition, there were banks in which the government had, usually by advancing funds, secured a decisive voice. In 1935 there were seven of these, not including the Bank of Canton which was under the personal control of T. V. Soong.[115] Through a total of thirteen

109. Calculated from figures given in TF:BFC, 217.
110. *Ibid.,* 175-76; YL:KHH, 75.   111. TF:BFC, 126.
112. *Ibid.,* 128.
113. CH (1937-45), 399; CPT:CKST, 15.
114. CYL:CK, 105-26.   115. CPT:CKST, 16.

banks the Kuomintang regime controlled 78 per cent of the combined resources of all modern banks in China.[116] The degree of concentration was also reflected in the executives. In 1935 seven men representing the seven leading commercial banks held among them at least fifty-three bank directorships.[117] The composition of the board was very similar for all the major banks.

This situation can easily be explained when we bear in mind the circumstances under which Chinese modern banks had started and under which they fell during Kuomintang domination. Because these institutions had been founded by individuals with political backing but no public support there were practically no shareholders except the management itself. Membership on the board was an honor mutually bestowed by fellow bankers. When the Kuomintang, by sheer political weight, imposed its control, the Bank of China, the Bank of Communications, and a few less important concerns became in effect treasuries to the head of the government, while the heads of seven leading commercial banks retained their autonomy by becoming government officials or by ingratiating themselves with leading political powers. Although personal rivalry existed among the bankers, their small number, their pre-Kuomintang common background, and their common interest in reducing government encroachment served to maintain harmony. As long as they were not recalcitrant, the government merely appointed a few superior heads— T. V. Soong, H. H. Kung, and later the Ch'en brothers—and left the bankers with a reasonable degree of autonomy. No major change took place in the power structure of the Chinese banking world from 1935 to 1949.

However, the number and size of the banks rapidly expanded. Between 1928 and 1937, 124 new banks were established, while only 23 were liquidated. The paid-up capital of the members of the Shanghai Bankers Association rose from 117 to 280 million Chinese dollars; between 1932 and 1937 the total capital of all modern banks increased from 214 to 434 million dollars.[118] The main stimulus seemed to be the steady flow of funds from rural areas to cities which accompanied the congregation of well-to-do Chinese in urban centers. One indication of this trend can be seen in the direction of Chinese internal remittances. In 1931 and 1932 no less than 47.4 per cent and 59.3 per

---

116. TF:BFC, 185-86. The thirteen banks include the Postal Remittance and Savings Bank, the Central Trust of China, the Sin Hua Savings Bank, but not the China Development Finance Corporation.

117. The men were K. P. Chen (10), Hsü Hsin-liu (14), Hu Chün (8), Chou Tso-min (6), Li Ming (7), Wu Ting-ch'ang (4), and Hsü Fu-ping (4). It might also be noted that of the seven only Hsü Fu-ping and Hu Chün were Chinese-trained, K. P. Chen having studied in America, Hsü Hsin-liu in England, and the other three in Japan.

118. TF:BFC, 185. Slightly different figures are found in CYL:CK, 66-67.

cent, respectively, of all remittances were from the rest of China to Shanghai.[119] Silver stock in Chinese and foreign banks of that city increased from 37 million Chinese dollars in 1920 to 171 million in 1928 and 594 million in May, 1934.[120] After that date it declined sharply, but not by returning to the interior. The world silver price had gone up as a result of American policy, and the Chinese stock followed the higher prices overseas. Before this exodus took place, however, deposits held by the twenty-four members of the Shanghai Bankers Association had increased from 497 million in 1921, to 953 million in 1927 and to 1,713 million in 1932.[121] The affluence of Shanghai stimulated modern banking activities.

Who were the depositors, and what did the banks do with these funds? While specific information is meager, the general pattern is clear. Individual depositors were the most important source of these funds. In 1936, for instance, the Bank of China and the Kincheng Banking Corporation reported that 63 to 66 per cent of their deposits came from private sources, 16 to 31 per cent from industry and commerce, and only 7 to 19 per cent from government organs.[122] The facts regarding the exact distribution of credits among users are obscure. The techniques by which banks financed the government varied greatly and cannot be identified from the published assets/liabilities figures of these concerns. It is probably safe to assume that all of the 2,600 million dollars of domestic borrowing of the Kuomintang regime up to 1936 were absorbed by the banks, which would account for about 46 per cent of the combined assets of all modern banks or some 70 per cent of the loans and investments made by these banks.[123]

Another important field of their activity was in real estate speculation, which was prohibited by the banking law of 1931 but which was nevertheless undertaken through various subterfuges. With such huge concentration of wealth in the two foreign settlements in Shanghai, it is to be expected that real estate values there would show steady increase over the years. In addition, Shanghai had historically served as a haven for wealthy Chinese fleeing from the civil wars. The first such case on record occurred in 1853 when hundreds of thousands came from neighboring areas occupied by the Taipings and Triads. A sharp rise in land value followed. By 1862 land "which had originally cost the foreigners fifty pounds sterling per acre was sold at ten

119. These were the remittances handled by the Bank of China (quoted in YHNC [1935]). According to other sources, the inward remittances to Shanghai exceeded the outward flow by nearly 90 per cent in 1932. See CKCTKM, 381, and *IB* (July 21, 1936), 8-9.
120. CHY (1935-36), 1474; CCC:CKN, 100-1.
121. CYL:CK, 70. The figures for 1927 and 1932 are listed as 976,000,000 and 1,974,000,000 respectively in CHY (1935-36), 1441.
122. CYL:CK, 71
123. TF:BFC, 184.

thousand pounds." Many Western merchants made huge profits by selling "every square foot of unoccupied ground." Even the British Consulate-General "sold some of its lovely acreage."[124] For some eight decades after that time, Shanghai was a sanctuary in the midst of political chaos in China. Industry developed, and real estate became a most popular form of speculation. The role of the banks in this field was described in a 1934 paper released by the Builder's Union of Shanghai.

> There are [in Shanghai] no less than 100,000 *mou* (a unit equivalent to one-sixth of an acre) in the busier and more prosperous quarters. If the average price be valued at 10,000 dollars, which is definitely an underestimate, the total value of land amounts to 1,000 million dollars. . . . According to P'u I Realty Company, new buildings in the past five years added up to some 500 million dollars in value. If we include all the old ones, the total value of buildings should be in the neighborhood of 2,000 million dollars. . . .
>
> The real estate conditions in Shanghai differ completely from those in the interior. There the transfer taxes are high and ownership seldom changes. People buy properties in order to pass them on to their descendants, and they do not buy unless they themselves have the money. In Shanghai, on the other hand, real estates are commercialized. Properties are purchased with an equity from 30 to 40 per cent of the price and a loan covering the rest. . . . Now it is calculated that out of a total value of 3,000 million dollars worth of land and buildings, properties owned outright by Chinese and foreign nationals and banks cannot exceed one-third of the total, leaving the other two-thirds subject to mortgage loans. If the average amount loaned be 60 per cent of the total value, no less than 1,200 million dollars are tied up in the real estate market. This sum has to come from Chinese and foreign firms in Shanghai.[125]

The report does not mention the specific parts played by different types of banking institutions. It was generally known, however, that Chinese modern banks were no less engaged in real estate operations than were the other firms. When real estate values in Shanghai fell after the conflict between Chinese and Japanese forces just outside the settlement in 1932, a banking crisis occurred which added to China's economic plight of the mid-thirties.[126] It was during this depression that the Kuomintang emerged as the controlling influence over the modern banks.

Of the rather small portion of funds that modern banks extended

124. HEO:SCS, 54.   125. CYL:CK, 84-85.
126. *Ibid.*, 87.

to industry and commerce, a high percentage went to textile mills. Industrial loans of the Shanghai Commercial and Savings Bank varied between 24 and 41 per cent of its total loans from 1931 through 1934, and of these industrial loans between 44 and 71 per cent were advances to cotton mills. [127] Figures published by the Bank of China are less explicit, but indicate that in 1934, 63 per cent of its industrial loans were to cotton mills.[128] Because Chinese mills were generally under-capitalized, their liability to the banks often far exceeded their capital.[129] Of the four forms of credit—unsecured overdraft, bills of exchange, loans secured by yarns and cloth, and mortgages on factory sites—the last was used for all the larger loans.[130] The customary pro-cedure was for the bank to assume control over the mill while lending to it about 50 per cent of the estimated worth of its site. The control included on-the-spot supervision over the operations, proprietory right over all the mill's properties, and exclusive right to make further loans if such were needed. Effective interest charges generally amounted to 15 per cent per annum.[131] As a consequence, except in boom times, the cotton mills often went bankrupt and were taken over by the banks. While the change of ownership was seldom publicized, a survey conducted by competent investigators revealed that between 1931 and 1937 no less than thirty mills, with a combined spindlage of 950,000 (or one-third of all Chinese-owned spindlage in China), passed through the hands of Chinese modern banks, often as a con-sortium with a specific debtor.[132] The fates of the mills varied: some were resold, some were dismantled, and some continued under the new owners. Among the creditors, there were a few foreign and Chinese native banks, but the Bank of China, with an interest in sixteen mills, was by far the most active.[133]

Direct control over industrial enterprises apparently led the modern banks to take the further step of launching new enterprises. In 1937 the Bank of China directly invested in two new cotton mills, one in Kunming with 5,200 spindles and one in Ch'ang-te with 30,000 spindles.[134] At the same time there were at least four syndicates organized by the leading banks to exercise control over a number of mills. Another device employed by some banks was the establishment of a subsidiary company that would operate freely in one or more industrial and commercial fields. A well-known example was the T'ung Ch'eng Company owned by the Kincheng Banking Corporation. During the Sino-Japanese War this company was active in various fields, including buying and hoarding scarce commodities. While no

127. TF:BFC, 164.   128. CYL:CK, 73.
129. YCP:CKMFC, 245-46.   130. *Ibid.*, 242-43.
131. *Ibid.*, 196.
132. Calculated from the data in YCP:CKMFC, 248-49.
133. *Ibid.*, 251-53.   134. *Ibid.*, 252.

details were divulged, it was widely known that the company made huge profits.

A pronounced feature of Chinese modern banks was their orientation toward urban markets and away from the farmers, which can be seen both in the locations of the banks and in their business operations. Early in 1935 the total paid-up capital of all Chinese modern banks was 265 million Chinese dollars, of which the members of the Shanghai Bankers Association held 130 million.[135] In terms of assets, only twelve banks then had resources of more than 100 million each; of these twelve, nine maintained their headquarters in Shanghai, one was based on Tientsin (but moved to Shanghai in 1936), one had a nominal headquarters in Nanking, and one operated out of Canton only because it was a provincial government bank.[136] If smaller banks with assets of more than thirty million are included, eight out of eleven such concerns were similarly based in Shanghai. If assets of even smaller banks are added, the combined resources of Chinese modern banks in Shanghai came close to 90 per cent of the total assets of all Chinese modern banks in the country.[137] The concentration indicates a lack of modern banking facilities over vast parts of China, especially the rural areas.

In spite of the fact that many banks were nominally agricultural banks, only one institution with very limited resources actually extended rural loans before 1933. In that year the Agricultural Bank of Kiangsu, which had started this activity in 1917, had an outstanding balance of C$1.6 million lent to farmers.[138] Several factors then began to draw the attention of other banks. One was the lack of suitable investment channels in the large cities. The Shanghai Commercial and Savings Bank established an agricultural department, and the Bank of China listed for the first time in its 1933 report agricultural loans amounting to 4.81 per cent of all loans outstanding.[139] In February, 1934, a consortium of five leading commercial banks started to operate in Shansi province and before the end of the year granted loans totaling C$2 million.[140] According to the 1935 Bank of China report, these operations reduced the rural interest rates from a range of 30 to 100 per cent per annum to a level of 20 to 30 per cent per annum.[141]

Another factor that favored the extension of agricultural credit was the anti-Communist campaign waged by the Kuomintang. In April,

135. CKCCNC (1935), D 87.

136. The head office of the Continental Bank was in Tientsin until 1936. The Farmers Bank of China was by law required to maintain its head office in Nanking.

137. Computed from data in CHY (1936-37), 784-87.

138. Li Ching-han, "Rural Finance and the Agricultural Co-operatives," EM, Vol. 33, No. 7, pp. 17-18.

139. See YHNC.   140. Li Ching-han, op. cit., 17-18.

141. CHY (1936-37), 801.

1933, Chiang Kai-shek ordered the formation of a Four Province Agricultural Bank especially to help the farmers and to weaken the Communist hold on them. By June, 1935, the bank had extended some C$10 million in loans through 1,147 agricultural co-operatives.[142] However, these efforts came far short of the peasants' needs. Reports emanating from the field cast doubt on the efficacy of these co-operatives, and a strong statement from Chiang Kai-shek's headquarters in April, 1935, condemning the banks for "reaping profit at the expense of the farmers" hardly contradicted these reports.[143] Moreover, the distribution of loans extended from 1933 through 1935 indicated that landowners and part-owners, who received 52 and 35 per cent of the total credit, were favored at the expense of tenant farmers, who received only 13 per cent. The short duration of the loans (up to one year only) eliminated the possibility of using them for long-term improvements. Lastly, the amount of co-operative credit was altogether insignificant. From 1933 through 1935, it was estimated that the credit distributed by all agricultural co-operatives in China amounted only to 1 per cent of the total agricultural credit and was granted to only 5 per cent of all the borrowing farmers.

The commercial banks were even less successful in this area than the government banks. Their loans were small, and not always granted to the farmers. In 1933, for instance, agricultural loans extended by the Bank of China included three different fields: loans against agricultural commodities, small loans to peasants, and loans to co-operatives. For that year, the second category amounted only to C$622,000 as compared to C$19.5 million in the first category, which probably was not rural credit at all.[144] The interest of the banks in their rural operations declined after mid-1934. The agricultural loans granted by the Shanghai Commercial and Savings Bank decreased from C$4.4 million in 1934 to 2.7 million in 1935.[145] A consortium of ten banks formed in 1935 with the aim of extending C$3 million in rural loans actually extended only one million. As stated in the *Bankers Weekly* of October, 1935, even though the bumper harvest in Shansi called for expansion of rural credit, the banks suspended all operations because their attention had again shifted back to Shanghai.[146] The back-to-the-people movement among the bankers was thus "much thunder but little rain."

However, the failure was due more to institutional factors than to the whims of bank executives. It has been noted that the banks were concentrated in urban areas and that their business practices

142. Li Ching-han, *op. cit.* 143. *Ibid.*, 18.

144. YHNC (1935), i/50. The corresponding figures for 1934 were C$1.1 million for the second category and C$76 million for the first (*ibid.*, i/81).

145. Wu Ch'eng-hsi, "Chinese Banking in 1935," EM (April 1, 1936), 85.

146. Wu Ch'eng-hsi, "An Evaluation of the Cooperatives in Chekiang," CC:CKN, 85.

were similar. Because of these factors, the banks had few staff members capable of handling rural operations. This deficiency was further aggravated by the reluctance of most Chinese city-dwellers to go into the countryside where living conditions were much poorer. Contemporary sources depict vividly the unfamiliarity of the bank personnel with rural surroundings and their resulting preference to deal with cooperatives rather than peasants.[147] The principles of modern banking were generally incompatible with Chinese rural conditions. Sound banking practice required adequate security against loans; the peasants had no securities to offer. The banks preferred that credit advanced be for productive purposes; a survey of four provinces from 1933 through 1935 revealed that only 27 per cent of all rural credit went into productive channels.[148] For permanent improvement of the farm the peasant needed long-term credit; commercial banks provided only loans of a seasonal nature. Operating not as a charity but for profit, these institutions were unable to extend loans to the poor, whose need was the greatest but whose ability to repay was the least.

For all of these reasons, rural operations were never more than a sideline for the banks. Although the movement toward rural markets resulted from a search for new investment opportunities, the banks stressed at the outset the humanitarian factor rather than the profit aspect.[149] As things turned out, the amount of credit extended was even smaller than originally planned. Consequently, as soon as a silver crisis developed in mid-1934, the banks completely lost interest in "doing something for the rural poor." In the ultimate analysis it was the deep gulf between two ways of life—urban and rural—that rendered a profitable association between commercial banks and rural communities difficult in China.

In reviewing Chinese modern banking, we see two periods with some overlapping features. In the earlier phase, modern banks in China were established by officials largely to further their own political influence. Not only did the initial capital come mainly from government funds, but the continued existence of the banks often depended on political support. The forms this support took were varied and unorthodox by Western standards. The banks depended for the most part on note-issues funneled into circulation through government spending; in turn the banks financed government deficits by granting loans and subscribing to bonds. Such borrowing was done at very high interest and brought large profits to the banks and bankers when all went well. On the other hand, as government finances deteriorated during the years of the early Republic, the banks

147. Ling Ho-cheng, "How Should Our Rural Financial System Be?" EM, Vol. 33, No. 7, p. 58.
148. TF:BFC, 207.
149. See the various bank reports in YHNC (1935).

led a precarious existence. In the eyes of their founders, however, the primary function of a bank was not to make money but to serve as a financial pillar to the regime in which they had a vital interest. To put the same thing differently, a sponsor eyed his bank as his political capital in much the same way as a warlord eyed his army as his. There was little thought to direct the funds into industrial and commercial markets, which had to be satisfied with facilities provided by native banks and, in the treaty ports, foreign banks. The intimate tie with politics was characteristic not only of the two government banks but also of the leading commercial banks, most of which were established primarily to increase the freedom of action of the same men who controlled the government banks. As the original sponsors gradually faded away from the political scene, the banks which had the good fortune to survive and even to prosper became almost the personal property of their original managers. The modern banking structure in China cannot be understood without some idea of this complex historical background.

The second period started in 1928. With the rise of the Kuomintang the capital was shifted from Peking to Nanking, near Shanghai. The modern banks, which had thrived on government financing, accordingly shifted their operations southward. Meanwhile, various economic and political factors converged to produce a boom in modern banking. A basic cause was the continual stream of men, talents, and wealth from the countryside, where modern banking was practically non-existent, to large cities, where modern institutions such as banks came into their own. The chief center of concentration was Shanghai, where deposits of modern banks increased by some 245 per cent between 1921 and 1932 and where the number of banks increased from 20 in 1919 to 34 in 1923, 63 in 1927, and 164 in 1937.[150] While the leading banks had always had branches in that port, the southward move of their top executives added new vigor to the Shanghai branches and resulted in an extention of their activities, including the financing of international trade and even real estate dealings for investment and speculative purposes. As time advanced, the native industries, especially those at Shanghai, became more accustomed to modern banking practices, and their dealings with the modern institutions increased. Another favorable factor was the gradual decline of foreign influences. In 1914 many Chinese lost heavily when a French bank, la Banque Industrielle de la Chine, failed.[151] It was a serious blow to foreign prestige in the eyes of Chinese investors who then began to view Chinese banks with more interest. But it was not until the late twenties that foreign privileges rapidly declined. After 1928 Western powers gave up a number of

150. CYL:CK, 70; LTY:EBC, 37-38.   151. LTY:EBC, 37-38.

concessions and leased territories in China, granted her tariff autonomy, and revised the judicial system in Shanghai to give the Chinese
judges more voice. It was under these circumstances that the custody
of customs receipts passed from foreign banks to the new Central
Bank of China, thus increasing vastly the resources of this institution.[152] In 1930 the Customs Gold Unit was introduced, and its
exchange with other currencies was fixed daily by the Central Bank.[153]
All of these innovations signified a new era for Chinese banking.

The most important change after 1927, however, was in the relations between the banks and the government. While this association
had always been close, with the rise of the Kuomintang the pattern of
relationship underwent a rather basic change. Previously, the banks
had been dominated by individual politicians, but were free from
government control. Indeed, in so far as the government was
financially insolvent, it had to depend on the banks for aid. As commercial or semi-commercial concerns, many of the banks enjoyed
stability and at least apparent prosperity. Furthermore, they had
branches in the port cities and could always claim foreign protection.
The Chinese central government, on the other hand, was generally
short-lived and had little power outside the capital. It really had no
effective political means to bring the banks to heel. This situation was
entirely changed after 1927. For a time, at least, the Kuomintang
represented a rising political influence with a coherent ideology that
symbolized the future. While it did not have unchallenged control
over all China, its position was much stronger than any previous
regime after 1916. At any rate, it was firmly entrenched in the two
provinces of Kiangsu and Chekiang, which were the immediate hinterland of Shanghai. As followers of Sun Yat-sen, many of the young
leaders—for example, T. V. Soong—had little connection with the
erstwhile ruling group in Peking. They were unencumbered by personal ties. Yet because of their urban, commercial background and
because of their familiarity with Western financial capitalism, they
had no difficulty in discerning the trade secrets of Chinese modern
bankers and beat them at their own game. They were further aided
by the official cult of state socialism, which readily justified the crushing of intransigent capitalists by political force.

All of these advantages would have been ineffective, however, if
the Kuomintang leaders had not been able to penetrate into the
foreign settlements in Shanghai, which were the financial center of
China and from which political rebels could and did operate with
great equanimity. The vital task of tightening the reins over prominent men within the foreign enclaves was accomplished by the Kuomintang through the active co-operation of Shanghai underworld leaders

152. TF:BFC, 100.   153. *Ibid.*, 102, 140.

—notably Tu Yung (Dou Yu-seng, 1887-1951), whose great influence over the detectives and police was tolerated, if not encouraged, by Western authorities. With its overwhelming political superiority and this added power over the personal security of prominent bankers, the Kuomintang easily obtained the latter's support.

The entente started almost immediately after Chiang's arrival in Shanghai in 1927. A few days later, Communists by the thousands were purged and slaughtered. Meanwhile, government borrowing from the banks steadily mounted, totaling some C$2,600 million between 1927 and 1935, equivalent to four times the revenue of the regime in 1934. There is evidence of the bankers' initial hesitation and occasional shock at the magnitude of the borrowing, but their services did not go unrewarded. First, they shared in the management of the issues as well as in the custody of the sinking fund. Second, the bonds were sold at a large discount: out of a face value of C$1,465 million issued between 1927 and 1934, the government actually received only C$809 million, the remainder being the profit, at least on paper, of the subscribing banks.[154] By reason of the same discount, the nominal interest rate of 7 to 8 per cent actually meant an annual return between 10 and 20 per cent in the years from 1927 through 1933.[155] The bonds also served as an active speculative medium. Contemporary sources suggest that speculators sometimes engineered civil wars in order to affect the short-run values of the bonds.[156] At any rate, persons close to the government had little difficulty in making a "kill." In the long run, the bonds steadily appreciated as the Nanking regime consolidated. The lowest quotations in Shanghai of the Seventeenth Year Long-Term Currency Loan were C$23.10 in 1932 and C$53.70 in 1936.[157] Such capital gains swelled the profits of the banks, since they were almost the sole subscribers.

As the banks purchased the bonds, they became irrevocably committed to the regime. After the reorganization of 1935, the Bank of China and the Bank of Communications were little more than government bureaus.[158] Several other commercial banks also came under official control. The "Northern Four" and the Chekiang Industrial Bank, the National Commercial Bank, and the Shanghai Commercial and Savings Bank survived as private institutions but only at the price of complete subservience to the government, which can be seen from the appointment of their top executives as cabinet ministers or as government representatives in various missions while retaining their positions in the banks.[159] Even excluding these seven banks, the government held at the end of 1935 a majority interest which controlled

154. *Ibid.*, 217.   155. *Ibid.*
156. MT:TY, 49-50.
157. CHY (1935-36), 1478; (1936-37), 768.
158. CPT:CKST, 15.   159. TF:BFC, 9; CPT:CKST, 15-17.

61 per cent of the combined resources of all Chinese banks.[160] This government domination yielded important political consequences. It alone enabled Chiang Kai-shek to fight his internal foes, to nationalize silver and institute a paper standard, and, finally, to resist Japan. Actually, the monopoly of the banking resources made credit for industry and commerce unavailable. Business prospered only in the hands of the privileged few, who by reason of their political connections, could obtain low-cost loans and government subsidies in various forms.[161] Known as "bureaucratic capitalists," these men reaped windfalls by speculation while genuine businesses were stifled. The structure was not unlike that of the old economy, with a small number of political leaders on top and large masses below; the only difference was that the art of economic manipulation had replaced the Confucian ethics as the operational code of the few. Within this system neither the peasants nor the urban business class could find a proper place. For this reason, democracy in the Western European and American sense never had a chance to develop in China. Instead, the country steadily drifted toward an opposite way of life, which, contrary to the predictions of Karl Marx, rose in China not among the proletariat but among the hard-pressed and misgoverned peasant masses.

160. TF:BFC, 186.

161. See, for instance, Wang, "Free Enterprise in China," PHR (November, 1960), 407-9.

By now it should be clear that an important and valuable way of viewing Chinese history in the last hundred years is to see it as the unfolding of Western cultural impact on an entirely different social arrangement, the traditional Chinese system. In the first chapter, I discussed the basic operating principles of that society. It was based on certain ethical values, of which the chief one was social harmony. The working of such a system dictated two occurrences: first, very slowly changing material conditions of life, and second, the social dominance of a group of literati whose duty was to defend and uphold the assumed values. Both these conditions broke down in the nineteenth century in the face of intensified Western impact. The slowly changing material conditions of life caused a kind of restraint on industrial and commercial activities as well as a discouragement of human endeavor in its attempts to conquer Nature. These restraints in turn placed China in a noncompetitive position in regard to the West, which had been freed from similar but milder moral and social shackles after the Renaissance, the Age of Invention, and the Industrial Revolution or revolutions.

At first the breakdown in China took the form of military defeats. In order to defend herself, China felt compelled to promote industrial enterprise and, later, to undertake the re-education of her educators, thus implicitly reversing the foundation of Chinese society. Once this process was started, there seemed hardly any possibility that the old order could be preserved. The pertinent question was not whether the old order would survive but rather the nature of the new order that was to replace it. Many Chinese would have preferred a society patterned on the West, especially on England and America. But such an individualistic order would probably have taken far longer to emerge than a system in which control was exercised from the center, and time was what the Chinese did not have, or at least what they felt they did not have. It is not too much to say that democracy in the Western sense of the term never had a chance in China.

Within this analysis the mechanism of change may be traced. The first point to note is the importance of the educated class. It was the intellectuals, not the peasants, who had to grapple consciously with the problems arising from Western penetration. The social and political nature of China's reaction to the West was to be determined by their attitudes, by whether they stubbornly resisted all change or adopted indiscriminate imitation. Broadly, there were four stages or periods in China's response to the West. In the first, from 1840 to 1860, only a few men anticipated the shattering experience that lay ahead for China. In the second, from 1860 to 1895, partial modernization was undertaken by a few officials in their capacity as foreign affairs experts. Such efforts were limited to technological innovation, and because these proved grossly inadequate for China's protection, social and political reform dominated the third phase, from 1895 to 1919. The outstanding events in this period are worth specific mention. First there was Yen Fu's attack on the monarchy as such and then Liang Ch'i-ch'ao's scathing criticism of the men in power. These two developments contributed heavily to the revolution of 1911, in which the Japanese-trained Chinese played an active part. Finally, between 1915 and 1919, a group of Chinese professors, some trained in Japan and some in the West, carried the revolution beyond the political border into the realm of values. They held that Confucianism had been the basic evil and that it must be discarded so that China could achieve true modernization.

The fourth phase, from 1919 to 1949, witnessed three attempts to fill in the vacuum left by the discredited Confucianism. One—the suggestion that China should be "totally Westernized"—was not really politically feasible and soon lost its appeal.[1] Another—the Kuomintang effort based on Sun Yat-sen's doctrines—held sway for

1. Confucianism and modern Western democracy would seem to be antithetic in historical as well as ideological senses. In the Western world it was the flourishing of trade from the eleventh century onward that led to the rise of a bourgeois middle class that, in turn, through a series of complex circumstances spreading over many centuries, became the main supporters of nationalism, capitalism, and democracy. In China, Confucianism hampered commercial developments and deprived the merchants of political influence. The two main social groups were the literati and the peasants, neither of which was best situated to sponsor a democratic political system. Ideologically, the gap between Confucianism and democracy is even more obvious. In Confucian society the masses are wards of the government; in democracy the government is decided by the masses. The basic assumption of democracy is that men are imperfect and that power corrupts; the foundation of Confucianism is the unbounded wisdom of the sage. Whereas democracy preaches tolerance of different views, Confucianism exalts conformity to one set of values. Even in method of operation the two systems are quite different: one depends on due process of law for the preservation of liberty and justice, while the other considers legal coercion as unworthy of good society. If nationalism and capitalism are historically inherent to Anglo-American democracy, acquisitiveness and the concept of political sovereignty are anathema to Confucian virtue. While the Confucian system begins at the center and inspires from above, democracy by its nature cannot be imposed on the masses. Thus the very effort to replace Confucianism with democracy indicates ignorance on the part of those who tried it. Without being aware of it, they were far more influenced by Confucian thought than by whatever Western culture they had assimilated. This can be seen from their own writings, which are filled with passionate words and scornful references to their opponents. Such emotionalism is consonant with the traditional insistence on distinguishing right from wrong in every issue, but it is a far cry from the democratic and scientific spirit that the writers themselves preached.

the twenty years between 1927 and 1949. A striking phenomenon of this experiment was the party's tendency to conform with the letter of Sun's teachings while ignoring their spirit. There were undoubtedly many reasons for this failure: for one thing, the inherent defects in Sun's doctrines were of such a nature that strict conformity with their wording tended to defeat the observance of their principle; for another, as I shall explain, the changed outlook of the Chinese officials was probably not conducive to the goal Sun had in mind. At any rate, it seems obvious that the Kuomintang failed and that its failure gave rise to a Communist regime, whose origin also lay in the May Fourth movement of 1919.

As far as this study is concerned, my immediate aim was to illustrate and evaluate the role of foreign-educated intellectuals. Because of the large number of men involved, the task of evaluation was necessarily a difficult one. A broad study of this type involves more hazards than biography, where conclusions can be based on minute investigation of a man's thought and actions. By the nature of this study my observations necessarily depend on the assumption that the men studied shared certain characteristics and that these were related to their actions. Furthermore, my evaluation is inevitably rather general, which means that it is likely to contain more value judgments than are ordinarily found in biographical studies.

As we have seen, the goal of the movement to study abroad was to nurture leadership in political, economic, and educational fields. Of these, the impact on economic development is perhaps the simplest to describe. Whereas the Japanese-trained accounted for a large proportion of China's top bankers, the Western-educated were heavily concentrated on the engineering side of economic endeavor. Probably because private industry was small, most of the engineers and technicians worked for the government. Although many of them rose to managerial positions, extremely few are known to have become entrepreneurs in their own right. The bankers, too, depended heavily on their connections with officialdom. In fact, most of them not only started out with political support but also continued to deal largely with the government until modern banking was practically nationalized in 1935. For these reasons, even though a class of businessmen and professionals came into existence, it had no political strength and failed to play a key role in China's industrialization.

Educationally, the most striking feature was perhaps the returned students' dominating position. From 1902 on, college professors in China were either foreigners or foreign-trained Chinese, and after 1922 all of the important teaching and administrative positions fell to men educated in the West.[2] To be sure, this monopoly did not

2. From 1907 to 1948 there were twenty-eight directors of higher education (two of whom held the same position twice) in the Ministry of Education. Of

mean that such men could do as they wished, for they still had to cope with a variety of social forces. Nevertheless, in a comparative sense they were almost in control of the situation. Under their administration, the Chinese educational system developed a number of striking characteristics. In the first place, it assigned far more importance to higher education than to lower; second, it stressed technology and science at the expense of the humanities; and third, it made extremely large use of foreign materials in the curriculum. Up to a point these characteristics merely reflected the fact that modern Chinese education started not as a means to enlighten the individual but as a device to strengthen China. To the degree that this was true, the peculiarities and variations may be attributed to policy. But there were features that did not result from choice. One of these was the glaring neglect of rural areas. Not only were rural educational facilities inadequate in number, but their quality was also extremely low. This situation restricted the peasants' opportunities to advance and better themselves and isolated the elite from the masses. Furthermore, in contrast to the old system, modern education was prohibitively expensive in terms of the average Chinese income. Before the Sino-Japanese war of 1937-45, few schools in China offered scholarships. With the concomitant decline in clan and village solidarity, which in former days helped to educate the poor, only the well-to-do could go to school.

Last was the change in the nature of education. Previously, the goal at all levels was to achieve moral and academic excellence. While this supposedly remained the basic purpose of elementary and secondary education, the aim of advanced training now became increasingly technical. The issue was further complicated in China by the disavowal of traditional values. As a consequence, there was a steady weakening of the moral sense and an increasing dedication to professional achievement. While the international standing of Chinese scientists rose perceptibly, their attachment to the masses became increasingly more remote. As a number of them recently admitted (under Communist prodding but not necessarily insincerely), they had never even tried to further science or technology in China.[3] Thus, scholars became experts in their own fields but paid almost no attention to national needs. Because all of this happened while the masses remained dependent on others to look after their interests, the educational impact of these developments had very ominous social consequences.

these, sixteen were Western-trained and five, Japanese-trained: details of seven others are unknown, but in all probability they were educated abroad. Most of the Chinese ministers of education since 1911 were Western-trained. Under the Kuomintang, from 1927 to 1952, the only exception was Chiang Kai-shek, who took nominal charge of the ministry for six months in 1930-31.

3. SHTK, *passim*, especially p. 39.

By comparison, the political role of the returned students is a more complicated story and needs to be described in stages. Broadly, one can speak of three periods, the first from 1895 to 1911, the second from 1915 to 1922, and the third from 1927 to 1949. In the first, the Japanese-educated played an important role, while the Western-trained with the exception of Yen Fu and perhaps Sun Yat-sen, were conspicuously insignificant. By 1919, however, at least one of them, Hu Shih, had become a key figure in the literary revolution and the campaign to discredit Confucianism. In subsequent years the number of Western-trained persons steadily increased, and under the Kuomintang many of them held important government positions.

Any brief comments on important political events are inevitably speculative. In my opinion, the outstanding feature of the revolution of 1911 was its futility, for neither the intellectuals nor the masses gained anything. Essentially the revolution represented the success of one man, Yüan Shih-kai, but even that success was extremely short-lived, leading as it did only to his ruin and death in 1916. Although no useful purpose could have been served by the prolongation of the Manchu dynasty, its downfall did not reflect any foresight or ability on the part of the revolutionaries. In regard to the May Fourth movement, the literary revolution would seem to be far more meaningful than the anti-Confucian campaign, but even here the true pioneers were Liang Ch'i-ch'ao, who had initiated a new style,[4] and numerous others who had actually used the colloquial medium in their propaganda before 1911.[5] With the benefit of hindsight, it seems that Hu Shih's originality has been exaggerated.

From a sociological point of view few things are as striking as the change in the attitude of the Chinese intellectuals between 1911 and 1927. Even though the earlier revolutionaries had many failings, most of them were dedicated to the pursuit of the common good. However misguided they might have been, they differed basically from the intellectuals of the 1930's. In a sense the men of 1911 were the last generation of the old elite who lived close to the land and had intimate connections with the peasantry. Although their power over the masses often led to abuses, these were kept within bounds by the men's attachment to their places of birth, the desire to leave a good name to their descendants, the moral restraints inspired by Confucianism, and the social stigmas attached to extravagant living. Nearly all these factors disappeared under Western impact. The new

4. As early as 1901, Liang attacked the literary medium and advocated the colloquial. See his article "The Colloquial Writing: A Prerequisite to Modernization" ("Lun pai-hua wei wei-hsin chih pen"), HHCSN, 1st series, I, 38-42.

5. Many provinces had a vernacular press before 1911. See, for instance, CTT: TMM, 42a; HHKM, IV, 332, VII, 318, 432; HHHIL, V, 504, for a description of such presses in Anhwei, Shantung, Ili, and Szechuan.

intellectuals often came from a mercantile background and invariably lived in the cities. Their family ties were relatively weak, and through neither religion nor education were they endowed with strong moral convictions. With the rise of industry and the professions they no longer had to seek employment in government service but were increasingly susceptible to the lure of high living so characteristic of modern industrialized society. As a consequence, material gain loomed large in life, and the old habit of hiding the urge to accumulate beneath a display of public virtue completely disappeared.

In terms of politics, this change was a decisive one. At the local level the absence of educated men from the rural areas rendered good government impossible. Reliable surveys of rural districts in the mid-1930's demonstrated clearly the deterioration of local government.[6] The old gentry virtually disappeared; their place was taken by petty militarists or their underlings, whose only concern was to loot the peasant to the maximum possible extent. These men were not infrequently known murderers, but there was little that the county government could do about them; indeed, there was a temptation for the magistrate to fall in with them in unsavory transactions. Much depended upon the locality: the riffraff were usually less active in areas close to the modern cities, where there was peace and order, and more obnoxious in the interior, where higher intellectuals were few and public opinion weak. In times of civil wars, usually confined to the rural areas, the situation reached its worst. The peasant had the choice of fleeing or staying on the land and taking the consequences. Either way he faced probable extinction.

Even at the national level, the political influence of the Western-educated men declined while their number and prominence increased. This came about largely because they had become more specialized in skill and individualized in attitude. Many of them probably had an implicit belief in democracy, but their convictions were insufficiently crystallized to form a basis for political action. Having no contact with the masses, they naturally depended on patronage from above. In this way, even though their nominal position might be exalted, their political role was limited to the execution of policies with which they had little sympathy. Thus, instead of serving as overseers of evil-doing monarchs as their predecessors had done, the modern intellectuals became willing tools of the existing power. This change was of vital importance to society, for it meant the removal of a safety valve in Chinese politics. When the masses became acutely dissatisfied with the regime, few men in the government were able to sense the

6. HCYNT, *passim*. This series of reports incurred the criticisms of some scholars, notably Fei Hsiao-t'ung, at the time it was published. However, the strictures were high-level discussions of the methodology involved rather than repudiations of the facts discovered.

grievances and make corrections.[7] By yielding their moral and political leadership, the Westernized intellectuals promoted, by default, the rise of totalitarian rule in China.

7. It is a striking fact that whereas the officials used to dwell constantly on the poverty of the masses and the need for the government to adopt alleviative measures, the modern bureaucrats practically never expressed such sentiments in their writings. The omission was certainly not due to any improvement in the lot of the peasants; it rather illustrates, I believe, the changed outlook of the officials.

APPENDIXES

LIST OF ABBREVIATIONS
AND BIBLIOGRAPHY

Expatriation: The Possible Inter-Generational Effect of Study Abroad

An interesting phenomenon in the matter of expatriation is the possible inter-generational effect of study abroad. In the course of this study, the biographical data of several thousand returned students have been examined. The extent of these data varies greatly, but in nearly all cases where details are available, we find study abroad to be more or less an "inherited" phenomenon, that is, a father who studied abroad tends to see that his son does also. The following are three sample cases.

Mr. C. was one of the original C.E.M. boys. After returning to China he worked in the telegraph service and also in the Kiangnan dockyard. His career was ordinary, although he became related by marriage to Charles Soon, the head of the famous Soong family. Mr. C. had two sons and two daughters, all of whom were educated in the West. The oldest daughter studied in the United States, married a Chinese diplomat, and had a son who was a Harvard-trained doctor teaching in 1956 in one of the better-known universities in the United States. Mr. C's second daughter was educated in England, married another returned student and had two sons, one of whom is in business in China and the other, an American citizen, is in business in New York. Mr. C's elder son was trained in America and became a very prominent surgeon in Shanghai. His wife was also American-educated, as is his only son, now pursuing graduate study in the United States. Mr. C's younger son was trained in England and also became a very prominent medical practitioner in Shanghai. His wife was educated in China. Of the four sons born to this couple, two, a pianist and a medical doctor, were Chinese-trained, and two, a pastor and an engineer, were American-educated. The last two are currently in the United States.

Mr. N. was also one of the original C.E.M. boys. After his return to China, he worked in the telegraph service and eventually became a district head of the service. He had four sons and three daughters. The first son was trained in England and had one daughter, who did not study abroad. Mr. N's second son studied at Yale on a partial Tsinghua scholarship. This son had three daughters. The eldest daughter went to the United States with her husband in 1946, both as students. They were naturalized in 1954. The other two daughters stayed in China; one married an American-trained doctor and the other a man trained in Japan. Mr. N's third son was sent to America as a Tsinghua graduate and had two daughters; one of them died at an early age, and the other is currently a student in Japan. Mr. N's fourth son was also sent to America as a Tsinghua graduate. He married a fellow Chinese student while in Chicago and had one son, who immigrated to the United States from Formosa in 1956, under the sponsorship of his American-citizen cousin. Of Mr. N's daughters, two were European-educated and one was trained in China.

Mr. S. went to America in 1894 as a student attaché of the Chinese legation. Until his retirement he always served in the Chinese diplomatic corps. He had two brothers: the elder, whom we shall designate as A, was the first Chinese consul-general in New York; the younger, whom we shall designate as B, graduated from the engineering school of Cornell in 1905. Brother A returned to China and became a government official. His two sons were both American-educated, one as a doctor and the other as an engineer. The engineer had no children, but the doctor had three sons. One of these sons was born in the United States, returned to China in his childhood, but went back again to the United States when he was fifteen years of age. He is now employed in the American civil service. The second and third sons, although not born in America, have become naturalized citizens and are currently serving in the United States army.

Mr. S's brother B was employed by the government after his return to China in 1905. For many years he was a railway engineer and at one time was connected with the Kailuan mines. His three sons, an architect, a doctor, and an engineer, were all American-trained. All of this group, including B, his sons and their wives, now reside in America. B and his wife left China in 1948, but his sons emigrated earlier.

Mr. S. himself has two sons and four daughters. All of them were reared abroad. The two boys received a thoroughly English education—at Winchester and Cambridge. Of the daughters one is a novelist who writes in English, two are married to Westerners, and the fourth, although married to a Chinese, resides in the United States.

These samples suggest that education abroad tended to pass from one generation to another in Chinese families. There seems to be a cumulative effect of long exposure to Western culture. In the third case history cited, alienation is very pronounced since most members of the third generation, beginning with the man who first received education abroad, are no longer Chinese citizens, not by reason of political persecution at home, but as a matter of choice. This case is not typical, but the peculiarity lies in the prominence of Mr. S. and his diplomatic profession, which afforded many opportunities to his children and relatives in traveling to the United States and in choosing their own destiny. Other Chinese, should they wish to emigrate to the United States, would be hampered by much greater restrictions on both sides of the ocean.

The other two cases seem fairly typical. In the case of the granddaughter of Mr. N, who together with her husband became naturalized in the United States, our data show clearly that the motivation was not political, but was rather admiration of Western culture and attraction of economic opportunity. No detailed information is available on how the foreign study of the C. and N. families was financed. A part of the funds no doubt came from their private income, but neither C. nor N. was excessively rich. In the case of N, the Tsinghua scholarships helped a great deal. In addition, it is possible that both families had some assistance from Western missionaries, since both C. and N. became converted to Christianity during their C.E.M. days. An important factor in both cases probably was the determination of the fathers to provide their children with an education abroad. With this determination and with their fairly prominent position in society, they succeeded in one way or another in sending most of their children abroad.

[Appendix B]

TABLE 10. *Fields of Chinese Students in America*

	1905[a]	1906-07[b]	1909[c]	1914[d]	1918[e]	1920-21[f]	1924[g]	1927[h]	1931-32[i]	1934-35[j]
Humanities	—	—	16.4	2.1	11.9	8.6	10.2	10.7	20.8	13.4
Literature	—	—	—	—	.5	—	.2	2.6	5.4	—
History	—	—	—	.3	.5	.9	2.1	1.6	1.0	1.6
Philosophy	—	—	.6	.1	1.0	1.0	—	1.7	.8	—
Library Science	—	—	—	—	.3	.2	—	.2	6.5	.8
Journalism	—	—	—	—	.2	—	.7	.2	.4	1.6
Fine Arts	—	—	—	.1	.3	1.0	2.3	.2	.1	—
General	—	—	15.8	1.6	9.1	5.5	4.9	4.2	6.6	9.4
Social Science	5.4	5.6	19.7	10.2	12.3	15.1	10.1	19.3	12.5	14.1
Law	1.5	—	8.2	1.7	2.6	1.5	5.5	2.3	1.7	1.6
Political Science	1.6	5.6	7.7	2.8	3.1	4.6		7.3	4.2	5.9
Economics	2.3	—	3.8	4.7	5.9	6.8	4.6	7.6	4.4	2.7
Sociology	—	—	—	1.0	.7	2.2	—	2.1	2.2	3.9
Business	5.4	8.6	9.3	4.0	10.5	10.1	14.0	14.1	10.8	12.4
Education	4.6	—	4.4	4.7	8.9	7.1	8.7	9.0	9.2	11.4
Education	4.6	—	2.2	3.5	5.8	5.6	7.5	6.0	6.5	7.2
Home Economics	—	—	—	—	.7	.2	.1	.1	.6	2.7
Religion	—	—	—	1.0	1.6	1.2	1.1	1.1	1.5	1.5
Music	—	—	2.2	—	.8	.1	—	1.8	.6	—
Social Work	—	—	—	.2	—	—	—	—	—	—
Engineering	23.8	27.2	33.9	30.8	28.2	38.3	36.3	23.7	22.4	30.1
Sciences	4.6	—	9.8	7.5	9.3	9.3	10.2	11.1	11.7	5.1
Medicine	4.6	—	2.2	4.8	7.9	6.0	6.8	7.6	7.8	9.5
Agriculture	4.6	—	4.3	6.0	4.3	5.2	3.5	3.3	4.2	3.9
Military Sciences	.8	—	—	.4	.5	.3	.2	1.2	.6	.1
Preparatory	46.2	58.6	—	29.5	6.2	—	—	—	—	—
Total	100.0	100.0	100.0	100.0	100.0	100.0	100.0	100.0	100.0	100.0
Subtotal										
no. students	130	162	183	747	1,058	862	1,225	1,272	933	931
Unknown	—	55	—	100	66	55	412	141	323	573
Total no. students	130	217	183	847	1,124	917	1,637	1,413	1,256	1,504

a. 1905, from John Fryer, *Admission of Chinese Students to American Colleges* (Washington, 1909), p. 180.

b. 1906-1907, from "Editorials," WCSJ, Vol. II, No. 2 (September-October, 1907), p. 2.

c. 1909, English Secretary's Report, CSM, Vol. V, No. 1 (November, 1909), p. 30.

d. 1914, compiled from the *Chinese Students' Directory*, 1914, published by the Chinese Students' Alliance of America.

e. 1918, from *Chinese Students' Directory*, 1918, published by C.S.A. in America.

f. 1920-21, from *Who's Who of the Chinese Students in America* (Berkeley, 1921).

g. 1924, from *The Handbook of Chinese Students in U.S.A.*, as quoted in Chang Tao-chih, "Conditions of Chinese Students in America and Our Future Policy of Study Abroad," CHCYC, Vol. XV, No. 9 (March, 1926).

1935-36	1936-37	1937-38	1941-42k	Nov. 1942l	1943m	1945n	1949-50o	1950-51	1951-52	1952-53	Total %	Total No.
22.8	12.4	15.0	6.5	5.8	6.8	7.0	14.3	13.2	11.9	10.5	11.7	3,690
.1	—	—	.4	1.4	3.1	2.2	2.3	2.7	3.0	3.2	3.5	1,112
—	—	—	.8	.8	1.5	1.3	1.3	1.2	1.2	1.7	1.0	314
.4	—	—	.6	—	.7	.7	.7	.8	1.0	.5	.6	181
.6	—	.5	.1	—	—	.3	.4	.5	.4	.7	.5	160
2.3	1.8	1.5	3.1	1.9	.3	.8	.7	.6	.3	.9	1.0	300
—	—	—	1.5	1.7	1.1	1.2	.3	.4	.6	.6	.6	182
19.4	10.6	13.0	—	—	—	.5	8.6	7.0	5.4	2.9	4.5	1,441
13.3	13.8	11.9	14.5	15.3	18.6	15.9	11.9	14.0	13.4	11.4	13.6	4,270
1.7	1.5	.6	1.0	1.3	2.1	1.8	.9	1.3	.9	1.5	1.5	461
3.4	3.9	3.3	4.5	4.3	5.6	5.1	4.4	3.9	4.7	3.8	4.3	1,348
4.9	5.6	5.2	4.3	4.8	7.1	6.0	4.9	5.9	5.1	3.8	5.2	1,636
3.3	2.8	2.8	4.7	4.9	3.8	3.0	1.8	3.0	2.7	2.3	2.6	825
7.0	8.6	7.8	8.6	7.9	6.5	6.9	7.5	8.5	7.7	8.6	8.6	2,708
16.1	17.8	17.8	13.1	8.0	8.3	7.2	15.7	14.7	12.9	11.3	12.2	3,840
11.5	12.6	12.3	6.5	4.6	5.0	4.7	6.2	6.2	5.4	4.3	6.8	2,137
2.7	2.1	2.5	2.3	2.0	.4	.6	2.8	1.9	1.4	1.6	1.6	493
1.5	2.2	1.9	2.3	—	.6	—	3.4	3.1	2.8	2.8	1.9	605
.4	.9	1.1	2.0	1.4	1.6	1.3	2.4	2.6	2.2	1.8	1.5	464
—	—	—	—	—	—	.7	.6	.9	1.0	1.1	.8	.4	141
23.0	22.4	25.5	· 28.4	39.1	34.8	41.1	27.5	25.8	25.5	26.9	28.7	9,023
6.6	10.4	6.3	13.6	15.7	14.5	10.9	14.8	15.0	17.4	18.6	12.3	3,872
7.3	11.1	11.0	13.1	5.2	6.5	7.6	5.1	5.9	8.4	10.2	7.8	2,455
3.6	3.4	4.6	2.1	2.9	2.8	2.4	3.2	2.9	2.8	2.5	3.3	1,045
.3	.1	.1	.1	.1	1.2	1.0	—	—	—	—	.3	87
—	—	—	—	—	—	—	—	—	—	—	1.5	442
100.0	100.0	100.0	100.0	100.0	100.0	100.0	100.0	100.0	100.0	100.0	100.0	—
1,585	1,909	2,221	1,545	1,042	1,259	2,372	3,634	3,351	2,773	2,238	—	31,432
299	253	117	204	15	38	650	290	274	224	410	—	4,499
1,884	2,162	2,338	1,749	1,057	1,297	3,022	3,924	3,625	2,997	2,648	—	35,931

h. 1927, from *The Handbook of Chinese Students in U.S.A.*, 1927.

i. 1931-32, from *The Handbook of Chinese Students in U.S.A.*, 1931-32.

j. 1934-38, from *Directory of the Chinese Students in America*, 1934-35, 1935-36, 1936-37, 1937-38, published by the Chinese Students' Christian Association in North America. This source includes Chinese students in Canada and Hawaii.

k. 1941-42, from CIB, Vol. VI, No. 4 (January, 1942), p. 2.

l. 1942, November from CIB, Vol. VII, No. 2 (November-December, 1942), p. 3.

m. 1943, from *Directory of Chinese University Graduates and Students in America*, 1943, published by the China Institute.

n. 1945, from *Directory of Chinese University Graduates and Students in America*, 1945.

o. 1949-53, from *Directory of Chinese Students in Colleges and Universities in the United States*, 1949, 1950, 1951, 1952, 1953, published by the China Institute.

TABLE 11. *Fields of Study of Chinese Students in Japan in Percentages*[a]

	1917	1918-21	1930[b]	1931	1932	1933	1934
Humanities	2.31	1.30	9.41	12.68	12.74	11.98	10.09
Social Sciences	9.96	24.84	23.37	40.94	39.15	27.65	40.92
Business	4.89	9.15	6.51	5.44	3.30	4.61	4.32
Education	5.90	.65	1.86	6.16	5.19	6.91	4.90
Engineering	25.74	23.53	10.79	12.68	11.32	15.21	11.24
Sciences	2.20	2.62	4.45	3.26	4.24	5.07	7.78
Medicine	14.39	11.11	4.45	13.41	13.68	20.74	8.65
Agriculture	4.60	2.12	2.68	5.43	10.38	7.83	12.10
Military Science	—	—	9.74	—	—	—	—
Preparatory	24.63	5.07	26.74	—	—	—	—
Others	5.38	19.61	—	—	—	—	—
Total	100.00	100.00	100.00	100.00	100.00	100.00	100.00

a. 1917 and 1918-21, from Chinese government statistics quoted in SHC:CTCK, 233-34, 240-41; 1930, from 19th CKTC; 1931, from 1st CYNC, II, 1111; 1932-34, from 21st, 22nd, and 23rd CKTC.

b. The 1930 figures came from an actual survey of Chinese students in Japan. The other figures refer to students going to Japan in a single year.

TABLE 12. *Fields of Study of Chinese Students in Great Britain and Ireland*

	1916	1917	Jan. '30-July '31	1932	1933	1934	1943	1945	1946-1947	1949-1950	1950-1951	1952-1953
Engineering	27.10	43.28	13.33	16.36	18.67	24.79	53.48	48.89	49.47	33.93	42.15	46.01
Science	6.50	11.94	15.56	12.73	5.33	22.31	8.02	7.78	13.25	14.11	14.05	7.97
Medicine	18.50	8.96	11.11	3.64	9.33	6.61	18.72	18.89	16.93	17.42	17.77	18.84
Agriculture	1.00	7.46	2.22	—	2.67	6.61	.53	.56	1.59	1.20	.41	.72
Humanities	2.40	4.48	13.33	16.36	14.67	14.05	3.74	6.11	5.81	7.92	5.44	6.89
Social Science	16.80	19.40	33.33	25.46	32.00	20.66	11.23	11.66	7.94	15.19	13.98	11.23
Education	—	—	—	16.36	10.67	4.14	2.14	2.78	2.91	4.80	2.07	3.99
Business	2.70	4.48	2.23	9.09	6.66	.83	2.14	2.78	1.32	2.10	1.24	1.81
Military	2.10	—	—	—	—	—	—	.55	.78	—	—	—
Preparatory	22.90	—	—	—	—	—	—	—	—	3.03	2.48	.73
Others	—	—	—	—	—	—	—	—	—	.30	.41	1.81
Total in per cent	100.00	100.00	100.00	100.00	100.00	100.00	100.00	100.00	100.00	100.00	100.00	100.00
Total in number	292	67	45	55	75	121	187	180	378	333	242	276
Including unknown	292	67	48	56	75	121	192	192	415	451	317	374

a. The 1916 figures are compiled from the data in TMTZ:CA, 28; the 1917 figures pertain to government students alone and are compiled from TCKNC, 1902-4; the 1930-34 figures pertain to students who applied for government permission to study in England and are compiled from various issues of CKTC; the 1943-53 figures are based on directories of Chinese students in Great Britain and Ireland.

[*Appendix C*]

TABLE 13. *Occupational Distribution of American-Trained Students*

	1917[a]	1919[a]	1922[b]	1925[a]	1934[c]	1937[b]
Education[d]	39.19	39.76	36.62	38.36	32.88	28.13
University	31.88	39.42	32.16	32.71		24.39
School	7.31	.34	4.46	5.65		3.74
Government service	35.59	22.82	20.74	15.41	42.00	29.34
Business	11.66	10.07	20.54	22.09	9.58	13.45
Bank		3.69	5.81	5.99		5.38
Commerce		6.38	12.02	4.46		4.60
Industry			2.71	11.64		3.47
Foreign employ	1.90	.34	1.94	3.94		4.60
Professionals	8.27	23.49	2.52	3.25	2.84	2.60
Social and religious work	3.39	3.52	.97	1.37	3.23	1.30
Others			16.67	15.58	9.47	20.58
Housewife				2.22		——
Deceased			5.43	——		6.25
Others			.58	——		——
Unknown			10.66	13.36	9.47	14.33
Total	100.00	100.00	100.00	100.00	100.00	100.00
Total in number of persons	472	596	516	584	2777	1152

a. 1917, from WWAR, 1916, and its 1917 supplement; 1919, from information in TMTZ:CA, 27-28, quoting a later edition of WWAR but giving only group figures and no detailed information about each individual; 1925, from the "Supplement of American Returned Students," WWCW, 1925.

b. 1922, adapted from SHC:CTCK, 260-62. Only Tsinghua graduates are included; 1937, from THTHL. Only Tsinghua graduates from the special preparatory course (*liu-mei yü-pei pan*) are included.

c. 1934, from a government survey published in SSHP, June 30, 1936. The survey covered all the foreign-trained who had responded to the government survey.

d. A word should be said of the terms used in the table. Under "University" are included all university teachers and presidents and other academic research workers. Under "School" are included all teachers and administrators below the college level. These two groups include all workers in the educational field irrespective of the nature of the institutions concerned—public, private, or foreign. For the other groups, classification is based on the category of employers rather than on the specific function of the individual. Thus an engineer is under "Government" if employed by it, under "Industry" if employed by a private industrial concern, and under "Professionals" if operating as an independent consulting engineer. Similarly, "Foreign employ" includes all who worked for foreigners or non-Chinese concerns, whether government, private, or international, in China or outside it. Under "Professionals" are included doctors who had private practices or worked in private hospitals, but not those who were in civil service and derived their main income from that source. Writers, lawyers, architects, and accountants are under "Professionals." "Social and religious work" refers to church work, Y.M.C.A., and all charitable activities. Perhaps the most ambiguous group is the "Unknown." The absence of information about a man's employment could mean one of two things, either he was unemployed or his occupation was unknown. Since most of the sources used here originated from Tsinghua University, which kept itself well-informed about students returned from America, it is probable that most of the men under "Unknown" were actually unemployed.

The classifications are the same for all years, except 1919, for which percentages are derived from the group figures given by the source quoted.

The data in this table are insufficient for a detailed analysis. The two major drawbacks are the unavailability of the original data for 1919 and the inclusion of other foreign-trained for 1934. It is almost certain that under "Professionals" for 1919 there were many engineers and doctors employed by the government, but we have no way to readjust the figures in line with our own classification for the other years. Another feature is the fluctuations in the percentages of businessmen, particularly the merchants and industrialists. This fact probably has much to do with the difference of coverage between the two groups of statistics used. The 1917, 1919, and 1925 figures refer to all American-trained, while the 1922 and 1937 refer only to Tsinghua graduates, among whom there were no girls. Another relevant factor is perhaps that frequent shift from one occupation to another was fairly common for the modern well-to-do Chinese; hence some fluctuations through the years are not too unexpected.

TABLE 14. *Employment and Academic Specialties of the American-Trained in China as of 1925*

Occupation[a]	Engineering	Sciences	Agriculture	Medicine	Social Sciences	Business	Education	Humanities	Military Science	Unknown	Totals
					(Fields of Study)						
Education[b]	28.7	62.5	69.5	26.3	31.9	30.4	59.5	50.0	33.3	31.3	38.4
University	26.3	53.6	52.8	26.3	29.0	25.0	54.1	31.3	33.3	25.4	32.7
School	2.4	8.9	16.7	—	2.9	5.4	5.4	18.7	—	5.9	5.7
Government Service	16.7	7.2	11.2	5.3	34.8	3.6	8.1	3.1	66.7	21.4	15.5
General	4.8	5.4	5.6	—	15.9	—	—	—	66.7	12.0	6.2
	—	—	—	—	—	3.6	5.4	—	—	4.7	—
Technicians	11.4	—	2.8	5.3	7.3	—	—	3.1	—	—	6.7
Diplomats	—	1.8	2.8	—	10.1	—	2.7	—	—	4.7	2.2
Militarists	.5	—	—	—	1.5	—	—	—	—	—	.4
Foreign employ	6.2	3.6	—	—	4.4	5.4	—	3.1	—	1.5	3.8
Bankers	—	—	2.7	—	8.7	42.8	—	6.3	—	2.9	6.0
Merchants	6.2	1.8	—	—	4.3	8.9	—	3.1	—	2.9	4.5
Industrialists	9.1	3.6	—	5.3	—	5.4	2.7	—	—	8.7	5.2
Industrial technicians (engineers)	15.8	1.8	2.8	—	—	—	—	3.1	—	—	6.3
Professionals	1.0	1.8	—	57.9	1.4	—	2.7	3.1	—	2.9	3.3
Rural Workers	—	—	—	—	—	—	2.7	3.1	—	—	—
Social and religious workers	—	—	—	—	—	—	—	6.2	—	—	1.4
Unknown	16.3	12.4	2.7	5.2	11.6	3.5	10.8	9.4	—	24.0	13.4
Housewives	—	5.3	11.1	—	1.5	—	10.8	12.6	—	1.5	2.2
Total each field	100.0	100.0	100.0	100.0	100.0	100.0	100.0	100.0	100.0	100.0	100.0
Student number	210	56	35	19	69	56	37	32	3	67	584[b]
Percent of total number of students	35.8	9.6	6.2	3.3	11.8	9.6	6.3	5.5	.5	11.5	100.0

a. See preceding Table 13, note d, for its explanation of terms, which is also applicable to this table.

b. There are six duplicates: four engineers of whom two were professors and government technicians, one was a professor and industrial technician, one was a professor and government officer; one agriculturist who was a school administrator and government officer; and one social scientist who was a professor and government officer.

TABLE 15. *Government Expenditure on Study Abroad and on Higher Education in China*

Year	Country of Study	No. of Students	Total Outlay in Chinese Currency	Per Student Cost
1909-10	China	749[a]	Tls. 328,742[b]	Tls. 439
	Abroad	2,969	1,695,719	571
	Japan	2,387[c]	818,741[d]	343
	U.S.A.	207[e]	300,978[f]	1,454
	Europe	375[g]	576,000[h]	1,536
1917	China	2,727[i]	$761,660[j]	$276
	Abroad	1,690	1,663,560	984
	Japan	1,084[k]	682,920[l]	630
	U.S.A.	500[m]	720,000[n]	1,440
	Europe	181[o]	260,640[p]	1,440
1931	China	21,996[q]	19,528,576[r]	887
	Abroad	947	1,649,916	1,742
	Japan	787[s]	925,512[t]	1,176
	U.S.A.	89[u]	451,764[v]	5,076
	Europe	71[u]	272,640[w]	3,840

a. 1st CYNC, sec. C, p. 12. The students were those of Peking University, Peiyang University, and Shansi University.

b. *Ibid.*

c. ECK:MEC, p. 29.

d. 450 yen per student per annum at 1.31 yen to Tl. 1. The exchange rates used are taken from TCKNC, 748; CY, 255; and 1st CYNC, sec. D, p. 66.

e. WCSJ (March, 1912), 738-39.

f. U.S. $960.00 per student per annum at U.S. $0.66 to Tl. 1.

g. ECK:MEC, 29. The figure was for 1910.

h. £192 per student per annum at 2s/6d to Tl. 1.

i. 1st CYNC, sec. C, p. 14.

j. *Ibid.*

k. SHC:CTCK, 233.

l. 840 yen per student per annum at 1 yen to C $0.75.

m. CSM (March, 1917), 239.

n. U.S. $960.00 per student per annum at U.S. $1.00 to C $1.50.

o. SHC:CTCK, 234.

p. £192 per student per annum at £1 to C $7.50.

q. Compiled from 1st CYNC, sec. D, pp. 32-33.

r. *Ibid.*; all government-operated colleges and technical schools are included.

s. Chin Lu-fu and Ch'en Chu-t'ung, "Recent Conditions of Our Students in Japan," CYTC, Vol. XXII, No. 4, pp. 92-93. The figure was probably incomplete and conservative.

t. 840 yen per student per annum at 1 yen to C $1.4.

u. The number of government students who left China in 1929-31.

v. U.S. $1,080 per student per annum at U.S. $1.00 to C $4.70.

w. £240 per student per annum at £1 to C $16.

List of Abbreviations and Bibliography

AC	*Agrarian China.* London: Institute of Pacific Relations, 1939.
AJ:CCI	Arnold, Julean H. *China: A Commercial and Industrial Handbook.* Washington, D.C., 1926.
AJS	*American Journal of Sociology.*
AMM	*American Mathematical Monthly,* 1894——.
AN	*Annals.* American Academy of Political and Social Science.
ANALECTS	*Confucius' Analects.* Translated by James Legge.
ARS:JTME	Anderson, Ronald S. *Japan: Three Epochs of Modern Education.* Washington, D.C., 1959.
AS	*The Asian Student.* San Francisco.
ASR	*American Sociological Review.*
BAC:RAEL	Bining, Arthur Cecil. *The Rise of American Economic Life.* New York, 1955.
BC:DHCC	Brandt, Conrad, Schwartz, Benjamin, and Fairbank, John. *A Documentary History of Chinese Communism.* Cambridge, 1952.
BDG	*Boston Daily Globe.*
BGH:CFE	Blakeslee, George H. *China and the Far East.* New York, 1913.
BGH:RDC	Blakeslee, George H. (ed.) *Recent Developments in China.* New York, 1913.
BHL:MPMC	Boorman, Howard L. (ed.) *Men and Politics in Modern China.* New York, 1960.
BHS:PDPO	Brunnert, H. S., and Hagelstrom, V. V. *Present Day Political Organization of China.* Taipeh, n.d.
BJOP:RE	Bland, J. O. P. *Recent Events and Present Policies in China.* Philadelphia, 1912.
BK:EMGS	Biggerstaff, Knight. *The Earliest Modern Government Schools in China.* Ithaca, 1961.
BPS:TP	Buck, Pearl S. *Tell the People: Talks with James Yen about the Mass Education Movement.* New York, 1945.
BSE	U.S. Office of Education. *Biennial Survey of Education.*
CA	U.S. House of Representatives. *Communism in Action.* 81st Congress, 1st Session, House Document No. 154, Part 3.
CAE:ILUS	Cook, Arthur E. *Immigration Laws of the United States.* Chicago, 1929.

CAW   *China at War.*

CB   *Current Biography.*

CBFE   *China Bulletin of the Far Eastern Joint Office, Division of Foreign Missions.* National Council of the Churches of Christ in the U.S.A.

CBY:ACW   Chao, Buwei Yang. *Autobiography of a Chinese Woman.* New York, 1947.

CC   Ch'un Ch'iu. Hongkong, 1957——.

CC:CKN   Ch'ien, Chia-chü (ed.). *Chung-kuo nung-ts'un ching-chi lun-wen chi.* Shanghai, 1956.

CC:CYS   Ch'en Ch'ing-chih. *Chung-kuo chiao-yü-shih.* Shanghai, 1936.

CCC:CKWK   Chang, Chin-chien. *Chung-kuo wen-kuan chih-tu shih.* Taipeh, 1955.

CCE:CC   Columbia, Cary-Elwes. *China and the Cross.* New York, 1956.

CCF:YF   Chou, Chen-fu. *Yen-fu ssu-hsiang shu-p'ing.* Shanghai, 1940.

CCF:YFSWH   Chou, Chen-fu. *Yen-fu shih-wen hsueh.* Peking, 1959.

CCH:LCM   Ch'en, Ch'un-hsuen. *Lo-chai man-pi.* Taipeh, 1962.

CCH:SC   Corbett, Charles Hodge. *Shantung Christian University.* New York, 1955.

CCKP   *Cheng-chih kuan-pao,* 1908-1911.

CCL:CG   Chang, Chung-li. *The Chinese Gentry.* Seattle, 1955.

CCL:CPSL   Chang, Ching-lu (comp.). *Chung-kuo chin-tai ch'u-pan shih-liao.* 2 vols. Shanghai, 1954.

CCR   *Current Chinese Readings.* Edited by Chi-chen Wang. New York, 1950.

CCSCY   Ch'en, Chien-shan, and others. *Chiao-yü tuan-p'ing.* Shanghai, 1925.

CCTI   *Ch'uan-cheng tsou-i hui-pien,* 1875-1902.

CCWHTK   *Ch'ing-chao wen-hsien t'ung-k'ao.*

CEC   *Christian Education in China: A Study Made by an Educational Commission Representing the Mission Boards and Societies Conducting Work in China.* New York: Committee of Reference and Counsel of the Foreign Missions Conference of North America, 1922.

CEH:CHE   Cressy, Earl H. *Christian Higher Education in China.* Shanghai, 1928.

CET:CC   Clark, Elmer T. *The Chiangs of China.* New York, 1943.

CFT:EW   Cheng, F. T. *East and West.* London, 1951.

CGB:CGF   Cressey, George B. *China's Geographical Foundations.* New York, 1934.

CH   *China Handbook.*

CHC   *China Critic.*
CHC:CKWH   Ch'en Hsü-ching. *Chung-kuo wen-hua te ch'u-lu.*
                Shanghai, 1934.
CHC:ESC   Chao, Cheng-hsin. "An Ecological Study of China
                from Segmentation to Integration." Unpublished
                Ph.D. dissertation, University of Michigan, 1933.
CHC:TMH   Ch'en, Hsi-ch'i. *T'ung Meng Hui ch'eng-li ch'ien te
                Sun Chung-shan.* Canton, 1957.
CHCYC   *Chung-hua chiao-yü chieh.* Shanghai, 1912-1937, 1947-
                1950.
CH:HDR   Cordier, Henri. *Histoire des relations de la Chine
                avec les puissances occidentales, 1860-1900.* 3 vols.
                Paris, 1901-1902.
CHJ:NTCC   Chang Hsiao-jo. *Nan-t'ung Chang Chi-chih hsien-
                sheng chuan-chi.* Shanghai, 1930.
CHL:TIT   Chou, Hsiu-luan. *Ti-i-tz'u shih-chieh ta-chan shih-
                ch'i chung-kuo min-tsu kung-yeh te fa-chan.* Shanghai,
                1958.
CHMK   *Chung-hua ming-kuo chu-jih liu-hsueh-sheng chien-tu-
                ch'u i-lan.* Nanking, 1929.
CHMKHC   *Chung-hua ming-kuo k'o-hsueh-chih.* 3 vols. Taipeh,
                1955.
CHMKT   *Chung-hua min-kuo t'ung-chi nien-chien, 1947.* Nan-
                king, 1948.
CHNC   *Chung-hua nien-chien.* Nanking.
CHS   *Ch'ien-Han-shu.*
CHY   *Chinese Yearbook.* Shanghai. 1935-1941.
CIB   *China Institute Bulletin.* New York, 1936-1947.
CJ:YSK   Ch'en, Jerome. *Yuan Shih-k'ai, 1859-1916.* Stanford,
                1961.
CKCC   *Chung-kuo ching-chi nien-chien.* Nanking.
CKCCNC   *Chung-kuo ching-chi nien-chien.* Hongkong, 1947.
CKCS   *Chung-kuo chien-she yueh-k'an.* Shanghai, 1919—.
CKCTKM   *Chung-kuo chin-tai kuo-min ching-chi-shih chiang-i.*
                Peking, 1958.
CKCTKS   *Chung-kuo chin-tai kung-yeh shih tzu-liao.* 4 vols.
                Shanghai, 1957.
CKCTLC   *Chung-kuo chin-tai-shih lun-ts'ung.* 10 vols. Taipeh,
                1956.
CKCTSSC   *Chung-kuo chin-tai shih-shih-chi.* Shanghai, 1961.
CKCYHI   *Ch'uan-kuo chiao-yü hui-i pao-kao.* Shanghai, 1928.
CKCYTT   *Chung-kuo chiao-yu tz'u-tien.* Edited by Yü Chia-chü
                and others. Shanghai, 1930.
CKHTS   *Chung-kuo hsien-tai-shih ts'ung-kan.* 4 vols. Taipeh,
                1960-1962.

CKHWH　　　　*Chung-kuo hsin-wen-hsueh ta-hsi.* 10 vols. Shanghai, 1935.

CKJM　　　　*Chung-kuo jen-ming ta-tz'u-tien.* Shanghai, 1940.

CKKCJML　　*Chung-kuo kung-ch'eng jen-min-lu.* N.p., 1941.

CKK:HH　　　Chang, Kuo-kan. *Hsin-hai ke-ming shih-liao.* Shanghai, 1958.

CKLT　　　　*Chung-kuo li-tai ming-jen chuan.* Edited by Chu Cho-ts'un. Shanghai, 1950.

CKN:IS　　　Chang, Kia-ngau. *The Inflationary Spiral: The Experience in China, 1939-1950.* New York, 1958.

CKS:CD　　　Chiang, Kai-shek. *China's Destiny.* Trans. by Wang Chung-hui. New York, 1947.

CKTC　　　　*Chuan-kuo kao-teng chiao-yü t'ung-chi.* Four issues (title varies) from 1928 to 1934: (1) 17th-20th Year, (2) 21st Year, (3) 22d Year, and (4) 23d Year. An abstract was issued for 1935 (24th Year).

CKY:CKWH　　Ch'en, Kao-yung. *Chung-kuo wen-hua wen-ti yen-chiu.* Shanghai, 1937.

CLF:CE　　　Ch'en, Li-fu. *Chinese Education during the War.* Chungking, 1942.

CM　　　　　*The Chinese Manual.* Shanghai, 1943-1944.

CM:CHS　　　Ch'ien, Mu. *Ch'in-han shih.* Hongkong, 1957.

CM:CKLS　　———. *Chung-kuo li-shih ching-shen.* Taipeh, 1954.

CM:CKLT　　———. *Chung-kuo li-tai cheng-chih te-shih.* Hongkong, 1952.

CM:HY　　　———. *Hsüeh-yüeh.* Hongkong, 1958.

CM:KSHL　　———. *Kuo-shih hsin-lun.* Hongkong, 1955.

CM:KSTK　　———. *Kuo-shih ta-kang.* 2 vols. Taipeh, 1952.

CM:TRM　　　Cameron, Meribeth E. *The Reform Movement in China, 1898-1912.* Sanford, 1931.

CML:TFW　　Chiang, Monlin. *Tides from the West.* New Haven, 1947.

CMS:JPWH　　Chang, Min-san (trans.). *Jih-pen wen-hua kei chung-kuo te ying-hsiang.* Shanghai. 1944.

CMY　　　　*Chinese Mission Yearbook.*

CPFE　　　　Clyde, Paul H. *The Far East.* 3d ed. Englewood Cliffs, 1958.

CPH:HW　　　Ch'en, pi-hsieh. *Hai-wai pin-fen lu.* Shanghai, 1937.

CPH:ST　　　Ch'en, Pearl Hsia. "The Social Thought of Lu Hsün." Unpublished Ph.D. dissertation, University of Chicago, 1953.

CPIWSM　　　*Ch'ou-pan i-wu shih-mo.* Peking, 1929-1931.

CPT:CKST　　Ch'en, Po-ta. *Chung-kuo ssu-ta chia-tsu.* Hongkong, 1947.

CPT:WHPF	Chien, Po-tsan (ed.). *Wu-hsü pien-fa.* 4 vols. Shanghai, 1953.
CR	*China Review.* London, 1931-1938.
CRR	*Chinese Recorder.*
CRS	China. Ministry of Economic Affairs. *Crop Reports* (Chinese title: *Nung-ch'ing pao-kao*). Nanking, 1933-1939.
CRYS:FPC	Cheng, Ronald Yu-soong. *The Financing of Public Education in China.* Shanghai, 1935.
CSAS	*Chinese Students and Alumni Service Newsletter.* Chicago.
CSC:CCA	Chou, Shu-chen. *Chou Chih-an hsien-sheng piehchuan.* Peking, 1948.
CSD	*Chinese Students' Directory.* Published by Chinese Students' Alliance in the United States.
CSH:CI	Chou, Shun-hsin. *The Chinese Inflation, 1937-1949.* New York, 1963.
CSI:MKT	Chia, Shih-i. *Min-kuo ts'ai-cheng-shih.* 1st series, 2 vols.; 2d series, 3 vols.; 3d series, 2 vols. Taipeh, 1962.
CSK	*Ch'ing-shih kao.*
CSM	*The Chinese Students' Monthly.* Published by the Chinese Students' Alliance in the United States, 1905-1930.
CSPSR	*Chinese Social and Political Science Review.* Peking, 1916-1941.
CST:CW	Coleridge, Samuel Taylor. *The Complete Works.* 7 vols. New York, 1871.
CSUS	*Chinese Students in the U.S., 1948-55.* New York: Committee on Educational Interchange Policy, 1956.
CTC:HPC	Chu Tzu-chia (pseu.). *Huang-p'u-chiang te cho-lang.* Hongkong, 1964.
CT:CKL	Ch'en, Ta. *Chung-kuo lao-kung wen-ti.* Shanghai, 1929.
CT:CKP	Ch'ien, Tai. *Chung-kuo pu-p'ing-teng t'iao-yueh chih yuan-ch'i chi-ch'i fei-ch'u chih ching-kuo.* Taipeh, 1961.
CT:CM	Ch'en, Ta. *Chinese Migrations with Special Reference to Labor Conditions.* Washington, 1923.
CTF:IPC	Carter, Thomas F. *The Invention of Printing in China.* Revised by L. Carrington Goodrich. 2d ed. New York, 1955.
CTH	*Ch'en Tu-hsiu te tsui-hou chien-chieh.* Hongkong, 1949.
CTH:CTH	Ch'en, T'ung-hsiao. *Ch'en Tu-hsiu P'ing-lun.* Peking, 1932.

CTS   *Chiu-t'ang-shu.*
CTST   *Chin-tai-shih tzu-liao* (a journal). No. 2. Peking, 1955.
CTT:TMM   Chow, Tse-tsung. *The May Fourth Movement.* Cambridge, 1960.
CWHK   *Chang wen-hsiang-kung ch'uan-chi.*
CWJ:SCC   Chen, William Juntung. "Some Controversies on Chinese Culture and Education." Unpublished Ph.D. dissertation, Columbia University, 1951.
CWR   *China Weekly Review.* Shanghai, 1917-1950.
CY   *China Yearbook.* H. G. W. Woodhead (ed.)., 1912-1937.
CYL:CK   Chang, Yueh-lan. *Chung-kuo yin-hang-yeh fa-chan-shih.* Shanghai, 1957.
CYL:WC   Chang, Yin-lin. *Wen-chi.* Taipeh, 1956.
CYNC   *Chiao-yü nien chien.* Published by the Ministry of Education of China. Two issues, 1st in 1934, 2d in 1948. Shanghai.
CYPKP   *Chiao-yü-pu kung-pao.* Nanking, 1929——?
CYTC   *Chiao-yü tsa-chih.* Shanghai, 1909-1948.
CYTTS   *Chiao-yü ta-tz'u-shu.* Shanghai, 1928.
CYWCC   *Chung-ying wen-chiao chi-chin wei-yuan-hui liu-ying t'ung-hsueh-lu.*
CYYCY   *Chung-yang yen-chiu-yuan yuan-shih lu.* Nanking, 1948.
CYYWH   *Chiao-yü yü wen-hua.* Taipeh, 1950——.
DCS   *Directory of Chinese Students in Colleges and Universities in the U.S.A.* New York: China Institute in America, 1951——.
DCU   *Directory of the Central Union of Chinese Students in Great Britain and Northern Ireland.* London.
DCUG   *Directory of Chinese University Graduates and Students in America.* New York: China Institute in America, 1943-1945.
DGH:CP   Danton, George H. *The Chinese People.* Boston, 1938.
DJA:LCJ   Dewey, John and Alice. *Letters from China and Japan.* New York, 1921.
DSPE   U.S. Department of State. *The Program of Emergency Aid to Chinese Students, 1949-55.* Washington, 1956.
DSR   ——. *Report to the Congress on the Chinese Emergency Aid Program.* Washington, 1955. (Mimeographed).
ECK:MEC   Edmunds, Charles K. *Modern Education in China.* Washington, 1919.
EDC   U.S. Office of Education. *Earned Degrees Conferred*

	by Higher Educational Institutions. Washington.
EM	*Eastern Miscellany* (Chinese title: *T'ung-fang ts-chih*). Shanghai, 1904-1937, 1943——.
EOW	*Education for One World.* New York, Institute of International Education.
ER	*Educational Review.* Shanghai.
ES	*Evening Star.* Washington.
EY	*Educational Yearbook of the International Institute of Teachers College of Columbia University.* New York.
FA:CEI	Feuerwerker, Albert. *China's Early Industrialization.* Cambridge, 1958.
FCR	*Free China Review.* Taipeh, 1951——.
FCY:TLC	Fang, Chao-ying, and Tu, Lien-che. *Ch'ing-ch'ao chin-shih t'i-ming pei-lu.* Harvard-Yenching Institute, 1941.
FEQ	*Far Eastern Quarterly.*
FH:CHCT	Fang, Hao. *Chung-hsi chiao-t'ung-shih.* 5 vols. Taipeh, 1954.
FHD:CIT	Fong, H. D. *Cotton Industry and Trade in China.* 2 vols. Tientsin, 1932.
FHT:HTCC	Fei, Hsiao-t'ung. *Hsiang-t'u ch'ung-chien.* Shanghai, 1948.
FH:WL	Fang, Hao. *Wen-lu.* Peking, 1948.
FJ:ACS	Fryer, John. *Admission of Chinese Students to American Colleges.* Washington, 1909.
FJK:CTI	Fairbank, John King. *Chinese Thought and Institutions.* Chicago, 1957.
FJK:USC	———. *The United States and China.* 2d ed. Cambridge, 1958.
FSA	*The Foreign Students in America.* New York: Commission on Survey of Foreign Students in the U.S.A., 1925.
FTY:CHMK	Feng, Tzu-yu. *Chung-hua min-kuo k'ai-kuo-ch'ien ke-ming shih.* 2 vols. Taipeh, 1954.
FTY:KMIS	Feng, Tzu-yu. *Ke-ming I-shih.* 2 vols. Taipeh, 1953.
FWL:CK	Fan, Wen-lan. *Chung-kuo chin-tai-shih.* Vol. I. Peking, 1953.
FYH:WSJS	Feng, Yü-hsiang. *Wo so-jen-shih te Chiang chieh-shih.* Hongkong, 1949.
FYL:HCP	Fung, Yu-lan. *History of Chinese Philosophy.* 2 vols. Translated by Derk Bodde. Princeton, 1952-1953.
GAH:CEA	Gregg, Alice H. *China and Educational Autonomy.* Syracuse, 1946.
GLC:LIC	Goodrich, L. Carrington. *Literary Inquisition of Ch'ien-lung.* Baltimore, 1935.

GP:TFA   Giquel, Prosper. *The Foochow Arsenal and Its Results*. Translated by H. Lang. Shanghai, 1874.

GSH:SCC   Gould, Sidney H. (ed.). *Sciences in Communist China*. Washington, D.C., 1961.

HA:ECCP   Hummel, Arthur (ed.). *Eminent Chinese of the Ching Period*. 2 vols. Washington, D.C., 1944.

HAN:SC   Holcombe, Arthur N. *The Spirit of the Chinese Revolution*. New York, 1930.

HAT:CL   Huang, Ai-ti. "Chinese Labor." Unpublished Master's thesis, University of Chicago, 1942.

HAWP   Yü, Pao-hsüen (ed.). *Huang-ch'ao hsü-ai Wen-pien*.

HCCS   *Huang-ch'ao ching-shih-wen-pien*. Comp. by Ho Ch'ang-ling. N.p., 1827.

HCC:TYJC   Huang, Ch'ing-ch'eng. *T'ung-yu jih-chi*.

HCC:WTS   Hsieh, Chao-chih. *Wu-tsa-tsu*.

HCH   *Hsin chung-hua*. Shanghai, 1933-1937, 1943——.

HCHSH, 1921   *Huan-ch'iu chung-kuo hsueh-sheng-hui nien-chien*. Shanghai, 1921.

HCHSH, 1923   *Huan-ch'iu chung-kuo hsueh-sheng-hui nien-k'an ti-erh-chi*. Shanghai, 1923.

HCHSH, 1925   *Huan ch'iu chung-kuo hsueh-cheng-hui erh-shih chou-nien chi-nien-ts'e*. Shanghai, 1925.

HCKJWC   *Hsin chung-kuo jen-wu chih*. 2 vols. Hongkong, 1950.

HCOAM   *How Chinese Officials Amass Millions*. New York, 1948.

HCS   *Handbook of Chinese Students in the United States*. New York: Chinese Students Handbook Company, 1922-1935.

HCT:HH   Hsüeh, Chün-tu. *Huang Hsing and the Chinese Revolution*. Sanford, 1961.

HCY:KTCK   Hu, Ch'iu-yuan. *Ku-tai chung-kuo wen-hua yü chung-kuo chih-shih fen-tz'u*. 2 vols. Hongkong, 1956.

HCY:OY   Hsü, Chien-yin. *Ou-yu tsa-lu*.

HCYNT   *Hsing-cheng yuan nung-ts'un fu-hsing wei-yuan hui ts'ung-shu*. 6 vols. Shanghai, 1934-1935.

HEO:SCS   Hauser, Ernest O. *Shanghai: City for Sale*. New York, 1940.

              Hsueh, Fu-ch'eng. *Ch'u-shih ying-fa i-pi ssu-kuo jih-chi*.
HFC:CSYF

HFHC   *Hsiao-fang-hu-chai yü-ti ts'ung-ch'ao*.

HGF:EC   Hudson, G. F. *Europe and China*. London, 1931.

HH   *Hsueh Heng*. Nanking.

HH:CKH   Hu, Hua. *Chung-kuo hsin-min chu chu-i ko-min-shih*. Peking, 1952.

HHCSN   *Hsin-hai ke-ming ch'ien shih-nien-chien shih-lun hsuen-chi.* 1st series, 2 vols; 2d series, 2 vols. Peking, 1962-1963.

HHHIL   *Hsin-hai ke-ming hui-i-lu.* 5 vols. Peking, 1961-1963.

HHKM   *Hsin-hai ke-ming.* 8 vols. Shanghai, 1957.

HICY:ITCP   Hsü, Immanuel C. Y. (trans.). *Intellectual Trends in the Ch'ing Period.* Cambridge, 1959.

HIS:CTTS   Hsiao, I-shan. *Ch'ing-tai t'ung-shih.* 5 vols. Taipeh, 1963.

HJAS   *Harvard Journal of Asiatic Studies.* Cambridge, 1936- ——.

HJ:TC   Hsü, Jun. *Tzu-chuan nien-p'u.*

HKC:CCY   Ho, Kan-chih. *Chung kuo ch'i-meng yun-tung-shih.* Shanghai, 1947.

HKC:CKC   Hsiao, Kung-ch'uan. *Chung-kuo cheng-chih ssu-hsiang-shih.* 6 vols. Taipeh, 1954.

HKCCN   *Hsü Kuang-ch'i chi-nien lun-wen-chi.* Peking, 1963.

HPC   *Papers on China.* Center for East Asian Studies, Harvard University.

HPT:PC   Ho, Ping-ti. *Studies on the Population of China, 1368-1953.* Cambridge, 1959.

HPTT   *Hsueh-pu tsou-tzu ch'i-yao.* Peking, 1905-1909.

HPY:FTC   Ho, Ping-yin. *The Foreign Trade of China.* Shanghai, 1935.

HPY:TJP   Hsieh, Ping-ying. *Tsai jih-pen yü-chung.* N.p., n.d.

HSIN   *Hsin Tien Ti.* Taipeh.

HSK:AS   Hsieh, Sung-kao. *My American Sketches.* Shanghai, 1925.

HS:LHJC   Hu, Shih. *Liu-hsueh jih-chi.* Shanghai, 1947-1948.

HSP   *Hsin Sheng Pao.* Taipeh.

HSSHPP   Hu shih Ssu-hsiang p'i-p'an. 8 vols. Peking, 1955-1956.

HS:SSTS   Hu, Shih. *Ssu-shih Tzu-shu.* Shanghai, 1935.

HS:TCR   ——. *The Chinese Renaissance.* Chicago, 1933.

HS:TWC   ——. *Ting Wen-chiang te chuan-chi.* Taipeh, 1956.

HS:WT   ——. *Wen-ts'un.* Shanghai, 1930.

HS:WT (1953)   ——. *Wen-ts'un.* 4 vols. Taipeh, 1953.

HSW:LCM   Hu, Sheng-wu, and Chin, Ch'ung-chi. *Lun Ch'ing-mo te li-hsien yun-tung.* Shanghai, 1959.

HT   *Hsiang-tao chou-pao.* Various places, 1922-1927.

HTH:EE   Huxley, Thomas H. *Evolution and Ethics and Other Essays.* New York, 1899.

HTS   *Hsin t'ang-shu.*

HTS:CK   Huang, Ta-shou. *Chung-kuo chin-tai-shih.* 3 vols. Taipeh, 1953-1955.

HTT   *Hsü t'ung-tien.*
HWHTK   *Hsü wen-hsien t'ung-k'ao.*
HY   *Hsin-yueh.* Shanghai, 1928-1933.
HY:CTY   Hsü, Ying and others, *Chan Tien-yu.* Peking, 1956.
HYHP   *Hsin-ya hsüeh-pao.* Hongkong, 1955——.
IB   *Information Bulletin.* Nanking, 1933-1937.
IHR:FY   Isaacs, Harold R. *Five Years of Kuomintang Re-
               action.* Shanghai, 1932.
IHR:TCR   ——. *The Tragedy of the Chinese Revolution.* Stan-
               ford, 1961.
IIEB   *Institute of International Education Bulletin.* New
               York.
INT   *Intercollegian.*
ISHK   Li Hung-chang. *I-shu han-kao.*
IYLJ:KT   I-yuan lao-jen. *Ku-tu pien-ch'ien chi-lueh.* Peking,
               1941.
JAS   *Journal of Asian Studies.* 1956——.
JKS:CY   Juan, Kui-sheng. *Ch'a-yü k'o-hua.* 2 vols. Shanghai,
               1959.
JMB:JSYS   Jansen, Marins B. *The Japanese and Sun Yat-sen.*
               Cambridge, 1954.
JMST   *Jen-min shou-ts'e.* Shanghai, 1950——.
JW   *Jen-wen.* Shanghai, 1930-1937, 1947-1948.
JY   *Japanese Yearbook.*
KC   *Kuan-ch'a.* Shanghai.
KCK:KSP   Ku, Chieh-kang and others. *Ku Shih pien.* 7 vols.
               Hongkong, 1963.
KCP:CWS   Kuo, Chan-p'o. *Chin wu-shih-nien chung-kuo ssu-
               hsiang-shih.* Peiping, 1935.
KFCC   *Kuo-fu ch'uan-chi.* 6 vols. Taipeh, 1961.
KFNP   *Kuo-fu nien-p'u ch'u-kao.* 2 vols. Taipeh, 1958.
KHSCK   *K'o-hsueh-shih chi-k'an.* Peking, 1958——.
KHYC   *Kuang-hsü yü-che hui-ts'un.*
KHYSK   *K'o-hsueh yü jen-sheng kuan.* Shanghai, 1923.
KKC:CKPHS   Ko Kung-chen. *Chung-kuo pao-hsueh-shih.* Peking,
               1955.
KKKM   *Kai-kuo kui-mo.* Taipeh, 1962.
KLTH   *Kuo-li ch'ing-hua ta-hsueh i-lan.* Peking, 1937.
KLY:APA   Kao, Lin-yin. "Academic and Professional Attain-
               ments of Native Chinese Students Graduating from
               Teachers College, Columbia University, 1909-1950."
               Unpublished Ph.D. dissertation, Teachers College,
               Columbia University, 1951.
KMJ:CT   Kuo, Mo-jo. *Ch'uang-tsao shih-nien.* Shanghai, 1932.
KMJ:KMCC   ——. *K'o-ming ch'un-ch'iu.* Shanghai, 1947.

KMR:AA   Konvitz, Milton R. *The Alien and the Asiatic in American Law.* Ithaca, 1946.

KMWH   *Ke-ming wen-hsien.* 24 vols. Taipeh, 1958-1961.

KT   *Kai-ts'ao.* Shanghai, 1919-1921.

KTI:CTCK   Kuo. T'ing-i (comp.). *Chin-tai chung-kuo shih-shih jih-chih.* 2 vols. Taipeh, 1963.

KWCP   *Kuo-wen chou-pao.* Tientsin and Shanghai, 1924-1937.

KWH:TCS   Kiang, Wen-han. *The Chinese Student Movement.* New York, 1948.

KWKC   *Ku-wen kuan-chih.*

KYC:GHE   Kiang, Ying-cheng. "The Geography of Higher Education in China." Unpublished Ph.D. dissertation, Teachers College, Columbia University, 1955.

KYT:CTSC   Kao, Yin-tsu. *Chung-hua ming-kuo ta-shih-chi.* Taipeh, 1957.

KYW:JCL   Ku, Yen-wu. *Jih-chih-lu.*

LAY   *Laymen's Foreign Inquiry Fact Finders' Report. Vol. V, Supplementary Series, Part Two, China.* New York, 1933.

LCC:YCC   Li, Ch'ang-chih. *Yin chung-kuo ti wen-i fu-hsing.* Shanghai, 1946.

LCC:YPSCC   Liang, Ch'i-ch'ao. *Yin-ping-shih ch'uan-chi.* 24 vols. Kunming, 1941.

LCC:YPSWC   Liang, Ch'i-ch'ao. *Yin-ping-shih wen-chi.* 16 vols. Kunming, 1941.

LCN:CKCP   Li, Chien-nung. *Chung-kuo chin po-nien shih.* 2 vols. Taipeh, 1962.

LCN:PHC   Li, Chien-nung. *The Political History of China, 1840-1928.* Translated by Ssu-yü Teng and Jeremy Ingalls. Princeton, 1956.

LCP:KSS   Liang, Chia-pin. *Kwangtung shih-san-hang k'ao.* Shanghai, 1937.

LEK:TPTK   Lo, Erh-kang. *Tai-p'ing t'ieh-kuo-shih Ts'ung-kao.* n.p., 1943.

LFC   L'institut Franco-Chinois de l'University de Lyon. *Reglement.* Lyon, April, 1928.

LH:CC   Lu Hsün. *Ch'uan-chi.* Shanghai, 1937.

LHH:CTY   Ling, Hung-hsün. *Chan Tien-yu hsien-sheng nien-p'u.* Taipeh, 1961.

LHH:YS   Liu, Hsi-hung. *Ying-shao jih-chi.*

LHL:CECN   Li, Ho-lin. *Chin erh-shih-nien chung-kuo wen-i ssu-ch'ao lun.* Shanghai, 1947.

LHL:KFTH   Lo, Hsiang-lin. *Kuo-fu chih ta-hsüeh shih-tai.* Taipeh, 1954.

LHS:CCCC   Liu, Hou-sheng. *Chang Ch'ien chüan-chi.* Shanghai, 1958.

LIB:EGC   Lewis, Ida Belle. *The Education of Girls in China.* New York, 1919.

LIC:CK   Liu, I-cheng. *Chung-kuo wen-hua-shih.* 3 vols. 2d ed. Taipeh, 1954.

LJ   *La Jeunesse* (Chinese title: *Hsin ch'ing-nien*).

LJKCC   Liang, Ch'i-ch'ao. *Liang Jen-kung chin-chu ti-i-ch'i.* Shanghai, 1925.

LJKHS   *Liang Jen-kung hsien-sheng nien-pu ch'ang-pien.* 3 vols. Taipeh, 1958.

LJR:LCC   Levenson, Joseph R. *Liang Ch'i-ch'ao and the Mind of Modern China.* Cambridge, 1953.

LK:LCH   Lo, Kuang. *Lu Cheng-hsiang chuan.* Hongkong, 1949.

LKP:CKKH   Li, Kuang-pi (ed.). *Chung-kuo k'o-hsueh chi-shu fa-ming ho k'o-hsueh chi-shu jen-wu lun-chi.* Peking, 1955.

LKS:HCMC   Latourette, Kenneth S. *A History of Christian Missions in China.* New York, 1929.

LKS:SH   ———. *A Short History of Modern China.* London, 1954.

LK:THJC   Li, Kui. *T'ung-hsing jih-chi.*

LM:SJ   Lamberton, Mary. *St. John's University, Shanghai, 1879-1951.* New York, 1955.

LNHP   *Ling-nan hsueh-pao.* Canton, 1929-1951.

LPC:KCHHC   Li, Pao-chia. *Kuan-ch'ang hsien-hsing chi.*

LPL:OY   Liu Ping-li. *Ou-yu san-chi.* Hongkong, 1954.

LSC:PSTC   Lee, Shao-ch'ang. *Pan-sheng tsa-chi.* Shanghai, 1941.

LSC:SIF   Lee, Shu-ching. "Social Implications of Farm Tenancy in China." Unpublished Ph.D. dissertation, University of Chicago, 1950.

LS:HH   Li, Shu. *Hsin-hai ke-ming ch'ien-hou te chung-kuo cheng-chih.* Peking, 1954.

LSK:CKH   Li, Shou-kung. *Chung-kuo hsien-tai-shih.* Taipeh, 1958.

LSYC   *Li-shih yen-chiu.* Peking.

LTC:CNI   Liu, Ta-chung. *China's National Income, 1931-36.* Washington, D.C., 1946.

LTCKP   *Li-tai chih-kuan piao.*

LTE:CFH   LaFargue, Thomas E. *China's First Hundred.* Pullman, 1942.

LTHH   *Liu-te hsueh-hui nien-chien.* Hamburg, 1927.

LT:STT   Li, T'ang. *Sung Tai-tsu.* Hongkong, 1964.

LTW:WS   Lo, Tun-wei. *Wu-shih-nien hui-i-lu.* Taipeh, 1953.

LTY:EBC	Lee, Tuh-yueh. "The Evolution of Banking in China." Unpublished Ph.D. dissertation, Graduate School of Banking, American Bankers Association, 1952.
LWCTK	Li, Hung-chang. *Li-wen-chung-kung tsou-kao.*
LYSNP	*San-shui Liang Yen-sun hsien-sheng nien-p'u.* 2 vols. N.p., n.d.
LYT:IL	Lin, Yutang. *The Importance of Living.* New York, 1940.
MENCIUS	*The Works of Mencius.* Translated by James Legge.
MFTG	Michael, Franz H., and Taylor, George E. *The Far East in the Modern World.* New York, 1956.
MHF:CA	MacNair, Harley F. *The Chinese Abroad.* Shanghai, 1933.
MHFLDF	MacNair, Harley F., and Lach, Donald F. *Modern Far Eastern International Relations.* New York, 1955.
MHF:MCH	MacNair, Harley F. (ed.). *Modern Chinese History: Selected Readings.* Shanghai, 1933.
MKFK	*Min-kuo fa-kui chi-k'an.* Shanghai, 1929.
MOC:WSTS	Mu, Ou-ch'u. *Wu-shih tzu-shu.* Shanghai, 1926.
MP:CN	Monroe, Paul. *A Nation in Evolution.* New York, 1928.
MS	*Ming-shih.*
MT:TY	Mao Tun. *Tzu Yeh.* Shanghai, 1933.
MYC:CCL	Ma, Yin-ch'u. *Ching-chi lun-wen-chi.* Shanghai, 1947.
MY:DMCJ	Mikami, Yoshio. *The Development of Mathematics in China and Japan.* Leipzig, 1913.
NAS	*North American Student.* 1913-1918.
NCH	*North China Herald.* Shanghai.
NCNAB	*New China News Agency Bulletin.*
NJ:SCC	Needham, Joseph. *Science and Civilization in China.* 4 vols. Cambridge, 1954-1962.
NL	*Nu-li.* Peking, 1922-1924.
NRJ	*National Reconstruction Journal.* New York.
NR:KCC	North, Robert C. *Kuomintang and Chinese Communist Elites.* Stanford, 1952.
NS	*Nan-shih.*
NSEQ	*Nankai Social and Economic Quarterly.*
NYHT	*Nan-yang Hsiung-ti yen-tsao kung-ssu shih-liao.* Shanghai, 1958.
NYT	*New York Times.*
OD	*Open Doors.* New York, Institute of International Education.
OR	*Ostasiatische Rundschau.* Hamburg, 1923-1944.
PCCP	*Pei-chuan chi-pu.* Peking, 1931.

PDK   *Phi Delta Kappan.*

PDS:CPF   Paauw, Douglas Seymour. "Chinese Public Finance During the Nanking Government Period." Unpublished Ph.D. dissertation, Harvard University, 1950.

PHR   *Pacific Historical Review.*

PHW:CKHPS   P'eng, Hsin-wei. *Chung-kuo huo-pi-shih.* Shanghai, 1958.

PI:WTC   P'u I. *Wo te ch'ien-pan-sheng.* 3 vols. Hongkong, 1964.

PKT:CHTY   P'an, Kuang-tan. *Cheng-hsueh tsui-yen.* Shanghai, 1948.

PLHK   Li Hung-chang. *Peng-liao han-kao.*

PM:WW   Perleberg, Max. *Who's Who in Modern China.* Hongkong, 1954.

PRL:RCM   Powell, Ralph L. *The Rise of Chinese Military Power, 1895-1912.* Princeton, 1955.

PRL:TC   Packard, Ruth L. "The Chinese Student Movement, 1935-1936." Unpublished Master's thesis, University of Chicago, 1941.

PTP:CKC   Pao, Tsun-p'eng. *Chung-kuo chin-tai ch'ing-nien yün-tung shih.* Taipeh, 1953.

PWL:AL   Phelps, William Lyon. *Autobiography and Letters.* Oxford, 1939.

QBCB   *Quarterly Bulletin of Chinese Bibliography.*

RAG:TSRS   Robinson, Arthur G. *The Senior Returned Students.* Tientsin, 1932.

RB:PC   Russell, Bertrand. *The Problem of China.* New York, 1922.

RCF:FIC   Remer, Charles F. *Foreign Investments in China.* New York, 1933.

RFW:PC   Riggs, Fred W. *Pressures on Congress.* New York, 1950.

RPS:IPC   Reinsch, Paul S. *Intellectual and Political Currents in the Far East.* Boston, 1911.

SA:CAD   Salter, Arthur. *China and the Depression.* Shanghai, 1934.

SA:PP   ———. *Personality in Politics.* London, 1947.

SBI:CCRM   Schwartz, Benjamin I. *Chinese Communism and the Rise of Mao.* Cambridge, 1961.

SCC:TN   *Shih Chih-chih hsien-sheng tsao-nien hui-i-lu.* Privately printed. N.p., n.d. 47 pp.

SC:HHKT   Sheng, Ch'eng. *Hai-wai kung-tu shih-nien chi-shih.* Shanghai, 1932.

SC:KMJ   Shih, Chien. *Kuo Mo-jo p'ing-lun.* Hongkong, 1954.

SC:SHS   Shih, Chün (comp.). *Chung-kuo chin-tai ssu-hsiang-shih ts'an-k'ao tzu-liao chien-pien.* Peking, 1957.

SCMI	*San Min Chu I.* Translated by Frank W. Price. Shanghai, 1927.
2d CYNC	See CYNC
SCSHC	*Sun Chung-shan hsuen-chi.* 2 vols. Peking, 1956.
SCT:CM	Sun, Ch'eng-tze. *Ch'un-ming meng-yü lu.* 70 *chüan.*
SCYN	*Shensi chiao-yü nien-pao.*
SHC:CKCY	Shu, Hsin-ch'eng. *Chung-kuo chiao-yü shih-liao.* 4 vols. Shanghai, 1928.
SHC:CKT	———. *Chiao-yü ts'ung-kao ti-i-chi.* Shanghai, 1925.
SHC:CTCK	———. *Chin-tai chung-kuo liu-hsueh shih.* Shanghai, 1927.
SHC:WHCY	———. *Wo ho chiao-yü.* Shanghai, 1945.
SHKH	*She-hui k'o-hsueh.* Peking, Tsinghua University.
SHKT	*Ssu-hsiang kai-tsao Wen-hsuen.* Peking, 1952.
SHYK	*She-shui yueh-k'an.* Published by the Shanghai Municipal Government, Bureau of Social Affairs.
SHS	*Shui-shih.*
SJA:CSD	Schumpeter, Joseph A. *Capitalism, Socialism, and Democracy.* 3d ed. New York, 1952.
SK:CNRS	Saneto, Kaishu. *Chūgokujin nihon ryugaku shikō.* Tokyo, 1939.
SK:KNBR	———. *Kindai nisshi bunka ron.* Tokyo, 1941.
SKJ	Shanghai Municipal Government, Bureau of Social Affairs. *Shang-hai kung-jen sheng-huo cheng-tu.* Shanghai, 1934.
SLH:CKSY	Sheng, Lang-hsi. *Chung-kuo shu-yuan chih-tu.* Shanghai, 1934.
SPH:JY	Shang, Pin-ho. *Jen-yin ch'un-chiu.* N.p., 1924.
SPL	*Szechuan Pao-lu yun-tung shih-liao.* Peking, 1959.
SPNC	*Shen-pao nien-chien.* Shanghai.
SPW:CKS	Sun, Pen-wen. *Chung-kuo she-hui wen-ti.* 3 vols. Shanghai, 1948.
SR:FC	Scott, Roderick. *Fukien Christian University.* New York, 1954.
SS	*Sung-shih.* Wan Yu Edition.
SSAS	Saggitarius (pseud.). *The Strange Apotheosis of Sun Yat-sen.* London, 1939.
SSCYHC	*Szechuan sheng chiao-yü hsing-cheng pao-kao shu.* Chengtu, 1914.
SSHP	*Shih-shih hsin-pao.* Shanghai.
SSWN	Chuang, Yü, and Ho, sheng-nai (ed.). *Tsui-chin san-shih-wu nien chih chung-kuo chiao-yü.* Shanghai, 1931.
STC:WC	Shen, Tsu-hsien, and Wu, Kai-sheng (comp.). *Jung-Means.* New York, 1942.

STH:JATT   Shen, Tsu-hsien, and Wu, Kai-sheng (comp.). *Jung-an ti-tzu-chi*. Taipeh, 1962.

STH:KH   Shen, Tsung-han. *K'e-nan ku-hsueh-chi*. Taipeh, 1955.

SURVEY   *A Survey of Chinese Students in American Universities and Colleges in the Past Hundred Years*. New York: China Institute in America, 1954.

SY:CK   Shang, Yueh. *Chung-kuo li-shih kang-yao*. Hongkong, 1957.

SYC:HY   Shen, Yu-chien. *Hsi-yu hui-i lu*. Shanghai, 1941.

SYCT   *Shang-hai yen-chiu tzu-liao*. 2 vols. Shanghai, 1936-1937.

SYL:CTKC   Shang, Yen-liu. *Ch'ing-tai k'o-chü kao-shih shu-lu*. Peking, 1958.

SYL:HTCC   Shen. Yun-lung. *Hsien-tai cheng-chih jen-wu shu-p'ing*. Hongkong, 1959.

SYS:IDC   Sun, Yat-sen. *The International Development of China*. Taipeh 1953.

TCHTHF   *Ta-ch'ing hsuen-t'ung hsin fa-ling*. 32 vols. Shanghai, 1910-1911.

TCJ:CCK   Ts'ao, Chü-jen. *Chiang Ching-kuo lun*. Hongkong, 1954.

TCJ:WTWS   ———. *Wen-t'an wu-shih nien*. Hongkong, n.d.

TCKHHF   *Ta-ch'ing kuang-hsü hsin-fa-ling*. 20 vols. Shanghai, 1910.

TCKNC   *Ti-i-hui chung-kuo nien-chien*. Shanghai, 1924.

TCP:CKC   Ting, Chih-p'in. *Chung-kuo chin ch'i-shih nien chiao-yü chi-shih*. Shanghai, 1935.

TCT:CSYF   Tseng, Chi-tse. *Ch'u-shih ying-fa jih-chi*.

TCT:SW   Tai, Chi-tao. *Sun Wen hsüeh-shuo chih che-hsüeh chi-ch'u*. Shanghai, 1925.

TCY:LCT   T'ao Chü-yin. *Lu chün-tzu chuan*. Shanghai, 1945.

TDCS   *Theses and Dissertations by Chinese Students in America*. New York: China Institute in America, 1927, 1928, 1936.

TF:BFC   Tamagna, Frank M. *Banking and Finance in China*. New York, 1942.

TFK:CKCC   Tseng, Fan-k'ang. *Chung-kuo cheng-chih chih-tu shih*. Taipeh, 1953.

THCC   *T'ao Hsing-chih hsien-sheng chi-nien ts'e*. N.p., n.d.

THCK   *Tsing-hua chou-k'an*. Peking, 1915-1937.

THM   *T'ien Hsia Monthly*. Shanghai, 1935-1941.

THP   *Tsinghua hsueh-pao*.

THTHL   *Tsinghua t'ung-hsueh-lu*. Peking: Tsinghua University, 1937.

TKL:CT	Ts'ai, Kuan-lo. *Ch'ing-tai ch'i-po min-jen-chüan.* 3 vols. Hongkong, 1963.
TKP	*Ta Kung Pao.* Shanghai.
TKY:CS	Ts'ui, Kuo-yin. *Ch'u-shih mei-jih-pi kuo jih-chi.*
TL:CKKS	Tsou, Lu. *Chung-kuo kuo-min-tang shih-kao.* Enlarged edition. Chungking, 1944.
TLK:SL	Tao, L. K. *The Standard of Living of Chinese Workers.* Shanghai, 1931.
TLL:CNC	T'ang, Leang-li. *China's New Currency System.* Shanghai, 1936.
TLL:RC	T'ang, Leang-li. *Reconstruction in China.* Shanghai, 1935.
TLNP	*Tsung-li nien-p'u ch'ang-pien ch'u-kao.* Nanking, 1932.
TLPL	*Tu-li p'ing-lun.* Peking, 1932-1937.
TLTC	*Ta-lu T'sa-chih.* Taipeh.
TMTZ:CA	Tyau, M. T. Z. *China Awakened.* New York, 1922.
TRE	*The Reorganization of Education in China.* Paris: International Institute of Intellectual Co-operation, 1932.
TSC:SCS	Ts'ui, Shu-ch'in. *Sun Chung-shan yü kung-ch'an chu-i.* Hongkong, 1954.
TSC:SMCI	Ts'ui, Shu-ch'in. *San-ming chu-i hsin-lun.* Taipeh, 1955.
TSH	*Ta Shang-hai ti nung-yeh.* Shanghai Municipal Government, Bureau of Social Affairs, 1933.
TSS:CTS	Tso, Shun-sheng. *Chin-tai-shih ssu-chiang.* Hongkong, 1962.
TSY:CKKS	Teng, Ssu-yü. *Chung-kuo k'ao-shih chih-tu shih.* Nanking, 1936.
TSY:CRW	Teng, Ssu-yü, and Fairbank, John K. (ed.). *China's Response to the West.* Cambridge, 1954.
TT	*T'ung-tien.* Wan Yu Edition.
TTHSCC	*Tsou-ting hsueh-hsiao chang-ch'eng.* Peking, 1904.
TTH:WIC	Tsien, Tsuen-hsuin. "Western Impact on China through Translation." Unpublished Master's thesis, University of Chicago, 1952.
TTNC	*T'ieh-tao nien-chien.* Nanking, 1932-1935.
TTP:MKMJ	T'ang Tsu-p'ei. *Min-kuo ming-jen hsiao-chüan.* Hongkong, 1961.
TTYLTT	Teng, T. Y., and Lew, T. T. *Education in China.* Peking, 1923.
TYF:CKY	Tseng, Yang-feng. *Chung-kuo yen-cheng-shih.* Shanghai, 1937.

TY:SHMC   Ting, Yi. *A Short History of Modern Chinese Litera-*
             ture. Peking, 1959.
TYT   *Tzu-yu t'an.* Taipeh, 1950——.
TYT:CKCY   T'an, Yü-tso. *Chung-kuo chung-yao yin-hang fa-chan-*
             shih. Taipeh, 1961.
UL:MAP   Untermeyer, Louis. *Modern American Poetry.* New
             York, 1950.
USFR   U.S. Department of State. *Foreign Relations of the*
             United States. Washington.
VCE:JJR   Vaughan, C. E. (ed.). *The Political Writings of J. J.*
             Rousseau. 2 vols. Cambridge, 1915.
WA:CR   Wylie, Alexander. *Chinese Researches.* Shanghai,
             1897.
WC:TK   Wang, Cheng. "The Kuomintang: A Sociological
             Study of Demoralization." Unpublished Ph.D. dis-
             sertation, Stanford University, 1953.
WCC:YCT   Wang, Chü-ch'ang. *Yen Chi-tao nien-p'u.* Shanghai,
             1936.
WCF:CKHW   Wang, Che-fu. *Chung-kuo hsin-wen-hsueh yun-tung*
             shih. Peking, 1951.
WCH:CC   Wu, Chih-hui. *Ch'üan-chi.* Shanghai, 1927.
WCH:HSLC   ———. *Hsueh-shu lun-chu.* Shanghai, 1925.
WCSI   *Wu-ch'ang Shou-i.* Taipeh, 1961.
WCSJ   *The World Chinese Students' Journal.* Shanghai,
             1906-1912.
WCS:TTCL   Wang, Ch'uan-shan. *Tu t'ung-chien lun.*
WCW:CPTS   Wang, Ching-wei. *China's Problems and Their Solu-*
             tions. Shanghai, 1934.
WCY:A   Wang, Ch'ung-yu. *Antimony.* London, 1908.
WCY:CKKYS   Wang, Ching-yü. *Chung-kuo chin-tai kung-yeh-shih*
             tzu-liao, 1895-1914. 2 vols. Peking, 1957.
WDY:HW   Wu, Daisy Yen. *Hsien Wu, 1893-1959.* Boston, 1959.
WFC:CYS   Wang, Feng-chieh. *Chung-kuo chiao-yü shih.* 4th
             ed. Shanghai, 1947.
WFG:CSM   Williston, Frank G. "The Chinese Student Move-
             ment, 1925-26." Unpublished Master's thesis, Uni-
             versity of Chicago, 1926.
WHCC   Wu, Hsiang, and Cheng, Chi. *Hsien-tai kuo-nei sheng-*
             li hsueh-che chih kung-hsien. Shanghai, 1954.
WHJP   *Wu-han jih-pao nien-chien.* Hankow, 1947.
WHTK   *Wen-hsien t'ung-k'ao.*
WIT:CC   Wen I-to. *Ch'uan-chi.* 4 vols. Shanghai, 1948.
WKCWLT   Wong, K. C., and Wu, Lien-teh. *History of Chinese*
             Medicine. 2d ed. Shanghai, 1936.

WLH:CKS   Wang, Li-hsi. *Chung-kuo she-hui shih lun-chan.* Shanghai, 1932.

WLTK   Chin, Hui-t'ien. *Wu-li t'ung-kao.*

WM:SYS   William, Maurice. *Sun Yat-sen Versus Communism.* Baltimore, 1932.

WNK:HSYT   Wang, Nien-k'un. *Hsueh-sheng yun-tung shih-yao chiang-hua.* Shanghai, 1951.

WOC   *In Commemoration of Twenty-fifth Anniversary, 1907-32.* Published by The Wing On Company, Hongkong, 1932.

WSC:EC   Wang, Shih-chieh. *Education in China.* Shanghai, 1933.

WSF:CCR   Wright, Stanley F. *China's Customs Revenue Since the Revolution of 1911.* Shanghai, 1935.

WSF:CSTA   Wright, Stanley F. *China's Struggle for Tariff Autonomy, 1843-1938.* Shanghai, 1938.

WS:YFC   Wang, Shih. *Yen-fu chuan.* Shanghai, 1957.

WTC:KLMK   Wei, Tzu-ch'u. *Ti-kuo chu-i yü kai-luan mei-kuang.* Shanghai, 1954.

WTC:TYM   Wang, Tsi C. "The Youth Movement of China." Unpublished Ph.D. dissertation, University of Chicago, 1925.

WTL:CKLT   Wang, T'ung-ling. *Chung-kuo li-tai tang-cheng shih.* Peking, 1931.

WWAS   *Who's Who of Academia Sinica.* (Chinese title: *Yuan-shih ti-ming lu*). Nanking, 1948.

WWAR   *Who's Who of American Returned Students.* Peking: Tsinghua College, 1917, with subsequent supplements.

WWCS   *Who's Who of Chinese Students in America.* Berkeley, 1921.

WWCW   *Who's Who in China.* Published by *China Weekly Review.* Shanghai, 1918-1950.

WY:CKHWH   Wang, Yao. *Chung-kuo hsin wen-hsüeh shih-kao.* Peking, 1951.

WYC:CIW   Wang, Y. C. "Chinese Intellectuals and the West." Unpublished Ph.D. dissertation, University of Chicago, 1957.

WYS:LSN   Wang, Yun-sheng. *Lu-shih-nien lai chung-kuo yü jin-pen.* 6 vols. Tientsin, 1932-1933.

YAN:CHH   Young, Arthur N. *China and the Helping Hand, 1937-1945.* Cambridge, 1963.

YBE   *Yearbook of Education.* London.

YCCA   *Yueh-chang ch'eng-an hui-lan.* Shanghai, 1905.

YCC:HI   Yü, Chia-chü. *Hui-i-lu.*

YCL:MKMJ   Yang, Chia-lo (ed.). *Min-kuo min-jen t'u-chien.* 2 vols. Shanghai, 1937.

YCP:CKMFC   Yen, Chung-p'ing. *Chung-kuo mien-fang-chih shih-kao.* Peking, 1955.

YCTIC   *Yen Chi-tao hsien-sheng i-chu.* Singapore, 1959.

YFL:YJC   Yüan, Fang-lai. *Yü Jih-chang chuan.* Shanghai, 1948.

YHC:CK   Yuan, Han-ch'ing. *Chung-kuo hua-hsueh-shih lun-wen-chi.* Peking, 1956.

YHNC   *Ch'uan-kuo Yin-hang nien-chien.* Shanghai.

YIMCCK   *Yen-i ming-chu ts'ung-k'an.* 8 vols. Shanghai, 1931.

YL:A   Yung, Liang. *Autobiography.* Shanghai, 1939.

YL:KHH   Yü Liang (pseud.). *Kung Hsiang-hsi.* Hongkong, 1955.

YSK   *Yuan Shih-kai ch'ieh-kuo-chi.* Taipeh, 1954.

YTF:TST   Yang, T'ing-fu. *T'an Ssu-t'ung nien-p'u.* Peking, 1957.

YTL:CWL   Yuan, T'ung-li. *China in Western Literature.* New Haven, 1958.

YTL:GDD   ———. *A Guide to Doctoral Dissertations by Chinese Students in America, 1905-1960.* Washington, D.C., 1961.

YW:MLCA   Yung, Wing. *My Life in China and America.* New York, 1909.

YWYT   *Yang-wu yun-tung.* 8 vols. Shanghai, 1961.

YYJ:HH   Yang, Yü-ju. *Hsin-hai ke-ming hsien-chu-chi.* Peking, 1957.

YYP:CKCY   Yang, Yin-p'u. *Chung-kuo chin-yung yen-chiu.* Shanghai, 1937.

INDEX

Index

A

Abdication, 4; edict, 294
Academia Sinica, 176, 384, 391, 415, 420; exchange program, 135; educational background of fellows, 180
Agrarian-bureaucratic system, origin of, 35
Agricultural Bank of Kiangsu, 490
Agriculture, 330, 360-61; under Confucianism, 7; farming-study tradition, 16; under Manchus, 31; foreign, 54; scientific farming, 361; farm problem, 458; taxation, 462; research, 474; bank loans, 491. *See also* Taxation, land
Agriculture and Commerce, Ministry of, 380
Air Force, interpreters, 133
Aisin Gioro P'u I, 15-16
Alcock, Rutherford, 428
Allen, Young J., 423
Alliance Society, 226, 247, 248, 250, 252, 272, 277n, 279, 280, 285, 290, 300, 303-4
American Bureau for Medical Aid to China, 136
American China Development Company, 264
American-European Returned Students' Association, Peking, 182
American-trained students, in 1872, 42-45; in 1896-1911, 71-73; goals of study, 74-75; 148-49; in 1901, 82; academic achievements, 84, 166; expatriation, 96-97, 187-90, 507-9; in 1912-27, 111-16; after Pearl Harbor, 137-40; social background, 154; native origins, 156-58; in education, 363
American Mathematical Monthly, 392
Anarchists, 337
Anderson, Carl, 390
Anderson, J. G., 381
Andreev, L., 405
Anhwei, 31; uprisings, 239-42; salt revenues, 432
Anhwei Normal College, 211

B

Aoyama, military school, 233
Arinori Mori, 363
Aristocracy, 342
Army, 86, 123, 287, 293, 294, 424; Japanese training, 68; role in revolution, 251; infiltration of, 279; reorganization of, 287, 297; as career, 376
Army Alliance Society, 280
Artsybashev, M., 405
Association for Universal Military Education, 233, 240, 246
Association of Provincial Councils, 258, 260, 262, 263; petitions Censorate-General, 256-57
Autocracy, 309, 323-24

Bank of Canton, 485
Bank of China, 442, 449, 450, 451, 452, 478-95 *passim*
Bank of Communications, 449, 450, 452, 478-86 *passim*, 495
Bankers Weekly, 491
Banking, 321, 447-53, 478-96; centralization of, 425; and internal debt, 438; bank failure, 449; government control, 449-51; relation to government, 482-86, 490-96, 499; crisis, 488; industrial loans, 489; rural loans, 490-92; foreign privilege, 493-94
Banque Industrielle de la Chine, 493
Barnett, J. D., 335
Belgium, technical study in, 54-55, 77, 159-60
Birkhoff, G., 391
Bismarck, Otto, 222, 327, 328; influence on Sun Yat-sen, 352-53
Blaschke, W., 391
Bluntschli, J. C., 222
Boxer indemnity, 426; French, 110; British, 414, 417, 453
Boxer indemnity scholarships, 389; American, 71-72, 78, 103, 162n, 383, 386, 393, 414; Japanese, 118-19; British, 129, 132, 140-41, 143, 151, 161-62
Boxer uprising, 51, 54, 93, 296